FEDERICO GARCÍA LORCA

COLLECTED POEMS

FEDERICO GARCÍA LORCA was born in 1898 in Fuente Vaqueros, a few miles outside Granada in the province of Andalusia, southern Spain. From an early age he was fascinated by Spain's mixed heritage, adapting its ancient folk songs, ballads, lullabies, and flamenco music into poems and plays. By the age of thirty, he had published five books of poems, culminating in 1928 with *Gypsy Ballads*, which brought him far-reaching fame. In 1929–30, he studied in New York City, where he wrote the poems—among his most socially engaging and compelling—that were to be published posthumously as *Poet in New York*. Upon returning to Spain he devoted much of his attention to theater, "the poetry which rises from the page . . . and becomes human." In 1936, at the outset of the Spanish Civil War, he was shot to death by anti-Republican rebels in Franco's army, and his books were banned and destroyed.

CHRISTOPHER MAURER, the editor of Lorca's *Selected Verse*, *Poet in New York*, and other works, is the author of numerous books and articles on Spanish poetry. He is head of the Department of Spanish, French, Italian, and Portuguese at the University of Illinois–Chicago.

Collected Poems

FEDERICO GARCÍA LORCA

—

COLLECTED POEMS

—

Revised edition, with an introduction and notes by Christopher Maurer

—

Translated by Catherine Brown, Cola Franzen, Angela Jaffray, Galway Kinnell, Will Kirkland, William Bryant Logan, Christopher Maurer, Robert Nasatir, Jerome Rothenberg, Greg Simon, Alan S. Trueblood, and Steven F. White

—

Farrar, Straus and Giroux

New York

Farrar, Straus and Giroux
18 West 18th Street, New York 10011

The translations in this edition were made possible by the General
Book and Library Division of the Spanish Ministry of Culture and
also, in part, by a grant from the Wheatland Foundation, New York.

Grateful acknowledgment is made to And, Antaeus, Northwest
Review, The Paris Review, Poetry New York, Quarry West,
Sequoia, Sulfur, Talus, and Cadmus Editions, where some of the
translations of these poems originally appeared, in somewhat different
form.

Library of Congress Cataloging-in-Publication Data
García Lorca, Federico, 1898–1936.
    [Poems. English & Spanish. Selections]
    Collected poems / Federico García Lorca ; revised edition, with
an introduction and notes by Christopher Maurer ; translated by
Catherine Brown . . . [et al.].
        p. cm.
    Rev. ed. of: Collected poems / Federico García Lorca. 1991.
(Poetical works of Federico García Lorca ; v. 2)
    Includes bibliographical references (p.   ) and indexes.
    Hardcover ISBN: 978-0-374-12615-5 (hardcover)
    Paperback ISBN: 978-0-374-52691-7 (pbk.)
    1. García Lorca, Federico, 1898–1936—Translations into
English. I. Maurer, Christopher. II. Brown, Catherine.
III. García Lorca, Federico, 1898–1936. Poems. English &
Spanish. v. 2. IV. Title.

PQ6613.A763 A225 2002
861'.62—dc21

                                        2001018779

www.fsgbooks.com

18   17   16   15

Contents

Preface

Since 1991, when this book was first published, Federico García Lorca has been transformed from Spain's best-known poet into a ubiquitous popular icon. In 1998, on the centenary of his birth, the poet who had feared "stupid Fame" and demanded silence for his poetry—"four white walls and a silence where the poet's voice can weep and sing"—captured renewed attention throughout the world. At symposia and literary commemorations from Barcelona to Cairo, from Peking to Buenos Aires, Lorca became what the English critic Paul Julian Smith described as a "site of struggle" between "pernicious and pervasive folkloric stereotypes" of his work and "feminist, gay, and deconstructive García Lorcas," and between the political "center" and the periphery. The King and Queen of Spain inaugurated the Año Lorca and Prince Felipe opened a major exposition. The Spanish Prime Minister, the conservative José María Aznar, recited the first few lines of one of the *Gypsy Ballads* and was pilloried in the press and in Congress for his "opportunistic" interest in a "Socialist" poet. Prominent musicians and writers—Lou Reed, Patti Smith, Derek Walcott, Bob Dylan, Ben Sidran, and Antonio Tabuchi—visited Lorca's house in Granada and offered personal tributes. In England, Lorca surpassed Bertolt Brecht as the most frequently performed foreign playwright.

The centenary also gave rise to a number of valuable publications. There were catalogues of expositions in Granada and Madrid; a new biography, by Leslie Stainton; a major book on Lorca's friend Salvador Dalí, by Ian Gibson; updated editions of many works by the Lorca scholar Mario Hernández; and a new four-volume edition of the *Obras completas* by Miguel García-Posada. Lorca's filmscript *Trip to the Moon* was filmed by Frederic Amat, and a TV documentary by John Healey gathered interviews with the poet's family and surviving friends. Lost manuscripts came to light, including *Poet in New York,* which had disappeared in 1936, as well as several missing suites. Translations and adaptations of Lorca's work multiplied, casting doubt on the observation by Ted Hughes, who translated *Blood Wedding,* that "Lorca cannot be Englished." All this seemed to offer ample justification for a revised edition of *The Collected Poems.*

This book—the most complete collection of Lorca's poetry available in English—includes all books of poems published during his lifetime and those that appeared posthumously. With the exception of the early *Book of Poems,* each book is given in its entirety. Also included is a selection from Lorca's uncollected poems and from several works that he mentions in interviews and in his correspondence, but which he did not live to complete: *Suites, Sonnets,* and *Odes. Poet in New York,* published separately and therefore absent from the first edition, has been included here, as have complete versions of the *Suites,* FAIRS, SUMMER HOURS, and SECRETS, and a more reliably ordered version of one of Lorca's most ambitious early sequences, IN THE GARDEN OF THE LUNAR GRAPEFRUITS. There are new translations by Angela Jaffray, Robert Nasatir, Jerome Rothenberg, and Galway Kinnell. The notes and bibliography have been updated, and a number of mistranslations and misprints in the first edition have been corrected. As in the first edition, I have excluded Lorca's juvenilia, prose poems, occasional verse, or minor works that, in my judgment, he did not finish or would not have published without thorough revision: all are available in the García-Posada edition of the *Obras completas.* The chapbook *Primeras canciones (First Songs),* published by a friend in 1936, has not been included here *as a book,* for it was itself an anthology of poems from different works. All of the poems in *Primeras canciones* are found in these pages, but as part of the work (e.g., *Suites* or *The Tamarit Divan*) to which they originally belonged.

The translators have taken a variety of approaches. Faithful, literal translation, an ideal impossible to define, seemed worth pursuing in this "total" view of Lorca's poetry. When, for stylistic reasons, the translators depart from the literal sense as perceived by the editor, alternate readings are offered in the notes. No one would suggest that these translations are "definitive" ones, or that other poets could not have offered a different, equally valid vision of Lorca: in the bibliography, I have listed a variety of other versions. Translation is a cumulative and provisional endeavor, in which no poet and no editor will ever have the final word.

I am deeply grateful to the translators; to editors Ethan Nosowsky, Jonathan Galassi, and Roslyn Schloss; and to Robert Nasatir, who worked both as translator and as editorial assistant. Thanks also to Jeffrey Miller of Cadmus Editions, Linn Blanchard, David Beltrán, William Kosmas, and Bill Swainson. For two decades now, the poet's sister Isabel García Lorca and his nephew, Manuel Fernández-Montesinos García, have allowed me to consult Lorca's manuscripts and have attended to my questions with kindness, patience, and courtesy, as have Mario Hernández and Andrew A. Anderson. Research funds were provided by Harvard University, Vanderbilt University, the University of Illinois at Chicago, the Spanish Ministry of Foreign Affairs, and the Program for Cultural Cooperation Between Spain's Ministry of Culture and United States Universities.

Deepest thanks to María Estrella Iglesias, to whom this edition is dedicated.

C.M.
University of Illinois at Chicago, 2001

Introduction

Federico García Lorca (1898–1936) was a charismatic and compli-
cated figure: preeminent poet of absence; renewer, with Miguel de
Unamuno and Ramón del Valle-Inclán, of the modern Spanish stage;
stern, inspired mediator—perhaps the most successful in modern Eu-
rope—of poetry and theater ("Theater," he once said, "is the poetry
that rises from the page and becomes human" [*OC* III:630]). And he
was much else besides: pianist, actor, director, lecturer, conversational-
ist, and maker of unforgettable drawings. Some of his friends thought
of him as a creative force of almost "cosmic" dimensions. He was an
"extraordinary creature," the poet Jorge Guillén once wrote. "And in
this case 'creature' means more than 'man' . . . [He was a] creature of
Creation, the crossroads of Creation, a man immersed in Creation
who partook of deep creative currents" (xvii). There *is* something el-
emental about Lorca. He seems to lead us urgently and directly to the
central mysteries of human existence. In the thirteen plays and nine
books of verse he was able to complete between 1917 and 1936—an
amazingly short career—he spoke unforgettably of all that most inter-
ests us: the otherness of nature, the demons of personal identity and
artistic creation, sex, childhood, and death.

Born in 1898, the eldest child of a wealthy farmer and an intelli-
gent, sensitive village schoolmistress, Lorca spent the first ten years
of his life in a southern village in the midst of the river plain—the
Vega—of Granada, the loveliest, most fertile countryside of Spain.
Reading his correspondence, whose lyrical intensity sometimes rivals
that of his poetry, one marvels that custom never blinded him to the
poignant beauty of those rural surroundings. "If you were here," he
writes to his friend the musicologist Adolfo Salazar in 1921 from As-
querosa, a village to which he returned often as a young man, "you
would be spinning like a top, trying to see in all four directions at
once.

*A few days ago, a greenish-purple moon came out over the Sierra Nevada, and
across the street from my house a woman sang a* berceuse *that was like a
golden streamer tangling itself in the landscape. At sunset, above all, one lives
in the midst of pure fantasy, in a half-effaced dream . . . there are times when
everything evaporates and we are left in a desert of pearly gray and pink and
dead silver. I cannot tell you how enormous this vega is, and this little white
village in the dark poplars. At night our flesh hurts from so many stars, and we*

are drunk on breeze and water. I doubt that even in India there are nights so charged with fragrance, so delirious. (EC 123)

Lorca's family was the wealthiest in Fuente Vaqueros, the poet's native village. But the family's liberal convictions and Federico's own curiosity as a child helped him to surmount social barriers and brought him into contact with the poverty and misery of rural Andalusia. A brief autobiography (*PrI* 447), probably written in 1918, records his anguish over the suffering of the rural poor. In one chapter he remembers having been told by the mother of one of his friends, "Don't come to see us tomorrow, because we have to do the washing."

What deep, mute tragedy! I couldn't visit them because they were naked. Trembling in the cold, they washed their rags—the only clothes they had . . . And when I returned home and looked at my closet, full of clean, fragrant clothing, I felt a great uneasiness, a cold weight in my heart.

On another occasion, he watches one of his friends, the six-year-old son of a goatherd, die a painful death from an undiagnosed ailment:

One day he felt a strange, gnawing pain in his stomach, and was unable to move. His parents attributed it to his having eaten too much green fruit, and left him to his punishment . . . But the pain only worsened . . . An old woman who lived nearby invented a remedy . . . cutting open a live toad and placing it on his stomach, and giving him mule dung cooked up with beetles.

Held down by several men, the screaming child is forced to swallow the revolting mixture. "Opening his mouth, which was full of bloody foam," he gives up the ghost. No consolation is offered to the boy's mother, only sarcasm from the woman who had concocted the medicine: "Such a delicate child! He wasn't fit to belong to a poor family" (*PrI* 390–91).

However melodramatic his account of these incidents, there is no doubt that Lorca was deeply troubled by social inequality. While living in the village he was always being reminded of his family's relative wealth (others dressed badly, but "on winter mornings I always went to school in a little red cape, with a black fur collar"). That feeling grew even more poignant when the family moved to Granada in 1910. Whenever he returned to the village as a young man, Lorca felt doubly estranged. In 1918 he writes:

The children who were in my grade school are field workers now, and when they see me, they almost don't dare to touch me with those great flinty hands of theirs, dirty from work. Why don't you come running and firmly shake my hand? Do you think the city has changed me? It hasn't. My body grew along with yours, and my heart beat to yours. Your hands are holier than mine. (PrI 439)

A longing for social justice, and bitter resentment of the Catholic Church for doing so little to alleviate suffering, are constant preoccupations in Lorca's earliest writing. "You are the miserable politicians of Evil," Lorca exclaims, condemning the Church in an essay of October 1917.

You are the exterminating angels of the light. You preach war in the name of the Lord of Hosts, and you teach men to hate whoever does not share your ideas . . . The world you have educated is a stupid one whose wings have been trimmed . . . We must rescue Jesus' idea from your ruinous machinations. ("Mística en que se trata de Dios" [Mystical Treatise on God], *PrI* 151)

Throughout his life, he would be haunted both by the failure of Rome to fulfill its evangelical mission (see "Cry to Rome" in *Poet in New York*) and by the poverty of the Spanish countryside. When the Second Republic was declared in 1931, Lorca traveled all over the country, both as lecturer and as director of a student theater troupe, La Barraca, to introduce drama, poetry, and modern painting to rural and provincial audiences. Some of his poetry and plays (*Poet in New York, Play Without a Title*) condemn the urban middle class's indifference to suffering. The popular success of one of his books, *The Gypsy Ballads*, seems to have helped him heal the social estrangement he had sometimes felt in childhood and adolescence. In a letter to his parents a year before his death, he tells of a reading of the *Ballads* in Barcelona:

The way I was received by the workers was extremely moving. It seemed so true, this contact with the real people. I was so moved I had a lump in my throat and could hardly speak . . . When I read "Ballad of the Spanish Civil Guard," the whole theater rose to its feet and shouted, "Long live the poet of the people!" And then I had to undergo more than an hour and a half of people standing in line to shake my hand: artisans, old workers, mechanics, children, students. It was the loveliest act I have experienced in my life. (EC 816)

GRANADA

Lorca's love of the countryside—"I am tied to the land," he once said, "in all my emotions" (*OC* III:526)—is an important element in his character. Equally important is his love of Granada. During his adolescence, Granada was one of the most charming of Spanish provincial capitals. In the 1920s, Gerald Brenan writes (230), it was

a quiet, sedate, self-contained country town, little troubled, except during the month of April, by tourists, and very different from the busy expanding place it is today. Its charm lay, of course, in its situation—the immense green plain, the snow-covered mountains, the elms and cypresses of the Alhambra hill, the streams of noisy, hurrying water. These made up something one could not expect to find anywhere else. But the city was also attractive for its own sake. Its streets and squares and vistas and public gardens might be too unobtrusive to catch the passing tourist's eye, but they had plenty in the way of character and variety to offer the resident. And then beyond them there was always the flat green countryside, with its great glittering olive trees and its clear racing streams bordered with blue iris and its groves of poplar poles by the river. There was a lyrical quality about the place, an elegance of site and detail, of tint and shape, that evoked Tuscany or Umbria rather than the harsh and tawny lion-skin of Spain.

More than a lyrical "setting" to be appreciated and savored, more than an exquisite backdrop, Lorca's Granada developed into a fruitful aesthetic idea, an image of his own character, sexuality, and poetry.

Central to that image is a sense of elegy and absence, the melancholy certainty that "life" is temporally and spatially *elsewhere*. Even the natural beauty of the city seemed evanescent and fleeting:

It is an astounding wealth. A wealth that stylizes everything, and where nothing can be captured. Granada is certainly not made to be painted, not even by an Impressionist. It is not pictorial, just as a river is not architectural. Everything flows, plays, and escapes. It is poetic, musical. A city of fugues without a skeleton. Melancholy with vertebrae. That is why I can't live here. (EC 385)

For at least a hundred years, since the days of Washington Irving, Gautier, and Dumas, it had been impossible to see Granada without seeing what it was *not*: what it had ceased to be. This feeling arose, in part, from an awareness of Granada's diminished role in history. The Alhambra had been the last redoubt of the Moors when they were definitively conquered and expelled by the Catholic monarchs in 1492: "a terrible moment," Lorca once remarked, "though they teach us the opposite in school. For an admirable civilization was lost, with poetry, astronomy, architecture, and delicacy that were unequaled in the world" (DS 130). The city's "colorful" Arabic heritage, and especially the legend of the Alhambra, had been the subject of much Spanish poetry, good and bad, from Romantic poets like José de Zorrilla to Modernist ones like Francisco Villaespesa and Salvador Rueda.

Turning his back on a long poetical tradition of sultans and moon-struck Moorish princesses, of turbans and pearly *alcázars*, of geraniums and carnations and Andalusian "passion," Lorca preferred to see Granada in contrast to the sensual urgency and plenitude of Seville ("Seville is Don Juan . . . it is man in the full complexity of his sensuality and emotion" [*SG* 67]). In one of the loveliest of Spain's traditional poems, a ballad steeped in Arab tradition, Granada is addressed as a bride by those who conquered her from the Moors:

If you would let me, Granada,
I would marry you.
As dowry and wedding gift,
I would give you Córdoba and Seville.

But in Lorca's peculiar vision, Granada is not ruled by a feminine spirit. The *genius loci* is the "effeminate archangel" depicted in *St. Michael (Granada)* in *The Gypsy Ballads*. That poem, inspired by a Baroque statue in a local shrine, dwells on the strangeness of an archangel who is usually seen as a warrior, but is dressed, here, like an "ephebe,"

his petticoats frozen
in spangles and lace.

The idea of enclosure—St. Michael is depicted "in the alcove of his tower"—arises often when Lorca speaks of his native city. Granada's timid soul, he insists, has always fled from the forces of nature—wind, driving rain, ocean, stars—and, with a love of small, intimate things, has taken refuge from the elements in the interior courtyard, the convent or monastery, the salon, the tiny chamber, the *carmen* (the walled house and garden thought by the Arabs to be an image of paradise). In his lecture "Paradise Closed to Many, Gardens Open to Few," on the masterpiece of the Baroque poet Pedro Soto de Rojas, Lorca writes that Rojas "encloses himself in his garden, and discovers water jets, dahlias, finches and gentle breezes" (*SG* 65).

To Lorca, Granada is not the unending firmament, but a single star framed in a window. Not the roar of the ocean, but the ocean one hears in a shell:

Someone brought me a seashell.

Singing inside
is a sea from a map.
My heart
fills up with water
and little tiny fish,
silvery, shadowy.

Someone brought me a seashell.

Even the wind seems tamer in Granada than elsewhere. Lorca writes of breezes that "dance on the fingertips" (SG 100), and one of the *Suites* evokes

The breeze
so wavy
like the hair of
certain girls.
Like the oceans made small
in certain old panels.

And all over Granada—and throughout Lorca's poetry—there is water. Not the abundant water of Versailles but "water with tempo, rather than murmur, water that is well measured and precise as it follows its geometrical, rhythmic course through the irrigation ditches" (SG 99).

Water
taps its silver
drum.

Water pent in wells, mortally still in river pools and reflecting ponds, scooped up and lifted on waterwheels, channeled through ditches and subterranean rivers (the paving-over of the Darro River in the early twentieth century left a psychological scar on the city); water pulsing skyward with swordlike movements and "rivers standing up": the water jets of the Generalife.

It would be tempting to gather all these images of Granada into an image of Lorca's sexuality: of his unremitting rejection and fear of heterosexual love. In his work, for example, pent-up water is often a symbol of death, of infertility and sexual frustration. It is in one of the letters—a note to Salvador Dalí's sister Ana María, written after an emotionally liberating vacation by the Mediterranean in Cadaqués—that he comes closest to linking the "tame" water of Granada with sexual repression and denial.

The weather is good, and the señoritas *of Granada go up to their white-washed terraces to see the mountains and not see the ocean . . . In the after-noon they dress in gauze and vaporous satiny things and go down to the promenade where the fountains flow like diamonds and there is an old anguish of roses and amorous melancholy . . . the* señoritas *of Granada have no love for the sea. They have enormous nacar shells with painted sailors and that is the way they see it; and great conch shells in their* salons, *and that is the way they hear it.* (EC 362)

Even the presence of kitsch seems revealing: the useless objects, the "enormous nacar shells with painted sailors" are as sad and deathly as the fragile, untouched bodies of the *señoritas*. It is hardly surprising that the heroine of Lorca's drama *Doña Rosita the Spinster*, an elegy of unrequited love set in turn-of-the-century Granada, is surrounded by useless objects, many of them in miniature.

The case of Doña Rosita, the aging spinster who waits in vain for the return of her lover from America, is paradigmatic. In Lorca's view, the inhabitant of Granada is better suited for meditation than for action. In Granada, "the day has only one immense hour, and that hour is spent drinking water, revolving on the axis of one's cane, and looking at the landscape . . . Two and two are never four in Granada. They are always two and two" (OC III:302).

As a young man, surrounded by a group of brilliant friends—the *tertulia* that gathered for conversation at the Alameda Café—Lorca protested energetically against this sense of historical "uselessness" and inaction. Two especially significant acts of rebellion were the *cante jondo* (deep song) festival he organized with the composer Manuel de Falla in 1922 and the short-lived literary magazine *gallo*, which he founded and directed in 1928.

The festival—an amateur competition designed to defend the aesthetic value of *cante jondo* (the Andalusian folk music also known as *flamenco*) and rescue it from commercial adulteration—created a controversy in the local and national press, for the question of deep song seemed to be bound up with the Spanish identity. Those who opposed it argued that the festival would only reinforce certain gypsyesque stereotypes about Spain and Spanish music. Falla and Lorca made their stand for *cante jondo* not as folklore but as living proof of Granada's "universality." Here, they argued, was an ancient musical tradition, one that had influenced French and Russian composers, from Glinka to Debussy, as well as modern Spaniards, from Albéniz and Granados to Robert Gerhard and Frederic Mompou (*SD* 10). Not even the Alhambra, Falla thought, was as truly universal.

The festival went off smoothly on the Feast of Corpus Christi 1922 but did not lead to the hoped-for renaissance: the commercialization of deep song grew more intense. But Lorca's encounter with *cante jondo* was of incalculable importance to him. It helped him face a variety of aesthetic problems and define his relation to "traditional" art, and it made him meditate for the first time on Granada's (and thus his own) place in Western culture. His experience as an organizer of *gallo* was less rewarding, but this too was a sign of his interest, as a young man, in discovering Granada's "universal meaning." By opening *gallo's* pages to experimental writing (e.g., that of Salvador Dalí) and to essays on contemporary aesthetics, he hoped to encourage his fellow citizens to "love Granada, but with our thought placed on Europe" (*OC* III:190).

ANDALUSIA

Lorca's vision of Granada forms part of a triptych: Granada, Córdoba, and Seville; and he sometimes complained that Granada was the least "Andalusian" of those three cities.

I, who am Andalusian, Andalusian through and through . . . I pine for Málaga, for Córdoba, for Sanlúcar la Mayor, for Algeciras, for Cádiz . . . for all that is intimately Andalusian. The true Granada is the one that no longer exists, the one that now seems dead, under the delirious, greenish gas lamps. The other Andalusia is alive: Málaga, for example. (*EC* 301)

Like Granada, Andalusia is a central image in Lorca's work and an element of his poetics. Even as a young man, he hoped that his poetry would put an end to the dominance of Castile (the arid central region of Spain) in Spanish literature. Of the three greatest living poets, two—Miguel de Unamuno and Antonio Machado—had made their mark as singers of the Castilian countryside and of Castile as a paradigm of the Spanish identity. The third, the Andalusian Juan Ramón Jiménez, who fostered Lorca's career as a young poet, offered an example of just the sort of "Andalusian universality" and literary catholicity to which Lorca himself aspired. Lorca's sense of Andalusian "mission" is apparent as early as the summer of 1922, when it occurs to him for the first time to compose a book of ballads. In July he writes to his friend Melchor Fernández Almagro:

This summer I want to write something calm and serene. I'm thinking of constructing some ballads with lagoons, ballads with mountains, ballads with stars: a limpid, mysterious work like a flower (arbitrary and perfect as a flower), all fragrance! I want to bring out of the shadows the little Arab girls who play in these villages, and to lead astray, in the groves of my lyricism, the ideal figures of the anonymous romancillos [six- and seven-syllable traditional ballads] . . . *This summer, if God helps me with his little doves* [of inspiration], *I will write a popular, extremely Andalusian work. I'm going to travel a bit through these marvelous villages, whose castles and whose people seem never to have existed for poets . . . And enough of Castile!!* (EC 148)

That battle cry—*¡¡Basta ya de Castilla!!*—signals a generational change in Spanish poetry. It is a sign of Lorca's exasperation and boredom with the lingering controversy over the national identity: the debate touched off in 1898 (the year of Lorca's birth) by Spain's humiliating defeat in the Spanish-American War. In his reply, Fernández Almagro applauds the poet's regional pride and complains of what the cult of Castilianism has meant "for the past twenty-five years":

vulgarity, the garbanzo-bean mentality, dust, adobe, teacher training courses . . . How lovely it would be if broken-down, sordid Castile allowed herself to be absorbed by northerners, who would give her strength and avarice, and by southerners, who would give her grace and refinement and the ability to dream. (EC 148)

Some of those hopes were to be realized, not only in Lorca's work but by other poets of his generation. The group of Spanish poets known as the "Generation of 1927" was proudly dominated by Andalusians: Lorca, Vicente Aleixandre, Luis Cernuda, Rafael Alberti, Emilio Prados, Manuel Altolaguirre. "Hegemony of the South," Jorge Guillén called it.

Lorca's image of Andalusia is, first and foremost, that of a historical melting pot, a fusion of diverse cultures: Oriental and Western, Greek and Roman, Arab and gypsy, Christian and Jewish. The poet considered *himself* a repository of these traditions, fancying at times that he had gypsy or Jewish blood. In Andalusia none of these cultural strata seems very far from the surface. Gerald Brenan (137–38) recalls how, in a mountain village in the Granada region in the early 1920s, he once entered a shop to buy some cigarettes "and was handed back with my change some unfamiliar coins.

On examining these at home I saw that they were Punic and Iberian. That is to say, they were the coins of Punic and Iberian cities minted under the Roman

Republic and thus the first coins to be minted in Spain except in the Greek cities of Catalonia.

Lorca's artistic vision of Andalusia is full of that easy interchange between past and present, and temporal *décalage* is a constant in his work. When, in *The Gypsy Ballads*, a blood feud breaks out among gypsies and a man is stabbed to death, one of the bystanders shrugs his shoulders and tells the Civil Guard:

Civil Guardsmen, Sirs,
it's the same as always:
four Romans are dead
and five Carthaginians.

Other poems play upon the same anachronistic mingling of past and present cultures (see PALIMPSESTS). The Córdoba portrayed in *St. Raphael* is a palimpsest of Arab and Roman cultures, and the Roman element extends all the way to the Baroque poet Don Luis de Góngora. In *Thamar and Amnon*, the gypsies (who came to Spain from Hindustan in the fifteenth century) mingle with biblical characters in a parched Holy Land that resembles Andalusia. In *Joke about Don Pedro*, Seville is confounded with Bethlehem.

There are certain other "timeless" elements that Lorca would identify both in the Andalusian character and in his own poetry. In the lecture on *cante jondo* he admires the "magnificent pantheism" of the traditional Andalusian lyric. "With deep spiritual feeling, the Andalusian entrusts Nature with his most intimate treasure, completely confident of being listened to" (*SD* 16). That intimacy is found throughout Lorca's work, from *Weathervane*, where he addresses the wind, to *Qasida of the Dark Doves*:

Through the laurel's branches
I saw two dark doves.
One was the sun,
the other the moon.
Little neighbors, I called,
where is my tomb?
In my tail, said the sun.
In my throat, said the moon.

An emotional extremism, an obsession with death, and an almost Oriental sense of fatalism are other elements Lorca deemed "Andalusian." "Our people cross their arms in prayer, look at the stars, and wait in vain for a sign of salvation," he writes (*SD* 11). But for all its gravity, Andalusia is also the domain of *gracia* and wit. In reading one of his own ballads, Lorca notices with satisfaction how "drama and dance are balanced on an intelligent needle of jest or irony" (*DS* 107).

MADRID

Granada and Andalusia are never more "present" to Lorca than when he remembers them from Madrid. At the age of twenty, he traveled to the capital to enroll in the Residencia de Estudiantes (Students' Residence), an experimental college, modeled on Oxford and Cambridge, designed to nurture a cultural elite to steer Spanish society toward liberal ideals. There, for the next several years, he lived in close contact with some of the best Spanish musicians, poets, painters, and scientists of his day. Rafael Alberti and Luis Buñuel were two of his closest friends, and the greatest writers of an earlier generation—Juan Ramón Jiménez, Miguel de Unamuno, and José Ortega y Gasset—returned often to the Residencia and supported its cultural activities. A stream of foreign visitors, some of whom Lorca heard and met—H. G. Wells, André Breton, G. K. Chesterton, Albert Einstein, Madame Curie, Paul Valéry, Howard Carter, Le Corbusier—reminded the "Residentes" that Spain was once again in intellectual dialogue with the rest of Europe.

In Madrid, Lorca witnessed an extraordinary flowering of arts and letters, the greatest since the age of Cervantes, Calderón, and Lope de Vega. Guillén (xxxviii) has recalled with nostalgia the "laborious hum" of the capital before the Civil War, and the rebirth of Spanish culture, both at home and abroad, from Pablo Ruiz Picasso to Juan Gris and Joan Miró, to Juan Ramón Jiménez; from Santiago Ramón y Cajal (the distinguished biologist) to Ramón María del Valle-Inclán to Ramón Gómez de la Serna.

It was at the Residencia that Lorca met Salvador Dalí, initiating a lasting friendship that deepened into passion and profoundly altered both men's vision of art. In his *Secret Life* (176), the painter recalled his first impressions of the poet:

[T]*he personality of Federico García Lorca produced an immense impression on me. The poetic phenomenon in its entirety and "in the raw" presented itself before me suddenly in flesh and bone, confused, blood-red, viscous and sublime, quivering with a thousand fires of darkness and of subterranean biology, like all matter endowed with the originality of its own form. I reacted, and immediately I adopted a rigorous attitude against the "poetic cosmos." I would say nothing that was indefinable, nothing of which a "contour" or a "law" could not be es-*

tablished . . . And when I felt the incendiary and communicative form of the poetry of the great Federico rise in wild, dishevelled flames I tried to beat them down with the olive branch of my premature anti-Faustian old age.

The first effects of Dalí's painting upon Lorca's poetics can be gauged by *Ode to Salvador Dalí*, in which Lorca praises his friend's unsentimental perspicacity with respect to nature: a poetics of classical "objectivity," a norm inimical to any sort of Romantic mystery. Interestingly, the art of Dalí drew Lorca both in the direction of classicism and, later, toward Surrealism. Among the fruits of that friendship are texts as diverse as *The Siren and the Carabineer* and *Two Lovers Murdered by a Partridge*.

Dividing his time between Granada and the Residencia, pursuing, by fits and starts, his studies at the University of Granada both in law and in philosophy and letters, Lorca wrote incessantly: poems, narrations, puppet plays, the libretto of a comic opera (for Manuel de Falla), dialogues, prose poems, occasional newspaper articles, memorable lectures on Góngora and on traditional song.

His career as a writer was a source of worry to his parents, especially to his father, Don Federico, an intensely practical man, who was always pushing his eldest son to learn something useful. Don Federico was not sure at first of his son's literary talent (he consulted with numerous friends before paying for the publication of *Impressions and Landscapes* and *Book of Poems*), and once his son moved to Madrid, he worried about Federico's friendships with stage directors, artists, actors, and actresses. At one point he seems to have ordered his son back to Granada from the Residencia de Estudiantes. Federico's correspondence with his parents throws much light on a problem that troubled the poet throughout his life: his sense of being "good for nothing but poetry," and his dependence on his parents. To his father's order to return to Granada, Federico replies:

I know perfectly well you want me by your side, but . . . what am I supposed to do in Granada? Listen to a lot of foolish conversation, and be the butt of envy and dirty tricks (naturally, this only happens to men of talent). Not that any of this matters to me—thank God, I am very much above it—but it is very, very annoying. One needn't argue with fools. And now, in Madrid, certain very respectable people are discussing me . . . and someday I will probably have a great name in literature . . . In Madrid I work, read and study. The atmosphere is marvelous. I see almost none of the people (and they are many) who come to visit me. When I go out, it is only to see Martínez Sierra [the playright and impresario] and go to the offices of España, *with a group of strong young intellectuals. But the real reason I can't leave Madrid isn't my books—though that is a powerful reason—but that I am in a* residence for students, *a place that* isn't just a boarding house. *It is extremely difficult to enter and if I myself managed to get in, thanks to my own talents and friendships and* simpatía, *beating out TEN other people who wanted to enter . . . [how can I leave?] . . . I beg you from the bottom of my heart to leave me here at least until the end of the year, and then I'll leave with my books published, and my conscience very clear, after having battled the Philistines and defended art: pure Art, true Art. You cannot change me. I was born a poet and an artist, just as others are born lame or blind, or handsome. Leave me my wings, I can assure you I will know how to use them . . . And don't consult about all this with friends who are lawyers, doctors, veterinarians, etc.—mediocre, nasty little people—but with Mother and the children. I believe I am right. You know how much I love you.* (EC 73–74)

Lorca's mother, whom he adored, was far more understanding and seldom needled him about his literary career: "For me [your literature] is more important than all the careers in the world. Better said, it is the best career of all, both for you and for me." She was a wonderful confidante, as aware of her son's genius as she was of his need to "acquire some culture" (*culturarte*); as eager to see his works in print as she was skeptical about his constant assurances that he was "studying hard." "I can see you've made yourself into a real student, at least in appearance," she tells him ironically, shortly after his move to Madrid.

You know that that way we'll stop bothering you. For my part, child, I must tell you I can't wait to read something of yours in print. In your handwriting, one can't read your poems without hitting a false note every other second. And frankly, one can't get any taste out of them. (EC 87)

Doña Vicenta's insistence that Lorca publish his poetry (he was often reluctant to see his works "dead on the page") is everywhere. She does what she can to soothe his writerly frustrations, reminds Federico not to expect understanding from people with old-fashioned ideas about poetry, and tries to reassure her husband that their son is going to amount to something as a writer.

What I would like you to tell me about is what you're thinking of doing with all the precious things you've got tucked away. Surely they aren't just to build up an archive. If all this is a secret, well and good. But if not, tell me and no one else, write me a little note and I'll keep it to myself and not show anyone. (*Ibid.*)

Always, the same advice: aim high and work hard.

You mustn't content yourself with the admiration of a few. That isn't enough. Many, many people must know of you—everyone . . . But you should give everything the time it requires, no more, so that you aren't, for example, waiting around for Tagore to arrive [he was to visit the Residencia] and neglecting your own things . . . As for your friends, I beg you not to lose more time with them than you need to rest. (EC 109–10)

The popular and critical success of *Songs* and *The Gypsy Ballads* (the latter brought out in 1928 by one of the most important publishing houses in Spain) must have delighted his parents. The *Ballads* (which can now be read in Czech, Japanese, Latin, and Esperanto) would become the best-selling book of poetry in twentieth-century Spain. But the success of the book (harshly criticized by Dalí and Buñuel) only depressed the poet himself, and a year after their publication he embarked on a year-long trip to New York and Havana.

Lorca arrived in New York in June 1929 and enrolled in English classes at Columbia University's summer school, but he spent much of the next eight months exploring the city with a group of Spanish and Mexican friends, working on his plays, writing a film script, and composing the poems published posthumously as *Poet in New York*. During that first summer he made an excursion to Eden Mills, Vermont, where he visited an American friend, Philip Cummings. In the fall he witnessed the crash of the stock market—an event that forever darkened his vision of the United States—and in spring 1930 spent two happy months in Cuba before returning to Spain.

Published in Mexico and New York in 1940 four years after Lorca's death, *Poet in New York* marks an abrupt change in his poetic work. Abandoning the shorter lines, rural ambience, and stylized imitation of popular verse that had characterized much of his early poetry, he creates a Whitmanesque protagonist who denounces the evils of modern civilization, above all in the United States: man's indifference to nature; the exploitation of certain parts of society (for example, the blacks); loss of religious faith; and indifference to the poetic word. In *Poet in New York*, a poetic "subject"—both prophet and redeemer—takes a dark lyrical journey through New York, Vermont, and Cuba, and predicts the apocalyptic destruction of urban society. The pain and emptiness mentioned so insistently by the protagonist of this book affect not only him—poet severed from the world of his childhood and stripped of his identity—but entire social groups, and mankind in general, a "world alone in a lonely sky."

The division of the book into ten sections creates the narrative illusion of a trip: the protagonist arrives in New York and becomes aware of his solitude; celebrates black people and condemns their oppressors; is overwhelmed by urban crowds; escapes to the New England countryside, only to encounter death and solitude once again; returns to the city, denouncing it anew; and finally flees to Cuba, where he unearths childhood memories and writes a euphoric "son," a poem based on Afro-Cuban dance rhythms. Along with FLIGHT FROM NEW YORK (TWO WALTZES TOWARD CIVILIZATION), which precedes the trip to Cuba, *Poet in New York* includes two of Lorca's odes. One, a paean to Walt Whitman, explores themes of homosexuality and homoeroticism, and the other, *Cry to Rome (From the Tower of the Chrysler Building)*, excoriates the Catholic Church for its indifference to the suffering of those who most need its help:

the blacks who empty the spittoons,
the boys who tremble beneath the pallid terror of executives,
the women who drown in mineral oil,
the multitudes with their hammers, violins, or clouds.

The book's faint narrative structure was reinforced by Lorca in a lecture-reading (*PNY* 185–201), given for the first time in 1932, where he interprets his own book, perhaps too narrowly, as a protest against mechanized, corrupt American society devoid of spiritual greatness. A series of delightful letters written by Lorca to his family from New York and Cuba (*PNY* 205–86) throws further light on some of the poems and cautions us against reading *Poet in New York* as autobiography.

At thirty-one he returned to Spain with a will to reform the Spanish theater: to foster amateur groups and repertory companies that would train new actors and find new audiences; to adapt and revive the classics; and, by means of his own writing, to remind the contemporary theater of its need for poetry, and of its roots in Greek tragedy, commedia dell'arte, Romanticism, and traditional art. He spoke frequently of the need to free the theater from the dictates of the middle class. He was listened to with interest, but time was running out.

The triumph of *Blood Wedding* in Madrid earned Lorca an invitation to Buenos Aires, and when he returned to Spain for the second time, after a wildly successful tour of Argentina and Uruguay in 1933–34, his plays and poems were attracting attention in France, Italy, and the United States. In the final, busiest years of his life, he wrote a cycle of love sonnets and his two gravest elegies: *Lament for*

Ignacio Sánchez Mejías (on the death in the bullring of a beloved friend) and the collection published posthumously as *The Tamarit Divan*. Regarded as Spain's most promising young playwright, Lorca had the feeling that his career in the theater was only beginning.

Then, in the summer of 1936, during the early days of the Spanish Civil War, the thirty-eight-year-old poet was hunted down by right-wing forces in Granada who accused him of being a "Russian spy" and of having "done more damage with his pen than others had with their guns" (Gibson, *Federico García Lorca*, 458). On the night of August 18–19, he was driven into the countryside and, with the authorization of one of Franco's generals, executed by a firing squad.

Elegy

"I am the enormous shadow of my tears," Lorca wrote in *The Tamarit Divan*, and the line is a splendid definition of his own work. He is the greatest of Spain's elegiac poets.

Elegy contrasts presence and absence. All language, of course, involves these terms: a present sign invokes an absent referent. But not all poets are as poignantly aware of this duality as Lorca. In this, of course, he is a Romantic, the poetic disciple of Gustavo Adolfo Bécquer, whose aesthetics rest on the conviction that no language will ever capture poetic emotion.

The comparison of presence and absence can adopt a number of forms: one contrasts what *is* and what *was*; how things *are* and how they *ought* to be (elegy often bears a formal resemblance to satire); what is *here* and what is *there* (the elegiac epistle). Whatever its terms, elegy compares modes of being. It feeds on desire: on the yearning to have what is absent or does not exist. And desire and elegy are the essence of Lorca's poetry. The poetic expression of desire is *itself* a presence of sorts. The verbal object—the memorable suggestion that there is something absent which we cannot apprehend—is accepted, by readers of elegiac poetry, *in lieu of* that "something." The poems are "here" to console us; their object eludes us.

Where, exactly, are the sources of Lorca's elegy? His earliest writing has its roots in a spiritual movement known in the Hispanic world as "Modernism," which begins in the last decade of the nineteenth century and expires around 1920. The characteristics of that movement are not easy to define with any precision. Valle-Inclán called it a "vivid yearning for personality, a desire to express sensations rather than ideas," and Juan Ramón Jiménez thought of Modernism as an enthusiasm for beauty. A passion for formal perfection in the tradition of the French Parnassians led to fresh experimentation with rhythm, meter, and rhyme. The language of Spanish poetry moved further from common speech than it had since the time of Góngora, and poetry was seen, more than ever, as a sacred way of life, the province of a chosen few; a holy "priesthood" in the midst of a rampantly materialistic bourgeoisie. Beauty was sought in the exotic, imaginary places that seemed to have pursued it as a way of life: the Orient, classical Greece, the world of Versailles or of modern Paris, Islamic Spain, the Middle Ages.

To the adolescent Lorca, who had come to literature from music, poetry seemed less a matter of verbal artistry or a quest for truth than a means of self-expression: a way of baring what Verlaine (one of his favorite poets) had called the "*paysage choisi*" of his own soul. Characteristically, he titles an early series of prose pieces *Estados sentimentales* (States of Emotion), another *Místicas* (Mystical Writings), and his first book, a collection of prose about his travels through Spain, *Impresiones y paisajes* (*Impressions and Landscapes*).

From his very earliest works, his tone is elegiac. Again and again, the young poet, who declares himself a "Romantic," a "redeemer of infinities," a "knight-errant of the spirit," a quixotic "dreamer," discovers, with a twinge of melancholy, that *nothing is as it should be* (the gist of all his poetry until 1920 or 1921). On more than one occasion he begs his readers not to laugh at him as he reveals his anguish. "I am a great Romantic," he writes apologetically to a friend in 1918, "and this is my greatest pride. In a century of zeppelins and of stupid deaths, I sit at my piano and weep as I dream of the mist of Handel, and I write verses that are very much my *own*, singing the same way to Christ as to Buddha, to Mohammad as to Pan" (*EC* 50). Only the world of nature, to which he draws near with "the Franciscan tenderness of [the French poet Francis] Jammes," and the works of a few great artists—Victor Hugo, Beethoven, Chopin, St. Teresa of Ávila, etc.—offer him any solace.

In the hundreds of essays and poems he composed between 1917 and 1918, he posits his faith in a spiritual "absolute" for which he can find no adequate name, but toward which all artistic endeavor, especially music and literature, seems to tend. The two most basic dualities in his early work are the struggle between the spirit and the flesh, and that between the "artist" and society (that "jungle of hatred and horror"). These terms, obviously, are closely related. The artist believes in the realm of the spirit ("the infinite," "the impossible," "the ideal," "poetry," "beauty," etc.), while society does not. Society is a torment to Lorca and to other "chaste, sublime dreamers" who accompany him.

Am I to blame for being a Romantic and a dreamer in a life that is all materialism and stupidity? Am I to blame for having a heart, and for having been born among people interested only in comfort and in money? What stigma has passion placed on my brow? I would like to pass by sighing, and not have anyone even notice me. For when others look at me with their superior smiles, their glances sully me. For my heart and my spirit are very high, and my eyes flee from theirs to contemplate the water, the clouds, or to look into my own heart. ("Meditación apasionada y sentimental," *PrI* 198)

In another essay, from the spring of 1917, he asks:

Who is it that is laughing? Who are you? I despise you all, I rise above your paltry thoughts. I am greater than you . . . Your hearts are full of indifference and your brains are taken up by mean and miserable things [while I] am made of impossible love . . . In life, the great problem is spiritual isolation, for men are so cruel that they love to embitter the lives of the few people who think and feel . . . There are many who scoff at love and at art, and these are the ones who achieve happiness on earth. Those who have a fiery heart and love truly . . . those are the ones who reap only sorrow and the unhappiness of the other life. I am one of them. And I will lean on the shepherd's staff of art, and will advance until my eyes open to the truth. ("Estado sentimental: La primavera" [State of Emotion: Spring], *PrI* 181)

To young Lorca, literature is the confession of an ineffable, incurable longing: "I only know . . . that my heart . . . has huge, impossible desires. My malady is one which cannot be cured." Literature is the melancholy record of one's failure to evade the cruelty of society, to conquer the flesh, to understand the meaning of human life, and to capture the spiritual absolute. Poetry resides less in the poem than in the heart: it is less a verbal construct than the invocation of things inherently "spiritual." Lorca himself identifies some of them in an essay of June 1917:

Fields full of melancholy and of hushed music . . . And old mansions with their coats of arms and their cloisters, and convents with their souls doing penance for carnal love, and fallen women with their nuances of Chopin, and children who peer at the infinite with their chaste eyes, and old musical instruments waiting for the hand that can make them speak, and the ruins of past civilizations, caressed lovingly by ivy and moss, and the moon with its painful clarity, and the day and the night and the skies and a page of the Bible . . . as long as all this exists, there will be dreamers in pain, and there will be lan-

guidness and there will be sighs, and civilization will pass by without staining our hearts. ("Mística en que se habla de la inspiración y de la tristeza de la ausencia" [Mystical Treatment of Inspiration and of the Sadness of Absence], *PrI* 111–12)

This vision of poetry prevails in *Book of Poems* (1921), an anthology (prepared with the help of his brother and paid for by his parents) of the best of his early work. Naturally, poetic feeling and beauty are treated as "givens," rather than illusions deliberately produced by written texts. Certain states of mind and certain natural phenomena (the sunset, autumn, music, the water of a fountain, roses, honey, the laurel tree, rain falling on provincial gardens) are intrinsically *poetic*: first, because they have been imbued with literary prestige by the post-Romantic poets (Baudelaire, Francis Jammes, Bécquer, Verlaine, Rubén Darío, the early Juan Ramón Jiménez) whom Lorca read as a young man, and second, because all of them awaken a yearning for the spiritual. In accordance with Hispanic Modernism, Lorca's earliest idea of the poet is of a seer, a medium, an idealistic, solitary figure embittered with "society," closer to the world of nature than to the world of men and uniquely able to feel the mysterious anguish of all things.

The poet is the medium
of Nature
who explains her greatness
by means of words.

The poet understands
all that is incomprehensible,
and things that hate each other
he calls friends.

He knows that all paths
are impossible
and thus he walks them
calmly in the night.
(*OC* I:200)

As in the juvenilia of many poets, Lorca's vision of elegy involves the comparison of personal past and present. Struggling with adolescence, the poet complains of having lost the faith and innocence of his childhood. In one poem, never published, he prays to escape from adolescence and to return to childhood:

Que la copa del semen
se derrame del todo,
que no quede en mi carne
ni sangre ni calor.
Quiero ser como un niño,
rosado y silencioso
que en los muslos de armiño
de su madre amoroso
escuchará un diálogo
de una estrella con Dios.
("Oración" [Prayer], *PI* 265)

(Let the goblet of my semen / spill over and empty completely, / so that my body will be left / without warmth or blood. / I want to be like a child / rosy and silent, / who, in the ermine thighs / of his loving mother, / can listen to a star / speaking with God.)

The matter of his own sexual development caused Lorca much anguish and made him feel even more distant from society, deepening the elegiac melancholy mentioned earlier. In May 1918, the month and year he writes the lines just quoted, he confides to his friend Adriano del Valle:

I am a poor, impassioned and silent fellow who, very nearly like the marvelous Verlaine, bears within a lily impossible to water, and to the foolish eyes of those who look upon me I seem to be a very red rose with the sexual tint of an April peony, which is not my heart's truth . . . My image and my verses give the impression of something very passionate . . . and yet, at the bottom of my soul, there's an enormous desire to be very childlike, very poor, very hidden. I see before me many problems, many entrapping eyes, many conflicts in the battle between head and heart and all my sentimental flowering seeks to enter a golden garden and I try hard because I like paper dolls and the playthings of childhood, and at times I lie down on my back on the floor to play games with my kid sister (she's my delight) . . . but the phantom that lives within us and hates us pushes me down the path . . . with each day that passes I have another doubt and another sadness. Sadness of the enigma of myself! (Selected Letters, tr. Gershator, 2)

Part of that "enigma" lay in Lorca's sexuality. When, exactly, the poet acknowledged to himself that he was gay, no one knows. But the juvenilia suggest that he was painfully aware, as early as the spring of 1918, that he was not like others of his age, and that he was tormented by the very idea of sex. In an essay written that March, he wonders rebelliously why one has to feel sexual desire at all:

Why is the flesh love? I don't know . . . I can only say that if my heart bleeds, it is because of that. If my eyes cry, it is because of that. If my soul resembles a withered flower, it is because of that.

Revealingly, the essay turns into a dialogue between Plato, who has "taken to heart what Socrates proclaimed," and Sappho, whose "great, ardent soul" yearns for the impossible. "I am the one," Plato remarks, "who loves ephebes."

Their breasts may be rigid, but they have the smell of genius . . . Their hair may be short, but they have the light and the aroma of oranges in their mouths . . . Sappho! Sappho! You are my sister in spirit, you are to your sex what I am to mine.

And Sappho replies:

Not all the maidens of Lesbos, so blonde and white, love me, but I love them. When I possess one of them, when I exhaust her with caresses, I am stung by the desire for another . . . They are so sweet and so warm . . . You cannot understand this sort of love . . . but I do . . . so much so . . . that I could not live without the caress of breasts . . . But I am so insatiable that my lovers fear my nights of furious passion. For them it is a step toward death. ("El poema de la carne. Nostalgia olorosa y ensoñadora" [Poem of the Flesh. Fragrant, Dreamlike Nostalgia], *PrI* 245–50)

Longing to escape the torment of sex—"the eternal preoccupation and the cause of all of humanity's terrible evils"—the young poet wishes he could turn into plant or star, breeze or butterfly; at certain moments "I yearn to be a flower, and to feel the ineffable bliss of having stamens and pistils, and to enjoy the reproductive act in a spiritual way" ("Mistica de la melancolía" [Mystical Treatise on Melancholy], *PrI* 72). More frequently he longs for the "impossible" or "distant woman," the virginal being, enamored of the ideal, who has had no experience of sex. He is always discovering that no happiness is possible for him, that no woman will ever satisfy his desire. "The woman you love is of white light, she is the epitome of beauty, the impossible."
    Melancholy, ennui, resentment of society: all these feelings are pres-

ent in *Book of Poems*, the "narrator" of which feels uniquely and hopelessly alienated: a modern-day Cyrano, Quijote, or Pierrot:

> *Weeping,*
> *I go down the street,*
> *grotesque, without solution,*
> *with the sadness of Cyrano*
> *and Quijote,*
> > *redeeming*
> *infinite impossibles*
> *with the rhythm of the clock.*

Rhetoric has clouded the voice he had as a child:

> *There is an ache in the flesh of my heart,*
> *in the flesh of my soul.*
> > *And when I speak*
> *my words bob in the air*
> *like corks on water.*

The very knowledge that he is a poet is enough to ruin his communion with the natural world:

> *Oh, what sorrow not to have*
> *the happy man's fantastical*
> *shirt—a tanned skin,*
> *the sun's carpet.*

> *(Flocks of letters*
> *wheel round my eyes.)*

> *Oh, what sorrow the ancient*
> *sorrow of poetry,*
> *this sticky sorrow*
> *so far from clean water!*

By the time *Book of Poems* appeared in print (summer 1921), Lorca had already surmounted this initial vision of elegiac poetry. In *New Songs* he had looked forward to a change in his poetics, praying for

> *A luminous and tranquil song*
> *full of thought,*

virgin to sadness and anguish,
virgin to reverie.

What would occupy him for the next two years, until 1923, were the possibilities, almost unexplored until then in Spanish poetry, of a new form: the sequence of short related poems. Drawing a structural idea from music, he had begun to work on his *Suites*. The title alludes vaguely both to the suites of modern composers like Debussy and to those of Renaissance or Baroque music: years later, Lorca spoke of gathering these sequences into a book entitled *El libro de las diferencias* (*The Book of Differences*), an unequivocal allusion to the theme and variations of Spanish Renaissance composers and instrumentalists like Alonso Mudarra, Luis de Narváez, and Antonio de Cabezón.

With exceptions like BARRAGE OF FIREWORK POEMS few of the suites really resemble a musical theme and variations. The "formal" intuition that underlies all of them is that a particular phenomenon—*cante jondo*, the sunset, the ocean, streams, the sky, stars, a village fair—can be better apprehended in a *series* of "moments," "etchings," "vignettes," or "views" than in discursive poetry of the sort that had prevailed in *Book of Poems*. Some of the series are temporal: one of the earliest, SUMMER HOURS, describes the coming of night, almost hour by hour, and the most ambitious of the entire series, IN THE GARDEN OF THE LUNAR GRAPEFRUITS, narrates an adolescent's voyage, from night until daybreak, into the unexplored "garden" or "forest" of his creative psyche. Others (e.g., MIRROR SUITE) are sets of aphorisms in the manner being cultivated in prose by writers like Gómez de la Serna, Juan Ramón Jiménez, and José Bergamín. Throughout the book, one senses a longing for concision and structural simplicity. Lorca's revision of *Bat*, from July 1921, is a dramatic example of the change in his poetics. Here are the first and second versions, side by side:

Bat

The bat
(elixir of shadow)
dissolves in the air.

Without bats
There would be no night.

Bat

The bat,
elixir of shadow,
true lover of the star,
nips at the heels of day.

They silence
its color
and make it
visible.

They nip the heel
of day
and awaken the dog
and the frog

. . . and they are the true
lovers of the star.

The first version "defines" the bat, the second sees *a* bat, at a specific moment. By the time Lorca revised this poem, he had discovered both the sequences of haiku (a form much discussed in literary reviews of the early 1920s and introduced into Hispanic literature by the Mexican Juan José Tablada) and the lyrics of the *cante jondo* repertoire, of which he would write, a year later, "it is wondrous and strange how the anonymous popular poet can condense all the highest emotional moments in human life into a three- or four-line stanza" (*SD* 11). Neither the haiku nor the deep-song repertoire has much to do with the wistful tonality of many of the suites, but both these forms had given Lorca a new glimpse of the possibilities of the short poem, then being explored abroad by Pound, e. e. cummings, William Carlos Williams, and many others.

The earnest melancholy of *Book of Poems* and the belief in the inherent poeticity of certain phenomena are permuted in *Suites* into gentle irony and mock sentimentality (e.g., WHITE ALBUM) as though the poet were smiling at the poetic persona he had worn in his earliest work. The natural world is still at the center of his attention, but it is treated more lightheartedly, as in THREE PRINTS OF THE SKY:

The stars
don't have a lover—

doesn't matter how pretty
the stars are!

They will wait for
their heartthrob—

to carry them off to
his perfect Venezia.

In *Suites* Lorca is at play with the natural elements, whimsically per-
sonifying them, or capturing them in miniature, true to the tradition
he thought characteristic of Granada, where people look at the world
"through the wrong end of the telescope" (SG 64).

   With these formal and tonal changes came a new vision of elegy.
Book of Poems involved a rather conventional elegiac contrast of what
is and what *was*. But the most interesting of the *Suites* contrast what *is*
and what *might have been.* This exploration of potential, unrealized
modes of being is developed on several levels. On the one hand, the
poet calls into question the ability of language to capture "reality."
Why, for example, must there be seven days of the week, and seven
colors?

(Why weren't there nine?
Why weren't there twenty?)

On the other hand, he confronts his own possibilities as a person:
modes of being that he himself has failed to realize. The adolescent
narrator of the LUNAR GRAPEFRUITS cycle sets out to explore

the ecstatic world, where all my possibilities live & all my lost landscapes. I
want to get in there, cold & sharp, to find a garden of flowerless seeds & blind
theories: in search of a love I never had but that once was mine.

In the "forest" of his poetic imagination, the narrator dreams of re-
turning to his "source," and recovering the state of pure potentiality
that existed before he was born (e.g., THE RETURN). All that we do
involves choice: exclusion of one possibility and realization of another.
Each step on the road of life turns into a crossroads: into a plexus of
roads not taken.

And steadily our feet
keep walking & creating
—like enormous fans—
these roads in embryo.

Dumb, embryonic life is imbued with the same awareness of potential
being.

Each seed thinks up
a genealogical tree—
covers the whole sky
with its stalks & roots.

Lost possibilities beckon to the narrator: the child he has not engendered, the woman he has not married, the wedding ring he might have worn. Everything around him exhibits the same poignant elegiac dividedness of being: reality and lost possibility. The minute one closes one's eyes to the colors and forms of the material world, one senses all that *might* have been. In the "garden"

The air's smeared over with
improbable vegetations.
Black & heavy branches.
Cinder-colored roses.

Like the poetic sequence, this sort of metaphysical elegy was something new to Spanish poetry (though it was later cultivated memorably by Jorge Luis Borges), and through the summer of 1923, Lorca was truly absorbed in his work and quite aware of its novelty and strangeness.

Over the next few years, other poetic sequences, ballads, and short lyrical poems poured from Lorca's pen, and his vision of elegy was modified still further. By 1926, five years had gone by since his first book, his parents were growing ever more impatient with his failure to publish (for the most part, his poems were transmitted orally, among an ever-widening circle of friends and enthusiasts), and he decided to winnow his manuscripts and distribute his poems in books.

The first to be published was *Songs*, a carefully assembled collection of seventy-seven lyrical poems written between 1921 and 1926, an anthology designed to show off, as Lorca once said, "all the strings of my lyre." Some of the poems in *Songs* were pulled from the unpublished manuscripts of *Suites*, and, naturally, the two books have similar themes. Like *Suites*, *Songs* is organized in sequences, though most of them were formed a posteriori rather than at the moment of composition, with one poem leading organically to another.

In *Songs*, Lorca's elegy crystallizes into an evocation of longing without object. The sign seems more "present" than before, in part because it is stunningly "concrete"; abstraction is carefully avoided. And the indeterminacy of the referent—the object of the poet's longing—makes it seem more "absent" than ever before.

Few poets are as inimical to abstraction as Lorca. One might say of him what he wrote of Góngora: "His fantasy counts on his five bodily senses; they obey him blindly, like five colorless slaves, and do not cheat him as they do other mortals" (DS 73). Abstract ideas—love, death, fatalism, sadness, desperation—are personified or qualified by adjectives and nouns that bring them into sensorial existence: "white-threaded sadness," "sweet rage," "deaf-mute weariness," "pomegranate-colored violence," "red-crested blasphemy." Emotions are almost always described as physiological sensations: the "fears of fine sand" one feels in the presence of the Civil Guard, or "the ivy of a shiver" of eroticism:

Amnon is softly moaning
on the sheets' cool chill.
The ivy of a shiver
covers burning flesh.

The same permutation from feeling to physiology is present in Lorca's dramatic works. In *Blood Wedding*, for instance, Leonardo describes his jealousy on hearing that his beloved will marry another:

The silver pins of your wedding
were making my blood turn black.
The dream was filling my flesh
with bitter, choking weeds.   (Tr. Dewell and Zapata, 59)

The critic Miguel García-Posada (OC 42) has noticed how Lorca corrects himself whenever he feels himself drifting toward abstraction. In an early draft of *Ballad of the Moon Moon*, for example, he had written:

Through the olive grove
came the dreamy gypsies.

The final version turns the gypsies into two of their essential elements:

Bronze and dream, the gypsies
Cross the olive grove.

Thus does the intangible—dream, the days, the sky, the breeze, song, the voice, the soul—come within reach of touch and sight.

Five voices answered,
as round as rings.

★

Soul,
turn orange-colored,
Soul,
turn the color of love.

Desire, here, can almost be touched. One remembers *Ode to Salvador Dalí:* "Your fancy [or fantasy] reaches only as far as your hands."

Robert Bly (101) once remarked that, like a small child, Lorca is always saying "what he wants, what he desires, what barren women desire, what water desires, what gypsies desire, what a bull desires just before he dies, what brothers and sisters desire." A part of Lorca's appeal is that the object of his desire is never specified. From *Songs* to *The Tamarit Divan,* his poetry tells of an uncentered, unsatisfiable longing. When the object is most clearly specified, Lorca will call attention to its ultimate indeterminacy. For all its sensual immediacy, Lorca's poetry is entirely alien to the spirit of *carpe diem,* for there is nothing to hold fast to, nothing but the poem itself, and the lingering ache of desire.

One image of that longing is the *Pena* referred to in the lyrics of the traditional deep song: a pain caused not only by death or by unreciprocated love but by hidden things. *The Gypsy Ballads,* Lorca would write, "have just one character":

Pain, dark and big as the summer sky, who percolates through the bone marrow and the sap of trees and has nothing to do with melancholy, nostalgia, or any other affliction or disease of the soul, being an emotion more heavenly than earthly. Andalusian pain, which is the struggle of the loving intelligence with the incomprehensible mystery that surrounds it. (DS 105)

That pain without object is already alluded to in *Poem of the Deep Song,* where Lorca says of the guitar:

It weeps for distant
things.
Hot Southern sands
yearning for white camellias.
Weeps arrow without target
evening without morning
and the first dead bird
on the branch.

In the *Ballads* it is personified by Soledad Montoya, who suffers without knowing why, saying only that her pain wells up from a "hidden source." Like the gypsy girl in *Sleepwalking Ballad*, Soledad seems to have vainly awaited the return of her lover. But as if insisting that *no* grief can be fully explained, Lorca avoids assigning any "cause" to her anguish. The same occurs in *Rider's Song*, in the well-known verses on Córdoba:

> Córdoba.
> Distant and lonely.
>
> Black pony, large moon,
> in my saddlebag, olives.
> Well as I know the roads,
> I shall never reach Córdoba.

The poet tells us neither the reason for that journey nor *why* it will not be completed. Here, as everywhere else in Lorca's work, yearning is neither explained nor fulfilled. It is only that things long to be "something else":

> Song would like to be light . . .
> ★
> In tears, the moon says:
> I want to be an orange.
> ★
> There are mountains
> that want to be
> water
> & that conjure up stars
> over their shoulders . . .
>
> And there are mountains
> that want to have
> wings
> & that conjure up clouds.

The horse longs to be a bee, and the bee a dog. Even the rose, epitome of tranquillity, searches for something that cannot be specified.

> The rose
> was not looking for the dawn:

almost eternal on its stem,
it looked for something else.

The *Tamarit Divan*, in which *Qasida of the Rose* appears, is the last
will and testament of an elegiac poet: the grave utterance of unsatisfied
desire in the shadow of death. The poet evokes a bitter love affair that
has all but ended and, as though speaking from the Garden of Gethse-
mane, anticipates and resigns himself to his own passion and death: a
death dark or luminous, alone or accompanied, but one that cannot be
avoided. In the *Divan*, love and death are all but indistinguishable: the
"bitter root" of all existence, the one trailing off inexplicably into the
other. To love what is fleeting is only to be reminded of death:

There is no one who can kiss
without feeling the smile of those without faces;
there is no one who can touch
an infant and forget the immobile skulls of horses.

Under the "lukewarm roses" of the nuptial bed, "the dead men moan,
awaiting their turn." Only death can still the poet's longing:

Everything else all passes away.
Now blush without name. Perpetual star.
Everything else is something else: sad wind,
while the leaves flee, whirling in flocks.

An Evocation of Style

Lorca's elegy is often an evocation of style. One of the hallmarks of his
art is its stylistic plurality: its persistent allusion to, and mimicry of,
other styles and other manners. He seems the most "direct" of poets,
and yet his work is elaborately "mannered."

Examples of stylistic allusion and pluralism abound in the poetry
but are easiest to identify in the theater. For example, the play entitled
The Love of Don Perlimplín for Belisa in Their Garden evokes a musical
form (the dialogue is punctuated by the music of Scarlatti) and at least
two genres of traditional literature: the puppet play and the *aleluya* (a
crudely engraved cartoon strip with captions in rhyming couplets).
Mariana Pineda (1927), a self-consciously "Romantic" drama in verse,
offers another example of stylistic plurality. When Lorca begins work
on that play, he considers making it "a sort of stylized poster of the
kind that blind men use to illustrate their ballads: a crime like the ones

sung about in ballads, so that the red blood [of the heroine] can blend with the red of the curtain" (*EC* 208). As work progresses, he decides to appeal to "all of the lovely old clichés of Romanticism" and give it the air, even the faded yellow tone, of an old lithograph. Some of the characters will strike characteristically Romantic poses ("Mariana sits down by the chair, her profile to the audience. Fernando is close by . . . They compose a picture of the period"), and these tableaux were ingeniously "framed," in the 1927 production, by the stage settings of Salvador Dalí. In its definitive version, the play is subtitled *Romance popular en tres estampas* (*Traditional Ballad in Three Engravings*).

And so it is throughout the dramatical works: *Yerma* is a "Tragic Poem," *Once Five Years Pass*, a "Legend of Time," *Doña Rosita*, a "Poem of Turn-of-the-Century Granada Divided into Various Gardens with Scenes of Song and Dance." *The Girl Who Waters the Basil and the Inquisitive Prince* is subtitled "Old Andalusian Tale in Three Engravings and a Chromolithograph." *Bernarda Alba*, a "Drama of Women in the Villages of Spain," is meant to suggest, according to a note at the end of the cast of characters, a photographic documentary: Lorca seems to be evoking the contrasts of black-and-white photography (*IGM* 235).

Lorca's titles and subtitles are statements of stylistic intention. They remind the reader that the play, poem, or drawing is executed and meant to be received "in the manner of" another artist, an earlier period, another literary genre or artistic medium. In his titles, correspondence, prefaces, and statements to the press, Lorca asks that his poems be read as songs, his drawings be construed as "theorems," and his plays as ballads, or ballets or poems or photographs. Few Spanish writers have ever crossed interartistic boundaries as insistently and as gracefully. And few have ever drawn on such a wealth of artistic forms. The traditional music gathered into songbooks by Renaissance courtiers; broadside ballads and the crude woodcuts which adorned them; the windless landscapes of Italian Renaissance painting; children's drawings; the piano repertoire of Beethoven and Chopin; Japanese poetry and Chinese theater; the comic films of Chaplin and Keaton; Picasso's drawings for the Ballets Russes: these are some of the artistic media Lorca drew upon, with increasing lucidity, in the stylization of his own work. By stylization I mean a work's allusion to another style, individual or collective: an allusion so persistent that it inscribes the work within another, secondary allusive system.

Among the styles alluded to are those associated with both secular and religious art. The Holy Mass, the litany, popular religious festivals, Jacobus de Voragine's *Golden Legend*, polychromed Baroque sculpture, the religious procession, are present throughout the poems and plays, and not simply as the cultural heritage of all Spaniards but also as vividly remembered structural paradigms that help to configure both individual texts and poetic sequences.

For example, Lorca refers to both *The Gypsy Ballads* and *Poem of the Deep Song* as *retablos*. He is thinking of the altar screens or "retables" that have long fascinated visitors to Spanish cathedrals, among them Richard Ford (I:59):

From the high altar rises a screen or reredos, called the retablo [and these], most elaborately designed, carved, painted and gilt estofado, are divided into compartments, either by niches or intercolumniations; the spaces are filled with paintings or sculpture, generally representing the life of the Virgin or of the Savior, or subjects taken from the Bible, or from the local legends and tutelars, and do the office of books to those who can see but cannot read.

When Lorca speaks of *The Gypsy Ballads* as a great *retablo* of Andalusia, he is referring not only to the book's thematic variety but also to the way it is organized. For example, the tripartite section devoted to the tutelary archangels of Granada, Seville, and Córdoba is said to have been inspired by the fact that statues of these three archangels—St. Michael, St. Gabriel, St. Raphael—are found in many Spanish churches.

A basic narrative device in Lorca's poetry is the vision of a procession of figures:

Detrás va Pedro Domecq
con tres sultanes de Persia.
(Behind them comes Pedro Domecq
and three Persian sultans.)

"This is a pilgrimage," Lorca remarks on copying out the ballad of St. Michael and sending it to his friend Jorge Guillén. He is alluding as much to its organization as to subject matter. As in the traditional Spanish ballads, a series of figures parades past the listener/reader.

The Catholic liturgy is alluded to even more often in Lorca's poetry than are religious sculpture or processions. The verbal, intellectual, and syntactical parallelism that permeates Lorca's poetry has usually been attributed to his familiarity with traditional verse and with the Galician-Portuguese love lyric. But it may also be related to the liturgy. In his great *Lament for Ignacio Sánchez Mejías*, the first section of which resembles a litany, the narrator officiates at a religious rite of his own invention.

An untitled manuscript fragment suggests that Lorca admired the Holy Mass less as a structural paradigm than as a stylized way of rendering deep emotion. In the fragment, he attempts to explain his recreation of a certain traditional ballad—"Elenita que borda corbatas" (see note to MIRROR SUITE, p. 900)—which he has choreographed for a stage presentation.

What I am trying to do is to get at the dramatic depths of the ballad, and set them in action. First of all, assign each line of verse to the proper voice, and then suggest the atmosphere [of the poem] with lovely figures. This is an extremely stylized evocation, with only the faintest indication of the action. A distant evocation, in which things are strangely transformed, in the manner of the Mass, which evokes the passion of Christ by means of his original words. This evocation ought to be based on slow movements and motionless faces . . . it ought to be the plastic algebra of a drama of passion and pain. (OC III:324)

"Algebra" as metaphor for style. The same phrase occurs in the sonnet to Manuel de Falla (p. 847): "Clean algebra of serene brow. / Discipline and passion . . ."

So far we have dealt with allusion to collective styles. The parody and pastiche of individual writers is not uncommon in Lorca's poetry, but it is not often a means of stylization. In *Songs*, for example, one can identify poems in the manner of Ramón del Valle-Inclán, of Lope de Vega, and of Juan Ramón Jiménez, as in the final poem of the book:

Day, what a hard time I have
letting you leave.
You go off filled with me.
You return and don't know me.

In 1928 Lorca invented an apocryphal poet and, parodying Hispanic Modernism, published some of his works in literary journals. The narration entitled "St. Lucy and St. Lazarus" renders tribute to the humoristic aphorisms of Ramón Gómez de la Serna, and "Uncertain Solitude" is a pastiche of Góngora. But to mimic another writer's style is not necessarily to stylize "in the manner of." In pastiche, the style is not *alluded* to, it tries to be present: it is *itself* the stylistic medium.

Many explanations might be offered for Lorca's habits of stylization. Some would be temperamental: his friends, his brother, and his biographers have written that he was a brilliant mime. Some would be circumstantial. He was trained as a classical pianist, and it is not surprising that, after he turned to literature in late adolescence, he tried to express musical ideas in his poems and prose (musical titles abound in his poems; at least fifty of them bear some allusion to song).

Stylization, parody, and pastiche can be ways of allaying the "anxiety of influence" and bearing "the burden of the past," the burden of one's *own* past, as when Lorca parodies himself and lapses playfully into "*lorquismo*," imitating his own youthful signature or executing a drawing in the manner of his adolescent self. And parody can also be a way of "mastering" one's rivals, as when (1928) Lorca composes an "*Antología moderna*" with an apocryphal introduction by the literary critic Enrique Díez-Canedo and parodies of the leading poets of his day: Juan Ramón Jiménez, Antonio Machado, Pedro Salinas, Jorge Guillén, José María Hinojosa, Salvador Dalí, José Bergamín, and Rafael Alberti.

Finally, stylization enables one to deal with the unbearably "picturesque." Being a poet in Granada, living a stone's throw from the Alhambra, was surely no easy matter. When he dealt with the most stereotypical of Andalusian themes—the smuggler, gypsy knife fights, the guitar, deep song—Lorca knew those subjects had been dealt with often by previous artists, both Spanish and foreign, from Merimée to Washington Irving to Salvador Rueda. Andalusia was a true palimpsest, not only of history but of literary styles. "I deserve at least a smile for my daring," he writes to the musicologist Adolfo Salazar in 1921, as he works on *Poem of the Deep Song*. And he retreats, in that book, to a safe aesthetic distance, and does his best to avoid what is known in Spanish as *una españolada*: broad brushstrokes of Spanish commonplace and color.

Poem of the Deep Song is usually read as an evocation of Andalusia through its most characteristic objects—oil lamp, taper, guitar, cave, scissors, prickly pear, etc.—but Lorca approaches all this from a certain distance. Several of the poems are labeled "*viñetas*" (vignettes), as though to remind us of a set of nineteenth-century engravings. What of this poem, *Surprise*?

They left him dead in the street
with a dagger in his breast.
No one knew him.
How the street-lamp trembled!

The syntax of this poem is reminiscent of traditional poetry. But what of the melodramatic tone? On the one hand, Lorca is gravely reminding the reader—as he does later on in the *Lament for Ignacio Sánchez Mejías*—of the terrifying anonymity of the dead. But he is also trying to capture the emotionally overwrought style of the *cante jondo* repertoire. In *Poema del cante jondo*, the voice is not always his "own." It is a shrill, high-pitched one, the *"falsete"* (see note, p. 897) he will use to address the Petenera:

Oh gypsy Petenera!
Oh Petenera!

Poetry about Andalusia deepens into metapoetry. Elegy, into an evocation of style.

Style and "Traditional" Poetry

Of all the stylistic "media" alluded to by Lorca, perhaps the most frequent is "traditional" (often called "popular") poetry.

From its beginnings, Spanish poetry shows a remarkable symbiosis of anonymous, traditional verse and "learned" creation, and nowhere has this phenomenon been more noticeable than in Andalusia. The very earliest poems in any Romance language are the eleventh-century *kharjas*: brief traditional songs used as refrains in the Arabic and Hebrew *muwashahas* of the learned poets of al-Andalus. As in the Galician-Portuguese lyric of the fourteenth century, in the *kharja* a maiden often confides in her mother:

¿Qué faré, mamma?
Mio al-habib est ad yana.
(What shall I do, mother?
My beloved is at the door.)

García Lorca knew nothing of these little poems in the Mozarabic dialect (the first *kharjas* were published in 1948, twelve years after his death), but he was an avid reader of other poets who had drawn on traditional verse, from the late Middle Ages (Juan Ruiz, Arcipreste de Hita) through the Renaissance (Gil Vicente) and Romanticism (Bécquer) to the poets of his own generation (Rafael Alberti). His encounter with the poetry and theater of Lope de Vega, who drew lovingly on traditional poetry, was especially significant, and the publication in 1925 of José Fernández Montesinos's anthology of Lope's lyrics in the "traditional" manner made a deep impression on him.

During his adolescence, Lorca had developed a considerable knowledge of traditional poetry, and when the ballad scholar Ramón Menéndez Pidal traveled to Granada in 1920, Lorca accompanied him to the gypsy quarter of the city and helped him record new versions.

By 1922, the year of his polemical lecture in defense of *cante jondo*, Lorca had mastered several regional songbooks and could play and sing by heart much of Felipe Pedrell's four-volume *Cancionero musical popular español*, a great treasury of Spanish traditional music: lullabies, wedding songs, ballads, religious chant, love lyrics, and the music sung by a variety of workers, from reapers to rag collectors and muleteers.

His studies at the Residencia de Estudiantes, in an ideological atmosphere where traditional art was studied and valued as a key to the Spanish "character," further nurtured his interest. It was at the Residencia, in 1928, that he first delivered his lecture on Spanish lullabies (*DS* 7–22).

The origins and aesthetic value of traditional poetry had long been a matter of debate among scholars and poets, both in Spain and abroad. The German Romantics (one was Jacob Grimm), who were first to study and collect traditional poetry in Spain, had distinguished between *Naturpoesie* and *Kunstpoesie*: anonymous "natural" folk poetry (*das Volk dichtet*), and the "art" poetry of learned individuals. *Naturpoesie* was viewed as the spontaneous product of a "pure and uncorrupted people," and it seemed to embody "the soul of the nation." Over the course of the nineteenth century, many would argue that traditional (or "natural" or "popular") poetry was merely "sunken culture": a tasteless deformation of certain nontraditional poems taken over by the people. The traditional Spanish love lyric, for example, was thought to have developed from the poetry of the troubadours. "Let no one allege that the brutish plowman is as capable of poetic thought and feeling as any enlightened man," writes a member of the Royal Spanish Academy around 1860. "It is thistles and weeds, not roses and carnations, that grow from the threshing floors . . . Rather than produce lovely poetic flowers, the people deface and make ugly" the poems created by learned poets.

While conceding the "learned" origin of traditional poetry, still other writers argued that "the people" often improve the poems they absorb. Thus, for example, the Sevillian poet Salvador Rueda, whose poetry and essays on popular art Lorca read as a young man:

It may be that it wasn't the people who wrote these poems. Perhaps they came, in different language, from the pens of [learned] poets. But it was the people who stripped them of rhetorical artifice and put them into its own language. (Rueda, n.p.)

By 1919, the year Lorca arrived in Madrid, Menéndez Pidal's research on the *pastourelle* had shown conclusively that not all traditional Spanish verse was of learned origin. But the aesthetic and ideological debate among poets and composers over how the "learned" poet could best imitate "traditional" art was still going on in earnest. Countless nineteenth- and early-twentieth-century Spanish poets, from Bécquer to Vicente Huidobro, had written pastiches of the traditional lyric, particularly the lyrics of deep song. By the end of the century, Antonio Machado y Álvarez, the father of the poet Antonio Machado, had tried to show the folly of this pseudotraditional approach. Even within his own family, his arguments had sometimes fallen on deaf ears. One of his sons, Manuel Machado, had published a collection of pastiches entitled *Cante hondo*, imitating both the meter and the images of the anonymous *flamenco* lyrics.

In his lecture on deep song, Lorca follows Machado y Álvarez and his more gifted son, Antonio, and argues with passion for stylization *in the manner of* deep song, rather than direct imitation.

Our people sing poems of Melchor de Palau, of Salvador Rueda, of Ventura Ruiz Aguilera, of Manuel Machado and others, but what a difference between the verse of these poets and the poems the people created themselves! It is the difference between a paper rose and a natural one! The poets who compose "popular" songs cloud the clear lymph of the true heart. How one notices in their poems the confident, ugly rhythm of the man who knows grammar!

Nothing but the very essence and this or that trill for its coloristic effect ought to be drawn straight from the people. We should never want to copy their ineffable modulations; we can do nothing but muddy them. Simply because of education. (SD 14)

Lorca himself was no exception: when he experimented, uncharacteristically, with a pastiche of the traditional ballad, the results were disastrous.

The musical terms that occur in Lorca's statement—"trill," "modulations," "coloristic" (he is thinking of tone color)—remind us that he wrote his lecture on *cante jondo* in collaboration with the composer Manuel de Falla. Falla's approach to the treatment of Spanish subjects, traditional art as a stylizing medium, and artistic stylization in general was decisive in Lorca's education as poet. Barely a year before Lorca set to work on *Poem of the Deep Song*, Falla had praised Claude Debussy's nonliteral use of folkloric material. While Falla's own master, Felipe Pedrell, had quoted literally from traditional song in some of his own musical works, in Debussy the traditional source is alluded to but seldom quoted directly.

The intense feeling of Spain crystallized in Evening in Granada *is something of a miracle if one considers that it was written by a foreigner, led only by his brilliant intuition. We are far away from those serenades,* madrileñas, *and* boleros *which the manufacturers of "Spanish music" used to give us. Here we are actually given Andalusia, the truth without the authenticity, as it were; for although not a single measure is taken from Spanish folklore, the whole piece, down to its smallest details, brings us Spain.*

"It is well known," Falla adds, "that Debussy always avoided repeating himself. 'It is necessary,' Debussy said, 'to adapt one's métier to the character one wants each work to have.' How right he was!" (Falla, 73). Those lines aptly summarize Lorca's own aesthetics. It must have fascinated him, as it did Falla, that the Spanish "style" in modern music had been created, in large part, by foreigners, few of whom had ever set foot in Andalusia. "I do not think any Spanish composer has ever succeeded in writing so authentic a *jota* [Aragonese regional dance] as Chabrier has," says Falla in another essay; and in still another: "Let us not forget . . . that Russian composers—Glinka and Rimsky-Korsakov among others—were the first to write Spanish symphonic music." Foreign composers like these would exemplify the ironic distance from one's surroundings and material—Andalusia, for example—that could be achieved through stylization. It is no coincidence that when Lorca sets out to write something "quintessentially Andalusian," *The Tragicomedy of Don Cristóbal and Mistress Rosita*, a play that alludes constantly to traditional song and to folklore, he finds himself lapsing into a playful parody of Victor Hugo's *Hernani*. For Granada was "the true acme of all European Romanticism" (*SG* 98).

Rather than imitate the imagery and meter of specific poems from the traditional repertoire, Lorca assimilated a collective style and a series of conventional formal features. The ones borrowed from traditional poetry are obvious: the use of parallelism, repetition, and the refrain (building blocks of all Lorca's verse, and of all poetry); the eight-syllable meter and feminine rhyme of the ballad; the expressive manipulation of verb tenses (e.g., in *The Gypsy Ballads*); and the musical nature of much traditional poetry (believing that "a ballad is not perfect unless it has its own melody to make it palpitate and give it blood and a severe or erotic air for its characters to move around in," Lorca wrote his own melodies for at least two of the *Ballads*) (*OC* I:799–800).

Rather more difficult to identify are the aesthetic qualities he admired in traditional poetry and hoped to capture in his own work. Foremost among them is a sense of mystery: the feeling of a story half told and half understood. The narrative poetry that "lives in variants" (Menéndez Pidal's memorable definition of the traditional ballad) is, like any other message transmitted orally, subject to transformation. By definition, there is no "correct" version of a traditional song. The very names of ballad characters vary from one version to another: Lorca liked to remember how the biblical name "Tamar" (a number of traditional ballads tell the story of Thamar and Amnon) had been altered by the people to "Altamare" or "Atlas Mares": "High Seas" (*DS* 122).

The poetic tale handed down orally from one generation to another, and transmitted across regional borders, comes to us in fragments. The ballads (thought by some to be fragments of longer epic poems) usually begin *in medias res* and reach us full of lacunae: their profiles, as Lorca once said, are "worn away by time."

Songs are like people. They live, they grow perfect, and some grow degenerate and come undone, until we are left with palimpsests, full of lacunae and senseless things. (*OC* III:483)

The feeling of "fragmentation," of narrative gaps, is the effect with which Lorca is experimenting in poems like *Joke about Don Pedro*, with its insertion of typographical and narrative lacunae. Judging from the lecture on lullabies, Lorca's own poetic imagination was awakened by the mysteries of songs rendered almost senseless by time. In Granada he had collected six different versions of this cradle song:

A la nana nana nana
a la nana de aquel
que llevó el caballo al agua
y lo dejó sin beber.
(Lullaby, lullaby,
of that man who led
his horse to the water
and didn't let him drink.)

His comment on the lullaby shows how fascinated he was by its narrative mystery. The child hears the lyrics repeated again and again, sung in a haunting minor key.

Silently, again and again, that man and his horse go down the road of dark boughs toward the river, and return to the spot where the song begins. The child will never see them face to face. In the penumbra of the lullaby, he will only imagine that man's dark suit, the horse's shiny rump. The characters in these songs never show their faces . . . But the melody makes that man and his horse intensely dramatic, and the strangeness of that man not watering his horse causes a rare, mysterious anguish. (DS 15)

Even the use of the demonstrative pronoun *aquel—that* man, rather than *the* man—struck Lorca as poetic. In an early poem reminiscent of Antonio Machado, the poet confides to a group of children:

el ella *del romance me sumía
en ensoñares claros.* (*OC* I:78)
(The she *of the ballad immersed me
in limpid daydreams.)*

Thus do English-speaking children sometimes wonder who "they" are in impersonal expressions like "They say . . ." What Lorca sought as a poet was the mystery and pathos encountered by Machado in the songs sung by children at play:

*On children's lips
the singing carries
a tale confused
but pain still clear,
the way clear water
carries a strain
of love long past
and leaves it unsaid.*   (Tr. Trueblood, 77)

The children's song fascinates both Lorca and Machado because it reconciles past and present, innocence and bitterness. It is an act of poetic faith similar to the one Lorca asks of both the poet and his readers. The poet must often "reject with vehemence any temptation to be understood" (*C* II:20). And the reader should emulate the child, who *believes* and sings without fully *understanding*. "Unlike us," Lorca observes in the lecture on lullabies,

the child's creative faith is still intact, and he does not yet carry the seed of destructive reason. He is innocent and therefore wise. He understands better than we do the ineffable key to poetic substance. (DS 15)

Poetry requires that faith and that innocence: "One must see with the eyes of a child and ask for the moon. Ask for the moon and believe they can place it in your hands" (*C* II:20).

By giving only the shadow of a "narration" to some of his ballads, Lorca was able to blend narrative and lyrical elements in a way that disconcerted his first readers. No one, for example, can be very certain of what "happens" in the dreamlike atmosphere of *Sleepwalking Ballad*. A gypsy smuggler, wounded in an encounter with the Civil Guard in the mountain ranges of Córdoba, seeks refuge in the house of the father of his beloved: that much seems clear, at least after a few readings. But what happens then is uncertain. Who is it that pronounces the poem's opening lines? And who is being addressed?

Green I want you green.
Green wind, green boughs.
Ship on the sea
And horse on the mountain.

Does the gypsy girl commit suicide? Why? Is she already dead when the smuggler arrives? "There *seems* to be a story, but there really isn't," remarked Salvador Dalí. Less intelligent readers—the journalist E. Gómez Baquero, for example—saw many of the poems as "artistically unfinished. Some give you the impression of a rough sketch, a first, provisional draft." With characteristic lucidity, Lorca described his own intentions:

The typical ballad had always been a narration, and it was the narrative element that made its physiognomy so charming, for when it grew lyrical without an echo of anecdote, it would turn into a song. I wanted to fuse the narrative ballad with the lyrical without affecting the quality of either. (DS 105)

Lyricism and narration, in what Lorca calls a "poignant dramatic atmosphere" (*DS* 106). And this too is something found in the traditional ballads. Some of them, especially those where dialogue is present, give us the feeling of a drama unfolding from one line to the next. In the traditional ballads, one does not *hear* a narration of how things happen, or an explanation of *why* they happen; one simply *sees* them happen. One of the seven Spanish popular songs Lorca recorded with "La Argentinita" in 1931 contains a marvelous example. A farm boy has been gored by a bull:

Friends, I am dying.
Friends, it's very bad.
I have three handkerchiefs in me
and this one makes four.

The wounding itself has not been mentioned. This dramatism, where visual detail replaces narrative explanation, is found not only in Lorca's ballads but throughout his work, in even the briefest of his lyrical compositions (e.g., *Hunter*). Lorca was so impressed by the dramatic qualities of the ballad that (as has already been noted) he sometimes "staged" ballads (e.g., those of Antonio Machado) and traditional songs in the theater. In his own plays, traditional songs have an important role. The lullaby of the horse who does not drink is glossed in *Blood Wedding*, where it foreshadows the death of Leonardo.

No doubt, Lorca also admired traditional poetry for appealing to all classes of Spanish society. The liberal ideology of the Residencia de Estudiantes had taught him respect for "popular" art and artisanry in all its forms, from songs to religious imagery to candy making. The lecture on lullabies shows his awareness of how traditional song cuts across socioeconomic boundaries, and of what he owes, as poet and as the son of a wealthy landowner, to the family maids.

Poor women feed this melancholy bread [the lullaby] not only to their own children; they also bring it into the homes of the rich. The rich child listens to the lullaby of the poor woman, who gives him, in her pure sylvan milk, the marrow of the country. / / For a long time now these wet nurses, maids, and other domestic servants have been doing the important job of carrying the ballad, the song, and the story into the houses of aristocrats and the bourgeoisie. Rich children know of Gerineldo, Don Bernardo, Tamar, and the Lovers of Teruel [characters in ballads] thanks to the admirable nannies and domestics who descend from the mountains or from far up the river to give us our first lesson in Spanish history, and brand our flesh with the harsh Iberian motto: "Alone you are; alone you will live." (DS 10–11)

The "fragmentary" quality mentioned earlier makes several of Lorca's ballads, and many of the lyrical poems, extremely difficult to understand. But the wide readership of the *Ballads* caused some critics to speak of Lorca as a "popular" poet (a term he himself rejected). In 1926, two years before the book was published, the poet Jorge Guillén wondered aloud, as he introduced Lorca at a poetry reading, "What miracle is this? What has happened?" Suddenly, "art for the few has become art for the many" (Guillén, liv).

The Avant-Garde: Symbol and Metaphor

Art for the few, art for the many. The problem was hotly debated by the Spanish avant-garde of the 1920s and 1930s, and it seemed more important than ever with the coming of the Second Republic and Spain's return to democracy in 1931.

In Madrid, Lorca came into contact with avant-garde currents that would change his work and help him define his own poetics. Although he never identified himself with any movement in particular and specifically dissociated himself from Ultraism, Surrealism, and the vanguard in general (*OC* III:368), his interest in contemporary painting and music and his friendships with Buñuel, Dalí, Falla, and others made him extraordinarily sensitive to the waves of aesthetic experimentation reaching Spain in the first three decades of the twentieth century.

There is much in Lorca's character that runs counter to the aesthetics of the avant-garde. Aware of his debt to Golden Age and to "traditional" Spanish poetry, Lorca had none of the *antipassatismo* that characterizes most, perhaps all, avant-garde art. The dividedness of *gallo*, the supposedly avant-garde literary magazine he directed in Granada, is symptomatic. While Dalí extols the "inescapable, paradigmatic beauty of the auto showroom and of aeronautics," Lorca and other *gallistas* are trying to raise money to publish editions of two Baroque poets and an album of traditional songs from Granada, and editorializing about the need to restore "the authentic Arabic houses of the Albaicín." Like Marinetti in Italy, Lorca lived in a huge museum—Granada—and sometimes felt oppressed by *el espanto turístico* (the horrors of tourism). But as noted earlier, his poetic reaction to the "picturesque" was very different. His poetry is rooted in time: the hours and seasons, the generative rhythms of nature, the notion (examined earlier) of the historical palimpsest. Nothing could be further from his poetics than the Futurists' longing for simultaneity or the Surrealists' immersion in a psychological "present." The mechanistic, urban utopias of Marinetti, or Dalí's cry to bombard the Gothic quarter of Barcelona, did not attract him (with the advent of the modern cinema, Lorca once observed, Futurism had lost its raison d'être). None of the icons of Futurism—automobile, propeller, shrapnel, locomotive—have any importance in his work. Nor did he share the avant-garde's sense of social alienation or its antagonism toward the public. There is much antibourgeois feeling in Lorca—we have seen it, for example, in his rebellion against the values of the commercial theater—but nowhere in his work do we find the nihilistic, Dadaist yearning for a radical subversion of language or of other social structures.

And yet the avant-garde helped Lorca examine at least two eternal aesthetic problems. Cubism, and related Hispanic movements like Creationism and Ultraism, invited him to ponder the relation between art and nature, the sign and reality. Surrealism nurtured his interest in the role of the irrational in the creation and interpretation of poetry. It was the avant-garde that made these problems seem especially urgent to poets of Lorca's generation, but in his struggle to resolve them, Lorca turned often, more than others, to tradition. A year before Lorca's death, the critic Ángel del Río (10) wrote perceptively of his friend's

internal continuity, with respect to his own work, and the historical continuity of his art in relation to the art of his time. Lorca has been the only poet of these last fifteen years whose roots are almost entirely Spanish. He has never broken—and more importantly, never tried *to break—with his immediate predecessors.*

One of Lorca's first encounters with avant-garde aesthetics arose from his friendship with the Chilean poet Vicente Huidobro, champion of Creationism, a doctrine that rebelled, in the wake of Cubism, against mimetic, representational art. "The poet," Huidobro insisted, "is a little God," whose role is not to imitate nature but to "create" another one without regard to the laws of verisimilitude. "Let us make poems as nature makes a tree," he wrote. "I have the right to want to see a flower that walks or a flock of sheep crossing a rainbow."

Oh Poets, why sing of roses!
Let them flower in your poems.   (Tr. Guss, 3)

It is not known exactly when Lorca met Huidobro. Between 1919 and 1921, the Chilean dedicated copies of two of his books to him, "in memory of so many unforgettable evenings of poetry and music" (Fernández-Montesinos, "Descripción," 54). In those slim volumes, *Poemas árticos* (*Arctic Poems*) and *Ecuatorial* (*Equatorial*), Lorca found "non-figurative" images analogous in intention to those of Cubism. The Cubists, Apollinaire had remarked in 1910, "still look at nature, but no longer imitate it . . . Verisimilitude no longer has any importance" (Fry, 114–15), and Picabia had concurred: "Almost all paintings have tried to re-create objects which exist in nature, and that is precisely what art must not be." In this spirit, Huidobro could boast:

I invented waterfalls
In the tops of trees.   (Tr. Guss, 51)

and offer images like these:

Biplanes in labor
      laying eggs in flight amid the mist

★

The new moon
        with its rigging battered
Anchored in Marseilles this morning
And the oldest sailors
Have found pearls shining
At the bottom of their pipes.   (Tr. Guss, 31–33)

It is not easy to identify Creationist images in Lorca's early work, perhaps because Creationism differs from other movements only in its intentions. Only rarely does one come upon lines that might have been written by Huidobro with the intention of "re-creating" nature:

Blind crowd—the perfumes
drifting past—
their feet propped up on uncut flowers.

But, as we shall see, the Chilean left a deep mark upon Lorca's writing *about* poetry.

Another current noticeable in Lorca's early verse is Ultraism, a movement of minor writers, headed by Lorca's friend Guillermo de Torre, who noisily and pedantically exalted "modernity" and attacked Hispanic Modernism and the "neurasthenic lyricism" of its archpoet, Rubén Darío. Like the Imagism of the English-speaking world, Ultraism attempted to rid poetry of anecdote and "Romantic sentiment" and reduce it to its essence: the metaphor (the more startling the metaphor, the better). Like the image of Creationism, the Ultraist metaphor often personifies nature, or compares it, shockingly, to man-made inventions (trolley car as spider spinning its thread, or Lorca's comparison of an agave plant to a jai-alai player). It scrambles the natural order, making objects function in unexpected ways (the crescent moon as telephone receiver). It compares abstract to material things or living to inanimate, and it makes large objects (the sea) fit within small ones (a bedroom or a bottle). In the wake of Futurism, the Ultraists also experimented with syntax, typography, punctuation, and the spatial disposition of the poem in order to express speed and simultaneity (experiments in which Lorca was never interested). The moon and stars—hallowed objects in Modernist poetry—had been treated with especial irreverence by the Ultraists. *Book of Poems* contains "Ultraist" metaphors like these:

The round silence of night,
one note on the stave
of the infinite.

★

The half moon, a fermata
somnolent and frozen,
marks a pause and splits
the midnight harmony.

★

White tortoise,
sleeping moon,
how slowly
you walk!
Closing
a shadowy eyelid,
you stare
like an archaeological
pupil.

★

. . . the oldest of stars
has damped its hurdy-gurdy

The section entitled SIX CAPRICCIOS in *Poem of the Deep Song* has often been characterized as Ultraist.

In his first years in Madrid, Lorca had also won the admiration of one of the most ingenious humorists Spain has ever known, Ramón Gómez de la Serna (1888–1963), the inventor of lyrical aphorisms he called *greguerías*. Defining his invention as "humorism + metaphor = *greguería*," Gómez de la Serna produced thousands of observations like these:

Tall pine trees are the feather dusters that serve to clean the sky.

★

The doorbell: navel of the wall.

★

Radiators are the feverish entrails of a house.

★

The stars were falling on the passersby like lighted cigarettes thrown from the terrace of the sky.

★

The rainbow is the scarf of the sky.

Such witticisms appealed to more than a few Spanish poets of the 1920s and early 1930s, and one can detect Gómez de la Serna's smiling presence in much of the poetry and prose that Lorca wrote between 1920 and 1927. When Lorca calls a country road a "Flammarion of footprints," or donkeys "Buddhas among fauna," or daylight a "vast Penelope," or mosquitoes "Pegasuses of dew," we know that he has discovered Gómez de la Serna and is distancing himself from the Modernism of Darío. The three avant-garde currents just mentioned, particularly Ultraism and the *greguería*, helped him surmount the poetics of *Book of Poems*—poetry as the expression of sentiment—and trained his eyes more disinterestedly on the world around him. In *Poem of the Deep Song* he turns, for the first time, from the "landscape of the soul" to the landscape of Andalusia. Like the lyrics of *cante jondo*, the avant-garde helped him prune and care for "the overluxuriant lyric tree left to us by the Romantics and post-Romantics" (*SD* 10).

In the development of his powers of metaphor, as with all else in his work, Lorca owes as much, probably more, to the Spanish tradition as to his contact with the avant-garde. In preparing for the three hundredth anniversary of the death of Don Luis de Góngora, an event commemorated in 1927 all over Spain and Latin America, Lorca had returned to the works of the great Baroque poet and had written an enthusiastic lecture analyzing his poetics (*DS* 59–85). Without fully understanding Góngora's poetry, Lorca found much to admire in him: meticulous workmanship and a thirst for poetic perfection; pride in his Andalusian origins; "aristocratic solitude" and scorn for the "vulgar" reader; a love of classical mythology; and a radically new vision of syntax and of the Spanish language. But above all Lorca loved the metaphorical splendor of Don Luis: the unimaginable clarity and complexity of his conceits. Góngora had "thought, without saying so, that the eternity of a poem depends on the quality and perfect fit of its images." And Lorca would do his best to emulate him throughout *The Gypsy Ballads*. Here, for example, is an image attributable to his study of Góngora's conceits:

> *Dense oxen of water*
> *charge at the boys*
> *bathing in the moons*
> *of their rippling horns.*

In these four lines from *Ballad of the Marked Man* some boys are swimming at night, struggling against the "charging" current of an irrigation canal. (A "water-ox," Lorca explains in the lecture on Góngora, is the popular Andalusian term for a "deep channel of water that flows slowly across a field: [the metaphorical name indicates] its combativeness, its strength and volume.") The crescent moon's reflection on the moving water has given the "water-ox" a pair of "rippling horns," and one can say that the boys are "bathing" in them.

But metaphor was only one pole of Lorca's image making. The other was symbolism, of two sorts: that which he inherited from modern poetry (Mallarmé, Maeterlinck, etc.); and the symbolism of the traditional lyric (traditional art seldom uses metaphor). The difference between metaphor and symbol need not be explained here. The latter involves an analogy, and has a solution, e.g.,

The rider was drawing closer
playing the drum of the plain

where, for a number of reasons—shape, resonance, color, etc.—"plain" is analogous to "drum." The symbol does not always involve analogical reasoning and is *not* apprehended as a riddle with a specific solution. In the best-known line of Lorca's poetry:

Green I want you green

"green" is, simply, a longed-for, indefinable state of mind, like Mallarmé's image of infinity: *azur*.

Metaphor and symbol govern the poet's relation to reality. There is, in much of Lorca's work, a strong Romantic feeling for the otherness of nature: a conviction that there is always something *out there*, totally alien to mankind, that cannot be apprehended by the imagination: the poetic unknown, the "life" that is stirring beyond our senses, and thus beyond the reach of metaphor.

The poet hears the flowing of great rivers. To his brow comes the coolness of the reeds that are trembling "nowhere." He wants to hear the dialogue of insects under the incredible boughs. He wants to penetrate to the music of the running of the sap inside the great tree trunks. He wants to understand the Morse code that speaks to the heart of the sleeping girl. (C II:16)

Metaphor plays a somewhat contradictory role in illumining this extrasensory reality or, at the very least, in reminding us of its existence. The reason, empowered by analogy, encounters what has not yet been named, and compares the known to the unknown, identifying or creating a new phenomenon. Metaphor, *by its very inadequacy*, by its provisional nature, by its inability to reach beyond the senses, somehow enhances that "otherness," reminding us of *all that the metaphor cannot capture*. As in the thought of certain mystics, the least adequate image can imply the greatest reverence for the unknown. We are never more aware of the ineffable than when the description is most precise and elaborate. The human reason is pushed to its limits, but there is always some mystery "left over." For Lorca, metaphor must have "two elements: form and a radius of action":

A central nucleus and the perspective surrounding it. The nucleus opens like a flower, startling us with its strangeness. But within the radius of light we learn the name of the flower and get to know its perfume. (DS 65)

What Lorca calls the "nucleus" is the impact of the comparison itself (A = B), the more unexpected, the better. The "radius" is the metaphor's analogical content: the sense data that make the comparison possible. The poetical impact of the "nucleus" reminds us of the unknown.

There is, of course, another point of view. Metaphor, especially the image based on personification, *deprives* the natural world of its otherness, bringing it irreverently into the realm of human reason. In his lecture on Góngora, Lorca had spoken enthusiastically of Góngora's "way of animating and vivifying Nature."

He needs the elements to be conscious. He hates what is deaf, he hates dark forces that have no limits . . . he transforms all that he touches . . . His sublime theogonic feeling gives personality to the forces of nature. (DS 80)

Two years later, that attitude toward the natural world would no longer seem satisfactory. The poetic "imagination"—even Góngora's prodigious imagination—does not really capture reality.

[It] travels and transforms things, endowing them with their purest sense, and it identifies relations which had never been suspected. But it always, always, always works with facts borrowed from the most clear and precise sort of reality. It falls within our human logic, controlled by reason, and cannot escape from it. Its special manner of creation needs order and limits. Imagination is what has invented the four points of the compass and what has discovered the intermediate causes of things. But it has never been able to abandon its hands in the senseless, illogical embers where inspiration is stirring, free and unfettered. Imagination is the first step, the foundation of all poetry . . . The poet uses it

to construct a tower against the natural elements and against mystery. The poet is unassailable; he orders and is heeded. But the best birds, the brightest lights always get away from him. (C II:14–15)

The lecture from which I have quoted, "Imagination, Inspiration, Evasion" (1928), is devoted to the role of reason ("imagination") and of irrationality ("inspiration") in the creation of poetry. In it, Lorca's meditation upon metaphor and symbol advanced a step further. Góngora's power of analogy had greatly attracted him: Don Luis is in perfect "control" of his "imaginative machinery." But in 1928, four years after Breton's first manifesto, the year of Dalí's conversion to Surrealism, Lorca is clearly disillusioned with the capacity of analogy and reason to capture much of the "unknown." Modern science can discover as much as or more than the metaphors of any "imaginative" poet. Nor is he content with the way readers *receive* metaphor: the enunciation of a riddle provokes one to decipher it analogically. Remembering the Creationism of Huidobro, but also the lesson of lullabies and children's songs, Lorca will defend the image that is *not* based on analogy, the "poetic fact" that is responded to and accepted but that cannot be easily explained. Searching for examples in his own work, Lorca quotes the two lines I have romanized here, from *Sleepwalking Ballad*, written four years earlier:

Up the two compadres climb,
up to the high railing,
leaving a trail of blood,
leaving a trail of tears.
Little tin-leaf lanterns
tremble on the roofs.
A thousand crystal tambourines
were wounding the dawn.

Of the meaning of these lines Lorca would later write,

I [can only] tell you that I saw [those tambourines] in the hands of angels and trees, but I will not be able to say more; certainly I cannot explain their meaning. And that is the way it should be. By means of poetry a man more rapidly approaches the cutting edge that the philosopher and the mathematician turn away from in silence. (DS 111–23)

It is in lines like these that metaphor crosses paths with the Creationist image. A new phenomenon—the "crystal tambourines"—seems to have been added to nature. A riddle, both auditory and visual, *seems* to have been posed. Are the "tambourines" the stars? Rain? Perhaps the silvery leaves of poplars or olive trees. The crystalline sound of running water, "wounding" the otherwise silent dawn? We are staring at the ghost of an analogy, a sort of poetic *trompe l'oeil*: a riddle unable to yield a convincing solution. The reader—the reader Lorca wanted to have in 1928—responds with faith rather than reason. Analogy confesses its own limitations.

In late 1928, a few months after he had given his lecture "Inspiration, Imagination, Evasion," an interviewer asked Lorca about his poetics. "A return to inspiration," he says. "Inspiration, pure instinct, the only reason of the poet. Logical poetry is unbearable to me. We've had enough of the lesson of Góngora. Instinct and passion, at least for now" (*OC* III:366). While poems like *Uncertain Solitude*, *The Siren and the Carabineer*, and some of the poems in *The Gypsy Ballads* had been written under the spell of Góngora, others—like some of the prose poems and narrations and *Poet in New York*—gave notice of a new manner. Lorca had lost his faith in the epistemological power of the metaphor.

But once again, tradition served as a restraint. Góngora had taught Lorca a lasting lesson in control and in clarity. In creating his poems, Don Luis had known how to reject "the jewels which his genius has placed randomly in his hands" (*C* I:17). It is not surprising that, even when praising "pure instinct," Lorca is unwilling to cultivate the automatism of the Surrealists. Poetic "evasion" can take many forms, he concedes in "Imagination, Inspiration, Evasion."

Surrealism employs dream, the ultra-real world of dreams, where one discovers true, authentic poetic norms. But no matter how pure it is, evasion by means of dream or the subconscious is not very clear. We Spaniards want profiles and visible mystery, form and sensuality. Surrealism can take hold in the north . . . but Spain, with her history, defends us from the strong liquor of dream. (*C* II:20–21)

A few years later, in 1933, in his lecture "Play and Theory of the Duende," Lorca makes a new attempt to examine the entire poetic process, from the conception of the poem to its interpretation by the reader, and once again he devises a poetics consistent with Spanish art. By now he sees poetry as a dialectical struggle between the forces of irrationality (personified in the *duende*, the impish earth spirit of Spanish folklore) and the forces of reason (personified in the classical Muse). His sympathy clearly lies with the *duende*. It is striking that in formulating his own aesthetic of the irrational, Lorca turns not to the language of Freud and Breton (much discussed in literary journals of the day) but to an expression drawn from colloquial Andalusian Spanish (in Andalusia people use the phrase *"tener duende"* of an artist with a certain ineffable, almost diabolical charm). To "have *duende*," to produce great art, to write the poem that will resist explanation and "baptize in dark water all who look at it," one must—Lorca argues—draw close to the earth, that is, acknowledge one's *own* death and the mortality of all things, and the limitations of reason and intelligence:

Intelligence is often the enemy of poetry, because it limits too much, and it elevates the poet to a sharp-edged throne where he forgets that ants could eat him or that a great arsenic lobster could fall suddenly on his head. (SD 51)

Of the works written after this stirring lecture—*Six Galician Poems, Lament for Ignacio Sánchez Mejías,* many of the sonnets, and, above all, *The Tamarit Divan*—none is devoid of metaphor. But what prevails is symbolic denomination: a higher realm of poetry where A is B not because of the sensorial properties they have in common but *just because: porque sí.* It is as though the "flower" of metaphor Lorca spoke of earlier had no petals of analogy, only a "nucleus." As though the flower were unopened. In lines like these, from the *Lament for Ignacio Sánchez Mejías,* metaphor (stone as "forehead" or "shoulder") is in harmony with symbol ("curved water," "trees of tears"):

The stone is a forehead where dreams groan
for lack of curving waters and frozen cypresses.
Stone is a shoulder for carrying away time
with its trees made of tears, and with ribbons and planets.

Or consider the symbolism of *Qasida of the Branches,* from *Divan*:

Through the groves of Tamarit
the leaden dogs have come,
to wait for the branches to fall,
for the branches to break by themselves.

There is no "correct" interpretation for these "leaden dogs," no riddle in hiding. And the "branches" have only the most general import: they "are" life, perhaps. They are, if one wants to remember the lecture on *duende*, "the branches we all wear, branches that do not have, will never have, any consolation."

Both Creationists and Ultraists had spoken of the metaphor as the truly universal element in poetry. Huidobro had written proudly that the same image can be understood in all languages:

La nuit vient des yeux d'autrui

La noche viene de los ojos ajenos

Night comes from others' eyes

For an Ultraist, poetry is what is *saved* in translation. At times, Lorca's symbolism grows so private, so opaque, that only the will to speak poetically—and to show the inadequacy of language—has any meaning. But at its best, it is truly universal. By means of certain archetypal symbols—the moon, blood, the elements—Lorca awakens resonances deep within the psyche of his readers as though appealing to mythic ways of thinking that "civilization" has all but obliterated. For all his stylization, his worldview is a primitivistic one. The Spanish historian of religion Ángel Álvarez de Miranda (49) has written (as have many other critics after him) that in Lorca's theater and poetry one finds "a religion, or, more exactly, a type of religiosity" akin to that of primitive, naturalistic man.

What we call [Lorca's] "poetry" coincides in all its essential elements with the themes, motives, and myths of ancient religions. This coincidence is due to the fact that both phenomena, poetry and religion, spring from the same coherent system of intuitions about the sacredness of organic life. And thus the essential content of Lorca's "poems" is a spontaneous, unconscious relapse into the mytholegomena that characterize naturalistic religion.

At the center of his cosmos is the moon, the Great Mother, the goddess who grants fertility, life, and death to all creation.

Life and death, speech and silence are the cardinal points of his elegiac world. Life in the shadow of death, speech in the shadow of the unknown: the natural mystery that seems inaccessible to speech and to reason. One of the myths Lorca's work evokes is that of Orpheus. His first and last words as a poet tell us of his longing to be *one* with nature; to be earth or tree, animal or "the little friend" of the wind; to die consumed by light, to mingle with the earth, to have flowers grow from his eyes and roses spill from his tongue; to comprehend the natural world and to lose himself in its rhythms. Poetry itself possesses a "religious," Orphic character, and what Lorca longs for is "A song to go to the soul of things / and the soul of winds, resting at last in the bliss / of the endless heart." His habits of stylization—his incessant evocation of other poets and periods and genres—remind us of the temporal and collective dimensions of poetry's struggle with the unknown. The moon is present in his work as a mysterious, numinous object; but present also is a poignant historical awareness of its aesthetic meaning. As a young man Lorca had seen *cante jondo* as "the scream of dead generations, a poignant elegy for lost centuries, the pathetic evocation of love under other moons and other winds" (*SD* 4). The same is true of his own deep song. Into his work he gathers the art of others. Poetry evokes its own power and its own helplessness and seems to carry us to the limit of understanding.

Christopher Maurer
Nashville, Tennessee 1990
Oak Park, Illinois 2001

Collected Poems

De

LIBRO DE
POEMAS

[*Muchacha con miriñaque y sortija, 1924*]

From

BOOK OF

POEMS

Translated by

Catherine Brown

[Girl with Hoop Skirt and Ring, 1924]

Veleta
Julio de 1920
(Fuente Vaqueros, Granada)

Viento del Sur.
Moreno, ardiente,
llegas sobre mi carne,
trayéndome semilla
de brillantes
miradas, empapado
de azahares.

Pones roja la luna
y sollozantes
10 los álamos cautivos, pero vienes
¡demasiado tarde!
¡Ya he enrollado la noche de mi cuento
en el estante!

Sin ningún viento,
¡hazme caso!
Gira, corazón;
gira, corazón.

Aire del Norte,
¡oso blanco del viento!,
20 llegas sobre mi carne
tembloroso de auroras
boreales,
con tu capa de espectros
capitanes,
y riyéndote a gritos
del Dante.
¡Oh pulidor de estrellas!
Pero vienes
demasiado tarde.
30 Mi almario está musgoso
y he perdido la llave.

Sin ningún viento,
¡hazme caso!
Gira, corazón;
gira, corazón.

Weathervane

July 1920
(Fuente Vaqueros, Granada)

    South wind.
Dark and burning,
soaked with orange blossoms,
you come over my flesh,
bringing me seed
of brilliant gazes.

    You turn the moon red,
make captive poplars moan,
but you've come
too late!
I've already scrolled up the night
of my tale on the shelf!

    Without any wind
—Look sharp!—
Turn, heart.
Turn, my heart.

    Northern air,
white bear of the wind!
You come over my flesh
shivering with boreal
auroras,
with your cape of phantom
captains,
laughing aloud at Dante.
Oh polisher of stars!
But you've come
too late.
My case is musty
and I've lost the key.

    Without any wind
—Look sharp!—
Turn, heart.
Turn, my heart.

Brisas, gnomos y vientos
de ninguna parte,
mosquitos de la rosa
de pétalos pirámides,
alisios destetados
entre los rudos árboles,
flautas en la tormenta,
¡dejadme!
Tiene recias cadenas
mi recuerdo,
y está cautiva el ave
que dibuja con trinos
la tarde.

Las cosas que se van no vuelven nunca,
todo el mundo lo sabe,
y entre el claro gentío de los vientos
es inútil quejarse.
¿Verdad, chopo, maestro de la brisa?
¡Es inútil quejarse!

Sin ningún viento,
¡hazme caso!
Gira, corazón;
gira, corazón.

Corazón nuevo
Junio de 1918
(Granada)

Mi corazón, como una sierpe,
se ha desprendido de su piel,
y aquí la miro entre mis dedos,
llena de heridas y de miel.

Los pensamientos que anidaron
en tus arrugas ¿dónde están?
¿Dónde las rosas que aromaron
a Jesucristo y a Satán?

Gnomes, breezes and winds
from nowhere.
Mosquitoes of the rose
with pyramid petals.
Trade winds weaned
among rough trees,
40   flutes in the storm,
begone!
My memory is chained;
captive the bird
that sketches the evening
in song.

    Things that go away never return—
everybody knows that.
And in the bright crowd of the winds
there's no use complaining!
50   Am I right, poplar, teacher of the breeze?
There's no use complaining!

    Without any wind
—Look sharp!—
Turn, heart.
Turn, my heart.

New Heart
June 1918
(Granada)

    Like a snake, my heart
has shed its skin.
I hold it there in my hand,
full of honey and wounds.

    The thoughts that nested
in your folds, where are they now?
Where the roses that perfumed
both Jesus Christ and Satan?

¡Pobre envoltura que ha oprimido
10 a mi fantástico lucero!
Gris pergamino dolorido
de lo que quise y ya no quiero.

Yo veo en ti fetos de ciencias,
momias de versos y esqueletos
de mis antiguas inocencias
y mis románticos secretos.

¿Te colgaré sobre los muros
de mi museo sentimental,
junto a los gélidos y oscuros
20 lirios durmientes de mi mal?

¿O te pondré sobre los pinos
—libro doliente de mi amor—
para que sepas de los trinos
que da a la aurora el ruiseñor?

¡Cigarra!

3 de agosto de 1918
(Fuente Vaqueros, Granada)
A María Luisa

¡Cigarra!
¡Dichosa tú!
Que sobre lecho de tierra
mueres borracha de luz.

Tú sabes de las campiñas
el secreto de la vida,
y el cuento del hada vieja
que nacer hierba sentía
en ti quedóse guardado.

10 ¡Cigarra!
¡Dichosa tú!
Pues mueres bajo la sangre
de un corazón todo azul.

Poor wrapper that damped
my fantastical star,
parchment gray and mournful
of what I loved once but love no more!

I see fetal sciences in you,
mummified poems, and bones
of my romantic secrets
and old innocence.

Shall I hang you on the wall
of my emotional museum,
beside the dark, chill,
sleeping irises of my evil?

Or shall I spread you over the pines
—suffering book of my love—
so you can learn about the song
the nightingale offers the dawn?

Cicada!

August 3, 1918
(Fuente Vaqueros, Granada)
          To María Luisa

Cicada!
Oh happy cicada!
On a bed of earth you die,
drunk with light.

You know from the fields
the secret of life;
you keep the tale
of that old fairy
who could hear the grass be born.

Cicada!
Oh happy cicada!
For you die under blood
of a deep blue heart.

9

La luz es Dios que desciende,
y el sol,
brecha por donde se filtra.

    ¡Cigarra!
¡Dichosa tú!
Pues sientes en la agonía
todo el peso del azul.

    Todo lo vivo que pasa
por las puertas de la muerte
va con la cabeza baja
y un aire blanco durmiente.
Con habla de pensamiento.
Sin sonidos . . .
Tristemente,
cubierto con el silencio
que es el manto de la muerte.

    Mas tú, cigarra encantada,
derramando son te mueres
y quedas trasfigurada
en sonido y luz celeste.

    ¡Cigarra!
¡Dichosa tú!
Pues te envuelve con su manto
el propio Espíritu Santo,
que es la luz.

    ¡Cigarra!
Estrella sonora
sobre los campos dormidos,
vieja amiga de las ranas
y de los oscuros grillos,
tienes sepulcros de oro
en los rayos tremolinos
del sol que dulce te hiere
en la fuerza del Estío,
y el sol se lleva tu alma
para hacerla luz.

The light is God descending,
and the sun
the chink it filters through.

Cicada!
Oh happy cicada!
For you feel in your throes
20   all the weight of the blue.

Everything alive that passes
through death's doors
goes head down, with
a white somnolent air.
With speech only thought.
Soundless . . . sadly,
cloaked with silence,
the mantle of death.

But you, cicada,
30   die enchanted, spilling music,
transfigured in sound
and heavenly light.

Cicada!
Oh happy cicada!
You are wrapped in the mantle
of the Holy Spirit,
who is light itself.

Cicada!
Sonorous star
40   over sleeping fields,
old friend of the frogs
and the shadowy crickets,
you have golden tombs
in turbulent sunbeams
that wound you, sweet
in the vigor of Summer.
The sun carries off your soul
to make it into light.

50   Sea mi corazón cigarra
     sobre los campos divinos.
     Que muera cantando lento
     por el cielo azul herido
     y cuando esté ya expirando
     una mujer que adivino
     lo derrame con sus manos
     por el polvo.

     Y mi sangre sobre el campo
     sea rosado y dulce limo
60   donde claven sus azadas
     los cansados campesinos.

     ¡Cigarra!
     ¡Dichosa tú!
     Pues te hieren las espadas invisibles
     del azul.

Mañana

7 de agosto de 1918
(Fuente Vaqueros, Granada)
                    A Fernando Marchesi

     Y la canción del agua
     es una cosa eterna.

     Es la savia entrañable
     que madura los campos.
     Es sangre de poetas
     que dejaron sus almas
     perderse en los senderos
     de la Naturaleza.

     ¡Qué armonías derrama
10   al brotar de la peña!
     Se abandona a los hombres
     con sus dulces cadencias.

Let my heart be a cicada
over heavenly fields.
Let it die singing slow,
wounded by the blue sky.
And, as it fades,
let this woman I foresee
scatter it through the dust
with her hands.

And let my blood on the field
make sweet and rosy mud
where weary peasants
sink their hoes.

Cicada!
Oh happy cicada!
For you are wounded by invisible swords
from the blue.

Morning
August 7, 1918
(Fuente Vaqueros, Granada)
To Fernando Marchesi

And the song of water
is a thing eternal.

It is the intimate sap
that ripens the fields,
the blood of poets
who loosed their souls
to wander all the ways
of Nature.

What harmonies it makes
as it gushes from the rock!
With sweet cadence
it gives itself to men.

La mañana está clara.
Los hogares humean
y son los humos brazos
que levantan la niebla.

Escuchad los romances
del agua en las choperas.
¡Son pájaros sin alas
20 perdidos entre hierbas!

Los árboles que cantan
se tronchan y se secan.
Y se tornan llanuras
las montañas serenas.
Mas la canción del agua
es una cosa eterna.

Ella es luz hecha canto
de ilusiones románticas.
Ella es firme y süave,
30 llena de cielo y mansa,
ella es niebla y es rosa
de la eterna mañana.
Miel de luna que fluye
de estrellas enterradas.
¿Qué es el santo bautismo,
sino Dios hecho agua
que nos unge las frentes
con su sangre de gracia?
Por algo Jesucristo
40 en ella confirmóse.
Por algo las estrellas
en sus ondas descansan.
Por algo Madre Venus
en su seno engendróse,
que amor de amor tomamos
cuando bebemos agua.
Es el amor que corre
todo manso y divino,
es la vida del mundo,
50 la historia de su alma.

The morning is bright.
Smoke rises from hearths
and lifts the fog in its arms.

Listen to the ballads
water sings under poplars:
they are wingless birds
lost in the grass!

20   Trees that sing
dry out and fall;
tranquil mountains
age into plains.
But the song of water
is a thing eternal.

It is light made song
of romantic illusions.
It is soft yet firm,
full of sky and gentle.
30   It is mist and rose
of eternal morning.
Moon-honey that flows
from buried stars.
What is holy baptism
but God become water,
anointing our foreheads
with blood of His grace?
For something was Jesus
confirmed in the water.
40   For something the stars
repose in its waves.
For something Mother Venus
was born in its breast:
it is love of love we drink
when we drink water.
It is love that flows
gentle and divine;
it is the life of the world,
the story of its soul.

Ella lleva secretos
de las bocas humanas,
pues todos la besamos
y la sed nos apaga.
Es un arca de besos,
de bocas ya cerradas,
es eterna cautiva,
del corazón hermana.

Cristo debió decirnos:
60 «Confesaos con el agua,
de todos los dolores,
de todas las infamias.
¿A quién mejor, hermanos,
entregar nuestras ansias
que a ella que sube al cielo
en envolturas blancas?»

No hay estado perfecto
como al tomar el agua.
Nos volvemos más niños
70 y más buenos: y pasan
nuestras penas vestidas
con rosadas guirnaldas.
Y los ojos se pierden
en regiones doradas.
¡Oh fortuna divina
por ninguno ignorada!
Agua dulce en que tantos
sus espíritus lavan,
no hay nada comparable
80 con tus orillas santas
si una tristeza honda
nos ha dado sus alas.

It carries the secrets
from human mouths,
for all of us kiss it
and extinguish our thirst.
It is an ark of kisses
from mouths now closed;
eternally captive, it is
sister to the heart.

Christ should have told us:
"Confess to the water
all of your suffering,
all of your shame.
Who better, brothers,
to hear our sorrows
than she who drifts skyward
clothed in white?"

There is no state so perfect
as ours, when we drink water.
We become more childlike,
more good, and our cares pass,
decked in rosy garlands.
And our eyes wander
through regions of gold.
Oh fortune divine
unknown to none!
Sweet water, who wash
the spirits of many,
nothing can match
your sacred banks
if a deep sadness
has given us its wings.

Canción otoñal
Noviembre de 1918
(Granada)

Hoy siento en el corazón
un vago temblor de estrellas
pero mi senda se pierde
en el alma de la niebla.
La luz me troncha las alas
y el dolor de mi tristeza
va mojando los recuerdos
en la fuente de la idea.

Todas las rosas son blancas,
10   tan blancas como mi pena,
y no son las rosas blancas,
que ha nevado sobre ellas.
Antes tuvieron el iris.
También sobre el alma nieva.
La nieve del alma tiene
copos de besos y escenas
que se hundieron en la sombra
o en la luz del que las piensa.
La nieve cae de las rosas
20   pero la del alma queda,
y la garra de los años
hace un sudario con ella.

¿Se deshelará la nieve
cuando la muerte nos lleva?
¿O después habrá otra nieve
y otras rosas más perfectas?

¿Será la paz con nosotros
como Cristo nos enseña?
¿O nunca será posible
30   la solución del problema?

¿Y si el Amor nos engaña?
¿Quién la vida nos alienta
si el crepúsculo nos hunde
en la verdadera ciencia

Autumn Song
November 1918
(Granada)

    Today in my heart
I feel a vague tremor of stars,
but my path is lost
in the soul of the mist.
The light clips my wings,
and my sorrow
is dipping memories
in the fountain of idea.

    All roses are white,
as white as my pain;
but roses are white only
because snow has fallen on them.
Before, they had the rainbow.
Snow also falls on the soul.
Soul snow has flakes:
scenes and kisses sunk
in the light or shadow
of the one who thinks them.
Snow falls from roses
but stays on the soul,
and the talon of years
weaves it into a shroud.

    Will the snow melt
when Death carries us off?
Or will there be, later,
other snow and other
more perfect roses?

    Will peace be with us
as Jesus teaches?
Or will the problem have
no possible solution?

    And if we're tricked by love?
Who will inspire us
if we're sunk by dusk

del Bien que quizá no exista
y del Mal que late cerca?

Si la esperanza se apaga
y la Babel se comienza,
¿qué antorcha iluminará
40 los caminos en la Tierra?

Si el azul es un ensueño,
¿qué será de la inocencia?
¿Qué será del corazón
si el Amor no tiene flechas?

Y si la muerte es la muerte,
¿qué será de los poetas
y de las cosas dormidas
que ya nadie las recuerda?
¡Oh sol de las esperanzas!
50 ¡Agua clara! ¡Luna nueva!
¡Corazones de los niños!
¡Almas rudas de las piedras!
Hoy siento en el corazón
un vago temblor de estrellas
y todas las rosas son
tan blancas como mi pena.

Canción menor
Diciembre de 1918
(Granada)

Tienen gotas de rocío
las alas del ruiseñor,
gotas claras de la luna
cuajadas por su ilusión.

Tiene el mármol de la fuente
el beso del surtidor,
sueño de estrellas humildes.

in the true knowledge
of Good that might not exist
and Evil that beats close by?

　　And if Hope is extinguished
and Babel begins,
40　　what torch can enlighten
the roads of the earth?

　　And if blue is an illusion,
what will become of innocence?
What will become of the heart
if Love has no arrows?

　　And if death is death,
what will become of poets
and sleeping things
that no one now remembers?
50　　Oh sun of hope!
Clear water! New moon!
Hearts of children!
Rough souls of the rocks!
Today in my heart
I feel a vague tremor of stars,
and all roses are white,
as white as my pain.

Minor Song
December 1918
(Granada)

　　There are dewdrops
on the nightingale's wings,
bright beads of moon
distilled by hope.

　　On the marble fountain
is the kiss of water,
dream of humble stars.

Las niñas de los jardines
me dicen todas adiós
10 cuando paso. Las campanas
también me dicen adiós.
Y los árboles se besan
en el crepúsculo. Yo
voy llorando por la calle,
grotesco y sin solución,
con tristeza de Cyrano
y de Quijote,
                        redentor
de imposibles infinitos
con el ritmo del reloj.
20 Y veo secarse los lirios
al contacto de mi voz
manchada de luz sangrienta,
y en mi lírica canción
llevo galas de payaso
empolvado. El amor
bello y lindo se ha escondido
bajo una araña. El sol
como otra araña me oculta
con sus patas de oro. No
30 conseguiré mi ventura,
pues soy como el mismo Amor,
cuyas flechas son de llanto,
y el carcaj el corazón.

Daré todo a los demás
y lloraré mi pasión
como niño abandonado
en cuento que se borró.

Elegía
Diciembre de 1918
(Granada)

Como un incensario lleno de deseos,
pasas en la tarde luminosa y clara

The girls in the gardens
all tell me goodbye
10 as I pass. The bells,
too, tell me goodbye.
And the trees kiss
in the dusk. Weeping,
I go down the street,
grotesque, without solution,
with the sadness of Cyrano
and Quijote,
                    redeeming
infinite impossibles
20 with the rhythm of the clock.
My voice is stained with bloody light,
and I see irises dry up
at its touch;
in my song
I wear the finery
of a white-faced clown. Love,
sweet Love, hides
under a spider. The sun,
another spider, hides me
30 under legs of gold.
I will not find my fortune,
for I am like Love himself,
whose arrows are tears,
and whose quiver is the heart.

I will give everything away
and weep my passion
like a lost child
in a forgotten tale.

Elegy
December 1918
(Granada)

Like a censer filled with desire,
you pass in the luminous evening

con la carne oscura de nardo marchito
y el sexo potente sobre tu mirada.

Llevas en la boca tu melancolía
de pureza muerta, y en la dionisiaca
copa de tu vientre la araña que teje
el velo infecundo que cubre la entraña
nunca florecida con las vivas rosas,
10   fruto de los besos.

                              En tus manos blancas
llevas la madeja de tus ilusiones,
muertas para siempre, y sobre tu alma
la pasión hambrienta de besos de fuego
y tu amor de madre que sueña lejanas
visiones de cunas en ambientes quietos,
hilando en los labios lo azul de la nana.

Como Ceres dieras tus espigas de oro
si el amor dormido tu cuerpo tocara,
y como la virgen María pudieras
20   brotar de tus senos otra Vía Láctea.

Te marchitarás como la magnolia.
Nadie besará tus muslos de brasa.
Ni a tu cabellera llegarán los dedos
que la pulsen como
                              las cuerdas de un arpa.

¡Oh mujer potente de ébano y de nardo!,
cuyo aliento tiene blancor de biznagas.
Venus del mantón de Manila que sabe
del vino de Málaga y de la guitarra.

¡Oh cisne moreno!, cuyo lago tiene
30   lotos de saetas, olas de naranjas
y espumas de rojos claveles que aroman
los nidos marchitos que hay bajo sus alas.

Nadie te fecunda. Mártir andaluza,
tus besos debieron ser bajo una parra

with your dark flesh of wilted nard
and sex omnipotent over your gaze.

    You have dead chastity's sadness on your lips,
and in the Dionysian goblet of your womb,
the spider weaves a barren veil for entrails
that have never bloomed with living roses,
the fruit of kisses.

                In your white hands
10 you hold a skein of dreams
now dead forever, and in your soul,
passion that hungers for kisses of fire,
and motherlove that dreams distant visions
of cradles and quiet, spinning
on your lips the blue of lullaby.

    Like Ceres, you would have given golden sheaves
if sleeping love had touched your body,
and like the Virgin, you could have
shot from your breast another Milky Way.

20   Like the magnolia, you will wither.
No one will kiss your ember thighs,
no fingers will run through your hair
as over harp strings.

    Oh woman mighty with ebony and nard,
whose breath is white as jasmine!
Venus in an embroidered shawl who knows
the guitar and sweet Málaga wine.

    Oh dark swan! whose lake holds lotuses
of *saetas*, waves of oranges, and spray
30 of red carnations that perfume
the wilted nests beneath its wings.

    No one makes you fertile. Andalusian martyr,
your kisses should have been beneath the vine,
filled with midnight silence
and the turbid rhythm of stagnant water.

plenos del silencio que tiene la noche
y del ritmo turbio del agua estancada.

Pero tus ojeras se van agrandando
y tu pelo negro va siendo de plata;
tus senos resbalan escanciando aromas
40   y empieza a curvarse tu espléndida espalda.

¡Oh mujer esbelta, maternal y ardiente!
Virgen dolorosa que tiene clavadas
todas las estrellas del cielo profundo
en su corazón, ya sin esperanza.

Eres el espejo de una Andalucía
que sufre pasiones gigantes y calla,
pasiones mecidas por los abanicos
y por las mantillas sobre las gargantas
que tienen temblores de sangre, de nieve
50   y arañazos rojos hechos por miradas.

Te vas por la niebla del Otoño, virgen
como Inés, Cecilia y la dulce Clara,
siendo una bacante que hubiera danzado
de pámpanos verdes y vid coronada.

La tristeza inmensa que flota en tus ojos
nos dice tu vida rota y fracasada,
la monotonía de tu ambiente pobre
viendo pasar gente desde tu ventana,
oyendo la lluvia sobre la amargura
60   que tiene la vieja calle provinciana,
mientras que a lo lejos suenan los clamores
turbios y confusos de unas campanadas.

Mas en vano escuchaste los acentos del aire.
Nunca llegó a tu oído la dulce serenata.
Detrás de tus cristales aún miras anhelante.
¡Qué tristeza tan honda tendrás dentro del alma
al sentir en el pecho ya cansado y exhausto
la pasión de una niña recién enamorada!

But the circles grow under your eyes
and your black hair turns to silver;
your breasts slip, spilling out perfume,
and your splendid spine begins to curve.

40 Oh slender woman, maternal and burning!
Our hopeless Lady of Sorrow, her heart
transfixed by all of the stars of deepest heaven.

You are the mirror of an Andalusia
that suffers silently gigantic passions
rocked by fans and by mantillas folded
over throats trembling with blood and snow
and scratched with the red trail of gazes.

You pass into the mist of autumn,
virginal like Agnes, sweet Clara, and Cecilia;
50 bacchante who could have danced,
crowned with grape leaves and green vines.

The immense sadness that floats in your eyes
tells us the failures of your broken life,
the monotony of being poor, of watching people
pass outside your window, hearing rain fall
on the bitterness of old provincial streets,
while, in the distance, rings out
the confused and turbid tumult of the bells.

But in vain you listened to the accents of the air,
60 and your ear never caught the sweet serenade.
You still look out from behind the curtains,
yearning. How deep the sadness in your soul,
to feel in your now exhausted breast
the passion of a young girl new in love!

Your body will go to the grave
intact of emotion.
A dawn song will break
over the dark earth.
From your eyes will grow two bloody carnations
70 and from your breasts, two snow-white roses.

Tu cuerpo irá a la tumba
70 intacto de emociones.
Sobre la oscura tierra
brotará una alborada.
De tus ojos saldrán dos claveles sangrientos
y de tus senos rosas como la nieve blancas.
Pero tu gran tristeza se irá con las estrellas
como otra estrella digna de herirlas y eclipsarlas.

Árboles
1919

¡Árboles!
¿Habéis sido flechas
caídas del azul?
¿Qué terribles guerreros os lanzaron?
¿Han sido las estrellas?

Vuestras músicas vienen del alma de los pájaros,
de los ojos de Dios,
de la pasión perfecta.
¡Árboles!
10 ¿Conocerán vuestras raíces toscas
mi corazón en tierra?

Madrigal
1919

Yo te miré a los ojos
cuando era niño y bueno.
Tus manos me rozaron
y me distes un beso.

(Los relojes llevan la misma cadencia,
y las noches tienen las mismas estrellas.)

Y se abrió mi corazón
como una flor bajo el cielo,

But your sadness will go off to the stars
like another star worthy to wound and eclipse them.

Trees
1919

　　Trees!
Were you once arrows
fallen from the blue?
What terrible warriors
cast you down? The stars?

　　Your music springs from the soul of birds,
from the eyes of God,
from perfect passion.
Trees!
10　Will your tough roots know
my heart in the soil?

Madrigal
1919

　　　　I looked into your eyes
　　　　when I was a boy and good.
　　　　Your hands brushed my skin
　　　　and you gave me a kiss.

　　(All clocks keep the same cadence,
all nights have the same stars.)

　　　　And my heart opened
　　　　like a flower under sky,

los pétalos de lujuria
10 y los estambres de sueño.

(Los relojes llevan la misma cadencia,
y las noches tienen las mismas estrellas.)

En mi cuarto sollozaba
como el príncipe del cuento
por Estrellita de Oro
que se fue de los torneos.

(Los relojes llevan la misma cadencia,
y las noches tienen las mismas estrellas.)

Yo me alejé de tu lado
20 queriéndote sin saberlo.
No sé cómo son tus ojos,
tus manos ni tus cabellos.
Sólo me queda en la frente
la mariposa del beso.

(Los relojes llevan la misma cadencia,
y las noches tienen las mismas estrellas.)

Aire de nocturno
1919

Tengo mucho miedo
de las hojas muertas,
miedo de los prados
llenos de rocío.
Yo voy a dormirme;
si no me despiertas,
dejaré a tu lado mi corazón frío.

            its petals of desire,
10   its stamens of dreams.

   (All clocks keep the same cadence,
all nights have the same stars.)

            Like the prince in the story,
            I sobbed in my room
            for the lady Estrellita,
            who went away from the joust.

   (All clocks keep the same cadence,
all nights have the same stars.)

            I went away from your side,
20   in love without knowing it.
            Now I don't know how your eyes
            look, nor your hands, nor your hair.
            I know only the butterfly
            of your kiss on my forehead.

   (All clocks keep the same cadence,
all nights have the same stars.)

Nocturne
1919

   I am afraid
of dead leaves,
of the fields
filled with dew.
I'll sleep now,
and if you don't wake me,
I'll leave my cold
heart by your side.

«¿Qué es eso que suena
muy lejos?»
10 «Amor,
el viento en las vidrieras,
¡amor mío!»

Te puse collares
con gemas de aurora.
¿Por qué me abandonas
en este camino?
Si te vas muy lejos
mi pájaro llora
y la verde viña
20 no dará su vino.

«¿Qué es eso que suena
muy lejos?»
«Amor,
el viento en las vidrieras,
¡amor mío!»

Tú no sabrás nunca,
esfinge de nieve,
lo mucho que yo
te hubiera querido
30 esas madrugadas
cuando tanto llueve
y en la rama seca
se deshace el nido.

«¿Qué es eso que suena
muy lejos?»
«Amor,
el viento en las vidrieras,
¡amor mío!»

"What is it that rustles so,
10 so far away?"
"Love.
The wind on the windows,
my love!"

I decked you with necklaces,
jewels of dawn.
Why have you left me
alone on this road?
If you go far away,
my bird will weep
20 and the green vineyard
will make no wine.

"What is it that rustles so,
so far away?"
"Love.
The wind on the windows,
my love!"

Snow sphinx,
you never will know
how I could have loved you
30 in the hard rains of dawn
when the nest comes undone
on the dry branch.

"What is it that rustles so,
so far away?"
"Love.
The wind on the windows,
my love!"

Canción primaveral

28 de marzo de 1919
(Granada)

I

Salen los niños alegres
de la escuela,
poniendo en el aire tibio
del Abril, canciones tiernas.
¡Qué alegría tiene el hondo
silencio de la calleja!
Un silencio hecho pedazos
por risas de plata nueva.

I I

Voy camino de la tarde
entre flores de la huerta
dejando sobre el camino
el agua de mi tristeza.
En el monte solitario
un cementerio de aldea
parece un campo sembrado
con granos de calaveras.
Y han florecido cipreses
como gigantes cabezas
que con órbitas vacías
y verdosas cabelleras
pensativos y dolientes
el horizonte contemplan.

¡Abril divino, que vienes
cargado de sol y esencias,
llena con nidos de oro
las floridas calaveras!

Spring Song
March 28, 1919
(Granada)

I

    Happy schoolchildren
pour into the street,
hanging tender songs
in the warm April air.
What joy for the deep
silence of the alley!
A silence shattered
by new-minted silver laughter.

II

    I go down paths of afternoon
among flowers in the orchard,
leaving along the way
the water of my sadness.
On the lonely hill,
a country graveyard
seems a field sown
with skull seed.
And cypresses have flowered
like gigantic heads
that, with empty sockets
and greening tresses,
pensive and sorrowful,
ponder the horizon.

    Oh divine April, who have come
laden with essences and sun,
fill the blooming skulls
with nests of gold!

Mar
Abril de 1919

El mar es
el Lucifer del azul.
El cielo caído
por querer ser la luz.

¡Pobre mar condenado
a eterno movimiento,
habiendo antes estado
quieto en el firmamento!

Pero de tu amargura
10   te redimió el amor.
Pariste a Venus pura,
y quedóse tu hondura
virgen y sin dolor.

Tus tristezas son bellas,
mar de espasmos gloriosos.
Mas hoy en vez de estrellas
tienes pulpos verdosos.

Aguanta tu sufrir,
formidable Satán.
20   Cristo anduvo por ti,
mas también lo hizo Pan.

La estrella Venus es
la armonía del mundo.
¡Calle el Eclesiastés!
Venus es lo profundo
del alma . . .

. . . Y el hombre miserable
es un ángel caído.
La tierra es el probable
30   paraíso perdido.

Ocean
April 1919

The ocean is
the Lucifer of blue.
The sky fallen
for wanting to be light.

Poor ocean, damned
to endless movement,
who once stood still
in the firmament!

But love redeemed you
10 from your bitterness.
You bore pure Venus,
and your depths were virgin
and felt no pain.

Your sadness is beautiful,
ocean of glorious spasms.
But today you have green octopi
instead of stars.

Suffer in patience,
formidable Satan.
20 Christ walked on you,
but so did Pan.

Venus, the star,
is the world's harmony
(Silence, Ecclesiastes!),
the depth of the soul . . .

. . . and wretched man
is a fallen angel.
The earth is probably
paradise lost.

Sueño
Mayo de 1919

Mi corazón reposa junto a la fuente fría.

    (Llénalo con tus hilos,
    araña del olvido.)

El agua de la fuente su canción le decía.

    (Llénalo con tus hilos,
    araña del olvido.)

Mi corazón despierto sus amores decía.

    (Araña del silencio,
    téjele tu misterio.)

10 El agua de la fuente lo escuchaba sombría.

    (Araña del silencio,
    téjele tu misterio.)

Mi corazón se vuelca sobre la fuente fría.

    (¡Manos blancas, lejanas,
    detened a las aguas!)

Y el agua se lo lleva cantando de alegría.

    (¡Manos blancas, lejanas,
    nada queda en las aguas!)

Tarde
Noviembre de 1919

Tarde lluviosa en gris cansado,
y sigue el caminar.
Los árboles marchitos.
                Mi cuarto, solitario.

Dream
May 1919

My heart is resting by the cool spring's banks.

> (Spin it full of thread,
> spider of forgetting.)

The spring waters whispered it their song.

> (Spin it full of thread,
> spider of forgetting.)

My heart awakened and told of its loves.

> (Spider of silence,
> weave it your mystery.)

The spring waters listened to it gravely.

> (Spider of silence,
> weave it your mystery.)

My heart tips over in the cooling spring.

> (Hold back the waters,
> oh distant white hands!)

And singing for joy, the waters float it away.

> (Nothing is left in the waters,
> oh distant white hands!)

Evening
November 1919

Rainy evening in exhausted gray,
and life goes on.
Drooping trees.
> My lonely room.

Y los retratos viejos
y el libro sin cortar . . .

Chorrea la tristeza por los muebles
y por mi alma.
Quizá,
no tenga para mí Naturaleza
el pecho de cristal.

10 Y me duele la carne del corazón
y la carne del alma.
Y al hablar,
se quedan mis palabras en el aire
como corchos sobre agua.

Sólo por tus ojos
sufro yo este mal,
tristezas de antaño
y las que vendrán.

Tarde lluviosa en gris cansado,
y sigue el caminar.

La sombra de mi alma
Diciembre de 1919
(Madrid)

La sombra de mi alma
huye por un ocaso de alfabetos,
niebla de libros
y palabras.

¡La sombra de mi alma!

He llegado a la línea donde cesa
la nostalgia,
y la gota de llanto se transforma,
alabastro de espíritu.

10 (¡La sombra de mi alma!)

And the old portraits
and the book with uncut pages . . .

    Sadness drips over the furniture,
over my soul.
              Perhaps
Nature's breast will not
be crystal clear for me.

10   There is an ache in the flesh of my heart,
in the flesh of my soul.
                   And when I speak,
my words bob in the air
like corks on water.

    Only for your eyes
do I feel this pain,
this sadness gone by,
and sadness to come.

    Rainy evening in exhausted gray,
and life goes on.

My Soul's Shadow
December 1919
(Madrid)

    My soul's shadow
flees through a sunset of alphabets,
mist of books
and words.

    My soul's shadow!

    I've arrived at the line
where nostalgia ceases,
and the drop of lament
becomes alabaster of spirit.

10   (My soul's shadow!)

El copo del dolor
se acaba,
pero queda la razón y la sustancia
de mi viejo mediodía de labios,
de mi viejo mediodía
de miradas.

Un turbio laberinto
de estrellas ahumadas
enreda mi ilusión
20   casi marchita.

¡La sombra de mi alma!

Y una alucinación
me ordeña las miradas.
Veo la palabra amor
desmoronada.

¡Ruiseñor mío!
¡Ruiseñor!
¿Aún cantas?

Hora de estrellas
1920

El silencio redondo de la noche
sobre el pentágrama
del infinito.

Yo me salgo desnudo a la calle,
maduro de versos
perdidos.
Lo negro, acribillado
por el canto del grillo,
tiene ese fuego fatuo,
10   muerto,
del sonido.
Esa luz musical

The skein of sorrow
runs out, but the substance
and the reason of my old
midday of lips remain,
my old midday of gazes.

A turbid labyrinth
of smoky stars
traps my near-wilted
illusion.

20   My soul's shadow!

And hallucination
milks my gazes.
I see the word "love"
worn away.

My nightingale!
Nightingale!
Are you still singing?

Hour of Stars
1920

The round silence of night,
one note on the stave
of the infinite.

Ripe with lost poems,
I step naked into the street.
The blackness riddled
by the singing of crickets:
sound,
that dead
10   will-o'-the-wisp,
that musical light

que percibe
el espíritu.

   Los esqueletos de mil mariposas
duermen en mi recinto.

   Hay una juventud de brisas locas
sobre el río.

El camino

   No conseguirá nunca
tu lanza
herir al horizonte.
La montaña
es un escudo
que lo guarda.

   No sueñes con la sangre de la luna
y descansa.
Pero deja, camino,
10   que mis plantas
exploren la caricia
de la rociada.

   ¡Quiromántico enorme!
¿Conocerás las almas
por el débil tatuaje
que olvidan en tu espalda?
Si eres un Flammarion
de las pisadas,
¡cómo debes amar
20   a los asnos que pasan
acariciando con ternura humilde
tu carne desgarrada!
Ellos solos meditan dónde puede
llegar tu enorme lanza.
Ellos solos, que son
los Bhudas de la Fauna,

perceived
by the spirit.

A thousand butterfly skeletons
sleep within my walls.

A wild crowd of young breezes
over the river.

The Road

Your lance
will never wound
the horizon.
The mountain
is a shield
that guards it.

Do not dream
of the blood of the moon,
just rest.
10 But, oh road, let
the soles of my feet
be caressed by the dew.

Enormous palmist!
Perhaps you read souls
in the faint tattoos
they leave forgotten on your back?
If you are a Flammarion
of footprints,
how you must love
20 the passing donkeys
who, with humble tenderness,
caress your riven flesh!
They alone consider
the aim of your enormous lance.
Buddhas among fauna,
they alone,
when old and wounded,

cuando viejos y heridos deletrean
tu libro sin palabras.

¡Cuánta melancolía
30   tienes entre las casas
del poblado!
¡Qué clara
es tu virtud! Aguantas
cuatro carros dormidos,
dos acacias,
y un pozo del antaño
que no tiene agua.

Dando vueltas al mundo,
no encontrarás posada.
40   No tendrás camposanto
ni mortaja,
ni el aire del amor renovará
tu sustancia.

Pero sal de los campos
y en la negra distancia
de lo eterno, si tallas
la sombra con tu lima
blanca, ¡oh, camino!,
¡pasarás por el puente
50   de Santa Clara!

El concierto interrumpido
1920

A Adolfo Salazar

Ha roto la armonía
de la noche profunda
el calderón helado y soñoliento
de la media luna.

Las acequias protestan sordamente,
arropadas con juncias,

spell out
your wordless book.

30   How melancholy you are
among the village houses!
How bright your virtue!
You patiently support
four sleeping wagons,
two acacias,
and an ancient well
that has no water.

In all your travels
round the world,
40   you find no shelter,
no cemetery, no shroud;
nor will the air of love
renew your being.

But come out of the fields
and if, in the black distance
of the eternal, you carve
the shadow with your
white file, oh road!
you'll go over the bridge
50   of Santa Clara.

The Interrupted Concert
1920

To Adolfo Salazar

The half moon, a fermata
somnolent and frozen,
marks a pause and splits
the midnight harmony.

Blanketed in sedge,
the ditches protest mutely,

y las ranas, muecines de la sombra,
se han quedado mudas.

En la vieja taberna del poblado
10 cesó la triste música,
y ha puesto la sordina a su aristón
la estrella más antigua.

El viento se ha sentado en los torcales
de la montaña oscura,
y un chopo solitario—el Pitágoras
de la casta llanura—
quiere dar, con su mano centenaria,
un cachete a la luna.

La balada del agua del mar
1920

A Emilio Prados
(cazador de nubes)

El mar
sonríe a lo lejos.
Dientes de espuma,
labios de cielo.

—¿Qué vendes, oh joven turbia,
con los senos al aire?

—Vendo, señor, el agua
de los mares.

—¿Qué llevas, oh negro joven,
10 mezclado con tu sangre?

—Llevo, señor, el agua
de los mares.

—¿Esas lágrimas salobres
de dónde vienen, madre?

and frogs, the muezzins of shadow,
have fallen silent.

In the old town tavern
10   the sad music stopped,
and the oldest of stars
has damped its hurdy-gurdy.

The wind has settled
in dark mountain hollows,
and a solitary poplar,
Pythagoras of chaste plains,
wants to lift up its hundred-year-old hand
and slap the moon in the face.

Seawater Ballad
1920

> *To Emilio Prados*
> *(hunter of clouds)*

The sea smiles
in the distance.
Teeth of foam,
lips of sky.

"What are you selling,
oh turbid girl,
with your breasts to the air?"

"I sell, sir, seawater."

"What are you carrying,
10   oh black youth,
mixed with your blood?"

"I carry, sir, seawater."

"Those salty tears:
where do they come from, mother?"

—Lloro, señor, el agua
de los mares.

—Corazón, ¿y esta amargura
seria, de dónde nace?

—¡Amarga mucho el agua
de los mares!

El mar
sonríe a lo lejos.
Dientes de espuma,
labios de cielo.

Deseo
1920

Sólo tu corazón caliente,
y nada más.

Mi paraíso un campo
sin ruiseñor
ni liras,
con un río discreto
y una fuentecilla.

Sin la espuela del viento
sobre la fronda,
ni la estrella que quiere
ser hoja.

Una enorme luz
que fuera
luciérnaga
de otra,
en un campo de
miradas rotas.

"I weep, sir, seawater."

"My heart, and this grave
bitterness: where is it born?"

"How bitter, seawater!"

The sea smiles
20 in the distance.
Teeth of foam,
lips of sky.

Desire
1920

Only your hot heart,
nothing more.

My paradise a field
without nightingales
or lyres,
with a little fountain
and a discreet stream.

Without the spur of the wind
on the branch,
10 without the star
yearning to be leaf.

An enormous light
that longs to be
mere firefly
of another,
in a field
of broken gazes.

Un reposo claro
y allí nuestros besos,
20 lunares sonoros
del eco,
se abrirían muy lejos.

Y tu corazón caliente,
nada más.

Hay almas que tienen . . .
8 de febrero de 1920

Hay almas que tienen
azules luceros,
mañanas marchitas
entre hojas del tiempo,
y castos rincones
que guardan un viejo
rumor de nostalgias
y sueños.

Otras almas tienen
10 dolientes espectros
de pasiones. Frutas
con gusanos. Ecos
de una voz quemada
que viene de lejos
como una corriente
de sombra. Recuerdos
vacíos de llanto
y migajas de besos.

Mi alma está madura
20 hace mucho tiempo,
y se desmorona
turbia de misterio.
Piedras juveniles,
roídas de ensueño,

A bright repose,
and there our kisses,
20   sonorous beauty marks
on Echo's face,
would open
far away.

And your hot heart,
nothing more.

Some Souls . . .
February 8, 1920

Some souls
have blue stars,
mornings pressed
between leaves of time,
and chaste corners
with an ancient
murmur of nostalgia
and dreams.

Other souls have
10   suffering phantoms
of passion. Fruits
worm-eaten. Echoes
of a burnt voice
that comes in
from a distance
like a current
of shadow. Memories
empty of lament.
Crumbs of kisses.

20   My soul has long
been ripe; it decays,
murky with mystery.
Childish stones
gnawed by illusion

caen sobre las aguas
de mis pensamientos.
Cada piedra dice:
«¡Dios está muy lejos!»

Elegía del silencio
Julio de 1920

Silencio, ¿dónde llevas
tu cristal empañado
de risas, de palabras
y sollozos del árbol?
¿Cómo limpias, silencio,
el rocío del canto
y las manchas sonoras
que los mares lejanos
dejan sobre la albura
10 serena de tu manto?
¿Quién cierra tus heridas
cuando sobre los campos
alguna vieja noria
clava su lento dardo
en tu cristal inmenso?
¿Dónde vas si al ocaso
te hieren las campanas
y quiebran tu remanso
las bandadas de coplas
20 y el gran rumor dorado
que cae sobre los montes
azules sollozando?

El aire del invierno
hace tu azul pedazos,
y troncha tus florestas
el lamentar callado
de alguna fuente fría.
Donde posas tus manos,
la espina de la risa
30 o el caluroso hachazo
de la pasión encuentras.

fall on the waters
of my thought.
Every stone says:
"God is far away!"

Elegy: To Silence
July 1920

    Silence, where are you taking
your windowpane misted
with laughter, with words,
and sobs from the trees?
Silence, how do you wash
the dew of song and the sonorous
stains of distant oceans
from the tranquil whiteness
of your cloak?
10 Who heals you when
some old waterwheel
in the fields
drives its slow dart
through your glass?
Where do you go if,
at sunset, you are wounded
by bells, and your backwaters
are broken by flocks of songs
and the great golden murmur
20 that falls on blue mountains
in tears?

    The winter air splinters
your blue, and the quiet lament
of some cool spring
cuts through your groves.
Wherever you lay your hands,
you find laughter's thorn
or the hot ax-blow of passion.
Even out among the stars,
30 the solemn buzzing of blue birds

Si te vas a los astros,
el zumbido solemne
de los azules pájaros
quiebra el gran equilibrio
de tu escondido cráneo.

Huyendo del sonido
eres sonido mismo,
espectro de armonía,
40   humo de grito y canto.
Vienes para decirnos
en las noches oscuras
la palabra infinita
sin aliento y sin labios.

Taladrado de estrellas
y maduro de música,
¿dónde llevas, silencio,
tu dolor extrahumano,
dolor de estar cautivo
50   en la araña melódica,
ciego ya para siempre
tu manantial sagrado?

Hoy arrastran tus ondas,
turbias de pensamiento,
la ceniza sonora
y el dolor del antaño.
Los ecos de los gritos
que por siempre se fueron.
El estruendo remoto
60   del mar, momificado.

Si Jehová se ha dormido,
sube al trono brillante,
quiébrale en su cabeza
un lucero apagado,
y acaba seriamente
con la música eterna,
la armonía sonora
de luz, y mientras tanto,
vuelve a tu manantial,

unsettles the poise
of your hidden skull.

    Fleeing from sound
you are sound itself:
ghost of harmony,
smoke of the cry and of song.
On dark nights you come to us
to whisper the infinite
word without breath,
40 without lips.

    Riddled with stars
and ripe with music,
Silence, where do you take
your extrahuman sorrow,
trapped in melodious spiderwebs,
your holy source
now dry forever?

    Today, cloudy with thought,
your waves drag
50 sonorous ash
and ancient sorrow.
The echoes of cries
now vanished forever,
the distant clamor
of a mummified ocean.

    If Jehovah has fallen
asleep, Silence,
ascend the radiant throne,
crack an extinguished star
60 over His head, and gravely
still the eternal music
of light. Then go back
to the source from which,
in the eternal night,
before God and Time,
you peacefully flowed.

donde en la noche eterna,
antes que Dios y el Tiempo,
manabas sosegado.

Encrucijada
Julio de 1920

¡Oh, qué dolor el tener
versos en la lejanía
de la pasión, y el cerebro
todo manchado de tinta!

¡Oh, qué dolor no tener
la fantástica camisa
del hombre feliz: la piel
—alfombra del sol—curtida!

(Alrededor de mis ojos
10   bandadas de letras giran.)

¡Oh, qué dolor el dolor
antiguo de la poesía,
este dolor pegajoso
tan lejos del agua limpia!

¡Oh dolor de lamentarse
por sorber la vena lírica!
¡Oh dolor de fuente ciega
y molino sin harina!

¡Oh, qué dolor no tener
20   dolor y pasar la vida
sobre la hierba incolora
de la vereda indecisa!

¡Oh el más profundo dolor,
el dolor de la alegría,
reja que nos abre surcos
donde el llanto fructifica!

Crossroad
July 1920

Oh, what sorrow to have
poems off in the distance
of passion, and a brain
all stained with ink!

Oh, what sorrow not to have
the happy man's fantastical
shirt—a tanned skin,
the sun's carpet.

(Flocks of letters
10   wheel round my eyes.)

Oh, what sorrow the ancient
sorrow of poetry,
this sticky sorrow
so far from clean water!

Oh, sorrow of sorrowing
to sip at the vein of lyric!
Oh, sorrow of dried-up fountains
and mills without flour!

Oh, what sorrow to have
20   no sorrow, to spend life
on the colorless grass
of the hesitant lane!

Oh, the deepest sorrow:
the sorrow of joy, a plow
cutting furrows for us
where weeping bears fruit!

(Por un monte de papel
asoma la luna fría.)
¡Oh dolor de la verdad!
30   ¡Oh dolor de la mentira!

Prólogo
24 de julio de 1920
(Vega de Zujaira)

Mi corazón está aquí,
Dios mío.
Hunde tu cetro en él, Señor.
Es un membrillo
demasiado otoñal
y está podrido.
Arranca los esqueletos
de los gavilanes líricos
que tanto, tanto lo hirieron,
10   y si acaso tienes pico
móndale su corteza
de Hastío.

Mas si no quieres hacerlo,
me da lo mismo
guárdate tu cielo azul,
que es tan aburrido,
el rigodón de los astros
y tu Infinito,
que yo pediré prestado
20   el corazón a un amigo.
Un corazón con arroyos
y pinos,
y un ruiseñor de hierro
que resista
el martillo
de los siglos.

Además, Satanás me quiere mucho,
fue compañero mío
en un examen de

(The cold moon rises
over a paper mountain.)
Oh, sorrow of truth!
30 Oh, sorrow of the lie!

Prologue
July 24, 1920
(Vega de Zujaira)

Here, my God,
is my heart.
Sink your scepter in it, Lord.
It is a quince
far too autumnal,
and rotten too.
Pluck out the skeletons
of lyrical hawks
that wounded it so deeply,
10 and if you happen to have
a beak, pare away the skin
of Ennui.

But if you don't want to,
that's fine with me.
Keep your boring old blue heaven
and its little rigadoon of stars.
Keep your Infinite too;
I'll borrow a heart
from a friend of mine.
20 A heart with rivulets
and pines,
and an iron nightingale
that stands up
to the hammer of ages.

Besides, Satan likes me a lot;
we took an exam in Lust together.
The rascal! He'll find me Marguerite—
I have his word.
Dark Marguerite,

30 lujuria, y el pícaro
buscará a Margarita
—me lo tiene ofrecido—,
Margarita morena,
sobre un fondo de viejos olivos,
con dos trenzas de noche
de Estío,
para que yo desgarre
sus muslos limpios.
Y entonces, ¡oh Señor!,
40 seré tan rico
o más que tú,
porque el vacío
no puede compararse
al vino
con que Satán obsequia
a sus buenos amigos.
Licor hecho con llanto.
¡Qué más da!
Es lo mismo
50 que tu licor compuesto
de trinos.

Dime, Señor,
¡Dios mío!
¿Nos hundes en la sombra
del abismo?
¿Somos pájaros ciegos
sin nidos?

La luz se va apagando.
¿Y el aceite divino?
60 Las olas agonizan.
¿Has querido
jugar como si fuéramos
soldaditos?
Dime, Señor,
¡Dios mío!
¿No llega el dolor nuestro
a tus oídos?
¿No han hecho las blasfemias
babeles sin ladrillos

on a ground of old olive trees,
with two braids
of Summer night,
so I can rip at her
immaculate thighs.
And then, oh Lord!
then I'll be as rich
or richer than you,
because the void
can't compare
to the wine
Satan gives
his good friends.
Liquor of lamentation.
But who cares!
It's the same as your
chirping liqueur.

   Tell me, Lord,
my God!
Do you sink us
in abyssal shadow?
Are we blind birds
and nestless?

   The light is fading.
And the holy oil?
The waves are dying.
Did you want
to play with us
like toy soldiers?
Tell me, Lord,
my God!
Doesn't our sorrow
reach your ears?
Haven't blasphemies
raised brickless Babels
to wound you, or do you just
enjoy the noise?
Are you deaf? Blind?
Or are you cross-eyed

70 para herirte, o te gustan
los gritos?
¿Estás sordo? ¿Estás ciego?
¿O eres bizco
de espíritu
y ves el alma humana
con tonos invertidos?

¡Oh Señor soñoliento!
¡Mira mi corazon
frío
80 como un membrillo
demasiado otoñal
que está podrido!

Si tu luz va a llegar,
abre los ojos vivos,
pero si continúas
dormido,
ven, Satanás errante,
sangriento peregrino,
ponme la Margarita
90 morena en los olivos,
con las trenzas de noche
de Estío,
que yo sabré encenderle
sus ojos pensativos
con mis besos manchados
de lirios.
Y oiré una tarde ciega
mi «¡Enrique! ¡Enrique!»
lírico,
100 mientras todos mis sueños
se llenan de rocío.

Aquí, Señor, te dejo
mi corazón antiguo,
voy a pedir prestado
otro nuevo a un amigo.
Corazón con arroyos
y pinos.
Corazón sin culebras

in spirit,
70 seeing double in the human soul?

    Oh nodding Lord!
Look at my heart,
cold as a quince:
too autumnal,
already rotten!

    If your light will come,
open living eyes;
but if you keep on
sleeping,
80 come here, wandering Satan,
you bloody pilgrim,
lay dark Marguerite down
for me among the olives
with the braids
of Summer night;
I'll know how to light fire
in those pensive eyes of hers
with my iris-stained
kisses.
90 And I'll hear, one blind evening,
my lyrical "Enrique!
Enrique!"
while all my dreams fill up
with dew.

    Here, Lord,
here's my old heart.
I'm going to borrow a new one
from a friend of mine.
Heart with rivulets
100 and pines.
Heart without vipers
or irises.
Robust, with the grace
of a young peasant
who crosses the river
in a single
bound.

65

ni lirios.
110 Robusto, con la gracia
de un joven campesino,
que atraviesa de un salto
el río.

Madrigal de verano
Agosto de 1920
(Vega de Zujaira)

Junta tu roja boca con la mía,
¡oh Estrella la gitana!
Bajo el oro solar del mediodía
morderé la Manzana.

En el verde olivar de la colina,
hay una torre mora
del color de tu carne campesina
que sabe a miel y aurora.

Me ofreces, en tu cuerpo requemado,
10 el divino alimento
que da flores al cauce sosegado
y luceros al viento.

¿Cómo a mí te entregaste, luz morena?
¿Por qué me diste llenos
de amor tu sexo de azucena
y el rumor de tus senos?

¿No fue por mi figura entristecida?
(¡Oh mis torpes andares!)
¿Te dio lástima acaso de mi vida,
20 marchita de cantares?

¿Cómo no has preferido a mis lamentos
los muslos sudorosos
de un San Cristóbal campesino, lentos
en el amor y hermosos?

Summer Madrigal
August 1920
(Vega de Zujaira)

Mix your red mouth with mine,
oh Estrella, gypsy girl!
And under the golden midday sun
I'll bite the Apple.

In the olive grove on the hill
stands a Moorish tower
the color of your peasant flesh
that tastes of dawn and honey.

Your scorched body is
10 celestial food that offers
flowers to the tranquil riverbed
and stars to the wind.

Why did you give yourself to me,
dark light? Why give me,
full of love, your lily sex,
the murmur of your breasts?

Was it for my mournful face?
(Oh, my awkward bearing!)
Perhaps you pitied
20 my wilted life of song?

Why did you choose my laments,
and not the sweaty thighs
of a peasant St. Christopher,
slow in love and handsome?

Danaide del placer eres conmigo.
Femenino silvano.
Huelen tus besos como huele el trigo
reseco del verano.

Entúrbiame los ojos con tu canto.
30 Deja tu cabellera
extendida y solemne como un manto
de sombra en la pradera.

Píntame con tu boca ensangrentada
un cielo del amor,
en un fondo de carne la morada
estrella de dolor.

Mi pegaso andaluz está cautivo
de tus ojos abiertos;
volará desolado y pensativo
40 cuando los vea muertos.

Y aunque no me quisieras te querría,
por tu mirar sombrío,
como quiere la alondra al nuevo día,
sólo por el rocío.

Junta tu roja boca con la mía,
¡oh Estrella la gitana!
Déjame bajo el claro mediodía
consumir la Manzana.

Cantos nuevos
Agosto de 1920
(Vega de Zujaira)

Dice la tarde:
            «¡Tengo sed de sombra!»
Dice la luna: «Yo, sed de luceros».
La fuente cristalina pide labios
y suspiros el viento.

A Danaid of pleasure you are
with me, feminine Silvanus.
Your kisses smell of
wheat parched in summer.

Cloud my eyes with your song.
30 Spread your hair,
solemn as a cloak of shadow
on the meadow.

Paint me a heaven of love
with your bloodied mouth,
and the violet star of pain
on a background of flesh.

Your open eyes have caught
my Andalusian Pegasus;
it will fly, desolate and pensive,
40 when it sees them dead.

Even if you did not love me,
I'd love you for your somber gaze
as the lark loves the new day—
only for the dew.

Mix your red mouth with mine,
oh Estrella, gypsy girl!
Let me, beneath the bright midday,
consume the Apple.

New Songs
August 1920
(Vega de Zujaira)

The afternoon says:
                        "I'm thirsty for shadow!"
And the moon: "I want stars."
The crystal fountain asks for lips,
the wind, for sighs.

Yo tengo sed de aromas y de risas.
Sed de cantares nuevos
sin lunas y sin lirios,
y sin amores muertos.

Un cantar de mañana que estremezca
10 a los remansos quietos
del porvenir. Y llene de esperanza
sus ondas y sus cienos.

Un cantar luminoso y reposado,
pleno de pensamiento,
virginal de tristezas y de angustias
y virginal de ensueños.

Cantar sin carne lírica que llene
de risas el silencio.
(Una bandada de palomas ciegas
20 lanzadas al misterio.)

Cantar que vaya al alma de las cosas
y al alma de los vientos
y que descanse al fin en la alegría
del corazón eterno.

Canción para la luna
Agosto de 1920

Blanca tortuga,
luna dormida,
¡qué lentamente
caminas!
Cerrando un párpado
de sombra, miras
cual arqueológica
pupila.
Que quizás sea . . .
10 (Satán es tuerto)
una reliquia,
viva lección

I'm thirsty for scents and for laughter.
Thirsty for new songs
without irises or moons,
without dead loves.

A morning song that can shiver
10 quiet backwaters
of the future and fill
their waves and silt with hope.

A luminous and tranquil song
full of thought,
virgin to sadness and anguish,
virgin to reverie.

A song skinned of lyric, filling
silence with laughter.
(A flock of blind doves
20 tossed into mystery.)

A song to go to the soul of things
and to the soul of winds,
resting at last in the bliss
of the eternal heart.

Song for the Moon
August 1920

White tortoise,
sleeping moon,
how slowly
you walk!
Closing
a shadowy eyelid,
you stare
like an archaeological
pupil.
10 Satan's one-eyed too . . .
Perhaps
it's a relic,

para anarquistas.
Jehová acostumbra
sembrar su finca
con ojos muertos
y cabecitas
de sus contrarias
milicias.
20 Gobierna rígido
la Fez divina
con su turbante
de niebla fría,
poniendo dulces
astros sin vida
al rubio cuervo
del día.
Por eso, luna,
¡luna dormida!,
30 vas protestando,
seca de brisas,
del gran abuso,
la tiranía
de ese Jehová
que os encamina
por una senda,
¡siempre la misma!,
mientras Él goza
en compañía
40 de Doña Muerte,
que es su querida . . .

Blanca tortuga,
luna dormida,
casta Verónica
del sol que limpias
en el ocaso
su faz rojiza.
Ten esperanza,
muerta pupila,
50 que el gran Lenín
de tu campiña
será la Osa
Mayor, la arisca

vivid lesson
for anarchists.
Jehovah has the habit
of sowing his lands
with lifeless eyes
and little heads
of enemy soldiers.
20 Turbaned
frigidly with mist,
he is the ruler
of Holy Fez,
tossing sweet
lifeless stars
to the blond crow
of morning.
And that is why, moon,
sleeping moon!,
30 dry of breezes,
you keep protesting
the abuses
of Jehovah, that despot,
who sends you packing
down the same old path
while He takes pleasure
with His beloved,
Lady Death . . .

White tortoise,
40 sleeping moon,
chaste Veronica
of the sun, you who
every evening,
wipe its reddened face.
Take hope,
dead pupil,
for your land's
great Lenin
will be Ursa
50 Major, the wild
beast of heaven
who'll calmly give
the farewell salute

fiera del cielo,
que irá tranquila
a dar su abrazo
de despedida,
al viejo enorme
de los seis días.

60   Y entonces, luna
blanca, vendría
el puro reino
de la ceniza.

(Ya habréis notado
que soy nihilista.)

In memoriam
Agosto de 1920

Dulce chopo,
dulce chopo,
te has puesto
de oro.
Ayer estabas verde,
un verde loco
de pájaros
gloriosos.
Hoy estás abatido
10   bajo el cielo de agosto
como yo bajo el cielo
de mi espíritu rojo.
La fragancia cautiva
de tu tronco
vendrá a mi corazón
piadoso.
¡Rudo abuelo del prado!
Nosotros,
nos hemos puesto
20   de oro.

to the enormous old man,
him of the six days.

   And then, white
moon, will come
the pure kingdom
of ash.

60   (As for me, I'm a nihilist;
you've all surely noticed.)

In Memoriam
August 1920

   Sweet poplar,
sweet poplar,
you have
turned gold.
Yesterday
you were green,
a green crazy
with glorious
birds.
10 Today you are downcast
under the August sky
as I am beneath
the sky of my red spirit.
My tender heart
will catch
the captive fragrance
of your trunk.
Rough grandfather
of the field!
20 You and I,
we have both
turned gold.

Se ha puesto el sol
Agosto de 1920

Se ha puesto el sol.
                    Los árboles
meditan como estatuas.
Ya está el trigo segado.
¡Qué tristeza
de las norias paradas!

Un perro campesino
quiere comerse a Venus, y le ladra.
Brilla sobre su campo de pre-beso,
como una gran manzana.

10   Los mosquitos—pegasos del rocío—
vuelan, el aire en calma.
La Penélope inmensa de la luz
teje una noche clara.

«Hijas mías, dormid, que viene el lobo»,
las ovejitas balan.
«¿Ha llegado el otoño, compañeras?»,
dice una flor ajada.

¡Ya vendrán los pastores con sus nidos
por la sierra lejana!
20   Ya jugarán las niñas en la puerta
de la vieja posada,
y habrá coplas de amor
que ya se saben
de memoria las casas.

Consulta
Agosto de 1920

¡Pasionaria azul!,
yunque de mariposas.

The Sun Has Set
August 1920

The sun has set,
                and trees,
like statues, meditate.
The wheat has all been cut.
What sadness
in the quiet waterwheels!

A country dog
hungers for Venus
and barks at her.
She shines above her pre-kiss field
10   like a great apple.

Mosquitoes—Pegasuses of dew—
wheel in the still air.
Light, that vast Penelope,
weaves a brilliant night.

"Sleep, my daughters,
for the wolf is coming,"
bleat the little sheep.
"Is it autumn yet, my friends?"
asks a crumpled flower.

20   Now shepherds will come with their nests
across the mountains, far away!
Now little girls will play
in the old inn's door,
and the houses will hear
love songs they've long known
by heart.

Inquiry
August 1920

Blue passionflower!
Anvil of butterflies.

¿Vives bien en el limo
de las horas?

(¡Oh poeta infantil,
quiebra tu reloj!)

Clara estrella azul,
ombligo de la aurora.
¿Vives bien en la espuma
de la sombra?

(¡Oh poeta infantil,
quiebra tu reloj!)

Corazón azulado,
lámpara de mi alcoba.
¿Lates bien sin mi sangre
filarmónica?

(¡Oh poeta infantil,
quiebra tu reloj!)

Os comprendo y me dejo
arrumbado en la cómoda
al insecto del tiempo.
Sus metálicas gotas
no se oirán en la calma
de mi alcoba.
Me dormiré tranquilo
como dormís vosotras,
pasionarias y estrellas,
que al fin la mariposa
volará en la corriente
de las horas
mientras nace en mi tronco
la rosa.

Do you live well
in the silt of the hours?

    (Oh childish poet,
smash your clock!)

    Pale blue star,
navel of dawn.
Do you live well
in the foam of the shadow?

    (Oh childish poet,
smash your clock!)

    Near-blue heart,
lamp of my room.
Do you beat well
without my philharmonic blood?

    (Oh childish poet,
smash your clock!)

    I understand you all.
I've left
in the dresser
the insect of time.
Its steely drops
will make no sound
in the calm of my room.
I will fall peacefully
asleep—as you do,
stars and passionflowers.
For, in the end,
the butterfly will sail
the current of the hours
while a rose is born
from my breast.

El lagarto viejo
26 de julio de 1920
(Vega de Zujaira)

En la agostada senda
he visto al buen lagarto
(gota de cocodrilo)
meditando.
Con su verde levita
de abate del diablo,
su talante correcto
y su cuello planchado,
tiene un aire muy triste
10 de viejo catedrático.
¡Esos ojos marchitos
de artista fracasado
cómo miran la tarde
desmayada!

¿Es este su paseo
crepuscular, amigo?
Usad bastón, ya estáis
muy viejo, Don Lagarto,
y los niños del pueblo
20 pueden daros un susto.
¿Qué buscáis en la senda,
filósofo cegato,
si el fantasma indeciso
de la tarde agosteña
ha roto el horizonte?

¿Buscáis la azul limosna
del cielo moribundo?
¿Un céntimo de estrella?
¿O acaso
30 estudiasteis un libro
de Lamartine, y os gustan
los trinos platerescos
de los pájaros?

(Miras al sol poniente,
y tus ojos relucen,

The Old Lizard
July 26, 1920
(Vega de Zujaira)

    In the sunbaked path
I've seen the good lizard
(drop of crocodile)
meditating.
Like a diabolical abbot
with his green waistcoat,
his perfect demeanor,
and his ironed collar;
melancholy, like
10   an old professor.
Those wilted eyes
of an artist manqué—
how they observe
the fainting afternoon!

    Is this your evening
stroll, my friend?
You should use a cane;
you're getting on now,
Mr. Lizard,
20   and the village children
could give you a scare.
Myopic philosopher,
what do you seek
along the path,
if the hesitant specter
of an August afternoon
has broken the horizon?

    Are you begging azure alms
from this dying sky?
30   A star-penny?
Maybe you studied
a book by Lamartine
and you just enjoy
the plateresque twitter of birds?

¡oh dragón de las ranas!,
con un fulgor humano.
Las góndolas sin remos
de las ideas, cruzan
40   el agua tenebrosa
de tus iris quemados.)

     ¿Venís quizá en la busca
de la bella lagarta,
verde como los trigos
de Mayo,
como las cabelleras
de las fuentes dormidas,
que os despreciaba, y luego
se fue de vuestro campo?
50   ¡Oh dulce idilio roto
sobre la fresca juncia!
¡Pero vivir! ¡qué diantre!
Me habéis sido simpático.
El lema de «me opongo
a la serpiente» triunfa
en esa gran papada
de arzobispo cristiano.

     Ya se ha disuelto el sol
en la copa del monte,
60   y enturbian el camino
los rebaños.
Es hora de marcharse,
dejad la angosta senda
y no continuéis
meditando,
que lugar tendréis luego
de mirar las estrellas
cuando os coman sin prisa
los gusanos.

70   ¡Volved a vuestra casa
bajo el pueblo de grillos!
¡Buenas noches, amigo
Don Lagarto!

(Looking at the setting sun,
your eyes gleam
—oh dragon of the frogs!—
with a human brilliance.
Oarless gondolas
40 of ideas ply murky water
in your burnt pupils.)

Maybe you're looking
for the pretty lizardess,
green like May wheat
or the hair of dormant fountains,
who spurned you
and left your field?
Oh sweet idyll, broken
on the cool sedge!
50 But that's life! What the hell!
You've been good to me.
The motto "I'm against
the serpent" triumphs
in that double chin, big
as a Christian archbishop's.

The sun has dissolved now
on the crest of the hill,
and returning flocks
stir up the dust.
60 It's time to go.
Leave this narrow path,
leave off your meditation.
You'll have time later
to look at the stars
as the worms consume you
slowly.

Back to your house
under the cricket village!
Good night, Mr. Lizard,
70 friend!

Ya está el campo sin gente,
los montes apagados
y el camino desierto.
Sólo de cuando en cuando
canta un cuco en la umbría
de los álamos.

Madrigal
Octubre de 1920
(Madrid)

Mi beso era una granada,
profunda y abierta;
tu boca era rosa
de papel.

El fondo un campo de nieve.

Mis manos eran hierros
para los yunques;
tu cuerpo era el ocaso
de una campanada.

10   El fondo un campo de nieve.

En la agujereada
calavera azul
hicieron estalactitas
mis te quiero.

El fondo un campo de nieve.

Llenáronse de moho
mis sueños infantiles,
y taladró a la luna
mi dolor salomónico.

20   El fondo un campo de nieve.

Not a soul in the fields now:
extinguished the mountains,
deserted the path.
From time to time
in the shadow of poplars
a cuckoo sings.

Madrigal
October 1920
(Madrid)

My kiss was a pomegranate,
open and deep;
your mouth a rose
of paper.

The background, a field of snow.

My hands were irons
for anvils;
your body, sunset
of a tolling bell.

10   The background, a field of snow.

The blue skull gaped.
Inside hung
my *I love you*'s,
stalactites.

The background, a field of snow.

My childish dreams
filled up with mildew,
and my spiral suffering
bored through the moon.

20   The background, a field of snow.

Ahora amaestro grave
a la alta escuela,
a mi amor y a mis sueños
(caballitos sin ojos).

Y el fondo es un campo de nieve.

El diamante
Noviembre de 1920
(Granada)

El diamante de una estrella
ha rayado el hondo cielo,
pájaro de luz que quiere
escapar del universo
y huye del enorme nido
donde estaba prisionero
sin saber que lleva atada
una cadena en el cuello.

Cazadores extrahumanos
10   están cazando luceros,
cisnes de plata maciza
en el agua del silencio.

Los chopos niños recitan
su cartilla; es el maestro
un chopo antiguo que mueve
tranquilo sus brazos muertos.
Ahora en el monte lejano
jugarán todos los muertos
a la baraja. ¡Es tan triste
20   la vida en el cementerio!

¡Rana, empieza tu cantar!
¡Grillo, sal de tu agujero!
Haced un bosque sonoro
con vuestras flautas. Yo vuelvo
hacia mi casa intranquilo.

Solemnly now I train
in the highest of schools
my love and my dreams
(ponies without eyes).

And the background is a field of snow.

Diamond
November 1920
(Granada)

The diamond of a star
has scratched the deep sky.
Bird of light that wants
to escape the universe,
it flees the great nest
that held it captive
but does not feel
the chain around its neck.

Extrahuman hunters
10   hunt the stars,
solid silver swans
in the water of silence.

The poplar children chant
their ABC's; the teacher
a serene old tree
waving its dead branches.
On the mountain, far away,
all the dead play cards.
How sad, the cemetery life!

20   Frog, strike up your song!
Cricket, come out of your hole!
Make a sonorous grove
with your flutes while I
restlessly turn home.

Se agitan en mi cerebro
dos palomas campesinas
y en el horizonte, ¡lejos!,
se hunde el arcaduz del día.
30 ¡Terrible noria del tiempo!

Noviembre
Noviembre de 1920

Todos los ojos
estaban abiertos
frente a la soledad
despintada por el llanto.
　　Tin
　　tan,
　　tin
　　tan.

Los verdes cipreses
10 guardaban su alma
arrugada por el viento,
y las palabras como guadañas
segaban almas de flores.
　　Tin
　　tan,
　　tin
　　tan.

El cielo estaba marchito.
¡Oh tarde cautiva por las nubes,
20 esfinge sin ojos!
Obeliscos y chimeneas
hacían pompas de jabón.
　　Tin
　　tan,
　　tin
　　tan.

Los ritmos se curvaban
y se curvaba el aire.

Two peasant doves
stir in my brain,
and the bucket of day
dips in the distant horizon.
Terrible waterwheel of time!

November
November 1920

All eyes were open
before the tearstained
solitude.
     Ding
     dong,
     ding
     dong.

The green cypresses
held fast to their
wind-wrinkled souls,
and words mowed
flower souls
like scythes.
     Ding
     dong,
     ding
     dong.

The sky wilted.
Oh afternoon in cloud captivity,
sphinx without eyes!
Obelisks and chimneys
were blowing soap bubbles.
     Ding
     dong,
     ding
     dong.

The rhythms curved
in the curving air,

Guerreros de niebla
30   hacían de los árboles
catapultas.
              Tin
              tan,
              tin
              tan.

    ¡Oh tarde,
tarde de mi otro beso!
Tema lejano de mi sombra,
¡sin rayo de oro!
40   Cascabel vacío.
Tarde desmoronada
sobre piras de silencio.
              Tin
              tan,
              tin
              tan.

La veleta yacente
Diciembre de 1920
(Madrid)

    El duro corazón de la veleta
entre el libro del tiempo.
(Una hoja la tierra
y otra hoja el cielo.)
Aplastóse doliente sobre letras
de tejados viejos.
Lírica flor de torre
y luna de los vientos,
abandona el estambre de la cruz
10   y dispersa sus pétalos,
para caer sobre las losas frías
comida por la oruga
de los ecos.

    Yaces bajo una acacia.
¡Memento!

as mist warriors
30 made catapults
of trees.
                Ding
                dong,
                ding
                dong.

    Oh afternoon,
afternoon of my other kiss!
Distant theme of my shadow,
without a golden ray!
40 Empty bell.
Afternoon collapsing
on pyres of silence.
                Ding
                dong,
                ding
                dong.

The Fallen Weathervane
December 1920
(Madrid)

    Hard heart of the weathervane
in the book of time.
(One leaf the earth,
the other the sky.)
Suffering, it smashed
on letters of old rooftiles.
Lyrical tower-blossom
and moon of the winds,
it leaves the cross, its stamen,
10 and scatters its petals.
Fallen on cold pavement,
eaten by the caterpillar echo.

    You lie under an acacia.
Memento!

No podías latir
porque eras de hierro . . .
Mas poseíste la forma,
¡conténtate con eso!
20 Y húndete bajo el verde
légamo,
en busca de tu gloria
de fuego,
aunque te llamen tristes
las torres desde lejos
y oigas en las veletas
chirriar tus compañeros.
Húndete bajo el paño
verdoso de tu lecho,
30 que ni la blanca monja,
ni el perro,
ni la luna menguante,
ni el lucero,
ni el turbio sacristán
del convento,
recordarán tus gritos
del invierno.
Húndete lentamente,
que si no, luego,
40 te llevarán los hombres
de los trapos viejos.
Y ojalá pudiera darte
por compañero
este corazón mío
¡tan incierto!

You had no heartbeat
because you were iron . . .
But you had form;
be happy for that!
Sink down deep
20   in the green ooze
and find your fiery glory,
though towers call sadly
from afar
and in weathervanes
you hear the creak of your companions.
Sink down deep
beneath the greening covers of your bed.
Not the white nun,
nor the dog,
30   nor the waning moon,
nor the morning star,
nor the dim sacristan
at the convent:
no one will remember
your winter cries.
Sink down slowly,
or else, later,
the ragmen will carry you away.
And I wish I could give you
40   my heart for a friend:
my uncertain heart!

POEMA DEL
CANTE JONDO

POEM OF

THE DEEP SONG

Translated by Cola Franzen, Christopher Maurer,

and Robert Nasatir

[Float of the Virgin of Sorrows, 1924]

Baladilla de los tres ríos

A Salvador Quintero

El río Guadalquivir
va entre naranjos y olivos.
Los dos ríos de Granada
bajan de la nieve al trigo.

¡Ay amor
que se fue y no vino!

El río Guadalquivir
tiene las barbas granates.
Los dos ríos de Granada,
10 uno llanto y otro sangre.

¡Ay amor
que se fue por el aire!

Para los barcos de vela
Sevilla tiene un camino;
por el agua de Granada
sólo reman los suspiros.

¡Ay amor
que se fue y no vino!

Guadalquivir, alta torre
20 y viento en los naranjales.
Dauro y Genil, torrecillas
muertas sobre los estanques.

¡Ay amor
que se fue por el aire!

¡Quién dirá que el agua lleva
un fuego fatuo de gritos!

¡Ay amor
que se fue y no vino!

Ballad of the Three Rivers

To Salvador Quintero

The river Guadalquivir
flows between orange and olive trees.
The two rivers of Granada
descend from snow to wheat.

Oh love
that left and did not return!

The river Guadalquivir
has garnet whiskers.
The two rivers of Granada:
one of tears, the other of blood.

Oh love
that left through the air!

Seville has a road
for sailboats;
only sighs row
on the waters of Granada.

Oh love
that left and did not return!

Guadalquivir, high tower
and wind in the orange groves.
Dauro and Genil, little towers
dead in the reflecting pools.

Oh love
that left through the air!

Who would guess that the water carries
a will-o'-the-wisp of shouts!

Oh love
that left and did not return.

POEM OF THE DEEP SONG

Lleva azahar, lleva olivas,
30 Andalucía, a tus mares.

¡Ay amor
que se fue por el aire!

Poema de la Siguiriya gitana

A Carlos Morla Vicuña

Paisaje

El campo
de olivos
se abre y se cierra
como un abanico.
Sobre el olivar
hay un cielo hundido
y una lluvia oscura
de luceros fríos.
Tiembla junco y penumbra
10 a la orilla del río.
Se riza el aire gris.
Los olivos
están cargados
de gritos.
Una bandada
de pájaros cautivos,
que mueven sus larguísimas
colas en lo sombrío.

La guitarra

Empieza el llanto
de la guitarra.
Se rompen las copas
de la madrugada.
Empieza el llanto

It carries olives and orange blossoms,
Andalusia, to your seas.

Oh, love
that left through the air!

TR. R.N.

Poem of the Gypsy Siguiriya
For Carlos Morla Vicuña

Landscape

The field
of olive trees
opens and closes
like a fan.
Above the olive grove
a foundering sky
and a dark rain
of cold stars.
Bulrush and penumbra tremble
10 at the river's edge.
The gray air ripples.
The olive trees
are laden
with cries.
A flock
of captive birds
moving their long long
tails in the gloom.

TR. C.F.

The Guitar

The weeping of the guitar
begins.
The goblets of dawn
are smashed.
The weeping of the guitar

de la guitarra.
Es inútil
callarla.
Es imposible
10   callarla.
Llora monótona
como llora el agua,
como llora el viento
sobre la nevada.
Es imposible
callarla.
Llora por cosas
lejanas.
Arena del Sur caliente
20   que pide camelias blancas.
Llora flecha sin blanco,
la tarde sin mañana,
y el primer pájaro muerto
sobre la rama.
¡Oh guitarra!
Corazón malherido
por cinco espadas.

El grito

La elipse de un grito
va de monte
a monte.

Desde los olivos,
será un arco iris negro
sobre la noche azul.

     ¡Ay!

Como un arco de viola,
el grito ha hecho vibrar
10   largas cuerdas del viento.

begins.
Useless
to silence it.
Impossible
10 to silence it.
It weeps monotonously
as water weeps
as the wind weeps
over snowfields.
Impossible
to silence it.
It weeps for distant
things.
Hot southern sands
20 yearning for white camellias.
Weeps arrow without target
evening without morning
and the first dead bird
on the branch.
Oh, guitar!
Heart mortally wounded
by five swords.

TR. C.F.

The Cry

The arc of a cry
travels from hill
to hill.

From the olive trees
a black rainbow
over the blue night.

Ay!

Like the bow of a viola
the cry has set the wind's
10 long strings to vibrating.

¡Ay!

(Las gentes de las cuevas
asoman sus velones.)

¡Ay!

El silencio

Oye, hijo mío, el silencio.
Es un silencio ondulado,
un silencio,
donde resbalan valles y ecos
y que inclina las frentes
hacia el suelo.

El paso de la Siguiriya

Entre mariposas negras,
va una muchacha morena
junto a una blanca serpiente
de niebla.

Tierra de luz,
cielo de tierra.

Va encadenada al temblor
de un ritmo que nunca llega;
tiene el corazón de plata
y un puñal en la diestra.

¿Adónde vas, Siguiriya,
con un ritmo sin cabeza?
¿Qué luna recogerá
tu dolor de cal y adelfa?

Ay!

(The people of the caves
bring out their oil lamps.)

Ay!

TR. C.F.

The Silence

Listen, my child, to the silence.
An undulating silence,
a silence
that turns valleys and echoes slippery,
that bends foreheads
toward the ground.

TR. C.F.

The Passage of the Siguiriya

Among black butterflies
goes a dark girl
beside a white serpent
of mist.

Earth of light,
sky of earth.

She goes chained to the tremor
of a rhythm that never arrives;
she has a heart of silver,
10 in her right hand a dagger.

Where are you going, Siguiriya,
with a headless rhythm?
What moon will gather up
your sorrow of lime and oleander?

Tierra de luz,
cielo de tierra.

Después de pasar

Los niños miran
un punto lejano.

Los candiles se apagan.
Unas muchachas ciegas
preguntan a la luna,
y por el aire ascienden
espirales de llanto.

Las montañas miran
un punto lejano.

Y después

Los laberintos
que crea el tiempo,
se desvanecen.

(Sólo queda
el desierto.)

El corazón,
fuente del deseo,
se desvanece.

(Sólo queda
10 el desierto.)

La ilusión de la aurora
y los besos,
se desvanecen.

Earth of light,
sky of earth.

TR. C.F.

Afterwards

The children gaze
at a distant spot.

The lamps are put out.
Some blind girls
ask questions of the moon
and spirals of weeping
rise through the air.

The mountains gaze
at a distant spot.

TR. C.F.

And Then

The labyrinths
that time creates
vanish.

(Only the desert
remains.)

The heart,
fountain of desire,
vanishes.

(Only the desert
remains.)

The illusion of dawn
and kisses
vanish.

POEM OF THE DEEP SONG

Sólo queda
el desierto.
Un ondulado
desierto.

Poema de la Soleá

A Jorge Zalamea

Tierra seca,
tierra quieta
de noches
inmensas.

(Viento en el olivar,
viento en la sierra.)

Tierra
vieja
del candil
10 y la pena.
Tierra
de las hondas cisternas.
Tierra
de la muerte sin ojos
y las flechas.

(Viento por los caminos.
Brisa en las alamedas.)

Pueblo

Sobre el monte pelado,
un calvario.
Agua clara
y olivos centenarios.
Por las callejas

Only the desert
remains.
Undulating
desert.

TR. C.F.

Poem of the Soleá
For Jorge Zalamea

Dry land,
quiet land
of immense
nights.

(Wind in the olive grove,
wind in the sierra.)

Old
land
of oil lamps
10 and sorrow.
Land
of deep cisterns.
Land
of death without eyes
and of arrows.

(Wind along the roadways.
Breeze in the poplars.)

TR. C.F.

Pueblo

On the bare hill,
a calvary.
Clear water
and hundred-year-old olive trees.
Through narrow streets

hombres embozados,
y en las torres
veletas girando.
Eternamente
10 girando.
¡Oh pueblo perdido
en la Andalucía del llanto!

Puñal

El puñal
entra en el corazón,
como la reja del arado
en el yermo.

No.
No me lo claves.
No.

El puñal,
como un rayo de sol,
10 incendia las terribles
hondonadas.

No.
No me lo claves.
No.

Encrucijada

Viento del Este,
un farol
y el puñal
en el corazón.
La calle

muffled men,
and on the towers
spinning weathervanes.
Eternally
10 spinning.
Oh lost pueblo
in the Andalusia of tears!

TR. R.N.

Dagger

The dagger
goes into the heart
like the blade of a plow
into barren land.

       No.
Don't run it through me.
       No.

The dagger
like a ray of sun
10 sets fire
to terrible
depths.

       No.
Don't run it through me.
       No.

TR. C.F.

Crossroads

East wind,
a street-lamp
and the dagger
in the heart.
The street

tiene un temblor
de cuerda
en tensión,
un temblor
10 de enorme moscardón.
Por todas partes
yo
veo el puñal
en el corazón.

¡Ay!

El grito deja en el viento
una sombra de ciprés.

(Dejadme en este campo
llorando.)

Todo se ha roto en el mundo.
No queda más que el silencio.

(Dejadme en este campo
llorando.)

El horizonte sin luz
10 está mordido de hogueras.

(Ya os he dicho que me dejéis
en este campo
llorando.)

Sorpresa

Muerto se quedó en la calle
con un puñal en el pecho.
No lo conocía nadie.

shudders
like a string
pulled tight,
the shudder
10 of an enormous horsefly.
Everywhere
I
see the dagger
in the heart.

TR. R.N.

Ay!

The shout leaves a cypress shadow
on the wind.

(Leave me in this field
crying.)

Everything has broken in the world.
Nothing but silence remains.

(Leave me in this field
crying.)

The lightless horizon
10 is bitten by bonfires.

(I have already told you to leave me
in this field
crying.)

TR. R.N.

Surprise

They left him dead in the street
with a dagger in his breast.
No one knew him.

¡Cómo temblaba el farol!
Madre.
¡Cómo temblaba el farolito
de la calle!
Era madrugada. Nadie
pudo asomarse a sus ojos
10 abiertos al duro aire.
Que muerto se quedó en la calle
que con un puñal en el pecho
y que no lo conocía nadie.

La Soleá

Vestida con mantos negros
piensa que el mundo es chiquito
y el corazón es inmenso.

Vestida con mantos negros.

Piensa que el suspiro tierno
y el grito, desaparecen
en la corriente del viento.

Vestida con mantos negros.

Se dejó el balcón abierto
10 y al alba por el balcón
desembocó todo el cielo.

*¡Ay yayayayay,
que vestida con mantos negros!*

Cueva

De la cueva salen
largos sollozos.

How the street-lamp trembled!
Mother.
How the little lamp trembled
in the street!
It was dawn. No one
was able to look into his eyes
10 open to the hard air.
And he was left dead in the street
with a dagger in his breast,
and no one knew him.

TR. R.N.

The Soleá

Dressed in black mantles
she thinks the world tiny
and the heart immense.

Dressed in black mantles.

She thinks the tender sigh
and the cry disappear
on the current of the wind.

Dressed in black mantles.

The balcony was left open
10 and at dawn the whole sky
flowed in through the balcony.

Ay yayayayay,
dressed in black mantles!

TR. R.N.

Cave

From the cave come
long sobs.

(Lo cárdeno
sobre lo rojo.)

El gitano evoca
países remotos.

(Torres altas y hombres
misteriosos.)

En la voz entrecortada
10 van sus ojos.

(Lo negro
sobre lo rojo.)

Y la cueva encalada
tiembla en el oro.

(Lo blanco
sobre lo rojo.)

Encuentro

Ni tú ni yo estamos
en disposición
de encontrarnos.
Tú . . . por lo que ya sabes.
¡Yo la he querido tanto!
Sigue esa veredita.
En las manos
tengo los agujeros
de los clavos.
10 ¿No ves cómo me estoy
desangrando?
No mires nunca atrás,
vete despacio
y reza como yo
a San Cayetano,
que ni tú ni yo estamos
en disposición
de encontrarnos.

(Purple
over red.)

The gypsy conjures
distant lands.

(Tall towers and mysterious
men.)

His eyes follow
10 the faltering voice.

(Black
over red.)

The whitewashed cave
trembles in the gold.

(White
over red.)

TR. C.F.

Encounter

Neither you nor I
are ready
to meet.
You . . . well, you know why.
I have loved her so much!
Follow that path.
I have holes
in my hands
from the nails.
10 Can't you see
how I'm losing my blood?
Don't ever look back,
go slowly
and pray like me
to San Cayetano,
for neither you nor I
are ready
to meet.

TR. C.M.

Alba

Campanas de Córdoba
en la madrugada.
Campanas de amanecer
en Granada.
Os sienten todas las muchachas
que lloran a la tierna
Soleá enlutada.
Las muchachas
de Andalucía la alta
y la baja.
Las niñas de España,
de pie menudo
y temblorosas faldas,
que han llenado de luces
las encrucijadas.
¡Oh campanas de Córdoba
en la madrugada,
y oh campanas de amanecer
en Granada!

Poema de la Saeta

A Francisco Iglesias

Arqueros

Los arqueros oscuros
a Sevilla se acercan.

Guadalquivir abierto.

Anchos sombreros grises,
largas capas lentas.

¡Ay, Guadalquivir!

Dawn

Bells of Córdoba
in the early hours.
Bells of dawn
in Granada.
They hear you,
all the girls who cry
for the tender *Soleá* in mourning.
The girls
of Andalusia the High
and the Low.
Young girls of Spain
with tiny feet
and trembling skirts
who've filled the crossroads
with lights.
Oh, bells of Córdoba
in the early hours,
and oh, bells of dawn
in Granada!

TR. R.N.

Poem of the Saeta

For Francisco Iglesias

Archers

Dark archers
approaching Seville.

Open Guadalquivir.

Wide gray sombreros,
long slow capes.

Oh, Guadalquivir!

Vienen de los remotos
países de la pena.

Guadalquivir abierto.

10 Y van a un laberinto.
Amor, cristal y piedra.

¡Ay, Guadalquivir!

Noche

Cirio, candil,
farol y luciérnaga.

La constelación
de la saeta.

Ventanitas de oro
tiemblan,
y en la aurora se mecen
cruces superpuestas.

Cirio, candil,
10 farol y luciérnaga.

Sevilla

Sevilla es una torre
llena de arqueros finos.

Sevilla para herir.
Córdoba para morir.

Una ciudad que acecha
largos ritmos,

They come from remote
countries of grief.

Open Guadalquivir!

10 And they enter a labyrinth.
Love, crystal and stone.

Oh Guadalquivir.

Night

Candle, oil lamp,
street–lamp and firefly.

The constellation
of the *saeta*.

Little golden windows
trembling;
and in the dawn,
crosses swaying,
one against the other.

10 Candle, oil lamp,
street–lamp and firefly.

Seville

Seville is a tower
full of fine archers.

Seville to wound.
Córdoba to die.

A city that lies in wait
for long rhythms,

y los enrosca
como laberintos.
Como tallos de parra
10   encendidos.

¡Sevilla para herir!

Bajo el arco del cielo,
sobre su llano limpio,
dispara la constante
saeta de su río.

¡Córdoba para morir!

Y loca de horizonte,
mezcla en su vino
lo amargo de Don Juan
20   y lo perfecto de Dionisio.

Sevilla para herir.
¡Siempre Sevilla para herir!

Procesión

Por la calleja vienen
extraños unicornios.
¿De qué campo,
de qué bosque mitológico?
Más cerca,
ya parecen astrónomos.
Fantásticos Merlines
y el Ecce Homo,
Durandarte encantado,
10   Orlando furioso.

and twists them
like labyrinths.
Like burning stems
10   of grapevines.

Seville to wound!

Under the arc of the sky,
over its clean plain,
she shoots the constant
saeta of her river.

Córdoba to die!

And crazy with horizon,
she mixes in her wine
the bitterness of Don Juan
20   and the perfection of Dionysus.

Seville to wound!
Always Seville to wound!

TR. R.N.

Procession

Along the side street come
strange unicorns.
From what field,
what mythological grove?
Close up
they resemble astronomers,
Fantastic Merlins
and the Ecce Homo.
Enchanted Durandarte.
10   Orlando furioso.

TR. C.F.

Paso

Virgen con miriñaque,
Virgen de la Soledad,
abierta como un inmenso
tulipán.
En tu barco de luces
vas
por la alta marea
de la ciudad,
entre saetas turbias
10 y estrellas de cristal.
Virgen con miriñaque,
tú vas
por el río de la calle,
¡hasta el mar!

Saeta

Cristo moreno
pasa
de lirio de Judea
a clavel de España.

¡Miradlo por dónde viene!

De España.
Cielo limpio y oscuro,
tierra tostada,
y cauces donde corre
10 muy lenta el agua.
Cristo moreno,
con las guedejas quemadas,
los pómulos salientes
y las pupilas blancas.

¡Miradlo por dónde va!

Float

Virgin in crinoline,
Virgin of Solitude,
open like an immense
tulip.
On your boat of light
you move
on the high tide
of the city,
among shadowy *saetas*
10 and stars of crystal.
Virgin in crinoline,
you move
down the river of the street
out to the sea!

> TR. R.N.

Saeta

Dark-skinned Christ
passes
from lily of Judea
to carnation of Spain.

Look here he comes!

Of Spain.
Sky clear and dark,
browned earth,
and stream beds where the water
10 barely trickles.
Dark-skinned Christ,
with long locks burnt
high cheekbones
and white pupils.

Look there he goes!

> TR. C.F.

123

Balcón

La Lola
canta saetas.
Los toreritos
la rodean,
y el barberillo,
desde su puerta,
sigue los ritmos
con la cabeza.
Entre la albahaca
10 y la hierbabuena,
la Lola canta
saetas.
La Lola aquella,
que se miraba
tanto en la alberca.

Madrugada

Pero como el amor
los saeteros
están ciegos.

Sobre la noche verde,
las saetas
dejan rastros de lirio
caliente.

La quilla de la luna
rompe nubes moradas
10 y las aljabas
se llenan de rocío.

¡Ay, pero como el amor
los saeteros
están ciegos!

Balcony

Lola
is singing *saetas*.
Would-be bullfighters
surround her,
and the little barber,
from his door,
follows the rhythms
with his head.
Between the basil
10 and the mint,
Lola is singing
saetas.
That very Lola
who used to look at herself
so long in the fountain.

TR. R.N.

Before Dawn

But like love
the archers
are blind.

Above the green night
arrows
leave traces of ardent
lily.

The keel of the moon
rips purple clouds
10 and the quivers
fill with dew.

Oh, but like love
the archers
are blind!

TR. C.F.

Gráfico de la Petenera

Campana
(Bordón)

En la torre
amarilla
dobla una campana.

Sobre el viento
amarillo
se abren las campanadas.

En la torre
amarilla
cesa la campana.

10 El viento con el polvo
hace proras de plata.

Camino

Cien jinetes enlutados,
¿dónde irán,
por el cielo yacente
del naranjal?
Ni a Córdoba ni a Sevilla
llegarán.
Ni a Granada la que suspira
por el mar.
Esos caballos soñolientos
10 los llevarán
al laberinto de las cruces
donde tiembla el cantar.
Con siete ayes clavados,
¿dónde irán
los cien jinetes andaluces
del naranjal?

Graphic of the Petenera

For Eugenio Montes

Bell

(Bass String)

In the yellow
tower
a bell tolls.

Over the yellow
wind
the bell–notes flower.

In the yellow
tower
the bell stops.

10   With dust the wind
shapes silver prows.

TR. C.F.

Road

One hundred horsemen in mourning,
where will they go,
under the recumbent sky
of the orange grove?
They will never get to Córdoba,
or Granada that sighs
for the sea.
Those sleepy horses
will carry them
10   to the labyrinth of crosses
where the song trembles.
Pierced by seven *ays*
where will they go,
the one hundred Andalusian horsemen
of the orange grove?

TR. R.N.

Las seis cuerdas

La guitarra
hace llorar a los sueños.
El sollozo de las almas
perdidas
se escapa por su boca
redonda.
Y como la tarántula,
teje una gran estrella
para cazar suspiros,
10 que flotan en su negro
aljibe de madera.

Danza
(En el huerto de la Petenera)

En la noche del huerto,
seis gitanas
vestidas de blanco
bailan.

En la noche del huerto,
coronadas
con rosas de papel
y biznagas.

En la noche del huerto,
10 sus dientes de nácar
escriben la sombra
quemada.

Y en la noche del huerto,
sus sombras se alargan
y llegan hasta el cielo
moradas.

The Six Strings

The guitar
makes dreams weep.
The sobs of lost
souls
escape through its round
mouth.
And like the tarantula
it weaves a large star
to trap the sighs
10 floating in its black
wooden cistern.

                    TR. C.F.

Dance
(In the Garden of the Petenera)

In the night of the garden,
six gypsy women
dance in white.

In the night of the garden,
crowned
with paper roses
and jasmine.

In the night of the garden,
their teeth—mother-of-pearl—
10 inscribe the burnt
darkness.

And in the night of the garden,
their shadows grow long
and purple
as they reach the sky.

                    TR. C.M.

Muerte de la Petenera

En la casa blanca muere
la perdición de los hombres.

Cien jacas caracolean.
Sus jinetes están muertos.

Bajo las estremecidas
estrellas de los velones,
su falda de moaré tiembla
entre sus muslos de cobre.

Cien jacas caracolean.
10 *Sus jinetes están muertos.*

Largas sombras afiladas
vienen del turbio horizonte,
y el bordón de una guitarra
se rompe.

Cien jacas caracolean.
Sus jinetes están muertos.

Falseta

¡Ay, Petenera gitana!
¡Yayay Petenera!
Tu entierro no tuvo niñas
buenas.
Niñas que le dan a Cristo muerto
sus guedejas,
y llevan blancas mantillas
en las ferias.
Tu entierro fue de gente
10 siniestra.
Gente con el corazón
en la cabeza,
que te siguió llorando

Death of the Petenera

In the white house
man's perdition is dying.

One hundred ponies caracole.
Their riders are all dead.

Under the shuddering stars
of the oil lamps,
her moiré skirt trembles
between her copper thighs.

One hundred ponies caracole.
10 *Their riders are all dead.*

Long, sharp shadows
come from the dark horizon,
and the bass string of a guitar
breaks.

One hundred ponies caracole.
Their riders are all dead.

TR. R.N.

Guitar Run

Oh gypsy Petenera!
Oh Petenera!
There were no good girls
at your burial.
Girls who give tresses
to dead Christ,
and wear white mantillas
to the fair.
Your burial was seen by
10 sinister people,
people with their hearts
in their heads,
who followed you crying

por las callejas.
¡Ay, Petenera gitana!
¡Yayay Petenera!

De profundis

Los cien enamorados
duermen para siempre
bajo la tierra seca.
Andalucía tiene
largos caminos rojos.
Córdoba, olivos verdes
donde poner cien cruces
que los recuerden.
Los cien enamorados
10 duermen para siempre.

Clamor

En las torres
amarillas
doblan las campanas.

Sobre los vientos
amarillos
se abren las campanadas.

Por un camino va
la Muerte, coronada
de azahares marchitos.
10 Canta y canta
una canción
en su vihuela blanca,
y canta y canta y canta.

through the side-streets.
Oh gypsy Petenera!
Oh Petenera!

TR. R.N.

De Profundis

The one hundred lovers
sleep forever
under the dry earth.
Andalucía has
long red roads.
Córdoba, green olive trees
where a hundred crosses
will help remember them.
The one hundred lovers
10   sleep forever.

TR. R.N.

Death Knell

In the yellow
towers
the bells toll.

Over the yellow
winds
the bell-notes flower.

Along a road goes
death, wearing a crown
of withered orange blossoms.
10   She sings and sings
a song
on her white *vihuela*,
sings and sings and sings.

POEM OF THE DEEP SONG

En las torres amarillas
cesan las campanas.

El viento con el polvo
hace proras de plata.

Dos muchachas
A Máximo Quijano

La Lola

Bajo el naranjo, lava
pañales de algodón.
Tiene verdes los ojos
y violeta la voz.

¡Ay, amor,
bajo el naranjo en flor!

El agua de la acequia
iba llena de sol.
En el olivarito
10 cantaba un gorrión.

¡Ay, amor,
bajo el naranjo en flor!

Luego, cuando la Lola
gaste todo el jabón,
vendrán los torerillos.

¡Ay, amor,
bajo el naranjo en flor!

In the yellow towers
the bells stop.

With dust the wind
shapes silver prows.

Two Girls

To Máximo Quijano

Lola

Under the orange tree,
she washes cotton diapers.
She has green eyes
and a violet voice.

Oh love,
under the orange blossoms!

The stream water
flowed full of sun.
A sparrow was singing
10 in the olive grove.

Oh love,
under the orange blossoms!

Later, when Lola
uses up all the soap,
the young *toreros* will come.

Oh love,
under the orange blossoms!

Amparo

Amparo,
¡qué sola estás en tu casa
vestida de blanco!

(Ecuador entre el jazmín
y el nardo.)

Oyes los maravillosos
surtidores de tu patio,
y el débil trino amarillo
del canario.

10 Por la tarde ves temblar
los cipreses con los pájaros,
mientras bordas lentamente
letras sobre el cañamazo.

Amparo,
¡qué sola estás en tu casa
vestida de blanco!

Amparo,
¡y qué difícil decirte:
yo te amo!

Viñetas flamencas

*A Manuel Torres, <<Niño de Jerez>>,
que tiene tronco de Faraón*

Retrato de Silverio Franconetti

Entre italiano
y flamenco,
¿cómo cantaría
aquel Silverio?
La densa miel de Italia,

Amparo

Amparo,
so alone in your house,
dressed in white!

(Dividing line between jasmine
and spikenard.)

You hear the marvelous
fountains of your patio,
and the delicate yellow trill
of the canary.

10   In the afternoon you see
the cypresses tremble with birds
while you slowly embroider
letters on canvas.

Amparo,
so alone in your house,
dressed in white!

And Amparo,
so difficult to say:
I love you!

TR. R.N.

Flamenco Vignettes

For Manuel Torres, "Niño de Jerez,"
descended from a line of Pharaohs

Portrait of Silverio Franconetti

Somewhere between Italian
and flamenco,
I wonder
how Silverio sang?
The dense honey of Italy

POEM OF THE DEEP SONG

con el limón nuestro,
iba en el hondo llanto
del siguiriyero.
Su grito fue terrible.
10   Los viejos
dicen que se erizaban
los cabellos
y se abría el azogue
de los espejos.
Pasaba por los tonos
sin romperlos.

Y fue un creador
y un jardinero.
Un creador de glorietas
20   para el silencio.

Ahora su melodía
duerme con los ecos.
Definitiva y pura.
¡Con los últimos ecos!

Juan Breva

Juan Breva tenía
cuerpo de gigante
y voz de niña.
Nada como su trino.
Era la misma
Pena cantando
detrás de una sonrisa.
Evoca los limonares
de Málaga la dormida,
10   y hay en su llanto dejos
de sal marina.
Como Homero, cantó
ciego. Su voz tenía
algo de mar sin luz
y naranja exprimida.

and our own lemon
were in that *siguiriyero*'s
deep wail.
His cry was terrible.
10 Old people say
it stood your hair on end
and opened the mercury
in mirrors.
He passed over the tones
without breaking them,
creator
and gardener.

Creator of bowers
for silence.

20 Now his melody
sleeps with the echoes.
Definitive, pure,
with the final echoes!

TR. C.M.

Juan Breva

Juan Breva had
a giant's body
and the voice of a girl.
Nothing like his trill.
Pain itself
singing
behind a smile.
He conjures up the lemon groves
of slumbrous Málaga,
10 his lament carries
hints of sea salt.
Like Homer he sang
blind. His voice had
something of sea without light,
and orange squeezed dry.

TR. C.F.

Café cantante

Lámparas de cristal
y espejos verdes.

Sobre el tablado oscuro,
la Parrala sostiene
una conversación
con la muerte.
La llama,
no viene,
y la vuelve a llamar.
10 Las gentes
aspiran los sollozos.
Y en los espejos verdes,
largas colas de seda
se mueven.

Lamentación de la muerte

A Miguel Benítez

Sobre el cielo negro,
culebrinas amarillas.

Vine a este mundo con ojos
y me voy sin ellos.
¡Señor del mayor dolor!
Y luego,
un velón y una manta
en el suelo.

Quise llegar adonde
10 llegaron los buenos.
¡Y he llegado, Dios mío! . . .
Pero luego,
un velón y una manta
en el suelo.

Cabaret

Glass lamps
and green mirrors.

On the dark stage
La Parrala carries on
a conversation
with death.
Calls her,
she doesn't come,
calls her again.
10 The people
swallow their sobs.
And in the green mirrors
long silken trains
begin to stir.

TR. C.F.

Death's Lament

For Miguel Benítez

Yellow lightning
in the black sky.

I came into this world with eyes,
and leave it without them.
God of Greatest Sorrow!
And in the end,
a taper and a blanket
on the floor.

I wanted to get where
10 the good people go,
and, my God, I did!
But in the end,
a taper and a blanket
on the floor.

Limoncito amarillo,
limonero.
Echad los limoncitos
al viento.
¡Ya lo sabéis! . . . Porque luego,
20 luego,
un velón y una manta
en el suelo.

Sobre el cielo negro,
culebrinas amarillas.

Conjuro

La mano crispada
como una Medusa
ciega el ojo doliente
del candil.

As de bastos.
Tijeras en cruz.

Sobre el humo blanco
del incienso, tiene
algo de topo y
10 mariposa indecisa.

As de bastos.
Tijeras en cruz.

Aprieta un corazón
invisible, ¿la veis?
Un corazón
reflejado en el viento.

As de bastos.
Tijeras en cruz.

Little yellow lemon,
lemon tree,
throw the lemons
to the breeze.
So now you know! For in the end,
20 the end:
a taper and a blanket
on the floor.

Yellow lightning
in the black sky.

TR. C.M.

Spell

The right hand
like a medusa
blinds the sickly eye
of the oil lamp.

Ace of spades.
Crossed scissors.

Above the white smoke
of the incense, it looks
something like a mole and
10 a hesitant butterfly.

Ace of spades.
Crossed scissors.

It clenches an
invisible heart, see it?
A heart
reflected in the wind.

Ace of spades.
Crossed scissors.

TR. C.F.

Memento

Cuando yo me muera,
enterradme con mi guitarra
bajo la arena.

Cuando yo me muera,
entre los naranjos
y la hierbabuena.

Cuando yo me muera,
enterradme, si queréis,
en una veleta.

10   ¡Cuando yo me muera!

Tres ciudades

A Pilar Zubiaurre

Malagueña

La muerte
entra y sale
de la taberna.

Pasan caballos negros
y gente siniestra
por los hondos caminos
de la guitarra.

Y hay un olor a sal
y a sangre de hembra
10   en los nardos febriles
de la marina.

La muerte
entra y sale,
y sale y entra

Memento

Whenever I die,
bury me with my guitar
beneath the sand.

Whenever I die,
among orange trees
and mint.

Whenever I die,
bury me if you wish
in a weathervane.

10 Whenever I die!

TR. C.F.

Three Cities

For Pilar Zubiaurre

Malagueña

Death
goes in and out
of the tavern.

Black horses
and sinister people
pass along the sunken roads
of the guitar.

There's an odor of salt
and female blood
10 in the feverish spikenard
along the shore.

Death
goes in and out,
out and in

la muerte
de la taberna.

Barrio de Córdoba
(Tópico nocturno)

En la casa se defienden
de las estrellas.
La noche se derrumba.
Dentro hay una niña muerta
con una rosa encarnada
oculta en la cabellera.
Seis ruiseñores la lloran
en la reja.

Las gentes van suspirando
10 con las guitarras abiertas.

Baile

La Carmen está bailando
por las calles de Sevilla.
Tiene blancos los cabellos
y brillantes las pupilas.

¡Niñas,
corred las cortinas!

En su cabeza se enrosca
una serpiente amarilla,
y va soñando en el baile
10 con galanes de otros días.

¡Niñas,
corred las cortinas!

of the tavern goes
death.

TR. C.F.

Neighborhood of Córdoba
(Nocturnal Theme)

Inside the house they take shelter
from the stars.
Night collapses.
Within, a dead girl,
a crimson rose
hidden in her hair.
Six nightingales on the railing
weep for her.

The people keep sighing
10 with gaping guitars.

TR. C.F.

Dance

Carmen is dancing
through the streets of Seville.
White is her hair
and her eyes shine.

Girls,
draw the curtains!

Around her head
a yellow serpent coils.
And as she dances she dreams
10 of swains of other days.

Girls,
draw the curtains!

Las calles están desiertas
y en los fondos se adivinan
corazones andaluces
buscando viejas espinas.

¡Niñas,
corred las cortinas!

Seis caprichos

A Regino Sainz de la Maza

Adivinanza de la guitarra

En la redonda
encrucijada,
seis doncellas
bailan.
Tres de carne
y tres de plata.
Los sueños de ayer las buscan,
pero las tiene abrazadas
un Polifemo de oro.
10 ¡La guitarra!

Candil

¡Oh, qué grave medita
la llama del candil!

Como un faquir indio
mira su entraña de oro
y se eclipsa soñando
atmósferas sin viento.

Cigüeña incandescente
pica desde su nido

The streets are empty.
In the deep recesses, hints of
Andalusian hearts
searching for old thorns.

Girls,
draw the curtains!

TR . C.F.

Six Capriccios

For Regino Sainz de la Maza

Riddle of the Guitar

At the round
crossway
six maidens
dance.
Three of flesh
and three of silver.
Dreams of yesterday seek them,
but a golden Polyphemus
holds them in his embrace.
10 Guitar!

TR . C.F.

Oil Lamp

Oh, how gravely the flame
of the oil lamp meditates!

Like an Indian fakir
it gazes at its golden entrails,
then goes into eclipse dreaming
atmospheres with no wind.

Incandescent stork
from its nest pecks

a las sombras macizas
10 y se asoma temblando
a los ojos redondos
del gitanillo muerto.

Crótalo

Crótalo.
Crótalo.
Crótalo.
Escarabajo sonoro.

En la araña
de la mano
rizas el aire
cálido
y te ahogas en tu trino
10 de palo.

Crótalo.
Crótalo.
Crótalo.
Escarabajo sonoro.

Chumbera

Laocoonte salvaje.

¡Qué bien estás
bajo la media luna!

Mútiple pelotari.

¡Qué bien estás
amenazando al viento!

at the massive shadows
10 and, trembling, approaches
the round eyes
of the dead gypsy boy.

TR. C.F.

Castanet

Castanet.
Castanet.
Castanet.
Sonorous scarab.

In the spider
of the hand
you crimp the warm
air,
and drown in your wooden
10 trill.

Castanet.
Castanet.
Castanet.
Sonorous scarab.

TR. C.F.

Prickly Pear

Wild Laocoön.

How grand you look
beneath the half-moon!

Multiplied ball player.

How grand you look
threatening the wind!

Dafne y Atis,
saben de tu dolor.
Inexplicable.

Pita

Pulpo petrificado.

Pones cinchas cenicientas
al vientre de los montes
y muelas formidables
a los desfiladeros.

Pulpo petrificado.

Cruz

La cruz.
(Punto final
del camino.)

Se mira en la acequia.
(Puntos suspensivos.)

Escena del teniente coronel
de la Guardia Civil

Cuarto de banderas

TENIENTE CORONEL: Yo soy el teniente coronel de la Guardia
Civil.
SARGENTO: Sí.
TENIENTE CORONEL: Y no hay quien me desmienta.
SARGENTO: No.

Daphne and Attis
know of your pain.
Inexplicable.

TR. C.F.

Agave

Petrified octopus.

You put dusty cinch straps
around the belly of the mountains
and formidable molars
along the defiles.

Petrified octopus.

TR. C.F.

Cross

The cross.
(Final point
of the road.)

Reflected in the waterway.
(Suspension points.)

TR. C.F.

Scene of the Lieutenant Colonel
of the Civil Guard

Flag Room

LT. COLONEL: I am the Lieutenant Colonel of the Civil Guard.
SERGEANT: Yes, sir.
LT. COLONEL: And no one contradicts me.
SERGEANT: Yes, sir.

TENIENTE CORONEL: Tengo tres estrellas y veinte cruces.

SARGENTO: Sí.

TENIENTE CORONEL: Me ha saludado el cardenal arzobispo de Toledo con sus veinticuatro borlas moradas.

SARGENTO: Sí.

TENIENTE CORONEL: Yo soy el teniente. Yo soy el teniente. Yo soy el teniente coronel de la Guardia Civil.

(Romeo y Julieta, celeste, blanco y oro, se abrazan sobre el jardín de tabaco de la caja de puros. El militar acaricia el cañón de su fusil lleno de sombra submarina.)

UNA VOZ (*fuera*):

Luna, luna, luna, luna,
del tiempo de la aceituna.
Cazorla enseña su torre
y Benamejí la oculta.

Luna, luna, luna, luna.
Un gallo canta en la luna.
Señor alcalde, sus niñas
están mirando a la luna.

TENIENTE CORONEL: ¿Qué pasa?

SARGENTO: ¡Un gitano!

(La mirada de mulo joven del gitanillo ensombrece y agiganta los ojirris del teniente coronel de la Guardia Civil.)

TENIENTE CORONEL: Yo soy el teniente coronel de la Guardia Civil.

SARGENTO: Sí.

TENIENTE CORONEL: ¿Tú quién eres?

GITANO: Un gitano.

TENIENTE CORONEL: ¿Y qué es un gitano?

GITANO: Cualquier cosa.

TENIENTE CORONEL: ¿Cómo te llamas?

GITANO: Eso.

TENIENTE CORONEL: ¿Qué dices?

GITANO: Gitano.

SARGENTO: Me lo encontré y lo he traído.

TENIENTE CORONEL: ¿Dónde estabas?

GITANO: En la puente de los ríos.

TENIENTE CORONEL: Pero ¿de qué ríos?

GITANO: De todos los ríos.

LT. COLONEL: I have three stars and twenty crosses.

SERGEANT: Yes, sir.

LT. COLONEL: The Cardinal Archbishop of Toledo greets me
with his twenty-four purple tassels.

SERGEANT: Yes, sir.

LT. COLONEL: I'm the Lieutenant. The Lieutenant. I'm the
Lieutenant Colonel of the Civil Guard.

*(Romeo and Juliet embrace in the tobacco garden of the cigar box under a
blue, white and gold sky. The soldier fondles the barrel of his rifle, full of
submarine darkness.)*

A VOICE (*backstage*):

Moon, moon, moon, moon,
at olive-picking time.
Cazorla shows its tower
and Benamejí hides its own.

Moon, moon, moon, moon.
A rooster is singing on the moon.
Mr. Mayor, your little girls
are looking at the moon.

LT. COLONEL: What's going on?

SERGEANT: A gypsy!

*(The gypsy boy's look—like that of a young mule—makes the eyes of
the Lieutenant Colonel of the Civil Guard grow wide and dark.)*

LT. COLONEL: I am the Lieutenant Colonel of the Civil Guard.

SERGEANT: Yes.

LT. COLONEL: And who are *you*?

GYPSY: A gypsy.

LT. COLONEL: And what is a gypsy?

GYPSY: Just about anything.

LT. COLONEL: What's your name?

GYPSY: Just that.

LT. COLONEL: What did you say?

GYPSY: Gypsy.

SERGEANT: I found him and brought him in.

LT. COLONEL: Where were you?

GYPSY: On the bridge of all rivers.

LT. COLONEL: What rivers?

GYPSY: All of them.

LT. COLONEL: And what were you doing there?

GYPSY: Making a tower of cinnamon.

TENIENTE CORONEL: ¿Y qué hacías allí?

GITANO: Una torre de canela.

TENIENTE CORONEL: ¡Sargento!

SARGENTO: A la orden, mi teniente coronel de la Guardia Civil.

GITANO: He inventado unas alas para volar, y vuelo. Azufre y rosa en mis labios.

TENIENTE CORONEL: ¡Ay!

GITANO: Aunque no necesito alas, porque vuelo sin ellas. Nubes y anillos en mi sangre.

TENIENTE CORONEL: ¡Ayyy!

GITANO: En enero tengo azahar.

TENIENTE CORONEL (*retorciéndose*): ¡Ayyyyy!

GITANO: Y naranjas en la nieve.

TENIENTE CORONEL: ¡Ayyyyy!, pun, pin, pam. (*Cae muerto.*)
(*El alma de tabaco y café con leche del teniente coronel de la Guardia Civil sale por la ventana.*)

SARGENTO: ¡Socorro!
(*En el patio del cuartel, cuatro guardias civiles apalean al gitanillo.*)

Canción del gitano apaleado

Veinticuatro bofetadas.
Veinticinco bofetadas;
después, mi madre, a la noche,
me pondrá en papel de plata.

Guardia Civil caminera,
dadme unos sorbitos de agua.
Agua con peces y barcos.
Agua, agua, agua, agua.

¡Ay, mandor de los civiles
10 que estás arriba en tu sala!
¡No habrá pañuelos de seda
para limpiarme la cara!

5 de julio 1925

LT. COLONEL: Sergeant!

SERGEANT: At your orders, my Lieutenant Colonel of the Civil
Guard!

GYPSY: I've invented wings to fly, and I fly. Sulphur and rose on
my lips!

LT. COLONEL: Ay!

GYPSY: Even though I don't need wings, for I fly without them.
Clouds and rings on my tongue.

LT. COLONEL: Ayyy!

GYPSY: In January I have orange blossoms.

LT. COLONEL (*squirming in irritation*): Ayyyy!

GYPSY: And oranges in the snow.

LT. COLONEL: Ayyyyy! Blam! Blam! (*He falls over dead.*)
(*The tobacco and coffee soul of the Lieutenant Colonel of the Civil
Guard flies through the window.*)

SERGEANT: Help!
(*In the courtyard of the barracks, four Civil Guards beat the gypsy boy.*)

Song of the Beaten Gypsy

Twenty-four times they hit me.
Twenty-five times in all.
Later, at night, my mother
will wrap me in silver foil.

Civil Guard of the roadways,
give me a sip of water.
Water with fish and ships.
Water, water, water, water.

Commander of the Civil Guard,
you, up alone in your room!
There'll never be enough silk
handkerchiefs to wipe my face!

July 5, 1925

TR. C.M.

Diálogo del Amargo

Campo

UNA VOZ:

Amargo.

Las adelfas de mi patio.

Corazón de almendra amarga.

Amargo.

(Llegan tres jóvenes con anchos sombreros.)

JOVEN 1.°: Vamos a llegar tarde.

JOVEN 2.°: La noche se nos echa encima.

JOVEN 1.°: ¿Y ése?

JOVEN 2.°: Viene detrás.

JOVEN 1.° *(en alta voz)*: ¡Amargo!

AMARGO *(lejos)*: Ya voy.

JOVEN 2.° *(a voces)*: ¡Amargo!

AMARGO *(con calma)*: Ya voy.

(Pausa)

JOVEN 1.°: ¡Qué hermosos olivares!

JOVEN 2.°: Sí.

(Largo silencio)

JOVEN 1.°: No me gusta andar de noche.

JOVEN 2.°: Ni a mí tampoco.

JOVEN 1.°: La noche se hizo para dormir.

JOVEN 2.°: Es verdad.

(Ranas y grillos hacen la glorieta del estío andaluz. El Amargo camina con las manos en la cintura.)

AMARGO: Ay yayayay.

Yo le pregunté a la muerte.

Ay yayayay.

(El grito de su canto pone un acento circunflejo sobre el corazón de los que lo han oído.)

JOVEN 1.° *(desde muy lejos)*: ¡Amargo!

JOVEN 2.° *(casi perdido)*: ¡Amargooo!

(Silencio)

(El Amargo está solo en medio de la carretera. Entorna sus grandes ojos verdes y se ciñe la chaqueta de pana alrededor del talle. Altas montañas le rodean. Su gran reloj de plata le suena oscuramente en el bolsillo a cada paso.)

(Un jinete viene galopando por la carretera.)

JINETE *(parando el caballo)*: ¡Buenas noches!

AMARGO: A la paz de Dios.

Dialogue of Amargo

Countryside

A VOICE:
> Amargo.
> The oleanders of my courtyard.
> Heart bitter as almond.
> Amargo.

(Three youths in wide-brimmed hats arrive.)

FIRST YOUTH: We're going to be late.

SECOND YOUTH: It's almost night.

FIRST YOUTH: What about him?

SECOND YOUTH: He's coming.

FIRST YOUTH (*loudly*): Amargo!

AMARGO (*from far away*): I'm coming!

SECOND YOUTH (*loudly*): Amargo!

AMARGO (*calmly*): I am coming.

> *(Pause)*

FIRST YOUTH: What beautiful olive groves.

SECOND YOUTH: Yes.

> *(Long silence)*

FIRST YOUTH: I don't like to travel at night.

SECOND YOUTH: Neither do I.

FIRST YOUTH: The night was made for sleeping.

SECOND YOUTH: True.

> *(Frogs and crickets raise the bower of the Andalusian summer. Amargo walks with his hands on his hips.)*

AMARGO: Ay, ay, ay
> I asked death a question.
> Ay, ay, ay!

> *(His piercing song puts a circumflex accent on the heart of his listeners.)*

FIRST YOUTH (*from far away*): Amargo!

SECOND YOUTH (*nearly lost*): Amargo!!

> *(Silence)*

> *(Amargo is alone in the middle of the road. Narrowing his green eyes, he fastens his corduroy jacket around his waist. He is surrounded by high mountains. His big silver watch ticks darkly in his pocket at every step.)*

> *(A rider comes galloping down the road.)*

RIDER (*reining in his horse*): Buenas noches!

AMARGO: Peace be to God.

JINETE: ¿Va usted a Granada?

AMARGO: A Granada voy.

JINETE: Pues vamos juntos.

AMARGO: Eso parece.

JINETE: ¿Por qué no monta en la grupa?

AMARGO: Porque no me duelen los pies.

JINETE: Yo vengo de Málaga.

AMARGO: Bueno.

JINETE: Allí están mis hermanos.

AMARGO (*displicente*): ¿Cuántos?

JINETE: Son tres. Venden cuchillos. Ése es el negocio.

AMARGO: De salud les sirva.

JINETE: De plata y de oro.

AMARGO: Un cuchillo no tiene que ser más que cuchillo.

JINETE: Se equivoca.

AMARGO: Gracias.

JINETE: Los cuchillos de oro se van solos al corazón. Los de plata
cortan el cuello como una brizna de hierba.

AMARGO: ¿No sirven para partir el pan?

JINETE: Los hombres parten el pan con las manos.

AMARGO: ¡Es verdad!

    (El caballo se inquieta.)

JINETE: ¡Caballo!

AMARGO: Es la noche.

    (El camino ondulante salomoniza la sombra del animal.)

JINETE: ¿Quieres un cuchillo?

AMARGO: No.

JINETE: Mira que te lo regalo.

AMARGO: Pero yo no lo acepto.

JINETE: No tendrás otra ocasión.

AMARGO: ¿Quién sabe?

JINETE: Los otros cuchillos no sirven. Los otros cuchillos son
blandos y se asustan de la sangre. Los que nosotros vendemos
son fríos. ¿Entiendes? Entran buscando el sitio de más calor y
allí se paran.

    *(El Amargo calla. Su mano derecha se le enfría como si agarrase un
pedazo de oro.)*

JINETE: ¡Qué hermoso cuchillo!

AMARGO: ¿Vale mucho?

JINETE: Pero ¿no quieres éste?

    (Saca un cuchillo de oro. La punta brilla como una llama de candil.)

RIDER: You going to Granada?

AMARGO: Yes, Granada.

RIDER: Then we'll go together.

AMARGO: Looks like it.

RIDER: Why don't you climb up on back?

AMARGO: I would, if my feet hurt.

RIDER: I've been in Málaga.

AMARGO: Good.

RIDER: My brothers are there.

AMARGO (*peevish*): How many of them?

RIDER: Three. They sell knives. It's their business.

AMARGO: May it bring them health.

RIDER: Silver and gold ones.

AMARGO: A knife is a knife. Needn't be more than that.

RIDER: You are mistaken.

AMARGO: Whatever you say.

RIDER: Knives of gold find the heart all by themselves. Silver ones
    cut the throat like a blade of grass.

AMARGO: Aren't they used for slicing bread?

RIDER: Men break bread with their hands.

AMARGO: Yes, that is true!

    (*The horse grows restless.*)

RIDER: Whoa!

AMARGO: Must be the night.

    (*The horse's shadow winds over the rolling road.*)

RIDER: Do you want a knife?

AMARGO: No.

RIDER: But look, I'm giving it to you.

AMARGO: But I won't accept it.

RIDER: You won't have another chance.

AMARGO: Who knows?

RIDER: Other knives are useless. Other knives are soft and scared
    of blood. The ones we sell are cold. Understand? They go in
    looking for the hottest spot, and there they stop.

    (*Amargo says nothing. His right hand grows as cold as if it were holding
    a piece of gold.*)

RIDER: What a beautiful knife!

AMARGO: Is it worth very much?

RIDER: But perhaps you'd rather have this one.

    (*He takes out a gold knife whose point shines like the flame of a candle.*)

AMARGO: I said no.

RIDER: Boy, climb up here with me!

        POEM OF THE DEEP SONG

AMARGO: He dicho que no.

JINETE: ¡Muchacho, súbete conmigo!

AMARGO: Todavía no estoy cansado.

(El caballo se vuelve a espantar.)

JINETE *(tirando de las bridas)*: Pero ¡qué caballo éste!

AMARGO: Es lo oscuro.

(Pausa)

JINETE: Como te iba diciendo, en Málaga están mis tres hermanos. ¡Qué manera de vender cuchillos! En la catedral compraron dos mil para adornar todos los altares y poner una corona a la torre. Muchos barcos escribieron en ellos sus nombres; los pescadores más humildes de la orilla del mar se alumbran de noche con el brillo que despiden sus hojas afiladas.

AMARGO: ¡Es una hermosura!

JINETE: ¿Quién lo puede negar?

(La noche se espesa como un vino de cien años. La serpiente gorda del Sur abre sus ojos en la madrugada, y hay en los durmientes un deseo infinito de arrojarse por el balcón a la magia perversa del perfume y la lejanía.)

AMARGO: Me parece que hemos perdido el camino.

JINETE: *(parando el caballo)*: ¿Sí?

AMARGO: Con la conversación.

JINETE: ¿No son aquéllas las luces de Granada?

AMARGO: No sé. El mundo es muy grande.

JINETE: Y muy solo.

AMARGO: Como que está deshabitado.

JINETE: Tú lo estás diciendo.

AMARGO: ¡Me da una desesperanza! ¡Ay yayayay!

JINETE: Porque si llegas allí, ¿qué haces?

AMARGO: ¿Qué hago?

JINETE: Y si te estás en tu sitio, ¿para qué quieres estar?

AMARGO: ¿Para qué?

JINETE: Yo monto este caballo y vendo cuchillos, pero si no lo hiciera, ¿qué pasaría?

AMARGO: ¿Qué pasaría?

(Pausa)

JINETE: Estamos llegando a Granada.

AMARGO: ¿Es posible?

JINETE: Mira cómo relumbran los miradores.

AMARGO: La encuentro un poco cambiada.

JINETE: Es que estás cansado.

AMARGO: Sí, ciertamente.

AMARGO: I'm not tired yet.

(*The horse spooks again.*)

RIDER: (*pulling on the reins*): What a horse.

AMARGO: It's the darkness.

(*Pause*)

RIDER: As I was telling you, my three brothers are in Málaga. How they sell knives! At the cathedral they bought two thousand of them to adorn all the altars and put a crown on the tower. Many a ship wrote its name on them. Down by the sea, the poorest fishermen get light from the luster of their sharp blades.

AMARGO: How beautiful it is!

RIDER: Who could deny it?

(*The night thickens like a hundred-year-old wine. The fat serpent of the South opens its eyes in the dawn, and sleepers feel the infinite urge to throw themselves out the window into the perverse magic of perfume and distance.*)

AMARGO: I think we've lost the road.

RIDER: (*stopping his horse*): Yes?

AMARGO: While we were talking.

RIDER: Aren't those the lights of Granada?

AMARGO: I don't know. The world is very big.

RIDER: And very lonely.

AMARGO: As though no one lived there.

RIDER: You're right.

AMARGO: It makes me despair. Ay yayayay!

RIDER: The thing is, if you get there, what do you do?

AMARGO: What do I do?

RIDER: And if you just stay still, what good is that?

AMARGO: What good?

RIDER: I ride this horse and sell knives, but if I didn't, what would happen?

AMARGO: What would happen?

(*Pause*)

RIDER: We're coming to Granada.

AMARGO: Is it possible?

RIDER: Look how the balconies are shining.

AMARGO: I find it a little changed.

RIDER: It's just that you're tired.

AMARGO: Yes, of course.

RIDER: Now you will not refuse to ride with me.

AMARGO: Wait a bit.

RIDER: Up with you! Quick! Come on up! We have to get there

JINETE: Ahora no te negarás a montar conmigo.

AMARGO: Espera un poco.

JINETE: ¡Vamos, sube! Sube de prisa. Es necesario llegar antes de que amanezca . . . Y toma este cuchillo. ¡Te lo regalo!

AMARGO: ¡Ay yayayay!

(El Jinete ayuda al Amargo. Los dos emprenden el camino de Granada. La sierra del fondo se cubre de cicutas y de ortigas.)

Canción de la madre del Amargo

Lo llevan puesto en mi sábana
mis adelfas y mi palma.

Día veintisiete de agosto
con un cuchillito de oro.

La cruz. ¡Y vamos andando!
Era moreno y amargo.

Vecinas, dadme una jarra
de azófar con limonada.

La cruz. No llorad ninguna.
El Amargo está en la luna.

9 julio 1925.

before the break of day. And take this knife. I'm giving it to you!

AMARGO: Ay yayayay!

(The Rider helps Amargo up, and the two of them take the road into Granada. In the background the mountains bristle with hemlocks and nettles.)

Song of Amargo's Mother

They carry him on my bed sheet,
my oleanders and my palm.

The twenty-seventh day of August
with a little knife of gold.

The cross, and that was that!
He was brown and bitter.

Neighbors, give me a brass
pitcher with lemonade.

The cross. Don't anyone cry.
Amargo is on the moon.

July 9, 1925

TR. C.M.

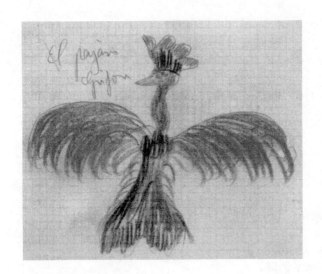

SUITES

[*El pájaro Grifón, ca. 1923*]

SUITES

Translated by

Jerome Rothenberg

Translator's Note & Dedication

As a type of "serial poetry" (Robin Blaser's and Jack Spicer's term), the "suites" come early in Lorca's career but already show a connection with the montage & vernacular methods of early European modernism. Many remained unpublished during his lifetime & were later reassembled from notebooks in Belamich's critical edition (1983). When I first attended to the several that had surfaced earlier, they struck me as a different kind of Lorca than I had known before—still characteristically his but with a coolness & (sometimes) quirkiness, a playfulness of mind & music that I found instantly attractive. The full run of suites shows other Lorca characteristics as well, but my attempt, as far as I could, has been to stress these, as if to pay homage by so doing to this most graceful & elegant of twentieth-century poets. Toward those ends I have moved where needed between the literal & playful, but I have tried throughout to stay within Lorca's range & to avoid effects not clearly signaled by his own. (Here Christopher Maurer has acted as my trusted guide, & I thank him warmly for his efforts.) Federico García Lorca was one of the first poets to lead me & others of my generation into poetry, & his "wit and intelligence" (his "salt" in that Spanish idiom that turns up elsewhere in his work) have remained an inspiration to me across the decades.

Finally, I would like to dedicate these translations to the memory of Paul Blackburn—a poet, a friend, & a powerful translator of Lorca—who was there before me.

Jerome Rothenberg

La suite de los espejos

Símbolo

Cristo
tenía un espejo
en cada mano.
Multiplicaba
su propio espectro.
Proyectaba su corazón
en las miradas
negras.
¡Creo!

El gran espejo

Vivimos
bajo el gran espejo.
¡El hombre es azul!
¡Hosanna!

Reflejo

Doña Luna.
(¿Se ha roto el azogue?)
No.
¿Qué muchacho ha encendido
su linterna?
Sólo una mariposa
basta para apagarte.
Calla . . . ¡pero es posible!
¡Aquella luciérnaga
es la luna!

Mirror Suite

Symbol

Christ,
a mirror
in each hand.
He multiplies
his shadow.
He projects his heart
through his black
looks.
I believe!

The Giant Mirror

We live beneath
a giant mirror.
Man is blue!
Hosanna!

Reflection

Lady Moon.
(Did someone shatter the quicksilver?)
No.
What child has flicked on
the lantern?
Even a butterfly could
blow you out.
Be quiet! . . . (Can it really!)
That glowworm
10   is the moon!

Rayos

Todo es abanico.
Hermano, abre los brazos.
Dios es el punto.

Réplica

Un pájaro tan sólo
canta.
El aire multiplica.
Oímos por espejos.

Tierra

Andamos
sobre un espejo
sin azogue,
sobre un cristal
sin nubes.
Si los lirios nacieran
al revés,
si las rosas nacieran
al revés,
10 si todas las raíces
miraran las estrellas
y el muerto no cerrara
sus ojos,
seríamos como cisnes.

Capricho

Detrás de cada espejo
hay una estrella muerta

Rays

Everything's a fan.
Brother, open up your arms.
God is the pivot.

Replica

Only a single bird
is singing.
The air is cloning it.
We hear through mirrors.

Earth

We walk on
an unsilvered
mirror,
a crystal surface
without clouds.
If lilies would grow
backwards,
if roses would grow
backwards,
10 if all those roots
could see the stars
& the dead not close
their eyes,
we would become like swans.

Capriccio

Behind each mirror
is a dead star

173

y un arco iris niño
que duerme.

Detrás de cada espejo
hay una calma eterna
y un nido de silencios
que no han volado.

El espejo es la momia
10 del manantial, se cierra
como concha de luz
por la noche.

El espejo
es la madre-rocío,
el libro que diseca
los crepúsculos, el eco hecho carne.

Sinto

Campanillas de oro.
Pagoda dragón.
Tilín tilín
sobre los arrozales.
Fuente primitiva,
fuente de la verdad.
A lo lejos,
garzas color de rosa
y un volcán marchito.

Los ojos

En los ojos se abren
infinitos senderos.
Son dos encrucijadas
de la sombra.

& a baby rainbow
sleeping.

Behind each mirror
is a blank forever
& a nest of silences
too young to fly.

The mirror is the wellspring
10 become mummy, closes
like a shell of light
at sunset.

The mirror
is the mother dew,
the book of desiccated
twilights, echo become flesh.

Shinto

Small golden bells.
Dragon pagoda.
Tinkle tinkle
over the ricefields.

Primal fountain.
Fountain of the real.

Far off,
pink-colored herons
& the spent volcano.

Eyes

In our eyes the roads
are endless.
Two are crossroads of
the shadow.

La muerte llega siempre
de esos campos ocultos.
(Jardinera que troncha
las flores de las lágrimas.)
Las pupilas no tienen
10 horizontes.
Nos perdemos en ellas
como en la selva virgen.
Al castillo de irás
y no volverás
se va por el camino
que comienza en el iris.
¡Muchacho sin amor,
Dios te libre de la yedra roja!
¡Guárdate del viajero,
20 Elenita que bordas
corbatas!

Initium

Adán y Eva.
La serpiente
partió el espejo
en mil pedazos,
y la manzana
fue la piedra.

Berceuse al espejo dormido

Duerme.
No temas la mirada
errante.
Duerme.

Ni la mariposa
ni la palabra
ni el rayo furtivo

Death always emerging
from those secret fields.
A woman working a garden:
teardrops like flowers
she breaks.
10 Horizonless pupils.
Virgin forests
we're lost in.
Castle of no return
that you reach
from the road that starts in the iris.
Oh boy without love, may God
set you free from red ivy.
And you, Elenita,
who sit there
20 embroidering neckties,
keep clear of that traveler.

Initium

Adam & Eve.
The serpent cracked
the mirror
in a thousand pieces,
& the apple
was his rock.

Berceuse for a Sleeping Mirror

    Sleep.
Do not fear the roaming
eye.
    Sleep.

The butterfly,
the word,
the furtive light

de la cerradura
te herirán.
Duerme.

Como mi corazón,
así tú,
espejo mío.
Jardín donde el amor
me espera.

Duérmete sin cuidado,
pero despierta
cuando se muera el último
beso de mis labios.

Aire

El aire
preñado de arcos iris
rompe sus espejos
sobre la fronda.

Confusión

¿Mi corazón
es tu corazón?
¿Quién me refleja pensamientos?
¿Quién me presta
esta pasión
sin raíces?
¿Por qué cambia mi traje
de colores?
¡Todo es encrucijada!
10   ¿Por qué ves en el cieno
tanta estrella?
¿Hermano, eres tú

in through the keyhole,
will not wound you.
10   Sleep.

As my heart is,
so you are,
my mirror.
Garden where my love
is waiting.

Sleep easy,
but awaken
when the last kiss dies against
my lips.

Air

The air
pregnant with rainbows
shatters its mirrors
over the grove.

Confusion

Is my heart
your heart?
Who is mirroring my thoughts?
Who lends me this un-
rooted passion?
Why are my clothes
changing color?
Everything is a crossroads!
Why does this slime
10   look so starry?
Brother, are you you

179

o soy yo?
¿Y estas manos tan frías
son de aquél?
Me veo por los ocasos,
y un hormiguero de gente
anda por mi corazón.

Remanso

El búho
deja su meditación,
limpia sus gafas
y suspira.
Una luciérnaga
rueda monte abajo
y una estrella
se corre.
El búho bate sus alas
10 y sigue meditando.

El jardín de las morenas

(FRAGMENTOS)

Pórtico

El agua
toca su tambor
de plata.

Los árboles
tejen el viento
y las rosas lo tiñen
de perfume.

or am I I?
And these cold hands,
are they his?
I see myself in sunsets
& a swarm of people
wanders through my heart.

The Pool

Horned owl
stops his meditations,
cleans his glasses,
sighs.
A firefly
spins downhill
& a star
slides by.
Old owl shakes his wings,
10 takes up his meditations.

Garden in Umber
or The Garden of the Brownhaired Girls
(FRAGMENTS)

Portico

Water
taps its silver
drum.

Trees
knit wind
that roses tint
with scent.

Una araña
inmensa
10 hace a la luna
estrella.

Acacia

¿Quién segó el tallo
de la luna?

(Nos dejó raíces
de agua.)

¡Qué fácil nos sería cortar las flores
de la eterna acacia!

Encuentro

María del Reposo,
te vuelvo a encontrar
junto a la fuentefría
del limonar.
¡Viva la rosa en su rosal!

María del Reposo,
te vuelvo a encontrar,
los cabellos de niebla
y ojos de cristal.
10 ¡Viva la rosa en su rosal!

María del Reposo,
te vuelvo a encontrar.
Aquel guante de luna que olvidé,
¿dónde está?
¡Viva la rosa en su rosal!

Gigantic
spider
10 turns moon
into star.

Acacia

Who cut down the moon's
stem?

(Left us roots
of water.)

How easy to pluck flowers from
this infinite acacia.

Encounter

María del Reposo,
again I encounter
thee near the coldspring
hard by the lemongrove.
(Long live the rose on its rosebush!)

María del Reposo,
again I encounter
thee with thy misty hair
& thy eyes of crystal.
10 (Long live the rose on its rosebush!)

María del Reposo,
again I encounter thee.
Thy moonglove forgotten,
ah where has it gone?
(And long live the rose on its rosebush!)

Limonar

Limonar.
Momento
de mi sueño.

Limonar.
Nido
de senos
amarillos.

Limonar.
Senos donde maman
10 las brisas del mar.

Limonar.
Naranjal desfallecido,
naranjal moribundo,
naranjal sin sangre.

Limonar.
Tú viste mi amor roto
por el hacha de un gesto.

Limonar.
Mi amor niño, mi amor
20 sin báculo y sin rosa.
Limonar.

Noche
(Suite para piano y voz emocionada)

Rasgos

Aquel camino
sin gente.
Aquel camino.

Lemongrove

Lemongrove.
Flash
in my dream.

Lemongrove.
Nest
of gold
bosoms.

Lemongrove.
Bosom where sucketh
10   the seabreeze.

Lemongrove.
Orangegrove growing faint,
orangegrove dying,
orangegrove bloodless.

Lemongrove.
You saw my love cracked
by the ax of a grimace.

Lemongrove,
o my child love, my love,
20   with no crozier, no rose.
O my lemongrove.

Night
(Suite for Piano and Poet's Voice)

Sketches

That road
got no people.
That road.

Aquel grillo
sin hogar.
Aquel grillo.

Y esta esquila
que se duerme.
Esta esquila . . .

Preludio

El buey
cierra sus ojos
lentamente . . .
(Calor de establo.)

Este es el preludio
de la noche.

Rincón del cielo

La estrella
vieja
cierra sus ojos turbios.

La estrella
nueva
quiere azular
la sombra.

(En los pinos del monte
hay luciérnagas.)

That weevil
got no home.
That weevil.

And this sheepbell
gone to sleep.
This sheepbell.

Prelude

The bullock
slowly
shuts his eyes.
Heat in the stable.

Prelude to
the night.

In a Corner of the Sky

The old
star
shuts her bleary eyes.

The new
star
wants to paint the night
blue.

(In the firtrees on the mountain:
fireflies.)

Total

La mano de la brisa
acaricia la cara del espacio
una vez
y otra vez.
Las estrellas entornan
sus párpados azules
una vez
y otra vez.

Un lucero

Hay un lucero quieto,
un lucero sin párpados.
—¿Dónde?
—Un lucero . . .
En el agua dormida
del estanque.

Franja

El camino de Santiago
(Oh noche de mi amor,
cuando estaba la pájara pinta
pinta
pinta
en la flor del limón.)

Una

Aquella estrella romántica
(para las magnolias,
para las rosas.)

The Whole Works

The wind's hand
caresses the forehead of space
again &
again.
The stars half-close
their blue eyelids
again &
again.

A Star

There is a tranquil star,
a star that has no eyelids.
—Where?
—A star . . .
In sleepy water.
In the pond.

Swath

O St. James Road.
O Milky Way.
(O night of love for me
when the yellow bird was painted
painted
painted
up in the lemontree.)

One

That romantic star
(one for the magnolias,
one for the roses).

Aquella estrella romántica
se ha vuelto loca.

Balalín,
balalán.

(Canta, ranita,
en tu choza
de sombra.)

Madre

La osa mayor
da teta a sus estrellas
panza arriba.
Gruñe
y gruñe.
¡Estrellas niñas, huid,
estrellitas tiernas!

Recuerdo

Doña Luna no ha salido.
Está jugando a la rueda
y ella misma se hace burla.
Luna lunera.

Hospicio

Y las estrellas pobres,
las que no tienen luz,

¡qué dolor,
qué dolor,
qué pena!

That romantic star
just went crazy.

Tralalee,
tralala.

(Sing, little frog,
in your shadowy
10 hut.)

Ursa Major

Bear mother
gives suck to the stars
astride her belly:
Grunt
grunt.
Run off, star babies,
tender little stars.

Memory

Our Lady Moon still hidden,
playing ring around a wheel.
She makes herself look silly.
Loony moon.

At the Poorhouse

And the poor stars
that have no light

—o sorrow,
sorrow,
o lamentation!—

están abandonadas
sobre un azul borroso.

¡Qué dolor,
qué dolor,
10 qué pena!

Cometa

En Sirio
hay niños.

Venus

Ábrete, sésamo
del día.
Ciérrate, sésamo
de la noche.

Abajo

El espacio estrellado
se refleja en sonidos.
Lianas espectrales.
Arpa laberíntica.

La gran tristeza

No puedes contemplarte
en el mar.
Tus miradas se tronchan
como tallos de luz.
Noche de la tierra.

end up stuck
in muddy blue.

O sorrow,
sorrow,
10   o lamentation!

Comet

There on Sirius
are babes.

Venus

Open sesame
by day.
Shut sesame
at night.

Below

Space & stars
reflected into sound.
Liana ghosts.
Harp labyrinths.

The Great Sadness

You can't look at yourself
in the ocean.
Your looks fall apart
like tendrils of light.
Night on earth.

Remansos

Ciprés
(Agua estancada.)

Chopo
(Agua cristalina.)

Mimbre
(Agua profunda.)

Corazón
(Agua de pupila.)

Remansillo

Me miré en tus ojos
pensando en tu alma.

Adelfa blanca.

Me miré en tus ojos
pensando en tu boca.

Adelfa roja.

Me miré en tus ojos
¡pero estabas muerta!

Adelfa negra.

Variación

El remanso del aire
bajo la rama del eco.

Backwaters

Cypress.
(Stagnant water.)

Poplar.
(Crystal water.)

Willow.
(Deep water.)

Heart.
(Eyeball water.)

Little Backwater

I saw myself in your eyes
& thinking about your soul.

   O oleander white.

I saw myself in your eyes
& thinking about your mouth.

   O oleander red.

I saw myself in your eyes
but saw that you were dead.

   O oleander black.

Variation

The backwater of air
under this echo's branches.

El remanso del agua
bajo fronda de luceros.

El remanso de tu boca
bajo espesura de besos.

Canción

    Ya viene la noche.

Golpean rayos de luna
sobre el yunque de la tarde.

    Ya viene la noche.

Un árbol viejo se abriga
con palabras de cantares.

    Ya viene la noche.

Si tú vinieras a verme
por los senderos del aire,

10   *Ya viene la noche.*

me encontrarías llorando
bajo los álamos grandes.
    ¡Ay morena!
Bajo los álamos grandes.

The backwater of water
under that frond of stars.

The backwater of your mouth
under our thickening kisses.

Song

    Night here already.

Moon's rays been striking
evening like an anvil.

    Night here already.

An old tree keeping warm
wrapped in words of songs.

    Night here already.

If you should come to see me
walking on the air—

10   *Night here already—*

you'd find me crying here
under the poplar trees.

    Ah, morena, my high brown!

Under the poplar trees.

Media luna

La luna va por el agua.
¿Cómo está el cielo tranquilo?
Va segando lentamente
el temblor viejo del río
mientras que una rana joven
la toma por espejito.

Caprichos

Sol

¡Sol!
¿Quién te llamó
sol?
A nadie le extrañaría,
digo yo,
ver en el cielo tres letras
en vez de tu cara
de oro.

Pirueta

Si muriera el alfabeto,
morirían todas las cosas.
Las palabras
son las alas.

La vida entera
depende
de cuatro letras.

Half Moon

Moon goes through the water.
How peaceable the sky is!
Slowly going gathering
old tremors from the river
while a young frog takes her
for a tiny mirror.

Capriccios

Sun

Sun!
Who was it named you
sun?
No one would be surprised,
I bet,
to see three letters in the sky
instead of your gold
face.

Pirouette

If the alphabet should die
then everything would die.
Whose words are
wings.

The whole of life
dependent on
four letters.

[*Árbol*]

Árbol.
La *ele* te da las hojas.

Luna.
La *u* te da el color.

Amor.
La *eme* te da los besos.

Momentos de canción

Canción con reflejo

En la pradera bailaba
mi corazón

(era la sombra
de un ciprés
sobre el viento)

y un árbol destrenzaba
la brisa del rocío.
¡La brisa!
Plata del tacto.

10 Yo decía: ¿recuerdas?

(No me importa
la estrella
ni la rosa.)

¿Recuerdas?

¡Oh palabra perdida!
¡Palabra
sin horizonte!

¿Recuerdas? . . .

[*Tree*]

Tree
The *tee* gives you leaves

Moon
the *oo* gives you color

Love
the *vee* gives you kisses

Moments of Song

Song with Reflections

Out on the prairie my heart
went dancing

(was a cypress's
shadow
out on the wind)

and a tree unbraiding
the breeze from the dew,
the breeze!
silver thing to the touch.

10   I said: do you remember?

(Not that I cared about
the star
or the rose.)

But, remember?

Word we have lost,
oh horizon-
less word!

Remember?

201

En la pradera bailaba
20   mi corazón.

(Era la sombra
de un ciprés
en el viento.)

Canción sin abrir

Sobre el río.
los cínifes.

Sobre el viento,
los pájaros.

(Tarde descarriada.)

¡Oh temblor
de mi corazón!

No temas,
me iré lejos
10   como un eco.

Me iré lejos
en un barco
sin vela
y sin remos.

¡Oh temblor
de mi corazón!

Sésamo

El reflejo
es lo real.
El río
y el cielo

Out on the prairie my heart
20 went dancing

(was a cypress's
shadow
out on the wind).

Unopened Song

Over the river
mosquitoes.

Over the windcurrents
birds.

(Evening adrift.)

Oh this quake
through my heart!

Have no fear,
I'll be going far off
10 like an echo.

I'll be going far off
in a boat
with no sails
& no oars.

Oh this quake
through my heart!

Sesame

The reflected is
the real.
The river
& sky

son puertas que nos llevan
a lo Eterno.
Por el cauce de las ranas
o el cauce de los luceros
se irá nuestro amor cantando,
10 la mañana del gran vuelo.
Lo real
es el reflejo.
No hay más que un corazón
y un solo viento.
¡No llorar! Da lo mismo
estar cerca
que lejos.
Naturaleza es
el Narciso eterno.

Canción bajo lágrimas

En aquel sitio,
muchachita de la fuente,
que hay junto al río,
te quitaré la rosa
que te dio mi amigo,
y en aquel sitio,
muchachita de la fuente,
yo te daré mi lirio.
¿Por qué he llorado tanto?
10 ¡Es todo tan sencillo! . . .
Esto lo haré ¿no sabes?
cuando vuelva a ser niño.
¡Ay! ¡ay!
Cuando vuelva a ser niño.

are portals that bear us
toward the eternal.
Through streambeds of frogs
or streambeds of stars
our love will go from us, singing
10   the dawn of the great escape.
The real is
the reflected.
There is only one heart
& one single wind.
Don't you weep! It's the same
from close up
as far out.
Nature: eternal
Narcissus.

Song Under Tears

In that place,
o sweet babe of the fountain,
out there by that brook,
I will take back the rose
my friend gave you.
Out there in that place,
o sweet babe of the fountain,
I will give you my lily.
Why have I cried for so long?
10   It's so simple! . . .
And it's just what I'll do, don't you know,
when I be a child once again,
tralala,
when I be a child once again.

Puesta de canción

(Adolfo en 1921)

Después de todo

(la luna
abre su cola
de oro)

. . . Nada . . .

(la luna
cierra su cola
de plata.)

Lejos,
10   una estrella
hiere al pavo real
del cielo.

Paisaje sin canción

Cielo azul.
Campo amarillo.

Monte azul.
Campo amarillo.

Por la llanura tostada
va caminando un olivo.

Un solo
olivo.

At Songfall
(Adolfo in 1921)

After all that

(the moon
opens its tail
of pure gold)

. . . nada . . .

(the moon
closes its tail
of pure silver)

Way out there
10 a star
wounds the peacock
up in the sky.

Landscape Minus Song

Blue sky.
Yellow field.

Blue hill.
Yellow field.

Through the parched prairie
one olive tree
wandering.

One single
tree.

Cuatro baladas amarillas

A Claudio Guillén

I

En lo alto de aquel monte
hay un arbolito verde.

Pastor que vas,
pastor que vienes.

Olivares soñolientos
bajan al llano caliente.

Pastor que vas,
pastor que vienes.

Ni ovejas blancas ni perro,
10   ni cayado ni amor tienes.

Pastor que vas.

Como una sombra de oro
en el trigal te disuelves.

Pastor que vienes.

II

La tierra estaba
amarilla.

Orillo, orillo,
pastorcillo.

Ni luna blanca
ni estrella lucían.

Orillo, orillo,
pastorcillo.

Four Ballads in Yellow

For Claudio Guillén

I

High up on the mountain
a little green tree

    & a shepherd who comes
    & a shepherd who goes.

Sleepy old olive trees
going down the warm valley

    & a shepherd who comes
    & a shepherd who goes.

Not white ewes nor a dog
10 nor a sheephook nor love

    for the shepherd who goes.

Like a shadow in gold
you dissolve in the wheat

    you shepherd who comes.

I I

The earth was
yellow.

    Catch as catch can,
    little shepherd man.

Not a white moon, no,
not a star aglow.

    Catch as catch can,
    little shepherd man.

Vendimiadora morena
10 corta el llanto de la viña.

  Orillo, orillo,
  pastorcillo.

I I I

  Dos bueyes rojos
  en el campo de oro.

Los bueyes tienen ritmo
de campanas antiguas
y ojos de pájaro.
Son para las mañanas
de niebla, y sin embargo,
horadan la naranja
del aire, en el verano.
10 Viejos desde que nacen,
no tienen amo.
Y recuerdan las alas
de sus costados.
Los bueyes
siempre van suspirando
por los campos de Ruth
en busca del vado,
del eterno vado,
borrachos de luceros
20 a rumiarse sus llantos.

  Dos bueyes rojos
  en el campo de oro.

I V

  Sobre el cielo
  de las margaritas ando.

Yo imagino esta tarde
que soy santo.
Me pusieron la luna
en las manos.

Brown grapepicking woman
10 gets tears from the vine.

> *Catch as catch can,*
> *little shepherd man.*

I I I

> *Two red bulls*
> *in one gold field.*

Bulls got a rhythm
like oldtime bells
& eyes like a bird's.
Made for foggy
mornings, & even so
they bore through the air–
orange, in summer.
10 Old from their birth
they don't have no boss
& think back to the wings
down their sides.
Two red bulls
that go around sighing
through fields of Ruth
for a shoal to cross over,
that eternal shoal,
drunk on starshine,
20 are chewing their cuds,
are chewing their sorrows.

> *Two red bulls*
> *in one gold field.*

I V

> *Over a sky*
> *made of daisies*
> *I walk.*

I imagine today
that I'm holy.

Yo la puse otra vez
en los espacios,
y el Señor me premió
10 con la rosa y el halo.

     Sobre el cielo
     de las margaritas ando.

Y ahora voy
por este campo.
A librar a las niñas
de galanes malos
y dar monedas de oro
a todos los muchachos.

     Sobre el cielo
20   *de las margaritas ando.*

Palimsestos

A José Moreno Villa

Ciudad

El bosque centenario
penetra en la ciudad
pero el bosque está dentro
del mar.

Hay flechas en el aire
y guerreros que van
perdidos entre ramas
de coral.

Sobre las casas nuevas
10 se mece un encinar
y tiene el cielo enormes
curvas de cristal.

That they placed the moon
in my hands.
That I set her back
into space.
10   And the Lord awarded me
a rose & a halo.

> *Over a sky*
> *made of daisies*
> *I walk.*

And now I move
down this field
rescuing maidens from
evil suitors,
giving gold coins
20   to all the young boys.

> *Over a sky*
> *made of daisies*
> *I walk.*

Palimpsests

For José Moreno Villa

City

A centenary forest
that invades the city
but is a forest set inside
the sea.

And arrows in the air
& warriors who wander
& are lost among its branching
coral boughs.

There, over the new houses,
10   an oakgrove has started moving,
& the sky's there with enormous
crystal curves.

Corredor

Por los altos corredores
se pasean dos señores

> (*Cielo*
> *nuevo.*
> *Cielo*
> *azul.*)

. . . se pasean dos señores
que antes fueron blancos monjes

> (*Cielo*
> *medio.*
> *Cielo*
> *morado.*)

. . . se pasean dos señores
que antes fueron cazadores

> (*Cielo*
> *viejo.*
> *Cielo*
> *de oro.*)

. . . se pasean dos señores
que antes fueron . . .

> (*Noche.*)

Aire

Lleno de cicatrices
está dormido.
Lleno de espirales
y de signos.
La estela del pájaro
y la estela del grito.

Corridor

Through the vaulted corridors
two gentlemen stroll by.

> (*New*
> *sky.*
> *Blue*
> *sky.*)

. . . two gentlemen stroll by
who once were two white monks.

> (*Mid*
> *sky.*
> *Mauve*
> *sky.*)

. . . two gentlemen stroll by
who once were two hunters.

> (*Old*
> *sky.*
> *Gold*
> *sky.*)

. . . two gentlemen stroll by
who once were . . .

> (*Night.*)

Air

Full of scars
& fast asleep.
And full of spirals,
signs.
The wake behind a bird
& the wake behind a scream.

215

Entre la polvareda
de palabras y ritmos
se suceden dos tonos,
10   negro y amarillo.

Madrigal

¡Oh Lucía de Granada!
Muchachita morena,
que vives al pie de Torres
Bermejas . . . ¿Si tus manos?
. . . tus manos . . .

      (luna llena)

¡Oh muchacha de abril!
¡Oh Melisendra!
La de las altas torres
10   y la rueca.
¡Si tus senos! . . . tus senos . . .

      (luna media)

¡Oh mujer de mi blanca
adolescencia!
La atigrada y fecunda
Eva.
En mis brazos te retuerces
como las ramas secas
de la encina, en la danza
20   de la hoguera.

¿Y mi corazón?
¿Era de cera?
¿Dónde está?
. . . ¿y mis manos?
¿y? . . .

      (luna ciega)

Out from the whirligig
of words & rhythms,
two sounds break loose:
10   a black, a yellow.

Madrigal

Oh Lucy of Granada!
my little brownhaired girl,
who lives down by the foot of the Red
Towers . . . what if your hands?
. . . your hands . . .

      (*full moon*)

Oh girl of April!
Melisendra!
You of the high towers
10   & the spindle.
What if your breasts! . . . your breasts . . .

      (*half moon*)

Oh woman of my snowwhite
adolescence!
Striped & fecund
Eve,
how in my arms you twist
like the dry branches
of an oaktree, in the bonfire's
20   dance.

(And my heart?
was it wax?
Where is it?
. . . & my hands?
&? . . .)

      (*blind moon*)

Primera página

A Isabel Clara, mi ahijada

> *Fuente clara.*
> *Cielo claro.*

¡Oh, cómo se agrandan
los pájaros!

> *Cielo claro.*
> *Fuente clara.*

¡Oh, cómo relumbran
las naranjas!

> *Fuente.*
> *Cielo.*

¡Oh, cómo el trigo
es tierno!

> *Cielo.*
> *Fuente.*

¡Oh, cómo el trigo
es verde!

Tres estampas del cielo

Dedicadas a la señorita Argimira López,
que no me quiso

I

Las estrellas
no tienen novio.

¡Tan bonitas
como son las estrellas!

Front Page

For Isabel Clara, my goddaughter

> *Clear fountain.*
> *Clear sky.*

Oh how the birds
grow bigger!

> *Clear sky.*
> *Clear fountain.*

Oh how the oranges
shine!

> *Fountain.*
> *Sky.*

Oh how the corn
is tender!

> *Sky.*
> *Fountain.*

Oh how the corn
is green!

Three Prints of the Sky

Dedicated to Señorita Argimira López,
who didn't love me

I

The stars
don't have a lover—

doesn't matter how pretty
the stars are!

Aguardan un galán
que las remonte
a su ideal Venecia.

Todas las noches salen
a las rejas
10 —¡oh cielo de mil pisos!—
y hacen líricas señas
a los mares de sombra
que las rodean.

Pero aguardar, muchachas,
que cuando yo me muera
os raptaré una a una
en mi jaca de niebla.

I I

Galán

En todo el cielo
hay un estrello.

Romántico y loco
con frac
de polvo
de oro.

¡Pero busca un espejo
para mirar su cuerpo!

¡Oh Narciso de plata
10 en lo alto del agua!

En todo el cielo
hay un estrello.

They will wait for
their heartthrob—
to carry them off to
his perfect Venezia.

Every night they'll slip out
10 to their railings
—o thousand-tiered sky—
& make lyrical gestures
at the ocean of shadows
around them.

But wait up, muchachas!
Because when I die
I will drag you away,
one by one,
on my cloudcovered pony.

II

Heartthrob

In that whole big sky
there is only one boy star.

Romantic & crazy.
With a top hat & tails
lined with gold
dust.

(But he tracks down a mirror,
he does, to gaze at his body.

Oh silver Narcissus,
10 riding high in the water.)

In that whole big sky
there is only one boy star.

Venus

Efectivamente,
tienes dos grandes senos
y un collar de perlas
en el cuello.

Un infante de bruma
te sostiene el espejo.

Aunque estás muy lejana,
yo te veo
llevar la mano de iris
10 a tu sexo
y arreglar indolente
el almohadón del cielo.

¡Te miramos con lupa
yo y el Renacimiento!

Estampas del mar
[A] Emilio y Manolo

El mar
quiere levantar
su tapa.

Gigantes de coral
empujan
con sus espaldas.

Y en las cuevas de oro
las sirenas ensayan
una canción que duerma
10 al agua.

¿Véis las fauces
y las escamas?

Venus

Sure enough,
you've got two big boobs
& a string of pearls
on your neck.

A child of the mist
holds your mirror.

Though you're very far off
I still see you,
placing a hand like a rainbow's
10   over your sex
or lazily punching the sky
into shape, like a pillow.

We're looking at you through a lens—
the renaissance & me.

Seaside Prints

[To] Emilio and Manolo

The sea
wants to blow
its lid.

Coral giants
heave with
their shoulders.

And in their gold caverns
the sirens
try out a song
10   that the water can sleep to.

Do you see its gullet
& scales?

Ante el mar
tomad vuestras lanzas.

Contemplación

Yo evoco
el capitel corintio,
la columna caída
y los pinos.
El mar clásico
canta siempre en Estío
y tiembla como el
capitel corintio.

Nocturno

Miro las estrellas
sobre el mar.
¡Las estrellas son de agua,
gotas de agua!

Miro las estrellas
sobre mi corazón.
¡Las estrellas son de aroma,
núcleos de aroma!

Miro la tierra
10 llena de sombra.

Guardias

En el reino del mar
hay dos guardas,
San Cristóbal
y Polifemo.

In front of the sea
raise your lances.

Contemplation

I evoke
the Corinthian capital,
the fallen column,
the pines.
The classical sea
that sings ever in summer
& like the Corinthian
capital, trembles.

Nocturne

I stare at the stars
that are over the ocean.
Oh stars made of water,
oh water drops.

I stare at the stars
that are over my heart.
Oh stars made of odors,
oh nuclei of odors.

I stare at the earth
10 filled with shadows.

The Guardsmen

In the kingdom of the sea
are two guards:
St. Christopher
& Polyphemus.

¡Tres ojos
sobre el viajero errante!

Dos estrellas del mar

En la torre
de la madrugada
María enseña a Venus
a tejer lana.
Venus le muestra todas
sus miradas
y María se asombra.

En la torre
de la madrugada.

Horas de Verano

Afilador.
(Las tres.)
El alma de Pan
en los labios
del afilador.

¡Qué tristeza
tan polvorienta!

Evoca
un verde remanso
10 y una cadera
entre las ramas.

El hombre lleva
la rueda
de Santa Catalina.

¡Qué tristeza!

Three eyes over
the vagabond rover.

The Sea with Two Stars

In Daybreak
Tower
Mary shows Venus
how to knit wool.
Venus shows Mary all
her best features.
And Mary's left speechless.

In Daybreak
Tower.

Summer Hours

Scissor man.
(3:00 p.m.)
Soul of Pan on
the lips of
the scissor man.

So much sadness
such dust!

He calls forth
a green pool
& a hip
in the branches.

Man who carries
a catherine
wheel.

Ah so much sadness!

Las cinco

(Potro)

Por la calle sin gente
pasa un caballo negro,
el caballo errabundo
de los malos sueños.

El aire del poniente
viene a lo lejos,
una ventana gime
con el viento.

Las seis

Los pájaros empujan
a la tarde
y llevan con sus picos
la cola azul del día.

El ocaso tatuado
de veletas
sostiene la barca
de la media luna.

Y en la fuente fría
10   canta la culebra.

Las siete

La primera estrella.
Todo mira hacia Venus
y ella como una niña
que se cae en el aljibe
tiembla y tiembla
como diciendo
"¿volveré mañana?"

5:00 p.m.
(Colt)

On a street without people
a black horse rides past,
a wandering horse
in dreams gone bad.

The air at sunset
comes from afar,
a window moaning
with the wind aloft.

6:00 p.m.

Birds jab at
the evening,
beaks carrying off
day's blue tail.

Sunset tattooed with
weathercocks
props up the half moon's
small boat.

And in the cold fountain
10   the little snake sings.

7:00 p.m.

First star out.
Everything looking toward Venus,
& she like a girl
who falls down a deep well,
shivers & shakes—
as if she was saying
"will I come back tomorrow?"

Las ocho

El cielo se arrancó
la venda
y el dragón de los mil ojos
nos lame con sus lenguas
de viento.

Venus se extravía
por la muchedumbre
y yo me acuerdo de una novia
que no he tenido nunca.

Las nueve

Azul sin sangre.
Aire de terciopelo.

¡Oh amiga mía!
Podemos
bajar a la cisterna del corazón,
podemos
por el río de las palabras
llegar a la isla
del beso.
10   Podemos
hundirnos en el olivar
sediento.

Vilano de noche

Sobre el agua
que late entre las zarzas
las estrellas
se alargan.

8:00 p.m.

Sky tears off
the blindfold
& the thousand-eyed dragon
licks us all over with
windtongues.

Venus wandering off
through the crowd
& I thinking back to a sweetheart
I never did have.

9:00 p.m.

A bloodless blue sky.
And a velvety breeze.

Oh my lady!

We can
make our way down to the cistern,
the heart, down
this river of words,
we can
come to
10   Kiss Island,
can
sink out of sight in
that burntover
olive grove.

Thistledown Night

Over the water
where they throb in the briars
the stars
open wide.

Ferias

Poema de la feria

Bajo el sol de la tuba
pasa la feria
suspirando a los viejos
pegasos cautivos.
La feria
es una rueda.
Una rueda de luces
sobre la noche.

10   Los círculos concéntricos
del tiovivo llegan
ondulando la atmósfera
hasta la luna
y hay un niño que pierden
todos los poetas
y una caja de música
sobre la brisa.

Caballitos

¡Oh qué pena de caballos
atravesados
por lanzas de caballeros
malos!

Venís a la tierra huyendo
de un cuento al revés, de un campo
lleno de viejos dragones
vencedores de los santos.

De misioneros del sueño
10   a los campos del diablo

Fairs

Poem at the Fairground

Tuba's a sun & beneath it
the fair's passing by,
see it breathing out old
Captive Pegasuses.
This fair
is a wheel.
A lightwheel high up
in the night.

See the carousel making
concentric circles,
see them snake through the atmosphere
up to the moon.
And a boy all the poets
have lost,
& a music box grinding away
on the breeze.

Wooden Horses

O sad little horses
the spears of the evil
horsemen
have pierced!

You came down to earth, fled
a story told backwards,
a field of old dragons,
the destroyers of saints.

Missionaries of dreams,
the Good Lord has sent you

el Señor os envió.
(Dios es un general malo).

¡Oh qué pena de caballos
atravesados
por lanzas de caballeros
malos!

Feria astral

Noche abierta.

Sobre el eje de la luna
gira el tiovivo de Dios.

Sirio el poeta
solloza lejos del tumulto.

Entre las estrellas niñas
baila la Osa Mayor.

Y en las crestas de las frondas
gira el cilindro de la brisa.

10 En la tienda de la aurora
una estrella viejecita
vende turrón de nieve.

Noche abierta.

Verbena

El que va a la verbena
entra en la casa
de las luciérnagas.

to the devil's own fields
(old God evil general).

O sad little horses
pierced
by spears
of evil knights.

Fair by Starlight

   Night open wide.

On moon's axis,
God's carousel spins.

A poet called Sirius
sobbing
apart from the crowd.

With his girl stars
the Big Bear
is dancing.

10 A wind like a cylinder
spinning
on top of the palms.

In dawn's kiosk
a little old star
sells snow nougats.

   Night open wide.

All Night Fair

When you go to the fair
in the evening
you step into a firefly house.

Chin
tata chin
tata chin.

A pesar de que . . .
no hay más verbena
que la de Cartagena.

10   Chin
tata chin
tata chin.

¡Qué locura de amor
y de pena!
Y este corazón mío,
¡cómo se deleita,
descubierto,
esperando la flecha!

        Chin
20   tata chin
tata chin.

Grito

Cínife,
mariposa
pájaro,
estrella.

¿Qué?

Estrella,
pájaro,
mariposa,
cínife.

Chin
tata chin
tata chin.

And no matter what . . .
there's no night fair more wild
than here in Cartagena.

10   Chin
      tata chin
      tata chin.

What crazy loving,
what pain!
And this heart of mine,
filled with delight,
lying open,
primed for love's arrow!

      Chin
20   tata chin
      tata chin.

Scream

Mosquito &
moth
bird
& star.

What?

Star &
bird
moth
& mosquito.

10 Ya en el suelo
mi corazón atravesado
vuela sobre las muchachas
de la feria.

Tambor

El tambor
es el corazón
de la feria.
Un corazón marchito
que late como si fuera
de un niño.

Ningún músico
lo ha visto.
El es el verdadero
10 Pierrot, que canta lírico
a la luna, que cabe
dentro de su anillo
con una melodía
de amor desconocido.

El tambor tiene una luz
de pergamino
(musical fuego fatuo)
y en las noches de estío
mil mariposas viejas
20 persiguen sus latidos.

El tambor es la nostalgia
del camino.
Suena a cielo con nubes
y a lejanía infinita.
En el barco encallado
del circo

238

10 And down on the ground
my pierced heart
see it fly up over the girls
at the fair.

Drum

The drum
is the heart
of the fair.
A shriveled-up heart
that beats like
the heart of a boy.

No musician
has seen it.
It's the true
10 Pierrot, crooning
a moon song,
slipped in under its ring
like a love lyric
nobody knows.

The drum has the brightness
of parchment
(a musical will-o'-the-wisp)
& on summery nights
a thousand black butterflies
20 follow its beats.

The drum's our nostalgia
for roads.
It's the sound of clouds in the sky
& infinite distance.
In the circus (a boat
run aground)
or out in the air

o en el aire campesino
¡late!
¡Oh ataúd de la luna
30   llena!

Rosas de papel

Aquel hombre
de la constelación inmensa,
Atlante,
de multicolor estrella,
va perdido entre las llagas
de las antorchas.
Aquel hombre
de la nube de risas
lleva
10   rosas para los vientos
de la infancia.
Y aquel hombre,
fantasma del otoño,
se reserva
las rosas de los niños
muertos
y se las manda
en una cometa.

Luna de feria

La luna
no se ve en las ferias.
¡Hay demasiadas lunas
sobre el césped!

Todo juega a ser luna.
La misma feria
es una luna herida
que cayó en la ciudad.

in the country,
it beats!
30 Oh coffin that holds
the full moon!

Paper Roses

That man,
an immense constellation,
Atlantis
a many-hued star,
wanders lost among wounds
made by torches.
That man
in a cloudburst of laughter
brings
10 roses to soft winds
of childhood.
And that man,
ghost of Autumn,
saves roses
to give to dead
children,
& sends them aloft
on a kite.

A Moon at the Fair

You don't see the moon
at these fairs.
There are too many moons
on the fairway!

They all play at being the moon.
And the old fair herself
is a moon that was wounded & fell
straight down on the city.

Lunas microscópicas
10 bailan en los cristales
y algunas se detienen
sobre los nubarrones
de la charanga.

La luna del azul
no se ve en las ferias.
Se vela suspirando:
"¡Me duelen los ojos!"

Canción morena

Me perdería
por tu país moreno,
María del Carmen.

Me perdería
por tus ojos sin nadie,
pulsando los teclados
de tu boca inefable.

En tu abrazo perpetuo
sería moreno el aire
10 y tendría la brisa
el vello de tu carne.

Me perdería
por tus senos temblantes,
por las hondas negruras
de tu cuerpo suave.

Me perdería
en tu país moreno,
María del Carmen.

Microscopic moons
10 are dancing in glasses
some stopped in their tracks
over the storm clouds
blown by the band.

You don't see a moon
at these fairs. No,
not in the sky.
You wait for it, sighing
       you say
"something's hurting my eyes!"

Song in Brown

I would lose myself
in your brown country,
María del Carmen,

would lose myself there
in your eyes (sans people),
would play on those keys,
your incredible mouth.

In our endless embrace
the air would be brown
10 & the breeze like
the down on your skin.

I would lose myself there
in your quivering breasts,
in your easy body's
deep darkness.

I would lose myself
in your brown country,
María del Carmen.

Columpio

La niña va en el columpio
de norte a sur
de sur a norte.
En la parábola
tiembla una estrella roja
bajo todas las estrellas.

Confusión

Sobre las casas despiertas
van serpentinas sonoras.

¡Rojas—amarillas—verdes!

La placeta está inundada
por los caños de los pitos.

¡Rojos—amarillos—verdes!

Las gentes van desacarriadas
por laberintos de música.

¡Azules—rosas—azules!

10 Y el reloj no tiene hora
ni las pupilas miradas.

¡Negras—negras—negras!

Ocaso de feria

Los balcones se cierran
para enjaular los besos.

¡Oh cuánta estrella,
cuánta estrella!

On the Swing

The girl on the swing
goes from north down to south,
from south up to north.
And on the parabola
a red star is trembling
beneath all the stars.

Confusion

Over wide awake houses
the streamers stream loudly

red—yellow—green!

The small square is flooded
with whistles & pipes

red—yellow—green!

The crowds run bewildered
thru musical mazes

blue—pink—blue!

And the clocks have no hours
the eyes have no sight

black—black—black!

Sunset at the Fair

The balconies shut
are cages for kisses.

     Oh all those stars,
     all those stars!

Se va apagando en el aire
un aristón moribundo.

¡Más estrellas,
más estrellas!

Pero los pobres pegasos
10 no pueden cerrar sus ojos.

¡Oh la única
estrella!

Variación
Trino (final)

Ante la feria desierta
el poeta suspira.

(El viento bate las lonas.)

Y por las frondas verdes
su pájaro se va.
Pájaro de Mambrún,
pájaro sin hogar,
cantando el pío pío,
cantando el pío pa.

Canciones bajo la luna

Luna llena
(Al salir)

Cuando sale la luna
se pierden las campanas
y aparecen las sendas
de lo impenetrable.

Fading out on the breeze
a dead hurdy-gurdy.

    More stars
    & more stars!

But poor little Pegasus
10 can't shut his eyes.

    Oh my one
    only star!

Variation
(The Final Trill)

Facing the deserted fair
the poet is sighing
(wind in his sails)
& over the fronds
his bird's flying off:
bird in the chimney,
bird got no home,
singing too-wit too-woo,
singing too-woo too-wit.

Sublunar Cantos

Full Moon
(At Moonrise)

When the moon comes out
the bells get lost
& the paths we can't cross
come in sight.

Cuando sale la luna
el mar cubre la tierra,
y el corazón se siente
isla del infinito.

La luna está más lejos
10   que el sol y las estrellas.
Es perfume y recuerdo,
pompa de azul marchito.

Colores

Sobre París la luna
tiene color violeta,
y se pone amarilla
en las ciudades muertas.

Hay una luna verde
en todas las leyendas.
Luna de telaraña
y de rota vidriera.
Y sobre los desiertos
10   es profunda y sangrienta.

Pero la luna blanca,
la luna verdadera,
sólo luce en los quietos
cementerios de aldea.

Capricho

En la red de la luna,
araña del cielo,
se enredan las estrellas
revoladoras.

When the moon comes out
ocean covers the earth
& heart feels like
infinity's island.

Moon more distant
10 than the sun & stars.
Is perfume & memory,
faded blue bubble.

Colors

Over Paris the moon's
got a violet color
& yellow
in the dead cities.

There's a green moon
that's moon of the legends,
a spiderweb moon
& a cracked stainedglass moon,
& over the deserts
10 a deep bloody moon.

But the white moon,
the true moon,
only shines on the soundless
graves in small towns.

Capriccio

In the net of moon,
the sky spider,
stars get entangled,
spinning around.

Salomé y la luna

La luna es una hermana
de Salomé (señora
que en una historia antigua
muerde una muerta boca).

Salomé era el ocaso.
Un ocaso
de ojos
y de labios.

La luna es el perpetuo
10 ocaso.
Tarde
continuada
y delirante.

El amor sin orillas
de Salomé al oro [?]
no fue por su palabra,
fue porque su cabeza,
medusa del desierto,
era una luna negra,
20 una luna imposible,
ahumada y soñolienta.

Salomé es la crisálida
y la luna el capullo,
crisálida de sombra
bajo un palacio oscuro.

La luna tiembla sobre el agua.
Salomé tiembla sobre el alma.
¡Oh sublime belleza,
querer hacer de un beso
30 una estrella!

Salome & the Moon

The moon is Salome's
sister. (Lady
who in the old story
gnaws a dead mouth.)

Salome was sunset.
Sunset
of eyes
& of lips.

Moon is perpetual
sunset.
Evening
unending &
frantic.

Love without bounds
of Salome for gold
—or for John—
was not for his word
but his head,
that desert medusa,
was now a black moon,
an impossible moon,
filled with smoke,
lost in sleep.

Salome the chrysalis
& moon the cocoon,
this shadowy chrysalis
beneath a dark palace.

Moon trembling over the water,
Salome over the soul.
Oh beauty sublime!
that would turn a kiss into
a star.

En el mediodía
o en la noche oscura,
si habláis de Salomé,
saldrá la luna.

[. . .]

Sombra

Pueblo

Entre tejado y tejado
va el alto río del cielo.
Sobre las acacias viejas
duermen pájaros errantes.

Y la torre sin campanas
(Santa Lucía de piedra)
se afirma en la tierra dura.

Memento

Cuando muramos
nos llevaremos
una serie de vistas
del cielo.

(Cielos de amanecer
y cielos nocturnos.)

Aunque me han dicho
que muertos
no se tiene
10 más recuerdo
que el de un cielo de Estío,
un cielo negro
estremecido
por el viento.

In the midst of the day
or the dark night,
if you speak of Salome
the moon will come out.

[. . .]

Shadow

Pueblo

Flows between roof & roof
the sky-high river.
Atop old acacias
migrant birds fast asleep.

And the tower with no bells
(St. Lucy in stone)
standing firm in hard earth.

Memento

When we die
we'll take with us
a series of shots
of the sky.

(Skies around daybreak
& skies in the night.)

Though they've told me
that dead
we don't have any memories
10 past a sky in midsummer,
a black sky
shaken up
by the wind.

Murciélago

El murciélago,
elixir de la sombra,
verdadero amante de la estrella,
muerde el talón del día.

Fin

Ya pasó
el fin del mundo
y ha sido
el juicio tremendo.
Ya ocurrió catástrofe
de los luceros.

El cielo de la noche
es un desierto,
un desierto de lámparas
10 sin dueño.

Muchedumbres de plata
se fueron
a la densa levadura
del misterio.

Y en el barco de la Muerte
vamos los hombres, sintiendo
que jugamos a la vida,
¡que somos espectros!

Mirando a los cuatro puntos
20 todo está muerto.
El cielo de la noche
es una ruina,
un eco.

Bat

Bat,
elixir of shadows,
true love of that star,
nips at day's heel.

End

End of the world
has already happened
& Terrible Judgment
has been.
Already demise of the stars
has occurred.

Night sky is
a wilderness—
a desert of lamps
10 with no owner.

Silver crowds
gone astray
in the thickening yeast of
the Mystery.

In the ship of Death
we are traveling, feeling
we're playing at life,
that we're ghosts!

Looking in all four directions
20 everything's dead.
Night sky is
a ruin,
an echo.

Osa mayor

(*Éramos siete.*
¿Dónde estamos?)

Juguete

Da tristeza
ver el carro
sin auriga
ni caballos.

Sobre el cielo
da una pena
suave verte soñando
con un camino de oro
y boreales caballos.

10 Sobre el negro cristalino
¿qué harás cuando tengas, carro,
con la lluvia de los tiempos
tus luceros oxidados?
¿No piensas nunca meterte
bajo techado?
Yo te unciría una noche
a dos grandes bueyes blancos.

Poniente

Sobre el cielo exquisito,
más allá del violado,
hay nubes desgarradas
como camelias grises,
y un deseo de alas
sobre las crestas frías.

Un ocaso teñido
de sombra como éste
dará una noche inmensa
10 sin brisa ni caminos.

Ursa Major

(We were seven.
Where are we?)

A Toy

Makes me feel sad,
seeing that cart
without any driver
or horses.

Over the sky
there's a lingering
sadness: to see how you're dreaming
a road paved with gold
& boreal horses.

10 Over that crystalline blackness
what will you do, cart,
when the rainy days have
rusted your stars?
Will you think, ever, to pack it in
under a roof?
One day I might yoke you
to two big white bulls.

Sundown

On this exquisite sky,
& long past the violet
the clouds lie shredded
like gray camellias—
a desire for wings
atop the cold mountains.

A sunset that's tinted
with shadows like this one
will call forth a vast night
10 sans breeze, sans highways.

Cumbre

Cuando llegue a la cumbre . . .

(Oh corazón desolado,
San Sebastián de Cupido.)

Cuando llegue a la cumbre . . .

¡Dejadme cantar!
Porque cantando
no veré los oteros sombríos
ni los rebaños
que en lo profundo van
10 sin pastores.
Cantando
veré la única estrella
que no existe.

Cuando llegue a la cumbre . . .
cantando.

Sauce

¡Jeremías
exquisito!

Las lágrimas asoman
por tus ojos fríos,
mas tu llanto no rueda
sobre el camino.

Abres bajo tus ramas
un abismo
y matizas con gestos
10 el color vespertino.

¡Oh Jeremías
exquisito!

Mountaintop

Coming up to the mountaintop . . .

(Desolate heart,
St. Sebastian of Eros.)

Coming up to the mountaintop . . .

Let me sing!
Because singing
I will not see the shadowy buttes
or the flock
in the depths
10 with no shepherds.
Singing
I will see the one star
that doesn't exist.

Coming up to the mountaintop . . .
singing.

Willow

Exquisite
Jeremiah!

Tears shine forth
through your very cold eyes
but your sobs do not roll
down this highway.

Under your branches you open
a gulf
& your gestures add shades to
10 the color of vespers.

O exquisite
Jeremiah!

El regreso

Yo vuelvo
por mis alas.

¡Dejadme volver!

¡Quiero morirme siendo
amanecer!

¡Quiero morirme siendo
ayer!

Yo vuelvo
por mis alas.

10 ¡Dejadme retornar!

Quiero morirme siendo
manantial.

Quiero morirme fuera
de la mar.

Corriente

El que camina
se enturbia.

El agua corriente
no ve las estrellas.

El que camina
se olvida.

Y el que se para
sueña.

The Return

I'm coming back
for my wings.

O let me come back!

I want to die where
it's dawn!

I want to die where
it's yesterday!

I'm coming back
for my wings.

10 O let me get back!

I want to die where
it's origin.

I want to die
out of sight
of the sea.

In Motion

You walk,
you get muddy.

Water in motion
will not see the stars.

You walk,
you go blank.

You stop walking,
you dream.

Hacia . . .

Vuelve,
¡corazón!
vuelve.

Por las selvas del amor
no verás gentes.
Tendrás claros manantiales.
En lo verde
hallarás la rosa inmensa
del siempre.

10   Y dirás: ¡Amor! ¡amor!
sin que tu herida
se cierre.

Vuelve,
¡corazón mío!
vuelve.

Recodo

Quiero volver a la infancia
y de la infancia a la sombra.

¿Te vas, ruiseñor?
Vete.

Quiero volver a la sombra
y de la sombra a la flor.

¿Te vas, aroma?
Vete.

Quiero volver a la flor
10   y de la flor
a mi corazón.

Towards . . .

Turn,
corazón!
turn.

Through forests where love is
you won't see a soul.
You will come on sweet waters.
Out where it's green
you will spot the great rose
named forever.

10 And will call out: Love! love!
without your wound
closing

Turn,
mi corazón!
turn.

Oxbow

I want to go back to childhood
& from childhood to shadow.

You going too, nightingale?
Better get going!

I want to go back to the shadow
& from the shadow to the flower.

You going too, perfume?
Better get going!

I want to go back to the flower
10 & from the flower
to my heart.

263   SUITES

¿Te vas, amor?
        ¡Adiós!

(¡A mi desierto corazón!)

Despedida

Me despediré
en la encrucijada
para entrar en el camino
de mi alma.

Despertando recuerdos
y horas malas
llegaré al huertecillo
de mi canción blanca
y me echaré a temblar como
10   la estrella de la mañana.

Ráfaga

Pasaba mi niña.
¡Qué bonita iba!
Con su vestidito
de muselina.
Y una mariposa
prendida.

¡Síguela, muchacho,
la vereda arriba!
Y si ves que llora
10   o medita,
píntale el corazón
con purpurina
y dile que no llore
si queda solita.

You going too, love?
Adios.

My bare heart.

Saying Goodbye

I'll be saying goodbye
at the crossroads,
heading off down that road
through my soul.

I'll arouse reminiscences,
stir up mean hours.
I'll arrive at the garden spot
in my song (my white song),
& I'll start in to shiver & shake
10   like the morning star.

Wind Gust

My girl coming by,
how sweet she looks walking!
with her cute muslin
dress
& a newly caught
butterfly.

Trail her, muchacho,
down every byway,
& if you once catch her crying
10   or thinking it over,
paint this onto her heart
& spray it with glitter
& tell her not to cry
if she should stay single.

La selva de los relojes

Entré
en la selva
de los relojes.

Frondas de tic-tac,
racimos de campanas
y bajo la hora múltiple,
constelaciones de péndulos.

Los lirios negros
de las horas muertas.
Los lirios negros
de las horas niñas.
¡Todo igual!
¿Y el oro del amor?

Hay una hora tan sólo.
¡Una hora tan sólo!
¡La hora fría!

Maleza

Me interné
por la hora mortal.
Hora de agonizante
y de últimos besos.
Grave hora en que sueñan
las campanas cautivas.

Relojes de cuco
sin cuco.
Estrella mohosa
y enormes mariposas
pálidas.

Entre el boscaje
de suspiros
el aristón

In the Forest of Clocks

I entered the forest
of clocks.

Leaves were ticking,
bells hung in clusters.
Under a manyfaced clock,
constellations and pendulums.

Black iris,
dead hours.
Black iris,
10 new hours.
All the same!
And love's golden hour?

There is only one hour,
one hour.
A very cold hour.

Chaparral

I plunged into my
hour of death.
My deathrattle hour.
Hour of last kisses.
Grave hour the captive bells
dream of.

Cuckoo clocks
without cuckoos.
Mildewing star
10 & enormous pale
butterflies.

From brambles
of sighs
the crank organ

sonaba
que tenía cuando niño.

¡Por aquí has de pasar,
corazón!
¡Por aquí,
20 corazón!

Vista general

Toda la selva turbia
es una inmensa araña
que teje una red sonora
a la esperanza.
¡A la pobre virgen blanca
que se cría con suspiros y miradas!

Él

La verdadera esfinge
es el reloj.
Edipo nacerá de una pupila.
Limita al norte
con el espejo
y al sur
con el gato.
Doña Luna es una Venus.
(Esfera sin sabor.)
10 Los relojes nos traen
los inviernos.
(Golondrinas hieráticas,
emigran el verano.)
La madrugada tiene
un pleamar de relojes
donde se ahoga el sueño.
Los murciélagos nacen
de las esferas
y el becerro los estudia

sounded
that I had as a child.

You must skip to my loo,
my darling,
skip to my loo,
20 my love.

Overview

The whole murky forest is one
giant spider
spinning a soundweb
for hope:
this poor lilywhite girl,
raised on glances & sighs.

He

The real sphinx
is a clock.
Oedipus will be born from its eye.
Its northern boundary
is mirror.
Its southern is cat.
Doña Luna is Venus.
Savorless sphere.
Clocks bring us
10 winter.
(Hieratic swallows,
they migrate in summer.)
Dawn is a floodtide
of clocks
where the dream is drowned.
Bats born from
spheres.
And the bullcalf scans them
heavy with thought.

preocupado.
¿Cuándo será el crepúsculo
de todos los relojes?
¿Cuándo esas lunas blancas
se hundirán por sus montes?

Eco del reloj

Me senté
en un claro del tiempo.
Era un remanso de silencio,
de un blanco
silencio.
Anillo formidable
donde los luceros
chocaban con los doce flotantes
números negros.

Meditación primera (y última)

El Tiempo
tiene color de noche.
De una noche quieta.
Sobre lunas enormes,
la Eternidad
está fija en las doce.
Y el Tiempo se ha dormido
para siempre en su torre.
Nos engañan

20 When will nightfall come
for all these clocks?
When will those white moons sink
under their hills?

Clock Echo

I sat down
in a clearing in time.
It was a pool of silence.
White silence.
Incredible ring
where the bright stars collide
with a dozen floating
black numbers.

First/Last Meditation

Time
is in night's colors.
Quiet night.
Over enormous moons,
eternity
is set at twelve.
Time's gone to sleep
forever
in his tower.

271

10 todos los relojes.
El Tiempo tiene ya
horizontes.

La hora esfinge

En tu jardín se abren
las estrellas malditas.
Nacemos bajo tus cuernos
y morimos.
¡Hora fría!
Pones un techo de piedra
a las mariposas líricas
y sentada en el azul
cortas alas
10 y límites.

•

[. . .]

Una . . . dos . . . y tres.
Sonó la hora en la selva.
El silencio
se llenó de burbujas
y un péndulo de oro
llevaba y traía
mi cara por el aire.

¡Sonó la hora en la selva!
Los relojes de bolsillo,
10 como bandadas de moscas,
iban y venían.

En mi corazón sonaba
el reloj sobredorado
de mi abuelita.

10   All clocks
    deceive us.
    Time at last has
    horizons.

The Sphinx Hour

In your garden the damned
stars open up.
We're born under your horns
& die there.
Cold hour!
You drop a stone roof
on these lyrical butterflies:
propped up in your sky
you cut off their wings
10 & confine them.

    •

[. . .]

One . . . two . . . three.
The hour struck in the forest.
The silence
filled up with bubbles.
A gold pendulum
carried my face
through the air.

The hour struck in the forest!
Pocket watches,
10 squadrons of flies,
came & went.

From my heart came the sound
of my grandmother's
goldplated watch.

Álbum blanco

A Claudio de la Torre

Eloísa López tenía un álbum sin escribir. Y se ha muerto. ¡Pobrecita! Pero yo se lo escribo con tinta blanca. Ruego a los lectores una oración por su alma. El arzobispo de Constantinopla se ha dignado conceder 100 días de indulgencia. ¡Ah! Si ustedes la hubiesen conocido . . .

Primera página
(Cerezo en flor)

En marzo
te marchas a la luna.
Dejas aquí tu sombra.
Las praderas se tornan
irreales.
Llueven pájaros blancos.
Y yo me pierdo en tu bosque
gritando:
¡Ábrete, sésamo!
10 ¿Seré niño?
Gritando:
¡Ábrete, sésamo!

Segunda página
(Cisne)

Ni Pan
ni Leda.

(Sobre tus alas
se duerme la luna llena.)

Ni bosque
ni siringa.

White Album

For Claudio de la Torre

Eloísa López kept an album in which she didn't write. And she died. Poor little thing! But I wrote something for her with white ink. I ask those who read it to pray for her soul. The Archbishop of Constantinople has deigned to grant 100 days of indulgence. Ah! if only you had known her . . .

First Page
(Cherry tree in flower)

In March
you go off to the moon.
Leave your shadow behind.
The prairies are turning
unreal.
They're raining white birds.
And I'm stuck in your forest
& cry
"Open sesame!"
10   (Could I still be a child?)
"Open sesame!"

Second Page
(Cygnus/ The Swan)

Not Pan
& not Leda.

(The full moon
sleeps over your wings.)

Not forest
& not syrinx.

(Por tu plumaje
resbala la noche fría.)

Ni carne rubia
10 ni besos.

(De escarcha y sueño remolcas
la barca de los muertos.)

Tercera página
(Inventos)

(Estrellas de la nieve)

Hay montañas
que quieren ser
de agua,
y se inventan estrellas
sobre la espalda.

(Nubes)

Y hay montañas
que quieren tener
alas,
y se inventan las nubes
blancas.

Cuarta página
(Nieve)

Las estrellas
se están desnudando.
Camisas de estrellas
caen sobre el campo.

(Through your feathers
cold night slipping by.)

Not blond flesh
10 & not kisses.

(Made of frost & of dreams, you
towing a boat for the dead.)

Third Page
(Conjurations)

(Snow stars)

There are mountains
that want to be
water
& that conjure up stars
over their shoulders.

(Clouds)

And there are mountains
that want to have
wings
& that conjure up clouds,
10 like white clouds.

Fourth Page
(Snow)

The stars
stripping down:
now blouses of stars
line the fields.

Quinta página
(Amanece)

La cresta del día
asoma.
Cresta blanca
de un gallo de oro.

La cresta de mi risa
asoma.
Cresta de oro
de un gallo de sombra.

Última página
Baladilla de Eloísa muerta
(Palabras de un estudiante)

Estabas muerta,
como al final
de todas las novelas.
Yo no te amaba, Eloísa.
¡Y eras tan tierna!
Con música de Bécquer
o de Espronceda,
tú me soñabas guapo
con melena,
10 y yo te daba besos
sin darme cuenta
de que no te decía:
¡oh labios de cereza!
Qué gran romántica
eras.
Bebías vinagre a escondidas
de tu abuela.
Te pusiste como una
celinda de primavera.
20 Y yo estaba enamorado
de otra. ¿No ves qué pena?
De otra que estaba escribiendo
un nombre sobre la arena.

Fifth Page
(At Dawn)

Day's crest
first appearing,
white crest
of a goldcolored cock.

Crest of my laugh
first appearing.
Gold crest
of a shadowy cock.

Final Page
Little ballad for dead Eloísa
(in the words of a student)

You were dead,
Eloísa,
like the dead at the end of all
novels.
I never did love you,
sweet as you were!
With music by Bécquer
or by Espronceda,
you dreamt of me handsome
10 & longhaired,
I who was kissing you
& was never aware
that I still had not told you
"oh lips like a cherry!"
What an awful romantic
you were,
drank down in secret
your grandmother's vinegar,
became like a tree,
20 a mockorange, in springtime.
And I was in love
with another.
     (See how it hurts?)

Cuando yo llegué a tu casa
estabas muerta
entre cirios y entre albahacas,
igual que en las novelas.
Rodeaban tu barquita
las niñas de tu escuela.
30 Habías bebido el vinagre
de la botella eterna.

Tilín talán
te lloraban
las campanas tiernas.

Talán tilín
en la tarde
con dolor de cabeza.
Quizás soñabas durmiendo
que eras Ofelia
40 sobre un lago azul de agua
calenturienta.

Tilín talán
¡que te lloren
las campanas tiernas!

¡Talán tilin
en la tarde
con dolor de cabeza!

With another I wrote out
a name in the sand.

When I got to your house
you were dead,
among candles & basil.
Just like in those novels.
30   Your poor boat encircled
by the girls from your school.
You had drunk of the vinegar,
the perpetual bottle.

Bim bom
the bells
were mourning you
tenderly.

Bim bom
in the evening
40   with an ache in your head.
Maybe you dreamed
of being Ophelia
on a blue lake
afloat in warm water.

Bim bom.
Let them mourn for you
tenderly!

Bim bom
in the evening
with an ache in your head!

Secretos

Fuente

Ante la fuente fría
Cristo medita
con una semilla
entre las manos.

(Está sediento el cauce
de la brisa.)

Ante la fuente clara
Cristo y su alma
luchan por la palabra
10 que duerme todavía.
¡Pero la fuente mana!

Pan

¡Ved qué locura!
Los cuernos de Pan
se han vuelto alas
y como una mariposa
enorme
vuela por su selva
de fuego.
¡Ved qué locura!

Leñador

En el crepúsculo
yo caminaba.
"¿Dónde vas?", me decían.

Secrets

Fountain

Cold fountain
before which Christ's
in meditation
a seed between
his hands.

(Parched channel
of the breeze)

Clear fountain
before which Christ
10 & Christ's soul struggle
for the word
still lost in sleep.
But the fountain's
pouring out.

Pan

Look how crazy!
Pan's horns
change to wings
& like a giant
butterfly
he's sailing through
a woods on fire.
Look how crazy!

Woodcutter

At dusk
I went out walking.
"Where to?" they asked me.

"A cazar estrellas claras."
Y cuando las colinas
dormían, regresaba
con todas las estrellas
en la espalda.
¡Todo el haz
10 de la noche blanca!

Espejo

Mi cintillo de oro
se perdió en el espejo.
(Quiero decir
que nunca existió.)

En los espejos se pierden
las cosas que no existen.

Mi cintillo era de oro:
¿de sol o de margaritas?

¿Qué mujer me lo dio?
10 Preguntárselo a mi espejo.

Por . . . más . . . que . . .
¡yo no tengo espejo!

Puerta abierta

Las puertas abiertas
dan siempre a una sima
mucho más profunda
si la casa es vieja.

La puerta
no es puerta

"Hunting the bright stars."
And when the hills
were sleeping, I returned
backpacking all
the stars.
A whole bag full of
10 night, white night!

Mirror

My golden ring
got lost in
the mirror. (I mean
to say: it never
did exist.)

In mirrors things get lost
that don't exist.

And was my ring's gold
the gold of suns or daisies?

10 What woman
gave it to me?
Ask my mirror.

No . . . matter . . . that . . .
I've got no mirror!

Open Door

Open doors
all give on a chasm
much deeper
the older the house is.

But a door
is no door

hasta que un muerto
sale por ella
y mira doliente, crucificada,
10   a la madrugada sanguinolenta.

¡Qué trabajo nos cuesta
traspasar los umbrales
de todas las puertas!
Vemos dentro una lámpara
ciega
o una niña que teme
las tormentas.

La puerta es siempre la clave
de la leyenda.
20   Rosa de dos pétalos
que el viento abre
y cierra.

Viaje

He visto las colas del viento,
las flores de la brisa.
He visto el pájaro Grifón
y la torre de Delgadina.

¿De dónde vienes,
de dónde?

He visto un camino azul
y unas niñas
que iban cantando el romance
10   de la verde oliva.

¿No sabes de dónde vengo,
niña mía?
Pues . . . de tu última
sonrisa.

until a dead man
comes through it,
looks around mournfully,
10 crucified
on the bloodspattered morning.

What sweat
to get past the thresholds
of all these damned doors!
Inside we see a blind
lamp,
see a girl hide in fear of
the weather.

The door is always the key
20 to the story.
Rose with two petals
blown open & shut
by the wind.

Journey

I have seen the wind's tails
the breeze's buds.
I have seen the griffon bird
& Delgadina's tower.

Where do you come from,
o where?

I have seen a blue road
& some girls
were singing the old ballad
10 of the olive tree in green.

Do you know where I come from,
my sweet girl?
Well . . . from your smile is where,
your last smile.

Botica

¿Esos venenos
son de la India?

¿Y esos perfumes
son de la Arabia?

(El boticario solloza
junto a su niño muerto.)

¿Aquél bálsamo cura
heridas de amor?

¿Y el agua sonrosada
de la juventud?

(El boticario se inclina
sobre su niño muerto.)

Dígame: ¿Alguna rosa
da un veneno violento?

¿Qué tiene esa redoma?
¿No ve usted cómo tiembla?

. . . .

(Entre los sollozos
se oye un batir de alas
dentro de todos los frascos.)

Doncellita

¿Por qué te recuerdo
bajo una lluvia de marzo
al salir del colegio?

Pajarita de las nieves
te llamaban. Un interno
te dio su rosa. Luego

Apothecary

Are those poisons
from India?

Those perfumes from Arabia?

(The apothecary sobbing
beside his dead son.)

Does that potion heal
the wounds of love?

And that rose-colored water
the wounds of youth?

10   (The apothecary bending
above his dead son.)

Tell me: which rose holds
the terrible poison?

And what does this vial hold?
Do you see how it's shaking?

. . . .

(Between sobs
comes a beating of wings
from his flasks.)

The Little Doncella

Why do I remember you
a rainy day in March,
coming out of the convent?

Little white snowbird
they called you. A schoolboy
once gave you his rose. Then

se te cayó la pluma
con que escribo los versos.
Tan pequeñita, y tú
10 ¡sin saberlo!

Seis canciones de anochecer

Horizonte

Sobre la verde bruma
se cae un sol sin rayos.

La ribera sombría
sueña al par que la barca
y la esquila inevitable
traba la melancolía.

En mi alma de ayer
suena un tamborcillo
de plata.

Pescadores

El árbol gigantesco
pesca con sus lianas
topos raros
de la tierra.

El sauce sobre el remanso
se pesca sus ruiseñores.
. . . pero en el anzuelo verde
del ciprés la blanca luna
no morderá . . . ni
10 tu corazón al mío,
morenita de Granada.

a feather dropped from you
with which I am writing these verses.
Such a small thing &
10   you will not know it!

Six Songs at Nightfall

Horizon

From above the green mist
old sun plunges down
sans sunrays.

And the shadowy shore
dreams in time to a boat
& a bell you can't miss
joins its sorrows.

In my leftover soul
there's the sound of a small
10   silver drum.

Fishermen

Gigantic tree,
with its lianas, fishes
rare moles
from the earth.

Above the pond the willow
fishes nightingales
. . . but on the cypress's green
fishhook, white moon
will not bite . . . nor will
10   your heart on mine,
oh brunette of Granada.

Solitario
(Zujaira)

Sobre el pianísimo
del oro . . .
mi chopo
solo.

Sin un pájaro
armónico.

Sobre el pianísimo
del oro . . .

El río a sus pies
10 corre grave y hondo
bajo el pianísimo
del oro . . .

Y yo con la tarde
sobre mis hombros
como un corderito
muerto por el lobo
bajo el pianísimo
del oro.

Delirio

Disuelta la tarde
y en silencio el campo,
los abejarucos
vuelan suspirando.
Los fondos deliran
azules y blancos.
El paisaje tiene
abiertos sus brazos.
¡Ay, señor, señor!
10 Esto es demasiado.

Solitaire
(Zujaira)

Over the pianissimo
of gold . . .
my lonely
poplar.

Without some harmonical
bird.

Over the pianissimo of gold . . .

The river at its feet
runs dark & deep
10 beneath the pianissimo
of gold . . .

And I with evening
on my shoulders
like a little lamb
the wolf has slain
beneath the pianissimo
of gold.

Delirium

Evening come apart
& the field gone silent.
The bee-eaters
flying past, sighing.
In the distances: wild
blues & whites.
The landscape with arms
spread wide open.
(Oh, lordy, lordy! if
10 this ain't too much.)

Memento
(Aire de llano)

La luna ya se ha muerto,
    do-re-mi
la vamos a enterrar
    do-re-fa
en una rosa blanca
    do-re-mi
con tallo de cristal.
    do-re-fa
Bajó hasta la chopera,
10   do-re-mi
se enredó en el zarzal.
    do-re-fa
¡Me alegro porque era
    do-re-mi
presumida de más!
    do-re-fa
No hubo para ella nunca
    do-re-mi
marido ni galán.
20   do-re-fa
¡Cómo se pondrá el cielo!
    do-re-mi
¡Ay, cómo se pondrá!
    do-re-fa
cuando llegue la noche
    do-re-mi
y no la vea en el mar.
    do-re-fa
¡Acudid al entierro!
30   do-re-mi
cantando el pío pa.
    do-re-fa
Se ha muerto la Mambruna
    do-re-mi
de la cara estelar.
    do-re-fa
Campanas de las torres,
    do-re-mi
¡doblar que te doblar!

Memento
(Prairie Air)

The moon is dead already
    do-re-mi
we're going to bury her now
    do-re-fa
in a chalk white rose
    do-re-mi
with a bright glass stalk
    do-re-fa.
She went down 'mongst the poplars
10   do-re-mi
got tangled in the briars
    do-re-fa.
I am happy about it because she
    do-re-mi
thought she was something special
    do-re-fa.
Nobody was good enough to be
    do-re-mi
her husband or her lover
20   do-re-fa.
How happy the sky is going to be
    do-re-mi
yes how happy the sky is going to be
    do-re-fa
when the night has come around
    do-re-mi
& doesn't see her in the ocean
    do-re-fa.
Let us all go to her funeral
30   do-re-mi
& let's sing the pío pa
    do-re-fa.
La Mambruna's stone cold dead
    do-re-mi
with her face that's like a star
    do-re-fa.
So let bells from their towers
    do-re-mi
ring like mad & ring like mad

do-re-mi
Culebras de las fuentes,
do-re-mi
¡cantar que te cantar!
do-re-fa

Última luz

En la confusión
azul
una hoguera lejana
(lanzada en el corazón
del monte).
Los pájaros juegan
al viento entre los chopos
y se ahondan
los cauces.

Países

Nieve

Campo sin caminos
y ciudad sin tejados.
El mundo está silencioso
y cándido.
Paloma gigantesca
de los astros.
¿Cómo no baja del azul
el eterno milano?

Mundo

Ángulo eterno,
la tierra y el cielo.
Con bisectriz de viento.

do-re-fa.
And let snakes at their fountains
　　　do-re-mi
sing like mad & sing like mad
　　　do-re-fa!

Last Light

In blue
confusion
distant bonfire
(skewering the mountain's
heart).
Birds who play at wind
amongst the poplars
& streambeds growing deeper
deeper down.

Countries

Snows

Field got no roads
& town got no roofs.
A silent & pale
world.
Gigantic dove
in the stars.
(Why don't he come down from the sky,
that perpetual buzzard?)

Worlds

Perpetual angle
of earth & sky,
with wind the bisector.

Ángulo inmenso,
el camino derecho,
con bisectriz de deseo.

Las paralelas se encuentran
en el beso.
¡Ah corazón
10   sin eco!
En ti empieza y acaba
el universo.

[. . .]

Suite del agua

País

En el agua negra,
árboles yacentes,
margaritas
y amapolas.

Por el camino muerto
van tres bueyes.

Por el aire,
el ruiseñor,
corazón del árbol.

Temblor

En mi memoria, turbia
con un recuerdo de plata,
piedra de rocío.

En el campo sin monte,
una laguna clara,
manantial apagado.

Enormous angle,
the road going straight,
with sex the bisector.

The parallels meet
in a kiss.
Oh heart without
10   echoes.
In you the beginning & end
of the All.

[. . .]

Water Suite

Homeland

Trees laid out
in black water,
daisies &
poppies.

Down the dead highway
come three oxen.

Nightingales
aloft,
heart of the tree.

Tremor

Dark to my mind,
with just a memory of silver,
a stone of dew.

In that field no mountain.
Only a clear lake,
a snuffed-out spring.

Acacia

¿Quién segó el tallo
de la luna?

(Nos dejó raíces
de agua.)

¿Qué fácil nos sería cortar las flores
de la eterna acacia!

Curva

Con un lirio en la mano
te dejo.
¡Amor de mi noche!
Y viudita de mi astro
te encuentro.

Domador de sombrías
mariposas,
sigo por mi camino.
Al cabo de mil años
10 me verás.
¡Amor de mi noche!
Por la vereda azul,
domador de sombrías
estrellas,
seguiré mi camino.
Hasta que el universo
quepa en mi corazón.

[. . .]

Acacia

Who cut down the moon's
stem?

(Left us roots
of water.)

How easy to pluck flowers from
this infinite acacia.

Curve

With a lily in your hand
I leave you,
o my night love!
Little widow of my single star
I find you.

Tamer of dark
butterflies!
I keep along my way.
After a thousand years are gone
10 you'll see me,
o my night love!

By the blue footpath,
tamer of dark
stars,
I'll make my way.
Until the universe
can fit inside
my heart.

[. . .]

Colmena

Vivimos en celdas
de cristal,
¡en colmena de aire!
Nos besamos a través
del cristal.
¡Maravillosa cárcel
cuya puerta
es la luna!

Cruz

Norte

Las estrellas frías
sobre los caminos.
Hay quien va y quien viene
por selvas de humo.
Las cabañas suspiran
bajo la aurora perpetua.
En el golpe
del hacha
valles y bosques tienen
10 un temblor de cisterna.
¡En el golpe
del hacha!

Sur

Sur:
espejismo,
reflejo.
Da lo mismo decir
estrella que naranja,
cauce que cielo.
¡Oh la flecha,

Beehive

We live in crystal
cells,
in a beehive made of air!
Kiss each other through
the glass.
Marvelous prisonhouse,
whose gateway is
the moon!

Cross

North

Cold stars
over our highways.
Those who come & those who go
through smoky forests.
The way the cabins breathe
beneath an endless dawn.
With each hit
the axe makes
valleys & forests quake
10   like cisterns.
With each hit
the axe makes!

South

South,
mirage,
reflection.
Might as well say star
as orange.
Riverbed as sky.

la flecha!
El Sur
10 es eso:
una flecha de oro,
sin blanco, sobre el viento.

Este

Escala de aroma
que baja
al Sur
(por grados conjuntos).

Oeste

Escala de luna
que asciende
al Norte
(cromática).

Tres Crepúsculos
(A Conchita, mi hermana)

I

La tarde está
arrepentida,
porque sueña
con el mediodía.
(Árboles rojos y nubes
sobre las colinas.)
La tarde soltó su verde
cabellera lírica
y tiembla dulcemente

Oh arrow
arrow!
is what the South
10 is:
golden arrow
with no bullseye,
rides the wind.

East

Diapason of fragrances
drops
South
(by set degrees).

West

Diapason of moon
climbs
North
(chromatic).

Three Crepuscular Poems

(For my sister Conchita)

I

The evening is
penitent,
still dreaming about
noon.
(Red trees & clouds
over the hills.)
The evening, loosening green
lyric hair,
is gently trembling

. . . le fastidia
ser tarde habiendo sido
mediodía.

II

¡Ahora empieza la tarde!
¿Por qué? ¿Por qué?
. . . Ahora mismo
he visto al día inclinarse
como un lirio.
La flor de la mañana
dobla el tallo
. . . ahora mismo . . .
La raíz de la tarde
10 surge de lo sombrío.

III

¡Adiós, sol!

Bien sé que eres la luna,
pero yo
no lo diré a nadie,
sol.
Te ocultas
detrás del telón
y disfrazas tu rostro
con polvos de arroz.
10 De día, la guitarra
del labrador;
de noche, la mandolina
de Pierrot.
¡Qué más da!

10   . . . vexed
to be the evening having once been
noon.

I I

Now the evening starts!
Why? Why?
. . . just now
I watched the day droop down
just like a morning flower.
A day lily
bending its stems
. . . just now . . .
the roots of evening
10 rising through the gloom.

I I I

(For Diane Rothenberg)

Adios, sun!

I know for sure that you're the moon,
but I
won't tell nobody,
sun.

You sneak
behind the curtain
& cover your face
with rice powder.

10 By day, the farmhand's
guitar,
by night, Pierrot's
mandolin.
I should care!

Tu ilusión
es crear el jardín
multicolor.
¡Adiós, sol!
No olvides lo que te ama
20 el caracol,
la viejecilla
del balcón,
y yo . . .
que juego al trompo con mi . . .
corazón.

[*Río azul*]

Río azul.
El barco de marfil
lleva las manzanas
de los besos muertos.
Manzanas de nieve
con el surco tembloroso de los labios.
Río azul.
Y el agua
es una mirada líquida,
10 un brazo de pupila
infinita.
Río azul.

Sueños

Todo mi sueño se cierra
como se debe cerrar
un lucero
viejo
que no quiere gastar
su última luz.

Your illusion,
sun, is to make
the garden
turn Technicolor.

Adios, sun!

20 And don't forget who loves you:
the snail,
the little old lady
on her balcony,
& me . . .
spinning my heart like a . . .
top.

[*Blue River*]

Blue river.
An ivory boat
carries apples.
Dead kisses.
Snow apples,
furrows atremble from lips.
Blue river.
And the water
stares out, liquid—
10 branch of an infinite
eye.
River blue.

Dreams

My whole dream shuts down tight
the way an old
star
might shut down
so as not to spill
its last light.

Todo mi sueño
pintado por fuera
con mi palabra
10 vana.

¡Mi sueño!
Granero de estrellas
con sus gusanos
de oro.

¡Mi sueño!
Paseo provinciano
con un banco
desierto.
Doña Distracción
20 hace girar
sus cien ojos
y una negra figura
se va por el camino
de la lluvia.

Todo mi sueño se cierra.

Las lianas del azul
tocan mi frente.
Ramas nebulosas
de los abetos
30 de Jehová.
Enturbian el horizonte
casto.

¡Divina confusión
del azul hundido!
Estrellas caídas
sobre la calva de la luna,
penachos de vegetación ideal.
Las otras estrellas
salen del cascarón
40 y la semilla de un cielo nuevo
se entierra en el infinito
frío.

The outside of
my whole dream painted
with my empty
10   words.

My dream!
My granary of stars
with its gold
worms.

My dream!
A smalltown promenade,
an empty bench.
My Lady Honeyhead
who rolls
20   her hundred eyes—
a shady form
moves down the highway
with the rain.

My whole dream shuts down tight.

Lianas from the blue
touch my forehead.
Hazy limbs
on Yahveh's old
firtrees
30   darken the virgin
horizon.

Divine perturbation
of the blue sky in ruins.
Stars fallen
on moon's balding head.
Tufts of unreal vegetation.
Other stars
burst their shells.
And a new heaven's seed
40   is embedding itself in a frost
that won't end.

¡Mi corazón
se llena
de alas!
El ejército
de los recuerdos
se pierde
en el camino
de la Muerte.
50 En la hoja
de rosa
de la tierra
paso bajo la ideal selva,
Pulgarcito sin cuento
y sin deseo.

Soledad

Abandono mi vestido
y estrujo mi corazón.
Mi corazón rezuma niebla.
Cuando la selva del azul oculte
la tierra,
mi corazón continuará
empapado de niebla.

Río azul.
Yo busco mi beso antiguo.
10 El beso de mi única hora.
Mi boca, lámpara
apagada,
busca su luz.

Río azul.
Pero había
montones de besos,
moldes de bocas borradas
y besos eternos

My heart
fills with
wings!
An army
of memories lost
on Death's road.
On the rose
leaf,
50 the earth,
under this unreal forest
I stride.
Little man
with no story to tell,
no desire.

Lonesome Blues

I toss off my clothes
& squeeze my heart dry.
Heart oozes mist.
When sky's woods hide
earth's,
my heart will still be
soaked with mist.

  Blue river.
I look for my long-ago kiss.
10 That kiss from my own
little hour.
My mouth, a dead
lamp,
still looks for its light.

  Blue river.
These great heaps
of kisses,
molds of botched mouths.
These unending kisses,

adheridos como caracoles
20 al mástil de marfil.

El barco se detiene.
Hay una tranquilidad sin ritmo
y yo subo a cubierta
con mi traje lírico.

Y los besos extraños,
pompas de jabón
que el alma fabrica,
me ahogan.
Mientras, el mío huye
30 por una fría
ceniza boreal.

Río azul.

[*Suite*]

[. . .]

Espera

Mi cuerpo viejo
con mi alma vieja
me esperan.

(Donde los ríos
abren sus manos.)

Sin lámpara,
sin luciérnaga—
¡en la tiniebla!

(Donde el brazo
10 del río
abre su mano.)

₂₀ like snails stuck tight to
an ivory mast.

And so the boat stops.
There's a rhythmless peace
& I scamper on deck
tricked out like a poet.

But those weird kisses,
choke me.
Soap bubbles,
the soul manufactures
₃₀ while mine's flying off
through the cold
northern ashes.

　　Blue river.

[*Suite*]

[. . .]

Those Who Wait

My old body
& my old soul
are waiting for me.

(Where the rivers
open their hands.)

Without lanterns
& glowworms—
with shadows.

(Where an arm of
₁₀ the river
opens its hand.)

315

Mi cuerpo viejo
me hace señas
detrás de una telaraña.

(¡Desde el ombligo
del mar!)

Paisaje visto con la nariz

Un temblor frío
cauterizado
por los gallos
enturbia la llanura.
En las casas
queman paja
de trigo.
Los arados
vendrán
10 al amanecer.

Esfera

Es lo mismo
río que surtidor.
Los dos
van a las estrellas.

Es lo mismo
picacho que hondonada.
A los dos
los cubre la sombra.

My old body
flashing me signs
from in back of a spiderweb.

(Signs from ocean's
umbilicus.)

Landscape Seen with the Nose

A cold tremor
burnt out of flesh by
the roosters
drops a cloud on the prairie.
In the house
someone's burning
the chaff.
The plows will come
with the dawn.

Sphere

It's the same if it's
river or geyser
because both go up
to the stars.

It's the same if it's
ridge or ravine
because both lie under
the shadow.

Ocaso

El sol
del ocaso
penetra por la entraña
como los rayos X.
Abre las fachadas
y despinta
el cristal del corazón.
¡Tened cuidado!
El aire entra en las salas
10   siniestras del secreto
y las palabras prisioneras
se asoman a las pupilas.
Por eso el prudente
gallo
encierra a sus gallinas
en el crepúsculo.

[. . .]

•

[. . . . .]
¿Qué pasará?
¿Qué no pasará?

Perejil colorado
y candil soñoliento.

¿Qué pasará?
¿Qué no pasará?

El ermitaño se duerme.
Se duerme
la princesa, se duerme
10   ¡el mismo cuento!

¿Qué pasará?
¿Qué no pasará?

Sundown

The sun
when it's sundown
digs into your gut
like an X-ray.
Opens up the façades
& discolors
the glass at your heart.
Be careful!
The air is invading your secret's
10 sinister rooms
& your words in bondage
loom up in your eyes.
And that's why the prudent
rooster
will lock up his hens
around twilight.

[. . .]

•

[. . . . .]
What's coming up?
What's not coming up?

Colorized parsley &
sleepy old oil lamps.

What's coming up?
What's not coming up?

Hermit gets sleepy
& princess
gets sleepy, even their story
10 gets sleepy!

What's coming up?
What's not coming up?

La palmera
(Poema tropical)

Límites

En el cielo la estrella,
y el pulpo abajo.
(La palmera de Satán
y la palmera de Zoroastro.)
La estrella flota
en el espacio.
El pulpo flota
en el Mediterráneo.
La palmera de Satán
10 y la palmera de Zoroastro
se mueven cuando agitan
los brazos.

La palmera

Entre el cielo y el agua
abres tu inmensa flor.
Rosa viva del viento
mediterráneo.

Te dan aire de negra
tus adornos de dátiles
y evocas la Gorgona
pensativa.

Eres junto a las olas
10 una araña-cigüeña
que teje sal y yodo
de los ritmos

y que sueña en la arena
bajo su pie escamado
un país de remansos
azules.

The Palm Tree
(A Tropical Poem)

Limits

Star in the sky—
& octopus below.
(Satan's palm tree
& Zoroaster's.)
The star floats
in space.
The octopus floats in
the Mediterranean.
Satan's palm tree
10 & Zoroaster's
sway
when their arms vibrate.

Palm Tree

Between water & sky
you expose your large flower.
Living rose of the mediterranean
wind.

With your hairdo of dates,
a Negress's graces,
you evoke a contemplative
gorgon.

You are there by the waves
10 like a spider-stork
weaving its rhythms of salt
& iodine

dreaming how under its
tentative foot   in the sand
there's a country of blue
oases.

Mediterráneo

¡Mar latino!
¡Palmeras
y olivos!

El grito de la palma
o el silencio del pino.
Siento como una inmensa
columna subir tu ruido
por encima de todos
los mares.
¡Mar latino!
Entre las torres blancas
y el capitel corintio
te cruzó patinando
la voz de Jesucristo.
¡Mar latino!

El gran falo del cielo
te dio su calor. Tu ritmo
fluye en ondas concéntricas
de Venus, que es tu ombligo.
¡Mar latino!

Guardas gestos inmortales
y eres
humilde. Yo he visto
salir marineros ciegos
y volver a su destino.
¡Oh Pedro de los mares!
¡Oh magnífico
desierto coronado
de palmeras y olivos!

Mediterranean

Latin sea!
palm trees
& olives!

The cry of the palm
or the pine tree's silence.
I feel your sound like
an overblown column
climbing higher than all other
seas.
10 Latin sea!
(Between whitewashed towers
& Corinthian capitals,
skidding across you,
came Jesus Christ's voice.)
Latin sea!

The sky's fat penis
gave you its heat. Your rhythm
flows out in concentric waves
from Venus, your omphalos.
20 Latin sea!

You strike immortal poses
& are humble. I have seen
blind sailors sail forth
& return to their lot.
Oh Peter, patron of seas!
Oh magnificent
desert crowned with
palm trees & olives.

La palma

La palma es el aire.
Ni el río ni Eva
logran plasmar curvas
tan perfectas.

La palma es el oro.
Ni el limón ni el trigo
logran ir más allá
del amarillo.

La palma es la Gracia.
10 En nuestras manos
llega a la cumbre azul
del desmayo.

Newton

En la nariz de Newton
cae la gran manzana,
bólido de verdades.
La última que colgaba
del árbol de la Ciencia.
El gran Newton se rasca
sus narices sajonas.
Había una luna blanca
sobre el encaje bárbaro
10 de las hayas.

En el bosque

Los gnomos
de los secretos
se mesan
los cabellos.

The Palm

The palm is air.
Neither river nor Eve
could form curves
so perfect.

The palm is gold.
Neither lemon nor wheat
could go further
from yellow.

The palm is Grace.
In our hands
it attains the blue summit
of swooning.

Newton

Onto the nose of Newton
a large apple falls.
A meteor of truths.
Last fruit to dangle from
the tree of Science.
And big Newton scratches
his Saxon nostrils.
A white moon over
these barbaric strings of lace:
the beech trees.

In the Woods

The gnomes
astride their secrets
tear
their beards out.

Amarran a la Muerte
y ordenan a los ecos
que despisten al hombre
con sus espejos.
En un rincón
10 está el secreto
revelado,
muerto.
Es un joven azul
con los pies de hierro,
que tiene entre las cejas
un lucero.
Lo lloran
sus compañeros.
El lago verde tiembla.
20 Hace viento.

Armonía

Las olas riman con el suspiro
y la estrella
con el grillo.
Se estremece en la córnea
todo el cielo frío,
y el punto es una síntesis
del infinito.

¿Pero quién une olas
10 con suspiros
y estrellas
con grillos?
Esperar que los Genios
tengan un descuido.
Las claves están flotando
entre nosotros mismos.

They tie up Death
& make the Echoes
mislead men
with mirrors.
In a corner
10 lies the secret,
in the open,
dead.
A blue boy
with iron feet—
a glowing star
between his eyebrows.
His companions
mourn him.
And the green lake trembles.
20 In the wind.

Harmony

Waves
rhyme with sighs
& stars with
crickets.
Atremble in the cornea
the whole cold sky.
A dot, a synthesis,
infinity's.

But who joins waves
10 with sighs?
And stars
with crickets?
Just hope these genies
may be missing something.
The proofs keep drifting by
among us.

El último paseo del filósofo

Newton
paseaba.
La muerte lo iba siguiendo
rasgueando su guitarra.
Newton
paseaba.
Los gusanos roían
su manzana.
Sonaba el viento en los árboles
10 y el río bajo las ramas.
Wordsworth hubiera llorado.
El filósofo tomaba
posturas inverosímiles
esperando otra manzana.
Corría por el camino
y tendíase junto al agua
para hundir su rostro en
la gran luna reflejada.
Newton
20 lloraba.

En un alto cedro dos
viejos búhos platicaban
y en la noche lentamente
el sabio volvía a su casa
soñando inmensas pirámides
de manzanas.

Réplica

Adán comió la manzana
de la virgen Eva.
Newton fue un segundo Adán
de la Ciencia.
El primero conoció
la belleza.
El segundo un Pegaso

The Philosopher's Last Walk

Newton
was taking a walk.
Death had followed him,
strumming his guitar.
Newton
was taking a walk.
The worms gnawed through
his apple.
The wind hummed in the trees,
the river beneath the branches.
(Wordsworth would have cried.)
The philosopher was striking
unimaginable poses,
was waiting for another apple.
He ran along the road.
He stretched out by the water.
He saw how his face would sink
in the big moon's reflection.
Newton
wept.

And high up on a cedar two
old owls yammered.
Slowly in the night the wise man
went back home.
He dreamt enormous pyramids
of apples.

Reply

Adam ate an apple
from the Virgin Eve.
Newton was a second Adam—
Science's.
The first knew
Beauty.
The second a Pegasus

cargado de cadenas.
Y no fueron culpables.
10   Las dos manzanas eran
sonrosadas
y nuevas
pero de amarga
leyenda.
¡Los dos senos cortados
de la niña inocencia!

Pregunta

¿Por qué fue la manzana
y no
la naranja
o la poliédrica
granada?
¿Por qué fue reveladora
esta fruta casta,
esta poma suave
y plácida?
10   ¿Qué símbolo admirable
duerme en sus entrañas?
Adán, Paris y Newton
la llevan en el alma
y la acarician sin
adivinarla.

Historietas del viento

[1]

El viento venía rojo
por el collado encendido
y se [ha] puesto verde verde
por el río.
Luego se pondrá violeta,
amarillo y . . .

bowed down by chains.
And neither one was guilty.
10   Their two apples
pink
& fresh
but with a bitter
history.
The severed breasts of
innocence, poor child.

Question

Why was it the apple
& not
the orange
or the polyhedral
pomegranate?
Why this virgin fruit
to clue them in,
this smooth & gentle
pippin?
10   What admirable symbol
lies dormant at its core?
Adam, Paris, Newton
carry it inside their souls
& fondle it without a clue
to what it is.

Vignettes of the Wind

[1]

The wind came in red
through the burntover pass
& changed into green
down by the river.
And will change into violet
yellow & (what?).

será sobre los sembrados
un arco iris tendido.

[II]

Viento estancado.
Arriba el sol.
Abajo
las algas temblorosas
de los álamos.
Y mi corazón
temblando.

Viento estancado
a las cinco de la tarde
10 sin pájaros.

[III]

La brisa
es ondulada
como los cabellos
de algunas muchachas.
Como los marecitos
de algunas viejas tablas.
La brisa
brota como el agua
y se derrama
10 —tenue bálsamo blanco—
por las cañadas,
y se desmaya
al chocar con lo duro
de la montaña.

Over fields sown with seed,
an elongated rainbow.

[II]

Stagnant wind.
Sun above you.
Below you
the tremulous algae of
aspens.
And my heart
trembling too.

Stagnant wind
at five in the afternoon
10   & no birds.

[III]

The breeze
so wavy
like the hair of
certain girls.
Like the oceans made small
in certain old panels.
The breeze
now gushes like water,
now overflows
10   —tenuous balsamic white—
through the canebrakes,
now faints,
where it crashes against
this rock of a mountain.

Escuela

Maestro
¿Qué doncella se casa
con el viento?

Niño
La doncella de todos
los deseos.

Maestro
¿Qué le regala
el viento?

Niño
Remolinos de oro
y mapas superpuestos.

Maestro
¿Ella le ofrece algo?

Niño
10   Su corazón abierto.

Maestro
Decid cómo se llama.

Niño
Su nombre es un secreto.

> (La ventana
> del colegio
> tiene una cortina
> de luceros.)

School

The Teacher
What maiden will marry
the wind?

The Child
The maiden of all
our desires.

The Teacher
What does the wind
give the maiden?

The Child
Whirlwinds of gold.
A pileup of maps.

The Teacher
And she gives him what?

The Child
10 Her heart laid bare.

The Teacher
Tell me her name.

The Child
Her name is a secret.

  (The window
  in the school
  has a curtain
  of stars.)

Cúco-cuco-cucó

A Enrique Díez-Canedo y a Teresa

El cuco divide la noche
con sus bolitas de cobre.

El cuco no tiene pico,
tiene dos labios de niño
que silban desde los siglos.

¡Gato,
esconde tu rabo!

El cuco va sobre el tiempo
flotando como un velero
10   y múltiple como un eco.

¡Urraca,
esconde tu pata!

Frente al cuco está la esfinge,
el símbolo de los cisnes
y la niña que no ríe.

¡Zorra,
esconde tu cola!

Un día se irá en el viento
el último pensamiento
20   y el penúltimo deseo.

¡Grillo,
vete bajo el pino!

Sólo el cuco quedará,
partiendo la eternidad
con bolitas de cristal.

Cúckoo-Cuckoo-Cuckóo

For Enrique Díez-Canedo & Teresa

The cuckoo divides the night
with its tiny copper pellets.

The cuckoo has no beak,
only two little lips like a child's
to whistle the centuries home.

Cat,
hide your cat tail!

The cuckoo flies over time,
floating in space like a sailboat
10 splitting apart like an echo.

Magpie,
hide your bird foot!

In front of the cuckoo 's the sphinx,
the symbol of the swan,
& the little girl who won't laugh.

Fox lady,
hide your fox tail!

One day it's all gone with the wind
the absolutely last thought
20 & the next to the last desire.

Cricket,
get under that pine!

For only the cuckoo will stay
splitting eternity
with its tiny crystal pellets.

La canción del cuco viejo

En el arca de Noé
canté.
Y en la fronda
de Matusalén.

Noé era un hombre bueno.
A Matusalén
le llegaba la barba
a los pies.

Lanzo mis silbidos
10   al cielo. Logré
que cayeran vacíos
otra vez.

Sobre la noche canto.
Cantaré
aunque estéis dormidos.
Cantaré
por todos los siglos
de los siglos. Amén.

Primer nocturno del cuco

A pesar de sus ojos
la noche va perdida.

(Sólo el cuco
permanece.)

En la cañavera lloran
vientos indecisos.

(Sólo el cuco
permanece.)

The Old Cuckoo's Song

In Noah's ark
I did sing.
And down on Methusaleh's farm.

For Noah was one good hombre.
And Methusaleh's
beard touched
the ground.

He launched my whistles
up to the sky. I got them
10   to fall down empty
just one more time.

Over the night I did sing.
I will sing
though you be asleep.
Por todos los siglos
de los siglos.
Time without end. Amen.

Cuckoo's First Nocturne

In despite of its eyes
the night's getting lost.

(For only the cuckoo
endureth.)

In the canebrake the sobbing
of uncertain winds.

(For only the cuckoo
endureth.)

¿Por aquí? ¿Por allí? El alma
10 ha perdido su olfato.

(Sólo el cuco
permanece.)

Segundo nocturno del cuco

El cuco dice que *Sí*.
¡Alégrate, colorín!
El ángel abre las puertas
de su jardín.

El cuco dice que *No*.
¡Canta, tierno ruiseñor!
Tendremos en cada ojo
una flor.
¡Oh qué maravillosa
10 resurrección!

¡Que No!
¡Que Sí!

(La noche
se iba por su confín.)

¡Que Sí!
¡Que No!

(Apurando sus gotas
va el reloj.)

Último nocturno

¡Oh qué estremecimiento!
El cuco ha llegado.
¡Huyamos!

Here? There? The soul
10 's lost power of smell.

(For only the cuckoo
endureth.)

Cuckoo's Second Nocturne

The cuckoo says Yes.
Get happy, goldfinch!
Angel opens the gates
to his garden.

The cuckoo says No.
Sing out, little nightingale!
With a flower
in each eye.
Oh what a great
10 resurrection!

And it's No!
And it's Yes!

(The night
back to the confines of Night.)

And it's Yes!
And it's No!

(Clock dribbles waterdrops
time winding down.)

Last Nocturne

Oh what a shuddering!
Cuckoo's come to town,
let's all of us clear out!

Si tú vieras a la amarga
adelfa sollozar,
¿qué harías, amor mío?

Pensaría en el mar.

Si tú vieses que la luna
te llama cuando se va,
¿qué harías, amor mío?

Suspirar.

Si yo te dijese un día
«Te amo» desde mi olivar,
¿qué harías, amor mío?

Clavarme un puñal.

¡Oh qué estremecimiento!
El cuco ha llegado.
¡Huyamos!

Ensueños del río

(Río Genil)

Las alamedas se van
pero dejan su reflejo

    (¡Oh qué bello
      momento!)

Las alamedas se van
pero nos dejan el viento.

El viento está amortajado
a lo largo, bajo el cielo.

    (¡Oh qué triste
      momento!)

If you should see the bitter
oleander sobbing,
what would you do, amor mío?

I would think about the ocean.

If you were to see the moon
call you as it floats away,
10   what would you do, amor mío?

Sigh.

And if one day I was to say:
"I love you" from my olive grove,
what would you do, amor mío?

Stick a dagger in myself.

Oh what a shuddering!
Cuckoo's come to town,
let's all of us clear out!

Daydreams of a River

(Río Genil)

The poplars are fading away
but leave their reflections.

    (What a beautiful
    time!)

The poplars are fading away
but leave us the wind.

The wind's shrouding everything
under the sun.

    (What a sad little
10   time!)

Pero ha dejado flotando,
sobre los ríos, sus ecos.

El mundo de las luciérnagas
ha invadido mis recuerdos.

(¡Oh qué bello
        momento!)

Y un corazón diminuto
me va brotando en los dedos.

·

El remanso tiene lotos
de círculos concéntricos.
Sobre mis sienes soporto
la majestad del silencio.

Maravillosos biseles
estremecen a los álamos.
Por las hierbas de la orilla
van los caracoles blancos.

Corriente lenta

Por el río se van mis ojos,
por el río . . .
Por el río se va mi amor,
por el río . . .
(Mi corazón va contando
las horas que está dormido).
El río trae hojas secas,
el río . . .
El río es claro y profundo,
el río . . .

But it leaves us its echoes,
afloat on the river.

The world of the fireflies
has invaded my thoughts

>   (What a beautiful
>   time!)

And a miniature heart
blossoms on my fingers.

•

This backwash has lotuses
spread in concentric circles.
On my temples I bear their
majestical silence.

Marvelous bevels shatter
the poplar trees.
Through the grass on the riverbank
little white snails come & go.

Lazy River

Down the river my eyes drift away
down the river . . .
Down the river my love drifts away
down the river . . .
(My heart goes on counting
how long it's asleep.)
The river is bearing dead leaves,
the river . . .
The river is crystal & deep,
the river . . .

(Mi corazón me pregunta
si puede cambiar de sitio.)

[. . .]

Madrigales

[I]

Como las ondas concéntricas
sobre el agua,
así en mi corazón
tus palabras.

Como un pájaro que choca
con el viento,
así sobre mis labios
tus besos.

Como fuentes abiertas
10   frente a la tarde,
así mis ojos negros
sobre tu carne.

II

Estoy preso
en tus círculos
concéntricos.
Como Saturno
llevo
los anillos
de mi sueño.
Y no acabo de hundirme
ni me elevo.

(And my heart asks me
can it change places.)

[. . .]

Madrigals

[I]

Like concentric waves
on the water,
your words
in my heart.

Like a bird that collides
with the wind,
your kiss
on my lips.

Like open fountains
10   fronting the night,
my dark eyes
on your skin.

II

I'm caught
in your concentric
circles.
Like Saturn
I lug around
rings
from my dreams.
I'm not totally sunk,
I'm not rising.
10   My love!

¡Amor mío!
Mi cuerpo
flota sobre el remanso
de los besos.

Meditaciones y alegorías del agua

Hace muchos años yo, soñador modesto y muchacho alegre, paso todos los veranos en la fresca orilla de un río. Por las tardes, cuando las admirables abejarucos cantan presintiendo el viento y la cigarra frota con rabia sus dos laminillas de oro, me siento junto a la viva hondura del remanso y echo a volar mis propios ojos que se posan asustados sobre el agua, o en las redondas copas de los álamos.

Bajo los mimbres picudos, junto a la lengua del agua, yo siento cómo toda la tarde abierta hunde mansamente con su peso la verde lámina del remanso [y] cómo las ráfagas de silencio ponen frío el asombrado cristal de mis ojos.

Los primeros días me turbó el espléndido espectáculo de los reflejos, las alamedas caídas que se ponen salomónicas al menor suspiro del agua, los zarzales y los juncos que se rizan como una tela de monja.

Pero yo no observé que mi alma se iba convirtiendo en prisma, que mi alma se llenaba de inmensas perspectivas y de fantasmas temblorosas. Una tarde miraba fijamente la verdura movible de las ondas y pude contemplar cómo un extraño pájaro de oro se curvaba sobre las ondas de un chopo reflejado; miré a la copa real que estaba inundada de sol poniente y sólo los invisibles pajarillos del viento jugaban entre las hojas; el pájaro de oro había desaparecido.

Una frescura maravillosa invadió todo mi cuerpo, envuelto en las últimas hebras de la cabellera crepuscular y una inmensa avenida luminosa atravesaba mi corazón. ¿Es posible? ¿Mi alma hace excursiones a las ondas en vez de visitar las estrellas?

La esquila de un rebaño ponía sus ecos oscuros en mi garganta y yo sentí la piel maravillosa de mi alma salpicada de gotitas cristalinas. ¿Cómo no has guardado, alma mía, el temblor de Venus o el violín de los vientos y has guardado en cambio el alga sonora de las cascadas y la inmensa flor del círculo concéntrico? . . . ¡Y vi todos mis recuerdos reflejados!

But my body's
afloat on this bayou,
your kisses.

Meditations & Allegories of Water

For many years now—being a smalltime dreamer & an easygoing
guy—I have spent my summers at a cool spot down along a river. In
the afternoons, when those amazing birds, the bee-eaters, start singing
in anticipation of the wind & an angry cicada rubs its two gold plates
together, I sit down beside a deep & active pool & move my eyes
around until they settle, frightened, on the water or the rounded tree-
tops of the nearby poplars.

Under some spiky osiers, up by the water's edge, I feel the after-
noon come open, gently pressing against the pool's green surface. A
silent air begins to freeze the astonished crystal in my eyes.

For the first few days the spectacle of what I saw reflected there en-
thralled me: the fallen poplar groves that changed to Solomonic
columns at the slightest stirring of the water, the brambles & the reeds
that curled up like a nun's cloth.

I didn't notice that my soul was changing to a prism, that it was fill-
ing with immense perspectives, trembling phantoms. One afternoon,
while staring at the mobile greenness of the waves, I saw how a
strange gold bird had curved itself around a reflected poplar. But when
I looked hard at the tree's real leaves awash with sunset, only some in-
visible small windbirds played in them. The golden bird had disap-
peared.

A marvelous coolness took hold of my body, as if to bind me with
the last strands of the sunset's hair, & a broad avenue of light ran
through my heart. How could this be? My soul on a trip through the
waves instead of a flight to the stars?

A sheep bell left dark echoes in my throat & I felt my soul's amaz-
ing skin being spattered by small crystal drops. O soul, why didn't
you stay true to Venus's quavering or to the wind's violin? why the
sonorous algae in the waterfalls & the enormous flower the concentric
circle makes? . . . And I saw all my memories reflected!

Barra

Yo volvía del secano. En lo hondo estaba la vega envuelta en su temblor azul. Por el aire yacente de la noche estival flotaban las temblorosas cintas de los grillos.

La música del secano tiene un marcado sabor amarillento.

Ahora comprendo cómo las cigarras son de oro auténtico y cómo un cantar puede hacerse ceniza entre los olivares.

Los muertos que viven en estos cementerios tan lejos de todo el mundo, deben ponerse amarillos como los árboles en noviembre.

Ya cerca de la vega parece que penetramos en una pecera verde, el aire es un mar de ondas azules, un mar hecho para la luna, y las ranas tocan sus múltiples flautas de caña seca.

Bajando del secano a la vega se tiene que cruzar un misterioso vado que pocas personas perciben, el Vado de los Sonidos. Es una frontera natural donde un silencio extraño quiere apagar dos músicas contrarias. Si tuviéramos la retina espiritual bien constituida podríamos apreciar cómo un hombre que baja teñido por el oro del secano se ponía verde al entrar en la vega, después de haber desaparecido en la turbia corriente musical de la divisoria.

Yo he querido seguir un momento el camino emocionante (de un lado las ranas, del otro los grillos) y he bebido fríos hilillos de silencio reciente entre los imperceptibles choques sonoros.

¿Qué hombre puede recorrer este camino largo sin que su alma se llene de un arabesco confuso? ¿Quién se atreve a decir «he andado un camino con la cabeza: un camino que no es de pájaro ni de pez ni de hombre, sino el camino de las orejas»?

¿Es éste el camino que va a *ninguna parte*, donde están los que han muerto esperando? Desde la cola del olivar hasta las avanzadas de los chopos, ¡qué admirables algas y lucecillas invisibles deben flotar!

Me he detenido ante la corriente y las largas antenas de mis oídos han explorado su profundidad. Por aquí es ancho y lleno [sic] de remolinos, pero en el monte se enterrará bajo las arenas azules del desierto. Ahora tiene la sublime confusión de los sueños olvidados.

La luna menguante como un ajo de oro pone un bozo adolescente a la comba del cielo.

Border

I was returning from the drylands. Down below a river valley trembled, a vega wrapped in blue. Out of the summer night, the sprawling air, some cricket ribbons, trembling, floated.

The desert music has a truly yellow taste.

I know now why cicadas are made of solid gold & how a song can turn to ashes in the olive groves.

Dead bodies living in these distant cemeteries must turn as yellow as November trees.

Getting close to the vega, we seem to have entered a green fishtank: the air is a sea of blue waves, an ocean made for the moon, where frogs play on multiple flutes of dry cane.

To get from the drylands to the vega, you cross a mysterious ford that few people notice: the Ford of Sounds. This ford forms a natural boundary where an eerie silence tries to stifle two contradictory musics. If our spiritual eyes were made for it, we would discern how a man, turned yellow by the golden wheat, changes to green on entering the vega, after disappearing in the murky flow of music at the border.

I tried for one moment to go down that awesome road (frogs on one side & crickets on the other). There amid sounds which clashed imperceptibly, I would sip cool little threads of newly made silence.

What man can travel this long road & not fill up his soul with crazy arabesques? Who would dare say "I walked along a path in my head, & it wasn't a path for birds or for fish or for men, but a path for our ears"?

Is this the path that leads to Nowhere, the home of those who died of waiting? From the rear of the olive grove to the advance line of poplars, what fantastic algae & little invisible lights float around us!

Here I pause beside the current & with my ears as antennae I explore its depths. The ford is wide & full of whirlpools, while in the mountains it is buried under the blue desert sand. Now it has the wonderful confusion of forgotten dreams.

The waning moon, like a clove of gold garlic, scatters down from a young boy's face on a curve in the sky.

Castillo de fuegos artificiales
quemado con motivo del cumpleaños
del poeta

Primera cohetería

Tú tú tú tú
yo yo yo yo
¿Quién? . . .
¡ni tú
ni yo!

Rueda Catalina

Doña Catalina
tenía un pelo de oro
entre su cabellera
de sombra.

(¿A quién espero,
Dios mío,
a quién espero?)

Doña Catalina
camina despacio
poniendo estrellitas
verdes en la noche.

(Ni aquí
ni allí,
sino aquí.)

Doña Catalina
se muere y le nace
una granadeta de luz
en la frente.

¡Chisssssssssssss!

Barrage of Firework Poems
on the Occasion of
the Poet's Birthday

First Launching

You you you you
me me me me
Who? . . .
not you!
not me!

Catherine Wheel

Doña Catalina
had a single gold hair
among her shadowy
tresses.

(For whom am I waiting,
dear God,
for whom am I waiting?)

Doña Catalina
walks slowly
10 scattering little green stars
in the night.

(Not here
& not there
but here.)

Doña Catalina:
a grenade of light
dies & is born
on her forehead.

Chssssssssssssss!

Cohetes

Seis lanzas de fuego
suben.
(La noche es una guitarra.)
Seis sierpes enfurecidas.
(Por el cielo vendrá San Jorge.)
Seis sopletes de oro y viento.
(¿Se agrandará la ampolla
de la noche?)

Jardín chino

En los bosquecillos
de grana y magnesio
saltan las princesitas
Chispas.

Hay una lluvia de naranjas
sobre el zig-zag de los cerezos
y entre comas vuelan azules
dragoncillos amaestrados.

Niña mía, este jardincillo
10 es para verlo en los espejitos
de tus uñas.
Para verlo en el biombo
de tus dientes.
Y ser como un ratoncito.

Girasol

Si yo amara a un cíclope
suspiraría
bajo esta mirada

Rockets

Six fiery spears
zoom up.
(The night's a guitar.)
Six fuming serpents.
(St. George will dive through the sky.)
Six torches of gold & of wind.
(Will they puff up the bell jars
of night?)

Chinese Garden

In the little woodlets
with their purples & magnesiums
the princesitas jumping
are baby sparkadillos.

There's a rain of oranges
above the zigzag cherryos—
& between commas comes a flight
of prancing blue dragondolas.

My little girl, this gardenette's
10 best looked at in the mirrorettes
that are thy fingernails.
And in those screens that are thy teeth.
As by a little mouselet.

Sunflower

If I did love a cyclops
I would swoon
beneath his stronger gaze

sin párpados.
¡Oh girasol de fuego!
El gentío lo mira
sin estremecimiento.
¡Ojo de la providencia
ante una muchedumbre
10   de Abeles!

¡Girasol girasol!
¡Ojo salvaje y puro
sin la ironía del guiño!

Girasol girasol.
¡Estigma ardiente sobre
los gentíos de feria!

Disco de rubíes

Gira y se estremece
como loco.
No sabe nada
¿y lo sabe todo?
¡Todas las flechas
a este corazón
redondo!

Todas las pupilas
a este corazón
10   redondo.
¡Lupa sangrienta entre
el misterio
y nosotros!

Capricho

¡Tris! . . .
¿Has cerrado
los ojos?

sans eyelids.
O fiery sunflower, ay!
The people stare at it
sans shuddering.
Eyeball of Providence
eyeing a crowdful of
10 Abels!

Sunflower sunflower!
Pure savage eyeball
sans winkage sans irony!

Sunflower sunflower!
Stigmata raging above
a fair full of peoples.

The Ruby Disc

gyrates & shakes
like crazy.
Knowing nothing—
knows it all?
All those arrows aimed
at this round
heart.
All those eyeballs aimed
at this round
10 heart.
A bloody lens between
the mystery
& us.

Capriccio

Zip! . . .
Did you just close
your eyes?

¡Triis! . . .
¿Más aún? Serás una
muchacha de brisa.
Yo soy un hombre.
　　¡Tras! . . .
Ya te vas, amor mío,
10　¿y tus ojos?
　　¡Traaas! . . .
Si los cierras yo tengo dos plumas.
¿Lo oyes? Dos plumas que miran
de mi pavo real.
　　¡Tris! . . .
¿Me has oído?
　　¡Traaas! . . .

Juego de lunas

La luna está redonda.
Alrededor, una noria
de espejos.
Alrededor, una rueda
de agua.
La luna se ha hecho láminas
como un pan de oro blanco.
La luna
se ha deshojado
10　en lunas.
Bandadas de fuentes
vuelan por el aire.
En cada fuente yace
una luna difunta.
La luna
se hace un bastón de luz
en el torrente claro.
La luna,
como una gran vidriera
20　rota, cae sobre el mar.
La luna
se va por un biombo

Ziiip! . . .
Even more? That's a
breezy young girl.
And I am an hombre.
    Zap!
Already you're gone, o my love,
& your eyes?
    Zaaap! . . .
If you close them, I have here two feathers,
you hear? two feathers staring out
from my peacock.
    Zip!
Did you hear me?
    Zaaap! . . .

A Game of Moons

Moon is round.
Roundabout it is a treadmill
built with mirrors.
Roundabout it is a wheel
like a waterwheel.
Moon's become a gilt leaf
like a loaf of white gold.
Moon sheds its petals
like moons.
Swarms of fountains
float through the sky.
In each fountain 's a moon
lying dead.
Moon
becomes a cane made of light
in bright torrents.
Moon
like a large stainedglass window
that breaks on the ocean.
Moon
through an infinite
screen.

infinito.
¿Y la Luna? ¿Y la Luna?

(Arriba,
no queda más que un aro
de cristalillos.)

Ruedas de fortuna

Abanico

El zodíaco
de la suerte
se abre en el abanico
rojo, amarillo y verde.

En la selva de los números
la niña se pierde
con los ojos cerrados.
¿El cuatro? ¿El cinco? ¿El siete?

Cada número guarda
pájaro o serpiente.
Sí, dice el cuatro.
No, dice el veinte.

El dedo de la niña
sobre el cielo de la suerte
pone la estrella de
más rico presente.

Ruleta

Rosa
de corola profunda.

¿Se te atraganta
la bolita?

And the moon? And the moon?
(Up above
nothing left but a ring
of small crystals.)

Wheels of Fortune

Fan

Chance's
zodiac
opens up, fanlike
red yellow green.

In the forest of numbers
a little girl lost
's got closed eyes
four? five? seven?

Each number's enclosing
a bird or a snake.
Yes says the four
No says the twenty.

On a sky ruled by chance
the little girl's finger
pins up her star—
most rich present.

Roulette

Rose
with the deepdown corolla.

Is it so hard to swallow
that pinball?

Tienes un cielo
de joyas falsas
y te deshojan manos
descarnadas.

Giras
10 sobre turbias pupilas
en el acre jardín
de las interrogaciones.
Giras
sonámbula y fría,
abriendo tu gran cola
de pavo real de números.

Caracol

Caracol,
estáte quieto.

Donde tú estés
estará el centro.

La piedra sobre el agua
y el grito en el viento
forman las imágenes
puras de tu sueño,
las circunferencias
10 imposibles [de] tu cuerpo.

Caracol col col col,
estáte quieto.

Donde tú estés
estará el centro.

You've got a sky
of fake jewels
& fleshless hands
strip you blind.

With blurred eyes
10 you whirl by
the bitter
inquisitor's garden.

Sleepless & cold
you whirl by.
Fanning out your great tail
like a peacock of numbers.

Caracols/ Snails

Caracol, now
hold still.

Where you are
will be center.

Stone over water
& cry in the wind
forming the pure
imagings in your dreams,
impossible circumferences
10 inside your body.

Caracol col col col
now be quiet.

Where you are
will be center.

Espiral

Mi tiempo
avanza en espiral.

La espiral
limita mi paisaje,
y me hace caminar
lleno de incertidumbre.

¡Oh línea recta! Pura
lanza sin caballero.
¡Cómo sueña tu luz
10 mi senda salomónica!

Balada del caracol blanco

Los niños juegan
bajo los álamos.
El río viejecito
va muy despacio
sentándose en las sillas
verdes de los remansos.
Mi niño ¿dónde está?
Quiere ser un caballo.
¡Tilín! ¡tilín! ¡tilín! Mi niño
10 ¡qué loquillo! cantando
quiere salirse
de mi corazón cerrado.

Caracolitos chicos,
caracoles blancos.

Spiral

My time
moves on in a spiral.

The spiral
limits my landscape,
leaves what is past in the shadows
& makes me advance
full of doubts.

Oh perfect straight line! Pure
spear without spearman.
10 How your light turns my solomonic
path into dream!

Ballade of White Caracols

The children play under
the poplar trees.
The little old river
runs very slowly,
seating itself on green
chairs, in the backwaters.
Where'd be my child, then?
Child who would change to a horse.
Tinkle tinkle! My child,
10 little madman! is singing,
would like to escape
my closed heart.

Sweet little tiny
white caracols.

Balada del caracol negro

Los niños sentados
escuchan un cuento.
El río traía
coronas de vientos
y una gran serpiente
desde un tronco viejo
miraba las nubes
redondas del cielo.
Niño mío chico,
¿dónde estás?
Te siento
en el corazón
¡y no es verdad! Lejos
esperas que yo saque
tu alma del silencio.

Caracoles grandes,
caracoles negros.

[*Epitafio a un pájaro*]

[. . . . .]
y sus ojos tuvieron
profundidad de siglos
mientras se le irisaba
la gran perla del pico
Adiós pájaro verde
Ya estarás en el Limbo
Visita de mi parte
a mi hermano Luisillo
en la pradera
con los mamoncillos
¡Adiós pájaro verde
tan grande y tan chico
¡Admirable quimera
del limón y el narciso!

Ballade of Black Caracols

The children, seated,
are hearing a story.
The river was bringing us
wind crowns,
& a snake a big snake
from a very old tree trunk
watched the round clouds
in the sky.
My child, my chico,
10 where are you? I feel you
here in my heart
but not so. Way out there
you're waiting for me, till I pluck
your soul from the silence.

Big caracols.
black caracols.

[*Epitaph for a Bird*]

[. . . . .]

and its eyes as deep
as centuries, beside
the iridescence, pearl–like,
of its beak
Adios green bird
You must already be in Limbo
Visit with my brother
Luisillo out there in the country
with his babes
10 Oh green bird adios,
so big so small
You incredible chimera,
lemon bird narcissus!

Acción de gracias

Gracias, Señor lejano.
Señor y Padre mío
que me das una inmensa
lección de lirismo.

¡Oh Santo, santo, santo
que muestras el divino
momento de la muerte
sin velos, a mi espíritu!

Dame la dignidad
10 del pájaro y el ritmo
de las alas abiertas
ante lo sombrío.

¡Oh Santo santo santo!
Esta noche te pido
agua para mis ojos,
sombra para mis gritos!

Memento

He acostado al cantor
sobre un gran crisantemo
y escribo su epitafio.

Memento.

La Tierra duerme bajo
su mantilla de viento
con mares encrespados
y con mares serenos.

Memento.

10 Ahora mismo se hacen
preguntas los luceros.
Tú sabes la respuesta
que no conocen ellos.

Thanksgiving

Thank thee dear distant
God & Father mine
who gives me unimagined
lessons in poesis.

Oh holy holy holy
who does show the godly
hour of death,
unveiled, unto my soul!

Give me the dignity
10 this dear bird had, the rhythm
of its open wings
before the dark.

Oh holy holy holy
whom I ask this night to grant me
water for my eyes, & oh
thy shadow for my cry.

Memento

I have laid out the singer
on a great chrysanthemum
& I have writ his epitaph.

Memento.

Earth sleeps beneath
her windy veil,
her stormy seas
gone into calm.

Memento.

10 Now should the stars
raise questions,
you will know the answers
they cannot comprehend.

Memento.

Yacerás esta noche
sobre un lírico lecho.
¿Qué niño durmió nunca
en una flor su sueño?

Memento.

20 Y esta noche enviaré
para velar tu cuerpo
la mariposa enorme
de mi único beso.

¡Memento!

Surtidores

Interior

Desde mi cuarto
oigo el surtidor.
Un dedo de la parra
y un rayo de sol
señalan hacia el sitio
de mi corazón.
Por el aire de agosto
se van las nubes, yo
sueño que no sueño
10 dentro del surtidor.

País

¡Surtidores de los sueños
sin aguas
y sin fuentes!

Memento.

You'll be laid out tonight
on a poet's bed.
What child ever dreamed
a dream inside a flower?

Memento.

20 And tonight I will send
as a guard for your body
the enormous butterfly
of my only kiss.

Memento!

Water Jets

Interior

From my room I hear
the water jet.
A finger of grapevine
& a trace of sunlight
pointing to the place
where my heart is.
Through the August air
the clouds roll by, I
dream I'm not dreaming
10 inside the water jet.

Homeland

Water jets in dreams
sans water
& sans fountains!

Se ven con el rabillo
del ojo, nunca frente
a frente.

Como todas las cosas
ideales, se mecen
en las márgenes puras
10   de la Muerte.

Aparte

La sangre de la noche
va por las arterias
de los surtidores.
¡Oh qué maravilla
de temblor!
Yo pienso
en ventanas abiertas,
sin pianos
y sin doncellas.

        •

[. . . . .]
¡Hace un instante!
Todavía la polvareda
se mece en el azul.
Hace un momento.
¡Dos mil siglos!
si mal no recuerdo.

Jardín

Hay cuatro caballeros
con espadas de agua
y está la noche oscura.

Are detected from the corner
of the eye, & never face
to face.

Like all ideal
things, swaying
at the perfect boundaries
10 of Death.

Aside

Night's blood
flows through the arteries
of water jets.
Oh what a gorgeous
quaking!
I think of
open windows,
sans pianos
& sans maids.

•

[. . . . .]
Only right then it was!
The cloud of dust still
swaying, in the blue.
Only just now it was.
Two thousand centuries!
if I remember right.

Garden

There are four caballeros
with four swords made of water
& a very dark night.

Las cuatro espadas hieren
el mundo de las rosas
y os herirán el corazón.
¡No bajéis al jardín!

Herbarios

I

Libro

El viajante de jardines
lleva un herbario.
En su tomo de olor, gira.

Por las noches vienen a sus ramas
las almas de los viejos pájaros.

Cantan en ese bosque comprimido
que requiere las fuentes del llanto.

Como las naricillas de los niños
aplastadas en el cristal opaco,
10   así las flores de este libro
sobre el cristal invisible de los años.

El viajante de jardines
abre el libro llorando,
y los colores errabundos
se desmayan sobre el herbario.

I I

El viajante del tiempo
trae el herbario de los sueños.

Yo
¿Dónde está el herbario?

The four swords are wounding
a world filled with roses
& will wound your hearts too.
Don't go down into that garden!

Herbals

I

Book

The voyager in gardens
carries an herbal with him.
On his manual of odors,
whirls around.

At night onto its branches come
the souls of ancient birds.

They sing in that tight forest,
so needful of a fount of tears.

Like the noses of small children
10 pressed to a dark windowpane
are the flowers in this book of flowers
against the years' blank glass.

The voyager in gardens
opens his book, begins to cry,
& the errant colors
in his herbal fade & die.

II

The voyager through time
carries the herbal book of dreams.

I
Where is the herbal?

El Viajante
Lo tienes en tus manos.

Yo
Tengo libres los diez dedos.

El Viajante
Los sueños bailan en tus cabellos.

Yo
¿Cuántos siglos han pasado?

El Viajante
Una sola hoja
tiene mi herbario.

Yo
10 ¿Voy al alba
o [a] la tarde?

El Viajante
El pasado está
inhabitable.

Yo
¡Oh jardín de la amarga fruta!

El Viajante
¡Peor es el herbario de la luna!

I I I

En mucho secreto, un amigo
me enseña el herbario de los ruidos.

(¡Chissss . . . silencio!
La noche cuelga del cielo.)

A la luz de un puerto perdido
vienen los ecos de todos los siglos.

The Voyager
You have it in your hands.

I
I have ten fingers free.

The Voyager
Dreams dance in your hair.

I
And how many centuries have passed?

The Voyager
My herbal is just an hour old.

I
Am I heading for evening or dawn?

The Voyager
10 The past's an unlivable world.

I
Oh, garden of bitter fruit.

The Voyager
Worse yet the herbal of moon.

III

In great secret, a friend
shows me the herbal of noise.

(Psst . . . Keep quiet!
Night's hanging down from the sky.)

In the light across a lost harbor
all the centuries' echoes rise.

(¡Chissss . . . silencio!
¡La noche oscila con el viento!)

(¡Chissss . . . silencio!
10 Viejas iras se enroscan en mis dedos.)

En el bosque de las toronjas de luna
(Poema extático)

Prólogo

Me voy a un largo viaje.

Sobre un espejo de plata encuentro, mucho antes de que amanezca, el maletín y la ropa que debo usar por las extrañísimas tierras y jardines teóricos.

Pobre y tranquilo, quiero visitar el mundo extático donde viven todas mis posibilidades y paisajes perdidos. Quiero entrar frío pero agudo en el jardín de las simientes no florecidas y de las teorías ciegas, en busca del amor que no tuve pero que era mío.

He buscado durante largos días por todos los espejos de mi casa el camino que conduce a ese jardín maravilloso y al fin, ¡por pura casualidad!, lo he encontrado.

Adopté muchos procedimientos. Por ejemplo, me puse a cantar procurando que mi voz se mantuviera larga y tensa sobre el aire, pero los espejos permanecían silenciosos. Hice complicadas geometrías con la palabra y el ritmo, llené los ojos de plata con mi llanto y hasta puse una pantalla a la lamparita que ilumina la gruta de mi cabeza, ¡pero todo fue inútil!

Una mañana velada, después que había desechado por imposible el proyecto de viaje y me hallaba libre de preocupaciones y de jardines invisibles, fui a peinarme ante un espejo y, sin preguntarle nada, su ancha cara de plata se llenó de un zigzag de cantos de ruiseñores, y en la profundidad del azogue surgió la clave clara y precisa, clave que naturalmente me está vedado revelar.

Yo emprendo sereno este viaje y desde luego me lavo las manos: contaré lo que vea, pero no me pidáis que explique nada. Pude haber ido al país de los muertos pero prefiero ir al país de lo que no vive, que no es lo mismo.

Desde luego que un alma *pura y completa* no sentiría esta curiosidad. Voy tranquilo. En el maletín llevo una buena provisión de luciérnagas.

(Psst . . . keep quiet!
Night's being swung by the wind.)

Pssst . . . keep quiet!
10 Old furies coil around my hands.

In the Forest of the Lunar Grapefruits
(A Static Poem)

Prologue

I am going on a long trip.

On a silver mirror I find, long before dawn, the satchel & the clothing I'll need for those exotic countries & theoretical gardens.

Poor & peaceful, I want to visit the ecstatic world, where all my possibilities live & all my lost landscapes. I want to get in there, cold & sharp, to find a garden of flowerless seeds & blind theories: in search of a love I never had but that once was mine.

Many's the long day that I searched—in every mirror in my house—for the road that leads to that marvelous garden. And at last— by pure chance!—I've found it.

I used many ploys. For a start I tried singing, keeping my voice big & tense in the air, but the mirrors stayed silent. I made complicated geometries with words & rhythms, I filled silvery eyes with my lament, I even placed a shade on the nightlight that illuminates the grotto in my head. But nothing helped.

One murky morning, after I had all but given up the idea of the trip & was feeling free of worries & invisible gardens, I went to comb my hair in front of a mirror, and without my asking it anything, its broad silver face filled up with a zigzag of nightingales singing, and in its mercurial depths the clear, precise key came to light—that key that I'm forbidden from revealing.

Now I'm setting out serenely on my voyage & truth to tell I'm washing my hands of it. I'll let you know what all I see there, just don't ask me to explain it. I could have gone to the country of the dead, but I prefer going to the country of the unliving, which is not the same.

And truth to tell a *pure & intact* soul would not feel this kind of curiosity. I'm going at it free & easy. In the satchel I've got a good supply of glowworms.

379

Antes de marchar siento un dolor agudo en el corazón. Mi familia duerme y toda la casa está en un reposo absoluto. El alba revelando torres y contando una a una las hojas de los árboles me pone un antifaz blanco y unos guantes de [. . . .]

Reflexión

Hombre que vas y vienes,
huye del río y el viento,
cierra los ojos y . . .
. . . y vendimia tus lágrimas.

Con el alma en un hilo,
olvida la pregunta.
No menees las hoces
de la interrogación.

La pregunta es la yedra
10   que nos cubre y despista.
Giran ante nuestros ojos
prismas y encrucijadas.

La respuesta es la misma
pregunta disfrazada.
Va como manantial
y vuelve como espejo.

[. . .]

Las tres brujas desengañadoras
(En la puerta del jardín)

Bruja 1.ª
¡Ay flauta del sapo
y luz del gusano!

Before taking off just now I felt a sharp pain in my heart. My family is sleeping & the whole house is in a state of absolute repose. The dawn reveals towers & one by one counts up the tree leaves. It slips a white mask on me & some kind of gloves [. . . .]

Reflection

You who come and go,
run from river & from wind,
close your eyes & . . .
. . . & gather in your tears.

With soul tied on a string,
forget the question.
No need to wield interrogator's
sickle.

Question is the ivy
10 that covers & disjuncts us,
right before our eyes it spins
prisms & a crossroads.

Answer is the same as
question, but disguised.
Starts as spring of water,
comes back around as mirror.

[. . .]

The Three Disillusioning Witches
(At the garden gate)

1st Witch
Aiie for the toad flute
& aiie for the worm light!

2.^a
¡Ay mares de fósforo
y bosques de acero!

3.^a
Nuestra enemiga la blanca
luz de los siete colores.

1.^a
Mis lágrimas darán el arco
negro de la luz negra.

2.^a
Vuelvan las cosas, vuelvan
a sus primeros planos.

3.^a
Reino de la semilla
y la tiniebla extática.

2.^a
Mundo sin ojos, mundo
sin laberinto, sin reflejo.

3.^a
Teorías. Altas torres
sin cimientos ni piedras.

1.^a
Flauta del sapo.
Luz del gusano.

Las tres
Cada cosa en su círculo.
Todos desconocidos.
El viento no contesta
las preguntas del árbol.

3.^a
¡Reino de la semilla
y la tiniebla extática!

2nd Witch
Aiie for the phosphorous sea
& aiie for the steel forests!

3rd Witch
Our enemy is the white
light with its seven colors.

1st Witch
My tears will spawn the black
rainbow of black light.

2nd Witch
Let things move back, move back
10 onto their primary planes.

3rd Witch
Kingdom of the seed
& the ecstatic dark.

2nd Witch
World without eyes, world
without labyrinths or reflections.

3rd Witch
Theories. Tall-rising towers
without foundations or stones.

1st Witch
Toad flute.
Worm light.

All Three
Each thing in its circle.
20 Everything unknown.
Wind that will not answer
questions from the tree.

3rd Witch
Kingdom of the seed
& the ecstatic dark.

2.ª
¡Ay flor equivocada
sobre el tallo ignorante!

1.ª
Hermanas, cegad las siete
pupilas del dragón blanco.

Las tres
Cada cosa en su círculo.
30 Todos desconocidos.
Cansados estamos, ¡bizcas!
de ir por el mismo sitio.

(Detrás de la puerta ríen
dos calaveras con alas.

Tres anchas risas, sin dientes
devoran mi fresca risa.)

Situación

La primera sierpe de viento
va entre alamedas sin savia.

Yo tengo una larga barba
de padre río.

Recuerdo viejas muchedumbres,
noches ciegas y pájaros sonámbulos.
Mi siglo como un río de agua gris
y mi laúd con las velas de plomo.

¡Qué cansancio de cielos en mis ojos!
10 Un calambre de alba permanente
aprisiona mi carne envejecida
con sus ramajes yertos y agitados.

2nd Witch
Ah poor mistaken flower
on its unknowing stem!

1st Witch
Sisters, blind the pupils in
the white dragon's seven eyes.

All Three
Each thing in its circle.
30 Everything unknown.
We are worn out, cockeyed,
gone to the same old place.

(Behind the door comes the laughter
of two skulls with wings.

Three huge smiles with no teeth
devour my cool little smile.)

Situation

The first windsnake twists
among the sapless poplars.

I have a huge beard,
just like old man river.

I recall the old crowds,
blind nights, sleepwalking birds.
My century's a graywater river
& my catboat is under lead sails.

Such ennui of skies on my eyeballs!
10 A spasm—perennial dawn—
imprisons my aged flesh
in its stiff, hectic branches.

Tan-tan
(Se iba la Tierra empedrada de cúpulas
bajo la cáscara azul de la atmósfera.)

¿Quién es?

(Entre una luz de leche y de luna
llego a la torre donde ya me esperan.)

Torre

Él estaba
con su corona
de carcajadas.
Larga barba amarilla.

Él
Te esperaba.

Yo
La ganzúa del Sueño
me abrió tu mansión.
        Vive
lo que no vivió nunca
ni vivirá. Mis ojos,
10   llenos de escarcha, copian
blancos bosques inmóviles.

Él
Dentro de cada estrella
hay un gusano de oro.
El dragón oculta una risa
de niño bajo un ala.

Yo
¡Ah bribón! ¡gran bribón!
Nada puedo ofrecerte.
¡Ni risa ni gusano!

Clang-clang
(The Earth was heading off, paved over with domes
under the atmosphere's eggshell blue.)

Who goes there?

(Between milklight & moonlight
I arrive at the tower where the others await me.)

Tower

He was there
with his crown of
loud heehaws.
Big yellow beard.

He
I was waiting for you.

I
The skeleton key to the Dream
opened your house for me.
          What now is alive
never lived
10   nor will live. My eyes,
filled with hoarfrost, mimic
white motionless forests.

He
Inside each star
's a gold worm.
Dragon hides smile of a child
'neath its wing.

I
Ah you beggar! Ah you bugger!
I've got nothing to offer you.
Not a smile, not a worm!

Él
Señor, tienes cien años.

Yo
20 Cien no, sobre los hombros
cada año una espada
larga de luz undosa.

Él
¿Cómo pasaste el río
de mariposas de agua?

Yo
Con la ganzúa del Sueño
y a pesar tuyo.

Él
Dame
tus labios.

Yo
¡Imposible!
¿Mi jardín de palabras?

Él
¿Tiemblas? Mira tu mundo.

Las Campanas (a lo lejos)
30 Tin tan
Tin tan

¡Ay, Navidad de tu casa!
La luna daba turquesas
a los ritmos de hojadelata.
Aquél nacía de barro.
¡Ay, Navidad de tu casa!

Nosotras te veíamos
sin corazón y sin cara
hacer puentes y látigos
40 grises con tu alma.

He
20 Mister, you're a hundred years old.

I
Not a hundred, no, on my shoulders
each year's a long
sword of quivering light.

He
How did you get past the river
& past the water butterflies?

I
With the key to the Dream—
in spite of your meddling.

He
                    Give me
your lips.

I
30   No. Can't be done!
Not my garden of words.

He
Are you trembling? Look at your world.

The Bells (in the distance)
                    Cling clang
                    Cling clang

Ah, that Christmas in your house!
The moon spawning turquoises
to a tinpan rhythm.
That one was born out of mud.
Ah, that Christmas in your house!

40 We bells saw you
    —heartless & faceless—
    making bridges and horsewhips
    turn gray like your soul.

Tin tan
Tin tan

¡Adiós! ¡adiós! y Memento,
¡pobre luz descarriada!
Gigantes nardos de tiniebla
rodean tu vieja casa.

Tin tan
Tin tan

Él
Alma tullida pero cristalina,
50 ¡mira el jardín!

Los viejos plenilunios
como discos inmensos de cristal
brillaban apoyados en la fronda.

Las Lámparas de la Torre (solas)
        ¡Ah! ¡Ah!
¿Cuándo dormiremos?
La sombra pesa sobre
nuestros ojos sin párpados.
¿Cuándo dormiremos?
Cortar nuestra flor
60 o darnos escafandra.
        ¡Ah! ¡Ah!

En el jardín de las toronjas de luna

Prólogo

Asy como la sombra nuestra vida se va,
que nunca más torna nyn de nos tornará
—Pero López de Ayala (*Consejos morales*)

Me he despedido de los amigos que más quiero para emprender un
corto pero dramático viaje. Sobre un espejo de plata encuentro mucho
antes de que amanezca el maletín con la ropa que debo usar en la ex-
traña tierra a que me dirijo.

Cling clang
Cling clang

Adios, adios, and Remember,
thou poor misguided light!
Gigantic spikenards of darkness
encircle thy ancient house.

50   Cling clang
Cling clang

He
Soul crippled but crystal clear,
come look at the garden!

The ancient full-moons
—like immense crystal discs—
sparkle propped in the foliage.

The Lights in the Tower (alone)
Ah! Ah!
When will we sleep?
The shadow weighs heavy, over
60 our lidless eyes.
When will we sleep?
Only cut off our flowers,
or get us a diving mask.
Ah! Ah!

In the Garden of the Lunar Grapefruits

Prologue
So like the shadow our life doth slip away
that never doth return nor us restore.
—Pero López de Ayala (*Consejos morales*)

I have taken leave of the friends I love the most & have set out on a
short dramatic journey. On a silver mirror I find, long before dawn,
the satchel with the clothing I'll need for the exotic country to which
I'm heading.

El perfume tenso y frío de la madrugada bate misteriosamente el inmenso acantilado de la noche.

En la página tersa del cielo temblaba la inicial de una nube, y debajo de mi balcón un ruiseñor y una rana levantan en el aire un aspa soñolienta de sonido.

Yo, tranquilo pero melancólico, hago los últimos preparativos, embargado por sutilísimas emociones de alas y círculos concéntricos. Sobre la blanca pared del cuarto, yerta y rígida como una serpiente de museo, cuelga la espada gloriosa que llevó mi abuelo en la guerra contra el rey don Carlos de Borbón.

Piadosamente descuelgo esa espada, vestida de herrumbre amarillenta como un álamo blanco, y me la ciño recordando que tengo que sostener una gran lucha invisible antes de entrar en el jardín. Lucha extática y violentísima con mi enemigo secular, el gigantesco dragón del Sentido Común.

Una emoción aguda y elegíaca por las cosas que no han sido, buenas y malas, grandes y pequeñas, invade los paisajes de mis ojos casi ocultos por unas gafas de luz violeta. Una emoción amarga que me hace caminar hacia este jardín que se estremece en las altísimas llanuras del aire.

Los ojos de todas las criaturas golpean como puntos fosfóricos sobre la pared del porvenir . . . lo de atrás se queda lleno de maleza amarilla, huertos sin frutos y ríos sin agua. Jamás ningún hombre cayó de espaldas sobre la muerte. Pero yo, por un momento, contemplando ese paisaje abandonado e infinito, he visto planos de vida inédita, múltiples y superpuestos como los cangilones de una noria sin fin.

Antes de marchar siento un dolor agudo en el corazón. Mi familia duerme y toda la casa está en un reposo absoluto. El alba, revelando torres y contando una a una las hojas de los árboles, me pone un crujiente vestido de encaje lumínico.

Algo se me olvida . . . no me cabe la menor duda . . . ¡tanto tiempo preparándome! y . . . Señor, ¿qué se me olvida? ¡Ah! Un pedazo de madera . . . uno bueno de cerezo sonrosado y compacto.

Creo que hay que ir bien presentado . . . De una jarra con flores puesta sobre mi mesilla me prendo en el ojal siniestro una gran rosa pálida que tiene un rostro enfurecido pero hierático.

Ya es la hora.

(En las bandejas irregulares de las campanadas, vienen los kikirikis de los gallos.)

The tight, cold scent of the sunrise beats weirdly on the huge escarpment we call night.

On the sky's stretched page a cloud's initial letter trembles, & below my balcony a nightingale & frog raise up a sleepy cross of sound.

I—tranquil, melancholy man—make my final preparations, impeded by those subtlest feelings aroused in me by wings & by concentric circles. On the white wall in my room, stiff & rigid like a snake in a museum, hangs the noble sword my grandfather carried in the war against Don Carlos the Pretender.

With reverence I take the sword down, coated with yellow rust like a white poplar, & I gird it on me while remembering that I'll have to go through an awful invisible fight before I enter the garden. An ecstatic & ferocious fight against my secular enemy, the giant dragon Common Sense.

A sharp & elegiac feeling for things that haven't been—good & evil, large & small—invades those landscapes in back of my eyes that my ultraviolet glasses have all but occulted. A bitter feeling that makes me travel toward this garden that shimmers on its skyhigh prairie.

The eyes of all creatures pound like phosphorescent points against the wall of the future . . . what was past stays filled with yellowing underbrush, orchards without any fruit, waterless rivers. No man ever fell backwards into death. But I, absorbed for now by this abandoned & infinite landscape, catch a glimpse of life's unpublished blueprints— multiplied, superposed, like buckets in an endless waterwheel.

Before taking off just now I felt a sharp pain in my heart. My family is sleeping & the whole house is in a state of absolute repose. The dawn reveals towers & one by one counts up the tree leaves. It slips a costume on me: crackling, made of spangled lace.

Must be something I've forgotten . . . can't be any doubt about it, so much time spent getting ready & . . . lord, what is it that escapes me? Ah, a piece of wood . . . a piece of good old cherry wood . . . rose-colored, tight-grained.

I believe in being well-groomed when I travel. . . . From a jar of flowers on my nightstand, I pick out a huge pale rose & pin it to my left lapel. It has a fierce but hieratic face.

And so the time has come.

(On the cockeyed trays of the bells' tongues come the cockadoo-dledoos of the roosters.)

Pórtico

NIÑO: *Yo voy por las plumas*
del pájaro Grifón.
ENANO: *Hijo mío, me es imposible*
ayudarte en esta empresa.
—*Cuento popular*

Tan-tan

El aire se había muerto.
Estaba inmóvil y arrugado.

Los pinos yacían en tierra.
Sus sombras de pie, ¡temblando!

Yo—Tú—Él
(en un solo plano)

Tan-tan

[. . .]

Momentos del Jardín

Marina

Cien negros navegantes
van en balsas de oro.

Sobre el mar en acecho
los corales emergen.

Yo, visir de una rara
Golconda de luceros,

calmo la sed de perlas
que tiene el agua y doy

pájaros y serpientes
10 a las ramas flotantes.

Portico

CHILD: *I am going in search of*
the griffon bird's wings.
DWARF: *My child, there is no way*
I can help you in this matter.
—Old folk tale

Clang clang

The air, having been killed,
lay motionless & shriveled.

The pinetrees, living, lay on the earth.
Their shadows uprisen, trembling!

I—You—He
(on a single plane)

Clang clang

[. . .]

Moments of the Garden

Seascape

One hundred black sailors
float on gold rafts.

Corals emerge
where seas lie in ambush.

Vizir of a strange
Golconda of stars,

I slake the thirst of the water
for pearls & I give

birds & serpents
10 to the floating boughs.

Perspectiva

Dentro de mis ojos
se abre el canto hermético
de las simientes que
no florecieron.

Todas sueñan un fin
irreal y distinto.
(El trigo sueña enormes
flores amarillentas.)

Todas sueñan extrañas
10 aventuras de sombra.
Frutos inaccesibles
y vientos amaestrados.

Ninguna se conoce.
Ciegas y desconocidas.
Les duelen sus perfumes
enclaustrados por siempre.

Cada semilla piensa
un árbol genealógico
que cubre todo el cielo
20 de tallos y racimos.

Por el aire se extienden
vegetaciones increíbles.
Ramas negras y grandes,
rosas color ceniza.

La luna casi ahogada
de flores y ramajes
se defiende con sus rayos
como un pulpo de plata.

Dentro de mis ojos
30 se abre el canto hermético
de las simientes que
no florecieron.

Perspective

From behind my eyes
hermetic song breaks open—
song of the seedling that
did not ever flower.

Each one dreams about an
unreal, quirky end.
(The wheat dreams it's got
enormous yellow flowers.)

All of them dreaming strange
10   adventures in the shade.
Fruits hanging out of reach
& domesticated winds.

None of them know each other,
blind & gone astray,
their perfumes paining them
but cloistered now forever.

Each seed thinks up
a genealogical tree—
covers the whole sky
20   with its stalks & roots.

The air's smeared over with
improbable vegetations.
Black & heavy branches.
Cinder-colored roses.

The moon nearly smothered
with flowers & with branches
fights them off with moonbeams
like an octopus in silver.

From behind my eyes
30   hermetic song breaks open—
song of the seedlings that
did not ever flower.

El jardín

Jamás nació, ¡jamás!
Pero pudo brotar.

Cada segundo se
profundiza y renueva.

Cada segundo abre
nuevas sendas distintas.

¡Por aquí! ¡Por allí!
Va mi cuerpo multiplicado.

Atravesando pueblos
o dormido en el mar.

¡Todo está abierto! Existen
llaves para las claves.

Pero el sol y la luna
nos pierden y despistan.

Y bajo nuestros pies
se enmarañan los caminos.

Aquí contemplo todo
lo que pude haber sido.

Dios o mendigo,
agua o vieja margarita.

Mis múltiples senderos
teñidos levemente

hacen una gran rosa
alrededor de mi cuerpo.

The Garden

was never born, never,
but could burst into life.

Every moment it's
deepened, restored.

Every moment it opens new
unheard-of pathways.

Over here! over there!
See my multiple bodies

passing through pueblos
or asleep in the ocean?

Everything open! Locks
to fit every key.

But the sun & moon
lose & delude us.

And under our feet
the highways are tangled.

Here I'll mull over all
I once could have been.

God or beggar,
water or old marguerite.

My multiple paths
barely stained

now form this enormous rose
encircling my body.

Como un mapa imposible,
el jardín de lo posible.

Cada segundo se
profundiza y renueva.

Jamás nació, ¡jamás!
30 ¡Pero pudo brotar!

Avenida

Las blancas Teorías
con los ojos vendados
danzaban por el bosque.

Lentas como cisnes
y amargas como adelfas.

Pasaron sin ser vistas
por los ojos del hombre,
como de noche pasan
inéditos los ríos,
10 como por el silencio
un rumor nuevo y único.

Alguna entre su túnica
lleva una gris mirada
pero de moribundo.
                Otras
agitan largos ramos
de palabras confusas.

No viven y están vivas.
Van por el bosque extático.
¡Enjambre de sonámbulas!

20 (Lentas como cisnes
y amargas como adelfas.)

Like an impossible map
the garden of the possible

every moment is
deepened, restored.

Was never born, never,
30 but could burst into life.

Avenue

Pallid white theories
with blindfolded eyes
would dance through the forest.

Sluggish like swans
& bitter like oleander.

They passed by, unseen
by a man's eyes,
as at nightfall the rivers
pass by, unreported.
10 As in the silence, a new-
fangled murmuring.

One of them inside her gown
has a gray heavy look
as of somebody dying.
                    Others
shake outsized branches of
disjuncted words.

They don't live, are alive,
pass through the ecstatic forest.
A swarm of sleepwalking women!

20 Sluggish like swans
& bitter like oleander.)

Paréntesis

Las doncellas dejan un olor
mental ausente de miradas.
El aire se queda indiferente,
camelia blanca de cien hojas.

Canción del jardinero inmóvil

Lo que no sospechaste
vive y tiembla en el aire.

Al tesoro del día
apenas si tocáis.

Van y vienen cargados
sin que los mire nadie.

Vienen rotos pero vírgenes
y hechos semilla salen.

Os hablan las cosas y
10   vosotros no escucháis.

El mundo es un surtidor
fresco, distinto y constante.

Al tesoro del día
apenas si tocáis.

Os veda el puro silencio,
el torrente de la sangre.

Pero dos ojos tenéis
para remontar los cauces.

Al tesoro del día
20   apenas si tocáis.

Parenthesis

Women leaving an odor behind them,
mental, stripped of appearances,
the air as indifferent as ever,
like a white camellia, a hundred blossoms.

Song of the Motionless Gardener

What you wouldn't have suspected
lives & trembles in the air.

Those treasures of the day
you keep just out of reach.

These come & go in truckloads
but no one stops to see them.

Banged up they come but virgin,
& gone back to seed they leave.

Things speak to you but no one
10   bothers to stop & listen.

The world's a waterspout of
objects, various & steady.

Those treasures of the day
you keep just out of reach.

The hot rush of your blood
drowning the virgin silence.

But the two good eyes you have
would draw you to the source.

Those treasures of the day
20   you keep just out of reach.

Lo que no sospechaste
vive y tiembla en el aire.

El jardín se enlazaba
por sus perfumes estancados.

Cada hoja soñaba
un sueño diferente.

Los puentes colgantes

¡Oh qué gran muchedumbre,
invisible y renovada,
la que viene a este jardín
a descansar para siempre!

Cada paso en la Tierra
nos lleva a un mundo nuevo.
Cada pie lo apoyamos
sobre un puente colgante.

Comprendo que no existe
10   el camino derecho.
Sólo un gran laberinto
de encrucijadas múltiples.

Constantemente crean
nuestros pies al andar
inmensos abanicos
de senderos en germen.

¡Oh jardín de las blancas
teorías! ¡Oh jardín
de lo que no soy pero
20   pude y debí haber sido!

What you wouldn't have suspected
lives & trembles in the air.

The garden joined together
by its putrefying perfumes.

Every leaf inside it dreaming
a different kind of dream.

Floating Bridges

Oh what a crush of people
invisible   reborn
make their way into this garden
for their eternal rest!

Every step we take on earth
brings us to a new world.
Every foot supported
on a floating bridge.

And I know that there is no
10   straight road in this world—
only a giant labyrinth
of intersecting crossroads.

And steadily our feet
keep walking & creating
—like enormous fans—
these roads in embryo.

Oh garden of white
theories! garden
of all I am not, all
20   I could & should have been!

Estampas del jardín

[1]

Las antiguas doncellas
que no fueron amadas
vienen con sus galanes
entre las quietas ramas.

Los galanes sin ojos
y ellas sin palabras
se adornan con sonrisas
como plumas rizadas.

Desfilan bajo grises
10 tulipanes de escarcha
en un blanco delirio
de luces enclaustradas.

La ciega muchedumbre
de los perfumes vaga
con los pies apoyados
sobre flores intactas.

¡Oh luz honda y oblicua
de las yertas naranjas!
Los galanes tropiezan
20 con sus rotas espadas.

II

La viuda de la luna
¿quién la olvidará?
Soñaba que la tierra
fuese de cristal.

Enfurecida y pálida,
quería dormir al mar,
peinando sus melenas
con gritos de coral.

Engravings of the Garden

[I]

Those antique virgins
still unloved,
walk with their loverboys
through silent leaves.

The boys, how eyeless
& how wordless they,
who cover themselves with smiles
like curlicues of feathers.

Strutting beneath the gray
10 & frosty tulips—
a white delirium
of cloistered lights.

Blind crowd—the perfumes
drifting past—
their feet propped up on
uncut flowers.

Oh deep & crooked light
from oranges gone numb!
And loverboys who stumble
20 over their broken swords.

I I

Widow of the moon—
who could forget her?
Dreaming that the earth
be crystal,

she, furious & pale,
would rock the sea to sleep,
comb out her tresses
with coral, like a cry.

Sus cabellos de vidrio
10 ¿quién los olvidará?
En su pecho los cien
labios de un manantial.

Alabardas de largos
surtidores la van
guardando por las ondas
quietas del arenal.

Pero la luna luna
¿cuándo volverá?
La cortina del viento
20 tiembla sin cesar.

La viuda de la luna
¿quién la olvidará?
Soñaba que la tierra
fuese de cristal.

Como el buen conde Arnaldo
¿quién te olvidará?
También soñaba toda
la tierra de cristal.

Tierra

Las niñas de la brisa
van con sus largas colas.

Cielo

Los mancebos del aire
saltan sobre la luna.

Hairs spun of glass—
who could forget them?
At her breast a hundred
lips, a single fountain.

Halberds from giant
jets spurt up,
keep guard of her by silent
waves, by dunes.

But moon, the moon,
when will the moon come back?
A curtain made of wind
that trembles on and on.

Widow of the moon—
who could forget her?
Dreaming that the earth
be crystal.

Like thee, good count Arnaldo,
who would forget thee too?
Thee, dreaming a whole earth
in crystal.

Earth

The girls of the breeze
go with long trains.

Sky

The boys of the air
jump over the moon.

Glorieta

Sobre el surtidor inmóvil
duerme un gran pájaro muerto.

Los dos amantes se besan
entre fríos cristales de sueño.

«La sortija, ¡dame la sortija!»
«No sé dónde están mis dedos».

«¿No me abrazas?» «Me dejé los brazos
cruzados y fríos en el lecho».

Bajo las hojas se arrastraba
10 un rayo de luna ciego.

Cancioncilla del niño que no nació

¡Me habéis dejado sobre una flor
de oscuros sollozos de agua!

El llanto que aprendí
se pondrá viejecito
arrastrando su cola
de suspiros y lágrimas.

Sin brazos, ¿cómo empujo
la puerta de la Luz?
Sirvieron a otro niño
10 de remos en su barca.

Pergola

A static jet of water,
over which
a large dead bird's
asleep.

Two lovers kissing
in among
Dream's icy
crystals.

"The ring, hand me the ring."
10   "I can't see where my fingers are."

"Why don't you hold me?"

          "No, my arms
are bent & freezing
on the bed."

And under the leaves,
a blind beam of moonlight
snaking along.

Little Song of the Unborn Child

On a flower of dark sobs
& waters you left me.

The lament that I learned
will be a shriveled old man
dragging sighs & tears
behind it like a tail.

If I have no arms,
how will I force daylight's door?
Those oars served another
10   child on his boat.

411   SUITES

Yo dormía tranquilo.
¿Quién taladró mi sueño?
Mi madre tiene ya
la cabellera blanca.

¡Me habéis dejado sobre una flor
de oscuros sollozos de agua!

El sátiro blanco

Sobre narcisos inmortales
dormía el sátiro blanco.

Enormes cuernos de cristal
virginizaban su ancha frente.

El sol como un dragón vencido
lamía sus largas manos de doncella.

Flotando sobre el río del amor
todas las ninfas muertas desfilaban.

El corazón del sátiro en el viento
10 se oreaba de viejas tempestades.

La siringa en el suelo era una fuente
con siete azules caños cristalinos.

Canción del muchacho de siete corazones

Siete corazones
tengo.
Pero el mío no lo encuentro.

En el alto monte, madre,
tropezábamos yo y el viento.

I was sleeping in peace.
Who ripped into my dream?
My mother has long had
a head of white hair.

On a flower of dark sobs
& waters you left me.

White Satyr

Atop deathless narcissuses
the white satyr slept.

Huge horns made of crystal
virginized his deep brows.

The sun, a tamed dragon,
licked his ladylike hands.

On the river of love
dead nymphs drifted by.

The satyr's heart in the wind
10 dried out from old storms.

The flute on the ground
was a fountain,
it had seven blue tubes
cut in glass.

Song of the Seven-Hearted Boy

Seven hearts
are the hearts that I have.
But mine is not there among them.

In the high mountains, mother,
where I sometimes ran into the wind,

Siete niñas de largas manos
me llevaron en sus espejos.

He cantado por el mundo
con mi boca de siete pétalos.
10 Mis galeras de amaranto
iban sin jarcias y sin remos.

He vivido los paisajes
de otras gentes. Mis secretos
alrededor de la garganta
¡sin darme cuenta! iban abiertos.

En el alto monte, madre,
(mi corazón sobre los ecos
dentro del álbum de una estrella)
tropezábamos yo y el viento.

20 Siete corazones
tengo.
Pero el mío no lo encuentro.

Olor blanco

¡Oh qué frío perfume
de jacintos!

Por los cipreses blancos
viene una doncella.
Trae sus senos cortados
[en] un plato de oro.

(Dos caminos.
Su larguísima cola
y la Vía Láctea.)

10 Madre
de los niños muertos
tiembla con el delirio
de los gusanos de luz.

seven girls with long hands
carried me around in their mirrors.

I have sung my way through this world
with my mouth with its seven petals.
10   My crimson-colored galleys
have cast off without rigging or oars.

I have lived my life in landscapes
that other men have owned.
And the secrets I wore at my throat,
unbeknownst to me, had come open.

In the high mountains, mother,
where my heart rises over its echoes
in the memory book of a star,
I sometimes ran into the wind.

20   Seven hearts
are the hearts that I have.
But mine is not there among them.

White Smell

Oh what cold perfumes
what hyacinths!

What maiden who comes
through white cypresses.
Carries her two severed breasts
on a platter of gold.

(Two highways.
Her very long train
& the milky way.)

10   Mother of stillborns
who shudders
with the frenzy of light-worms.

¡Oh qué frío perfume
de jacintos!

Encuentro

Flor de sol.
Flor de río.

Yo
¿Eras tú? Tienes el pecho
iluminado y no te he visto.

Ella
¡Cuántas veces te han rozado
las cintas de mi vestido!

Yo
Sin abrir, oigo en tu garganta
las blancas voces de mis hijos.

Ella
Tus hijos flotan en mis ojos
como diamantes amarillos.

Yo
¿Eras tú? ¿Por dónde arrastrabas
esas trenzas sin fin, amor mío?

Ella
En la luna. ¿Te ríes? Entonces,
alrededor de la flor del narciso.

Yo
En mi pecho se agita sonámbula
una sierpe de besos antiguos.

Ella
Los instantes abiertos clavaban
sus raíces sobre mis suspiros.

Oh what cold perfumes
what hyacinths!

Encounter

Sun flower.
River flower.

I
Was it you? Your breast so blazing
with light I lost sight of you.

She
And my dress with its ribbons—
how many times did it brush you?

I
In your throat I can hear, unopened,
my children's white voices.

She
Your children afloat in my eyes
10 are yellow like diamonds.

I
Was it you? Where were you dragging
your unending tresses, my love?

She
On the moon—are you laughing?
then circling Narcissus' flower.

I
In my breast a snake that won't sleep
but quakes with old kisses.

She
The moments fell open & fastened
their roots on my sighs.

Yo

Enlazados por la misma brisa

20 frente a frente ¡no nos conocimos!

Ella

El ramaje se espesa, vete pronto.

¡Ninguno de los dos hemos nacido!

Flor de sol.

Flor de río.

Arco de lunas

Un arco de lunas negras

sobre el mar sin movimiento.

Mis hijos que no han nacido

me persiguen.

«¡Padre, no corras, espera!

El más chico viene muerto».

Se cuelgan de mis pupilas.

Canta el gallo.

El mar hecho piedra ríe

10 su última risa de olas.

«¡Padre, no corras!»

Mis gritos

se hacen nardos.

I
Joined by one breeze
20 face to face, we were strangers!

She
The branches are burgeoning,
                    go from me!
Neither of us has been born.

    Sun flower.
    River flower.

Moonbow

A bow of black moons
over the motionless sea.

My unborn children
track me down.

"Father, don't run from us, wait,
the youngest of us is dying."

They hang themselves from my eyes.
The cock starts to crow.

The sea, turned to stone, is laughing
10 a last laugh made of waves.

"Father, don't run from us!" . . .
                    And my screams
turning to spikenards.

Duna

Sobre la extensa duna
de la luz antiquísima
me encuentro despistado
sin cielo ni camino.

El Norte moribundo
apagó sus estrellas.
Los cielos naufragados
se ondulaban sin prisa.

Por el mar de la luz
10 ¿dónde voy? ¿A quién busco?
Aquí gime el reflejo
de las lunas veladas.

¡Ay, mi fresco pedazo
de madera compacta,
vuélveme a mi balcón
y a mis pájaros vivos!

El jardín seguirá
moviendo sus arriates
sobre la ruda espalda
20 del silencio encallado.

¡Amanecer y repique!

El sol con sus cien cuernos
levanta el cielo bajo.

El mismo gesto repiten
los toros en la llanura.

La pedrea estremecida
de los viejos campanarios

Dune

Atop that vast dune
—most ancient light—
I find myself lost
with no sky, no road.

The North near to death
had switched off its stars.
The skies were shipwrecked,
slowly rising & falling.

Through a sea made of light
10 I go where? I seek whom?
A reflection that cries here
—of moons hidden by veils.

May the cool piece of tight-grained
wood in my hand
take me back to my balcony—
my still living birds.

Then the garden will follow,
will be moving its borders
on the coarse-grained shoulders
20 of a silence run aground.

Wake Up / Ring Out

Sun with his hundred horns
lifts the downed sky.

Same motion repeated by
the bulls on the prairie.

Spectacular rain of stones
around the old bell towers

despierta y pone en camino
al gran rebaño del viento.

En el río ahora comienzan
10 las batallas de los peces.

Alma mía, niño y niña,
¡¡silencio!!

arouses the wind, drives
its vast herd down the road.

In the river the wars
10 of the fish are beginning.

My soul, boy & girl,
be silent, *silent!*

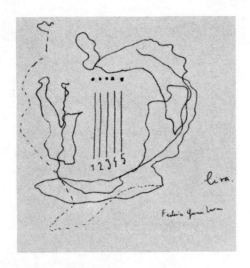

APÉNDICE:
SUITES

[Lira, 1927]

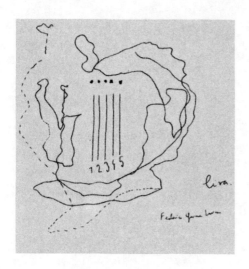

APPENDIX

TO SUITES

Translated by

Jerome Rothenberg

[Lyre, 1927]

Viaje

La boca del ocaso
muerde el yeso del monte.
Una estrella niña
se ha escapado
por el azul.

Melancolía vieja

El paisaje tiene
telarañas de siglos.
Archivo de crepúsculos
y de noches.

Salutación

Desde la sombra mía
entre mis lirios, lleno
de esta melancolía
de hombre bueno
que ha visto desangrar un amor naciente
(blanco cisne sin alas) lentamente
y que quiere cortar la desolada
rosa espectral que finge la alborada,
echo al vuelo mi lírica campana
10 esta hermosa mañana
de viento
soñoliento . . .

Mi tristeza incurable
se carmina y aprende
vuestro amor admirable.
Esta tristeza invade
mi corazón dormido

Train Ride

Sundown's mouth bites
mountain's chalk.
A girl star
's run away in
her blue sky.

Old Melancholy

Landscape's got
a century of cobwebs.
Storage bin for sunsets
& for nights.

A Salutation

From my shadow
among lilies, filled up
with the melancholy
of the good man
who saw the bleeding of
a newborn love (white,
wingless swan) by inches
& who wants to clip the lonely
spectral rose the dawn
10 pretends to be,
I set my lyric bell to ringing
on this lovely morning
with its dreamy
wind . . .

How terminal my sadness,
daubs itself with rouge & learns
your wondrous love.
This sadness that invades

    APPENDIX TO SUITES

que vive por casualidad
gris y gris

20 Carbonilla en los ojos,
y las uñas de Satán
escarbándome el pecho.
Satán,
mi amigo de la infancia.
El topo del tren
roe las raíces del viento
y avanza.

Lejanía de campanas.
Arados yacentes.
30 Besanas líricas.

Cabecea la tarde
y ha cesado
el dominó de los colores

Una guitarra dice
"Mi madera es ciprés".
Soñolencia en do sostenido para fagot y cuerdas.
Vaivenes.
Y en los paso [a] nivel
cortes de mangas.

Después
(Sobre el prado indeciso)

He llegado a la puerta
del *Luego*.
¡Dadme la guitarra!
Todo el mundo está blanco.
¡Dadme la guitarra!
Me iré a contar los pinos
de aquella montaña
o las arenas
de la mar salada.
10 He dejado en el viento

my sleepy heart
20   alive by chance
gray   gray

Coaldust in my eyes
& Satan's fingernails
scratching my breast.
Satan,
my old boyhood friend.
The train, a mole,
gnaws at the wind's roots
& goes on.

30   Distances of bells.
Plows dormant.
Lyric furrows.

Evening nodding out
the domino of colors
faded

A guitar that says
"My wood is cypress."
Somnolence in G sharp for bassoon & strings.
Vibrations.
40   And at the railroad crossings
an arm gives you the shaft.

Afterwards
(On the undecidable prairie)

I've pulled up to the doorway
of *Then.*
Hand me down my guitar!
The whole world is white.
Hand me down my guitar!
I'm off to count pines
on that mountain,
sands
in the saltsavored sea.

procesiones de lágrimas
y voy a divertirme
por las playas del alma.

(Llevo gafas de oro
y un frac color naranja)

Las tres

¡Ya se está levantando
el aire del Poniente!

La tierra está cubierta
por un mar amarillo.
Hay un hombre de oro
bañándose en el río
y ha naufragado el sol
en azul derretido.

—Ya se está levantando
10 el aire del Poniente.—

Desde aquí

Decid a mis amigos
que he muerto.

El agua canta siempre
bajo el temblor del bosque.

Decid a mis amigos
que he muerto.
(¡Cómo ondulan los chopos
la gasa del sonido!)

Decid que me he quedado
10 con los ojos abiertos

10   Left the vale of tears
back in the wind
gone to have a sweet time
find a beach for my soul.

(I've got goldrimmed glasses
& an orangecolored tux)

3:00 p.m.

The air from the west
will already be stirring.

A yellow sea's
covering earth.
And a man made of gold's
bathing down by the river,
while sun's come to ruin
in the molten blue sky.

—The air from the west
10   will already be stirring.—

From Out Here

Tell my friends
that I'm dead.

The water sings endlessly
down where the forest is rumbling.

Tell my friends
that I'm dead.
(The poplars are waving
gauzes of sound!)

Tell them I'm out here
10   with my eyes wide open,

y que cubría mi cara
el inmortal pañuelo
del azul.

¡Ay!

y que me fui sin pan
a mi lucero.

Tarde

Ha llegado la hora
de ser sinceros
la hora de los llantos
sin consuelo
la última hora antes
del gran silencio.
Quitarse los vestidos
la carne los huesos
y arrojad de vosotros
10   el corazón enfermo.
¡Llanto y Salud amigos!
Esperad a los vientos
cargados de semillas
y paisajes inéditos.
Floreced, y arrancaos
la floración de nuevo,
vestidos inefables
corazón carne y huesos.
Llanto y Salud amigos
20   Frente al mar de los vientos
para ser vivos siempre
ser murientes eternos.

my face covered up
by this deathless bandana,
the sky.

     Ah!

Gone off without bread
to my own shining star.

Evening

It's now the hour
for being sincere
the hour for groans
without letup
the last hour before
the big silence.
Step out of your clothes
flesh & bones
puke up
10 your sick hearts.
With groans & greetings amigos!
Watch out for those winds
stuffed with seeds
& unpublished landscapes
Blossom, & tear out
your blossoms anew
unspeakably dressed
heart   flesh   bones.
With groans & greetings amigos!
20 In front of the sea of the wind
be always alive, be
eternally dying.

Diurno

Ciudad

[A] *Guillermo de Torre*

La torre dice: «hasta aquí»
y el ciprés: «yo más allá».

Hombres y mujeres hacen
la Babel de las palabras.

Avanzan por los tejados
violentos zig-zag y elipses.

La ciudad adorna su frente
con plumas de humo y silbidos.

Todos buscan lo que no
10 podrán encontrar jamás

y la hierba crece ante
el pórtico del Allí.

II

Reacción

¡Corazón mío, vete
con las sabias tortugas,
corazón mío, por
un Sahara de luz!

De pontifical
con sus capas pluviales
las tortugas enseñan
lo inútil de los pies.

Saben las falsedades
10 de horizontes celestes

Day Poems

The City
[To] Guillermo de Torre

The tower says: "up to here"
& the cypress: "me up to there."

Men & women are making
a babel out of words.

Raging across the rooftops
frantic zigzags, ellipses.

The city covers its forehead
with smoky feathers & screams.

(They all look for what
10   they can't find.)

And the grass grows in front of
the portico of Up There.

I I

The Reaction

My heart go away
with your know-it-all turtles

my heart go & find
a Sahara of light!

y dedican su vida
a estudiar una estrella
con la que
impregnan el carey.

Corazón mío, vete
con las sabias tortugas.
Hélice para el cuerpo
y alas para el espíritu
no te harán falta cuando
20 sientas andar la tierra.

Corazón mío, apaga
tu vieja sed de límite.

De *Narciso*

Puerta

Arco de rosas.
Arco de pájaros.
Repique de luna.

Yo

Yo
Gallito de oro,
dime tu secreto

Decked out like the pope
10 with their pluvial capes
turtles can teach us
the uselessness of feet.

They can cut through the flimflam
of celestial horizons
& dedicate their lives
to studying a star
a star with which
to impregnate their shells.

My heart go away
20 with your know-it-all turtles

A spiral for your body
& wings for your soul
you aren't going to need them
when you feel the ground shake!

My heart put to rest
your old hunger for limits.

From *Narcissus*

Door

Arch of roses.
Arch of birds.
Moonbeams clanging.

I

I
Little gold rooster,
tell me your secret.

Gallo
Levanta con tu grito
la losa de la noche.

Yo
¿Qué quieres de mí
que no me dejas, Sueño?

Sueño
Doce cisnes de oro
y doce lunas negras.

Yo
Quiero días y noches
10 claros y sin secretos.

Sueño
[. . . . .]

Rooster
Let your shout lift
the tombstone of night.

I
What do you want from me, Dream,
that you won't let me be?

Dream
A dozen gold swans
& a dozen black moons.

I
I want clear days & nights,
10 & no secrets.

Dream
[. . . . .]

CANCIONES

1921–1924

A Pedro Salinas, Jorge Guillén
y Melchorito Fernández Almagro

[*Leyenda japonesa, 1926*]

SONGS

1921–1924

*To Pedro Salinas, Jorge Guillén,
and Melchorito Fernández Almagro*

Translated by Alan S. Trueblood

[*Japanese Legend, 1926*]

Teorías

Canción de las siete doncellas

(Teoría del arco iris)

Cantan las siete
doncellas.

(Sobre el cielo un arco
de ejemplos de ocaso.)

Alma con siete voces,
las siete doncellas.

(En el aire blanco,
siete largos pájaros.)

Mueren las siete
doncellas.

(¿Por qué no han sido nueve?
¿Por qué no han sido veinte?)

El río las trae.
Nadie puede verlas.

Nocturno esquemático

Hinojo, serpiente y junco.
Aroma, rastro y penumbra.
Aire, tierra y soledad.

(La escala llega a la luna.)

Theories

Song of the Seven Maidens
(Theory of the Rainbow)

Singing,
the seven maidens.

(Across the sky in a bow,
a choice of sunsets.)

One soul with seven voices,
the seven maidens.

(In the white air
seven long birds.)

Dying, the seven
10 maidens.

(Why weren't there nine?
Why weren't there twenty?)

The river brings them.
No one can see them.

Nocturne in Outline

Fennel, serpent, and rushes.
Aroma, trail, and half-shadow.
Air, earth, and apartness.

(The ladder stretches to the moon.)

La canción del colegial

Sábado.
(Puerta de jardín.)

Domingo.
(Día gris.
Gris.)

Sábado.
(Arcos azules.
Brisa.)

Domingo.
10 (Mar con orillas.
Metas.)

Sábado.
(Semilla,
estremecida.)

Domingo.
(Nuestro amor se pone
amarillo.)

•

El canto quiere ser luz.
En lo oscuro el canto tiene,
hilos de fósforo y luna.
La luz no sabe qué quiere.
En sus límites de ópalo,
se encuentra ella misma,
y vuelve.

Schoolboy's Song

Saturday.
(Garden gate.)

Sunday.
(Gray day.
Gray.)

Saturday.
(Blue archway.
Breeze.)

Sunday.
10 (Sea and seashore.
Goals.)

Saturday.
(Seed
quivering.)

Sunday.
(Our love turns
yellow.)

•

Song would like to be light.
Song in the dark shows
filaments of phosphorus and moon.
Light doesn't know what it wants.
At its opaline edge
it meets up with itself
and returns.

445

Tiovivo

A José Bergamín

Los días de fiesta
van sobre ruedas.
El tiovivo los trae
y los lleva.

Corpus azul.
Blanca Nochebuena.

Los días, abandonan
su piel, como las culebras,
con la sola excepción
10   de los días de fiesta.

Estos son los mismos
de nuestras madres viejas.
Sus tardes son largas colas
de moaré y lentejuelas.

Corpus azul.
Blanca Nochebuena.

El tiovivo gira
colgado de una estrella.
Tulipán de las cinco
20   partes de la tierra.

Sobre caballitos
disfrazados de panteras
los niños se comen la luna
como si fuera una cereza.

¡Rabia, rabia, Marco Polo!
Sobre una fantástica rueda,
los niños ven lontananzas
desconocidas de la tierra.

Corpus azul.
30   Blanca Nochebuena.

Merry-go-round

For José Bergamín

Holidays
travel on wheels.
The merry-go-round brings them
and takes them away.

Blue Corpus Christi.
White Christmas Eve.

Days shed their skins
just like snakes,
with the single exception
10 of holidays.

These haven't changed
since our old mothers' time.
Their afternoons are long trains
of moiré and sequins.

Blue Corpus Christi.
White Christmas Eve.

The merry-go-round turns,
suspended from a star.
Tulip of the five
20 corners of the earth.

On wooden horses
disguised as panthers
children gobble the moon
as they would a cherry.

Now hear *this*, Marco Polo:
From their fabulous wheel
children see far-off places
nowhere in this world.

Blue Corpus Christi.
30 White Christmas Eve.

Balanza

La noche quieta siempre.
El día va y viene.

La noche muerta y alta.
El día con un ala.

La noche sobre espejos
y el día bajo el viento.

Canción con movimiento

Ayer.

(Estrellas
azules.)

Mañana.

(Estrellitas
blancas.)

Hoy.

(Sueño: flor adormecida
en el valle de la enagua.)

10   Ayer.

(Estrellas
de fuego.)

Mañana.

(Estrellas
moradas.)

Hoy.

Balance

Night always still.
Day comes and goes.

Night dead and lofty.
Day wingèd.

Night over mirrors
and day beneath the wind.

Song with Movement

Yesterday.

(Stars
blue.)

Tomorrow.

(Stars
white and tiny.)

Today.

(My dream: flower asleep
in the petticoat's valley.)

10   Yesterday.

(Stars
afire.)

Tomorrow.

(Stars
lavender.)

Today.

(Este corazón, ¡Dios mío!
¡Este corazón que salta!)

Ayer.

20   (Memoria
de estrellas.)

Mañana.

(Estrellas
cerradas.)

Hoy . . .

(¡Mañana!)

¿Me marearé quizá
sobre la barca?

¡Oh los puentes del Hoy
en el camino de agua!

Refrán

Marzo
pasa volando.

Y enero sigue tan alto.

Enero,
sigue en la noche del cielo.

Y abajo Marzo es un momento.

Enero.
Para mis ojos viejos.

(This heart, heavens!
This heart's pounding!)

Yesterday.

20 (Remembering
stars.)

Tomorrow.

(Stars
closed up.)

Today.

(Tomorrow!)

Might I be sick
in the boat?

Oh, Today and its bridges
30 on the highroad of water!

Proverb

March
goes flying by.

And January stays aloft.

January
stays on in the night of the sky.

And March is one moment below.

January.
For my old eyes.

Marzo.
10 Para mis frescas manos.

Friso

A Gustavo Durán

TIERRA
    Las niñas de la brisa
van con sus largas colas.

CIELO
    Los mancebos del aire
saltan sobre la luna.

Cazador

    ¡Alto pinar!
Cuatro palomas por el aire van.

    Cuatro palomas
vuelan y tornan.
Llevan heridas
sus cuatro sombras.

    ¡Bajo pinar!
Cuatro palomas en la tierra están.

Fábula

    Unicornios y cíclopes.

    Cuernos de oro
y ojos verdes.

    Sobre el acantilado,
en tropel gigantesco
ilustran el azogue
sin cristal, del mar.

    Unicornios y cíclopes.

March.
10   For my fresh hands.

Frieze

To Gustavo Durán

EARTH
    The girls of the breeze
pass in their trailing gowns.

SKY
    The youths of the air
jump over the moon.

Hunter

    Tall pine grove!
Four doves ply the air.

    Four doves
fly off and return.
There are wounds
in their four shadows.

    Low pine grove!
Four doves are on the ground.

Fable

    Unicorns and cyclops.

    Gold horns
and green eyes.

    On the headland
in a gigantic throng
they luster the glassless
quicksilver of the sea.

    Unicorns and cyclops.

Una pupila
10 y una potencia.

¿Quién duda la eficacia
terrible de esos cuernos?

¡Oculta tus blancos,
Naturaleza!

•

Agosto,
contraponientes
de melocotón y azúcar,
y el sol dentro de la tarde,
como el hueso en una fruta.

La panocha guarda intacta,
su risa amarilla y dura.

Agosto.
Los niños comen
10 pan moreno y rica luna.

Arlequín

Teta roja del sol.
Teta azul de la luna.

Torso mitad coral,
mitad plata y penumbra.

Cortaron tres árboles
A Ernesto Halffter

Eran tres.

(Vino el día con sus hachas.)

One eye
10   and one potency.

Who can question the awful
efficacy of those horns?

Conceal your bull's eyes,
Nature!

●

August.
Facing the sunset
peaches and sugar,
and the sun inside the evening
like the stone in a fruit.

The ear of corn holds intact
its hard yellow laughter.

August.
Children eat
10   dark bread and tasty moon.

Harlequin

Red teat of the sun.
Blue teat of the moon.

Torso half coral,
half silver and penumbra.

Three Trees Were Cut Down
To Ernesto Halffter

There were three.

(Day came with its axes.)

Eran dos.

(Alas rastreras de plata.)

Era uno.

Era ninguno.

(Se quedó desnuda el agua.)

Nocturnos de la ventana

A la memoria de José de Ciria y Escalante. Poeta

1

Alta va la luna.
Bajo corre el viento.

(Mis largas miradas,
exploran el cielo.)

Luna sobre el agua.
Luna bajo el viento.

(Mis cortas miradas
exploran el suelo.)

Las voces de dos niñas
10   venían. Sin esfuerzo,
de la luna del agua,
me fui a la del cielo.

2

Un brazo de la noche
entra por mi ventana.

There were two.

(Silver wings dragging.)

There was one.

There were none.

(The water stripped bare.)

Nocturnes from the Window

To the memory of José de Ciria y Escalante. Poet

1

High rides the moon.
The wind rushes low.

(Long glances of mine
explore the sky.)

Moon on the water.
Moon beneath the wind.

(Short glances of mine
explore the earth.)

The voices of two little girls
10 drew near. Without trying,
from the water's moon
I moved up to the sky's.

2

An arm of the night
comes in through my window.

Un gran brazo moreno
con pulseras de agua.

Sobre un cristal azul
jugaba al río mi alma.

Los instantes heridos
por el reloj . . . pasaban.

3

Asomo la cabeza
por mi ventana, y veo
cómo quiere cortarla
la cuchilla del viento.

En esta guillotina
invisible, yo he puesto
las cabezas sin ojos
de todos mis deseos.

Y un olor de limón
10 llenó el instante inmenso,
mientras se convertía
en flor de gasa el viento.

4

Al estanque se le ha muerto
hoy una niña de agua.
Está fuera del estanque,
sobre el suelo amortajada.

De la cabeza a sus muslos
un pez la cruza, llamándola.
El viento le dice «Niña»,
mas no puede despertarla.

El estanque tiene suelta
10 su cabellera de algas
y al aire sus grises tetas
estremecidas de ranas.

A great dusky arm
with bracelets of water.

On blue crystal
my soul was playing river.

The instants stricken
by the clock . . . kept passing.

3

Leaning out my window,
I see how eager
to slice off my head
the wind's cleaver is.

In this guillotine
none can see, I have placed
the eyeless heads
of all my desires.

And a breath of lemon
10 filled the vast moment
as the wind became
a flower of gauze.

4

Today the pond has lost
a water girl to death.
She is outside the pond
in a shroud on the grass.

From her head to her thighs
a fish crosses and calls her.
The wind calls out "Child"
but cannot wake her.

The pond has unwound
10 the long algae of its hair,
expressing gray teats
quivering with frogs.

«Dios te salve» rezaremos
a Nuestra Señora de Agua
por la niña del estanque
muerta bajo las manzanas.

Yo luego pondré a su lado
dos pequeñas calabazas
para que se tenga a flote,
20   ¡ay! sobre la mar salada.

Residencia de Estudiantes. 1923

Canciones para niños

A la maravillosa niña Colomba Morla Vicuña,
dormida piadosamente el día 12 de agosto de 1928

Canción china en Europa
A mi ahijada Isabel Clara

La señorita
del abanico,
va por el puente
del fresco río.

Los caballeros
con sus levitas,
miran el puente
sin barandillas.

La señorita
10   del abanico
y los volantes,
busca marido.

Los caballeros
están casados,
con altas rubias
de idioma blanco.

God preserve you. We will pray
to Our Lady of Water
for the maiden of the pond
beneath the apple boughs, dead.

Then I'll place at her side
two small calabash gourds
to keep her afloat—
20 alas, on salt seas.

Residencia de Estudiantes, 1923

Songs for Children
To the wonderful little girl Colomba Morla Vicuña,
who rested in the Lord August 12, 1928

Song of China in Europe
To my godchild Isabel Clara

The young lady
with the fan
is taking the bridge
across the river.

The gentlemen
in frock coats
are looking at the bridge
with no railings.

The young lady
10 with the fan
and the flounces
seeks a husband.

The gentlemen
are married
to tall blondes
of white speech.

Los grillos cantan
por el Oeste.

(La señorita,
20 va por lo verde.)

Los grillos cantan
bajo las flores.

(Los caballeros,
van por el Norte.)

Cancioncilla sevillana

A Solita Salinas

Amanecía
en el naranjel.
Abejitas de oro
buscaban la miel.

¿Dónde estará
la miel?

Está en la flor azul,
Isabel.
En la flor,
10 del romero aquel.

(Sillita de oro
para el moro.
Silla de oropel
para su mujer.)

Amanecía,
en el naranjel.

Westward
crickets chirp.

(The young lady
20 walks the green.)

Crickets chirp
under flowers.

(Northward
the gentlemen go.)

Sevillian Ditty

To Solita Salinas

Daybreak
in the orange grove.
Little gold bees
were out after honey.

And where can
the honey be?

It's in the blue blossom,
Isabel.
In the bloom
10 of that rosemary plant.

(A little gold seat
for the Moor.
A seat that glitters
for his wife.)

Daybreak
in the orange grove.

Caracola

A Natalita Jiménez

Me han traído una caracola.

Dentro le canta
un mar de mapa.
Mi corazón
se llena de agua
con pececillos
de sombra y plata.

Me han traído una caracola.

•

*A Mademoiselle Teresita Guillén
tocando su piano de seis notas*

El lagarto está llorando.
La lagarta está llorando.

El lagarto y la lagarta
con delantalitos blancos.

Han perdido sin querer
su anillo de desposados.

¡Ay, su anillito de plomo,
ay, su anillito plomado!

Un cielo grande y sin gente
10 monta en su globo a los pájaros.

El sol, capitán redondo,
lleva un chaleco de raso.

¡Miradlos qué viejos son!
¡Qué viejos son los lagartos!

Seashell

To Natalita Jiménez

Someone brought me a seashell.

Singing inside
is a sea from a map.
My heart
fills up with water
and little tiny fish,
silvery, shadowy.

Someone brought me a seashell.

•

To Mlle. Teresita Guillén
playing her six-note piano

Mr. Lizard is crying.
Mrs. Lizard is crying.

Mr. and Mrs. Lizard
in little white aprons.

They've gone and lost
their wedding ring.

Oh, their little lead ring!
Their little leaden ring, oh!

A big peopleless sky
10 lifts the birds in its balloon.

The sun, a roly-poly captain,
wears a satin vest.

How old they are, just look!
How old the lizards are!

¡Ay cómo lloran y lloran,
¡ay!, ¡ay!, cómo están llorando!

Canción cantada

En el gris,
el pájaro Grifón
se vestía de gris.
Y la niña Kikirikí
perdía su blancor
y forma allí.

Para entrar en el gris
me pinté de gris.
¡Y cómo relumbraba
10   en el gris!

Paisaje

A Rita, Concha, Pepe y Carmencica

La tarde equivocada
se vistió de frío.

Detrás de los cristales
turbios, todos los niños,
ven convertirse en pájaros
un árbol amarillo.

La tarde está tendida
a lo largo del río.
Y un rubor de manzana
10   tiembla en los tejadillos.

Canción tonta

Mamá.
Yo quiero ser de plata.

Oh, how they do weep,
and, oh, how they are weeping!

Song Sung

In the gray
the griffon bird
was wearing gray.
And the Cock-a-doodle girl
was losing her whiteness
and her shape.

To enter the gray
I painted myself gray.
And how I glistened
10 in the gray!

Landscape

To Rita, Concha, Pepe, and Carmencica

By mistake the evening
had dressed in cold.

Through the mist on the panes
all the children
watch a yellow tree
change into birds.

Evening is stretched out
all down the river.
And the flush of an apple
10 shivers over tile roofs.

Silly Song

Mommy.
I want to be all silver.

Hijo,
tendrás mucho frío.

Mamá.
Yo quiero ser de agua.

Hijo,
tendrás mucho frío.

Mamá.
10 Bórdame en tu almohada.

¡Eso sí!
¡Ahora mismo!

Andaluzas

A Miguel Pizarro
(en la irregularidad simétrica del Japón)

Canción de jinete (1860)

En la luna negra
de los bandoleros,
cantan las espuelas.

Caballito negro.
¿Dónde llevas tu jinete muerto?

. . . Las duras espuelas
del bandido inmóvil
que perdió las riendas.

Caballito frío.
10 ¡Qué perfume de flor de cuchillo!

En la luna negra,
sangraba el costado
de Sierra Morena.

Caballito negro.
¿Dónde llevas tu jinete muerto?

    Son,
you'll be awfully cold.

    Mommy.
I want to be all water.

    Son,
you'll be awfully cold.

    Mommy.
10 Sew me onto your cushion.

    That I will!
This very moment!

Andalusian Songs

To Miguel Pizarro
(in the symmetrical irregularity of Japan)

Rider's Song (1860)

    In the dark of the moon,
the highwaymen's moon,
spurs sing out.

    Dark little horse.
Whither away with your dead rider?

    . . . The harsh spurs
of the motionless highwayman
who lost hold of the reins.

    Cold little horse.
10 What a fragrance of knife in bloom!

    In the dark of the moon
blood flowed from the flank
of Sierra Morena.

    Dark little horse.
Whither away with your dead rider?

La noche espolea
sus negros ijares
clavándose estrellas.

Caballito frío.
20 ¡Qué perfume de flor de cuchillo!

En la luna negra,
¡un grito! y el cuerno
largo de la hoguera.

Caballito negro.
¿Dónde llevas tu jinete muerto?

Adelina de paseo

La mar no tiene naranjas,
ni Sevilla tiene amor.
Morena, qué luz de fuego.
Préstame tu quitasol.

Me pondrá la cara verde
zumo de lima y limón.
Tus palabras—pececillos—
nadarán alrededor.

La mar no tiene naranjas.
10 Ay amor.
¡Ni Sevilla tiene amor!

•

Zarzamora con el tronco gris,
dame un racimo para mí.

Sangre y espinas. Acércate.
Si tú me quieres, yo te querré.

Night sinks spurs
in her dark flanks,
pinning down stars.

Cold little horse.
20 What a fragrance of knife in bloom!

In the dark of the moon
a cry! And the long horn
of the bonfire.

Dark little horse.
Whither away with your dead rider?

Adelina Out Walking

The sea has no oranges
nor Seville any love.
Dark girl, such fiery light!
Lend me your parasol.

Juice of lemon and lime
will turn my face green.
Your words—little fish—
will swim roundabout.

The sea has no oranges.
10 Oh the pity, love.
Nor Seville any love!

•

Bramble gray of stalk,
give me a cluster just for me.

Blood and thorns. Come closer.
If you love me, I'll love you too.

471

Deja tu fruto de verde y sombra
sobre mi lengua, zarzamora.

Qué largo abrazo te daría
en la penumbra de mis espinas.

Zarzamora, ¿dónde vas?
A buscar amores que tú no me das.

•

Mi niña se fue a la mar,
a contar olas y chinas,
pero se encontró, de pronto,
con el río de Sevilla.

Entre adelfas y campanas
cinco barcos se mecían,
con los remos en el agua
y las velas en la brisa.

¿Quién mira dentro la torre
enjaezada, de Sevilla?
Cinco voces contestaban
redondas como sortijas.

El cielo monta gallardo
al río, de orilla a orilla.
En el aire sonrosado,
cinco anillos se mecían.

Tarde

*(¿Estaba mi Lucía con
los pies en el arroyo?)*

Tres álamos inmensos
y una estrella.

Leave the green and dark of your fruit,
bramble, on my tongue.

What a long hug I'd give you
in the half-shade of my thorns.

Bramble, why are you leaving?
10 To look for the love you withhold.

•

My girl went down to the sea
to count waves and pebbles
and what should she encounter
but the river of Seville!

Amid rosebay and bells,
five boats were riding
with oars in the water
and sails to the wind.

Who's that looking into
10 Seville's filigreed tower?
Five voices replied
as round as any ring.

The sky bestrides the river
smartly, from bank to bank.
In the rose-colored air
five rings were riding.

Evening

*(Was my Lucy dangling
her feet in the stream?)*

Three looming poplars,
one star.

473

El silencio mordido
por las ranas, semeja
una gasa pintada
con lunaritos verdes.

En el río,
un árbol seco,
ha florecido en círculos
10 concéntricos.

Y he soñado sobre las aguas,
a la morenita de Granada.

Canción de jinete

Córdoba.
Lejana y sola.

Jaca negra, luna grande,
y aceitunas en mi alforja.
Aunque sepa los caminos
yo nunca llegaré a Córdoba.

Por el llano, por el viento,
jaca negra, luna roja.
La muerte me está mirando
10 desde las torres de Córdoba.

¡Ay, qué camino tan largo!
¡Ay, mi jaca valerosa!
¡Ay, que la muerte me espera,
antes de llegar a Córdoba!

Córdoba.
Lejana y sola.

The silence bitten
by frogs resembles
a gauze veil speckled
with little green dabs.

A stark tree
in the river
has broken out in concentric
10 circles of bloom.

And on the waters I dreamed
of a nut-brown Granada maiden.

Rider's Song

Córdoba.
Distant and lonely.

Black pony, large moon,
in my saddlebag, olives.
Well as I know the roads,
I shall never reach Córdoba.

Over the plain, through the wind,
black pony, red moon.
Death keeps a watch on me
10 from Córdoba's towers.

Oh, such a long way to go!
And, oh, my spirited pony!
Ah, but death awaits me
before I ever reach Córdoba.

Córdoba.
Distant and lonely.

¡Es verdad!

¡Ay, qué trabajo me cuesta
quererte como te quiero!

Por tu amor me duele el aire,
el corazón
y el sombrero.

¿Quién me compraría a mí,
este cintillo que tengo
y esta tristeza de hilo
blanco, para hacer pañuelos?

10   ¡Ay qué trabajo me cuesta
quererte como te quiero!

    •

Arbolé arbolé
seco y verdé.

La niña del bello rostro
está cogiendo aceituna.
El viento, galán de torres,
la prende por la cintura.

Pasaron cuatro jinetes,
sobre jacas andaluzas
con trajes de azul y verde,
10   con largas capas oscuras.

«Vente a Córdoba, muchacha.»
La niña no los escucha.

Pasaron tres torerillos
delgaditos de cintura,
con trajes color naranja
y espadas de plata antigua.

It's True

    Oh what a hard time I have
loving you as I love you.

    On account of your love
I have an air ache,
a heart ache, a hat ache.

    Someone please buy
this hatband of mine
and this fine-spun white sadness
perfect for kerchiefs!

10   Oh, what a hard time I have
loving you as I love you.

•

    Tree, lifeless tree,
tree live green.

    The girl fair of face
is picking olives.
The wind, the towers' beau,
clasps her by the waist.

    Four riders came by
on Andalusian ponies
in suits of blue and green
10   with long dark capes.

    "Come along to Córdoba, child."
The girl pays no heed.

    Three bullfighting youngsters
came by, slim of waist,
in bright orange suits
with swords of antique silver.

«Vente a Sevilla, muchacha.»
La niña no los escucha.

Cuando la tarde se puso
morada, con luz difusa,
pasó un joven que llevaba
rosas y mirtos de luna.

«Vente a Granada, muchacha».
Y la niña no lo escucha.

La niña del bello rostro
sigue cogiendo aceituna,
con el brazo gris del viento
ceñido por la cintura.

Arbolé arbolé
seco y verdé.

.

Galán,
galancillo.
En tu casa queman tomillo.

Ni que vayas, ni que vengas,
con llave cierro la puerta.

Con llave de plata fina.
Atada con una cinta.

En la cinta hay un letrero:
«Mi corazón está lejos».

No des vueltas en mi calle.
¡Déjasela toda al aire!

Galán,
galancillo.
En tu casa queman tomillo.

"Child, come along to Seville."
The girl pays no heed.

20   When evening turned mauve,
with far-scattered light,
a young man came by
with roses and moonbeam myrtle.

"Child, come along to Granada."
And the girl pays no heed.

The girl fair of face
goes on picking olives
with the wind's gray arm
clasping her by the waist.

Tree, lifeless tree,
30   tree live green.

•

Suitor,
suitor of mine.
At your house they're burning thyme.

Come or go as you please,
I'll stay under lock and key.

A key made of fine silver.
On a ribbon for good measure.

On the ribbon words are written:
"My heart is not smitten."

10   Don't roam my street day and night.
Only the wind has that right.

Suitor,
suitor of mine.
At your house they're burning thyme.

Tres retratos con sombra

Verlaine

La canción,
que nunca diré,
se ha dormido en mis labios.
La canción,
que nunca diré.

Sobre las madreselvas
había una luciérnaga,
y la luna picaba
con un rayo en el agua.

Entonces yo soñé,
la canción,
que nunca diré.

Canción llena de labios
y de cauces lejanos.

Canción llena de horas
perdidas en la sombra.

Canción de estrella viva
sobre un perpetuo día.

Baco

Verde rumor intacto.
La higuera me tiende sus brazos.

Como una pantera, su sombra,
acecha mi lírica sombra.

La luna cuenta los perros.
Se equivoca y empieza de nuevo.

Three Portraits with Shading

Verlaine

The song
I'll never speak,
on the tip of my tongue fell asleep.
The song
I'll never speak.

On the honeysuckle
a firefly blinked
and the moon was pricking
the water with a beam.

It was then I dreamed
the song
I'll never speak.

Song filled with lips,
flowing from far away.

Song filled with hours
whiled away in the shade.

Song of stars alive
in perpetual daytime skies.

Bacchus

Green sound intact.
The fig tree's arms open to me.

Its shadow, like a panther,
stalks my lyrical shadow.

The moon is counting dogs.
She slips and starts over.

Ayer, mañana, negro y verde,
rondas mi cerco de laureles.

¿Quién te querría como yo,
si me cambiaras el corazón?

. . . Y la higuera me grita y avanza
terrible y multiplicada.

Juan Ramón Jiménez

En el blanco infinito,
nieve, nardo y salina,
perdió su fantasía.

El color blanco, anda,
sobre una muda alfombra
de plumas de paloma.

Sin ojos ni ademán
inmóvil sufre un sueño.
Pero tiembla por dentro.

En el blanco infinito,
¡qué pura y larga herida
dejó su fantasía!

En el blanco infinito.
Nieve. Nardo. Salina.

Venus
Así te vi.

La joven muerta
en la concha de la cama,
desnuda de flor y brisa
surgía en la luz perenne.

Yesterday, tomorrow, black and green,
you haunt my laurel wreath.

No one would love you like me
10   if you'd only change my heart!

   . . . And the fig tree shouts and comes at me
in frightful proliferation.

Juan Ramón Jiménez

In the infinity of white,
snow, spikenard, and salt flat,
his fantasy went astray.

The color white moves
over a soundless carpet
of pigeon feathers.

Eyeless, no gesture, stock-still,
he is haunted by a dream.
But inwardly he quivers.

10   In the infinity of white
what a clean, long gash
his fantasy left!

In the infinity of white.
Snow. Spikenard. Salt flat.

Venus

I saw you thus.

The dead maiden
in the shell of the bed,
stripped of blossom and breeze,
ascended in unending light.

483

Quedaba el mundo,
lirio de algodón y sombra,
asomado a los cristales
viendo el tránsito infinito.

La joven muerta,
10   surcaba el amor por dentro.
Entre la espuma de las sábanas
se perdía su cabellera.

Debussy

Mi sombra va silenciosa
por el agua de la acequia.

Por mi sombra están las ranas
privadas de las estrellas.

La sombra manda a mi cuerpo
reflejos de cosas quietas.

Mi sombra va como inmenso
cínife color violeta.

Cien grillos quieren dorar
10   la luz de la cañavera.

Una luz nace en mi pecho,
reflejado, de la acequia.

Narciso

Niño.
¡Que te vas a caer al río!

En lo hondo hay una rosa
y en la rosa hay otro río.

The world was left behind,
a lily of cotton and shadow,
watching through the panes
the infinite passage.

The dead maiden
10 plied love from within.
In the foam of the sheets
her long hair disappeared.

Debussy

My shadow glides in silence
over the watercourse.

On account of my shadow
the frogs are deprived of stars.

The shadow sends my body
reflections of quiet things.

My shadow moves like a huge
violet-colored mosquito.

A hundred crickets are trying
10 to gild the glow of the reeds.

A glow arises in my breast,
the one mirrored in the water.

Narcissus

Boy!
You'll fall into the river!

Deep down there's a rose
with another river inside.

¡Mira aquel pájaro! ¡Mira
aquel pájaro amarillo!

    Se me han caído los ojos
    dentro del agua.

  ¡Dios mío!
10 ¡Que se resbala! ¡Muchacho!

     . . . y en la rosa estoy yo mismo.

Cuando se perdió en el agua,
comprendí. Pero no explico.

Juegos

Dedicados a la cabeza de Luis Buñuel
En gros plan

Ribereñas
(Con acompañamiento de campanas)

  Dicen que tienes cara
(balalín)
de luna llena.
(balalán)

  ¿Cuántas campanas oyes? -
(Balalín.)
No me dejan.
  (¡Balalán!)

  Pero tus ojos . . . ¡Ah! . . .
10 (balalín)

Look at that bird! Just look
at that yellow bird!

    My eyes have dropped
    into the water.

  Good Lord!
10 He's slipping! Boy!

    . . . and I'm inside the rose myself.

When he vanished into the water,
I understood. But I shan't explain.

Games

Dedicated to the head of Luis Buñuel
En gros plan

Songs of the Riverbank
(To an accompaniment of bells)

  They say your face
(ding dong)
is simply a moonface.
(dong ding)

  How many bells do you hear?
(Ding dong.)
They don't let me.
  (Dong ding!)

  But your eyes . . . Aha!
10 (ding dong)
. . . eye pouches, I mean . . .
(dong ding)
and that golden laugh
(ding dong)

. . . perdona, tus ojeras . . .
(balalán)
y esa risa de oro
(balalín)
y esa . . . no puedo, esa . . .
(balalán)

Su duro miriñaque
las campanas golpean.

¡Oh, tu encanto secreto . . . tu . . .

20 (balalín
lín
lín
lín . . .)

Dispensa.

A Irene García
(criada)

En el soto,
los alamillos bailan
uno con otro.
Y el arbolé,
con sus cuatro hojitas
baila también.

¡Irene!
Luego vendrán las lluvias
y las nieves.
10 Baila sobre lo verde.

and your . . . it's beyond me, your . . .
(dong ding)

    The bells keep striking
their hard hoop skirts.

    Oh, your secret charm . . . your . . .

20 (dong ding
    ding
    ding
    ding . . .)

    Forgive me.

To Irene García
(a servant)

    In the grove
young poplars are dancing
each with another.
And that tree
with the handful of leaves
is dancing along.

    Irene!
Soon the rains will come
and the snows.
10 Dance on the green.

Sobre lo verde verde,
que te acompaño yo.

¡Ay, cómo corre el agua!
¡Ay, mi corazón!

En el soto,
los alamillos bailan
uno con otro.
Y el arbolé,
con sus cuatro hojitas
20 baila también.

Al oído de una muchacha

No quise.
No quise decirte nada.

Vi en tus ojos
dos arbolitos locos.
De brisa, de risa y de oro.

Se meneaban.

No quise.
No quise decirte nada.

●

Las gentes iban
y el otoño venía.

Las gentes,
iban a lo verde.
Llevaban gallos
y guitarras alegres.
Por el reino
de las simientes.

On the green greensward,
I'll be your partner.

Oh, how the water flows!
Ah, my heart knows!

In the grove
young poplars are dancing
each with another.
And that tree
with the handful of leaves
20 is dancing along.

Whispered to a Girl

I was not willing.
Not willing to tell you a thing.

I could see in your eyes
two saplings giddy.
With breezes, with laughter, with gold.

They were swaying.

I was not willing.
Not willing to tell you a thing.

•

People were leaving
and autumn coming.

People
were off to the green world.
They took cocks
and merry guitars.
Into the realm
of seeds.

El río soñaba,
corría la fuente.
¡Salta,
corazón caliente!

     Las gentes,
iban a lo verde.

     El otoño venía
amarillo de estrellas,
pájaros macilentos
y ondas concéntricas.
Sobre el pecho almidonado,
la cabeza.
¡Párate,
corazón de cera!

     Las gentes iban
y el otoño venía.

Canción del mariquita

     El mariquita se peina
con su peinador de seda.

     Los vecinos se sonríen
en sus ventanas postreras.

     El mariquita organiza
los bucles de su cabeza.

     Por los patios gritan loros,
surtidores y planetas.

     El mariquita se adorna
con un jazmín sinvergüenza.

     La tarde se pone extraña
de peines y enredaderas.

The river was dreaming,
10 on ran the fountain.
Leap up,
warm heart!

People
were off to the green world.

Autumn was coming
yellow with stars,
sickly birds
and concentric ripples.
Hanging his head
20 on his starched breast.
Stop beating,
wax heart!

People were leaving
and autumn coming.

Song of the Fairy

The fairy fixes his hair
in his silk dressing gown.

The neighbors smile
at back windows.

The fairy arranges
the curls on his head.

In patios shriek parrots,
jets of water, and planets.

The fairy pretties himself
10 with some shameless jasmine.

The afternoon turns peculiar
with combs and coiling vines.

493

El escándalo temblaba
rayado como una cebra.

¡Los mariquitas del Sur,
cantan en las azoteas!

Árbol de canción

Para Ana María Dalí

Caña de voz y gesto,
una vez y otra vez
tiembla sin esperanza
en el aire de ayer.

La niña suspirando
lo quería coger;
pero llegaba siempre
un minuto después.

¡Ay, sol! ¡Ay, luna, luna!
10 Un minuto después.
Sesenta flores grises
enredaban sus pies.

Mira cómo se mece
una vez y otra vez,
virgen de flor y rama,
en el aire de ayer.

•

Naranja y limón.

¡Ay, la niña
del mal amor!

Limón y naranja.

Scandal was shuddering,
streaked like a zebra.

The fairies of the south
sing on roof terraces.

Tree of Song
For Ana María Dalí

A reed in voice and gesture
again and again
quivers forlorn
in yesterday's breeze.

The girl, with a sigh,
was trying to catch it
but she always arrived
a minute too late.

O sun! Moon, O moon!
10 A minute too late.
Sixty gray flowers
trammeled her feet.

She sees it swaying
again and again,
innocent of flower and branch,
in yesterday's breeze.

•

Orange and lemon.

Oh, the girl
unhappy in love!

Lemon and orange.

¡Ay de la niña,
de la niña blanca!

Limón.

(¡Cómo brillaba
el sol!)

10 Naranja.

(¡En las chinas
del agua!)

La calle de los mudos

Detrás de las inmóviles vidrieras
las muchachas juegan con sus risas.

(En los pianos vacíos,
arañas titiriteras.)

Las muchachas hablan con sus novios
agitando sus trenzas apretadas.

(Mundo del abanico,
el pañuelo y la mano.)

Los galanes replican haciendo,
10 alas y flores con sus capas negras.

Canciones de luna
A José F. Montesinos

La luna asoma

Cuando sale la luna
se pierden las campanas
y aparecen las sendas
impenetrables.

Alas for the girl,
the pale girl!

Lemon.

(How the sun was glinting!)

Orange.

10   (Off the pebbles
in the water!)

The Street of the Mute

Behind the unmoving glass doors
the girls play with their laughter.

(On the empty pianos,
puppeteer spiders.)

To talk with their suitors, the girls
shake their tight-knit braids.

(World of the fan,
the hand, and the handkerchief.)

In reply the suitors' black capes
10   describe flourishes and wings.

Moon Songs
To José F. Montesinos

The Moon Appears

At the rise of the moon
bells fade out
and impassable paths
appear.

Cuando sale la luna,
el mar cubre la tierra
y el corazón se siente
isla en el infinito.

Nadie come naranjas
10 bajo la luna llena.
Es preciso comer,
fruta verde y helada.

Cuando sale la luna
de cien rostros iguales,
la moneda de plata
solloza en el bolsillo.

Dos lunas de tarde

1

(A Laurita, amiga de mi hermana)

La luna está muerta, muerta;
pero resucita en la primavera.

Cuando en la frente de los chopos
se rice el viento del sur.

Cuando den nuestros corazones
su cosecha de suspiros.

Cuando se pongan los tejados
sus sombreritos de yerba.

La luna está muerta, muerta;
10 pero resucita en la primavera.

2

(A Isabelita, mi hermana)

La tarde canta
una «berceuse» a las naranjas.

At the rise of the moon
the sea overspreads the land
and the heart feels like an island
in the infinite.

No one eats oranges
10 in the full moon's light.
Fruit must be eaten
green and ice-cold.

At the rise of the moon
with its hundred faces alike,
silver coins
sob away in pockets.

Two Evening Moons

1

(To Laurita, my sister's friend)

The moon is dead, is dead
but in spring will come back to life.

When across the poplars' faces
the south wind is rippling.

When our hearts have yielded
their harvest of sighs.

When tiled roofs are wearing
their little grass hats.

The moon is dead, is dead
10 but in spring will come back to life.

2

(To Isabelita, my sister)

The evening is singing
a *berceuse* to the oranges.

Mi hermanita canta:
«La tierra es una naranja».

La luna llorando dice:
«Yo quiero ser una naranja».

No puede ser, hija mía,
aunque te pongas rosada.
Ni siquiera limoncito.
10   ¡Qué lástima!

Lunes, miércoles y viernes

Yo era.

Yo fui.

Pero no soy.

Yo era . . .

(¡Oh fauce maravillosa
la del ciprés y su sombra!
Ángulo de luna llena.
Ángulo de luna sola.)

Yo fui . . .

10   La luna estaba de broma
diciendo que era una rosa.
(Con una capa de viento
mi amor se arrojó a las olas.)

Pero no soy . . .

(Ante una vidriera rota
coso mi lírica ropa.)

My little sister is singing:
"The earth is an orange."

In tears, the moon says:
"I want to be an orange."

No way, my child,
even if you turned rosy.
Not even a nice lemon.
Oh, what a pity!

Monday, Wednesday, and Friday

I was.

I had been.

But not I am.

I was . . .

(Oh marvelous jaws—
jaws of the cypress and its shadow!
Angle of a full moon.
Angle of a lone moon.)

I had been . . .

10   The moon in a joking mood
was calling itself a rose.
(With the wind as cape
my love flung itself into the waves.)

But not I am . . .

(By a broken windowpane
I mend my lyric clothing.)

Murió al amanecer

Noche de cuatro lunas
y un solo árbol,
con una sola sombra
y un solo pájaro.

Busco en mi carne las
huellas de tus labios.
El manantial besa al viento
sin tocarlo.

Llevo el No que me diste,
en la palma de la mano,
como un limón de cera
casi blanco.

Noche de cuatro lunas
y un solo árbol.
En la punta de una aguja,
está mi amor ¡girando!

Primer aniversario

La niña va por mi frente.
¡Oh, qué antiguo sentimiento!

¿De qué me sirve, pregunto,
la tinta, el papel y el verso?

Carne tuya me parece,
rojo lirio, junco fresco.

Morena de luna llena.
¿Qué quieres de mi deseo?

Dead at Daybreak

    Night of four moons
and a single tree
with a single shadow
and a single bird.

    On my flesh I seek the
imprint of your lips.
The jet of spray kisses the wind
without even touching it.

    I bear the "No" you handed me
10 in the palm of my hand
like a wax lemon
nearly white.

    Night of four moons
and a single tree.
On the point of a needle
stands my love—whirling round!

First Anniversary

    The girl moves across my brow.
Oh, how ancient a feeling!

    What use to me, I ask,
is paper, ink, and verse?

    To me it's like your flesh,
red lily, fresh rushes.

    Dark, full-moon girl.
What can you want with my desire?

Segundo aniversario

La luna clava en el mar
un largo cuerno de luz.

Unicornio gris y verde,
estremecido pero extático.

El cielo flota sobre el aire
como una inmensa flor de loto.

(¡Oh, tú sola paseando
la última estancia de la noche!)

Flor

A Colin Hackforth

El magnífico sauce
de la lluvia, caía.

¡Oh la luna redonda
sobre las ramas blancas!

Eros con bastón (1925)
(A Pepín Bello)

Susto en el comedor

Eras rosa.
Te pusiste alimonada.

¿Qué intención viste en mi mano
que casi te amenazaba?

Quise las manzanas verdes.
No las manzanas rosadas . . .

Second Anniversary

The moon fastens on the sea
a long horn of light.

Unicorn gray and green,
trembling yet ecstatic.

The sky floats on the air
like a giant lotus flower.

(O you, girl, pacing alone
the final chamber of night!)

Flower
To Colin Hackforth

The magnificent willow
of the rain was falling.

Oh, round moon
on white branches!

Eros with a Cane (1925)
(To Pepín Bello)

Fright in the Dining Room

You were rose color.
You turned lemon.

What design did you see in my hand
that seemed to be threatening you?

The apples I wanted were the green.
Not the rosy apples . . .

alimonada . . .

(Grulla dormida la tarde,
puso en tierra la otra pata.)

Lucía Martínez

Lucía Martínez.
Umbría de seda roja.

Tus muslos como la tarde
van de la luz a la sombra.
Los azabaches recónditos
oscurecen tus magnolias.

Aquí estoy, Lucía Martínez.
Vengo a consumir tu boca
y arrastrarte del cabello
10   en madrugada de conchas.

Porque quiero, y porque puedo.
Umbría de seda roja.

La soltera en misa

Bajo el moisés del incienso,
adormecida.

Ojos de toro te miraban.
Tu rosario llovía.

Con ese traje de profunda seda,
no te muevas, Virginia.

Da los negros melones de tus pechos
al rumor de la misa.

lemon . . .

(The afternoon, a crane asleep,
put its other foot down.)

Lucía Martínez

Lucía Martínez.
Shadowy in red silk.

Like the evening, your thighs
move from light into shadow.
Hidden veins of jet
darken your magnolias.

Here I am, Lucía Martínez.
I've come to devour your mouth
and drag you off by the hair
10   into the seashells of daybreak.

Because I want to and I can.
Shadowy in red silk.

The Unmarried Woman at Mass

Under the cradle of the incense
you have dozed off.

Eyes of bulls looked you over.
Your rosary was raining.

In that dress of yours, deep in silk,
don't stir, Virginia.

Yield the black melons of your breasts
to the drone of the mass.

Interior

Ni quiero ser poeta,
ni galante.
¡Sábanas blancas donde te desmayes!

No conoces el sueño
ni el resplandor del día.
Como los calamares,
ciegas desnuda en tinta de perfume.
Carmen.

Nu

Bajo la adelfa sin luna
estabas fea desnuda.

Tu carne buscó en mi mapa
el amarillo de España.

Qué fea estabas, francesa,
en lo amargo de la adelfa.

Roja y verde, eché a tu cuerpo
la capa de mi talento.

Verde y roja, roja y verde.
10   ¡Aquí somos otra gente!

Serenata
(Homenaje a Lope de Vega)

Por las orillas del río
se está la noche mojando
y en los pechos de Lolita
se mueren de amor los ramos.

Interior

I want to be neither a poet
nor a ladies' man.
White sheets for you to pass out in!

You know neither sleep
nor the brightness of day.
Like the squid, in your nakedness,
you are blinding, with perfume for ink.
Carmen.

Nu

Beneath the moon-dark rosebay
you looked ugly naked.

Your flesh sought on my map
the yellow of Spain.

How ugly you looked, woman of France,
in the bitterness of the rosebay.

Red and green, over your body,
I threw the cape of my talent.

Green and red, red and green.
10   Here we're a different breed!

Serenade
(Homage to Lope de Vega)

Down on the riverbanks
the night has gone wading
and against Lolita's breasts,
for love, bouquets are fading.

Se mueren de amor los ramos.

La noche canta desnuda
sobre los puentes de marzo.
Lolita lava su cuerpo
con agua salobre y nardos.

10   Se mueren de amor los ramos.

La noche de anís y plata
relumbra por los tejados.
Plata de arroyos y espejos.
Anís de tus muslos blancos.

Se mueren de amor los ramos.

En Málaga

Suntuosa Leonarda.
Carne pontifical y traje blanco,
en las barandas de «Villa Leonarda».
Expuesta a los tranvías y a los barcos.
Negros torsos bañistas oscurecen
la ribera del mar. Oscilando
—concha y loto a la vez—
viene tu culo
de Ceres en retórica de mármol.

Trasmundo
A Manuel Angeles Ortiz

Escena

Altas torres.
Largos ríos.

Hada
Toma el anillo de bodas
que llevaron tus abuelos.

For love, bouquets are fading.

The naked night is singing
across the bridges of March.
Lolita washes her body
in brackish water and nard.

10   For love, bouquets are starved.

The night, all anise and silver,
glints off the rooftop tiles.
Silver of streams and mirrors.
Anise of your white thighs.

For love, the bouquets die.

In Málaga

Sumptuous Leonarda.
Pontifical flesh and white gown
at the balustrades of "Villa Leonarda."
Exhibited to tramcars and ships.
Black torsos of bathers darken
the seashore. Swaying
—conch shell and lotus at once—
your behind comes along
like Ceres in a rhetoric of marble.

Back of the World
To Manuel Ángeles Ortiz

Scene

Tall towers.
Long rivers.

Fairy
Take the wedding ring
your grandparents wore.

Cien manos, bajo la tierra,
lo están echando de menos.

Yo
    Voy a sentir en mis manos
una inmensa flor de dedos
y el símbolo del anillo.
10 No lo quiero.

    Altas torres.
Largos ríos.

Malestar y noche

    Abejaruco.
En tus árboles oscuros.
Noche de cielo balbuciente
y aire tartamudo.

    Tres borrachos eternizan
sus gestos de vino y luto.
Los astros de plomo giran
sobre un pie.
               Abejaruco.
En tus árboles oscuros.

10   Dolor de sien oprimida
con guirnalda de minutos.
¿Y tu silencio? Los tres
borrachos cantan desnudos.

    Pespunte de seda virgen
tu canción.
              Abejaruco.
Uco uco uco uco.
              Abejaruco.

A hundred hands beneath the sod
are wishing they had it.

I
   I'd be feeling on my hands
a vast flowering of fingers
and the symbol of the ring.
10 I don't want it.

   Tall towers.
Long rivers.

Disquiet and Night

   Bee-eating bird.
In the dark of your trees.
Night of skies slurred
and tongue-tied air.

   Three drunks perpetuate
motions of wine and grief, blurred.
The leaden stars pirouette
on one foot.
          Bee-eating bird.
In the dark of your trees.

10 Aching of temples confined
in a garland of minutes deferred.
What of your silence? The three
naked drunks are singing.

   A backstitch in virgin silk:
your song.
          Bee-eating bird.
Heard, slurred, blurred, deferred.
          Bee-eating bird.

El niño mudo

El niño busca su voz.
(La tenía el rey de los grillos.)
En una gota de agua
buscaba su voz el niño.

No la quiero para hablar;
me haré con ella un anillo
que llevará mi silencio
en su dedo pequeñito.

En una gota de agua
10 buscaba su voz el niño.

(La voz cautiva, a lo lejos,
se ponía un traje de grillo.)

El niño loco

Yo decía: «Tarde.»
Pero no era así.
La tarde era otra cosa
que ya se había marchado.

(Y la luz encogía
sus hombros como una niña.)

«Tarde.» ¡Pero es inútil!
Ésta es falsa, ésta tiene
media luna de plomo.
10 La otra no vendrá nunca.

(Y la luz como la ven todos,
jugaba a la estatua con el niño loco.)

Aquélla era pequeña
y comía granadas.
Ésta es grandota y verde, yo no puedo

The Voiceless Child

    The child goes seeking his voice.
(The king of the crickets had it.)
In a drop of water
the child sought his voice.

    Not that I want it to talk with;
I'll turn it into a ring
for my silence to wear
on its little finger.

    In a drop of water
10 the child sought his voice.

    (Far off, the captive voice
was dressing in cricket's clothes.)

The Crazy Boy

    I said: "Afternoon."
But it wasn't so.
The afternoon was something else
already gone by.

    (And the light kept shrugging
its shoulders like a girl.)

    "Afternoon!" But it's no use!
This one is false, this one contains
a half moon of lead.
10 The real one won't ever come.

    (And the light as you and I see it
was playing statue with the crazy boy.)

    The other one was small
and liked to eat pomegranates.
This one is gawky and green and I can't

515

tomarla en brazos ni vestirla.
¿No vendrá? ¿Cómo era?

(Y la luz que se iba, dio una broma.
Separó al niño loco de su sombra.)

Desposorio

Tirad ese anillo
al agua.

(La sombra apoya sus dedos
sobre mi espalda.)

Tirad ese anillo. Tengo
más de cien años. ¡Silencio!

¡No preguntadme nada!

Tirad ese anillo
al agua.

Despedida

Si muero,
dejad el balcón abierto.

El niño come naranjas.
(Desde mi balcón lo veo.)

El segador siega el trigo.
(Desde mi balcón lo siento.)

¡Si muero,
dejad el balcón abierto!

pick it up in my arms or dress it.
Won't that one come? What was it like?

(And the departing light played a trick.
It split the crazy boy from his shadow.)

Marriage Vow

Throw that ring
in the water.

(Fingers of shadow are pressing
against my back.)

Throw away that ring. I am
over a hundred years old. Be still!

Ask me no questions.

Throw that ring
in the water.

Leave-taking

If I die,
leave the balcony open.

The boy is eating oranges.
(From my balcony I can see him.)

The reaper is reaping the wheat.
(From my balcony I can hear him.)

If I die,
leave the balcony open!

Suicidio

*(Quizá fue por no saberte
la geometría)*

El jovencito se olvidaba.
Eran las diez de la mañana.

Su corazón se iba llenando
de alas rotas y flores de trapo.

Notó que ya no le quedaba,
en la boca más que una palabra.

Y al quitarse los guantes, caía,
de sus manos, suave ceniza.

Por el balcón se veía una torre.
10 El se sintió balcón y torre.

Vio, sin duda, cómo le miraba
el reloj detenido en su caja.

Vio su sombra tendida y quieta,
en el blanco diván de seda.

Y el joven rígido, geométrico,
con un hacha rompío el espejo.

Al romperlo, un gran chorro de sombra,
inundó la quimérica alcoba.

Amor

(con alas y flechas)

Cancioncilla del primer deseo

En la mañana verde,
quería ser corazón.
Corazón.

Suicide

*(Maybe it was because you hadn't
mastered geometry)*

The lad was going blank.
It was ten in the morning.

His heart was growing full
of broken wings and rag flowers.

He noticed there remained
just one word on his lips.

And when he took off his gloves
a soft ash fell from his hands.

A tower showed through the balcony door.
10 He felt he was balcony and tower.

No doubt he saw how the clock,
stopped in its case, surveyed him.

He saw his shadow quiet and prone
on the white silk divan.

And the stiff, geometrical youth
smashed the mirror with a hatchet.

When it broke, a great burst of shadow
flooded the illusory room.

Love

(with wings and arrows)

Ditty of First Desire

In the green morning
I wanted to be a heart.
A heart.

Y en la tarde madura
quería ser ruiseñor.
Ruiseñor.

(Alma,
ponte color naranja.
Alma,
10   ponte color de amor.)

En la mañana viva,
yo quería ser yo.
Corazón.

Y en la tarde caída
quería ser mi voz.
Ruiseñor.

¡Alma,
ponte color naranja!
¡Alma,
20   ponte color de amor!

En el instituto y en la universidad

La primera vez
no te conocí.
La segunda, sí.

Dime
si el aire te lo dice.

Mañanita fría
yo me puse triste,
y luego me entraron
ganas de reírme.

10   No te conocí.
Sí me conociste.
Sí te conocí.
No me conociste.

And in the ripe evening
I wanted to be a nightingale.
A nightingale.

(Soul,
turn orange-colored.
Soul,
10 turn the color of love.)

In the vivid morning
I wanted to be myself.
A heart.

And at the evening's end
I wanted to be my voice.
A nightingale.

Soul,
turn orange-colored.
Soul,
20 turn the color of love.

In School and at the University

The first time
I didn't know you.
The second I did.

Tell me,
does the breeze tell you?

Early one morning
I grew sad
and then I was seized
with an urge to laugh.

10 I didn't know you.
You did know me.
I did know you.
You didn't know me.

521

Ahora entre los dos
se alarga impasible,
un mes, como un
biombo de días grises.

La primera vez
no te conocí.
20   La segunda, sí.

Madrigalillo

Cuatro granados
tiene tu huerto.

(Toma mi corazón
nuevo.)

Cuatro cipreses
tendrá tu huerto.

(Toma mi corazón
viejo.)

Sol y luna.
10   Luego . . .
¡ni corazón,
ni huerto!

Eco

Ya se ha abierto
la flor de la aurora.

(¿Recuerdas
el fondo de la tarde?)

Now between us two
a month unfeelingly
unfolds just like a
screen of gray days.

The first time
I didn't know you.
20   The second I did.

Brief Madrigal

Four pomegranate trees
grow in your garden.

(Take my heart—
the new one.)

Four cypress trees
will grow in your garden.

(Take my heart—
the old one.)

Sun and moon.
10   Whereupon . . .
neither heart
nor garden!

Echo

The flower of dawn
has already opened.

(Do you recall
the depths of evening?)

El nardo de la luna
derrama su olor frío.

(¿Recuerdas
la mirada de agosto?)

Idilio

A Enrique Durán

Tú querías que yo te dijera
el secreto de la primavera.

Y yo soy para el secreto
lo mismo que es el abeto.

Árbol cuyos mil deditos
señalan mil caminitos.

Nunca te diré, amor mío,
por qué corre lento el río.

Pero pondré en mi voz estancada
10 el rielo ceniza de tu mirada.

¡Dame vueltas, morenita!
Ten cuidado con mis hojitas.

Dame más vueltas alrededor,
jugando a la noria del amor.

¡Ay! No puedo decirte, aunque quisiera,
el secreto de la primavera.

•

Narciso.
Tu olor.
Y el fondo del río.

The spikenard moon
pours down its cold scent.

(Do you remember
the gaze of August?)

Idyll
To Enrique Durán

You wanted me to tell you
the secret of spring.

When it comes to secrets, I
am exactly like the fir.

A tree whose thousand little fingers
point to a thousand byways.

My love, I'll never tell you
why the river runs so slow.

But upon my voice's still waters
10 I'll place the flickering ash of your glance.

Circle about me, dark beauty.
Watch out for my prickly needles.

Circle about me some more,
playing the draw-wheel of love.

Oh, I couldn't tell you if I wished
the secret of spring.

•

Narcissus.
The smell of you.
And the river bottom.

Quiero quedarme a tu vera.
Flor del amor.
Narciso.

Por tus blancos ojos cruzan
ondas y peces dormidos.
Pájaros y mariposas
10 japonizan en los míos.

Tú diminuto y yo grande.
Flor del amor.
Narciso.

Las ranas ¡qué listas son!
Pero no dejan tranquilo
el espejo en que se miran
tu delirio y mi delirio.

Narciso.
Mi dolor.
20 Y mi dolor mismo.

Granada y 1850

Desde mi ventana
oigo el surtidor.

Un dedo de parra
y un rayo de sol,
señalan hacia el sitio
de mi corazón.

Por el aire de Agosto
se van las nubes. Yo,
sueño que no sueño
10 dentro del surtidor.

I want to stay on your banks.
Flower of love.
Narcissus.

Moving across your white eyes
are waves and sleeping fish.
Birds and butterflies
10   are Japanning in mine.

You so tiny and I large.
Flower of love.
Narcissus.

These frogs—how quick they are!
But they never stop ruffling
the mirror that holds in reflection
your madness and my madness.

Narcissus.
My pain.
20   And the pain itself.

Granada 1850

From my window
I can hear the fountain's fall.

A finger of grapevine
and a beam of sunlight
point to the spot
where my heart is.

In the August air
the clouds go by.
I dream I'm not dreaming
10   inside the fountain.

Preludio

Las alamedas se van,
pero dejan su reflejo.

Las alamedas se van,
pero nos dejan el viento.

El viento está amortajado
a lo largo bajo el cielo.

Pero ha dejado flotando
sobre los ríos, sus ecos.

El mundo de las luciérnagas
10 ha invadido mis recuerdos.

Y un corazón diminuto
me va brotando en los dedos.

•

Sobre el cielo verde,
un lucero verde
¿qué ha de hacer, amor,
¡ay!, sino perderse?

Las torres fundidas
con la niebla fría,
¿cómo han de mirarnos
con sus ventanitas?

Cien luceros verdes
10 sobre un cielo verde,
no ven a cien torres
blancas, en la nieve.

Prelude

The poplar lanes move on
but leave their reflection.

The poplar lanes move on
but leave us the wind.

The wind lies shrouded
full length beneath the sky.

But floating on the rivers
it has left its echoes.

The world of fireflies
10   has invaded my memories.

And a tiny little heart
is sprouting at my fingertips.

•

Against the green sky
a green day-star.
Oh love, what can it do
but fade away?

Those towers fused
with the chill mist—
how will they see us
with their tiny windows?

A hundred green day-stars
10   against a green sky
can't see a hundred towers,
white in the snow.

Y esta angustia mía
para hacerla viva,
he de decorarla
con rojas sonrisas.

Soneto

Largo espectro de plata conmovida
el viento de la noche suspirando,
abrió con mano gris mi vieja herida
y se alejó: yo estaba deseando.

Llaga de amor que me dará la vida
perpetua sangre y pura luz brotando.
Grieta en que Filomela enmudecida
tendrá bosque, dolor y nido blando.

¡Ay, qué dulce rumor en mi cabeza!
10 Me tenderé junto a la flor sencilla
donde flota sin alma tu belleza.

Y el agua errante se pondrá amarilla,
mientras corre mi sangre en la maleza
mojada y olorosa de la orilla.

Canciones para terminar
A Rafael Alberti

De otro modo

La hoguera pone al campo de la tarde,
unas astas de ciervo enfurecido.
Todo el valle se tiende; por sus lomos,
caracolea el vientecillo.

El aire cristaliza bajo el humo.
Ojo de gato triste y amarillo.
Yo en mis ojos paseo por las ramas.
Las ramas se pasean por el río.

And to bring to life
this heartache of mine,
I'll have to adorn it
with red smiles.

Sonnet

A specter trailing restless silver,
the night wind with its sighing,
reopened my old wound in its gray hands,
moved on, and left me there desiring.

Wound of love, source to sustain my life
with blood always new and light unblemished.
Cleft in which the tongueless Philomel
will find her nest, her grove, her grief replenished.

Ah, so sweet a sound inside my head!
10 I shall lie down beside the simple flower
on which your soulless beauty soars.

Then the meandering water will turn yellow
as my blood keeps flowing through the marshy,
moist and fragrant growth along the shores.

Songs to End With
To Rafael Alberti

In Another Manner

The bonfire gives the evening land
the antlers of a raging stag.
The valley stretches away. A little breeze
zigzags among the furrows.

Air crystallizes in the smoke
—a cat's eye sad and yellow.
My eyes and I glide along the branches.
The branches do their gliding on the river.

531

Llegan mis cosas esenciales.
10 Son estribillos de estribillos.
Entre los juncos y la baja-tarde,
¡qué raro que me llame Federico!

Canción de noviembre y abril

El cielo nublado
pone mis ojos blancos.

Yo, para darles vida,
les acerco una flor
amarilla.

No consigo turbarlos.
Siguen yertos y blancos.

(Entre mis hombros vuela
mi alma dorada y plena.)

10 El cielo de abril
pone mis ojos de añil.

Yo, para darles alma,
les acerco una rosa
blanca.

No consigo infundir
lo blanco en el añil.

(Entre mis hombros vuela
mi alma impasible y ciega.)

•

Agua, ¿dónde vas?

Riyendo voy por el río
a las orillas del mar.

Things essential to me come to hand.
10 Refrains of other refrains.
Between the rushes and the dropping day,
how strange my having Federico for a name!

Song of November and April

The cloudy sky
turns my eyes white.

To bring them to life
I hold a flower to them—
a yellow one.

I'm unable to stir them.
They stay blankly white.

(In between my shoulders
flits my soul, full and golden.)

10 The April sky
turns my eyes indigo.

To give them a soul
I hold a rose to them—
a white one.

I'm unable to infuse
the indigo with white.

(In between my shoulders
fits my soul, blind and stolid.)

•

Whither bound, water?

I'm chuckling my way
downstream to the seashore.

533

Mar, ¿adónde vas?

Río arriba voy buscando
fuente donde descansar.

Chopo, y tú ¿qué harás?

No quiero decirte nada.
Yo . . . ¡temblar!

10   ¿Qué deseo, qué no deseo,
por el río y por la mar?

(Cuatro pájaros sin rumbo
en el alto chopo están.)

El espejo engañoso

Verde rama exenta
de ritmo y de pájaro.

Eco de sollozo
sin dolor ni labio.
Hombre y Bosque.

Lloro
frente al mar amargo.
¡Hay en mis pupilas
dos mares cantando!

Canción inútil

Rosa futura y vena contenida,
amatista de ayer y brisa de ahora mismo,
¡quiero olvidarlas!

Sea, whither bound?

Upstream to discover
springs to repose in.

Aspen, what about you?

I've nothing to tell you.
It's . . . quaking for me!

10   What do I want or not want
by river, by sea?

(Four aimless birds
are on the tall aspen.)

The Cheating Mirror

Green branch barren
of rhythm and bird.

Echo of a sob
with no pain or lips.
Man and Woods.

I shed tears
beside the salt sea.
In my pupils
are two seas singing.

Useless Song

Rose of the future and lode withheld,
yesterday's amethyst and breeze of right now:
I want to forget them!

Hombre y pez en sus medios, bajo cosas flotantes,
esperando en el alga o en la silla su noche,
¡quiero olvidarlos!

Yo.
¡Sólo yo!
Labrando la bandeja
donde no irá mi cabeza.
¡Sólo yo!

Huerto de marzo

Mi manzano,
tiene ya sombra y pájaros.

¡Qué brinco da mi sueño
de la luna al viento!

Mi manzano,
da a lo verde sus brazos.

¡Desde marzo, cómo veo
la frente blanca de enero!

Mi manzano . . .
(viento bajo).

Mi manzano . . .
(cielo alto).

Dos marinos en la orilla
A Joaquín Amigo

1.º

Se trajo en el corazón
un pez del Mar de la China.

Man and fish in their elements, under things floating,
in algae or in armchair awaiting their night:
I want to forget them!

I.
Only I!
At work on the tray
which won't carry my head.
Only I!

Orchard, March

My apple tree
now has birds and a shadow.

What a hop my dream takes
from the moon to the wind!

My apple tree
gives its arms up to green.

Viewed from March, what a sight—
the white brow of January!

My apple tree . . .
(Wind down low.)

My apple tree . . .
(Sky far up.)

Two Sailors Ashore

To Joaquín Amigo

First

In his heart he brought back
a fish from the China Sea.

A veces se ve cruzar
diminuto por sus ojos.

Olvida siendo marino
los bares y las naranjas.

Mira al agua.

2.º

Tenía la lengua de jabón.
Lavó sus palabras y se calló.

Mundo plano, mar rizado,
cien estrellas y su barco.

Vio los balcones del Papa
y los pechos dorados de las cubanas.

Mira al agua.

Ansia de estatua

Rumor.
Aunque no quede más que el rumor.

Aroma.
Aunque no quede más que el aroma.

Pero arranca de mí el recuerdo
y el color de las viejas horas.

Dolor.
Frente al mágico y vivo dolor.

Batalla.
10 En la auténtica y sucia batalla.

¡Pero quita la gente invisible
que rodea perenne mi casa!

At times one sees the tiny form
flitting across his eyes.

Sailor and all, he forgets
Oranges and bars.

He gazes at the water.

Second

He had a tongue of soap.
He washed his words and stopped speaking.

Level world, crinkled sea,
a hundred stars and his ship.

He has seen the Pope's balconies
and the gilt breasts of Cuban women.

He gazes at the water.

Straining Toward Statue

Sound.
Even if only sound remains.

Smell.
Even if only smell remains.

But root out of me the memory
and the color of the old days.

Pain.
As against the keen, magic pain.

Battle.
10 In the honest, filthy battle.

But remove the invisible people
forever surrounding my house!

Canción del naranjo seco

A Carmen Morales

Leñador.
Córtame la sombra.
Líbrame del suplicio
de verme sin toronjas.

¿Por qué nací entre espejos?
El día me da vueltas.
Y la noche me copia
en todas sus estrellas.

Quiero vivir sin verme.
10 Y hormigas y vilanos,
soñaré que son
mis hojas y mis pájaros.

Leñador.
Córtame la sombra.
Líbrame del suplicio
de verme sin toronjas.

Canción del día que se va

¡Qué trabajo me cuesta
dejarte marchar, día!
Te vas lleno de mí,
vuelves sin conocerme.
¡Qué trabajo me cuesta
dejar sobre tu pecho
posibles realidades
de imposibles minutos!

En la tarde, un Perseo
10 te lima las cadenas,
y huyes sobre los montes
hiriéndote los pies.
No pueden seducirte

540

Song of the Dead Orange Tree

To Carmen Morales

Woodcutter.
Cut down my shadow.
Deliver me from the torment
of bearing no fruit.

Why was I born among mirrors?
Day turns round and round me.
And night copies me
in all her stars.

Let me live unmirrored.
10   And then let me dream
that ants and thistledown
are my leaves and my birds.

Woodcutter.
Cut down my shadow.
Deliver me from the torment
of bearing no fruit.

Song of Departing Day

Day, what a hard time I have
letting you leave.
You go off filled with me.
You return and don't know me.
What a hard time I have
leaving in your bosom
possible concretions
of impossible minutes.

In the evening a Perseus
10   files away your chains,
and you flee over hills
where you cut your feet.
Powerless to lure you

mi carne ni mi llanto,
ni los ríos en donde
duermes tu siesta de oro.

Desde Oriente a Occidente
llevo tu luz redonda.
Tu gran luz que sostiene
20 mi alma, en tensión aguda.
Desde Oriente a Occidente,
¡qué trabajo me cuesta
llevarte con tus pájaros
y tus brazos de viento!

are my flesh and my tears
and the rivers on which
you sleep your golden siesta.

From East to West
I bear your round light.
Your vast light that keeps
20   my soul highly tensed.
From East to West
what a hard time I have
bearing you with your birds
and your windy arms.

PRIMER
ROMANCERO
GITANO
1924–1927

THE

GYPSY

BALLADS

1924–1927

Translated by

Will Kirkland and Christopher Maurer

[*Soledad Montoya, 1930*]

1

Romance de la luna, luna

A Conchita García Lorca

La luna vino a la fragua
con su polisón de nardos.
El niño la mira, mira.
El niño la está mirando.
En el aire conmovido
mueve la luna sus brazos
y enseña, lúbrica y pura,
sus senos de duro estaño.
—Huye luna, luna, luna.
10 Si vinieran los gitanos,
harían con tu corazón
collares y anillos blancos.
—Niño, déjame que baile.
Cuando vengan los gitanos,
te encontrarán sobre el yunque
con los ojillos cerrados.
—Huye luna, luna, luna,
que ya siento sus caballos.
—Niño, déjame, no pises
20 mi blancor almidonado.

El jinete se acercaba
tocando el tambor del llano.
Dentro de la fragua el niño
tiene los ojos cerrados.
Por el olivar venían,
bronce y sueño, los gitanos.
Las cabezas levantadas
y los ojos entornados.

Cómo canta la zumaya,
30 ¡ay, cómo canta en el árbol!
Por el cielo va la luna
con un niño de la mano.

Dentro de la fragua lloran,
dando gritos, los gitanos.

Ballad of the Moon Moon

To Conchita García Lorca

The moon came to the forge
wearing a bustle of nards.
The boy is looking at her.
The boy is looking hard.
In the troubled air
the wind moves her arms,
showing, lewd and pure,
her hard, tin breasts.
"Run, moon moon moon.
10 If the gypsies came,
they would make of your heart
necklaces and white rings."
"Child, let me dance.
When the gypsies come,
they will find you on the anvil
with your little eyes shut tight."
"Run, moon moon moon.
I can hear their horses.
Child, let me be, don't walk
20 on my starchy white."

The rider was drawing closer
playing the drum of the plain.
In the forge the child
has his eyes shut tight.
Bronze and dream, the gypsies
cross the olive grove.
Their heads held high,
their eyes half open.

Ay how the nightjar sings!
30 How it sings in the tree!
The moon goes through the sky
with a child in her hand.

In the forge the gypsies
wept and cried aloud.

El aire la vela, vela.
El aire la está velando.

2

Preciosa y el aire
A Dámaso Alonso

Su luna de pergamino
Preciosa tocando viene,
por un anfibio sendero
de cristales y laureles.
El silencio sin estrellas,
huyendo del sonsonete,
cae donde el mar bate y canta
su noche llena de peces.
En los picos de la sierra
10 los carabineros duermen
guardando las blancas torres
donde viven los ingleses.
Y los gitanos del agua
levantan, por distraerse,
glorietas de caracolas
y ramas de pino verde.

★

Su luna de pergamino
Preciosa tocando viene.
Al verla se ha levantado
20 el viento, que nunca duerme.
San Cristobalón desnudo,
lleno de lenguas celestes,
mira a la niña tocando
una dulce gaita ausente.

—Niña, deja que levante
tu vestido para verte.
Abre en mis dedos antiguos
la rosa azul de tu vientre.

The air is watching, watching.
The air watched all night long.

TR. C.M.

2

Preciosa and the Wind

To Dámaso Alonso

Playing her parchment moon
Preciosa comes along
an amphibious path
of laurel trees and glass.
Silence without a star
flees the throbbing sound
and falls where the ocean beats,
singing its night full of fish.
On the mountain peaks
10 sleep the Civil Guard
watching the white towers
where the English live.
And the gypsies of the water
just to pass the time,
raise pergolas of river plants
and branches of green pine.

★

Playing her parchment moon
Preciosa comes along.
The wind, who never sleeps,
20 sees her and starts to rise:
nude Saint Christopher
full of heavenly tongues
watches the child play
a sweet absent flute.

Let me see you, child;
let me lift your dress.
Open in my old fingers
the blue rose of your womb.

Preciosa tira el pandero
30 y corre sin detenerse.
El viento-hombrón la persigue
con una espada caliente.

Frunce su rumor el mar.
Los olivos palidecen.
Cantan las flautas de umbría
y el liso gong de la nieve.

¡Preciosa, corre, Preciosa,
que te coge el viento verde!
¡Preciosa, corre, Preciosa!
40 ¡Míralo por dónde viene!
Sátiro de estrellas bajas
con sus lenguas relucientes.

★

Preciosa, llena de miedo,
entra en la casa que tiene
más arriba de los pinos,
el cónsul de los ingleses.

Asustados por los gritos
tres carabineros vienen,
sus negras capas ceñidas
50 y los gorros en las sienes.

El inglés da a la gitana
un vaso de tibia leche,
y una copa de ginebra
que Preciosa no se bebe.

Y mientras cuenta, llorando,
su aventura a aquella gente,
en las tejas de pizarra
el viento, furioso, muerde.

Preciosa throws away
30   her tambourine and runs.
The wind giant pursues her
with a hot sword.

The sea contracts its sound.
The olive trees turn pale.
Flutes of shadow sing
and the snow's smooth gong.

Hurry, Preciosa, hurry!
Or the wind will get you.
Run, Preciosa, run!
40   The wind is close behind,
satyr of low stars
with his shiny tongues.

*

Fearful Preciosa
goes into the house
the English consul has
up above the pines.

Frightened by her cries,
come three Civil Guards,
black capes wrapped tight,
50   hats pulled on hard.

The Englishman gives the gypsy
a glass of lukewarm milk
and a tumbler of gin
which Preciosa does not drink.

And while she cries and tells
those people her adventure,
the furious wind is biting
on the tiles of the roof.

TR. C.M.

3

Reyerta

A Rafael Méndez

En la mitad del barranco
las navajas de Albacete,
bellas de sangre contraria,
relucen como los peces.
Una dura luz de naipe
recorta en el agrio verde
caballos enfurecidos
y perfiles de jinetes.
En la copa de un olivo
10 lloran dos viejas mujeres.
El toro de la reyerta
se sube por las paredes.
Ángeles negros traían
pañuelos y agua de nieve.
Ángeles con grandes alas
de navajas de Albacete.
Juan Antonio el de Montilla
rueda muerto la pendiente,
su cuerpo lleno de lirios
20 y una granada en las sienes.
Ahora monta cruz de fuego
carretera de la muerte.

★

El juez, con guardia civil,
por los olivares viene.
Sangre resbalada gime
muda canción de serpiente.
Señores guardias civiles:
aquí pasó lo de siempre.
Han muerto cuatro romanos
30 y cinco cartagineses.

3

The Feud

To Rafael Méndez

Halfway down the gorge
knives of Albacete,
beautiful with enemy blood,
shine like fish.
In the sour green
the hard light of a card
cuts out enraged horses
and profiles of riders.
Two old women cry
10 in an olive tree.
The bull of the feud
climbs right up the walls.
Black angels were bringing
handkerchiefs and snow water;
angels with big wings
of Albacete knives.
Juan Antonio de Montilla
rolls dead down the slope,
his body full of irises,
20 a pomegranate in his temples.
Now he rides a cross of fire
down the road of death.

★

Through the olive groves
come judge and Civil Guard.
The sliding blood is moaning
the mute song of a snake.
Civil Guardsmen, Sirs,
it's the same as always:
four Romans are dead
30 and five Carthaginians.

La tarde loca de higueras
y de rumores calientes,
cae desmayada en los muslos
heridos de los jinetes.
Y ángeles negros volaban
por el aire de poniente.
Ángeles de largas trenzas
y corazones de aceite.

4

Romance sonámbulo

A Gloria Giner y a Fernando de los Ríos

Verde que te quiero verde.
Verde viento. Verdes ramas.
El barco sobre la mar
y el caballo en la montaña.
Con la sombra en la cintura,
ella sueña en su baranda,
verde carne, pelo verde,
con ojos de fría plata.
Verde que te quiero verde.
10 Bajo la luna gitana,
las cosas la están mirando
y ella no puede mirarlas.

★

Verde que te quiero verde.
Grandes estrellas de escarcha
vienen con el pez de sombra
que abre el camino del alba.
La higuera frota su viento
con la lija de sus ramas,
y el monte, gato garduño,
20 eriza sus pitas agrias.
Pero ¿quién vendrá? ¿Y por dónde?...
Ella sigue en su baranda,
verde carne, pelo verde,
soñando en la mar amarga.

The afternoon, grown wild
with figs and hot murmurs,
swoons and falls into
the rider's wounded thighs.
And black angels were soaring
through the western sky.
Angels with long tresses
and hearts of olive oil.

TR. C.M.

4

Sleepwalking Ballad

To Gloria Giner and Fernando de los Ríos

Green I want you green.
Green wind, green boughs.
Ship on the sea
and horse on the mountain.
With shadow at her waist
she dreams at her railing,
green flesh, green hair,
and eyes of cold silver.
Green I want you green.
10 Under the gypsy moon
things are looking at her,
and she cannot return their gaze.

★

Green I want you green.
Great stars of frost
come with the shadow-fish
that opens the road for dawn.
The fig tree rubs its wind
on the sandpaper of its boughs,
and the hill, a wildcat,
20 bristles with maguey spears.
But who will come? From where?
She stays at her railing,
green flesh, green hair,
dreaming of the bitter sea.

—Compadre, quiero cambiar
mi caballo por su casa,
mi montura por su espejo,
mi cuchillo por su manta.
Compadre, vengo sangrando,
30 desde los puertos de Cabra.
—Si yo pudiera, mocito,
este trato se cerraba.
Pero yo ya no soy yo,
ni mi casa es ya mi casa.
—Compadre, quiero morir
decentemente en mi cama.
De acero, si puede ser,
con las sábanas de holanda.
¿No ves la herida que tengo
40 desde el pecho a la garganta?
—Trescientas rosas morenas
lleva tu pechera blanca.
Tu sangre rezuma y huele
alrededor de tu faja.
Pero yo ya no soy yo,
ni mi casa es ya mi casa.
—Dejadme subir al menos
hasta las altas barandas,
¡dejadme subir!, dejadme
50 hasta las verdes barandas.
Barandales de la luna
por donde retumba el agua.

★

Ya suben los dos compadres
hacia las altas barandas.
Dejando un rastro de sangre.
Dejando un rastro de lágrimas.
Temblaban en los tejados
farolillos de hojalata.
Mil panderos de cristal
60 herían la madrugada.

"Compadre, I want to trade
my horse for your house,
my saddle for your mirror,
my knife for your blanket.
Compadre, I've come here bleeding
30 from the passes of Cabra."
"If I could, young man,
I'd make that deal with you.
But I am no longer I,
and my house is no longer mine."
"Compadre, I want to die
decently in bed.
A steel one, if possible,
with real linen sheets.
Don't you see this wound
40 from my chest to my throat?"
"Three hundred brown roses
cover your white shirt.
Your blood oozes and smells
around your sash.
But I am no longer I,
and my house is no longer mine."
"Let me climb, at least,
up to the high railings.
Let me climb! Let me,
50 up to the green rails!
Big railings of the moon
where the water roars."

★

Up the two compadres climb,
up to the high rails,
leaving a trail of blood,
leaving a trail of tears.
Little tin-leaf lanterns
tremble on the roofs.
A thousand crystal tambourines
60 were wounding the early hours.

Verde que te quiero verde,
verde viento, verdes ramas.
Los dos compadres subieron.
El largo viento, dejaba
en la boca un raro gusto
de hiel, de menta y de albahaca.
—¡Compadre! ¿Dónde está, dime,
dónde está tu niña amarga?
—¡Cuántas veces te esperó!
70 ¡Cuántas veces te esperara,
cara fresca, negro pelo,
en esta verde baranda!

★

Sobre el rostro del aljibe
se mecía la gitana.
Verde carne, pelo verde,
con ojos de fría plata.
Un carámbano de luna
la sostiene sobre el agua.
La noche se puso íntima
80 como una pequeña plaza.
Guardias civiles borrachos
en la puerta golpeaban.
Verde que te quiero verde.
Verde viento. Verdes ramas.
El barco sobre la mar.
Y el caballo en la montaña.

5

La monja gitana
A José Moreno Villa

Silencio de cal y mirto.
Malvas en las hierbas finas.
La monja borda alhelíes
sobre una tela pajiza.

Green I want you green,
green wind, green boughs.
Up the two compadres climbed.
The long wind was leaving
a strange taste in their mouth
of basil, gall and mint.
"Compadre, where is she?
Where is your bitter girl?"
"How often she awaited you,
70 how often did she wait,
fresh face, black hair,
on this rail of green."

★

The gypsy girl was rocking
on the rain-well's face.
Green flesh, green hair
and eyes of cold silver.
An icicle of the moon
holds her over the water.
The night became as intimate
80 as a village square.
Drunken Civil Guards
were pounding on the door.
Green I want you green.
Green wind. Green boughs.
Ship on the sea
and horse on the mountain.

TR. C.M.

5

The Gypsy Nun
To José Moreno Villa

Silence of myrtle and lime.
Mallows bloom in meadow grasses.
The nun embroiders gillyflowers
on a flaxen cloth.

Vuelan en la araña gris
siete pájaros del prisma.
La iglesia gruñe a lo lejos
como un oso panza arriba.
¡Qué bien borda! ¡Con qué gracia!
10 Sobre la tela pajiza,
ella quisiera bordar
flores de su fantasía.
¡Qué girasol! ¡Qué magnolia
de lentejuelas y cintas!
¡Qué azafranes y qué lunas,
en el mantel de la misa!
Cinco toronjas se endulzan
en la cercana cocina.
Las cinco llagas de Cristo
20 cortadas en Almería.
Por los ojos de la monja
galopan dos caballistas.
Un rumor último y sordo
le despega la camisa,
y al mirar nubes y montes
en las yertas lejanías,
se quiebra su corazón
de azúcar y yerbaluisa.
¡Oh, qué llanura empinada
30 con veinte soles arriba!
¡Qué ríos puestos de pie
vislumbra su fantasía!
Pero sigue con sus flores,
mientras que de pie, en la brisa,
la luz juega el ajedrez
alto de la celosía.

6

La casada infiel

A Lydia Cabrera y a su negrita

Y que yo me la llevé al río
creyendo que era mozuela,
pero tenía marido.

Through the gray chandelier
fly the prism's seven birds.
The church growls in the distance
like a bear turned on its back.
How finely she embroiders! And with such grace!
10 She is longing to embroider
flowers of her fantasies
on the flaxen cloth.
What a sunflower! What magnolias
of sequins and ribbons!
What crocuses, what moons
across the altar cloth!
In the nearby kitchen,
five grapefruit sweetening:
the five wounds of Christ,
20 picked in Almería.
Through the nun's eyes
two gypsy bandits gallop.
A dull and distant noise
lifts the shirtwaist from her back,
and seeing clouds and mountains
across the rigid distances,
her heart of lemon verbena
and sugar breaks in two.
Oh what a rising plain
30 with twenty suns above!
What rivers on their feet
her fantasy has glimpsed!
But she continues with her flowers,
while, standing in the wind,
the light plays chess
across the jalousies.

TR. W.K.

6

The Unfaithful Wife

To Lydia Cabrera and her black girl

So I took her to the river.
I thought she wasn't married,
but she had a husband.

Fue la noche de Santiago
y casi por compromiso.
Se apagaron los faroles
y se encendieron los grillos.
En las últimas esquinas
toqué sus pechos dormidos,
y se me abrieron de pronto
como ramos de jacintos.
El almidón de su enagua
me sonaba en el oído,
como una pieza de seda
rasgada por diez cuchillos.
Sin luz de plata en sus copas
los árboles han crecido
y un horizonte de perros
ladra muy lejos del río.

★

Pasadas las zarzamoras,
los juncos y los espinos,
bajo su mata de pelo
hice un hoyo sobre el limo.
Yo me quité la corbata.
Ella se quitó el vestido.
Yo el cinturón con revólver.
Ella sus cuatro corpiños.
Ni nardos ni caracolas
tienen el cutis tan fino,
ni los cristales con luna
relumbran con ese brillo.
Sus muslos se me escapaban
como peces sorprendidos,
la mitad llenos de lumbre,
la mitad llenos de frío.
Aquella noche corrí
el mejor de los caminos,
montado en potra de nácar
sin bridas y sin estribos.
No quiero decir, por hombre,
las cosas que ella me dijo.
La luz del entendimiento
me hace ser muy comedido.

It was St. James' eve,
and almost as if agreed.
The streetlights went out,
the crickets went on.
At the far edge of town
I touched her sleeping breasts.
10 They opened to me suddenly
like fronds of hyacinth.
The starch of her petticoat
made a sound in my ears
like a piece of silk
being ripped by ten knives.
Silver light gone from their leaves,
the trees have grown bigger,
and a horizon of dogs
barks far from the river.

★

20 Out beyond the brambles,
the hawthorns and reeds,
beneath her mane of hair
I made a hollow in the sedge.
I took off my necktie.
She took off her dress.
I, my belt and pistol.
She, four bodices.
No silken shell or spikenard
is finer than her skin,
30 nor did moons or mirrors
ever glow like this.
Her thighs eluded me
like startled fish,
one half filled with fire,
the other half with cold.
That night the road I ran
was the finest of them all,
without a bridle or stirrup
on a filly made of pearl.
40 As a man, I won't repeat
the things she said to me.
The light of understanding
has made me more discreet.

Sucia de besos y arena
yo me la llevé del río.
Con el aire se batían
las espadas de los lirios.

Me porté como quien soy.
Como un gitano legítimo.
50 Le regalé un costurero
grande, de raso pajizo,
y no quise enamorarme
porque, teniendo marido,
me dijo que era mozuela
cuando la llevaba al río.

7

Romance de la pena negra
A José Navarro Pardo

Las piquetas de los gallos
cavan buscando la aurora,
cuando por el monte oscuro
baja Soledad Montoya.
Cobre amarillo, su carne
huele a caballo y a sombra.
Yunques ahumados, sus pechos
gimen canciones redondas.
—Soledad: ¿por quién preguntas
10 sin compaña y a estas horas?
—Pregunte por quien pregunte,
dime: ¿a ti qué se te importa?
Vengo a buscar lo que busco,
mi alegría y mi persona.
—Soledad de mis pesares,
caballo que se desboca,
al fin encuentra la mar
y se lo tragan las olas.
—No me recuerdes el mar,
20 que la pena negra brota
en las tierras de aceituna
bajo el rumor de las hojas.

I took her from the river
soiled with kisses and sand.
The sabers of the irises
were stabbing at the breeze.

I behaved as what I am.
As a true-born gypsy.
50 I gave her a sewing basket
made of straw-gold satin,
and refused to fall in love
because she had a husband,
though she said she wasn't married
when I took her to the river.

TR. W.K.

7

Ballad of Black Pain

To José Navarro Pardo

Pickaxes of the roosters
are digging for the dawn
when down the dark hill
comes Soledad Montoya.
Yellow copper, her flesh
smells of horses and darkness.
Smoky anvils, her breasts
weep round songs.
"Soledad, who do you ask for
10 so late and so alone?"
"No matter who it is,
what is it to you?
I want whatever I want,
my person and my joy."
"Soledad of my sorrows,
the horse that runs away
finds the sea at last
and is swallowed by the waves."
"Don't remind me of the sea,
20 for the black pain springs
from the lands of the olive
under rustling leaves."

—¡Soledad, qué pena tienes!
¡Qué pena tan lastimosa!
Lloras zumo de limón
agrio de espera y de boca.
—¡Qué pena tan grande! Corro
mi casa como una loca,
mis dos trenzas por el suelo
30   de la cocina a la alcoba.
¡Qué pena! Me estoy poniendo
de azabache, carne y ropa.
¡Ay, mis camisas de hilo!
¡Ay, mis muslos de amapola!
—Soledad: lava tu cuerpo
con agua de las alondras,
y deja tu corazón
en paz, Soledad Montoya.

                        ★

      Por abajo canta el río:
40   volante de cielo y hojas.
Con flores de calabaza
la nueva luz se corona.
¡Oh pena de los gitanos!
Pena limpia y siempre sola.
¡Oh pena de cauce oculto
y madrugada remota!

8

San Miguel
(Granada)
      A Diego Buigas de Dalmáu

San Miguel

      Se ven desde las barandas,
por el monte, monte, monte,
mulos y sombras de mulos
cargados de girasoles.

"Soledad, what pain you have,
what dreadful pain!
You cry lemon juice,
bitter from waiting and the mouth."
"Ay, what pain! I walk
madly around my house,
from kitchen to bedroom,
30   my tresses on the floor.
Ay, what pain! My clothes
and flesh are turning black.
Ay, my linen nightgowns!
Ay, my poppy thighs!"
"Soledad, wash your body
in water of the larks.
Soledad Montoya, let
peace into your heart."

★

Downstream the river sings:
40   veil of leaves and sky
and the new light crowns
itself in pumpkin flowers.
Oh pain, pain of the gypsies,
clean pain, always alone,
pain from a hidden spring
and from a distant dawn!

TR. C.M.

8.

St. Michael
(Granada)

To Diego Buigas de Dalmáu

St. Michael

You can see them from the railings
on the mount, the mount, the mount,
mules and shadows of mules
carrying sunflower seed.

Sus ojos en las umbrías
se empañan de inmensa noche.
En los recodos del aire
cruje la aurora salobre.

Un cielo de mulos blancos
10 cierra sus ojos de azogue,
dando a la quieta penumbra
un final de corazones.
Y el agua se pone fría
para que nadie la toque.
Agua loca y descubierta
por el monte, monte, monte.

★

San Miguel, lleno de encajes
en la alcoba de su torre,
enseña sus bellos muslos
20 ceñidos por los faroles.

Arcángel domesticado
en el gesto de las doce,
finge una cólera dulce
de plumas y ruiseñores.
San Miguel canta en los vidrios,
Efebo de tres mil noches,
fragante de agua colonia
y lejano de las flores.

★

El mar baila por la playa
30 un poema de balcones.
Las orillas de la luna
pierden juncos, ganan voces.
Vienen manolas comiendo
semillas de girasoles,
los culos grandes y ocultos
como planetas de cobre.
Vienen altos caballeros
y damas de triste porte,
morenas por la nostalgia

Their eyes, in the shady places,
cloud over with huge night.
The salty dawn is rustling
in riverbends of breeze.

A sky of white mules
10 closes its quicksilver eyes,
making the calm penumbra
a resting place for hearts.
And the water turns cold
so no one will touch it.
Wild, uncovered water
on the mount, the mount, the mount.

★

St. Michael, full of lace
in the alcove of his tower,
shows his lovely thighs
20 ringed in lantern light.

Domesticated archangel
pointing to twelve o'clock
feigns a sweet anger
of plumes and nightingales.
St. Michael sings in the glass,
ephebe of three thousand nights,
fragrant with cologne,
and far away from flowers.

★

On the beach the sea is dancing
30 a poem of balconies.
The shores of the moon
gain voices and lose reeds.
Manolas in bright costume
are eating sunflower seeds,
their huge bottoms hidden
like copper planets.
Tall gentlemen come by
and ladies of sad mien,
dusky with nostalgia

de un ayer de ruiseñores.
Y el obispo de Manila,
ciego de azafrán y pobre,
dice misa con dos filos
para mujeres y hombres.

★

San Miguel se estaba quieto
en la alcoba de su torre,
con las enaguas cuajadas
de espejitos y entredoses.

San Miguel, rey de los globos
50 y de los números nones,
en el primor berberisco
de gritos y miradores.

9

San Rafael
(Córdoba)

A Juan Izquierdo Croselles

San Rafael

Coches cerrados llegaban
a las orillas de juncos
donde las ondas alisan
romano torso desnudo.
Coches que el Guadalquivir
tiende en su cristal maduro,
entre láminas de flores
y resonancias de nublos.
Los niños tejen y cantan
10 el desengaño del mundo
cerca de los viejos coches
perdidos en el nocturno.
Pero Córdoba no tiembla
bajo el misterio confuso,
pues si la sombra levanta
la arquitectura del humo,

for a yesterday of nightingales.
The Bishop of Manila,
saffron-blind and poor,
says a double-edged mass
for the men and women.

★

St. Michael was resting calmly
in the alcove of his tower,
his petticoats frozen
in spangles and lace.

St. Michael, king of balloons
50 and of uneven numbers,
in the berberesque grace
of shouts and miradors.

TR. C.M.

9

St. Raphael
(Córdoba)

To Juan Izquierdo Croselles

St. Raphael

Closed coaches were coming
to the reeds along the shore
where, smoothed by the waves,
lies a nude Roman torso.
Coaches the Guadalquivir
lays across its ripened mirror,
between the resonating clouds
and laminae of flowers.
Young boys weave and sing
10 the truth about the world
near the ancient coaches
lost in the night.
But Córdoba doesn't tremble
before the swirling mystery,
for though the shadows raise
an architecture of smoke,

un pie de mármol afirma
su casto fulgor enjuto.
Pétalos de lata débil
20   recaman los grises puros
de la brisa, desplegada
sobre los arcos de triunfo.
Y mientras el puente sopla
diez rumores de Neptuno,
vendedores de tabaco
huyen por el roto muro.

I I

   Un solo pez en el agua
que a las dos Córdobas junta.
Blanda Córdoba de juncos.
30   Córdoba de arquitectura.
Niños de cara impasible
en la orilla se desnudan,
aprendices de Tobías
y Merlines de cintura,
para fastidiar al pez
en irónica pregunta
si quiere flores de vino
o saltos de media luna.
Pero el pez que dora el agua
40   y los mármoles enluta,
les da lección y equilibrio
de solitaria columna.
El Arcángel aljamiado
de lentejuelas oscuras,
en el mitin de las ondas
buscaba rumor y cuna.

★

   Un solo pez en el agua.
Dos Córdobas de hermosura.
Córdoba quebrada en chorros.
50   Celeste Córdoba enjuta.

a marble foot affirms
its radiance, chaste and spare.
Petals of frail tin
20 are scaled on pure grays
of the wind, unfurled
over the triumphal arches.
And while the bridge is blowing
ten of Neptune's whispers,
tobacco vendors flee
through the broken wall.

II

Only one fish in the water,
joining two Córdobas:
soft Córdoba of reeds,
30 Córdoba of architecture.
Boys with impassive faces
undressing on the shore,
apprentices to Tobias,
wizards of the waist,
ask ironic questions
just to tease the fish:
do you want wine flowers
or leaps like half a moon?
But the fish that gilds the water
40 and drapes mourning on the marble
teaches them the equilibrium
of a solitary column.
The archangel, half Arab,
with a flourish of dark sequins,
was seeking hush and cradle
in the hubbub of the waves.

★

Only one fish in the water.
Two Córdobas of splendor.
Córdoba broken into gushers.
50 Córdoba celestial and spare.

                    TR. W.K.

San Gabriel
(Sevilla)
A D. Agustín Viñuales

San Gabriel

Un bello niño de junco,
anchos hombros, fino talle,
piel de nocturna manzana,
boca triste y ojos grandes,
nervio de plata caliente,
ronda la desierta calle.
Sus zapatos de charol
rompen las dalias del aire,
con los dos ritmos que cantan
10   breves lutos celestiales.
En la ribera del mar
no hay palma que se le iguale,
ni emperador coronado,
ni lucero caminante.
Cuando la cabeza inclina
sobre su pecho de jaspe,
la noche busca llanuras
porque quiere arrodillarse.
Las guitarras suenan solas
20   para San Gabriel Arcángel,
domador de palomillas
y enemigo de los sauces.
—San Gabriel: el niño llora
en el vientre de su madre.
No olvides que los gitanos
te regalaron el traje.

I I

Anunciación de los Reyes,
bien lunada y mal vestida,
abre la puerta al lucero
30   que por la calle venía.
El Arcángel San Gabriel,

10

St. Gabriel
(Seville)

To D. Agustín Viñuales

St. Gabriel

A beautiful reed of a child,
shoulders wide, slim at the hip,
skin of an apple at night,
sad mouth and big eyes,
a nerve of hot silver,
walks the empty streets.
His shoes of patent leather
break the dahlias of the wind
with two cadences that sing
in brief celestial mourning.
All along the seashore
no palm can be his equal,
no crowned emperor,
nor passing star.
When he drops his head
against his jasper breast
the night looks round for plains
because it wants to kneel.
Guitars play by themselves
for St. Gabriel Archangel,
tamer of little doves
and envy of the willows.
"St. Gabriel: The baby's crying
in his mother's womb.
Don't forget the gypsies
gave that suit to you."

II

Annunciation de los Reyes,
rich in moons and poorly dressed,
opens the door to the star
that was shining down the street.
The Archangel St. Gabriel,

entre azucena y sonrisa,
biznieto de la Giralda,
se acercaba de visita.
En su chaleco bordado
grillos ocultos palpitan.
Las estrellas de la noche,
se volvieron campanillas.
—San Gabriel: aquí me tienes
40 con tres clavos de alegría.
Tu fulgor abre jazmines
sobre mi cara encendida.
—Dios te salve, Anunciación.
Morena de maravilla.
Tendrás un niño más bello
que los tallos de la brisa.
—¡Ay San Gabriel de mis ojos!
¡Gabrielillo de mi vida!
Para sentarte yo sueño
50 un sillón de clavellinas.
—Dios te salve, Anunciación,
bien lunada y mal vestida.
Tu niño tendrá en el pecho
un lunar y tres heridas.
—¡Ay San Gabriel que reluces!
¡Gabrielillo de mi vida!
En el fondo de mis pechos
ya nace la leche tibia.
—Dios te salve, Anunciación.
60 Madre de cien dinastías.
Áridos lucen tus ojos,
paisajes de caballista.

★

El niño canta en el seno
de Anunciación sorprendida.
Tres balas de almendra verde
tiemblan en su vocecita.

Ya San Gabriel en el aire
por una escala subía.
Las estrellas de la noche
70 se volvieron siemprevivas.

between a lily and a smile,
great-grandson of the Giralda,
was coming on his visit.
Hidden crickets pulse
in his embroidered vest.
The stars of night were turning
into tiny bellflowers.
"Here I am, St. Gabriel,
40   with three nails of delight.
Your radiance opens jasmines
on my burning face."
"God bless you, Annunciation,
dark wonder of a woman.
You will have a child more beautiful
than new shoots of the wind."
"Ay, St. Gabriel, light of my eyes!
Dearest Gabe, joy of my life!
I dream of giving you
50   a throne of carnations."
"God bless you, Annunciation,
rich in moons and poorly dressed.
On his breast your child will bear
a dark spot and three wounds."
"Ay, my radiant St. Gabriel!
Dearest Gabe, joy of my life!
Deep in my breasts
the warm milk is born."
"God bless you, Annunciation,
60   mother of a hundred dynasties.
Your eyes gleam like the arid
landscapes of horse and rider."

★

The child sings at the breast
of amazed Annunciation.
Three green–almond bullets
quiver in his little voice.

Up a ladder through the air
St. Gabriel was climbing.
And the stars of night
70   turned into everlastings.

TR. W.K.

Prendimiento de Antoñito el Camborio en el camino de Sevilla

A Margarita Xirgu

Antonio Torres Heredia,
hijo y nieto de Camborios,
con una vara de mimbre
va a Sevilla a ver los toros.
Moreno de verde luna,
anda despacio y garboso.
Sus empavonados bucles
le brillan entre los ojos.
A la mitad del camino
10 cortó limones redondos,
y los fue tirando al agua
hasta que la puso de oro.
Y a la mitad del camino,
bajo las ramas de un olmo,
Guardia Civil caminera
lo llevó codo con codo.

★

El día se va despacio,
la tarde colgada a un hombro,
dando una larga torera
20 sobre el mar y los arroyos.
Las aceitunas aguardan
la noche de Capricornio,
y una corta brisa ecuestre
salta los montes de plomo.
Antonio Torres Heredia,
hijo y nieto de Camborios,
viene sin vara de mimbre
entre los cinco tricornios.

—Antonio, ¿quién eres tú?
30 Si te llamaras Camborio,
hubieras hecho una fuente
de sangre con cinco chorros.
Ni tú eres hijo de nadie,

The Taking of Little Tony Camborio
on the Seville Highway

To Margarita Xirgu

Antonio Torres Heredia,
son and grandson of Camborios,
goes to Seville with a rod of willow
to see the bulls.
Brown as a green moon,
he walks slow and proud.
His ringlets, peacock blue,
gleam between his eyes.
The journey half over,
10 he cut some round lemons,
and threw them in the water
until it turned gold.
And the journey half over,
a squad of Civil Guardsmen,
beneath a spreading elm,
took him by the arm.

★

The day moves slowly away,
over the creeks and the sea,
the afternoon draped from its shoulder
20 like a torero, his back to the bull.
The olives are ripe
for Capricorn night;
a quick equestrian breeze
leaps the hills of lead.
Antonio Torres Heredia,
son and grandson of Camborios,
comes without his willow rod
between the five tricorn hats.

"Antonio, who are you?
30 If you were really a Camborio,
you would have made a fountain
of blood, with five gushers.
You're not even a son-of-a-no-one.

ni legítimo Camborio.
¡Se acabaron los gitanos
que iban por el monte solos!
Están los viejos cuchillos
tiritando bajo el polvo.

★

A las nueve de la noche
40 lo llevan al calabozo,
mientras los guardias civiles
beben limonada todos.
Y a las nueve de la noche
le cierran el calabozo,
mientras el cielo reluce
como la grupa de un potro.

12

Muerte de Antoñito el Camborio
A José Antonio Rubio Sacristán

Voces de muerte sonaron
cerca del Guadalquivir.
Voces antiguas que cercan
voz de clavel varonil.
Les clavó sobre las botas
mordiscos de jabalí.
En la lucha daba saltos
jabonados de delfín.
Bañó con sangre enemiga
10 su corbata carmesí,
pero eran cuatro puñales
y tuvo que sucumbir.
Cuando las estrellas clavan
rejones al agua gris,
cuando los erales sueñan
verónicas de alhelí,
voces de muerte sonaron
cerca del Guadalquivir.

You're not a true Camborio.
They're gone, all the gypsies
who walked the hills alone!
All of their old knives
are shivering beneath the dust."

★

    At nine o'clock that evening
40 they put him in a cell,
while all the Civil Guardsmen
were drinking lemonade.
And at nine o'clock that evening
they locked him in the cell,
while the sky was gleaming
like the haunches of a colt.

TR. W.K.

12

The Death of Little Tony Camborio

To José Antonio Rubio Sacristán

    Voices of death were heard
near the Guadalquivir.
Voices of old surrounding
the voice of a virile carnation.
He pierced their boots
with the sharp bites of a boar.
In the fight he took
soapy dolphin leaps.
He bathed his scarlet tie
10 in the enemy's blood,
but there were four blades
and he had to go down.
When stars drive their lances
into bulls of gray water,
when calves are dreaming
veronicas of gillyflowers,
voices of death were heard
near the Guadalquivir.

—Antonio Torres Heredia,
20 Camborio de dura crin,
moreno de verde luna,
voz de clavel varonil:
¿quién te ha quitado la vida
cerca del Guadalquivir?
—Mis cuatro primos Heredias,
hijos de Benamejí.
Lo que en otros no envidiaban,
ya lo envidiaban en mí.
Zapatos color corinto,
30 medallones de marfil,
y este cutis amasado
con aceituna y jazmín.
—¡Ay Antonio el Camborio
digno de una Emperatriz!
Acuérdate de la Virgen
porque te vas a morir.
—¡Ay Federico García,
llama a la Guardia Civil!
Ya mi talle se ha quebrado
40 como caña de maíz.

★

Tres golpes de sangre tuvo,
y se murió de perfil.
Viva moneda que nunca
se volverá a repetir.
Un ángel marchoso pone
su cabeza en un cojín.
Otros de rubor cansado,
encendieron un candil.
Y cuando los cuatro primos
50 llegan a Benamejí,
voces de muerte cesaron
cerca del Guadalquivir.

"Antonio Torres Heredia,
20   stiff-maned Camborio,
brown from green moon,
voice of a virile carnation,
who took your life
near the Guadalquivir?"
"My four Heredia cousins,
sons of Benamejí.
What they never envied in others,
they always envied in me.
Plum-colored shoes,
30   medallions of ivory,
this well-kneaded skin
of jasmine and olive."
"Ay, Little Tony Camborio,
worthy of an empress!
Think about the Virgin.
It's time for you to die."
"Ay, Federico García,
call out the Civil Guard!
My body has been broken
40   like a stalk of corn."

★

Three times his blood gushed out,
and he died in a fine silhouette:
live coin that will never
be matched by another.
A swaggering angel puts
his head upon a pillow.
Others with faint color
light an oil lamp for him.
And when the four cousins
50   return to Benamejí
voices of death were no longer heard
near the Guadalquivir.

TR. W.K.

Muerto de amor

A Margarita Manso

—¿Qué es aquello que reluce
por los altos corredores?
—Cierra la puerta, hijo mío,
acaban de dar las once.
—En mis ojos, sin querer,
relumbran cuatro faroles.
—Será que la gente aquella
estará fregando el cobre.

★

Ajo de agónica plata
10 la luna menguante, pone
cabelleras amarillas
a las amarillas torres.
La noche llama temblando
al cristal de los balcones
perseguida por los mil
perros que no la conocen,
y un olor de vino y ámbar
viene de los corredores.

★

Brisas de caña mojada
20 y rumor de viejas voces
resonaban por el arco
roto de la media noche.
Bueyes y rosas dormían.
Sólo por los corredores
las cuatro luces clamaban
con el furor de San Jorge.
Tristes mujeres del valle
bajaban su sangre de hombre,
tranquila de flor cortada
30 y amarga de muslo joven.
Viejas mujeres del río
lloraban al pie del monte,
un minuto intransitable

13

Dead from Love

To Margarita Manso

"What is that shining
along the high hallways?"
"My son, close the door,
eleven is striking."
"In my eyes, unbidden,
four lights are burning."
"It must be those people
scrubbing their copper."

★

Garlic clove of dying silver,
10   the waning moon drapes
lengths of yellow hair
on yellow towers.
Night knocks trembling
on the windows of the balcony,
chased by the thousand
dogs that do not know her.
A smell of wine and ambergris
is coming from the hallways.

★

Breezes from wet reeds
20   and the sound of ancient voices
were resonating through
the broken arch of midnight.
Rose and ox were sleeping.
Only those four lights
were screaming in the hallways
with the fury of St. George.
Sad women of the valley
were bringing down their blood of man,
calm issue of plucked flower,
30   and bitterness of young thigh.
Old women of the river,
at the bottom of the hill,
cry an impassable minute

de cabelleras y nombres.
Fachadas de cal ponían
cuadrada y blanca la noche.
Serafines y gitanos
tocaban acordeones.
—Madre, cuando yo me muera
40 que se enteren los señores.
Pon telegramas azules
que vayan del Sur al Norte.

★

Siete gritos, siete sangres,
siete adormideras dobles
quebraron opacas lunas
en los oscuros salones.
Lleno de manos cortadas
y coronitas de flores,
el mar de los juramentos
50 resonaba, no sé dónde.
Y el cielo daba portazos
al brusco rumor del bosque,
mientras clamaban las luces
en los altos corredores.

14

El emplazado

Para Emilio Aladrén

¡Mi soledad sin descanso!
Ojos chicos de mi cuerpo
y grandes de mi caballo,
no se cierran por la noche
ni miran al otro lado
donde se aleja tranquilo
un sueño de trece barcos.
Sino que limpios y duros
escuderos desvelados,
10 mis ojos miran un norte
de metales y peñascos
donde mi cuerpo sin venas
consulta naipes helados.

of long hair and names.
The whitewashed walls were turning
the night white and square.
Gypsies and seraphim
played accordions.
"Mother, when I die

40 I want the gentlemen to know.
Send blue telegrams
from South to North."

★

Seven shouts and seven bloods,
seven double poppy blooms
break the opaque mirrors
in the darkened rooms.
Full of severed hands
and little flower crowns,
the sea of oaths resounded,

50 where, I do not know.
And the sky was slamming doors
to rough noises of the woods,
while the lights were screaming
along the high hallways.

TR. W.K.

14

Ballad of the Marked Man
To Emilio Aladrén

My aloneness with no rest!
The small eyes of my body
and the great ones of my horse
do not close at night
or look aside to see
a dream of thirteen boats
receding peacefully.
But clean and hard
as watchful squires,

10 my eyes look toward a north
of crags and metals
where my veinless body
consults the frozen cards.

Los densos bueyes del agua
embisten a los muchachos
que se bañan en las lunas
de sus cuernos ondulados.
Y los martillos cantaban
sobre los yunques sonámbulos
20 el insomnio del jinete
y el insomnio del caballo.

★

El veinticinco de junio
le dijeron a el Amargo:
—Ya puedes cortar, si gustas,
las adelfas de tu patio.
Pinta una cruz en la puerta
y pon tu nombre debajo,
porque cicutas y ortigas
nacerán en tu costado,
30 y agujas de cal mojada
te morderán los zapatos.
Será de noche, en lo oscuro,
por los montes imantados
donde los bueyes del agua
beben los juncos soñando.
Pide luces y campanas.
Aprende a cruzar las manos,
y gusta los aires fríos
de metales y peñascos.
40 Porque dentro de dos meses
yacerás amortajado.

★

Espadón de nebulosa
mueve en el aire Santiago.
Grave silencio, de espalda,
manaba el cielo combado.

★

El veinticinco de junio
abrió sus ojos Amargo,

Dense oxen of water
charge at the boys
bathing in the moons
of their rippling horns.
Hammers were singing
on somnambulistic anvils
20   insomnia of rider,
insomnia of horse.

★

On the twenty-fifth of June
they told El Amargo:
"The time has come to cut
the oleanders in your courtyard.
Paint a cross on your door
and put your name beneath it,
for nettle and hemlock
will grow from your side,
30   and needles of wet lime
will gnaw through your shoes.
It will be at night, in darkness,
in the magnetic mountains
where the water oxen
drink the reeds and dream.
Ask for lights and bells.
Learn to cross your hands
and taste the freezing winds
of crags and metals:
40   before two months are gone
you will lie in shrouds."

★

Santiago swings his sword,
a nebula, across the sky.
Somber silence flowed
out of arching heaven.

★

On the twenty-fifth of June
El Amargo opened his eyes,

y el veinticinco de agosto
se tendió para cerrarlos.
50   Hombres bajaban la calle
para ver al emplazado,
que fijaba sobre el muro
su soledad con descanso.
Y la sábana impecable,
de duro acento romano,
daba equilibrio a la muerte
con las rectas de sus paños.

15

Romance de la Guardia Civil Española

A Juan Guerrero.
Cónsul general de la poesía

Los caballos negros son.
Las herraduras son negras.
Sobre las capas relucen
manchas de tinta y de cera.
Tienen, por eso no lloran,
de plomo las calaveras.
Con el alma de charol
vienen por la carretera.
Jorobados y nocturnos,
10   por donde animan ordenan
silencios de goma oscura
y miedos de fina arena.
Pasan, si quieren pasar,
y ocultan en la cabeza
una vaga astronomía
de pistolas inconcretas.

          ★

¡Oh ciudad de los gitanos!
En las esquinas banderas.
La luna y la calabaza
20   con las guindas en conserva.
¡Oh ciudad de los gitanos!
¿Quién te vio y no te recuerda?

and the twenty-fifth of August
he lay down and closed them.
50 Men were coming down the street
to see the man who was to die,
who threw across the wall
his aloneness, now at rest.
And the spotless sheet,
with its strong accent of Rome,
gave equilibrium to death
by the straightness of its folds.

TR. W.K.

15

Ballad of the Spanish Civil Guard

To Juan Guerrero.
Consul General of Poetry

Black are the horses,
the horseshoes are black.
Glistening on their capes
are stains of ink and of wax.
Their skulls—and this is why
they do not cry—are cast in lead.
They ride the roads
with souls of patent leather.
Hunchbacked and nocturnal,
10 they command, where they appear,
the silence of dark rubber
and fears of fine sand.
They go as they will,
and hidden in their heads
is a vague astronomy
of phantasmagoric pistols.

★

Oh city of the gypsies!
Corners hung with banners.
The moon and pumpkins,
20 and cherries in preserve.
Oh city of the gypsies!
Who could see and not remember you?

Ciudad de dolor y almizcle,
con las torres de canela.

★

Cuando llegaba la noche,
noche que noche nochera,
los gitanos en sus fraguas
forjaban soles y flechas.
Un caballo malherido
30 llamaba a todas las puertas.
Gallos de vidrio cantaban
por Jerez de la Frontera.
El viento vuelve desnudo
la esquina de la sorpresa,
en la noche platinoche,
noche que noche nochera.

★

La Virgen y San José
perdieron sus castañuelas,
y buscan a los gitanos
40 para ver si las encuentran.
La Virgen viene vestida
con un traje de alcaldesa
de papel de chocolate
con los collares de almendras.
San José mueve los brazos
bajo una capa de seda.
Detrás va Pedro Domecq
con tres sultanes de Persia.
La media luna soñaba
50 un éxtasis de cigüeña.
Estandartes y faroles
invaden las azoteas.
Por los espejos sollozan
bailarinas sin caderas.
Agua y sombra, sombra y agua
por Jerez de la Frontera.

City of musk and sorrow,
city of cinnamon towers.

★

    As the night was coming,
the night so nightly night,
the gypsies at their forges
were shaping suns and arrows.
A badly wounded stallion
₃₀ knocked at every door.
Glass roosters were singing
in Jerez de la Frontera.
The naked wind turns
the corner of surprise,
in the night silvernight,
the night so nightly night.

★

    The Virgin and St. Joseph
have lost their castanets,
and are looking for the gypsies
₄₀ to see if they can find them.
Here comes the Virgin, dressed
just like a mayor's wife,
in silver chocolate foil
with necklaces of almonds.
St. Joseph swings his arms
beneath a cape of silk.
Behind them comes Pedro Domecq
and three Persian sultans.
The half moon was dreaming
₅₀ an ecstasy of storks.
And streamers and lamps
took over terraced roofs.
A dancer without hips
sobbed in every mirror.
Water and shadow, shadow and water
in Jerez de la Frontera.

★

¡Oh ciudad de los gitanos!
En las esquinas banderas.
Apaga tus verdes luces
60   que viene la benemérita.
¡Oh ciudad de los gitanos!
¿Quién te vio y no te recuerda?
Dejadla lejos del mar
sin peines para sus crenchas.

★

Avanzan de dos en fondo
a la ciudad de la fiesta.
Un rumor de siemprevivas,
invade las cartucheras.
Avanzan de dos en fondo.
70   Doble nocturno de tela.
El cielo, se les antoja,
una vitrina de espuelas.

★

La ciudad, libre de miedo,
multiplicaba sus puertas.
Cuarenta guardias civiles
entran a saco por ellas.
Los relojes se pararon,
y el coñac de las botellas
se disfrazó de noviembre
80   para no infundir sospechas.
Un vuelo de gritos largos
se levantó en las veletas.
Los sables cortan las brisas
que los cascos atropellan.
Por las calles de penumbra
huyen las gitanas viejas
con los caballos dormidos
y las orzas de monedas.
Por las calles empinadas
90   suben las capas siniestras,
dejando detrás fugaces
remolinos de tijeras.

Oh city of the gypsies!
Corners hung with flags.
Put your green lights out:
60 the Civil Guard is coming.
Oh city of the gypsies!
Who could see and not remember you?
Let her be, far from the sea,
with no combs to hold her hair.

★

They are riding two abreast
to the celebrating city.
The murmur of everlastings
invades their cartridge belts.
They are riding two abreast.
70 A night of doubled serge.
The sky, they like to fancy,
is a showcase full of spurs.

★

The city, free of fear,
was multiplying doors.
Forty Civil Guardsmen
pour through to sack and burn.
The clocks came to a stop
and the brandy bottles
masqueraded as November
80 so as not to stir suspicions.
A flight of long screams
rose from the weathercocks.
Sabers slash at breezes
trampled under hoof.
Through the half-lit streets
old gypsy women flee
with their sleepy horses
and enormous jars of coins.
Up the steep streets
90 climb the sinister capes,
leaving behind them
brief whirlwinds of shears.

En el Portal de Belén
los gitanos se congregan.
San José, lleno de heridas,
amortaja a una doncella.
Tercos fusiles agudos
por toda la noche suenan.
La Virgen cura a los niños
100 con salivilla de estrella.
Pero la Guardia Civil
avanza sembrando hogueras,
donde joven y desnuda
la imaginación se quema.
Rosa la de los Camborios,
gime sentada en su puerta
con sus dos pechos cortados
puestos en una bandeja.
Y otras muchachas corrían
110 perseguidas por sus trenzas,
en un aire donde estallan
rosas de pólvora negra.
Cuando todos los tejados
eran surcos en la tierra,
el alba meció sus hombros
en largo perfil de piedra.

★

¡Oh ciudad de los gitanos!
La Guardia Civil se aleja
por un túnel de silencio
120 mientras las llamas te cercan.

¡Oh ciudad de los gitanos!
¿Quién te vio y no te recuerda?
Que te busquen en mi frente.
Juego de luna y arena.

In the manger of Bethlehem
all the gypsies gather.
St. Joseph, badly wounded,
lays a shroud upon a girl.
Sharp and stubborn, rifles
crackle in the night.
The Virgin mends the children
100 with saliva from a star.
But the Civil Guard advances,
sowing giant fires,
where, young and naked,
imagination burns.
Rosa, the Camborio,
sits moaning at her door
with her severed breasts
before her on a tray.
Other girls were running
110 chased by their braids,
in a wind exploding
with roses of black powder.
When all the tiled roofs
were furrows in the earth,
dawn heaved its shoulders
in a silhouette of stone.

★

Oh city of the gypsies!
The Civil Guardsmen ride away
through a tunnel of silence
120 while the flames encircle you.

Oh city of the gypsies!
Who could see you and not remember you?
Let them find you on my brow:
play of sand and moon.

                              TR. W.K.

Tres romances históricos

16

Martirio de Santa Olalla

A Rafael Martínez Nadal

I

Panorama de Mérida

Por la calle brinca y corre
caballo de larga cola,
mientras juegan o dormitan
viejos soldados de Roma.
Medio monte de Minervas
abre sus brazos sin hojas.
Agua en vilo redoraba
las aristas de las rocas.
Noche de torsos yacentes
10 y estrellas de nariz rota,
aguarda grietas del alba
para derrumbarse toda.
De cuando en cuando sonaban
blasfemias de cresta roja.
Al gemir la santa niña
quiebra el cristal de las copas.
La rueda afila cuchillos
y garfios de aguda comba.
Brama el toro de los yunques,
20 y Mérida se corona
de nardos casi despiertos
y tallos de zarzamora.

II

El martirio

Flora desnuda se sube
por escalerillas de agua.

Three Historical Ballads

16

Martyrdom of St. Eulalia

To Rafael Martínez Nadal

I

Panorama of Mérida

    A full-tailed stallion rears
and races down the street.
Old soldiers far from Rome
play at cards or sleep.
A half hill of Minervas
opens its leafless arms.
Suspended water gilds
the edges of the stones.
A night of scattered torsos
10 and stars of broken noses
waits for cracks of dawn
to completely tumble down.
Now and then red-crested
blasphemy resounds.
The blessed girl's moaning
breaks the crystal goblets.
Knives and meat hooks
are sharpened on the wheel.
The roaring anvil bulls begin
20 and Mérida is crowned
with half-awakened spikenard
and shoots of tangled thorns.

I I

The Martyrdom

    Naked Flora climbs
the little cascade stairs.

El Cónsul pide bandeja
para los senos de Olalla.
Un chorro de venas verdes
le brota de la garganta.
Su sexo tiembla enredado
como un pájaro en las zarzas.
Por el suelo, ya sin norma,
brincan sus manos cortadas
que aún pueden cruzarse en tenue
oración decapitada.
Por los rojos agujeros
donde sus pechos estaban
se ven cielos diminutos
y arroyos de leche blanca.
Mil arbolillos de sangre
le cubren toda la espalda
y oponen húmedos troncos
al bisturí de las llamas.
Centuriones amarillos,
de carne gris, desvelada,
llegan al cielo sonando
sus armaduras de plata.
Y mientras vibra confusa
pasión de crines y espadas,
el Cónsul porta en bandeja
senos ahumados de Olalla.

III

Infierno y gloria

Nieve ondulada reposa.
Olalla pende del árbol.
Su desnudo de carbón
tizna los aires helados.
Noche tirante reluce.
Olalla muerta en el árbol.
Tinteros de las ciudades
vuelcan la tinta despacio.
Negros maniquís de sastre
cubren la nieve del campo
en largas filas que gimen

The Consul asks a tray
to put Eulalia's breasts on.
A gusher of green veins
blossoms from her throat.
Her trembling sex is tangled
30   like a bird in thorns.
On the ground, directionless,
leap her severed hands,
able still to join
in sweet, decapitated prayer.
In the crimson holes
where her breasts were,
streams of white milk
and miniature heavens are seen.
A thousand tiny trees of blood
40   spread across her back,
their damp trunks holding off
the scalpel of the flames.
Centurions in yellow
with graying, sleepless flesh,
arrive in heaven, clanging
suits of silver armor.
While through the fevered
throb of sword and mane
the Consul carries on his tray
50   Eulalia's smoke-dark breasts.

I I I

Inferno and Glory

Undulating snow lies still.
Eulalia hangs from the tree.
The carbon of her nakedness
smears the freezing wind.
Night pulls taut and gleams.
Eulalia, dead in the tree.
The inkwells of the cities
slowly spill their ink.
Black tailors' mannequins
60   cover snowy fields
in long lines that moan

su silencio mutilado.
Nieve partida comienza.
Olalla blanca en el árbol.
Escuadras de níquel juntan
los picos en su costado.

★

Una Custodia reluce
sobre los cielos quemados,
entre gargantas de arroyo
70 y ruiseñores en ramos.
¡Saltan vidrios de colores!
Olalla blanca en lo blanco.
Ángeles y serafines
dicen: Santo, Santo, Santo.

17

Burla de don Pedro a caballo
(Romance con lagunas)
A Jean Cassou

Por una vereda
venía Don Pedro.
¡Ay, cómo lloraba
el caballero!
Montado en un ágil
caballo sin freno,
venía en la busca
del pan y del beso.
Todas las ventanas
10 preguntan al viento
por el llanto oscuro
del caballero.

Primera laguna

Bajo el agua
siguen las palabras.
Sobre el agua
una luna redonda

their mutilated silence.
Broken snow begins again.
Eulalia, white in the tree.
Squads of nickel join
their sharp beaks in her side.

★

A golden Shrine of Christ
shines in burned-out skies,
from gorges in the hills
70 to nightingales in branches.
Bits of stained glass leap.
Eulalia white on white.
The Angels and the Seraphim
sing: Holy, Holy, Holy.

TR. W.K.

17

Joke about Don Pedro on Horseback
(Ballad with Lacunae and Lagoons)
To Jean Cassou

Along a trail
Don Pedro came.
Oh how that gentleman
was weeping!
Upon a nimble
horse, without a bit,
he came in search of
bread and kisses.
All the windows
10 ask the wind
about the dark cries
of that gentleman.

First Lacuna

Under the water
the words continue.
On top of the water
a round moon

se baña,
dando envidia a la otra
¡tan alta!
20 En la orilla,
un niño,
ve las lunas y dice:
¡Noche; toca los platillos!

Sigue

A una ciudad lejana
ha llegado Don Pedro.
Una ciudad lejana
entre un bosque de cedros.
¿Es Belén? Por el aire
yerbaluisa y romero.
30 Brillan las azoteas
y las nubes. Don Pedro
pasa por arcos rotos.
Dos mujeres y un viejo
con velones de plata
le salen al encuentro.
Los chopos dicen: No.
Y el ruiseñor: Veremos.

Segunda laguna

Bajo el agua
siguen las palabras.
40 Sobre el peinado del agua
un círculo de pájaros y llamas.
Y por los cañaverales,
testigos que conocen lo que falta.
Sueño concreto y sin norte
de madera de guitarra.

Sigue

Por el camino llano
dos mujeres y un viejo
con velones de plata

is bathing,
filling with envy
the other—so high!
20 And on the bank,
a child
sees the moons and says:
"Nighttime, play your cymbals!"

It Continues

Don Pedro has come
to a distant city.
A distant city
in a forest of cedar.
Is it Bethlehem? Lemon verbena
and rosemary float in the wind.
30 Terraces and clouds
are gleaming. Don Pedro
rides through broken arches.
An old man and two women
come out to meet him
bearing silver lamps.
The poplars say, "No."
And the nightingale, "We'll see."

Second Lacuna

Under the water
the words continue.
40 Over the water's combed hair.
is a circle of birds and flames.
And in the canebrakes,
witnesses who know what's missing.
A specific, aimless dream
of guitar wood.

It Continues

Down the level road
an old man and two women
bearing silver lamps

van al cementerio.
50 Entre los azafranes
han encontrado muerto
el sombrío caballo
de Don Pedro.
Voz secreta de tarde
balaba por el cielo.
Unicornio de ausencia
rompe en cristal su cuerno.
La gran ciudad lejana
está ardiendo
60 y un hombre va llorando
tierras adentro.
Al Norte hay una estrella.
Al Sur un marinero.

Última laguna

    Bajo el agua
están las palabras.
Limo de voces perdidas.
Sobre la flor enfriada,
está Don Pedro olvidado
¡ay!, jugando con las ranas.

TR. W.K.

18

Thamar y Amnón

Para Alfonso García Valdecasas

    La luna gira en el cielo
sobre las tierras sin agua
mientras el verano siembra
rumores de tigre y llama.
Por encima de los techos
nervios de metal sonaban.
Aire rizado venía
con los balidos de lana.
La tierra se ofrece llena
10 de heridas cicatrizadas,

are going to the cemetery.
50 They have found
Don Pedro's somber horse
among the saffron
flowers, dead.
Secret voice of afternoon
was bleating in the sky.
Unicorn of absence
breaks his horn on glass.
The great and distant
city burns, while
60 far inland
a man is crying.
To the north, a star.
To the south, a sailor.

Last Lacuna

Under the water
the words remain.
Silt of lost voices.
Don Pedro forgotten,
on the chilled flower, ay!
and playing with the frogs.

18

Thamar and Amnon

For Alfonso García Valdecasas

The moon circles the sky
over dry lands,
while the summer sows
rumbling of tiger and flame.
Above the rooftops
metal nerves were ringing.
A wind full of curls
came with woolly bleatings.
The earth offers itself
10 covered with scars

o estremecida de agudos
cauterios de luces blancas.

★

Thamar estaba soñando
pájaros en su garganta,
al son de panderos fríos
y cítaras enlunadas.
Su desnudo en el alero,
agudo norte de palma,
pide copos a su vientre
20 y granizo a sus espaldas.
Thamar estaba cantando
desnuda por la terraza.
Alrededor de sus pies,
cinco palomas heladas.
Amnón delgado y concreto,
en la torre la miraba,
llenas las ingles de espuma
y oscilaciones la barba.
Su desnudo iluminado
30 se tendía en la terraza,
con un rumor entre dientes
de flecha recién clavada.
Amnón estaba mirando
la luna redonda y baja,
y vio en la luna los pechos
durísimos de su hermana.

★

Amnón a las tres y media
se tendió sobre la cama.
Toda la alcoba sufría
40 con sus ojos llenos de alas.
La luz maciza sepulta
pueblos en la arena parda,
o descubre transitorio
coral de rosas y dalias.
Linfa de pozo oprimida
brota silencio en las jarras.
En el musgo de los troncos
la cobra tendida canta.

or shuddering from the sharp
and cauterizing light.

★

Thamar was dreaming
of birds in her throat
to a tune of cold tambourines
and moonstruck zithers.
Her nakedness at roof edge,
sharp pole star of a palm,
asks snowflakes for her belly
20 and hailstones for her back.
Thamar was singing
naked on the terrace.
Circled round her feet,
five frozen doves.
Amnon, thin and hard,
watched her from the tower,
loins full of foam,
and beard, of small vibrations.
His gleaming nakedness
30 stretched out on the terrace,
biting back the murmur
of a just-struck arrow.
Amnon was looking
at the moon, low and round,
and saw in the moon
the hard breasts of his sister.

★

At half past three, Amnon
lay down on the bed.
The whole room was suffering
40 with his wing-filled eyes.
The solid light entombs
villages in ocher sand
or reveals a transitory
choir of dahlias and roses.
Pent-up lymph of wells
spurts silence in the jars.
In the moss of tree limbs
the uncoiled cobra sings.

Amnón gime por la tela
50 fresquísima de la cama.
Yedra del escalofrío
cubre su carne quemada.
Thamar entró silenciosa
en la alcoba silenciada,
color de vena y Danubio,
turbia de huellas lejanas.
—Thamar, bórrame los ojos
con tu fija madrugada.
Mis hilos de sangre tejen
60 volantes sobre tu falda.
—Déjame tranquila, hermano.
Son tus besos en mi espalda
avispas y vientecillos
en doble enjambre de flautas.
—Thamar, en tus pechos altos
hay dos peces que me llaman
y en las yemas de tus dedos
rumor de rosa encerrada.

★

Los cien caballos del rey
70 en el patio relinchaban.
Sol en cubos resistía
la delgadez de la parra.
Ya la coge del cabello,
ya la camisa le rasga.
Corales tibios dibujan
arroyos en rubio mapa.

★

¡Oh, qué gritos se sentían
por encima de las casas!
Qué espesura de puñales
80 y túnicas desgarradas.
Por las escaleras tristes
esclavos suben y bajan.
Émbolos y muslos juegan
bajo las nubes paradas.
Alrededor de Thamar
gritan vírgenes gitanas

Amnon is softly moaning
on the sheets' cool chill.
The ivy of a shiver
covers burning flesh.
Thamar enters silently
the silence of the room,
the color of vein and Danube,
dark from distant signs.
"Erase my eyes, Thamar,
with your appointed dawn.
The threads of my blood
weave ruffles on your dress."
"Brother, leave me. Please.
Your kisses on my back
are wasps and puffs of wind,
flutes in double swarms."
"From your high breasts, Thamar,
two fish are calling me,
and on your fingertips
murmur of a cloistered rose."

★

The hundred horses of the king
whinnied in the courtyard.
Cubes of sun pressed hard
on the thinness of the vine.
Now he takes her by the hair,
now he tears her underthings.
Warm corals drawing little creeks
across a map of blonde.

★

Oh, what shouts were heard
over all the houses!
What thickets of knives
and tunics torn.
On the stairways, saddened
slaves go up and down.
Thighs and pistons play
beneath the halted clouds.
Around Thamar
virgin gypsies shout,

y otras recogen las gotas
de su flor martirizada.
Paños blancos, enrojecen
90   en las alcobas cerradas.
Rumores de tibia aurora
pámpanos y peces cambian.

                 ★

    Violador enfurecido,
Amnón huye con su jaca.
Negros le dirigen flechas
en los muros y atalayas.
Y cuando los cuatro cascos
eran cuatro resonancias,
David con unas tijeras
100   cortó las cuerdas del arpa.

and others gather up the drops
of her martyred flower.
White cloth turns to red
90 behind the bedroom doors.
Warm sunrise full of noises,
exchanged by fish and vines.

★

    Ravisher enraged,
Amnon flees on his pony.
Negroes loose their arrows on him
from parapets and towers.
And when the four hooves
had become four echoes,
King David took a scissors
100 and cut the strings of his harp.

TR. W.K.

[ODAS]

[SLAVDOR ADIL *(Peintre), ca. 1925*]

[ODES]

Translated by

William Bryant Logan,

Greg Simon, and

Steven F. White

[SLAVDOR ADIL *(Peintre), ca. 1925*]

Oda a Salvador Dalí

Una rosa en el alto jardín que tú deseas.
Una rueda en la pura sintaxis del acero.
Desnuda la montaña de niebla impresionista.
Los grises oteando sus balaustradas últimas.

Los pintores modernos en sus blancos estudios,
cortan la flor aséptica de la raíz cuadrada.
En las aguas del Sena un *ice-berg* de mármol
enfría las ventanas y disipa las yedras.

El hombre pisa fuerte las calles enlosadas.
10 Los cristales esquivan la magia del reflejo.
El Gobierno ha cerrado las tiendas de perfume.
La máquina eterniza sus compases binarios.

Una ausencia de bosques, biombos y entrecejos
yerra por los tejados de las casas antiguas.
El aire pulimenta su prisma sobre el mar
y el horizonte sube como un gran acueducto.

Marineros que ignoran el vino y la penumbra,
decapitan sirenas en los mares de plomo.
La Noche, negra estatua de la prudencia, tiene
20 el espejo redondo de la luna en su mano.

Un deseo de formas y límites nos gana.
Viene el hombre que mira con el metro amarillo.
Venus es una blanca naturaleza muerta
y los coleccionistas de mariposas huyen.

★

Cadaqués, en el fiel del agua y la colina,
eleva escalinatas y oculta caracolas.
Las flautas de madera pacifican el aire.
Un viejo dios silvestre da frutas a los niños.

Sus pescadores duermen, sin ensueño, en la arena.
30 En alta mar les sirve de brújula una rosa.
El horizonte virgen de pañuelos heridos,
junta los grandes vidrios del pez y de la luna.

Ode to Salvador Dalí

A rose in the high garden you desire.
A wheel in the pure syntax of steel.
The mountain stripped bare of Impressionist fog.
The grays watching over the last balustrades.

The modern painters in their white ateliers
clip the square root's sterilized flower.
In the waters of the Seine a marble iceberg
chills the windows and scatters the ivy.

Man treads firmly on the cobbled streets.
10 Windows elude the magic of reflections.
The Government has closed the perfume stores.
The machine perpetuates its binary beat.

An absence of forests and screens and brows
roams across the roofs of the old houses.
The air polishes its prism on the sea
and the horizon rises like a great aqueduct.

Sailors who know no wine and no penumbra
behead the sirens on the seas of lead.
Night, black statue of prudence, holds
20 the moon's round mirror in her hand.

A desire for forms and limits overwhelms us.
Here comes the man who sees with a yellow ruler.
Venus is a white still life
and the butterfly collectors run away.

★

Cadaqués, at the fulcrum of water and hill,
lifts flights of stairs and hides seashells.
Wooden flutes pacify the air.
An ancient woodland god gives the children fruit.

Her fishermen sleep dreamless on the sand.
30 On the high seas a rose is their compass.
The horizon, virgin of wounded handkerchiefs,
links the great crystals of fish and moon.

617

Una dura corona de blancos bergantines
ciñe frentes amargas y cabellos de arena.
Las sirenas convencen, pero no sugestionan,
y salen si mostramos un vaso de agua dulce.

★

¡Oh Salvador Dalí, de voz aceitunada!
No elogio tu imperfecto pincel adolescente
ni tu color que ronda la color de tu tiempo,
40   pero alabo tus ansias de eterno limitado.

Alma higiénica, vives sobre mármoles nuevos.
Huyes la oscura selva de formas increíbles.
Tu fantasía llega donde llegan tus manos,
y gozas el soneto del mar en tu ventana.

El mundo tiene sordas penumbras y desorden,
en los primeros términos que el humano frecuenta.
Pero ya las estrellas ocultando paisajes,
señalan el esquema perfecto de sus órbitas.

La corriente del tiempo se remansa y ordena
50   en las formas numéricas de un siglo y otro siglo.
Y la Muerte vencida se refugia temblando
en el círculo estrecho del minuto presente.

Al coger tu paleta, con un tiro en un ala,
pides la luz que anima la copa del olivo.
Ancha luz de Minerva, constructora de andamios,
donde no cabe el sueño ni su flora inexacta.

Pides la luz antigua que se queda en la frente,
sin bajar a la boca ni al corazón del hombre.
Luz que temen las vides entrañables de Baco
60   y la fuerza sin orden que lleva el agua curva.

Haces bien en poner banderines de aviso,
en el límite oscuro que relumbra de noche.
Como pintor no quieres que te ablande la forma
el algodón cambiante de una nube imprevista.

El pez en la pecera y el pájaro en la jaula.
No quieres inventarlos en el mar o en el viento.

A hard diadem of white brigantines
encircles bitter foreheads and hair of sand.
The sirens convince, but they don't beguile,
and they come if we show a glass of fresh water.

★

Oh Salvador Dalí, of the olive-colored voice!
I do not praise your halting adolescent brush
or your pigments that flirt with the pigment of your times,
40 but I laud your longing for eternity with limits.

Sanitary soul, you live upon new marble.
You run from the dark jungle of improbable forms.
Your fancy reaches only as far as your hands,
and you enjoy the sonnet of the sea in your window.

The world is dull penumbra and disorder
in the foreground where man is found.
But now the stars, concealing landscapes,
reveal the perfect schema of their courses.

The current of time pools and gains order
50 in the numbered forms of century after century.
And conquered Death takes refuge trembling
in the tight circle of the present instant.

When you take up your palette, a bullet hole in its wing,
you call on the light that brings the olive tree to life.
The broad light of Minerva, builder of scaffolds,
where there is no room for dream or its hazy flower.

You call on the old light that stays on the brow,
not descending to the mouth or the heart of man.
A light that the loving vines of Bacchus
60 and the chaotic force of curving water fear.

You do well when you post warning flags
along the dark limit that shines in the night.
As a painter, you refuse to have your forms softened
by the shifting cotton of an unexpected cloud.

The fish in the fishbowl and the bird in the cage.
You refuse to invent them in the sea or the air.

Estilizas o copias después de haber mirado,
con honestas pupilas sus cuerpecillos ágiles.

Amas una materia definida y exacta
70   donde el hongo no pueda poner su campamento.
Amas la arquitectura que construye en lo ausente
y admites la bandera como una simple broma.

Dice el compás de acero su corto verso elástico.
Desconocidas islas desmiente ya la esfera.
Dice la línea recta su vertical esfuerzo
y los sabios cristales cantan sus geometrías.

★

Pero también la rosa del jardín donde vives.
¡Siempre la rosa, siempre, norte y sur de nosotros!
Tranquila y concentrada como una estatua ciega,
80   ignorante de esfuerzos soterrados que causa.

Rosa pura que limpia de artificios y croquis
y nos abre las alas tenues de la sonrisa.
(Mariposa clavada que medita su vuelo.)
Rosa del equilibrio sin dolores buscados.
¡Siempre la rosa!

★

¡Oh Salvador Dalí de voz aceitunada!
Digo lo que me dicen tu persona y tus cuadros.
No alabo tu imperfecto pincel adolescente,
pero canto la firme dirección de tus flechas.

90   Canto tu bello esfuerzo de luces catalanas,
tu amor a lo que tiene explicación posible.
Canto tu corazón astronómico y tierno,
de baraja francesa y sin ninguna herida.

Canto el ansia de estatua que persigues sin tregua,
el miedo a la emoción que te aguarda en la calle.
Canto la sirenita de la mar que te canta
montada en bicicleta de corales y conchas.

Pero ante todo canto un común pensamiento
que nos une en las horas oscuras y doradas.

You stylize or copy once you have seen
their small, agile bodies with your honest eyes.

You love a matter definite and exact,
70 where the toadstool cannot pitch its camp.
You love the architecture that builds on the absent
and admit the flag simply as a joke.

The steel compass tells its short, elastic verse.
The sphere denies unknown islands.
The straight line tells of its upward struggle
and the learned crystals sing their geometries.

★

But also the rose of the garden where you live.
Always the rose, always, our north and south!
Calm and ingathered like an eyeless statue,
80 not knowing the buried struggle it provokes.

Pure rose, which cleanses us of artifice and rough sketches,
opening for us the slender wings of the smile.
(Pinned butterfly that ponders its flight.)
Rose of balance, with no self-inflicted pains.
Always the rose!

★

Oh Salvador Dalí, of the olive-colored voice!
I speak of what your person and your paintings tell me.
I do not praise your halting adolescent brush,
but I sing the steady aim of your arrows.

90 I sing your fair struggle of Catalan lights,
your love of what might be made clear.
I sing your astronomical and tender heart,
a never-wounded deck of French cards.

I sing your restless longing for the statue,
your fear of the feelings that await you in the street.
I sing the small sea siren who sings to you,
riding her bicycle of corals and conches.

But above all I sing a common thought
that joins us in the dark and golden hours.

No es el Arte la luz que nos ciega los ojos.
Es primero el amor, la amistad o la esgrima.

Es primero que el cuadro que paciente dibujas
el seno de Teresa, la de cutis insomne,
el apretado bucle de Matilde la ingrata,
nuestra amistad pintada como un juego de oca.

Huellas dactilográficas de sangre sobre el oro,
rayen el corazón de Cataluña eterna.
Estrellas como puños sin halcón te relumbren,
mientras que tu pintura y tu vida florecen.

110 No mires la clepsidra con alas membranosas,
ni la dura guadaña de las alegorías.
Viste y desnuda siempre tu pincel en el aire
frente a la mar poblada con barcos y marinos.

Soledad

Homenaje a Fray Luis de León

Difícil delgadez:
¿Busca el mundo una blanca,
total, perenne ausencia?
—Jorge Guillén

Soledad pensativa
sobre piedra y rosal, muerte y desvelo,
donde libre y cautiva,
fija en su blanco vuelo,
canta la luz herida por el hielo.

Soledad con estilo
de silencio sin fin y arquitectura,
donde la flauta en vilo
del ave en la espesura,
10   no consigue clavar tu carne oscura.

En ti dejo olvidada
la frenética lluvia de mis venas,
mi cintura cuajada:

100 The light that blinds our eyes is not art.
Rather it is love, friendship, crossed swords.

   Not the picture you patiently trace,
but the breast of Theresa, she of sleepless skin,
the tight-wound curls of Mathilde the ungrateful,
our friendship, painted bright as a game board.

   May fingerprints of blood on gold
streak the heart of eternal Catalunya.
May stars like falconless fists shine on you,
while your painting and your life break into flower.

110   Don't watch the water clock with its membraned wings
or the hard scythe of the allegory.
Always in the air, dress and undress your brush
before the sea peopled with sailors and with ships.

TR. W.B.L.

Solitude

In homage to Fray Luis de León

> *Difficult slenderness:*
> *Does the world seek a white,*
> *whole, everlasting absence?*
> *—Jorge Guillén*

   Thoughtful solitude
upon rosebush and stone, death and waking,
where free and captive,
fixed in her white flight,
the light sings wounded by the ice.

   Solitude with style
of endless silence and architecture,
where the suspended flute
of the bird in the thicket
10 cannot pierce your dark flesh.

   In you I leave behind,
forgotten, the frantic rain of my veins,
my hardened waist;

y rompiendo cadenas,
rosa débil seré por las arenas.

Rosa de mi desnudo
sobre paños de cal y sordo fuego,
cuando roto ya el nudo,
limpio de luna, y ciego,
20   cruce tus fijas ondas de sosiego.

★

En la curva del río
el doble cisne su blancura canta.
Húmeda voz sin frío
fluye de su garganta,
y por los juncos rueda y se levanta.

Con su rosa de harina
niño desnudo mide la ribera,
mientras el bosque afina
su música primera
30   en rumor de cristales y madera.

Coros de siemprevivas
giran locos pidiendo eternidades.
Sus señas expresivas
hieren las dos mitades
del mapa que rezuma soledades.

El arpa y su lamento
prendido en nervios de metal dorado,
tanto dulce instrumento
resonante o delgado,
40   buscan ¡oh soledad! tu reino helado.

Mientras tú, inaccesible
para la verde lepra del sonido,
no hay altura posible
ni labio conocido,
por donde llegue a ti nuestro gemido.

and breaking chains
I will become a weak rose on the sands.

 Rose of my naked form
on cloth of lime and soundless fire;
once the knot is broken,
clean of moon and blind,
20 I'll sail upon your fixed waves of repose.

★

 At the river's bend
the double swan is singing her own whiteness.
A wet voice, not cold,
flows from her throat
and wheels around and rises in the reeds.

 With his rose of flour
a naked boy is measuring the banks,
while the forest tunes
its primordial music
30 to murmuring of crystals and of wood.

 Choirs of immortelles
circle, begging for eternities.
Their clear gestures
wound the two halves
of the map that oozes solitudes.

 The harp and its lament
caught in nerves of golden metal,
such sweet instruments,
slender or resounding,
40 seek—oh solitude!—your frozen kingdom.

 And you, whom the green
leprosy of sound can never reach,
there's no created height
nor any known lip
through which our moans might come at last to you.

TR. W.B.L.

Oda al Santísimo Sacramento del Altar
Homenaje a Manuel de Falla

Exposición

> *Pange, lingua, gloriosi*
> *corporis mysterium.*

Cantaban las mujeres por el muro clavado
cuando te vi, Dios fuerte, vivo en el Sacramento,
palpitante y desnudo como un niño que corre
perseguido por siete novillos capitales.

Vivo estabas, Dios mío, dentro del ostensorio.
Punzado por tu Padre con agujas de lumbre.
Latiendo como el pobre corazón de la rana
que los médicos ponen en el frasco de vidrio.

Piedra de soledad donde la hierba gime
10 y donde el agua oscura pierde sus tres acentos,
elevan tu columna de nardo bajo nieve
sobre el mundo de ruedas y falos que circula.

Yo miraba tu forma deliciosa flotando
en la llaga de aceites y paño de agonía,
y entornaba mis ojos para darle en el dulce
tiro al blanco de insomnio sin un pájaro negro.

Es así, Dios anclado, como quiero tenerte.
Panderito de harina para el recién nacido.
Brisa y materia juntas en expresión exacta
20 por amor de la carne que no sabe tu nombre.

Es así, forma breve de rumor inefable,
Dios en mantillas, Cristo diminuto y eterno,
repetido mil veces, muerto, crucificado
por la impura palabra del hombre sudoroso.

Cantaban las mujeres en la arena sin norte,
cuando te vi presente sobre tu Sacramento.
Quinientos serafines de resplandor y tinta
en la cúpula neutra gustaban tu racimo.

Ode to the Most Holy Sacrament of the Altar
In homage to Manuel de Falla

Exposition

*Pange, lingua, gloriosi
corporis mysterium.*

The women were singing by the spiked wall,
All-Powerful God, when I saw you
alive in the Sacrament, vibrant, naked,
like a boy running from seven capital bulls.

You, my God, alive inside the monstrance.
Pierced by your Father's needles of fire.
Beating like the poor heart of a frog
kept in a glass container by the doctors.

Oh stone of loneliness where the grass moans
10 and the dark water forfeits its three accents,
they lift your column of spikenard under snow
above the turning world of wheel and phallus.

I watched while your delicious form floated
on the annointed wound and the death cloth.
I narrowed my eyes to hit it: sweet bull's-eye
of insomnia without a black bird.

Anchored God, this is the way I want you.
Small flour tambourine for the newborn child.
Breath of wind and matter exactly joined
20 for love of the flesh that doesn't know your name.

Like this, concise form of ineffable murmurs,
swaddling-clothed God, tiny eternal Christ,
said a thousand times, who died, crucified
by the impure words of sweating men.

The women were singing in the aimless sands
when I saw your presence above your Sacrament.
Five hundred brilliant, inky seraphim
tasted your grapes in the neutral dome.

¡Oh Forma sacratísima, vértice de las flores,
donde todos los ángulos toman sus luces fijas,
donde número y boca construyen un presente
cuerpo de luz humana con músculos de harina!

¡Oh Forma limitada para expresar concreta
muchedumbre de luces y clamor escuchado!
¡Oh nieve circundada por témpanos de música!
¡Oh llama crepitante sobre todas las venas!

Mundo

> *Agnus Dei qui tollis peccata mundi.*
> *Miserere nobis.*

Noche de los tejados y la planta del pie
silbaba por los ojos secos de las palomas.
Alga y cristal en fuga ponen plata mojada
los hombros de cemento de todas las ciudades.

La gillette descansaba sobre los tocadores
con su afán impaciente de cuello seccionado.
En la casa del muerto los niños perseguían
una sierpe de arena por el rincón oscuro.

Escribientes dormidos en el piso catorce.
Ramera con los senos de cristal arañado.
Cables y media luna con temblores de insecto.
Bares sin gente. Gritos. Cabezas por el agua.

Para el asesinato del ruiseñor venían
tres mil hombres armados de lucientes cuchillos.
Viejas y sacerdotes lloraban resistiendo
una lluvia de lenguas y hormigas voladoras.

Noche de rostro blanco. Nula noche sin rostro.
Bajo el sol y la luna. Triste noche del mundo.
Dos mitades opuestas y un hombre que no sabe
cuándo su mariposa dejará los relojes.

Debajo de las alas del dragón hay un niño.
Caballitos de cadmio por la estrella sin sangre.

Oh, most holy Form, vertex of flowers,
30 where each angle takes its own fixed light,
where number and mouth build this laid-out body
of human light and muscles of flour.

Oh, Form whose limits express the concrete
multitude of lights and heard cries!
Oh, snow surrounded by icebergs of music!
Oh, flame crackling over all our veins!

World
> *Agnus Dei qui tollis peccata mundi.*
> *Miserere nobis.*

A night of rooftops and soles of the feet
was whistling through the dry eyes of doves.
Fleeing glass and seaweed turn to wet silver
40 the cement shoulders of the cities.

The razor rested on the dressing tables,
waiting impatiently to section necks.
Children were chasing a sand serpent
in a dark corner of the dead man's house.

The scribes fast asleep on the fourteenth floor.
The prostitute with her breasts of scratched glass.
Cables and half moon with insect tremors.
Empty taverns. Screams. Heads in the water.

In order to murder the nightingale,
50 three thousand men came, armed with shining knives.
Old women and priests cried while fighting off
a cloudburst of tongues and flying ants.

White-faced night. Non-night without a face.
Under sun and moon. Sad night of the world.
Opposing halves and a man who does not know
when his butterfly will leave the clocks.

There is a child under the dragon's wings.
Ponies of cadmium by the bloodless star.

El unicornio quiere lo que la rosa olvida
60 y el pájaro pretende lo que las aguas vedan.

Sólo tu Sacramento de luz en equilibrio
aquietaba la angustia del amor desligado.
Sólo tu Sacramento, manómetro que salva
corazones lanzados a quinientos por hora.

Porque tu signo es clave de llanura celeste
donde naipe y herida se entrelazan cantando,
donde la luz desboca su toro relumbrante
y se afirma el aroma de la rosa templada.

Porque tu signo expresa la brisa y el gusano.
70 Punto de unión y cita del siglo y el minuto.
Orbe claro de muertos y hormiguero de vivos
con el hombre de nieves y el negro de la llama.

Mundo, ya tienes meta para tu desamparo.
Para tu horror perenne de agujero sin fondo.
¡Oh Cordero cautivo de tres voces iguales!
¡Sacramento inmutable de amor y disciplina!

Demonio
> *Quia tu es, Deus, fortitudo mea:*
> *quare me repulisti? et quare tristis*
> *incedo, dum affligit me inimicus?*

Honda luz cegadora de materia crujiente,
luz oblicua de espadas y mercurio de estrella
anunciaban el cuerpo sin amor que llegaba
80 por todas las esquinas del abierto domingo.

Forma de la belleza sin nostalgia ni sueño.
Rumor de superficies libertadas y locas.
Médula de presente. Seguridad fingida
de flotar sobre el agua con el torso de mármol.

Cuerpo de belleza que late y que se escapa;
un momento de venas y ternura de ombligo.
Belleza encadenada sin línea en flor, ni centro,
ni puras relaciones de número y sonrisa.

The unicorn wants what the rose forgets,
and the bird seeks what the waters have banned.

Only your Sacrament of balanced light
quieted the anguish of unbound love.
Only your Sacrament, manometer
that saves hearts hurled at five hundred miles an hour.

For your sign is the key to the starry plain
where the card and wound are entwined in song,
where the light pours out its resplendent bull
and the scent of the warm rose grows strong.

Your sign expresses the breeze and the worm.
Junction where the age and the moment call.
Clear orb of the dead, anthill of the living,
with the man of the snows and the black of the flame.

World, now there's a goal for your helplessness.
For your perennial horror of black holes.
Oh, captive Lamb of three equal voices!
Changeless Sacrament of love and discipline!

Devil

    Quia tu es, Deus, fortitudo mea:
    quare me repulisti? et quare tristis
    incedo, dum affligit me inimicus?

The deep blinding light of crackling matter,
the sword's slanting light, and the star's mercury
proclaimed the loveless body's arrival
on all the corners of the open Sunday.

Beauty's form without nostalgia or dream.
Murmur of crazy surfaces set free.
The present's marrow. False sense of safety:
to float on water with a marble torso.

Beauty's body throbs and makes its escape.
A moment of veins and navel's tenderness.
Beauty chained with no blossoming line or center,
no pure relations of number and smile.

Vedlo llegar, oriente de la mano que palpa.
90 Vendaval y mancebo de rizos y moluscos.
Fuego para la carne sensible que se quema.
Níquel para el sollozo que busca a Dios volando.

Las nubes proyectaban sombras de cocodrilo
sobre un cielo incoloro batido por motores.
Altas esquinas grises y letras encendidas
señalaban las tiendas del enemigo Bello.

No es la mujer desnuda, ni el duro adolescente
ni el corazón clavado con besos y lancetas.
No es ser dueño de todos los caballos del mundo
100 ni descubrir el anca musical de la luna.

El encanto secreto del enemigo es otro.
Permanecer. Quedarse con la luz del minuto.
Permanecer clavados en su belleza triste
y evitar la inocencia de las aguas nacidas.

Que al balido reciente y a la flor desnortada
y a los senos sin huellas de la monja dormida
responda negro toro de límites maduros
con la fe de un momento sin pudor ni mañana.

Para vencer la carne fuerte del enemigo,
110 mágico prodigioso de fuegos y colores,
das tu cuerpo celeste con tu sangre divina
en este Sacramento definido que canto.

Desciendes a materia para hacerte visible
a los ojos que observan tu vida renovada
y vencer sin espadas, en unidad sencilla,
al enemigo bello de las mil calidades.

¡Alegrísimo Dios! ¡Alegrísima Forma!
Aleluya reciente de todas las mañanas.
Misterio facilísimo de razón o de sueño,
120 si es fácil la belleza visible de la rosa.

¡Aleluya, aleluya del zapato y la nieve!
Alba pura de acantos en la mano incompleta.

See him arrive, east for the groping hand.
90   Gale winds and young man with curls and mollusks.
Fire for sensitive flesh consumed by fire.
Chrome for the sob that flies in search of God.

The clouds were casting crocodile shadows
on a colorless sky beaten by motors.
High gray corners and letters in flames
betrayed the beautiful enemy's tents.

It's not naked women, hard teenagers,
or the heart pierced by kisses and lancets.
It's not owning every horse in the world,
100 or finding the moon's musical haunches.

So, what is the enemy's secret charm?
To survive. To command the flash of light.
To fasten ourselves to his sad beauty
and avoid the innocence of spring water.

Let the shapely contours of the black bull
and his instant, shameless faith in no tomorrow
answer the new bleating, the drifting flower,
and the trackless breasts of the sleeping nun.

To vanquish the strong flesh of the enemy,
110 prodigious magician of fires and colors,
you offer your divine body and blood
in this definite Sacrament that I sing.

You descend into matter to appear
to the eyes that observe your renewed life,
vanquishing, in simple unity, swordless,
the beautiful enemy's thousand facets.

Most joyful God! Most joyful Form!
New alleluia of each and every day.
Such a simple mystery of reason or dream,
120 if the rose's visible beauty is simple.

Alleluia, alleluia of shoe and snow.
Pure acanthus dawn in the unfinished hand.

¡Aleluya, aleluya de la norma y el punto
sobre los cuatro vientos sin afán deportivo!

Lanza tu Sacramento semillas de alegría
contra los perdigones de dolor del Demonio
y en el estéril valle de luz y roca pura
la aguja de la flauta rompe un ángel de vidrio.

Carne
> *Qué bien os quedasteis,*
> *galán del cielo,*
> *que es muy de galanes*
> *quedarse en cuerpo.*
> —Lope de Vega, *Auto de los cantares*

Por el nombre del Padre, roca, luz y fermento.
130 Por el nombre del Hijo, flor y sangre vertida,
en el fuego visible del Espíritu Santo
Eva quema sus dedos teñidos de manzana.

Eva gris y rayada con la púrpura rota
cubierta con las mieles y el rumor del insecto.
Eva de yugulares y de musgo baboso
en el primer impulso torpe de los planetas.

Llegaban las higueras con las flores calientes
a destrozar los blancos muros de disciplina.
El hacha por el bosque daba normas de viento
140 a la pura dinamo clavada en su martirio.

Hilos y nervios tiemblan en la sección fragante
de la luna y el vientre que el bisturí descubre.
En el diván de raso los amantes aprietan
los tibios algodones donde duermen sus huesos.

¡Mirad aquel caballo cómo corre! ¡Miradlo
por los hombros y el seno de la niña cuajada!
¡Mirad qué tiernos ayes y qué son movedizo
oprimen la cintura del joven embalado!

¡Venid, venid! Las venas alargarán sus puntas
150 para morder la cresta del caimán enlunado

Alleluia, alleluia of point and standard
over the four unsporting winds.

Your Sacrament scatters seeds of joy
against the Devil's buckshot of pain,
and in the barren valley of light and pure stone,
the flute's needle breaks an angel of glass.

Flesh

> *How handsome you are,*
> *heavenly gallant,*
> *for gallants are always*
> *removing their capes.*
> —Lope de Vega, *Auto de los cantares*

In the name of the Father, rock, light, and ferment.
130 In the name of the Son, flower, and spilled blood,
in the visible fire of the Holy Spirit,
Eve burns her own apple-stained fingers.

Eve, gray and streaked with torn crimson,
covered with honey and buzzing insects.
Eve of jugulars and dripping moss,
in the first sluggish impulse of the planets.

The fig trees with their hot flowers
were destroying the white walls of discipline.
The woodsman's axe gave the wind's standards
140 to the pure dynamo nailed in its martyrdom.

Threads and nerves trembled in the moon's fragrant
phase, and in the womb found by the scalpel.
On the satin couch, the lovers compress
warm cotton swabs where their bones are sleeping.

Look at that galloping horse! Look at it
on the shoulders and breast of the girl taking shape!
Look what tender sighs and moving sound
press upon the waist of the bundled youth!

Come, come and watch the veins uncoiling
150 to bite the lunar caiman's cockscomb

mientras la verde sangre de Sodoma reluce
por la sala de un yerto corazón de aluminio.

Es preciso que el llanto se derrame en la axila,
que la mano recuerde blanda goma nocturna.
Es preciso que ritmos de sístole y diástole
empañen el rubor inhumano del cielo.

Tienen en lo más blanco huevecillos de muerte
(diminutos madroños de arsénico invisible)
que secan y destruyen el nervio de luz pura
160 por donde el alma filtra lección de beso y ala.

Es tu cuerpo, galán, tu boca, tu cintura,
el gusto de tu sangre por los dientes helados.
Es tu carne vencida, rota, pisoteada
la que vence y relumbra sobre la carne nuestra.

Es el yerto vacío de lo libre sin norte
que se llena de rosas concretas y finales.
Adán es luz y espera bajo el arco podrido
las dos niñas de sangre que agitaban sus sienes.

¡Oh Corpus Christi! ¡Oh Corpus de absoluto silencio
170 donde se quema el cisne y fulgura el leproso!
¡Oh blanca Forma insomne!
¡Ángeles y ladridos contra el rumor de venas!

while the green blood of Sodom glows
in the parlor of a stiff aluminum heart.

The tears must flow from the armpit,
the hand should remember soft nocturnal rubber.
The rhythms of systole and diastole
should cloud the inhuman blush of the sky.

In their whitest place, they have death's little eggs
(tiny red berries of invisible arsenic)
that wither and destroy the nerve of pure light
160 where the soul filters a lesson of kiss and wing.

It's your body, gallant, your mouth, your waist,
the taste of your blood through frozen teeth.
It's your vanquished flesh, broken, trampled,
that defeats and dazzles our own flesh.

It's the stiff emptiness of all that drifts freely,
full of concrete and final roses.
Adam is light, waiting under the rotten arch
for the two girls of blood who beat in his temples.

Oh, Body of Christ! Oh, Body of absolute silence,
170 where the swan burns and the leper shines!
Oh blank, sleepless Form!
Angels and dogs barking against the whisper of veins.

TR. G.S. AND S.F.W.

POETA EN
NUEVA YORK

A Bebé y Carlos Morla

*Los poemas de este libro están escritos en la ciudad de Nueva York,
el año 1929–1930, en que el poeta vivió como estudiante
en Columbia University. —F.G.L.*

[*Autorretrato en Nueva York, 1929–32*]

POET IN NEW YORK

To Bebé and Carlos Morla

*The poems in this book were written in the city of New York during
the year 1929–1930, when the poet lived as a student
at Columbia University. —F.G.L.*

Translated by Greg Simon and Steven F. White

[*Self-portrait in New York, 1929–32*]

I
Poemas de la soledad en Columbia University

Furia color de amor,
amor color de olvido.
—LUIS CERNUDA

Vuelta de paseo

Asesinado por el cielo.
Entre las formas que van hacia la sierpe
y las formas que buscan el cristal
dejaré crecer mis cabellos.

Con el árbol de muñones que no canta
y el niño con el blanco rostro de huevo.

Con los animalitos de cabeza rota
y el agua harapienta de los pies secos.

Con todo lo que tiene cansancio sordomudo
10   y mariposa ahogada en el tintero.

Tropezando con mi rostro distinto de cada día.
¡Asesinado por el cielo!

1910
(Intermedio)

Aquellos ojos míos de mil novecientos diez
no vieron enterrar a los muertos,
ni la feria de ceniza del que llora por la madrugada,
ni el corazón que tiembla arrinconado como un caballito de mar.

Aquellos ojos míos de mil novecientos diez
vieron la blanca pared donde orinaban las niñas,
el hocico del toro, la seta venenosa
y una luna incomprensible que iluminaba por los rincones
los pedazos de limón seco bajo el negro duro de las botellas.

I
Poems of Solitude at Columbia University

Rage, love's color,
love, the color of oblivion.
—LUIS CERNUDA

After a Walk

Cut down by the sky.
Between shapes moving toward the serpent
and crystal-craving shapes,
I'll let my hair grow.

With the amputated tree that doesn't sing
and the child with the blank face of an egg.

With the little animals whose skulls are cracked
and the water, dressed in rags, but with dry feet.

With all the bone-tired, deaf-and-dumb things
10   and a butterfly drowned in the inkwell.

Bumping into my own face, different each day.
Cut down by the sky!

1910
(Intermezzo)

Those eyes of mine in nineteen-ten
saw no one dead and buried,
no village fair of ash from the one who weeps at dawn,
no trembling heart cornered like a sea horse.

Those eyes of mine in nineteen-ten
saw the white wall where little girls pissed,
the bull's muzzle, the poisonous mushroom,
and an incomprehensible moon illuminating dried lemon rinds
under the hard black bottles in corners.

10 Aquellos ojos míos en el cuello de la jaca,
en el seno traspasado de Santa Rosa dormida,
en los tejados del amor, con gemidos y frescas manos,
en un jardín donde los gatos se comían a las ranas.

Desván donde el polvo viejo congrega estatuas y musgos.
Cajas que guardan silencio de cangrejos devorados.
En el sitio donde el sueño tropezaba con su realidad.
Allí mis pequeños ojos.

No preguntarme nada. He visto que las cosas
cuando buscan su curso encuentran su vacío.
20 Hay un dolor de huecos por el aire sin gente
y en mis ojos criaturas vestidas ¡sin desnudo!

Nueva York, agosto 1929

Fábula y rueda de los tres amigos

Enrique,
Emilio,
Lorenzo.
Estaban los tres helados:
Enrique por el mundo de las camas,
Emilio por el mundo de los ojos y las heridas de las manos,
Lorenzo por el mundo de las universidades sin tejados.

Lorenzo,
Emilio,
10 Enrique.
Estaban los tres quemados:
Lorenzo por el mundo de las hojas y las bolas de billar,
Emilio por el mundo de la sangre y los alfileres blancos,
Enrique por el mundo de los muertos y los periódicos abandonados.

Lorenzo,
Emilio,
Enrique.
Estaban los tres enterrados:
Lorenzo en un seno de Flora,

Those eyes of mine on the pony's neck,
on the pierced breast of Santa Rosa as she sleeps,
on the rooftops of love, with moans and cool hands,
on a garden where cats devour frogs.

Attic where the ancient dust assembles statues and moss.
Boxes that keep the silence of devoured crabs.
In the place where the dream was colliding with its reality.
My little eyes are there.

Don't ask me any questions. I've seen how things
that seek their way find their void instead.
There are spaces that ache in the uninhabited air
and in my eyes, completely dressed creatures—no one naked there!

New York, August 1929

Fable of Three Friends to Be Sung in Rounds

Enrique,
Emilio,
Lorenzo.
The three of them were frozen:
Enrique in the world of beds,
Emilio in the world of eyes and wounded hands,
Lorenzo in the world of roofless universities.

Lorenzo,
Emilio,
Enrique.
The three of them were burned:
Lorenzo in the world of leaves and billiard balls,
Emilio in the world of blood and white pins,
Enrique in the world of the dead and discarded newspapers.

Lorenzo,
Emilio,
Enrique.
The three of them were buried:
Lorenzo in Flora's breast,

₂₀ Emilio en la yerta ginebra que se olvida en el vaso,
Enrique en la hormiga, en el mar y en los ojos vacíos de los pájaros.

Lorenzo,
Emilio,
Enrique.
Fueron los tres en mis manos
tres montañas chinas,
tres sombras de caballo,
tres paisajes de nieve y una cabaña de azucenas
por los palomares donde la luna se pone plana bajo el gallo.

₃₀ Uno
y uno
y uno.
Estaban los tres momificados,
con las moscas del invierno,
con los tinteros que orina el perro y desprecia el vilano,
con la brisa que hiela el corazón de todas las madres,
por los blancos derribos de Júpiter donde meriendan muerte los
    borrachos.

Tres
y dos
₄₀ y uno.
Los vi perderse llorando y cantando
por un huevo de gallina,
por la noche que enseñaba su esqueleto de tabaco,
por mi dolor lleno de rostros y punzantes esquirlas de luna,
por mi alegría de ruedas dentadas y látigos,
por mi pecho turbado por las palomas,
por mi muerte desierta con un solo paseante equivocado.

Yo había matado la quinta luna
y bebían agua por las fuentes los abanicos y los aplausos.
₅₀ Tibia leche encerrada de las recién paridas
agitaba las rosas con un largo dolor blanco.
Enrique,
Emilio,
Lorenzo.
Diana es dura,
pero a veces tiene los pechos nublados.

₂₀ Emilio in the forgotten shot of gin,
Enrique in the ant, the sea, the empty eyes of the birds.

Lorenzo,
Emilio,
Enrique.
In my hands the three of them were
three Chinese mountains,
three shadows of horses,
three snowy landscapes and a shelter of lilies
by the dovecotes where the moon lies flat beneath the rooster.

₃₀ One
and one
and one.
The three of them were mummified
with winter flies,
with the inkwells that dogs piss and thistledown despises,
with the breeze that chills every mother's heart,
by Jupiter's white wreckage, where the drunks lunch on death.

Three
and two
₄₀ and one.
I saw them lose themselves, weeping and singing,
in a hen's egg,
in the night that showed its tobacco skeleton,
in my sorrow, full of faces and piercing lunar shrapnel,
in my joy of serrated wheels and whips,
in my breast that is troubled with doves,
in my deserted death with a lone mistaken passerby.

I had killed the fifth moon,
and the fans and applause were drinking water from the fountains.
₅₀ Warm milk inside the new mothers
was stirring the roses with a long white sorrow.
Enrique,
Emilio,
Lorenzo.
Diana is hard,
but sometimes her breasts are banked with clouds.

Puede la piedra blanca latir en la sangre del ciervo
y el ciervo puede soñar por los ojos de un caballo.

Cuando se hundieron las formas puras
60 bajo el cri cri de las margaritas,
comprendí que me habían asesinado.
Recorrieron los cafés y los cementerios y las iglesias.
Abrieron los toneles y los armarios.
Destrozaron tres esqueletos para arrancar sus dientes de oro.
Ya no me encontraron.
¿No me encontraron?
No. No me encontraron.
Pero se supo que la sexta luna huyó torrente arriba,
70 y que el mar recordó ¡de pronto!
los nombres de todos sus ahogados.

Tu infancia en Menton

Sí, tu niñez: ya fábula de fuentes.
—JORGE GUILLÉN

Sí, tu niñez: ya fábula de fuentes.
El tren y la mujer que llena el cielo.
Tu soledad esquiva en los hoteles
y tu máscara pura de otro signo.
Es la niñez del mar y tu silencio
donde los sabios vidrios se quebraban.
Es tu yerta ignorancia donde estuvo
mi torso limitado por el fuego.
Norma de amor te di, hombre de Apolo,
10 llanto con ruiseñor enajenado,
pero, pasto de ruina, te afilabas
para los breves sueños indecisos.
Pensamiento de enfrente, luz de ayer,
índices y señales del acaso.
Tu cintura de arena sin sosiego
atiende sólo rastros que no escalan.
Pero yo he de buscar por los rincones
tu alma tibia sin ti que no te entiende,
con el dolor de Apolo detenido
20 con que he roto la máscara que llevas.

The white stone can throb in deer blood
and the deer can dream through the eyes of a horse.

When the pure shapes sank
60 under the chirping of daisies,
I knew they had murdered me.
They combed the cafés, graveyards, and churches for me,
pried open casks and cabinets,
destroyed three skeletons in order to rip out their gold teeth.
But they couldn't find me anymore.
They couldn't find me.
No. They couldn't find me.
But they discovered the sixth moon had fled against the torrent,
70 and the sea—suddenly!—remembered
the names of all its drowned.

Your Childhood in Menton

> Yes, your childhood: now a fable of fountains.
> —JORGE GUILLÉN

Yes, your childhood: now a fable of fountains.
The train and the woman who fills the sky.
Your shy loneliness in hotels
and your pure mask of another sign.
The sea's childhood and your silence
where the crystals of wisdom shattered.
Your rigid ignorance where
my torso was circumscribed by fire.
What I gave you, Apollonian man, was the standard of love,
10 fits of tears with an estranged nightingale.
But ruin fed upon you, you whittled yourself to nothing
for the sake of fleeting, aimless dreams.
Thoughts before you, yesterday's light,
traces and signs of what might be . . .
Your waist of restless sand
follows only trails that do not climb.
But in every corner I must look for your warm soul
that is without you and doesn't understand you,
with the sorrow of Apollo stopped in his tracks,
20 the sorrow with which I shattered your mask.

Allí, león, allí, furia de cielo,
te dejaré pacer en mis mejillas;
allí, caballo azul de mi locura,
pulso de nebulosa y minutero.
He de buscar las piedras de alacranes
y los vestidos de tu madre niña,
llanto de media noche y paño roto
que quitó luna de la sien del muerto.
30 Sí, tu niñez: ya fábula de fuentes.
Alma extraña de mi hueco de venas,
te he de buscar pequeña y sin raíces.
¡Amor de siempre, amor, amor de nunca!
¡Oh, sí! Yo quiero. ¡Amor, amor! Dejadme.
No me tapen la boca los que buscan
espigas de Saturno por la nieve
o castran animales por un cielo,
clínica y selva de la anatomía.
Amor, amor, amor. Niñez del mar.
40 Tu alma tibia sin ti que no te entiende.
Amor, amor, un vuelo de la corza
por el pecho sin fin de la blancura.
Y tu niñez, amor, y tu niñez.
El tren y la mujer que llena el cielo.
Ni tú, ni yo, ni el aire, ni las hojas.
Sí, tu niñez: ya fábula de fuentes.

II
Los Negros
Para Ángel del Río

Norma y paraíso de los negros

Odian la sombra del pájaro
sobre el pleamar de la blanca mejilla
y el conflicto de luz y viento
en el salón de la nieve fría.

It's there, lion, there, sky's fury,
where I'll let you graze on my cheeks;
there, blue horse of my insanity,
pulse of the nebula and hand that counts the minutes.
There I'll look for the scorpions' stones
and the clothes of the girl who was your mother,
midnight tears and torn cloth
that wiped moonlight from the temples of the dead man.
30 Yes, your childhood: now a fable of fountains.
Strange soul, tiny and adrift, ripped
from the emptied space of my veins—I must look until I find you.
The same love as ever, but never the same!
Yes, I do love! Love! Leave me alone, all of you.
And don't try to cover my mouth, you who seek
the wheat of Saturn in snowfields,
or castrate animals on behalf of a sky,
anatomy's clinic and jungle.
Love, love, love. The sea's childhood.
40 Your warm soul that is without you and doesn't understand you.
Love, love, the flight of the doe
through the endless breast of whiteness.
And your childhood, love, your childhood.
The train and the woman who fills the sky.
Not you, not me, not the air, not the leaves.
Yes, your childhood: now a fable of fountains.

II
The Blacks

For Ángel del Río

Standards and Paradise of the Blacks

They hate the bird's shadow
on the white cheek's high tide
and the conflict of light and wind
in the great cold hall of snow.

Odian la flecha sin cuerpo,
el pañuelo exacto de la despedida,
la aguja que mantiene presión y rosa
en el gramíneo rubor de la sonrisa.

Aman el azul desierto,
10 las vacilantes expresiones bovinas,
la mentirosa luna de los polos,
la danza curva del agua en la orilla.

Con la ciencia del tronco y el rastro
llenan de nervios luminosos la arcilla
y patinan lúbricos por aguas y arenas
gustando la amarga frescura de su milenaria saliva.

Es por el azul crujiente,
azul sin un gusano ni una huella dormida,
donde los huevos de avestruz quedan eternos
20 y deambulan intactas las lluvias bailarinas.

Es por el azul sin historia,
azul de una noche sin temor de día,
azul donde el desnudo del viento va quebrando
los camellos sonámbulos de las nubes vacías.

Es allí donde sueñan los torsos bajo la gula de la hierba.
Allí los corales empapan la desesperación de la tinta,
los durmientes borran sus perfiles bajo la madeja de los caracoles
y queda el hueco de la danza sobre las últimas cenizas.

El rey de Harlem

Con una cuchara
le arrancaba los ojos a los cocodrilos
y golpeaba el trasero de los monos.
Con una cuchara.

Fuego de siempre dormía en los pedernales
y los escarabajos borrachos de anís
olvidaban el musgo de las aldeas.

They hate the unbodied arrow,
the punctual handkerchief of farewell,
the needle that sustains a rosy tension
in the seed-bearing spikes of their smiles.

They love the deserted blue,
10   the swaying bovine faces,
the deceitful moon of both poles,
and water's bent dance on the shoreline.

They use the science of tree trunk and rake
to cover the clay with luminous nerves,
and as they glide with easy desire over water and sand,
they taste the bitter freshness of their millenary spit.

It's in the crackling blue,
blue without a single worm or sleeping footprint,
where the ostrich eggs stay forever
20   and the untouched rains dance and stroll.

It's in the blue that has no history,
blue of a night without fear of day,
blue where the nude of the wind breaks up
camels of empty clouds moving in their sleep.

It's there the torsos dream beneath the hungry grass,
there the coral absorbs the ink's desperation,
the sleepers erase their profiles under the skein of snails,
and the emptied space of the dance stays above the last of the ashes.

The King of Harlem

With a spoon
he dug out the crocodiles' eyes,
and swatted the monkeys on their asses.
With a spoon.

Age-old fire slept in the flints
and the beetles drunk on anisette
forgot about the moss of the villages.

Aquel viejo cubierto de setas
iba al sitio donde lloraban los negros
10 mientras crujía la cuchara del rey
y llegaban los tanques de agua podrida.

Las rosas huían por los filos
de las últimas curvas del aire,
y en los montones de azafrán
los niños machacaban pequeñas ardillas
con un rubor de frenesí manchado.

Es preciso cruzar los puentes
y llegar al rumor negro
para que el perfume de pulmón
20 nos golpee las sienes con su vestido
de caliente piña.

Es preciso matar al rubio vendedor de aguardiente,
a todos los amigos de la manzana y de la arena;
y es necesario dar con los puños cerrados
a las pequeñas judías que tiemblan llenas de burbujas,
para que el rey de Harlem cante con su muchedumbre,
para que los cocodrilos duerman en largas filas
bajo el amianto de la luna,
y para que nadie dude la infinita belleza
30 de los plumeros, los ralladores, los cobres y las cacerolas de las cocinas.

¡Ay, Harlem! ¡Ay, Harlem! ¡Ay, Harlem!
No hay angustia comparable a tus rojos oprimidos,
a tu sangre estremecida dentro del eclipse oscuro,
a tu violencia granate, sordomuda en la penumbra,
a tu gran rey prisionero, con un traje de conserje.

★ ★ ★

Tenía la noche una hendidura y quietas salamandras de marfil.
Las muchachas americanas
llevaban niños y monedas en el vientre
y los muchachos se desmayaban en la cruz del desperezo.

40 Ellos son.
Ellos son los que beben el whisky de plata junto a los volcanes
y tragan pedacitos de corazón por las heladas montañas del oso.

The old man covered with mushrooms
was on his way to the place where the blacks wept
while the king's spoon cracked
and the vats of putrid water arrived.

The roses fled along the blades
of the air's last curves,
and on the piles of saffron
the children flattened tiny squirrels
with faces flushed in their strained frenzy.

It's necessary to cross the bridges
and reach the murmuring blacks
so the perfume of their lungs
can buffet our temples with its covering
of hot pineapple.

It's necessary to kill the blond vendor of firewater
and every friend of apple and sand,
and it's necessary to use the fists
against the little Jewish women who tremble, filled with bubbles,
so the king of Harlem sings with his multitude,
so crocodiles sleep in long rows
beneath the moon's asbestos,
and so no one doubts the infinite beauty
of feather dusters, graters, copper pans, and kitchen casseroles.

Ay, Harlem! *Ay*, Harlem! *Ay*, Harlem!
There is no anguish like that of your oppressed reds,
or your blood shuddering with rage inside the dark eclipse,
or your garnet violence, deaf and dumb in the penumbra,
or your grand king a prisoner in the uniform of a doorman.

★ ★ ★

The night was cracked, and there were motionless ivory salamanders.
American girls
were carrying babies and coins in their wombs,
and the boys stretched their limbs and fainted on the cross.

They are the ones.
The ones who drink silver whisky near the volcanoes
and swallow pieces of heart by the bear's frozen mountains.

653

Aquella noche el rey de Harlem, con una durísima cuchara,
le arrancaba los ojos a los cocodrilos
y golpeaba el trasero de los monos.
Con una cuchara.

Los negros lloraban confundidos
entre paraguas y soles de oro,
los mulatos estiraban gomas, ansiosos de llegar al torso blanco,
50 y el viento empañaba espejos
y quebraba las venas de los bailarines.

Negros, Negros, Negros, Negros,

la sangre no tiene puertas en vuestra noche boca arriba.
No hay rubor. Sangre furiosa por debajo de las pieles.
Viva en la espina del puñal y en el pecho de los paisajes,
bajo las pinzas y las retamas de la celeste luna de cáncer.

Sangre que busca por mil caminos muertes enharinadas y ceniza de nardo,
cielos yertos, en declive, donde las colonias de planetas
rueden por las playas con los objetos abandonados.

60 Sangre que mira lenta con el rabo del ojo,
hecha de espartos exprimidos, néctares de subterráneos.
Sangre que oxida al alisio descuidado en una huella
y disuelve a las mariposas en los cristales de la ventana.

Es la sangre que viene, que vendrá
por los tejados y azoteas, por todas partes,
para quemar la clorofilia de las mujeres rubias,
para gemir al pie de las camas, ante el insomnio de los lavabos,
y estrellarse en una aurora de tabaco y bajo amarillo.

¡Hay que huir!,
70 huir por las esquinas y encerrarse en los últimos pisos,
porque el tuétano del bosque penetrará por las rendijas
para dejar en vuestra carne una leve huella de eclipse
y una falsa tristeza de guante desteñido y rosa química.

That night the king of Harlem, with an unbreakable spoon,
dug out the crocodiles' eyes
and swatted the monkeys on their asses.
With a spoon.

The blacks cried in confusion
among umbrellas and gold suns,
the mulattoes stretched rubber, thinking anxiously of turning their
    torsos white,
50 and the wind tarnished mirrors
and shattered the veins of the dancers.

Blacks, Blacks, Blacks, Blacks,

the blood has no doors in your recumbent night.
No blush in your face. Blood rages beneath skin.
Alive in the dagger's spine and the landscapes' breast,
under the pincers and Scotch broom of cancer's celestial moon.

Blood that searches a thousand roads for deaths dusted with flour and
    ashes of spikenards,
rigid, descending skies in which the colonies of planets
can wheel with the litter on the beaches.

60 Blood that looks slowly from the corner of an eye,
blood wrung from hemp and subway nectars.
Blood that rusts the careless trade wind in a footprint
and dissolves butterflies in windowpanes.

Blood flows, and will flow
on rooftops everywhere,
and burn the blond women's chlorophyll,
and groan at the foot of the beds near the washstands' insomnia,
and burst into an aurora of tobacco and low yellow.

There must be some way out of here,
70 some street to flee down, some locked room on the top floor to hide
    in,
because the forest's marrow will slip through the cracks
to leave on your skin a faint trace of an eclipse
and a false sorrow of faded glove and chemical rose.

Es por el silencio sapientísimo
cuando los camareros y los cocineros y los que limpian con la lengua
las heridas de los millonarios
buscan al rey por las calles o en los ángulos del salitre.

Un viento sur de madera, oblicuo en el negro fango,
escupe a las barcas rotas y se clava puntillas en los hombros.
80 Un viento sur que lleva
colmillos, girasoles, alfabetos
y una pila de Volta con avispas ahogadas.

El olvido estaba expresado por tres gotas de tinta sobre el monóculo.
El amor, por un solo rostro invisible a flor de piedra.
Médulas y corolas componían sobre las nubes
un desierto de tallos, sin una sola rosa.

A la izquierda, a la derecha, por el Sur y por el Norte,
se levanta el muro impasible
para el topo y la aguja del agua.
90 No busquéis, negros, su grieta
para hallar la máscara infinita.
Buscar el gran sol del centro
hechos una piña zumbadora.
El sol que se desliza por los bosques
seguro de no encontrar una ninfa.
El sol que destruye números y no ha cruzado nunca un sueño,
el tatuado sol que baja por el río
y muge seguido de caimanes.

Negros, Negros, Negros, Negros,

100 Jamás sierpe ni cebra ni mula
palidecieron al morir.
El leñador no sabe cuándo expiran
los clamorosos árboles que corta.
Aguardad bajo la sombra vegetal de vuestro rey
a que cicutas y cardos y ortigas turben postreras azoteas.

Entonces, negros, entonces, entonces,
podréis besar con frenesí las ruedas de las bicicletas,

Through the all-knowing silence,
waiters, cooks, and those whose tongues lick clean
the wounds of millionaires
seek the king in the streets or on the sharp angles of saltpeter.

A wooden wind from the south, slanting through the black mire,
spits on the broken boats and drives tacks into shoulders.
80 A south wind that carries
tusks, sunflowers, alphabets,
and a battery with drowned wasps.

Oblivion was expressed by three drops of ink on the monocle.
Love, by a single, invisible, stone-deep face.
And above the clouds, bone marrow and corollas
composed a desert of stems without a single rose.

To the left and right, south and north,
the wall rises, impassable
for the mole and the needle made of water.
90 Blacks, don't look for some kind of crack
to find the infinite mask.
Look for the great central sun.
Turn into a swarm of buzzing pineapple.
The sun that slides through the forests,
sure that a nymph will not be there.
The sun that destroys numbers, and has never crossed a dream,
the tattooed sun that descends the river
and bellows just ahead of the crocodiles.

Blacks, Blacks, Blacks, Blacks,

100 No serpent, no zebra or mule
ever turned pale in the face of death.
The woodcutter doesn't know when the clamorous trees
that he cuts down expire.
Wait in your king's jungle shade
until hemlock, thistles, and nettles disturb the last rooftops.

Then, blacks, and only then
will you be able to frantically kiss bicycle wheels,

poner parejas de microscopios en las cuevas de las ardillas
y danzar al fin sin duda, mientras las flores erizadas
110 asesinan a nuestro Moisés casi en los juncos del cielo.

¡Ay, Harlem disfrazada!
¡Ay, Harlem, amenazada por un gentío de trajes sin cabeza!
Me llega tu rumor,
me llega tu rumor atravesando troncos y ascensores,
a través de láminas grises,
donde flotan tus automóviles cubiertos de dientes,
a través de los caballos muertos y los crímenes diminutos,
a través de tu gran rey desesperado,
cuyas barbas llegan al mar.

Iglesia abandonada
(Balada de la Gran Guerra)

Yo tenía un hijo que se llamaba Juan.
Yo tenía un hijo.
Se perdió por los arcos un viernes de todos los muertos.
Lo vi jugar en las últimas escaleras de la misa
y echaba un cubito de hojalata en el corazón del sacerdote.
He golpeado los ataúdes. ¡Mi hijo! ¡Mi hijo! ¡Mi hijo!
Saqué una pata de gallina por detrás de la luna, y luego
comprendí que mi niña era un pez
por donde se alejan las carretas.
10 Yo tenía una niña.
Yo tenía un pez muerto bajo la ceniza de los incensarios.
Yo tenía un mar ¿de qué? Dios mío. ¡Un mar!
Subí a tocar las campanas, pero las frutas tenían gusanos
y las cerillas apagadas
se comían los trigos de la primavera.
Yo vi la transparente cigüeña de alcohol
mondar las negras cabezas de los soldados agonizantes
y vi las cabañas de goma
20 donde giraban las copas llenas de lágrimas.
En las anémonas del ofertorio te encontraré, ¡corazón mío!,
cuando el sacerdote levante la mula y el buey con sus fuertes brazos,
para espantar los sapos nocturnos que rondan los helados paisajes del cáliz.
Yo tenía un hijo que era un gigante,

place pairs of microscopes in squirrel lairs,
and dance fearlessly at last while the bristling flowers
110 cut down our Moses in the bulrushes that border heaven.

Ay, Harlem in disguise!
Ay, Harlem, threatened by a mob of headless suits!
I hear your murmur,
I hear it moving through tree trunks and elevator shafts,
through gray sheets
where your cars float covered with teeth,
through dead horses and petty crimes,
through your grand, despairing king
whose beard reaches the sea.

Abandoned Church
(Ballad of the Great War)

Once I had a son named John.
Once I had a son.
He was lost in the arches, one Friday, Day of the Dead.
I saw him playing on the last raised steps of the Mass
and he lowered a tin bucket into the priest's deep heart.
I pounded on the coffins. My son! My son! My son!
I pulled a chicken leg from behind the moon and suddenly
realized that my girl had become a fish
where carts recede in the distance.
10 Once I had a little girl.
Once I had a dead fish beneath the ashes of the censers.
Once I had a sea. Of what? My God. A sea!
I climbed up to ring the bells, but the fruit was wormy
and the snuffed-out tapers
had eaten the spring wheat.
I saw the transparent stork of alcohol
picking clean the black heads of dying soldiers
and I saw the shelters of rubber
20 where the spinning goblets brimmed with tears.
I'll find you, my dear son, in anemones of the offertory
when the priest lifts the mule and the ox with his powerful arms,
to frighten nocturnal toads that roam the chalice's frozen landscape.
Once I had a son who was a giant,

pero los muertos son más fuertes y saben devorar pedazos de cielo.
Si mi niño hubiera sido un oso,
yo no temería el sigilo de los caimanes,
ni hubiese visto al mar amarrado a los árboles
para ser fornicado y herido por el tropel de los regimientos.
30 ¡Si mi niño hubiera sido un oso!
Me envolveré sobre esta lona dura para no sentir el frío de los
    musgos.
Sé muy bien que me darán una manga o la corbata;
pero en el centro de la misa yo romperé el timón y entonces
vendrá a la piedra la locura de pingüinos y gaviotas
que harán decir a los que duermen y a los que cantan por las
    esquinas:
Él tenía un hijo.
Un hijo. Un hijo. Un hijo
que no era más que suyo, porque era su hijo.
Su hijo. Su hijo. Su hijo.

III
Calles y sueños

A Rafael R. Rapún

Un pájaro de papel en el pecho
dice que el tiempo de los besos no ha llegado.
—VICENTE ALEIXANDRE

Danza de la muerte

El mascarón. Mirad el mascarón
cómo viene del África a New York.

Se fueron los árboles de la pimienta,
los pequeños botones de fósforo.
Se fueron los camellos de carne desgarrada
y los valles de luz que el cisne levantaba con el pico.

Era el momento de las cosas secas:
de la espiga en el ojo y el gato laminado;

but the dead are more powerful and can devour pieces of the sky.
If my boy had been a bear,
I wouldn't fear the crocodiles lying in ambush,
or have seen the sea lashed to the trees
for the brutal pleasure of the regiments.
30 If only my boy had been a bear!
I'll lie down and wrap myself in this rough canvas so I won't feel the
    cold moss.
I know very well that I'll be given shirt sleeves or a tie;
but in the middle of Mass I'll break the rudder and then
the insanity of penguins and gulls will come to the stone
and make those who sleep and sing on street corners say:
Once he had a son.
A son. A son. A son
who was his alone, because he was his son.
His son. His son. His son.

III
Streets and Dreams

To Rafael R. Rapún

A paper bird inside the breast
says the time for kisses is still not here.
—VICENTE ALEIXANDRE

Dance of Death

The mask. Look how the mask
comes from Africa to New York.

They are gone, the pepper trees,
the tiny buds of phosphorus.
They are gone, the camels with torn flesh,
and the valleys of light the swan lifted in its beak.

It was the time of parched things,
the wheat spear in the eye, the laminated cat,

del óxido de hierro de los grandes puentes
10 y el definitivo silencio del corcho.

Era la gran reunión de los animales muertos
traspasados por las espadas de la luz.
La alegría eterna del hipopótamo con las pezuñas de ceniza
y de la gacela con una siempreviva en la garganta.

En la marchita soledad sin onda
el abollado mascarón danzaba.
Medio lado del mundo era de arena,
mercurio y sol dormido el otro medio.

El mascarón. ¡Mirad el mascarón!
20 *Arena, caimán y miedo sobre Nueva York.*

Desfiladeros de cal aprisionaban un cielo vacío
donde sonaban las voces de los que mueren bajo el guano.
Un cielo mondado y puro, idéntico a sí mismo,
con el bozo y lirio agudo de sus montañas invisibles.

Acabó con los más leves tallitos del canto
y se fue al diluvio empaquetado de la savia,
a través del descanso de los últimos desfiles
levantando con el rabo pedazos de espejo.

Cuando el chino lloraba en el tejado
30 sin encontrar el desnudo de su mujer,
y el director del banco observaba el manómetro
que mide el cruel silencio de la moneda,
el mascarón llegaba a Wall Street.

No es extraño para la danza
este columbario que pone los ojos amarillos.
De la esfinge a la caja de caudales hay un hilo tenso
que atraviesa el corazón de todos los niños pobres.
El ímpetu primitivo baila con el ímpetu mecánico,
ignorantes en su frenesí de la luz original.
40 Porque si la rueda olvida su fórmula,
ya puede cantar desnuda con las manadas de caballos;
y si una llama quema los helados proyectos
el cielo tendrá que huir ante el tumulto de las ventanas.

the time of tremendous, rusting bridges
10   and the deathly silence of cork.

It was the great gathering of dead animals
pierced by the swords of light.
The endless joy of the hippopotamus with cloven feet of ash
and of the gazelle with an immortelle in its throat.

In the withered, waveless solitude,
the dented mask was dancing.
Half of the world was sand,
the other half mercury and dormant sunlight.

The mask. Look at the mask!
20   *Sand, crocodile, and fear above New York.*

Canyons of lime imprisoned an empty sky,
where the voices of those who die under the guano were heard.
A pure and well-peeled sky, identical with itself,
with the down and the keen-edged iris of its invisible mountains—

it finished off the slender stems of song
and was swept away toward channels of sap,
through the stillness of the last parades,
lifting pieces of mirror with its tail.

While the Chinaman wept on the roof,
30   not finding the nude of his wife,
and the bank director examined the manometer
that measures the cruel silence of money,
the mask arrived on Wall Street.

It isn't a strange place for the dance,
these cemetery niches that turn the eyes yellow.
Between the sphinx and the bank vault, there is a taut thread
that pierces the heart of all poor children.
The primitive impetus dances with the mechanical impetus,
unaware, in their frenzy, of the original light.
40   Because if the wheel forgets its formula,
it will sing nude with herds of horses;
and if a flame burns the frozen blueprints,
the sky will have to flee before the tumult of windows.

No es extraño este sitio para la danza. Yo lo digo.
El mascarón bailará entre columnas de sangre y de números,
entre huracanes de oro y gemidos de obreros parados
que aullarán, noche oscura, por tu tiempo sin luces.
¡Oh salvaje Norteamérica!, ¡oh impúdica!, ¡oh salvaje!
Tendida en la frontera de la nieve.

50 *El mascarón. ¡Mirad el mascarón!*
¡Qué ola de fango y luciérnagas sobre Nueva York!

★ ★ ★

Yo estaba en la terraza luchando con la luna.
Enjambres de ventanas acribillaban un muslo de la noche.
En mis ojos bebían las dulces vacas de los cielos
y las brisas de largos remos
golpeaban los cenicientos cristales del Broadway.

La gota de sangre buscaba la luz de la yema del astro
para fingir una muerta semilla de manzana.
El aire de la llanura, empujado por los pastores,
60 temblaba con un miedo de molusco sin concha.

Pero no son los muertos los que bailan.
Estoy seguro.
Los muertos están embebidos devorando sus propias manos.
Son los otros los que bailan con el mascarón y su vihuela.
Son los otros, los borrachos de plata, los hombres fríos,
los que duermen en el cruce de los muslos y llamas duras,
los que buscan la lombriz en el paisaje de las escaleras,
los que beben en el banco lágrimas de niña muerta
o los que comen por las esquinas diminutas pirámides del alba.

70 ¡Que no baile el Papa!
¡No,
que no baile el Papa!
Ni el Rey,
ni el millonario de dientes azules,
ni las bailarinas secas de las catedrales,
ni constructores, ni esmeraldas, ni locos, ni sodomitas.
Sólo este mascarón.
Este mascarón de vieja escarlatina.
¡Sólo este mascarón!

This isn't a strange place for the dance, I tell you.
The mask will dance among columns of blood and numbers,
among hurricanes of gold and groans of the unemployed,
who will howl, in the dead of night, for your dark time.
Oh, savage, shameless North America!
Stretched out on the frontier of snow.

50 *The mask. Look at the mask!*
Such a wave of mire and fireflies above New York!

★ ★ ★

I was on the terrace, wrestling with the moon.
Swarms of windows riddled one of the night's thighs.
Placid sky-cattle drank from my eyes
and the breezes on long oars
struck the ashen store windows on Broadway.

The drop of blood looked for light in the star's yolk
so as to seem a dead apple seed.
The prairie air, driven by the shepherds,
60 trembled in fear like a mollusk without its shell.

But I'm sure there are no dancers
among the dead.
The dead are engrossed in devouring their own hands.
It's the others who dance with the mask and its *vihuela*.
Others, drunk on silver, cold men,
who sleep where thighs and hard flames intersect,
who seek the earthworm in the landscape of fire escapes,
who drink a dead girl's tears at the bank
or eat pyramids of dawn on tiny street corners.

70 But don't let the Pope dance!
No,
don't let the Pope dance!
Nor the King,
nor the millionaires with blue teeth,
nor the barren dancers of the cathedrals,
nor builders, nor emeralds, nor madmen, nor sodomites.
Only this mask.
This mask of ancient scarlet fever.
Only this mask!

Que ya las cobras silbarán por los últimos pisos.
Que ya las ortigas estremecerán patios y terrazas.
Que ya la Bolsa será una pirámide de musgo.
Que ya vendrán lianas después de los fusiles
y muy pronto, muy pronto, muy pronto.
¡Ay, Wall Street!

El mascarón. ¡Mirad el mascarón!
¡Cómo escupe veneno de bosque
por la angustia imperfecta de Nueva York!

Diciembre 1929

Paisaje de la multitud que vomita
(Anochecer de Coney Island)

La mujer gorda venía delante
arrancando las raíces y mojando el pergamino de los tambores.
La mujer gorda,
que vuelve del revés los pulpos agonizantes.
La mujer gorda, enemiga de la luna,
corría por las calles y los pisos deshabitados
y dejaba por los rincones pequeñas calaveras de paloma
y levantaba las furias de los banquetes de los siglos últimos
y llamaba al demonio del pan por las colinas del cielo barrido
10 y filtraba un ansia de luz en las circulaciones subterráneas.
Son los cementerios. Lo sé. Son los cementerios
y el dolor de las cocinas enterradas bajo la arena.
Son los muertos, los faisanes y las manzanas de otra hora
los que nos empujan en la garganta.

Llegaban los rumores de la selva del vómito
con las mujeres vacías, con niños de cera caliente,
con árboles fermentados y camareros incansables
que sirven platos de sal bajo las arpas de la saliva.
Sin remedio, hijo mío. ¡Vomita! No hay remedio.
20 No es el vómito de los húsares sobre los pechos de la prostituta,
ni el vómito del gato que se tragó una rana por descuido.
Son los muertos que arañan con sus manos de tierra
las puertas de pedernal donde se pudren nublos y postres.

Cobras shall hiss on the top floors.
Nettles shall shake courtyards and terraces.
The Stock Exchange shall become a pyramid of moss.
Jungle vines shall come in behind the rifles
and all so quickly, so very, very quickly.
Ay, Wall Street!

The mask. Look at the mask!
And how it spits its forest poison
through New York's imperfect anguish!

December 1929

Landscape of a Vomiting Multitude
(Dusk at Coney Island)

The fat lady came first,
tearing out roots and moistening drumskins.
The fat lady
who turns dying octopuses inside out.
The fat lady, the moon's antagonist,
was running through the streets and deserted buildings
and leaving tiny skulls of pigeons in the corners
and stirring up the furies of the last centuries' feasts
and summoning the demon of bread through the sky's clean-swept hills
10 and filtering a longing for light into subterranean tunnels.
The graveyards, yes, the graveyards
and the sorrow of the kitchens buried in sand,
the dead, pheasants and apples of another era,
pushing into our throat.

There were murmurings from the jungle of vomit
with the empty women, with hot wax children,
with fermented trees and tireless waiters
who serve platters of salt beneath harps of saliva.
There's no other way, my son, vomit! There's no other way.
20 It's not the vomit of hussars on the breasts of their whores,
nor the vomit of a cat choking down a frog,
but the dead who scratch with clay hands
on flint gates where clouds and desserts decay.

La mujer gorda venía delante
con las gentes de los barcos, de las tabernas y de los jardines.
El vómito agitaba delicadamente sus tambores
entre algunas niñas de sangre
que pedían protección a la luna.
¡Ay de mí! ¡Ay de mí! ¡Ay de mí!
30 Esta mirada mía fue mía, pero ya no es mía.
Esta mirada que tiembla desnuda por el alcohol
y despide barcos increíbles
por las anémonas de los muelles.
Me defiendo con esta mirada
que mana de las ondas por donde el alba no se atreve.
Yo, poeta sin brazos, perdido
entre la multitud que vomita,
sin caballo efusivo que corte
los espesos musgos de mis sienes.
40 Pero la mujer gorda seguía delante
y la gente buscaba las farmacias
donde el amargo trópico se fija.
Sólo cuando izaron la bandera y llegaron los primeros canes
la ciudad entera se agolpó en las barandillas del embarcadero.

Nueva York, 29 de diciembre de 1929

Paisaje de la multitud que orina
(Nocturno de Battery Place)

Se quedaron solos.
Aguardaban la velocidad de las últimas bicicletas.
Se quedaron solas.
Esperaban la muerte de un niño en el velero japonés.
Se quedaron solos y solas.
Soñando con los picos abiertos de los pájaros agonizantes,
con el agudo quitasol que pincha
al sapo recién aplastado,
bajo un silencio con mil orejas
10 y diminutas bocas de agua
en los desfiladeros que resisten
el ataque violento de la luna.
Lloraba el niño del velero y se quebraban los corazones

The fat lady came first
with the crowds from the ships, taverns, and parks.
Vomit was delicately shaking its drums
among a few little girls of blood
who were begging the moon for protection.
Who could imagine my sadness?
30   The look on my face was mine, but now isn't me.
The naked look on my face, trembling in alcohol
and launching incredible ships
through the anemones of the piers.
I protect myself with this look
that flows from waves where no dawn would go,
I, poet without arms, lost
in the vomiting multitude,
with no effusive horse to shear
the thick moss from my temples.
40   But the fat lady went first
and the crowds kept looking for the pharmacies
where the bitter tropics could be found.
Only when a flag went up and the first dogs arrived
did the entire city rush to the railings of the boardwalk.

New York, December 29, 1929

Landscape of a Pissing Multitude
(Battery Place Nocturne)

The men kept to themselves.
They were waiting for the swiftness of the last cyclists.
The women kept to themselves.
They were expecting the death of a boy on a Japanese schooner.
They all kept to themselves—
dreaming of the open beaks of dying birds,
the sharp parasol that punctures
a recently flattened toad,
beneath silence with a thousand ears
10   and tiny mouths of water
in the canyons that resist
the violent attack of the moon.
The boy on the schooner was crying and hearts were breaking

angustiados por el testigo y la vigilia de todas las cosas
y porque todavía en el suelo celeste de negras huellas
gritaban nombres oscuros, salivas y radios de níquel.
No importa que el niño calle cuando le claven el último alfiler.
Ni importa la derrota de la brisa en la corola del algodón.
Porque hay un mundo de la muerte con marineros definitivos
20   que se asomarán a los arcos y os helarán por detrás de los árboles.
Es inútil buscar el recodo
donde la noche olvida su viaje
y acechar un silencio que no tenga
trajes rotos y cáscaras y llanto,
porque tan sólo el diminuto banquete de la araña
basta para romper el equilibrio de todo el cielo.
No hay remedio para el gemido del velero japonés,
ni para estas gentes ocultas que tropiezan con las esquinas.
El campo se muerde la cola para unir las raíces en un punto
30   y el ovillo busca por la grama su ansia de longitud insatisfecha.
¡La luna! Los policías. ¡Las sirenas de los transatlánticos!
Fachadas de crin, de humo, anémonas, guantes de goma.
Todo está roto por la noche,
abierta de piernas sobre las terrazas.
Todo está roto por los tibios caños
de una terrible fuente silenciosa.
¡Oh gentes! Oh mujercillas. ¡Oh soldados!
Será preciso viajar por los ojos de los idiotas,
campos libres donde silban mansas cobras deslumbradas,
40   paisajes llenos de sepulcros que producen fresquísimas manzanas,
para que venga la luz desmedida
que temen los ricos detrás de sus lupas,
el olor de un solo cuerpo con la doble vertiente de lis y rata
y para que se quemen estas gentes que pueden orinar alrededor de
    un gemido
o en los cristales donde se comprenden las olas nunca repetidas.

Asesinato
(Dos voces de madrugada en Riverside Drive)

—*¿Cómo fue?*
—Una grieta en la mejilla.
¡Eso es todo!

in anguish over everything's witness and vigil,
and because on the sky-blue ground of black footprints,
obscure names, saliva, and chrome radios were still crying.
It doesn't matter if the boy grows silent when stuck with the last pin,
or if the breeze is defeated in cupped cotton flowers,
because there is a world of death whose perpetual sailors
20   will appear in the arches and freeze you from behind the trees.
It's useless to look for the bend
where night loses its way
and to wait in ambush for a silence that has no
torn clothes, no shells, and no tears,
because even the tiny banquet of a spider
is enough to upset the entire equilibrium of the sky.
There is no cure for the moaning from a Japanese schooner,
nor for those shadowy people who stumble on the curbs.
The countryside bites its own tail in order to gather a bunch of roots
30   and a ball of yarn looks anxiously in the grass for unrealized longitude.
The moon! The police. The foghorns of the ocean liners!
Facades of horse hair, of smoke, anemones, rubber gloves.
Everything is shattered in the night
that spreads its legs on the terraces.
Everything is shattered in the tepid faucets
of a terrible silent fountain.
Oh, crowds! Loose women! Soldiers!
We will have to journey through the eyes of idiots,
open country where the tame cobras hiss in a daze,
40   landscapes full of graves that yield the freshest apples,
so that uncontrollable light will arrive
to frighten the rich behind their magnifying glasses—
the odor of a single corpse from the double source of lily and rat—
and so that fire will consume those crowds still able to piss around a
    moan
or on the crystals in which each inimitable wave is understood.

Murder
(*Two Early Morning Voices on Riverside Drive*)

"*How did it happen?*"
"A gash on the cheek.
That's all!

Una uña que aprieta el tallo.
Un alfiler que bucea
hasta encontrar las raicillas del grito.
Y el mar deja de moverse.
—*¿Cómo, cómo fue?*
—Así.
10   —*¡Déjame! ¿De esa manera?*
—Sí.
El corazón salió solo.
—*¡Ay, ay de mí!*

Navidad en el Hudson

¡Esa esponja gris!
Ese marinero recién degollado.
Ese río grande.
Esa brisa de límites oscuros.
Ese filo, amor, ese filo.
Estaban los cuatro marineros luchando con el mundo.
Con el mundo de aristas que ven todos los ojos.
Con el mundo que no se puede recorrer sin caballos.
Estaban uno, cien, mil marineros
10   luchando con el mundo de las agudas velocidades,
sin enterarse de que el mundo
estaba solo por el cielo.

El mundo solo por el cielo solo.
Son las colinas de martillos y el triunfo de la hierba espesa.
Son los vivísimos hormigueros y las monedas en el fango.
El mundo solo por el cielo solo
y el aire a la salida de todas las aldeas.

Cantaba la lombriz el terror de la rueda
y el marinero degollado
20   cantaba al oso de agua que lo había de estrechar;
y todos cantaban aleluya,
aleluya. Cielo desierto.
Es lo mismo, ¡lo mismo!, aleluya.

A fingernail that pinches the stem.
A pin that dives
until it finds the roots of a scream.
And the sea stops still."
"How, how did it happen?"
"Like this."
10   *"Really! Like that?"*
"Yes.
The heart came out on its own."
"I'm done for!"

Christmas on the Hudson

That gray sponge!
That sailor whose throat was just cut.
That great river.
Those dark boundaries of the breeze.
That keen blade, my love, that keen blade.
The four sailors wrestled with the world.
With that sharp-edged world that all eyes see.
With the world no one can know without horses.
One, a hundred, a thousand sailors
10   wrestling with the world of keen-edged velocities,
unaware that the world
was alone in the sky.

The world alone in the lonely sky.
Hills of hammers and the thick grass's triumph.
Teeming anthills and coins in the mire.
The world alone in the lonely sky,
and the air where all the villages end.

The earthworm sang its terror of the wheel,
and the sailor whose throat was slashed
20   sang to the water-bear that held him close;
and they were all singing alleluia,
alleluia. Deserted sky.
It's all the same—the same!—alleluia.

He pasado toda la noche en los andamios de los arrabales
dejándome la sangre por la escayola de los proyectos,
ayudando a los marineros a recoger las velas desgarradas,
y estoy con las manos vacías en el rumor de la desembocadura.
No importa que cada minuto
un niño nuevo agite sus ramitos de venas,
30 ni que el parto de la víbora, desatado bajo las ramas,
calme la sed de sangre de los que miran el desnudo.
Lo que importa es esto: hueco. Mundo solo. Desembocadura.
Alba no. Fábula inerte.
Sólo esto: desembocadura.
Oh esponja mía gris.
Oh cuello mío recién degollado.
Oh río grande mío.
Oh brisa mía de límites que no son míos.
Oh filo de mi amor, oh hiriente filo.

Nueva York, 27 de diciembre de 1929

Ciudad sin sueño
(Nocturno del Brooklyn Bridge)

No duerme nadie por el cielo. Nadie, nadie.
No duerme nadie.
Las criaturas de la luna huelen y rondan las cabañas.
Vendrán las iguanas vivas a morder a los hombres que no sueñan
y el que huye con el corazón roto encontrará por las esquinas
al increíble cocodrilo quieto bajo la tierna protesta de los astros.

No duerme nadie por el mundo. Nadie, nadie.
No duerme nadie.
Hay un muerto en el cementerio más lejano
10 que se queja tres años
porque tiene un paisaje seco en la rodilla;
y el niño que enterraron esta mañana lloraba tanto
que hubo necesidad de llamar a los perros para que callase.

No es sueño la vida. ¡Alerta! ¡Alerta! ¡Alerta!
Nos caemos por las escaleras para comer la tierra húmeda
o subimos al filo de la nieve con el coro de las dalias muertas.

I stood all night on scaffolding in the boroughs,
leaving my blood on the stucco projects,
helping the sailors lower their ripped sails,
and I stand with empty hands in the murmur of the river's mouth.
It doesn't matter if every minute
a newborn child waves the little branches of its veins,
30 or if a newborn viper, set free beneath the branches,
calms the blood lust of those who look at the nude.
What matters is this: emptied space. Lonely world. River's mouth.
Not dawn. Idle fable.
This alone: river's mouth.
Oh, my gray sponge!
Oh, my throat just cut open!
Oh, my great river!
Oh, my breeze's boundaries that are not mine!
Oh, the keen blade of my love, oh, the cutting blade!

New York, December 27, 1929

Sleepless City
(Brooklyn Bridge Nocturne)

Out in the sky, no one sleeps. No one, no one.
No one sleeps.
Lunar creatures sniff and circle the dwellings.
Live iguanas will come to bite the men who don't dream,
and the brokenhearted fugitive will meet on street corners
an incredible crocodile resting beneath the tender protest of the stars.

Out in the world, no one sleeps. No one, no one.
No one sleeps.
There is a corpse in the farthest graveyard
10 complaining for three years
because of an arid landscape in his knee;
and a boy who was buried this morning cried so much
they had to call the dogs to quiet him.

Life is no dream. Watch out! Watch out! Watch out!
We fall down stairs and eat the moist earth,
or we climb to the snow's edge with the choir of dead dahlias.

Pero no hay olvido ni sueño:
carne viva. Los besos atan las bocas
en una maraña de venas recientes
y al que le duele su dolor le dolerá sin descanso
y el que teme la muerte la llevará sobre los hombros.

Un día
los caballos vivirán en las tabernas
y las hormigas furiosas
atacarán los cielos amarillos que se refugian en los ojos de las vacas.
Otro día
veremos la resurrección de las mariposas disecadas
y aun andando por un paisaje de esponjas grises y barcos mudos
veremos brillar nuestro anillo y manar rosas de nuestra lengua.
¡Alerta! ¡Alerta! ¡Alerta!
A los que guardan todavía huellas de zarpa y aguacero,
a aquel muchacho que llora porque no sabe la invención del puente
o a aquel muerto que ya no tiene más que la cabeza y un zapato,
hay que llevarlos al muro donde iguanas y sierpes esperan,
donde espera la dentadura del oso,
donde espera la mano momificada del niño
y la piel del camello se eriza con un violento escalofrío azul.

No duerme nadie por el cielo. Nadie, nadie.
No duerme nadie.
Pero si alguien cierra los ojos,
¡azotadlo, hijos míos, azotadlo!
Haya un panorama de ojos abiertos
y amargas llagas encendidas.
No duerme nadie por el mundo. Nadie, nadie.
Ya lo he dicho.
No duerme nadie.
Pero si alguien tiene por la noche exceso de musgo en las sienes,
abrid los escotillones para que vea bajo la luna
las copas falsas, el veneno y la calavera de los teatros.

But there is no oblivion, no dream:
raw flesh. Kisses tie mouths
in a tangle of new veins
20   and those in pain will bear it with no respite
and those who are frightened by death will carry it on their
    shoulders.

One day
horses will live in the taverns
and furious ants
will attack the yellow skies that take refuge in the eyes of cattle.
Another day
we'll witness the resurrection of dried butterflies,
and even when walking in a landscape of gray sponges and silent ships,
we'll see our ring shine and roses spill from our tongues.
30   Watch out! Watch out! Watch out!
Those still marked by claws and cloudburst,
that boy who cries because he doesn't know bridges exist,
or that corpse that has nothing more than its head and one shoe—
they all must be led to the wall where iguanas and serpents wait,
where the bear's teeth wait,
where the mummified hand of a child waits
and the camel's fur bristles with a violent blue chill.

Out in the sky, no one sleeps. No one, no one.
No one sleeps.
40   But if someone closes his eyes,
whip him, my children, whip him!
Let there be a panorama of open eyes
and bitter inflamed wounds.
Out in the world, no one sleeps. No one. No one.
I've said it before.
No one sleeps.
But at night, if someone has too much moss on his temples,
open the trap doors so he can see in moonlight
the fake goblets, the venom, and the skull of the theaters.

Panorama ciego de Nueva York

Si no son los pájaros
cubiertos de ceniza,
si no son los gemidos que golpean las ventanas de la boda,
serán las delicadas criaturas del aire
que manan la sangre nueva por la oscuridad inextinguible.
Pero no, no son los pájaros.
Porque los pájaros están a punto de ser bueyes.
Pueden ser rocas blancas con la ayuda de la luna
y son siempre muchachos heridos
10   antes de que los jueces levanten la tela.

Todos comprenden el dolor que se relaciona con la muerte,
pero el verdadero dolor no está presente en el espíritu.
No está en el aire, ni en nuestra vida,
ni en estas terrazas llenas de humo.
El verdadero dolor que mantiene despiertas las cosas
es una pequeña quemadura infinita
en los ojos inocentes de los otros sistemas.

Un traje abandonado pesa tanto en los hombros
que muchas veces el cielo los agrupa en ásperas manadas;
20   y las que mueren de parto saben en la última hora
que todo rumor será piedra y toda huella latido.
Nosotros ignoramos que el pensamiento tiene arrabales
donde el filósofo es devorado por los chinos y las orugas
y algunos niños idiotas han encontrado por las cocinas
pequeñas golondrinas con muletas
que sabían pronunciar la palabra amor.

No, no son los pájaros.
No es un pájaro el que expresa la turbia fiebre de laguna,
ni el ansia de asesinato que nos oprime cada momento,
30   ni el metálico rumor de suicidio que nos anima cada madrugada.
Es una cápsula de aire donde nos duele todo el mundo,
es un pequeño espacio vivo al loco unísón de la luz,
es una escala indefinible donde las nubes y rosas olvidan
el griterío chino que bulle por el desembarcadero de la sangre.
Yo muchas veces me he perdido
para buscar la quemadura que mantiene despiertas las cosas
y sólo he encontrado marineros echados sobre las barandillas

Blind Panorama of New York

If it isn't the birds
covered with ash,
if it isn't the cries beating against the windows of the wedding,
it is the delicate creatures of the air
that spill fresh blood in the inextinguishable darkness.
But no, it isn't the birds,
because the birds will soon become oxen.
They could become white rocks with the moon's help
and they are always wounded boys
before the judges lift the cloth.

Everyone understands the pain that accompanies death,
but genuine pain doesn't live in the spirit,
nor in the air, nor in our lives,
nor on these terraces of billowing smoke.
The genuine pain that keeps everything awake
is a tiny, infinite burn
on the innocent eyes of other systems.

An abandoned suit weighs so heavily on the shoulders
that the sky often shrugs them into rugged togetherness.
And those who die in childbirth learn in their last hour
that every murmur will be stone and every footstep will throb.
We forget that the mind has boroughs
where Chinese and caterpillars devour the philosopher.
And some feebleminded children in the kitchens have discovered
tiny swallows on crutches
that could pronounce the word love.

No, it isn't the birds.
A bird can't express the cloudy fever of a lagoon
or the urge to murder someone that oppresses us every moment,
or the metallic hum of suicide that revives us every morning.
It's a capsule of air where we suffer the whole world,
a tiny space alive in the crazy unison of light,
an indefinable ladder on which clouds and roses forget
the Chinese howl that boils over on the waterfront of the blood.
I've often lost myself
in order to find the burn that keeps everything awake
and all I've found are sailors leaning over the railings

y pequeñas criaturas del cielo enterradas bajo la nieve.
Pero el verdadero dolor estaba en otras plazas
40 donde los peces cristalizados agonizaban dentro de los troncos;
plazas del cielo extraño para las antiguas estatuas ilesas
y para la tierna intimidad de los volcanes.

No hay dolor en la voz. Sólo existen los dientes,
pero dientes que callarán aislados por el raso negro.
No hay dolor en la voz. Aquí sólo existe la Tierra.
La Tierra con sus puertas de siempre
que llevan al rubor de los frutos.

Nacimiento de Cristo

Un pastor pide teta por la nieve que ondula
blancos perros tendidos entre linternas sordas.
El Cristito de barro se ha partido los dedos
en los filos eternos de la madera rota.

¡Ya vienen las hormigas y los pies ateridos!
Dos hilillos de sangre quiebran el cielo duro.
Los vientres del demonio resuenan por los valles
golpes y resonancias de carne de molusco.

Lobos y sapos cantan en las hogueras verdes
10 coronadas por vivos hormigueros del alba.
La mula tiene un sueño de grandes abanicos
y el toro sueña un toro de agujeros y de agua.

El niño llora y mira con un tres en la frente.
San José ve en el heno tres espinas de bronce.
Los pañales exhalan un rumor de desierto
con cítaras sin cuerdas y degolladas voces.

La nieve de Manhattan empuja los anuncios
y lleva gracia pura por las falsas ojivas.
Sacerdotes idiotas y querubes de pluma
20 van detrás de Lutero por las altas esquinas.

and tiny sky creatures buried under the snow.
But on other plazas, there was genuine pain
40 where crystallized fish were dying inside tree trunks;
plazas of blue sky alien to the unscathed statues of antiquity
and to the intimate tenderness of volcanoes.

There is no pain in the voice. Only the teeth exist,
but isolated teeth that will be silenced by black satin.
There is no pain in the voice. Only the Earth exists here.
The Earth and its timeless doors
which lead to the blush of the fruit.

The Birth of Christ

A shepherd begs to be suckled in snow that drifts
white dogs stretched out between shaded lanterns.
The little clay Christ has split its fingers
on the eternally keen edges of the splintered wood.

Here come the ants and the feet stiff with cold!
Two small threads of blood break up the hard sky.
The demon's intestines fill the valleys
with the blows and resonances of mollusk flesh.

Wolves and toads sing in green bonfires
10 crowned by the flaming anthills of dawn.
The mule has a dream of enormous fans
and the bull dreams a pierced bull and water.

The child with a three on its forehead cries and stares.
St. Joseph sees three bronze thorns in the hay.
And the swaddling clothes exhale a desert's rumbling
with stringless zithers and beheaded voices.

The snow of Manhattan blows against billboards
and carries pure grace through the fake Gothic arches.
Idiot clergymen and cherubim in feathers
20 follow Luther in a line around the high corners.

La aurora

La aurora de Nueva York tiene
cuatro columnas de cieno
y un huracán de negras palomas
que chapotean las aguas podridas.
La aurora de Nueva York gime
por las inmensas escaleras
buscando entre las aristas
nardos de angustia dibujada.
La aurora llega y nadie la recibe en su boca
porque allí no hay mañana ni esperanza posible:
a veces las monedas en enjambres furiosos
taladran y devoran abandonados niños.
Los primeros que salen comprenden con sus huesos
que no habrá paraíso ni amores deshojados:
saben que van al cieno de números y leyes,
a los juegos sin arte, a sudores sin fruto.
La luz es sepultada por cadenas y ruidos
en impúdico reto de ciencia sin raíces.
Por los barrios hay gentes que vacilan insomnes
como recién salidas de un naufragio de sangre.

IV
Poemas del Lago Eden Mills
A Eduardo Ugarte

Poema doble del Lago Eden

> *Nuestro ganado pace, el viento espira.*
> —GARCILASO

Era mi voz antigua
ignorante de los densos jugos amargos.
la que vino lamiendo mis pies
bajo los frágiles helechos mojados.

Dawn

Dawn in New York has
four columns of mire
and a hurricane of black pigeons
splashing in the putrid waters.
Dawn in New York groans
on enormous fire escapes
searching between the angles
for spikenards of drafted anguish.
Dawn arrives and no one receives it in his mouth
10 because tomorrow and hope are impossible there:
sometimes the furious swarming coins
penetrate like drills and devour abandoned children.
Those who go out early know in their bones
there will be no paradise or loves that bloom and die:
they know they will be mired in numbers and laws,
in mindless games, in fruitless labors.
The light is buried under chains and noises
in an impudent challenge of rootless science.
And crowds stagger sleeplessly through the boroughs
20 as if they had just escaped a shipwreck of blood.

IV
Poems of Lake Eden Mills
To Eduardo Ugarte

Double Poem of Lake Eden

> *Our cattle graze, the wind sends forth its breath.*
> —GARCILASO

It was the voice I had before,
ignorant of the dense and bitter sap,
the one that came lapping at my feet
beneath the moist and fragile ferns.

¡Ay, voz antigua de mi amor!
Ay, voz de mi verdad.
Ay, voz de mi abierto costado,
cuando todas las rosas manaban de mi lengua
y el césped no conocía la impasible dentadura del caballo.

10 Estás aquí bebiendo mi sangre,
bebiendo mi humor de niño pasado,
mientras mis ojos se quiebran en el viento
con el aluminio y las voces de los borrachos.

Dejarme pasar la puerta
donde Eva come hormigas
y Adán fecunda peces deslumbrados.
Dejarme pasar, hombrecillos de los cuernos,
al bosque de los desperezos
y los alegrísimos saltos.

20 Yo sé el uso más secreto
que tiene un viejo alfiler oxidado
y sé del horror de unos ojos despiertos
sobre la superficie concreta del plato.

Pero no quiero mundo ni sueño, voz divina,
quiero mi libertad, mi amor humano
en el rincón más oscuro de la brisa que nadie quiera.
¡Mi amor humano!

Esos perros marinos se persiguen
y el viento acecha troncos descuidados.
30 ¡Oh voz antigua, quema con tu lengua
esta voz de hojalata y de talco!

Quiero llorar porque me da la gana,
como lloran los niños del último banco,
porque yo no soy un hombre, ni un poeta, ni una hoja,
pero sí un pulso herido que sonda las cosas del otro lado.

Quiero llorar diciendo mi nombre,
rosa, niño y abeto a la orilla de este lago,
para decir mi verdad de hombre de sangre
matando en mí la burla y la sugestión del vocablo.

Ay, my love's voice from before
ay, voice of my truth,
ay, voice of my open side,
when all the roses spilled from my tongue
and the grass hadn't felt the horse's impassable teeth!

10 Here you are drinking my blood,
drinking the humor of the child I was,
while my eyes are shattered by aluminum
and drunken voices in the wind.

Let me pass through the arch
where Eve devours ants
and Adam impregnates the dazzling fish.
Little men with horns, let me return
to the grove of easy living
and the somersaults of pure joy.

20 I know the best secret way
to use an old rusty pin,
and I know the horror of eyes wide-awake
on the concrete surface of a plate.

But I want neither world nor dream, divine voice,
I want my liberty, my human love
in the darkest corner of the breeze no one wants.
My human love!

Those sea-dogs chase each other
and the wind lies in ambush for careless tree trunks.
30 Oh, voice of before, let your tongue burn
this voice of tin and talc!

I want to cry because I feel like it—
the way children cry in the last row of seats—
because I'm not a man, not a poet, not a leaf,
only a wounded pulse that probes the things of the other side.

I want to cry saying my name,
rose, child, and fir on the shore of this lake,
to speak truly as a man of blood
killing in myself the mockery and the suggestive power of the word.

40 No, no. Yo no pregunto, yo deseo,
    voz mía libertada que me lames las manos.
    En el laberinto de biombos es mi desnudo el que recibe
    la luna de castigo y el reloj encenizado.

    Así hablaba yo.
    Así hablaba yo cuando Saturno detuvo los trenes
    y la bruma y el Sueño y la Muerte me estaban buscando.
    Me estaban buscando
    allí donde mugen las vacas que tienen patitas de paje
    y allí donde flota mi cuerpo entre los equilibrios contrarios.

Cielo vivo

Yo no podré quejarme
si no encontré lo que buscaba.
Cerca de las piedras sin jugo y los insectos vacíos
no veré el duelo del sol con las criaturas en carne viva.

Pero me iré al primer paisaje
de choques, líquidos y rumores
que trasmina a niño recién nacido
y donde toda superficie es evitada,
para entender que lo que busco tendrá su blanco de alegría
10 cuando yo vuele mezclado con el amor y las arenas.

Allí no llega la escarcha de los ojos apagados
ni el mugido del árbol asesinado por la oruga.
Allí todas las formas guardan entrelazadas
una sola expresión frenética de avance.

No puedes avanzar por los enjambres de corolas
porque el aire disuelve tus dientes de azúcar,
ni puedes acariciar la fugaz hoja del helecho
sin sentir el asombro definitivo del marfil.

Allí bajo las raíces y en la médula del aire,
20 se comprende la verdad de las cosas equivocadas.
El nadador de níquel que acecha la onda más fina
y el rebaño de vacas nocturnas con rojas patitas de mujer.

40 No, no, I'm not asking, I'm telling you what I want,
my liberated voice lapping at my hands.
In the labyrinth of folding screens my nakedness receives
the punishing moon and the clock covered with ash.

I was speaking that way.
I was speaking that way when Saturn stopped the trains
and the fog and the Dream and Death were looking for me.
Looking for me
where cattle with the little feet of a page bellow
and my body floats between contrary equilibriums.

Living Sky

I won't be able to complain
though I never found what I was looking for.
Near the dried-up stones and the husks of insects,
I won't see the sun's duel with the creatures of flesh and blood.

But I'll go to the first landscape
of shocks, fluids, and murmurs
that seeps into a newborn child,
and where all surfaces are avoided,
so I'll know that my search has a joyful target
10 when I'm flying, jumbled with love and sandstorms.

There, the frost of snuffed-out eyes won't reach,
nor the bellowing of a tree, murdered by the caterpillar.
There, all the shapes intertwine and have
the same frenetic, forward expression.

You can't pass through the swarming corollas—
the air dissolves your teeth of sugar.
And you can't caress the elusive fern
without feeling the utter astonishment of ivory.

There, under roots and in the medulla of the air,
20 mistaken things are understood as true.
The finest wave about to pounce on the chrome swimmer
and the flock of nocturnal cattle with a woman's little red feet . . .

Yo no podré quejarme
si no encontré lo que buscaba,
pero me iré al primer paisaje de humedades y latidos
para entender que lo que busco tendrá su blanco de alegría
cuando yo vuele mezclado con el amor y las arenas.

Vuelo fresco de siempre sobre lechos vacíos.
Sobre grupos de brisas y barcos encallados.
30 Tropiezo vacilante por la dura eternidad fija
y amor al fin sin alba. Amor. ¡Amor visible!

Eden Mills, Vermont, 24 de agosto de 1929

V
En la cabaña del farmer

(Campo de Newburgh)

A Concha Méndez y Manuel Altolaguirre

El niño Stanton

—*Do you like me?*
—*Yes, and you?*
—*Yes, yes.*

Cuando me quedo solo
me quedan todavía tus diez años,
los tres caballos ciegos,
tus quince rostros con el rostro de la pedrada
y las fiebres pequeñas heladas sobre las hojas del maíz.
Stanton. Hijo mío. Stanton.
10 A las doce de la noche el cáncer salía por los pasillos
y hablaba con los caracoles vacíos de los documentos.
El vivísimo cáncer lleno de nubes y termómetros
con su casto afán de manzana para que lo piquen los ruiseñores.
En la casa donde hay un cáncer
se quiebran las blancas paredes en el delirio de la astronomía

I won't be able to complain
though I never found what I was looking for;
but I'll go to the first fluid landscape of heartbeats
so I'll know that my search has a joyful target
when I'm flying, jumbled with love and sandstorms.

I'm used to the cool air when I fly over empty beds.
Over squalls and ships run aground.
30 I stumble sleepily through eternity's fixed hardness
and love at the end without dawn. Love. Visible love!

Eden Mills, Vermont, August 24, 1929

V

In the Farmer's Cabin

(In the Newburgh Countryside)
To Concha Méndez and Manuel Altolaguirre

Little Stanton

> *"Do you like me?"*
> *"Yes, and you?"*
> *"Yes, yes."*

When I'm by myself
your ten years stay with me.
So do the three blind horses,
your fifteen faces with the face after the stoning
and tiny frozen fevers on leaves of corn.
Stanton, my son, Stanton.
10 At twelve midnight, cancer wandered through the corridors
and spoke with the documents' empty snails,
cancer springing to life, full of clouds and thermometers,
with an apple's chaste longing to be pecked by nightingales.
In the house where there is cancer,
the white walls shatter in the delirium of astronomy

y por los establos más pequeños y en las cruces de los bosques
brilla por muchos años el fulgor de la quemadura.
Mi dolor sangraba por las tardes
cuando tus ojos eran dos muros.
20   Cuando tus manos eran dos países
y mi cuerpo rumor de hierba.
Mi agonía buscaba su traje,
polvorienta, mordida por los perros,
y tú la acompañaste sin temblar
hasta la puerta del agua oscura.
¡Oh mi Stanton, idiota y bello entre los pequeños animalitos!
Con tu madre fracturada por los herreros de las aldeas,
con un hermano bajo los arcos,
otro comido por los hormigueros,
30   ¡y el cáncer sin alambradas latiendo por las habitaciones!
Hay nodrizas que dan a los niños
ríos de musgo y amargura de pie
y algunas negras suben a los pisos para repartir filtro de rata.
Porque es verdad que la gente
quiere echar las palomas a las alcantarillas
y yo sé lo que esperan los que por la calle
nos oprimen de pronto las yemas de los dedos.

Tu ignorancia es un monte de leones, Stanton.
El día que el cáncer te dió una paliza
40   y te escupió en el dormitorio donde murieron los huéspedes en la
    epidemia
y abrió su quebrada rosa de vidrios secos y manos blandas
para salpicar de lodo las pupilas de los que navegan,
tú buscaste en la hierba mi agonía,
mi agonía con flores de terror,
mientras que el agrio cáncer mudo que quiere acostarse contigo
pulverizaba rojos paisajes por las sábanas de amargura
y ponía sobre los ataúdes
helados arbolitos de ácido bórico.
Stanton, vete al bosque con tus arpas judías,
50   vete para aprender celestiales palabras
que duermen en los troncos, en nubes, en tortugas,
en los perros dormidos, en el plomo, en el viento,
en lirios que no duermen, en aguas que no copian,
para que aprendas, hijo, lo que tu pueblo olvida.
Cuando empiece el tumulto de la guerra

and the burn glows brightly for many years
in the tiny stables, in forests where paths intersect.
My sorrow bled in the afternoons
when your eyes became two walls,
20 when your hands became two countries
and my body murmured like grass.
My agony went looking for its clothes,
dusty, bitten by dogs,
and you went with it, without trembling,
to the threshold of dark water.
Oh, Stanton, idiotic and beautiful among the little animals,
your mother hammered to pieces by the village blacksmiths,
one brother under the arches
and the other one eaten by the anthills,
30 and cancer, free of barbed wire, beating in the rooms like a heart!
There are wet nurses who give children
rivers of moss and bitter feet,
and black women who spread love potions made from rats in the
    bedrooms upstairs.
Because it's true, there are people
who want to dump doves in the sewers
and I know what else they want—the people
hanging out in the street who suddenly squeeze our fingertips.

Your ignorance is a mountain of lions, Stanton.
The day cancer gave you a beating,
40 and spit on you in the bedroom where the guests died in the
    epidemic,
and opened its broken rose of dry glass and soft hands
to spatter mud in the eyes of sailors—
you looked for my agony in the grass,
my agony and its flowers of pure fear,
while the speechless, acid cancer that wants to go to bed with you
pulverized red landscapes on the bedsheets of bitterness
and placed on the coffins
little frozen trees of boric acid.
Stanton, go to the woods with your jew's-harp,
50 go to learn celestial words
that sleep in tree trunks, clouds, and turtles,
in sleeping dogs, in lead and wind,
in irises that don't sleep and waters that copy nothing.
Go to learn, my son, what your people forget.

dejaré un pedazo de queso para tu perro en la oficina.
Tus diez años serán las hojas
que vuelan en los trajes de los muertos,
diez rosas de azufre débil
60 en el hombro de mi madrugada.
Y yo, Stanton, yo solo, en olvido,
con tus caras marchitas sobre mi boca,
iré penetrando a voces las verdes estatuas de la Malaria.

Vaca

A Luis Lacasa

Se tendió la vaca herida.
Árboles y arroyos trepaban por sus cuernos.
Su hocico sangraba en el cielo.

Su hocico de abejas
bajo el bigote lento de la baba.
Un alarido blanco puso en pie la mañana.

Las vacas muertas y las vivas,
rubor de luz o miel de establo,
balaban con los ojos entornados.

10 Que se enteren las raíces
y aquel niño que afila su navaja
de que ya se pueden comer la vaca.

Arriba palidecen
luces y yugulares.
Cuatro pezuñas tiemblan en el aire.

Que se entere la luna
y esa noche de rocas amarillas
que ya se fue la vaca de ceniza.

Que ya se fue balando
20 por el derribo de los cielos yertos,
donde meriendan muerte los borrachos.

When the thunder of war begins,
I'll leave a piece of cheese for your dog in the office.
Your ten years will be the leaves
flying in the clothes of the dead,
ten roses of powerless sulfur
60 on the shoulder of my dawn.
And I, Stanton, by myself, forgotten,
your withered faces on my mouth—
I'll go shouting my way through the green statues of Malaria.

Cow

To Luis Lacasa

The wounded cow lay down,
trees and streams climbing over its horns.
Its muzzle bled in the sky.

Its muzzle of bees
under the slow mustache of slobber.
A white cry brought the morning to its feet.

Cows, dead and alive,
blushing light or honey from the stables,
bellowed with half-closed eyes.

10 Tell the roots
and that child sharpening his knife:
now they can eat the cow.

Above them, lights
and jugulars turn pale.
Four cloven hoofs tremble in the air.

Tell the moon
and that night of yellow rocks:
now the cow of ash has gone.

Now it has gone bellowing
20 through the wreckage of the rigid skies
where the drunks lunch on death.

Niña ahogada en el pozo
(Granada y Newburgh)

Las estatuas sufren con los ojos por la oscuridad de los ataúdes,
pero sufren mucho más por el agua que no desemboca . . . ,
que no desemboca.

El pueblo corría por las almenas rompiendo las cañas de los
    pescadores.
¡Pronto! ¡Los bordes! ¡De prisa! Y croaban las estrellas tiernas.
. . . que no desemboca.

Tranquila en mi recuerdo, astro, círculo, meta,
lloras por las orillas de un ojo de caballo.
. . . que no desemboca.

10 Pero nadie en lo oscuro podrá darte distancias,
sino afilado límite: porvenir de diamante.
. . . que no desemboca.

Mientras la gente busca silencios de almohada,
tú lates para siempre definida en tu anillo.
. . . que no desemboca.

Eterna en los finales de unas ondas que aceptan
combate de raíces y soledad prevista.
. . . que no desemboca.

¡Ya vienen por las rampas! ¡Levántate del agua!
20 ¡Cada punto de luz te dará una cadena!
. . . que no desemboca.

Pero el pozo te alarga manecitas de musgo,
insospechada ondina de su casta ignorancia.
. . . que no desemboca.

No, que no desemboca. Agua fija en un punto.
Respirando con todos sus violines sin cuerdas.
En la escala de las heridas y los edificios deshabitados.
¡Agua que no desemboca!

Little Girl Drowned in the Well
(Granada and Newburgh)

Statues suffer the darkness of coffins with their eyes,
but they suffer even more from water that never reaches the sea . . .
that never reaches the sea.

The townspeople ran along the battlements, breaking the fishermen's
  poles.
Quickly! To the edge! Hurry! And the tender stars sounded like
  bullfrogs.
. . . that never reaches the sea.

At peace in my memory, heavenly body, circumference, boundary,
you cry on the shores of a horse's eye.
. . . that never reaches the sea.

10 But no one in the darkness will be able to give you distances,
only sharpened limits: diamond future.
. . . that never reaches the sea.

While the people look for pillowed silences,
you pulsate forever, defined by your ring.
. . . that never reaches the sea.

You'll always be undying at the end of waves that accept
the combat of roots and anticipated solitude.
. . . that never reaches the sea.

They're coming up the ramps! Arise from the water!
20 Every point of light will toss you a chain!
. . . that never reaches the sea.

But the well pulls you back with small mossy hands,
you, unforeseen nymph of its chaste ignorance.
. . . that never reaches the sea.

No, that never reaches the sea. Water fixed in one place,
breathing with all its unstrung violins
on the musical scale of wounds and deserted buildings.
Water that never reaches the sea!

VI
Introducción a la muerte

(Poemas de la soledad en Vermont)

Para Rafael Sánchez Ventura

Muerte

A Isidoro de Blas

Qué esfuerzo,
qué esfuerzo del caballo
por ser perro,
qué esfuerzo del perro por ser golondrina,
qué esfuerzo de la golondrina por ser abeja,
qué esfuerzo de la abeja por ser caballo.
Y el caballo,
¡qué flecha aguda exprime de la rosa!,
¡qué rosa gris levanta de su belfo!
10 Y la rosa,
qué rebaño de luces y alaridos
ata en el vivo azúcar de su tronco;
y el azúcar,
¡qué puñalitos sueña en su vigilia!;
y los puñales diminutos,
¡qué luna sin establos!, ¡qué desnudos!,
piel eterna y rubor, andan buscando.
Y yo, por los aleros,
qué serafín de llamas busco y soy.
20 Pero el arco de yeso,
¡qué grande, qué invisible, qué diminuto!,
sin esfuerzo.

VI
Introduction to Death

(Poems of Solitude in Vermont)

For Rafael Sánchez Ventura

Death

To Isidoro de Blas

How hard they try!
How hard the horse tries
to become a dog.
How hard the dog tries to become a swallow.
How hard the swallow tries to become a bee.
How hard the bee tries to become a horse.
And the horse,
what a sharp arrow it squeezes from the rose,
what an ashen rose rising from its lips!
10 And the rose,
what a flock of lights and cries
knotted in the living sugar of its trunk.
And the sugar,
what daggers it dreams in its vigils!
And these miniature daggers,
what a moon without stables, what nakedness,
undying and rosy flesh they seek out!
And I, on the roof's edge,
what a burning angel I look for and am.
20 But the plaster arch,
how vast, how invisible, how minute,
without even trying!

Nocturno del hueco

Para ver que todo se ha ido,
para ver los huecos y los vestidos,
¡dame tu guante de luna,
tu otro guante de hierba,
amor mío!

Puede el aire arrancar los caracoles
muertos sobre el pulmón del elefante
y soplar los gusanos ateridos
de las yemas de luz o de las manzanas.

10 Los rostros bogan impasibles
bajo el diminuto griterío de las hierbas
y en el rincón está el pechito de la rana,
turbio de corazón y mandolina.

En la gran plaza desierta
mugía la bovina cabeza recién cortada
y eran duro cristal definitivo
las formas que buscaban el giro de la sierpe.

Para ver que todo se ha ido
dame tu mudo hueco, ¡amor mío!
20 *Nostalgia de academia y cielo triste.*
¡Para ver que todo se ha ido!

Dentro de ti, amor mío, por tu carne,
¡qué silencio de trenes boca arriba!
¡cuánto brazo de momia florecido!
¡qué cielo sin salida, amor, qué cielo!

Es la piedra en el agua y es la voz en la brisa
bordes de amor que escapan de su tronco sangrante.
Basta tocar el pulso de nuestro amor presente
para que broten flores sobre los otros niños.

30 *Para ver que todo se ha ido.*
Para ver los huecos de nubes y ríos.

Nocturne of Emptied Space

I

If you want to see that nothing is left,
see the emptied spaces and the clothes,
give me your lunar glove,
your other glove of grass,
my love!

The air can tear dead snails
from the elephant's lung
and blow on the stiff, cold worms
from budding light or apples.

10 Faces erased of all emotion sail
beneath the faint uproar of the grass
and the frog's little breast is in the corner
with a clouded heart and mandolin.

On the great deserted plaza,
the cow's freshly severed head kept bellowing
and shapes that looked for the serpent's coiling
crystallized completely.

If you want to see that nothing is left,
give me your speechless, emptied space, my love,
20 *schoolboy nostalgia and sad sky!*
If you want to see that nothing is left!

Inside you, my love, in your flesh,
the silence of derailed trains!
So many mummies' arms in bloom!
What a dead-end sky, my love, what a sky!

Stone in water, voice on the breeze—
love's limits burst free from their bleeding trunk.
Feeling the pulse of our love today is enough
to make flowers spring from other children.

30 *If you want to see that nothing is left,*
see the emptied spaces of clouds and rivers,

Dame tus ramos de laurel, amor.
¡Para ver que todo se ha ido!

Ruedan los huecos puros, por mí, por ti, en el alba
conservando las huellas de las ramas de sangre
y algún perfil de yeso tranquilo que dibuja
instantáneo dolor de luna apuntillada.

Mira formas concretas que buscan su vacío.
Perros equivocados y manzanas mordidas.
40 Mira el ansia, la angustia de un triste mundo fósil
que no encuentra el acento de su primer sollozo.

Cuando busco en la cama los rumores del hilo
has venido, amor mío, a cubrir mi tejado.
El hueco de una hormiga puede llenar el aire,
pero tu vas gimiendo sin norte por mis ojos.

No, por mis ojos no, que ahora me enseñas
cuatro ríos ceñidos en tu brazo.
En la dura barraca donde la luna prisionera
devora a un marinero delante de los niños.

50 *Para ver que todo se ha ido,*
¡amor inexpugnable, amor huido!
No, no me des tu hueco,
¡que ya va por el aire el mío!
¡Ay de ti, ay de mí, de la brisa!
Para ver que todo se ha ido.

I I

Yo.
Con el hueco blanquísimo de un caballo,
crines de ceniza. Plaza pura y doblada.

Yo.
60 Mi hueco traspasado con las axilas rotas.
Piel seca de uva neutra y amianto de madrugada.

Toda la luz del mundo cabe dentro de un ojo.
Canta el gallo y su canto dura más que sus alas.

give me your laurel boughs, my love.
If you want to see that nothing is left!

The pure spaces spin through me, through you, at dawn,
preserving the tracks of the bloody branches
and some profile of tranquil plaster that depicts
the punctured moon's instant sorrow.

Look at the concrete shapes in search of their void.
Mistaken dogs and half-eaten apples.
40 Look at this sad fossil world, with its anxiety and anguish,
a world that can't find the accent of its very first sob.

When I search the bed for murmuring thread,
I know you've come, my love, to cover my roof.
The emptied space of an ant can fill the air,
but you moan with nothing to guide you through my eyes.

No, not through my eyes, because now you show me
four rivers wrapped tightly around your arm,
in the rough lean-to where the imprisoned moon
devours a sailor in front of the children.

50 *If you want to see that nothing is left,*
my impenetrable love, now that you have gone,
don't give me your emptied space. No.
Mine is already traveling through the air!
Who will pity you, or me, or the breeze?
If you want to see that nothing is left.

II

Me.
With the white, white space of a horse,
ashen-maned. Pure and folded plaza.

Me.
60 My emptied space pierced with what remains of my armpits.
Like a neutered grape's shriveled skin and asbestos at dawn.

All the world's light fits inside an eye.
The rooster crows and his song lasts longer than his wings.

Yo.
Con el hueco blanquísimo de un caballo.
Rodeado de espectadores que tienen hormigas en las palabras.

En el circo del frío sin perfil mutilado.
Por los capiteles rotos de las mejillas desangradas.

Yo.
70 Mi hueco sin ti, ciudad, sin tus muertos que comen.
Ecuestre por mi vida definitivamente anclada.

Yo.

No hay siglo nuevo ni luz reciente.
Sólo un caballo azul y una madrugada.

Paisaje con dos tumbas *y un perro asirio*

Amigo:
levántate para que oigas aullar
al perro asirio.
Las tres ninfas del cáncer han estado bailando,
hijo mío.
Trajeron unas montañas de lacre rojo
y unas sábanas duras donde estaba el cáncer dormido.
El caballo tenía un ojo en el cuello
y la luna estaba en un cielo tan frío
10 que tuvo que desgarrarse su monte de Venus
y ahogar en sangre y ceniza los cementerios antiguos.

Amigo,
despierta, que los montes todavía no respiran
y las hierbas de mi corazón están en otro sitio.
No importa que estés lleno de agua de mar.
Yo amé mucho tiempo a un niño
que tenía una plumilla en la lengua
y vivimos cien años dentro de un cuchillo.
Despierta. Calla. Escucha. Incorpórate un poco.
20 El aullido

Me.
With the white, white space of a horse.
Ringed by onlookers with their ant-teeming words.

In the circus of cold weather with no mutilated profile.
Among the chipped columns of cheeks bled white.

Me.
70   My emptied space without you, city, without your voracious dead.
Rider through my life finally at anchor.

Me.

No new age. No enlightenment.
Only a blue horse and dawn.

Landscape with Two Graves
and an Assyrian Dog

Friend,
get up and listen
to the Assyrian dog howl.
Cancer's three nymphs have been dancing,
my son.
They carried mountains of red sealing wax
and stiff bed sheets to the place where cancer slept.
The horse had an eye in its neck
and the moon was in a sky so cold
10   that she had to tear open her mound of Venus
and drown the ancient graveyards in blood and ashes.

Friend,
wake up, the mountains still aren't breathing
and the grass of my heart is somewhere else.
It doesn't matter if you're full of seawater.
For a long time I loved a child
who had a tiny feather on his tongue,
and we lived inside a knife for a hundred years.
Wake up. Be still. Listen. Sit up in your bed.
20   The howling

es una larga lengua morada que deja
hormigas de espanto y licor de lirios.
Ya viene hacia la roca. ¡No alargues tus raíces!
Se acerca. Gime. No solloces en sueños, amigo.

¡Amigo!
Levántate para que oigas aullar
al perro asirio.

Ruina

A Regino Sáinz de la Maza

Sin encontrarse.
Viajero por su propio torso blanco.
¡Así iba el aire!

Pronto se vió que la luna
era una calavera de caballo
y el aire una manzana oscura.

Detrás de la ventana,
con látigos y luces, se sentía
la lucha de la arena con el agua.

10   Yo ví llegar las hierbas
y les eché un cordero que balaba
bajo sus dientecillos y lancetas.

Volaba dentro de una gota
la cáscara de pluma y celuloide
de la primer paloma.

Vienen las hierbas, hijo.
Ya suenan sus espadas de saliva
por el cielo vacío.

Mi mano, amor. ¡Las hierbas!
20   Por los cristales rotos de la casa
la sangre desató sus cabelleras.

is a long purple tongue that releases
terrifying ants and the liquor of irises.
Here it comes toward the rock. Don't spread out your roots!
It approaches. Moans. Friend, don't sob in your dreams.

Friend!
Get up and listen
to the Assyrian dog howl.

Ruin

To Regino Sáinz de la Maza

Never finding itself,
traveling through its own white torso,
the air made its way!

Soon it was clear that the moon
was a horse's skull,
and the air, a dark apple.

Behind the window,
with whips and lights, I felt
sand struggling with water.

10 I saw all the blades of grass arrive
and I threw a bleating lamb
to their little teeth and lancets.

The first dove, encased
in feathers and plastic,
flew inside a single drop.

Here comes the grass, son.
Its spit-swords ring
through the empty sky.

Hold my hand, my love. The grass!
20 Through the house's broken windows,
the blood unleashed its waves of hair.

Tu sólo y yo quedamos.
Prepara tu esqueleto para el aire.
Yo sólo y tú quedamos.

Prepara tu esqueleto.
Hay que buscar de prisa, amor, de prisa,
nuestro perfil sin sueño.

Amantes asesinados por una perdiz

Hommage à Guy de Maupassant

—Los dos lo han querido, —me dijo su madre—. Los dos . . .

—No es posible, señora, —dije yo—. Usted tiene demasiado temperamento y a su edad ya se sabe por qué caen los alfileres del rocío.

—Calle usted, Luciano, calle usted . . . No, no, Luciano, no.

—Para resistir este nombre necesito contener el dolor de mis recuerdos. ¿Y usted cree que aquella pequeña dentadura y esa mano de niño que se han dejado olvidadas dentro de la ola me pueden consolar de esta tristeza?

—Los dos lo han querido —me dijo su prima—. Los dos.

Me puse a mirar el mar y lo comprendí todo.

¿Será posible que del pico de esa paloma cruelísima que tiene corazón de elefante salga la palidez lunar de aquel transatlántico que se aleja?

—Recuerdo que tuve que hacer varias veces uso de mi cuchara para defenderme de los lobos. Yo no tenía culpa ninguna, usted lo sabe. ¡Dios mío! Estoy llorando.

—Los dos lo han querido —dije yo—. Los dos. Una manzana será siempre un amante, pero un amante no podrá ser jamás una manzana.

—Por eso se han muerto, por eso. Con veinte ríos y un solo invierno desgarrado.

—Fue muy sencillo. Se amaban por encima de todos los museos.
Mano derecha,
con mano izquierda.
Mano izquierda,
con mano derecha.
Pie derecho,
con pie derecho.
Pie izquierdo,
con nube.
Cabello,
con planta de pie.

Only you and I are left.
Prepare your skeleton for the air.
We're the only ones who remain.

Prepare your skeleton.
Hurry, love, hurry, we've got to look
for our sleepless profile.

Two Lovers Murdered by a Partridge

Hommage à Guy de Maupassant

"They both wanted it," his mother told me. "Both of them."

"My dear woman," I said, "that's impossible. You're too emotional, and at your age you should know why the dewdrops settle on the ground like pins."

"Be quiet, Luciano, be quiet. No, no, Luciano, no."

"In order to make that name bearable, I need to restrain my painful memories. And you think I could be consoled for my sadness by that tiny set of teeth, and that child's hand, forgotten inside the wave?"

"They both wanted it," his cousin told me. "Both of them."

I contemplated the sea and suddenly I understood everything.

"Could it be that the moonlit pallor of that departing ocean liner comes from the beak of that cruel dove with an elephant's heart?"

"I remember I had to use my spoon several times to ward off the wolves. I wasn't to blame for anything. You know that. My God, I'm crying!"

"They both wanted it," I said. "Both of them. An apple will always be a lover, but a lover can't ever be an apple."

"That's why they died. That's why. At the age of twenty rivers and a single shredded winter."

"It was very simple. They made love above and beyond the museums."

Right hand
with left hand.
Left hand
with right hand.
Right foot
with right foot.
Left foot
with cloud.
Hair
with sole of the foot.

Planta de pie,
con mejilla izquierda.

¡Oh mejilla izquierda! ¡Oh noroeste de barquitos y hormigas de mercurio . . . ! Dame el pañuelo, Genoveva; voy a llorar . . . Voy a llorar hasta que de mis ojos salga una muchedumbre de siemprevivas . . .

Se acostaban.

No había otro espectáculo más tierno.

¿Me ha oído usted?

¡Se acostaban!

Muslo izquierdo,
con antebrazo izquierdo.

Ojos cerrados,
con uñas abiertas.

Cintura, con nuca
y con playa.

Y las cuatro orejitas eran cuatro ángeles en la choza de la nieve. Se querían. Se amaban. A pesar de la Ley de la gravedad. La diferencia que existe entre una espina de rosa y una *Star* es sencillísima.

Cuando descubrieron esto, se fueron al campo.

Se amaban.

¡Dios mío! Se amaban ante los ojos de los químicos.

Espalda, con tierra,
tierra, con anís.

Luna, con hombro dormido.

Y las cinturas se entrecruzaban con un rumor de vidrios.

Yo vi temblar sus mejillas cuando los profesores de la Universidad les traían hiel y vinagre en una esponja diminuta. Muchas veces tenían que espantar a los perros que gemían por las yedras blanquísimas del lecho. Pero ellos se amaban.

Eran un hombre y una mujer,
o sea,
un hombre
y un pedacito de tierra,
un elefante
y un niño,
un niño y un junco.

Eran dos mancebos desmayados
y una pierna de níquel.

¡Eran los barqueros!

Sí.

Eran los terribles barqueros del Guadiana que machacan con sus remos todas las rosas del mundo.

Sole of the foot
with left cheek.

Oh, left cheek! Oh, northwest of little boats and ants of mercury! Give me the handkerchief, Genoveva; I'm going to cry . . . I'm going to cry until a bunch of immortelles emerges from my eyes . . .

They were going to bed.

There was no other spectacle so tender . . .

Did you hear me?

They were going to bed!

Left thigh
with left forearm.

Closed eyes
with open fingernails.

Waist with nape,
and with shoreline.

And the four little ears were four angels in a snowy cabin. They yearned. They made love. Defying the law of gravity. The difference between a rose thorn and a *Star* is very simple.

When they figured this out, they left for the countryside.

They made love.

My God! They made love while the chemists watched.

Their backs with the earth,
earth with anise.

Moon with a sleeping shoulder.

And their waists entwined, whispering like glass.

. I saw their cheeks tremble when the professors brought them gall and vinegar in a tiny sponge. Many times they had to scare away the dogs that howled in the pure white ivy of the bed. But they made love.

They were man and woman,
in other words,
a man
and a little piece of earth,
an elephant
and a child,
a child and a bulrush.

They were two young men who had fainted
and a chrome-plated leg.

They were boatmen!

Yes.

They were the terrible boatmen of the Guadiana, who crush all the world's roses with their oars.

El viejo marinero escupió el tabaco de su boca y dio grandes voces para espantar a las gaviotas. Pero ya era demasiado tarde.

Cuando las mujeres enlutadas llegaron a casa del Gobernador, éste comía tranquilamente almendras verdes y pescados fríos en un exquisito plato de oro. Era preferible no haber hablado con él.

En las islas Azores.

Casi no puedo llorar.

Yo puse dos telegramas, pero desgraciadamente ya era tarde.

Muy tarde.

Sólo sé deciros que dos niños que pasaban por la orilla del bosque vieron una perdiz que echaba un hilito de sangre por el pico.

Esta es la causa, querido capitán, de mi extraña melancolía.

Luna y panorama de los insectos
(Poema de amor)

> *La luna en el mar riela,*
> *en la lona gime el viento*
> *y alza en blando movimiento*
> *olas de plata y azul.*
> —ESPRONCEDA

Mi corazón tendría la forma de un zapato
si cada aldea tuviera una sirena.
Pero la noche es interminable cuando se apoya en los enfermos
y hay barcos que buscan ser mirados para poder hundirse tranquilos.

Si el aire sopla blandamente
mi corazón tiene la forma de una niña.
Si el aire se niega a salir de los cañaverales
mi corazón tiene la forma de una milenaria boñiga de toro.

¡Bogar! Bogar, bogar, bogar,
hacia el batallón de puntas desiguales,
hacia un paisaje de acechos pulverizados.
Noche igual de la nieve, de los sistemas suspendidos
y la luna.
¡La luna!
Pero no la luna.
La raposa de las tabernas.

The old sailor spit tobacco from his mouth, and yelled to frighten away the gulls. But it was too late.

When the women in mourning arrived at the governor's mansion, he was quietly eating green almonds and cold fish from an exquisite gold plate. It would have been better not to have spoken with him.

In the Azores.

I'm nearly unable to cry.

I sent two telegrams, but unfortunately it was too late.

Very late.

I can only tell you that two children, passing by the edge of the forest, saw a partridge that trailed a little thread of blood from its beak.

That's the reason, my dear captain, for my strange melancholia.

Moon and Panorama of the Insects
(Love Poem)

> The moon shimmers on the sea,
> the wind moans in the sail
> and raises gently swelling
> blue and silver waves.
> —ESPRONCEDA

My heart would take the shape of a shoe
if a siren lived in every village.
But the night never ends when it leans on the sick,
and there are ships that want to be seen in order to sink in peace.

If the wind blows softly,
my heart takes the shape of a girl.
If the wind won't leave the cane fields,
my heart takes the shape of a millenary cow pie.

Row! Row, row, row,
10 toward the army of jagged points,
toward a landscape of pulverized ambushes.
Equal night of the snow, the discontinued systems,
and the moon.
The moon!
But not the moon.
The taverns' vixen.

El gallo japonés que se comió los ojos.
Las hierbas masticadas.

No nos salvan las solitarias en los vidrios,
20 ni los herbolarios donde el metafísico
encuentra las otras vertientes del cielo.
Son mentira las formas. Sólo existe
el círculo de bocas del oxígeno.
Y la luna.
Pero no la luna.
Los insectos.
Los muertos diminutos por las riberas.
Dolor en longitud.
Yodo en un punto.
30 Las muchedumbres en el alfiler.
El desnudo que amasa la sangre de todos,
y mi amor que no es un caballo ni una quemadura.
Criatura de pecho devorado.
¡Mi amor!

Ya cantan, gritan, gimen: *Rostro. ¡Tu rostro! Rostro.*
Las manzanas son unas.
Las dalias son idénticas.
La luz tiene un sabor de metal acabado
y el campo de todo un lustro cabrá en la mejilla de la moneda.
40 *Pero tu rostro cubre los cielos del banquete.*
¡Ya cantan!, ¡gritan!, ¡gimen!,
¡cubren!, ¡trepan!, ¡espantan!

Es necesario caminar, ¡de prisa!, por las ondas, por las ramas,
por las calles deshabitadas de la Edad Media que bajan al río,
por las tiendas de las pieles donde suena un cuerno de vaca herida,
por las escalas, ¡sin miedo!, por las escalas.
Hay un hombre descolorido que se está bañando en el mar;
es tan tierno que los reflectores le comieron jugando el corazón,
y en el Perú viven mil mujeres, ¡oh insectos!, que noche y día
50 hacen nocturnos y desfiles entrecruzando sus propias venas.

Un diminuto guante corrosivo me detiene. ¡Basta!
En mi pañuelo he sentido el tris
de la primera vena que se rompe.
Cuida tus pies, ¡amor mío!, ¡tus manos!,

The Japanese rooster that ate its own eyes.
The cud.

The lonely women in store windows won't save us,
20 nor herbariums where the metaphysician
meets the other slopes of the sky.
Shapes are a lie. What is there?
The circle of mouths of the oxygen.
And the moon.
But not the moon.
The insects,
little dead things lining the shores,
sorrow on longitude,
iodine on stitched flesh,
30 the crowd on the head of a pin,
the naked man who kneads everyone's blood,
and my love who is neither horse nor burn,
creature whose breast was consumed.
My love!

Now they sing, scream, moan: *A face. Your face! A face.*
The apples are one,
the dahlias identical,
the light tastes like worn-out metal
and the countryside of half a decade will fit on the cheek of a coin.
40 *But your face covers the skies of the feast.*
Now they sing, scream, moan,
cover everything, climb, terrify!

We've got to move—Hurry up!—through the waves, the branches,
the deserted streets of the Middle Ages going down to the river,
the stores of hides where a wounded cow's horn bellows,
up the ladders—Don't be scared!—up the ladders.
A discolored man is bathing in the sea;
he's so tender that searchlights ate him as he gambled away his heart,
and a thousand women live in Peru—Oh, insects!—night and day
50 they weave nocturnes and parades among their own veins.

One tiny corrosive glove stops me. That's enough!
I feel the crackle of the first
broken vein on my handkerchief.
Watch out for your hands and feet, my love,

ya que yo tengo que entregar mi rostro.
¡Mi rostro, mi rostro, ay, mi comido rostro!

Este fuego casto para mi deseo,
esta confusión por anhelo de equilibrio,
este inocente dolor de pólvora en mis ojos,
60 aliviará la angustia de otro corazón
devorado por las nebulosas.

No nos salva la gente de las zapaterías,
ni los paisajes que se hacen música al encontrar las llaves oxidadas.
Son mentira los aires. Sólo existe
una cunita en el desván
que recuerda todas las cosas.
Y la luna.
Pero no la luna.
Los insectos.
70 Los insectos solos,
crepitantes, mordientes, estremecidos, agrupados,
y la luna
con un guante de humo sentada en la puerta de sus derribos.
¡¡La luna!!

Nueva York, 4 de enero de 1930

VII
Vuelta a la ciudad
Para Antonio Hernández Soriano

New York
(Oficina y denuncia)

A Fernando Vela

Debajo de las multiplicaciones
hay una gota de sangre de pato;
debajo de las divisiones

714

since I must give up my face,
my face, my face, yes, my half-eaten face!

This chaste, burning desire of mine,
this confusion from longing for equilibrium,
this innocent sorrow of gunpowder in my eyes,
60   will lighten the anguish of another heart
consumed by the nebulae.

The people in shoe stores won't save us,
nor the landscapes becoming music when they find the rusted keys.
Breezes are a lie. Only a small cradle
exists, in the attic,
that remembers everything.
And the moon.
But not the moon.
The insects.
70   Just the insects,
crackling, biting, quivering, swarming,
and the moon
with a smoking glove in the doorway of its wreckage.
The moon!!

New York, January 4, 1930

VII
Return to the City

For Antonio Hernández Soriano

New York
(Office and Denunciation)

To Fernando Vela

Under the multiplications,
a drop of duck's blood;
under the divisions,

hay una gota de sangre de marinero;
debajo de las sumas, un río de sangre tierna.
Un río que viene cantando
por los dormitorios de los arrabales,
y es plata, cemento o brisa
en el alba mentida de New York.
Existen las montañas. Lo sé.
Y los anteojos para la sabiduría.
Lo sé. Pero yo no he venido a ver el cielo.
He venido para ver la turbia sangre,
la sangre que lleva las máquinas a las cataratas
y el espíritu a la lengua de la cobra.
Todos los días se matan en New York
cuatro millones de patos,
cinco millones de cerdos,
dos mil palomas para el gusto de los agonizantes,
un millón de vacas,
un millón de corderos
y dos millones de gallos,
que dejan los cielos hechos añicos.
Más vale sollozar afilando la navaja
o asesinar a los perros en las alucinantes cacerías,
que resistir en la madrugada
los interminables trenes de leche,
los interminables trenes de sangre
y los trenes de rosas maniatadas
por los comerciantes de perfumes.
Los patos y las palomas,
y los cerdos y los corderos
ponen sus gotas de sangre
debajo de las multiplicaciones,
y los terribles alaridos de las vacas estrujadas
llenan de dolor el valle
donde el Hudson se emborracha con aceite.
Yo denuncio a toda la gente
que ignora la otra mitad,
la mitad irredimible
que levanta sus montes de cemento
donde laten los corazones
de los animalitos que se olvidan
y donde caeremos todos
en la última fiesta de los taladros.

a drop of sailor's blood;
under the additions, a river of tender blood.
A river that sings and flows
past bedrooms in the boroughs—
and it's money, cement, or wind
in New York's counterfeit dawn.
10 I know the mountains exist.
And wisdom's eyeglasses,
too. But I didn't come to see the sky.
I'm here to see the clouded blood,
the blood that sweeps machines over waterfalls
and the soul toward the cobra's tongue.
Every day in New York, they slaughter
four million ducks,
five million hogs,
two thousand pigeons to accommodate the tastes of the dying,
20 one million cows,
one million lambs,
and two million roosters
that smash the skies to pieces.
It's better to sob while honing the blade
or kill dogs on the delirious hunts
than to resist at dawn
the endless milk trains,
the endless blood trains
and the trains of roses, manacled
30 by the dealers in perfume.
The ducks and the pigeons,
and the hogs and the lambs
lay their drops of blood
under the multiplications,
and the terrified bellowing of the cows wrung dry
fills the valley with sorrow
where the Hudson gets drunk on oil.
I denounce everyone
who ignores the other half,
40 the half that can't be redeemed,
who lift their mountains of cement
where the hearts beat
inside forgotten little animals
and where all of us will fall
in the last feast of pneumatic drills.

Os escupo en la cara.
La otra mitad me escucha
devorando, orinando, volando en su pureza,
como los niños de las porterías
50 que llevan frágiles palitos
a los huecos donde se oxidan
las antenas de los insectos.
No es el infierno, es la calle.
No es la muerte. Es la tienda de frutas.
Hay un mundo de ríos quebrados y distancias inasibles
en la patita de ese gato quebrada por un automóvil,
y yo oigo el canto de la lombriz
en el corazón de muchas niñas.
Oxido, fermento, tierra estremecida.
60 Tierra tú mismo que nadas por los números de la oficina.
¿Qué voy a hacer, ordenar los paisajes?
¿Ordenar los amores que luego son fotografías?
Que luego son pedazos de madera y bocanadas de sangre.
No, no; yo denuncio.
Yo denuncio la conjura
de estas desiertas oficinas
que no radian las agonías,
que borran los programas de la selva,
y me ofrezco a ser comido por las vacas estrujadas
70 cuando sus gritos llenan el valle
donde el Hudson se emborracha con aceite.

Cementerio judío

Las alegres fiebres huyeron a las maromas de los barcos
y el judío empujó la verja con el pudor helado del interior de la
    lechuga.

Los niños de Cristo dormían,
y el agua era una paloma,
y la madera era una garza,
y el plomo era un colibrí,
y aun las vivas prisiones de fuego
estaban consoladas por el salto de la langosta.

I spit in all your faces.
The other half hears me,
devouring, pissing, flying in their purity,
like the supers' children in lobbies
50 who carry fragile twigs
to the emptied spaces where
the insect antennae are rusting.
This is not hell, but the street.
Not death, but the fruit stand.
There is a world of broken rivers and distances just beyond our grasp
in the cat's paw smashed by a car,
and I hear the earthworm's song
in the hearts of many girls.
Rust, fermentation, quaking earth.
60 You yourself are the earth as you drift in office numbers
What shall I do now? Set the landscapes in order?
Order the loves that soon become photographs,
that soon become pieces of wood and mouthfuls of blood?
No, no: I denounce it all.
I denounce the conspiracy
of these deserted offices
that radiate no agony,
that erase the forest's plans,
and I offer myself as food for the cows wrung dry
70 when their bellowing fills the valley
where the Hudson gets drunk on oil.

Jewish Cemetery

The fevers fled with great joy to the hawsers of mooted ships
and the Jew pushed against the gate chastely the way lettuce grows
    coldly from its center.

Christ's children slept,
and the water was a dove,
and the wood was a heron,
and the lead was a hummingbird,
and even the living prisons of fire
were consoled by the locust's leap.

Los niños de Cristo bogaban y los judíos llenaban los muros
10 con un solo corazón de paloma
por el que todos querían escapar.
Las niñas de Cristo cantaban y las judías miraban la muerte
con un solo ojo de faisán,
vidriado por la angustia de un millón de paisajes.

Los médicos ponen en el níquel sus tijeras y guantes de goma
cuando los cadáveres sienten en los pies
la terrible claridad de otra luna enterrada.
Pequeños dolores ilesos se acercan a los hospitales
y los muertos se van quitando un traje de sangre cada día.

20 Las arquitecturas de escarcha,
las liras y gemidos que se escapan de las hojas diminutas
del otoño, mojando las últimas vertientes,
se apagaban en el negro de los sombreros de copa.

La hierba celeste y sola de la que huye con miedo el rocío
y las blancas entradas de mármol que conducen al aire duro
mostraban su silencio roto por las huellas dormidas de los zapatos.

El judío empujó la verja;
pero el judío no era un puerto
y las barcas de nieve se agolparon
30 por las escalerillas de su corazón:
las barcas de nieve que acechan
un hombre de agua que las ahogue.
Las barcas de los cementerios
que a veces dejan ciegos a los visitantes.

Los niños de Cristo dormían
y el judío ocupó su litera.
Tres mil judíos lloraban en el espanto de las galerías
porque reunían entre todos con esfuerzo media paloma,
porque uno tenía la rueda de un reloj
40 y otro un botín con orugas parlantes
y otro una lluvia nocturna cargada de cadenas
y otro la uña de un ruiseñor que estaba vivo;
y porque la media paloma gemía
derramando una sangre que no era la suya.

Christ's children rowed and the Jews packed the walls
10   with a single dove's heart
through which all of them wished to escape.
Christ's little girls sang and the Jewish women looked at death
with a pheasant's solitary eye,
glazed by the anguish of a million landscapes.

The doctors put their scissors and surgical gloves on the chrome table
when the feet of the corpses feel
the terrible brightness of another buried moon.
Tiny unscathed pains approach the hospitals
and the dead take off a suit of blood every day.

20   The architecture of frost,
the lyres and moans that escape from the small leaves
in autumn, drenching the farthest slopes,
were extinguished in the blackness of their top hats.

The dew retreats in fear from blue, forsaken grass,
and the white marble entrances that lead to hard air
were showing their silence broken by sleeping footprints.

The Jew pushed against the gate;
but the Jew was not a port
and the boats of snow piled up
30   on the gangways of his heart:
the boats ready to ambush
a man of water who can drown them.
The boats of the cemeteries
that sometimes blind the visitors.

Christ's children slept
and the Jew lay down in his berth.
Three thousand Jews wept in the galleries of terror
because it was all they could do to gather half a dove among
    themselves,
because one of them had the wheel from a clock
40   and another a boot laced with talking caterpillars
and another a nocturnal rain burdened with chains
and another the claw of a nightingale that was still alive;
and because the half-dove moaned,
spilling blood that was not its own.

Las alegres fiebres bailaban por las cúpulas humedecidas
y la luna copiaba en su mármol
nombres viejos y cintas ajadas.
Llegó la gente que come por detrás de las yertas columnas
y los asnos de blancos dientes
50 con los especialistas de las articulaciones.
Verdes girasoles temblaban
por los páramos del crepúsculo
y todo el cementerio era una queja
de bocas de cartón y trapo seco.
Ya los niños de Cristo se dormían
cuando el judío, apretando los ojos,
se cortó las manos en silencio
al escuchar los primeros gemidos.

Nueva York, 18 de enero de 1930

Crucifixión

La luna pudo detenerse al fin por la curva blanquísima de los
   caballos.
Un rayo de luz violenta que se escapaba de la herida
proyectó en el cielo el instante de la circuncisión de un niño muerto.

La sangre bajaba por el monte y los ángeles la buscaban,
pero los cálices eran de viento y al fin llenaba los zapatos.
Cojos perros fumaban sus pipas y un olor de cuero caliente
ponía grises los labios redondos de los que vomitaban en las esquinas.
Y llegaban largos alaridos por el Sur de la noche seca.
Era que la luna quemaba con sus bujías el falo de los caballos.
10 Un sastre especialista en púrpura
había encerrado a las tres santas mujeres
y les enseñaba una calavera por vidrios de la ventana.
Los niños en el arrabal rodeaban a un camello blanco
que lloraba asustado porque al alba
tenía que pasar sin remedio por el ojo de una aguja.
¡Oh cruz! ¡Oh clavos! ¡Oh espina!
¡Oh espina clavada en el hueso hasta que se oxiden los planetas!
Como nadie volvía la cabeza, el cielo pudo desnudarse.
Entonces se oyó la gran voz y los fariseos dijeron:

The fevers danced with great joy on the humid domes,
and the moon inscribed in its marble
ancient names and worn ribbons.
Those who dine behind the rigid columns arrived,
so did the donkeys with their white teeth
50 and the specialists in the body's joints.
Green sunflowers trembled
in the highlands of dusk
and the whole cemetery began to complain
with cardboard mouths and dry rags.
Christ's children were going to sleep
when the Jew, squeezing his eyes shut,
silently cut off his hands
as he heard the first moans begin.

New York, January 18, 1930

Crucifixion

The moon could rest in the end along the pure white curve of the
    horses.
A violent beam of light that escaped from the wound
projected the instant of a dead child's circumcision on the sky.

Blood flowed down the mountain and angels looked for it,
but the chalices became wind and finally filled the shoes.
Crippled dogs puffed on their pipes and the odor of hot leather
grayed the round lips of those who vomited on street corners.
And long southern howls arrived with the arid night.
It was the moon burning the horses' phallus with its candles.
10 A tailor, who specialized in purple,
had locked up three saintly women
and was showing them a skull through the window glass.
In the borough, boys circled a white camel
that wept because at dawn
there was no other way except through the needle's eye.
Oh, cross! Oh, nails! Oh, thorn!
Oh, thorn driven to the bone until the planets rust to pieces!
Since no one turned to look, the sky could undress.
Then the great voice was heard, and the pharisees said:

"Esa maldita vaca tiene las tetas llenas de leche."
La muchedumbre cerraba las puertas
y la lluvia bajaba por las calles decidida a mojar el corazón
mientras la tarde se puso turbia de latidos y leñadores
y la oscura ciudad agonizaba bajo el martillo de los carpinteros.
"Esa maldita vaca
tiene las tetas llenas de perdigones",
dijeron los fariseos.
Pero la sangre mojó sus pies y los espíritus inmundos
estrellaban ampollas de laguna sobre las paredes del templo.
Se supo el momento preciso de la salvación de nuestra vida.
Porque la luna lavó con agua
las quemaduras de los caballos
y no la primera vida que callaron en la arena.
Entonces salieron los fríos cantando sus canciones
y las ranas encendieron sus lumbres en la doble orilla del río.
"Esa maldita vaca, maldita, maldita, maldita,
no nos dejará dormir", dijeron los fariseos,
y se alejaron a sus casas por el tumulto de la calle
dando empujones a los borrachos y escupiendo la sal de los sacrificios
mientras la sangre los seguía con un balido de cordero.

Fue entonces
y la tierra despertó arrojando temblorosos ríos de polilla.

Nueva York, 18 de octubre de 1929

VIII
Dos odas

A mi editor, Armando Guibert

Grito hacia Roma
(Desde la torre del Chrysler Building)

Manzanas levemente heridas
por finos espadines de plata,
nubes rasgadas por una mano de coral

20 That wicked cow has teats full of milk.
The multitude locked their doors
and rain flowed down the streets, determined to drench their hearts
while the evening clouded over with heartbeats and woodcutters
and the darkened city agonized under the carpenters' hammer.
"That wicked cow
has teats full of bird shot,"
said the pharisees.
But blood drenched their feet and unclean spirits
splattered drops of blistered ponds on the temple walls.
30 Someone found out precisely when our lives would be saved
because the moon washed the burns
of the horses with water
and not the first life they silenced in the sand.
Then the chills went out singing their songs
and frogs ignited fires on the river's double shore.
"That wicked cow, wicked, wicked, wicked,
won't let us sleep," said the pharisees,
and they withdrew to their houses through the riotous street,
pushing drunks aside and spitting sacrificial salt
40 while the blood followed them like a bleating lamb.

That's how it was
and the awakened earth cast off trembling rivers of moths.

New York, October 18, 1929

VIII
Two Odes
To my publisher, Armando Guibert

Cry to Rome
(From the Tower of the Chrysler Building)

Apples barely grazed
by slender, silver rapiers,
clouds torn apart by a coral hand

que lleva en el dorso una almendra de fuego,
peces de arsénico como tiburones,
tiburones como gotas de llanto para cegar una multitud,
rosas que hieren
y agujas instaladas en los caños de la sangre,
mundos enemigos y amores cubiertos de gusanos
10 caerán sobre ti. Caerán sobre la gran cúpula
que unta de aceite las lenguas militares,
donde un hombre se orina en una deslumbrante paloma
y escupe carbón machacado
rodeado de miles de campanillas.

Porque ya no hay quien reparta el pan y el vino,
ni quien cultive hierbas en la boca del muerto,
ni quien abra los linos del reposo,
ni quien llore por las heridas de los elefantes.
No hay más que un millón de herreros
20 forjando cadenas para los niños que han de venir.
No hay más que un millón de carpinteros
que hacen ataúdes sin cruz.
No hay más que un gentío de lamentos
que se abren las ropas en espera de la bala.
El hombre que desprecia la paloma debía hablar,
debía gritar desnudo entre las columnas
y ponerse una inyección para adquirir la lepra
y llorar un llanto tan terrible
que disolviera sus anillos y sus teléfonos de diamante.
30 Pero el hombre vestido de blanco
ignora el misterio de la espiga,
ignora el gemido de la parturienta,
ignora que Cristo puede dar agua todavía,
ignora que la moneda quema el beso de prodigio
y da la sangre del cordero al pico idiota del faisán.

Los maestros enseñan a los niños
una luz maravillosa que viene del monte;
pero lo que llega es una reunión de cloacas
donde gritan las oscuras ninfas del cólera.
40 Los maestros señalan con devoción las enormes cúpulas sahumadas;
pero debajo de las estatuas no hay amor,
no hay amor bajo los ojos de cristal definitivo.

that carries a fiery almond on its back,
arsenic fish like sharks,
sharks like wailing drops that blind the masses,
roses that wound
and needles that lace the blood's plumbing,
enemy worlds and loves covered with worms
will fall on you. Will fall on the great dome
that anoints the military tongues with oil,
where a man pisses on a dazzling dove
and spits pulverized coal
surrounded by thousands of hand bells.

Because there is no one to bestow the bread or the wine,
or make grass grow in the mouths of the dead,
or spread the linen of rest and peace,
or weep for the wounded elephants.
There are only a million blacksmiths
who forge chains for tomorrow's children.
Only a million carpenters
who make coffins with no cross.
Only a crowd of laments
unbuttoning their clothes, waiting for the bullets.
The man who scorns the dove should have spoken,
screamed naked between the columns,
and injected himself with leprosy
and shed tears terrible enough
to dissolve his rings and diamond telephones.
But the man dressed in white
knows nothing of the mystery of the wheat ear,
or the moans of a woman giving birth,
or the fact that Christ can still give water,
or the money that burns the prodigy's kiss
and gives the blood of the lamb to the pheasant's idiot beak.

The schoolteachers show the children
a marvelous light coming from the mountain;
but what arrives is a junction of sewers
where cholera's nymphs scream in the shadows.
The teachers point devoutly to the enormous domes filled with
  burning incense;
but beneath the statues there is no love,
no love beneath the final crystal eyes.

El amor está en las carnes desgarradas por la sed,
en la choza diminuta que lucha con la inundación;
el amor está en los fosos donde luchan las sierpes del hambre,
en el triste mar que mece los cadáveres de las gaviotas
y en el oscurísimo beso punzante debajo de las almohadas.

Pero el viejo de las manos traslúcidas
    dirá: amor, amor, amor,
50 aclamado por millones de moribundos;
    dirá: amor, amor, amor,
    entre el tisú estremecido de ternura;
    dirá: paz, paz, paz,
    entre el tirite de cuchillos y melones de dinamita;
    dirá: amor, amor, amor,
    hasta que se le pongan de plata los labios.

Mientras tanto, mientras tanto, ¡ay!, mientras tanto,
    los negros que sacan las escupideras,
    los muchachos que tiemblan bajo el terror pálido de los directores,
60 las mujeres ahogadas en aceites minerales,
    la muchedumbre de martillo, de violín o de nube,
    ha de gritar aunque le estrellen los sesos en el muro,
    ha de gritar frente a las cúpulas,
    ha de gritar loca de fuego,
    ha de gritar loca de nieve,
    ha de gritar con la cabeza llena de excremento,
    ha de gritar como todas las noches juntas,
    ha de gritar con voz tan desgarrada
    hasta que las ciudades tiemblen como niñas
70 y rompan las prisiones del aceite y la música.
    Porque queremos el pan nuestro de cada día,
    flor de aliso y perenne ternura desgranada,
    porque queremos que se cumpla la voluntad de la Tierra
    que da sus frutos para todos.

Oda a Walt Whitman

Por el East River y el Bronx
    los muchachos cantaban enseñando sus cinturas,
    con la rueda, el aceite, el cuero y el martillo.

Love is in the flesh shredded by thirst,
in the tiny thatched hut struggling against the flood;
love is in the pits where the serpents of famine writhe,
in the sad sea where the dead gulls drift
and in the obscurest kiss bristling beneath the pillows.

But the old man with translucent hands
will say: Love, love, love,
50   acclaimed by millions of the dying;
he will say: Love, love, love,
amidst the gold lamé that trembles with tenderness;
he will say: Peace, peace, peace,
among the shivering of knives and melons of dynamite;
he will say: Love, love, love,
until his lips have turned to silver.

Meanwhile, yes, meanwhile
the blacks who empty the spittoons,
the boys who tremble beneath the pallid terror of executives,
60   the women who drown in mineral oil,
the multitudes with their hammers, violins, or clouds—
they'll scream even if they bash their brains against the wall,
scream in front of the domes,
scream driven crazy by fire,
scream driven crazy by snow,
scream with their heads full of excrement,
scream as if all the nights converged,
scream with such a heartrending voice
until the cities tremble like little girls
70   and knock down the prisons of oil and music.
Because we demand our daily bread,
alder in bloom and perennially harvested tenderness,
because we demand that Earth's will be done,
that its fruits be offered to everyone.

Ode to Walt Whitman

By the East River and the Bronx
boys were singing, exposing their waists,
with the wheel, with oil, leather, and the hammer.

Noventa mil mineros sacaban la plata de las rocas
y los niños dibujaban escaleras y perspectivas.

Pero ninguno se dormía,
ninguno quería ser el río,
ninguno amaba las hojas grandes,
ninguno la lengua azul de la playa.

10 Por el East River y el Queensborough
los muchachos luchaban con la industria,
y los judíos vendían al fauno del río
la rosa de la circuncisión
y el cielo desembocaba por los puentes y los tejados
manadas de bisontes empujadas por el viento.

Pero ninguno se detenía,
ninguno quería ser nube,
ninguno buscaba los helechos
ni la rueda amarilla del tamboril.

20 Cuando la luna salga
las poleas rodarán para turbar al cielo;
un límite de agujas cercará la memoria
y los ataúdes se llevarán a los que no trabajan.

Nueva York de cieno,
Nueva York de alambres y de muerte.
¿Qué ángel llevas oculto en la mejilla?
¿Qué voz perfecta dirá las verdades del trigo?
¿Quién el sueño terrible de tus anémonas manchadas?

Ni un solo momento, viejo hermoso Walt Whitman,
30 he dejado de ver tu barba llena de mariposas,
ni tus hombros de pana gastados por la luna,
ni tus muslos de Apolo virginal,
ni tu voz como una columna de ceniza;
anciano hermoso como la niebla,
que gemías igual que un pájaro
con el sexo atravesado por una aguja.
Enemigo del sátiro,
enemigo de la vid
y amante de los cuerpos bajo la burda tela.

Ninety thousand miners taking silver from the rocks
and children drawing stairs and perspectives.

But none of them could sleep,
none of them wanted to be the river,
none of them loved the huge leaves
or the shoreline's blue tongue.

10 By the East River and the Queensboro
boys were battling with industry
and the Jews sold to the river faun
the rose of circumcision,
and over bridges and rooftops, the mouth of the sky emptied
herds of bison driven by the wind.

But none of them paused,
none of them wanted to be a cloud,
none of them looked for ferns
or the yellow wheel of the tambourine.

20 As soon as the moon rises
the pulleys will spin to upset the sky;
a border of needles will besiege memory
and the hearses will bear away those who don't work.

New York, mire,
New York, wires and death.
What angel is hidden in your cheek?
Whose perfect voice will sing the truths of wheat?
Who, the terrible dream of your stained anemones?

Not for a moment, Walt Whitman, lovely old man,
30 have I failed to see your beard full of butterflies,
nor your corduroy shoulders frayed by the moon,
nor your thighs as pure as Apollo's,
nor your voice like a column of ash;
old man, beautiful as the mist,
you moaned like a bird
with its sex pierced by a needle.
Enemy of the satyr,
enemy of the vine,
and lover of bodies beneath rough cloth . . .

Ni un solo momento, hermosura viril
que en montes de carbón, anuncios y ferrocarriles,
soñabas ser un río y dormir como un río
con aquel camarada que pondría en tu pecho
un pequeño dolor de ignorante leopardo.

Ni un solo momento, Adán de sangre, Macho,
hombre solo en el mar, viejo hermoso Walt Whitman,
porque por las azoteas,
agrupados en los bares,
saliendo en racimos de las alcantarillas,
50 temblando entre las piernas de los chauffeurs
o girando en las plataformas del ajenjo,
los maricas, Walt Whitman, te señalan.

¡También ése! ¡También! Y se despeñan
sobre tu barba luminosa y casta
rubios del norte, negros de la arena,
muchedumbre de gritos y ademanes
como los gatos y como las serpientes,
los maricas, Walt Whitman, los maricas,
turbios de lágrimas, carne para fusta,
60 bota o mordisco de los domadores.

¡También ése! ¡También! Dedos teñidos
apuntan a la orilla de tu sueño,
cuando el amigo come tu manzana
con un leve sabor de gasolina
y el sol canta por los ombligos
de los muchachos que juegan bajo los puentes.

Pero tú no buscabas los ojos arañados,
ni el pantano oscurísimo donde sumergen a los niños,
ni la saliva helada,
70 ni las curvas heridas como panza de sapo
que llevan los maricas en coches y en terrazas
mientras la luna los azota por las esquinas del terror.

Tú buscabas un desnudo que fuera como un río.
Toro y sueño que junte la rueda con el alga,
padre de tu agonía, camelia de tu muerte,
y gimiera en las llamas de tu ecuador oculto.

Not for a moment, virile beauty,
who among mountains of coal, billboards, and railroads,
dreamed of becoming a river and sleeping like a river
with that comrade who would place in your breast
the small ache of an ignorant leopard.

Not for a moment, Adam of blood, Macho,
man alone at sea, Walt Whitman, lovely old man,
because on penthouse roofs,
gathered at bars,
emerging in bunches from the sewers,
trembling between the legs of chauffeurs,
or spinning on dance floors wet with absinthe,
the faggots, Walt Whitman, point you out.

He's one, too! That's right! And they land
on your luminous chaste beard,
blonds from the north, blacks from the sands,
crowds of howls and gestures,
like cats or like snakes,
the faggots, Walt Whitman, the faggots,
clouded with tears, flesh for the whip,
the boot, or the teeth of the lion tamers.

He's one, too! That's right! Stained fingers
point to the shore of your dream
when a friend eats your apple
with a slight taste of gasoline
and the sun sings in the navels
of boys who play under bridges.

But you didn't look for scratched eyes,
nor the darkest swamp where someone submerges children,
nor frozen saliva,
nor the curves slit open like a toad's belly
that the faggots wear in cars and on terraces
while the moon lashes them on the street corners of terror.

You looked for a nude like a river.
Bull and dream who would join wheel with seaweed,
father of your agony, camellia of your death,
who would groan in the blaze of your hidden equator.

Porque es justo que el hombre no busque su deleite
en la selva de sangre de la mañana próxima.
El cielo tiene playas donde evitar la vida
80 y hay cuerpos que no deben repetirse en la aurora.

Agonía, agonía, sueño, fermento y sueño.
Este es el mundo, amigo, agonía, agonía.
Los muertos se descomponen bajo el reloj de las ciudades,
la guerra pasa llorando con un millón de ratas grises,
los ricos dan a sus queridas
pequeños moribundos iluminados,
y la vida no es noble, ni buena, ni sagrada.

Puede el hombre, si quiere, conducir su deseo
por vena de coral o celeste desnudo:
90 mañana los amores serán rocas y el Tiempo
una brisa que viene dormida por las ramas.

Por eso no levanto mi voz, viejo Walt Whitman,
contra el niño que escribe
nombre de niña en su almohada,
ni contra el muchacho que se viste de novia
en la oscuridad del ropero,
ni contra los solitarios de los casinos
que beben con asco el agua de la prostitución,
ni contra los hombres de mirada verde
100 que aman al hombre y queman sus labios en silencio.

Pero sí contra vosotros, maricas de las ciudades,
de carne tumefacta y pensamiento inmundo.
Madres de lodo. Arpías. Enemigos sin sueño
del Amor que reparte coronas de alegría.

Contra vosotros siempre, que dais a los muchachos
gotas de sucia muerte con amargo veneno.
Contra vosotros siempre,
Fairies de Norteamérica,
Pájaros de La Habana,
110 *Jotos* de Méjico,
Sarasas de Cádiz,
Apios de Sevilla,
Cancos de Madrid,

Because it's all right if a man doesn't look for his delight
in tomorrow morning's jungle of blood.
The sky has shores where life can be avoided
80   and there are bodies that shouldn't repeat themselves in the dawn.

Agony, agony, dream, ferment and dream.
This is the world, my friend, agony, agony.
Bodies decompose beneath the city clocks,
war passes by in tears, followed by a million gray rats,
the rich give their mistresses
small illuminated dying things,
and life is neither noble, nor good, nor sacred.

Man is able, if he wishes, to guide his desire
through a vein of coral or a nude as blue as the sky:
90   tomorrow, loves will become stones, and Time
a breeze that drowses in the branches.

That's why I don't raise my voice, old Walt Whitman,
against the little boy who writes
the name of a girl on his pillow,
nor against the boy who dresses as a bride
in the darkness of the wardrobe,
nor against the solitary men in casinos
who drink prostitution's water with revulsion,
nor against the men with that green look in their eyes
100 who love other men and burn their lips in silence.

But yes against you, urban faggots,
tumescent flesh and unclean thoughts.
Mothers of mud. Harpies. Sleepless enemies
of the love that bestows crowns of joy.

Always against you, who give boys
drops of foul death with bitter poison.
Always against you,
Fairies of North America,
Pájaros of Havana,
110 *Jotos* of Mexico,
Sarasas of Cádiz,
Apios of Seville,
Cancos of Madrid,

Floras de Alicante,
Adelaidas de Portugal.

¡Maricas de todo el mundo, asesinos de palomas!
Esclavos de la mujer. Perras de sus tocadores.
Abiertos en las plazas con fiebre de abanico
o emboscados en yertos paisajes de cicuta.

120 ¡No haya cuartel! La muerte
mana de vuestros ojos
y agrupa flores grises en la orilla del cieno.
¡No haya cuartel! ¡¡Alerta!!
Que los confundidos, los puros,
los clásicos, los señalados, los suplicantes
os cierren las puertas de la bacanal.

Y tú, bello Walt Whitman, duerme a orillas del Hudson
con la barba hacia el polo y las manos abiertas.
Arcilla blanda o nieve, tu lengua está llamando
130 camaradas que velen tu gacela sin cuerpo.

Duerme: no queda nada.
Una danza de muros agita las praderas
y América se anega de máquinas y llanto.
Quiero que el aire fuerte de la noche más honda
quite flores y letras del arco donde duermes
y un niño negro anuncie a los blancos del oro
la llegada del reino de la espiga.

IX
Huida de Nueva York
(Dos valses hacia la civilización)

Pequeño vals vienés

En Viena hay diez muchachas,
un hombro donde solloza la muerte

Floras of Alicante,
Adelaidas of Portugal.

Faggots of the world, murderers of doves!
Slaves of women. Their bedroom bitches.
Opening in public squares like feverish fans
or ambushed in rigid hemlock landscapes.

120 No quarter given! Death
spills from your eyes
and gathers gray flowers at the mire's edge.
No quarter given! Attention!
Let the confused, the pure,
the classical, the celebrated, the supplicants
close the doors of the bacchanal to you.

And you, lovely Walt Whitman, stay asleep on the Hudson's banks
with your beard toward the pole, openhanded.
Soft clay or snow, your tongue calls for
130 comrades to keep watch over your unbodied gazelle.

Sleep on, nothing remains.
Dancing walls stir the prairies
and America drowns itself in machinery and lament.
I want the powerful air from the deepest night
to blow away flowers and inscriptions from the arch where you sleep,
and a black child to inform the gold-craving whites
that the kingdom of grain has arrived.

IX
Flight from New York
(Two Waltzes toward Civilization)

Little Viennese Waltz

In Vienna there are ten little girls,
a shoulder for death to cry on,

y un bosque de palomas disecadas.
Hay un fragmento de la mañana
en el museo de la escarcha.
Hay un salón con mil ventanas.

¡Ay, ay, ay, ay!
Toma este vals con la boca cerrada.

Este vals, este vals, este vals,
de sí, de muerte y de coñac
que moja su cola en el mar.

Te quiero, te quiero, te quiero,
con la butaca y el libro muerto,
por el melancólico pasillo,
en el oscuro desván del lirio,
en nuestra cama de la luna
y en la danza que sueña la tortuga.

¡Ay, ay, ay, ay!
Toma este vals de quebrada cintura.

En Viena hay cuatro espejos
donde juegan tu boca y los ecos.
Hay una muerte para piano
que pinta de azul a los muchachos.
Hay mendigos por los tejados.
Hay frescas guirnaldas de llanto.

¡Ay, ay, ay, ay!
Toma este vals que se muere en mis brazos.

Porque te quiero, te quiero, amor mío,
en el desván donde juegan los niños,
soñando viejas luces de Hungría
por los rumores de la tarde tibia,
viendo ovejas y lirios de nieve
por el silencio oscuro de tu frente.

¡Ay, ay, ay, ay!
Toma este vals del "Te quiero siempre."

and a forest of dried pigeons.
There is a fragment of the morning
in the museum of winter frost.
There is a thousand-windowed dance hall.

Ay, ay, ay, ay!
Take this close-mouthed waltz.

Little waltz, little waltz, little waltz,
10 of itself, of death, and of brandy
that dips its tail in the sea.

I love you, I love you, I love you,
with the armchair and the book of death,
down the melancholy hallway,
in the iris's darkened garret,
in our bed that is the moon's bed,
and in that dance the turtle dreams of.

Ay, ay, ay, ay!
Take this broken-waisted waltz.

20 In Vienna there are four mirrors
in which your mouth and the echoes play.
There is a death for piano
that paints the little boys blue.
There are beggars on the roof.
There are fresh garlands of tears.

Ay, ay, ay, ay!
Take this waltz that dies in my arms.

Because I love you, I love you, my love,
in the attic where the children play,
30 dreaming ancient lights of Hungary
through the noise, the balmy afternoon,
seeing sheep and lilies of snow
through the dark silence of your forehead.

Ay, ay, ay, ay!
Take this "I will always love you" waltz.

En Viena bailaré contigo
con un disfraz que tenga
cabeza de río.
¡Mira qué orillas tengo de jacintos!
40   Dejaré mi boca entre tus piernas,
mi alma en fotografías y azucenas,
y en las ondas oscuras de tu andar
quiero, amor mío, amor mío, dejar,
violín y sepulcro, las cintas del vals.

Vals en las ramas

Cayó una hoja
y dos
y tres.
Por la luna nadaba un pez.
El agua duerme una hora
y el mar blanco duerme cien.
La dama
estaba muerta en la rama.
La monja
10   cantaba dentro de la toronja.
La niña
iba por el pino a la piña.
Y el pino
buscaba la plumilla del trino.
Pero el ruiseñor
lloraba sus heridas alrededor.
Y yo también
porque cayó una hoja
y dos
20   y tres.
Y una cabeza de cristal
y un violín de papel.
Y la nieve podría con el mundo
si la nieve durmiera un mes,
y las ramas luchaban con el mundo,
una a una,
dos a dos
y tres a tres.

In Vienna I will dance with you
in a costume with
a river's head.
See how the hyacinths line my banks!
40 I will leave my mouth between your legs,
my soul in photographs and lilies,
and in the dark wake of your footsteps,
my love, my love, I want to leave
violin and grave, the ribbons of the waltz.

Waltz in the Branches

One leaf fell,
a second
and a third.
A fish swam on the moon.
The water sleeps for only an hour,
but the white sea sleeps for a hundred.
There was a dead lady
in the branch of the tree.
The nun in her habit
10 sang inside the pomegranate.
This girl of mine
reached the pinecone from the pine.
And the pine went along
to look for the tiny feather's song.
But the wounded nightingale cried
throughout the countryside.
And I did too,
because the first leaf fell,
a second
20 and a third.
And a head of crystal
and a paper fiddle.
And the snow could make its way in the world,
if the snow slept for a month,
and the branches wrestled with the world,
one by one,
two by two
and three by three.

¡Oh duro marfil de carnes invisibles!
30   ¡Oh golfo sin hormigas del amanecer!
Con el muuu de las ramas,
con el ay de las damas,
con el croo de las ranas
y el gloo amarillo de la miel.
Llegará un torso de sombra
coronado de laurel.
Será el cielo para el viento
duro como una pared
y las ramas desgajadas
40   se irán bailando con él.
Una a una
alrededor de la luna,
dos a dos
alrededor del sol,
y tres a tres
para que los marfiles se duerman bien.

X

El poeta llega a La Habana

A don Fernando Ortiz

Son de negros en Cuba

Cuando llegue la luna llena iré a Santiago de Cuba,
iré a Santiago
en un coche de agua negra.
Iré a Santiago.
Cantarán los techos de palmera.
Iré a Santiago.
Cuando la palma quiere ser cigüeña,
iré a Santiago.
Y cuando quiere ser medusa el plátano,
10   iré a Santiago.
Iré a Santiago
con la rubia cabeza de Fonseca.

Oh, the hard ivory of invisible flesh!
30 Oh, the dawn's abyss with no ants!
With the swish of the trees,
with the sighs of the ladies,
with the croaking frogs
and the honey's yellow glug.
A shadow's torso will arrive,
wearing a laurel crown.
For the wind, the sky will
be as hard as a wall
and all the downed branches
40 will leave as they dance.
One by one
around the moon,
two by two
around the sun,
and three by three
so the ivory can sleep.

X

The Poet Arrives in Havana

To Don Fernando Ortiz

Blacks Dancing to Cuban Rhythms

As soon as the full moon rises, I'm going to Santiago, Cuba,
I'm going to Santiago
in a coach of black water.
I'm going to Santiago.
The thatched roofs will sing.
I'm going to Santiago.
When the palm wants to be a stork,
I'm going to Santiago.
When the banana tree wants to be a sea wasp,
10 I'm going to Santiago.
I'm going to Santiago
with Fonseca's blond head.

Iré a Santiago.
Y con el rosa de Romeo y Julieta
iré a Santiago.
Mar de papel y plata de moneda.
Iré a Santiago.
¡Oh Cuba! ¡Oh ritmo de semillas secas!
Iré a Santiago.
20 ¡Oh cintura caliente y gota de madera!
Iré a Santiago.
Arpa de troncos vivos. Caimán. Flor de tabaco.
Iré a Santiago.
Siempre he dicho que yo iría a Santiago
en un coche de agua negra.
Iré a Santiago.
Brisa y alcohol en las ruedas,
iré a Santiago.
Mi coral en la tiniebla,
30 iré a Santiago.
El mar ahogado en la arena,
iré a Santiago.
Calor blanco, fruta muerta,
iré a Santiago.
¡Oh bovino frescor de cañavera!
¡Oh Cuba! ¡Oh curva de suspiro y barro!
Iré a Santiago.

I'm going to Santiago.
And with Romeo and Juliet's rose
I'm going to Santiago.
Paper sea and silver coins.
I'm going to Santiago.
Oh, Cuba, oh, rhythm of dried seeds!
I'm going to Santiago.
20 Oh, fiery waist, oh, drop of wood!
I'm going to Santiago.
Harp of living tree trunks. Crocodile. Tobacco plant in bloom!
I'm going to Santiago.
I always said I'd go to Santiago
in a coach of black water.
I'm going to Santiago.
Wind and rum on the wheels,
I'm going to Santiago.
My coral in the darkness,
30 I'm going to Santiago.
The sea drowned in the sand,
I'm going to Santiago.
White heat, rotting fruit,
I'm going to Santiago.
Oh, the bovine coolness of sugar cane!
Oh, Cuba! Oh, curve of sigh and clay!
I'm going to Santiago.

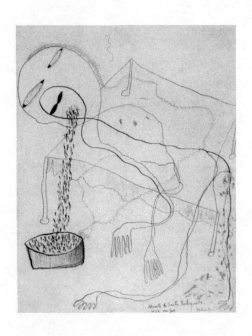

VIAJE A
LA LUNA

[Muerte de Santa Radegunda, 1929]

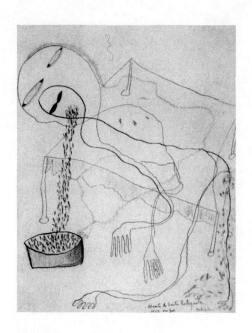

TRIP TO
THE MOON

Translated by

Greg Simon and

Steven F. White

[*Death of St. Radegunda, 1929*]

1

White bed against a gray wall. Above the bedcovers, a dance begins between numbers 13 and 22. First there are only two, but then others appear until they cover the bed like tiny ants.

2

An invisible hand pulls back the covers.

3

Large feet running fast in oversized socks, patterned with black and white diamonds.

4

Frightened head staring at a point and fades out to a wire head, against a background of water.

5

Double-exposed letters that read *Help Help Help*, moving up and down above a woman's genitals.

6

The camera pans down a long corridor with a window at the end.

7

View of Broadway at night with tic-tac movement. Fade-out to the previous scene.

8

Six legs oscillating at high speed.

9

The legs fade out to a group of trembling hands.

10

The trembling hands fade out to a double exposure of a crying little boy.

11

And the crying boy, to a double exposure of a woman who beats him.

12

This scene fades out to the long corridor, which the camera traverses again, at high speed.

13

At the end, a close-up of an eye, double-exposed above fish, which fades out to the following . . .

14

Fast fall down a roller coaster in blue, with double-exposed letters that read *Help! Help!*

15

Each of the two titles *Help! Help!* fades out to a footprint.

16

And each footprint, into a silkworm on a leaf against a white background.

17

A large dead head emerges from the silkworms, and from the dead head, a moonlit sky.

18

The moon is cut open, and a drawing of a head appears, vomiting, blinking, and fading out to . . .

19

Two boys who walk and sing with their eyes closed.

20

Heads of the singing boys, filled with blots of ink.

21

Ink drops thrown against a white frame. (All these scenes [move] rapidly and with well-marked rhythms.) And here a sign saying *Wrong way.*

22
Door.

23
A man in a white robe emerges. From the opposite side, a boy comes out in a bathing suit with large squares of black and white.

24
Close-up of the plaid bathing suit above a double exposure of a fish.

25
The man in the robe holds out a harlequin costume, but the boy refuses it. Then the robed man grabs him by the throat, the boy screams, but the man in the robe covers his mouth with the harlequin costume.

26
Close-up of hands tightly squeezing the harlequin costume.

27
Everything fades out to double-exposed sea serpents from the aquarium, these into crabs from the same aquarium, and these into other rhythmic fish.

28
A live fish in a close-up, held and squeezed to death by a person's hand, and advancing with its little mouth open until the lens is covered.

29
Inside the fish's little mouth, a close-up of two fish, leaping in agony. These become a kaleidoscope in which one hundred fish leap and throb in agony.

30
Title: TRIP TO THE MOON

Room. Two women dressed in black sit and cry with their heads on a table with a lamp. They lift their hands to the sky. Shots of their breasts and hands. Their long hair has fallen over their faces, and their hands are made of wire coils.

31
The women continue to lower and raise their arms to the sky.

32

A frog falls onto the table.

33

Huge double-exposed frog looming above a background of furiously waving orchids.

The orchids go away, and there appears a drawing of a woman's enormous head, vomiting, changing from negative to positive and positive to negative at high speed.

34

A door slams violently, and another door, and another, and another, over a double exposure of the women who raise and lower their arms. As each door closes, a title appears that reads . . . *Elena, Helena, elhena, eLHeNa.*

35

The women go quickly to the door.

36

With a greatly accelerated rhythm, the camera descends the stairs and, in a double exposure, ascends them also.

37

The stairs ascended and descended, triple-exposed.

38

Double-exposed iron bars that pass over a drawing: "The Death of St. Radegunda."

39

A woman in mourning falls down the stairs.

40

Close-up of her.

41

Another very realistic view of her. She wears a kerchief on her head, Spanish style. Shot of her bleeding nostrils.

42

Her head face down, double-exposed on a drawing of veins with big grains of salt to make them stand out.

43
From below, the camera focuses on and climbs the stairs. At the top, the nude of a boy appears. His head is like an anatomical doll, with muscles, veins, and tendons. The circulatory system is drawn on his naked body, and he drags a harlequin costume.

44
Shot of him from the waist up. He looks from side to side. This fades out to a street at night.

45
Once in the street at night, there are three figures in overcoats who show signs of being cold. They wear their collars turned up. One lifts his head and looks upward, and the moon appears on-screen; another looks up at the moon, and a close-up of a bird's head appears; its neck is wrung until it dies in front of the lens; the third looks at the moon, and a drawing of the moon appears on-screen, against a white background, and fades out to genitals, and then the genitals fade out to a screaming mouth.

46
The three run away through the street.

47
The veined man appears in the street, and stretches his arms out like a cross. He leaps forward on-screen.

48
Fade-out to a crossing of fast trains, triple-exposed.

49
The trains fade out to a double exposure of piano keyboards, and hands playing them.

50
Fade-out to a bar where several boys are dressed in tuxedos. The waiter pours wine for them, but they can't lift it to their mouths. The glasses become very heavy and the boys struggle anxiously, as in a dream. A nearly naked girl enters with a harlequin and they dance in slow motion. Everyone tries to drink, but can't. The waiter continues to fill the glasses, even though they are already full.

51

The veined man appears, gesticulating and making desperate signs and movements which express life and accelerated rhythm. All the men become very drowsy.

52

A head stares stupidly. It approaches the screen [sic]. And fades out to a frog. The veined man crushes the frog in his fingers.

53

A sponge appears and a blindfolded head.

54

Fade-out to a street where the girl dressed in white flees with a harlequin.

55

A vomiting head. And immediately all the people in the bar vomit.

56

The preceding fades out to an elevator where a small black boy vomits. The harlequin and the naked girl go up in the elevator.

57

They go up in the elevator and embrace.

58

Shot of a sensual kiss.

59

The boy bites the girl's neck and pulls violently on her hair.

60

A guitar appears, and a hand quickly cuts the strings with scissors.

61

The girl defends herself against the boy, and he, furiously, gives her another deep kiss, and covers her eyes with his thumbs, as if to plunge them in.

62
The girl screams, and the boy, back turned, removes his sport coat and a wig, and the veined man appears.

63
Then she fades out to a white plaster bust, and the veined man kisses her passionately.

64
Shot of the plaster bust with lip and hand prints.

65
Again the words *Elena elena elena elena* appear.

66
These words fade out into faucets violently gushing water.

67
And these faucets into the veined man, lying dead among discarded newspapers and herrings.

68
A bed appears, and hands that cover a corpse.

69
A boy in a white robe and rubber gloves comes in, and a girl dressed in black. They paint a mustache with ink on a terrible dead man's head. And they kiss with much laughter.

70
A cemetery emerges from them and they are seen kissing over a grave.

71
Shot of a vulgar cinematic kiss with other characters.

72
And finally a quick shot of the moon and trees in the wind.

"Infancia y muerte"

———

Poemas de

TIERRA

Y LUNA

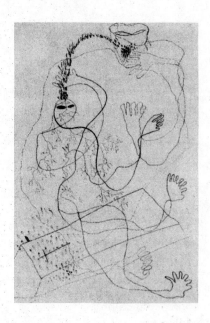

"Childhood and Death"

—

Poems from

EARTH

AND MOON

Translated by

Greg Simon and

Steven F. White

[*Two Figures over a Tomb, ca. 1929–31*]

Infancia y muerte

Para buscar mi infancia, ¡Dios mío!,
comí naranjas podridas, papeles viejos, palomares vacíos
y encontré mi cuerpecito comido por las ratas
en el fondo del aljibe con las cabelleras de los locos.
Mi traje de marinero
no estaba empapado con el aceite de las ballenas,
pero tenía la eternidad vulnerable de las fotografías.
Ahogado, sí, bien ahogado, duerme, hijito mío, duerme,
niño vencido en el colegio y en el vals de la rosa herida,
10   asombrado con el alba oscura del vello sobre los muslos,
asombrado con su propio hombre que masticaba tabaco en su
    costado siniestro.
Oigo un río seco lleno de latas de conserva,
donde cantan las alcantarillas y arrojan las camisas llenas de sangre,
un río de gatos podridos que fingen corolas y anémonas
para engañar a la luna y que se apoye dulcemente en ellos.
Aquí, solo con mi ahogado,
aquí, solo con la brisa de musgos fríos y tapaderas de hojalata,
aquí, solo, veo que ya me han cerrado la puerta.
Me han cerrado la puerta y hay un grupo de muertos
20   que juega al tiro al blanco y otro grupo de muertos
que busca por la cocina las cáscaras de melón
y un solitario, azul, inexplicable muerto,
que me busca por las escaleras, que mete las manos en el aljibe
mientras los astros llenan de ceniza las cerraduras de las catedrales
y las gentes se quedan de pronto con todos los trajes pequeños.

Para buscar mi infancia, ¡Dios mío!,
comí limones estrujados, establos, periódicos marchitos,
pero mi infancia era una rata que huía por un jardín oscurísimo,
una rata satisfecha, mojada por el agua simple,
30   una rata para el asalto de los grandes almacenes
y que llevaba un anda de oro entre sus dientes diminutos.

Tierra y luna

Me quedo con el transparente hombrecillo
que come los huevos de la golondrina.

Childhood and Death

So I could look for my childhood, my God!—
I ate rotten oranges, old papers, empty dovecotes,
and found my little body eaten by the rats
at the bottom of a well with the lunatics' hair.
My sailor's suit
wasn't soaked with whale oil,
but it did have the vulnerable eternity of photographs.
Drowned, yes, completely drowned, sleep, my child, sleep.
Child defeated in grade school and in the waltz of the wounded rose,
10   amazed by the dark dawning of the thighs' soft hair,
amazed by his own man chewing tobacco in his left side.
I hear a dry river full of tin cans
where the sewers sing and hurl shirts full of blood.
A river of rotten cats that pretend to be corollas and anemones
to deceive the moon, so it will rest gently on them.
Alone here with my drowned boy.
Alone here with the breeze of cold moss and tin lids.
Alone, here, I see they have closed the door on me.
The door has been closed on me and some of the dead
20   go target shooting, and others
look in the kitchen for melon rinds,
and a single, blue, inexplicable dead one
looks for me on the stairs, plunges his hands into the well
while the stars cover cathedral locks with ashes
and everyone's suit is suddenly too small for him.

So I could look for my childhood, my God!—
I ate squeezed lemons, stables, withered newspapers.
But my childhood was a rat that scurried through a dark, dark garden,
a satisfied rat, soaked in simple water,
30   a rat to attack the great warehouses,
carrying a golden streamer between its tiny teeth.

Earth and Moon

I'll stick with the transparent little man
who eats the swallow's eggs.

Me quedo con el niño desnudo
que pisotean los borrachos de Brooklyn.
Con las criaturas mudas que pasan bajo los arcos.
Con el arroyo de venas ansioso de abrir sus manecitas.

Tierra tan solo. Tierra.
Tierra para los manteles estremecidos,
para la pupila viciosa de nube,
10   para las heridas recientes y el húmedo pensamiento.
Tierra para todo lo que huye de la tierra.

No es la ceniza en vilo de las cosas quemadas,
ni los muertos que mueven sus lenguas bajo los árboles.
Es la tierra desnuda que bala por el cielo
y deja atrás los grupos ligeros de ballenas.

Es la tierra alegrísima, imperturbable nadadora,
la que yo encuentro en el niño y en las criaturas que pasan los arcos.
Viva tierra de mi pulso y del baile de los helechos
que deja a veces por el aire un duro perfil de Faraón.

20   Me quedo con la mujer fría
donde se queman los musgos inocentes.
Me quedo con los borrachos de Brooklyn
que pisan al niño desnudo.
Me quedo con los signos desgarrados
de la lenta comida de los osos.

Pero entonces bajó la luna despeñada por las escaleras
poniendo las ciudades de hule celeste y talco sensitivo,
llenando de pies de mármol la llanura sin recodos
y olvidando bajo las sillas diminutas carcajadas de algodón.

30   ¡Oh Diana, Diana! Diana vacía,
convexa resonancia donde la abeja se vuelve loca!
Mi amor es paso, tránsito, larga muerte gustada,
nunca la piel ilesa de tu desnudo huido.

Es Tierra, ¡Dios mío!, tierra lo que vengo buscando.
Embozo de horizonte, latido y sepultura.
Es dolor que se acaba y amor que se consume.
Torre de sangre abierta con las manos quemadas.

I'll stick with the naked child
trampled by the drunks of Brooklyn.
With the speechless creatures passing under the arches.
With the stream of veins, anxious to open their little hands.

Only Earth. Earth.
Earth for trembling tablecloths,
for a cloud's vicious eyeball,
10 for recent wounds and dampened thoughts.
Earth for everything that flees from earth.

It isn't the suspended ashes of charred things,
nor the dead who move their tongues beneath the trees.
It's naked earth bleating through the sky,
leaving light colonies of whales behind.

It's the joyful earth, imperturbable swimmer,
that I find in children and creatures passing the arches.
Living earth of my pulse and the dance of the ferns
that sometimes leaves a Pharaoh's hard profile in the air.

20 I'll stick with the cold woman
where innocent moss goes up in flames.
I'll stick with Brooklyn's drunks
who trample the naked child.
I'll stick with the shredded signs
of the bears' slow meal.

But then the moon tumbled down the stairs,
covering the cities with blue oilcloth and sentient talc,
filling the uncurved plain with marble feet
and forgetting, beneath the chairs, tiny peals of cotton laughter.

30 Oh Diana, Diana, empty Diana!
The bee goes insane in your convex resonance.
My love is a footstep, passage, long death that I relish,
never the unharmed skin of your nakedness in flight.

It's earth. My God! Earth, that I come looking for.
Muffled horizon, heartbeat, and tomb.
It's sorrow that runs out, love that consumes itself.
Charred hands opening a tower of blood.

Pero la luna subía y bajaba las escaleras
repartiendo lentejas desangradas en los ojos,
40   dando escobazos de plata a los niños de los muelles
y borrando mi apariencia por el término del aire.

Pequeño poema infinito

Para Luis Cardoza y Aragón

Equivocar el camino
es llegar a la nieve
y llegar a la nieve
es pacer durante varios siglos las hierbas de los cementerios.

Equivocar el camino
es llegar a la mujer,
la mujer que no teme la luz,
la mujer que mata dos gallos en un segundo,
la luz que no teme a los gallos
10   y los gallos que no saben cantar sobre la nieve.

Pero si la nieve se equivoca de corazón
puede llegar el viento Austro,
y como el aire no hace caso de los gemidos,
tendremos que pacer otra vez las hierbas de los cementerios.
Yo vi dos dolorosas espigas de cera
que enterraban un paisaje de volcanes
y vi dos niños locos
que empujaban llorando las pupilas de un asesino.

Pero el dos no ha sido nunca un número
20   porque es una angustia y su sombra,
porque es la demostración del otro infinito que no es suyo
y es las murallas del muerto
y el castigo de la nueva resurrección sin finales.

Los muertos odian el número dos,
pero el número dos adormece a las mujeres,
y como la mujer teme la luz,
la luz tiembla delante de los gallos
y los gallos sólo saben volar sobre la nieve,
30   tendremos que pacer sin descanso las hierbas de los cementerios.

But the moon went up and down the stairs,
handing out bloodless lentils in the eyes,
40   striking the children on the piers with silver brooms,
erasing my apparition from the boundary of air.

Little Infinite Poem

For Luis Cardoza y Aragón

To take the wrong road
is to arrive at snow
and to arrive at snow
is to graze for several centuries on graveyard weeds.

To take the wrong road
is to arrive at woman,
woman unafraid of light,
woman killing two roosters a second,
light unafraid of roosters,
10   and roosters that can't sing on snow.

But if snow chooses the wrong heart,
the South Wind can come,
and since air pays no attention to moaning,
we'll have to graze once more on graveyard weeds.
I saw two sad, waxen spikes of wheat
that buried a volcanic landscape,
and two crazy children
who wept as they pushed a murderer's eyeballs.

But two has never been a number.
20   It is anguish and its shadow,
it is the demonstration of somebody else's infinity,
and the dead man's walls,
and the punishment of the new, unending resurrection.

Dead men hate the number two,
but the number two lulls women to sleep
and since women fear light,
and light trembles before roosters,
and roosters only fly above the snow—
we'll have to graze on graveyard weeds forever.

Omega
(Poema para muertos)

Las hierbas.

Yo me cortaré la mano derecha.
Espera.

Las hierbas.

Tengo un guante de mercurio y otro de seda.
Espera.

¡Las hierbas!

No solloces. Silencio. Que no nos sientan.
Espera.

10   ¡Las hierbas!

Se cayeron las estatuas
al abrirse la gran puerta.

¡¡Las hierbaaas!!

Canción de la muerte pequeña

Prado mortal de lunas
y sangre bajo tierra.
Prado de sangre vieja.

Luz de ayer y mañana.
Cielo mortal de hierba.
Luz y noche de arena.

Me encontré con la muerte.
Prado mortal de tierra.
Una muerte pequeña.

Omega
(Poem for the Dead)

The weeds.

I'll cut my right hand off.
Wait.

The weeds.

I have one glove of mercury and another of silk.
Wait.

The weeds!

No sobbing. Silence. They must not hear us.
Wait.

10   The weeds!

The statues fell down
as the great door swung open.

The weeeeds!!

Song of a Little Death

Mortal field of moons
and subterranean blood.
Field of ancient blood.

Past and future light.
Mortal sky of grass.
Light and night of sand.

I came face to face with death.
Mortal field of land.
A little death.

10 El perro en el tejado.
    Sola mi mano izquierda
    atravesaba montes sin fin
    de flores secas.

    Catedral de ceniza.
    Luz y noche de arena.
    Una muerte pequeña.

    Una muerte y yo un hombre.
    Un hombre solo, y ella
    una muerte pequeña.

20 Prado mortal de lunas.
    La nieve gime y tiembla
    por detrás de la puerta.

    Un hombre, ¿y qué? Lo dicho.
    Un hombre solo y ella.
    Prado, amor, luz y arena.

El poeta pide ayuda a la Virgen

    Pido a la divina Madre de Dios,
    reina celeste de todo lo criado,
    me dé la pura luz de los animalitos
    que tienen una sola letra en su vocabulario.
    Animales sin alma. Simples formas.
    Lejos de la despreciable sabiduría del gato.
    Lejos de la profundidad ficticia de los buhos.
    Lejos de la escultórica sapiencia del caballo.
    Criaturas que aman sin ojos,
10 con un solo sentido de infinito ondulado
    y que se agrupan en grandes montones
    para ser comidas por los pájaros.
    Pido la sola dimensión
    que tienen los pequeños animales planos,
    para narrar cosas cubiertas de tierra
    bajo la dura inocencia del zapato.
    No hay quien llore porque comprenda

766

The dog on the roof.
Only my left hand
crossed the unending
slopes of dry flowers.

Cathedral of ash.
Light and night of sand.
A little death.

A death and the man I am.
A man alone with her,
a little death.

Mortal field of moons.
The snow moans and trembles
on the other side of the door.

A man. So what? That's all.
A man alone with her.
Field, love, light, and sand.

The Poet Prays to the Virgin for Help

I pray to the Divine Mother of God,
Heavenly Queen of all living things,
that she grant me the pure light of the little animals
that have a single letter in their vocabulary.
Animals without souls. Simple shapes.
Far from the cat's despicable knowledge.
Far from the owl's fictitious profundity.
Far from the horse's sculptural wisdom.
Creatures that love without eyes,
10 with a single sense of infinity's waves,
and that gather in great piles
to be eaten by the birds.
Grant me the single dimension
that flat little animals have
so that I can tell of things covered with earth
beneath the hard innocence of the shoe.
There is no one to weep because he understands

el millón de muertecitas que tiene el mercado.
Esa muchedumbre china de las cebollas decapitadas
20 y ese gran sol amarillo de viejos peces aplastados.

Tú, Madre siempre terrible, ballena de todos los cielos;
tú, Madre siempre bromista, vecina del perejil prestado:
sabes que yo comprendo la carne mínima del mundo
para poder expresarlo.

the millions of tiny deaths at the marketplace,
the Chinese multitude of headless onions,
20 and that great yellow sun of old, flattened fish.

You, Mother, forever to be feared, whale of all the skies;
you, Mother, forever joking, neighbor of the borrowed parsley:
you know that to speak of the world
I must understand its slightest flesh.

DIVÁN
DEL TAMARIT

[Agua sexual, 1934]

THE TAMARIT DIVAN

Translated by

Catherine Brown

[*Sexual Water, 1934*]

Gacelas

Gacela primera
Del amor imprevisto

Nadie comprendía el perfume
de la oscura magnolia de tu vientre.
Nadie sabía que martirizabas
un colibrí de amor entre los dientes.

Mil caballitos persas se dormían
en la plaza con luna de tu frente,
mientras que yo enlazaba cuatro noches
tu cintura, enemiga de la nieve.

Entre yeso y jazmines, tu mirada
era un pálido ramo de simientes.
Yo busqué, para darte, por mi pecho
las letras de marfil que dicen *siempre*.

Siempre, siempre: jardín de mi agonía,
tu cuerpo fugitivo para siempre,
la sangre de tus venas en mi boca,
tu boca ya sin luz para mi muerte.

Gacela II
De la terrible presencia

Yo quiero que el agua se quede sin cauce.
Yo quiero que el viento se quede sin valles.

Quiero que la noche se quede sin ojos
y mi corazón sin la flor del oro;

que los bueyes hablen con las grandes hojas
y que la lombriz se muera de sombra;

que brillen los dientes de la calavera
y los amarillos inunden la seda.

Ghazals

I
Ghazal of Love Unforeseen

No one understood the perfume, ever:
the dark magnolia of your belly.
No one ever knew you martyred
love's hummingbird between your teeth.

A thousand Persian ponies fell asleep
in the moonlit plaza of your brow,
while four nights through I bound
your waist, the enemy of snow.

Between plaster and jasmine
10   your glance, pale branch of seed.
I searched my breast to give you
the ivory letters saying: Ever.

Ever, ever, my agony's garden,
your elusive form forever:
blood of your veins in my mouth,
your mouth now lightless for my death.

II
Ghazal of the Terrible Presence

I want there to be no channel for the water.
I want there to be no valleys for the wind.

I want there to be no eyes for the night,
no flower of gold for my heart;

and I want the oxen to talk to big leaves,
and the earthworm to die of shadow,

and I want teeth in the skull to gleam,
and the yellows to wash over the silk.

Puedo ver el duelo de la noche herida
luchando enroscada con el mediodía.

Resisto un ocaso de verde veneno
y los arcos rotos donde sufre el tiempo.

Pero no ilumines tu limpio desnudo
como un negro cactus abierto en los juncos.

Déjame en un ansia de oscuros planetas,
pero no me enseñes tu cintura fresca.

Gacela III
Del amor desesperado

La noche no quiere venir
para que tú no vengas,
ni yo pueda ir.

Pero yo iré,
aunque un sol de alacranes me coma la sien.

Pero tú vendrás
con la lengua quemada por la lluvia de sal.

El día no quiere venir
para que tú no vengas,
ni yo pueda ir.

Pero yo iré
entregando a los sapos mi mordido clavel.

Pero tú vendrás
por las turbias cloacas de la oscuridad.

Ni la noche ni el día quieren venir
para que por ti muera
y tú mueras por mí.

I can see the struggle of wounded night
10 wrestling in coils with midday.

I can endure a sunset green with poison
and the broken arches where time suffers.

But do not show me your immaculate nude
like a black cactus open in the reeds.

Leave me in longing for shadowy planets,
but do not show me the cool of your waist.

III
Ghazal of Desperate Love

Night does not want to come
so that you cannot come,
so that I cannot go.

But I will go,
though a sun of scorpions feed on my temples.

But you will come,
with your tongue burnt by the shower of salt.

Day does not want to come
so that you cannot come,
10 so that I cannot go.

But I will go,
and cede to the toads my bitten carnation.

But you will come,
through the murky sewers of darkness.

Night and day do not want to come
so that I die for you
and you for me.

Gacela IV
Del amor que no se deja ver

Solamente por oír
la campana de la Vela
te puse una corona de verbena.

Granada era una luna
ahogada entre las yedras.

Solamente por oír
la campana de la Vela
desgarré mi jardín de Cartagena.

Granada era una corza
10   *rosa por las veletas.*

Solamente por oír
la campana de la Vela
me abrasaba en tu cuerpo
sin saber de quién era.

Gacela V
Del niño muerto

Todas las tardes en Granada,
todas las tardes se muere un niño.
Todas las tardes el agua se sienta
a conversar con sus amigos.

Los muertos llevan alas de musgo.
El viento nublado y el viento limpio
son dos faisanes que vuelan por las torres
y el día es un muchacho herido.

No quedaba en el aire ni una brizna de alondra
10   cuando yo te encontré por las grutas del vino.
No quedaba en la tierra ni una miga de nube
cuando te ahogabas por el río.

Un gigante de agua cayó sobre los montes
y el valle fue rodando con perros y con lirios.

IV
Ghazal of the Love That Hides from Sight

Just to hear
the bell of the Vela
I made you a crown of verbena.

Granada was a moon
drowned in the ivy.

Just to hear
the bell of the Vela
I clawed at my Cartagena garden.

Granada was a doe
10   *pink among weathervanes.*

Just to hear
the bell of the Vela
I burned in your body
without knowing whose it was.

V
Ghazal of the Dead Child

Every afternoon in Granada
a child dies, every afternoon.
Every afternoon the water sits down
to talk things over with its friends.

The dead wear wings of moss.
The wind cloudy and the wind clean
are two pheasants that circle the towers
and the day is a wounded boy.

No strand of lark remained in the air
10   when I found you there in the wine caves.
No crumb of cloud remained on the land
when you were drowning in the river.

A giant of water fell down the mountains
and the valley rolled by with irises and dogs.

Tu cuerpo, con la sombra violeta de mis manos,
era, muerto en la orilla, un arcángel de frío.

Gacela VI
De la raíz amarga

Hay una raíz amarga
y un mundo de mil terrazas.

Ni la mano más pequeña
quiebra la puerta del agua.

¿Dónde vas, adónde, dónde?
Hay un cielo de mil ventanas
—batalla de abejas lívidas—
y hay una raíz amarga.

Amarga.

10   Duele en la planta del pie,
el interior de la cara,
y duele en el tronco fresco
de noche recién cortada.

¡Amor, enemigo mío,
muerde tu raíz amarga!

Gacela VII
Del recuerdo de amor

No te lleves tu recuerdo.
Déjalo solo en mi pecho,

temblor de blanco cerezo
en el martirio de enero.

Me separa de los muertos
un muro de malos sueños.

Doy pena de lirio fresco
para un corazón de yeso.

Your body, shadowed violet by my hands,
dead on the bank, was an archangel of cold.

VI
Ghazal of the Bitter Root

There is a bitter root
and a world of a thousand terraces.

Not even the tiniest hand
breaks down the door of the waters.

Where are you going, where?
There is a sky of one thousand windows
—a battle of livid bees—
and there is a bitter root.

Bitter.

10   It hurts in the sole of the foot,
the inside of the face,
and it hurts in the cool trunk
of the new-cut night.

Love, my enemy,
bite your bitter root!

VII
Ghazal of the Memory of Love

Don't take your memory with you.
Leave it alone in my breast,

a shudder of cherry trees
in white January martyrdom.

A wall of bad dreams
divides me from the dead.

For a plaster heart
I give fresh lily pain.

Toda la noche, en el huerto
10　mis ojos, como dos perros.

Toda la noche, comiendo
los membrillos de veneno.

Algunas veces el viento
es un tulipán de miedo;

es un tulipán enfermo,
la madrugada de invierno.

Un muro de malos sueños
me separa de los muertos.

La hierba cubre en silencio
20　el valle gris de tu cuerpo.

Por el arco del encuentro
la cicuta está creciendo.

Pero deja tu recuerdo,
déjalo solo en mi pecho.

Gacela VIII
De la muerte oscura

Quiero dormir el sueño de las manzanas,
alejarme del tumulto de los cementerios.
Quiero dormir el sueño de aquel niño
que quería cortarse el corazón en alta mar.

No quiero que me repitan que los muertos no
　　pierden la sangre;
que la boca podrida sigue pidiendo agua.
No quiero enterarme de los martirios que da la hierba,
ni de la luna con boca de serpiente
que trabaja antes del amanecer.

All night in the orchard
my eyes, like two dogs.

All through the night
eating quinces of poison.

Sometimes the wind
is a tulip of fear;

and a sickly tulip
the winter dawn.

A wall of bad dreams
divides me from the dead.

Grass covers in silence
your body's gray vale.

Hemlock grows round
the arch of the meeting.

But leave me your memory,
leave it alone in my breast.

VIII
Ghazal of Dark Death

I want to sleep the sleep of apples,
far away from the uproar of cemeteries.
I want to sleep the sleep of that child
who wanted to cut his heart out on the sea.

I don't want to hear that the dead lose no blood,
that the decomposed mouth is still begging for water.
I don't want to find out about grass-given martyrdoms,
or the snake-mouthed moon that works before dawn.

I want to sleep just a moment,
a moment, a minute, a century.
But let it be known that I have not died:

Quiero dormir un rato,
un rato, un minuto, un siglo;
pero que todos sepan que no he muerto;
que hay un establo de oro en mis labios;
que soy el pequeño amigo del viento Oeste;
que soy la sombra inmensa de mis lágrimas.

Cúbreme por la aurora con un velo
porque me arrojará puñados de hormigas,
y moja con agua dura mis zapatos
para que resbale la pinza de su alacrán.

20 Porque quiero dormir el sueño de las manzanas
para aprender un llanto que me limpie de tierra;
porque quiero vivir con aquel niño oscuro
que quería cortarse el corazón en alta mar.

Gacela IX
Del amor maravilloso

Con todo el yeso
de los malos campos,
eras junco de amor, jazmín mojado.

Con sur y llama
de los malos cielos,
eras rumor de nieve por mi pecho.

Cielos y campos
anudaban cadenas en mis manos.

Campos y cielos
10 azotaban las llagas de mi cuerpo.

Gacela X
De la huida

Me he perdido muchas veces por el mar
con el oído lleno de flores recién cortadas,

that there is a stable of gold in my lips,
that I am the West Wind's little friend,
that I am the enormous shadow of my tears.

Wrap me at dawn in a veil,
for she will hurl fistfuls of ants;
sprinkle my shoes with hard water
so her scorpion's sting will slide off.

Because I want to sleep the sleep of apples
20 and learn a lament that will cleanse me of earth;
because I want to live with that dark child
who wanted to cut his heart out on the sea.

IX
Ghazal of Marvelous Love

Despite all the gypsum
of bad fields
you were reed of love, wet jasmine.

Despite south wind and flame
of bad skies
you were murmur of snow in my breast.

Skies and fields
knotted chains on my hands.

Fields and skies
10 lashed the wounds on my flesh.

X
Ghazal of the Flight

I have often been lost on the sea
with my ear full of fresh-cut flowers,

con la lengua llena de amor y de agonía.
Muchas veces me he perdido por el mar,
como me pierdo en el corazón de algunos niños.

No hay nadie que, al dar un beso,
no sienta la sonrisa de la gente sin rostro,
ni hay nadie que, al tocar un recién nacido,
olvide las inmóviles calaveras de caballo.

10 Porque las rosas buscan en la frente
un duro paisaje de hueso
y las manos del hombre no tienen más sentido
que imitar a las raíces bajo tierra.

Como me pierdo en el corazón de algunos niños,
me he perdido muchas veces por el mar.
Ignorante del agua, voy buscando
una muerte de luz que me consuma.

Gacela XI
Del amor con cien años

Suben por la calle
los cuatro galanes.

Ay, ay, ay, ay.

Por la calle abajo
van los tres galanes.

Ay, ay, ay.

Se ciñen el talle
esos dos galanes.

Ay, ay.

10 ¡Cómo vuelve el rostro
un galán y el aire!

with my tongue full of agony and love.
Often I have been lost on the sea,
as I am lost in the heart of certain children.

There is no one who can kiss
without feeling the smile of those without faces;
there is no one who can touch
an infant and forget the immobile skulls of horses.

10 Because roses search the forehead
for a hard landscape of bone,
and human hands have no more sense
than to mimic roots beneath the soil.

As I am lost in the heart of certain children,
I have often been lost on the sea.
Not knowing water, I keep looking
to be consumed in luminous death.

XI
Ghazal of the Hundred-Year-Old Love

Up the street
go the four young blades.

Ay, ay, ay, ay.

Down the street
go the three young blades.

Ay, ay, ay.

They cinch in their waists,
those two young blades.

Ay, ay.

10 How he turns his face,
one young blade and the breeze!

Ay.

Por los arrayanes
se pasea nadie.

Casidas

Casida primera
Del herido por el agua

Quiero bajar al pozo,
quiero subir los muros de Granada,
para mirar el corazón pasado
por el punzón oscuro de las aguas.

El niño herido gemía
con una corona de escarcha.
Estanques, aljibes y fuentes
levantaban al aire sus espadas.
¡Ay qué furia de amor, qué hiriente filo,
10 qué nocturno rumor, qué muerte blanca!
¡Qué desiertos de luz iban hundiendo
los arenales de la madrugada!
El niño estaba solo
con la ciudad dormida en la garganta.
Un surtidor que viene de los sueños
lo defiende del hambre de las algas.
El niño y su agonía, frente a frente,
eran dos verdes lluvias enlazadas.
El niño se tendía por la tierra
20 y su agonía se curvaba.

Quiero bajar al pozo,
quiero morir mi muerte a bocanadas,
quiero llenar mi corazón de musgo,
para ver al herido por el agua.

Ay.

Through the myrtle groves
nobody goes walking.

Qasidas

I
Qasida of One Wounded by Water

I want to go down to the well,
I want to go up on the walls of Granada,
to behold the heart pierced
by the dark awl of water.

The wounded child was moaning,
crowned with frost.
Pools, cisterns, and fountains
raised their swords in the air.
Oh, what a frenzy of love, how cutting the edge!
10   What nocturnal murmur, what white death!
What luminous deserts
sank the sandpits of dawn!
The child was alone,
the city asleep in his throat.
A water jet springing from dreams
protects him from the hunger of algae.
The child and his agony, face to face,
were two green rains interlaced.
The child stretched out on the ground;
20   his agony curved in the air.

I want to go down to the well;
I want to die my death by mouthfuls.
I want to fill my heart with moss
to see the one wounded by water.

Casida II
Del llanto

He cerrado mi balcón
porque no quiero oír el llanto,
pero por detrás de los grises muros
no se oye otra cosa que el llanto.

Hay muy pocos ángeles que canten,
hay muy pocos perros que ladren,
mil violines caben en la palma de mi mano.

Pero el llanto es un perro inmenso,
el llanto es un ángel inmenso,
10   el llanto es un violín inmenso,
las lágrimas amordazan al viento,
y no se oye otra cosa que el llanto.

Casida III
De los ramos

Por las arboledas del Tamarit
han venido los perros de plomo
a esperar que se caigan los ramos,
a esperar que se quiebren ellos solos.

El Tamarit tiene un manzano
con una manzana de sollozos.
Un ruiseñor agrupa los suspiros
y un faisán los ahuyenta por el polvo.

Pero los ramos son alegres,
10   los ramos son como nosotros.
No piensan en la lluvia y se han dormido,
como si fueran árboles, de pronto.

Sentados con el agua en las rodillas
dos valles esperaban al Otoño.
La penumbra con paso de elefante
empujaba las ramas y los troncos.

II
Qasida of the Weeping

I have closed off my balcony,
for I do not want to hear the weeping.
But out there, beyond gray walls,
nothing is heard but the weeping.

There are very few angels who sing.
There are very few dogs who bark.
A thousand violins fit in the palm of my hand.

But the weeping is an enormous dog,
the weeping is an enormous angel,
10   the weeping is an enormous violin,
tears have muzzled the wind,
and nothing is heard but the weeping.

III
Qasida of the Branches

Through the groves of Tamarit
the leaden dogs have come,
to wait for the branches to fall,
for the branches to break by themselves.

At Tamarit there's an apple tree
with an apple of sobs.
A nightingale gathers up sighs,
a pheasant drives them off through the dust.

But the branches are happy;
10   the branches are like us.
They don't think of rain,
and they've dropped off to sleep,
as if they were trees, just like that.

Sitting with their knees in water
two valleys awaited the Fall.
The half-light with elephant step
was leaning on trunks and on branches.

Por las arboledas del Tamarit
hay muchos niños de velado rostro
a esperar que se caigan mis ramos,
20   a esperar que se quiebren ellos solos.

Casida IV
De la mujer tendida

Verte desnuda es recordar la Tierra,
la Tierra lisa, limpia de caballos.
La Tierra sin un junco, forma pura
cerrada al porvenir: confín de plata.

Verte desnuda es comprender el ansia
de la lluvia que busca débil talle,
o la fiebre del mar de inmenso rostro
sin encontrar la luz de su mejilla.

La sangre sonará por las alcobas
10   y vendrá con espadas fulgurantes,
pero tú no sabrás dónde se ocultan
el corazón de sapo o la violeta.

Tu vientre es una lucha de raíces,
tus labios son un alba sin contorno.
Bajo las rosas tibias de la cama
los muertos gimen esperando turno.

Casida V
Del sueño al aire libre

Flor de jazmín y toro degollado.
Pavimento infinito. Mapa. Sala. Arpa. Alba.
La niña sueña un toro de jazmines
y el toro es un sangriento crepúsculo que brama.

Si el cielo fuera un niño pequeñito,
los jazmines tendrían mitad de noche oscura,

Through the groves of Tamarit
are many children with faces veiled
20   to wait for my branches to fall,
for my branches to break by themselves.

IV
Qasida of the Woman Prone

To see you naked is to remember the Earth,
the smooth Earth, clean of horses,
the Earth without reeds, pure form,
closed to the future, confine of silver.

To see you naked is to understand the desire
of rain that looks for the delicate waist,
or the fever of the broad-faced sea
that cannot find the light of its cheek.

Blood will ring through the bedrooms
10   and will come with flaming swords,
but you will not know the hiding places
of the violet or the heart of the toad.

Your womb is a struggle of roots.
Your lips are a dawn without contour.
Under the lukewarm roses of the bed
the dead men moan, awaiting their turn.

V
Qasida of the Dream in Open Air

Jasmine flower and bull beheaded.
Infinite pavement. Chart. Hall. Harp. Dawn.
The girl dreams of a jasmine bull
and the bull is a bloody sunset bellowing.

If the sky were a little boy,
the jasmines would be half dark night,

y el toro circo azul sin lidiadores,
y un corazón al pie de una columna.

Pero el cielo es un elefante,
el jazmín es un agua sin sangre,
y la niña es un ramo nocturno
por el inmenso pavimento oscuro.

Entre el jazmín y el toro
o garfios de marfil o gente dormida.
En el jazmín un elefante y nubes
y en el toro el esqueleto de la niña.

Casida VI
De la mano imposible

Yo no quiero más que una mano,
una mano herida, si es posible.
Yo no quiero más que una mano,
aunque pase mil noches sin lecho.

Serí un pálido lirio de cal,
sería una paloma amarrada a mi corazón,
sería el guardián que en la noche de mi tránsito
prohibiera en absoluto la entrada a la luna.

Yo no quiero más que esa mano
para los diarios aceites y la sábana blanca de mi agonía.
Yo no quiero más que esa mano
para tener un ala de mi muerte.

Lo demás todo pasa.
Rubor sin nombre ya. Astro perpetuo.
Lo demás es lo otro; viento triste,
mientras las hojas huyen en bandadas.

the bull a blue arena without matadors,
and a heart at the foot of a column.

But the sky is an elephant,
10   the jasmine a water without blood,
and the girl a nocturnal branch
across the pavement, infinitely dark.

Between the jasmine and the bull
either ivory hooks or sleeping people.
In the jasmine, an elephant and clouds
and in the bull, the skeleton of the girl.

VI
Qasida of the Impossible Hand

I want nothing else, only a hand,
a wounded hand, if possible.
I want nothing else, only a hand,
though I spend a thousand nights without a bed.

It would be a pale lily of lime,
a dove tethered fast to my heart.
It would be the guard who, on the night of my death,
would block entrance absolutely to the moon.

I want nothing else, only that hand,
10   for the daily unctions and my agony's white sheet.
I want nothing else, only that hand,
to carry a wing of my own death.

Everything else all passes away.
Now blush without name. Perpetual star.
Everything else is something else: sad wind,
while the leaves flee, whirling in flocks.

Casida VII
De la rosa

La rosa
no buscaba la aurora:
casi eterna en su ramo,
buscaba otra cosa.

La rosa
no buscaba ni ciencia ni sombra:
confín de carne y sueño,
buscaba otra cosa.

La rosa
10 no buscaba la rosa:
inmóvil por el cielo,
buscaba otra cosa.

Casida VIII
De la muchacha dorada

La muchacha dorada
se bañaba en el agua
y el agua se doraba.

Las algas y las ramas
en sombra la asombraban,
y el ruiseñor cantaba
por la muchacha blanca.

Vino la noche clara,
turbia de plata mala,
10 con peladas montañas
bajo la brisa parda.

La muchacha mojada
era blanca en el agua
y el agua, llamarada.

Vino el alba sin mancha,
con cien caras de vaca,

VII
Qasida of the Rose

The rose
was not looking for the dawn:
almost eternal on its stem,
it looked for something else.

The rose
was not looking for science or shadow:
confine of flesh and of dream
it looked for something else.

The rose
10   was not looking for the rose.
Through the sky, immobile,
it looked for something else.

VIII
Qasida of the Golden Girl

The golden girl
bathed in the water
and the water turned gold.

Algae and branches
in shadow surprised her,
and the nightingale sang
for the white girl.

The clear night came,
dim with bad silver,
10   with mountains bare
beneath dun breeze.

The wet girl
was white in the water
and the water, a blaze.

The dawn came spotless
with a hundred cow faces,

yerta y amortajada
con heladas guirnaldas.

La muchacha de lágrimas
20   se bañaba entre llamas,
y el ruiseñor lloraba
con las alas quemadas.

La muchacha dorada
era una blanca garza
y el agua la doraba.

Casida IX
De las palomas oscuras

Por las ramas del laurel
vi dos palomas oscuras.
La una era el sol,
la otra la luna.
Vecinitas, les dije,
¿dónde está mi sepultura?
En mi cola, dijo el sol.
En mi garganta, dijo la luna.
Y yo que estaba caminando
10   con la tierra por la cintura
vi dos águilas de nieve
y una muchacha desnuda,
La una era la otra
y la muchacha era ninguna.
Aguilitas, les dije,
¿dónde está mi sepultura?
En mi cola, dijo el sol.
En mi garganta, dijo la luna.
Por las ramas del laurel
20   vi dos palomas desnudas.
La una era la otra
y las dos eran ninguna.

with frozen garlands,
stiff and shrouded.

The girl of tears
20 was bathing in flames,
and the nightingale wept
with burned wings.

The golden girl
was a white heron
and the water turned her gold.

IX
Qasida of the Dark Doves

Through the laurel's branches
I saw two dark doves.
One was the sun,
the other the moon.
Little neighbors, I called,
where is my tomb?
In my tail, said the sun.
In my throat, said the moon.
And I who was walking
10 with the earth at my waist,
saw two snowy eagles
and a naked girl.
The one was the other
and the girl was neither.
Little eagles, I called,
where is my tomb?
In my tail, said the sun.
In my throat, said the moon.
Through the laurel's branches
20 I saw two naked doves.
The one was the other
and both of them were neither.

Gacela del mercado matutino

Por el arco de Elvira
quiero verte pasar,
para saber tu nombre
y ponerme a llorar.

¿Qué luna gris de las nueve
te desangró la mejilla?
¿Quién recoge tu semilla
de llamarada en la nieve?
¿Qué alfiler de cactus breve
10   asesina tu cristal? . . .

Por el arco de Elvira
voy a verte pasar,
para beber tus ojos
y ponerme a llorar.

¡Qué voz para mi castigo
levantas por el mercado!
¡Qué clavel enajenado
en los montones de trigo!
¡Qué lejos estoy contigo,
20   qué cerca cuando te vas!

Por el arco de Elvira
voy a verte pasar,
para sentir tus muslos
y ponerme a llorar.

Ghazal of the Market in the Morning

Through the Arch of Elvira
I want to see you go,
so that I can learn your name
and break into tears.

What gray moon of nine o'clock
drew the blood from your cheek?
Who takes in your seed,
burst of flame in the snow?
What needle of a small cactus
10   murders your crystal?

Through the Arch of Elvira
I want to see you go,
so that I can drink in your eyes
and break into tears.

What cries to punish me
you raise in the market!
What a carnation, estranged
in the mounds of wheat!
How far, when I am with you!
20   How near, when you depart!

Through the Arch of Elvira
I want to see you go,
to feel your thighs
and break into tears.

TR. C.M.

       THE TAMARIT DIVAN

SEIS POEMAS
GALEGOS

[Rua das Gaveas, 1934]

SIX GALICIAN

POEMS

Translated by

Catherine Brown

[Rua das Gaveas, 1934]

Madrigal â cibdá de Santiago

Chove en Santiago
meu doce amor.
Camelia branca do ar
brila entebrecido o sol.

Chove en Santiago
na noite escura.
Herbas de prata e sono
cobren a valeira lúa.

Olla a choiva pol-a rúa,
10 laio de pedra e cristal.
Olla no vento esvaído
soma e cinza do teu mar.

Soma e cinza do teu mar,
Santiago, lonxe do sol;
ágoa de mañán anterga
trema no meu corazón.

Romaxe de Nosa Señora da Barca

¡Ay ruada, ruada, ruada
da Virxe pequena
e a súa barca!

A Virxe era de pedra
e a súa coroa de prata.
Marelos os catro bois
que no seu carro a levaban.

Pombas de vidro traguían
a choiva pol-a montana.
10 Mortos e mortas de néboa
pol-os sendeiros chegaban.

¡Virxe, deixa a túa cariña
nos doces ollos das vacas

Madrigal for the City of Santiago

Rain falls on Santiago,
my sweet love.
White camellia of the air,
the veiled sun shines.

Rain falls on Santiago
in the dark of night.
Grasses of silver and dream
cover the vacant moon.

10   Look at the rain in the street,
lament of stone and of glass.
See on the languishing wind
shadow and ash of your ocean.

Shadow and ash of your ocean,
Santiago, far from the sun;
water of ancient morning
trembles in my heart.

Ballad of Our Lady of the Boat

Oh, the Virgin,
the pilgrimage to see
the little Virgin and her boat!

The Virgin was stone
and her crown was silver.
Four straw-colored oxen
were pulling her cart.

Glass doves swept rain
down from the mountain,
10   and down paths and trails
came the misty dead.

Virgin, leave us your face
in the sweet eyes of cows

e leva sobr'o teu manto
as froles da amortallada!

Pol-a testa de Galicia
xa ven salaiando a i-alba.
A Virxe mira pr'o mar
dend'a porta da súa casa.

20 *¡Ay ruada, ruada, ruada*
da Virxe pequena
e a súa barca!

Cántiga do neno da tenda

Bos Aires ten unha gaita
sobor do Río da Prata,
que a toca o vento do norde
coa súa gris boca mollada.
¡Triste Ramón de Sismundi!
Xunto â rúa d'Esmeralda
c'unha basoira de xesta
sacaba o polvo das caixas.
Ao longo das rúas infindas
10 os galegos paseiaban
soñando un val imposíbel
na verde riba da pampa.
¡Triste Ramón de Sismundi!
Sintéu a muiñeira d'ágoa
mentres sete bois de lúa
pacían na súa lembranza.
Foise pr'a veira do río,
veira do Río da Prata.
Sauces e cabalos múos
20 creban o vidro das ágoas.
Non atopóu o xemido
malencónico da gaita,
non víu ô inmenso gaiteiro
coa boca frolida d'alas;
triste Ramón de Sismundi,
veira do Río da Prata,

and wear on your cloak
the flowers of mourning!

The dawn comes, sighing
over the face of Galicia.
From the door of her house
the Virgin looks at the sea.

20   *Oh, the Virgin,*
the pilgrimage to see
the little Virgin and her boat!

Song of the Shop Boy

Buenos Aires has a bagpipe
over the river La Plata,
and the north wind plays it
with a damp gray mouth.
Unhappy Ramón de Sismundi!
In a shop by Esmeralda Street
he swept the dust from boxes
with a little straw broom.
Down the infinite streets
10   wandered other Galicians,
dreaming impossible valleys
on the green shore of the pampa.
Unhappy Ramón de Sismundi!
He heard a watery song from home
while seven lunar oxen
grazed on his nostalgia.
He went down to the banks
of the river, down
to the banks of La Plata.
20   Willows and mute horses
shattered the glass of the waters.
He did not find
the bagpipes' drone,
did not see the great piper
whose mouth bloomed with wings.
Unhappy Ramón de Sismundi
saw, on the banks of La Plata,

víu na tarde amortecida
bermello muro de lama.

Noiturnio do adoescente morto

Imos silandeiros orela do vado
pra ver ô adoescente afogado.

Imos silandeiros veiriña do ar,
antes que ise río o leve pr'o mar.

Súa i-alma choraba, ferida e pequena
embaixo os arumes de pinos e d'herbas.

Ágoa despenada baixaba de lúa
cobrindo de violas a montana núa.

O vento deixaba camelias de soma
10   na lumieira murcha da súa triste boca.

¡Vinde mozos loiros do monte e do prado
pra ver ô adoescente afogado!

¡Vinde xente escura do cume e do val
antes que ise río o leve pr'o mar!

O leve pr'o mar de curtiñas brancas
onde van e vên vellos bois de ágoa.

¡Ay, cómo cantaban os albres do Sil
sobre a verde lúa, coma un tamboril!

¡Mozos, imos, vinde, aixiña, chegar
20   *porque xa ise río o leva pr'o mar!*

Canzón de cuna pra Rosalía Castro, morta

¡Érguete, miña amiga,
que xa cantan os galos do día!

only the fainting afternoon,
and the reddish wall of silt.

Nocturne of the Drowned Youth

Let us go down, silent, to the bank of the ford
to look at the youth who drowned there, in the water.

Let us go down, silent, to the shore of the air
before this river takes him down to the sea.

His soul was weeping, wounded and small,
under needles of pine and of grasses.

Water descended, flung down from the moon,
and covered the naked mountain with violets.

The wind laid camellias of shadow
10   in the wilted light of his unhappy mouth.

Come, blind boys of the mountains and fields,
come look at the youth who drowned there, in the water.

Come, dark folk of the peaks and the valleys,
before this river takes him down to the sea.

It takes him down to the white-curtained sea,
where old water-oxen come and go slowly.

Oh, how the trees by the river were singing
over the sunken green drum of the moon!

Boys, let us go; come, hurry, away!
20   *for now this river takes him down to the sea.*

Lullaby in Death for Rosalía de Castro

Arise, my friend,
for the roosters are crowing!

¡Érguete, miña amada,
porque o vento muxe coma unha vaca!

Os arados van e vên
dende Santiago a Belén.
Dende Belén a Santiago
un anxo ven en un barco.
Un barco de prata fina
10   que trai a door de Galicia.
Galicia deitada e queda,
transida de tristes herbas.
Herbas que cobren teu leito
e a negra fonte dos teus cabelos.
Cabelos que van ô mar
onde as nubens teñen seu nidio pombal.

¡Érguete, miña amiga,
que xa cantan os galos do día!
¡Érguete, miña amada,
20   *porque o vento muxe como unha vaca!*

Danza da lúa en Santiago

¡Fita aquel branco galán,
fita seu transido corpo!

É a lúa que baila
na Quintana dos mortos.

Fita seu corpo transido,
negro de somas e lobos.

Nai: A lúa está bailando
na Quintana dos mortos.

¿Quén fire poldro de pedra
10   na mesma porta do sono?

¡É a lúa! ¡É a lúa
na Quintana dos mortos!

Arise, my love,
for the wind, like a cow, is lowing!

The plows come and go
from Santiago to Bethlehem.
From Bethlehem to Santiago
comes an angel in a boat.
A boat of fine silver
10   bears the pain of Galicia.
Galicia stretched out and silent,
harrowed with unhappy grasses.
Grasses that cover your bed
and the black fountain of your hair.
Hair that flows to the sea,
to the shining dovecote of clouds.

Arise, my friend,
for the roosters are crowing!
Arise, my love,
20   *for the wind, like a cow, is lowing!*

Dance of the Moon in Santiago

Look at that white cavalier,
look at his wasted body!

It is the moon that dances
in the courtyard of the dead.

Look at his wasted body,
black with shadow and wolves.

Mother, the moon is dancing
in the courtyard of the dead.

Who wounds the stone colt
10   at the portals of sleep?

It's the moon! It's the moon
in the courtyard of the dead!

809

¿Quén fita meus grises vidros
cheos de nubens seus ollos?

É a lúa, é a lúa
na Quintana dos mortos.

Déixame morrer no leito
soñando na frol d'ouro.

Nai: A lúa está bailando
na Quintana dos mortos.

¡Ai filla, c'o ar do ceo
vólvome branca de pronto!

Non é o ar, é a triste lúa
na Quintana dos mortos.

¿Quén xime co-este xemido
d'inmenso boi malencónico?

Nai: É a lúa, é a lúa
na Quintana dos mortos.

¡Sí, a lúa, a lúa
coroada de toxo,
que baila, e baila, e baila
na Quintana dos mortos!

Who looks in my gray windows
with his eyes full of clouds?

It's the moon, it's the moon
in the courtyard of the dead.

Let me die here in bed,
the flower of gold in my dreams.

Mother, the moon is dancing
20   in the courtyard of the dead.

Oh, daughter, the air from the sky
has suddenly turned me white!

It isn't the air; it's the unhappy moon
in the courtyard of the dead.

Who moans with that moan
of an ox, huge and sad?

Mother, it's the moon, it's the moon
in the courtyard of the dead.

Yes, it's the moon, the moon
30   with its crown of gorse
that dances, dances, dances
in the courtyard of the dead!

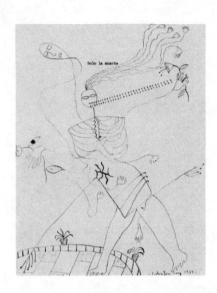

LLANTO POR

IGNACIO SÁNCHEZ MEJÍAS

A mi querida amiga
Encarnación López Júlvez

[*Imagen de la muerte, 1934*]

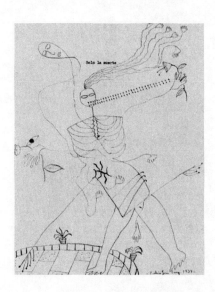

LAMENT FOR

IGNACIO SÁNCHEZ MEJÍAS

To my dear friend
Encarnación López Júlvez

Translated by Galway Kinnell

[Image of Death, 1934]

1. La cogida y la muerte

A las cinco de la tarde.
Eran las cinco en punto de la tarde.
Un niño trajo la blanca sábana
a las cinco de la tarde.
Una espuerta de cal ya prevenida
a las cinco de la tarde.
Lo demás era muerte y sólo muerte
a las cinco de la tarde.

10 El viento se llevó los algodones
a las cinco de la tarde.
Y el óxido sembró cristal y níquel
a las cinco de la tarde.
Ya luchan la paloma y el leopardo
a las cinco de la tarde.
Y un muslo con un asta desolada
a las cinco de la tarde.
Comenzaron los sones de bordón
a las cinco de la tarde.
Las campanas de arsénico y el humo
20 *a las cinco de la tarde.*
En las esquinas grupos de silencio
a las cinco de la tarde.
¡Y el toro solo corazón arriba!
a las cinco de la tarde.
Cuando el sudor de nieve fue llegando
a las cinco de la tarde,
cuando la plaza se cubrió de yodo
a las cinco de la tarde,
la muerte puso huevos en la herida
30 *a las cinco de la tarde.*
A las cinco de la tarde.
A las cinco en punto de la tarde.

Un ataúd con ruedas es la cama
a las cinco de la tarde.
Huesos y flautas suenan en su oído
a las cinco de la tarde.
El toro ya mugía por su frente
a las cinco de la tarde.

1. The Goring and the Death

At five in the afternoon.
It was exactly five in the afternoon.
A boy brought the linen sheet
at five in the afternoon.
A basket of lime standing ready
at five in the afternoon.
Everything else was death, only death,
at five in the afternoon.

Wind scattered bits of gauze
at five in the afternoon.
Oxide sowed glass and nickel
at five in the afternoon.
Now the dove battles with the leopard
at five in the afternoon.
And a thigh with a desolate horn
at five in the afternoon.
Now began the drums of a dirge
at five in the afternoon.
And the bells of arsenic and smoke
at five in the afternoon.
Silence gathered on every corner
at five in the afternoon.
And the bull alone with lifted heart!
at five in the afternoon.
When sweat of snow began
at five in the afternoon,
and the bull-ring was drenched in iodine
at five in the afternoon,
death laid its eggs in the wound
at five in the afternoon.
At five in the afternoon.
At exactly five in the afternoon.

The bed is a coffin on wheels
at five in the afternoon.
Bones and flutes play in his ear
at five in the afternoon.
The bull's bellowings stay at his forehead
at five in the afternoon.

El cuarto se irisaba de agonía
40   *a las cinco de la tarde.*
A lo lejos ya viene la gangrena
a las cinco de la tarde.
Trompa de lirio por las verdes ingles
a las cinco de la tarde.
Las heridas quemaban como soles
a las cinco de la tarde,
y el gentío rompía las ventanas
a las cinco de la tarde.
A las cinco de la tarde.
50   ¡Ay qué terribles cinco de la tarde!
¡Eran las cinco en todos los relojes!
¡Eran las cinco en sombra de la tarde!

2. La sangre derramada

¡Que no quiero verla!

Dile a la luna que venga,
que no quiero ver la sangre
de Ignacio sobre la arena.

¡Que no quiero verla!

La luna de par en par,
caballo de nubes quietas,
60   y la plaza gris del sueño
con sauces en las barreras.

¡Que no quiero verla!
Que mi recuerdo se quema.
¡Avisad a los jazmines
con su blancura pequeña!

¡Que no quiero verla!

La vaca del viejo mundo
pasaba su triste lengua
sobre un hocico de sangres

The room turned iridescent in his agony
40 *at five in the afternoon.*
Now in the distance gangrene appears
at five in the afternoon.
A white lily in the green groins
at five in the afternoon.
The wounds burned like suns
at five in the afternoon.
And the crowd breaking the windows
at five in the afternoon.
At five in the afternoon.
50 Ah, that terrible five in the afternoon!
It was five by all the clocks!
It was five in the shade of the afternoon!

2. *The Spilled Blood*

I don't want to see it!

Tell the moon to come,
for I don't want to see
Ignacio's blood on the sand.

I don't want to see it!

The wide-open moon.
A horse of unmoving clouds,
60 and the gray bull-ring of dream
with willows at its *barreras.*

I don't want to see it!
Remembering burns.
Send word to the jasmines
to bring their tiny whiteness!

I don't want to see it!

The cow of the ancient world
ran her sad tongue
over a muzzle filled with all the blood

70 derramadas en la arena,
  y los toros de Guisando,
  casi muerte y casi piedra,
  mugieron como dos siglos
  hartos de pisar la tierra.
  No.
  ¡Que no quiero verla!

  Por las gradas sube Ignacio
  con toda su muerte a cuestas.
  Buscaba el amanecer,
80 y el amanecer no era.
  Busca su perfil seguro,
  y el sueño lo desorienta.
  Buscaba su hermoso cuerpo
  y encontró su sangre abierta.
  ¡No me digáis que la vea!
  No quiero sentir el chorro
  cada vez con menos fuerza;
  ese chorro que ilumina
  los tendidos y se vuelca
90 sobre la pana y el cuero
  de muchedumbre sedienta.
  ¿Quién me grita que me asome?
  ¡No me digáis que la vea!

  No se cerraron sus ojos
  cuando vio los cuernos cerca,
  pero las madres terribles
  levantaron la cabeza.
  Y a través de las ganaderías
  hubo un aire de voces secretas,
100 que gritaban a toros celestes
  mayorales de pálida niebla.

  No hubo príncipe en Sevilla
  que comparársele pueda,
  ni espada como su espada
  ni corazón tan de veras.
  Como un río de leones
  su maravillosa fuerza,
  y como un torso de mármol

70 ever spilled on sand,
   and the bulls of Guisando,
   half death and half stone,
   bellowed, like two centuries
   fed up with treading the earth.
   No.
   I don't want to see it!

   Ignacio climbs the steps
   carrying all his death on his shoulders.
   He was looking for daybreak,
80 and daybreak was no more.
   He seeks his confident profile
   and drowsiness disorients him.
   He was looking for his beautiful body
   and found his upwelling blood.
   Don't ask me to see it!
   I don't want to feel the gush
   each time with less force,
   the gush that lights up
   the rows of seats and spills
90 over the corduroy and leather
   of a thirsting crowd.
   Who cries to me to come forward?
   I don't want to see it!

   His eyes didn't shut
   when the horns drew near,
   but the terrified mothers
   lifted their heads to see.
   And through the cattle-ranches
   rose a breeze of secret chants,
100 ranchers of pale mist
   crying out to the bulls of heaven.

   Never was there a prince in Seville
   who was his equal,
   never a sword like his sword,
   or a heart with the truth of his.
   His prodigious strength
   was like a river of lions,
   and his stately reserve

su dibujada prudencia.
110 Aire de Roma andaluza
le doraba la cabeza
donde su risa era un nardo
de sal y de inteligencia.
¡Qué gran torero en la plaza!
¡Qué buen serrano en la sierra!
¡Qué blando con las espigas!
¡Qué duro con las espuelas!
¡Qué tierno con el rocío!
¡Qué deslumbrante en la feria!
120 ¡Qué tremendo con las últimas
banderillas de tiniebla!

Pero ya duerme sin fin.
Ya los musgos y la hierba
abren con dedos seguros
la flor de su calavera.
Y su sangre ya viene cantando:
cantando por marismas y praderas,
resbalando por cuernos ateridos,
vacilando sin alma por la niebla,
130 tropezando con miles de pezuñas,
como una larga, oscura, triste lengua,
para formar un charco de agonía
junto al Guadalquivir de las estrellas.

¡Oh blanco muro de España!
¡Oh negro toro de pena!
¡Oh sangre dura de Ignacio!
¡Oh ruiseñor de sus venas!

No.
¡Que no quiero verla!
140 Que no hay cáliz que la contenga,
que no hay golondrinas que se la beban,
no hay escarcha de luz que la enfríe,
no hay canto ni diluvio de azucenas,
no hay cristal que la cubra de plata.
No.
¡¡Yo no quiero verla!!

like a torso of marble.
110 The aura of Andalusian Rome
was a golden mist around his head,
and his smile a spikenard
of wit and intelligence.
What a bullfighter in the ring!
What a countryman in the sierra!
How gentle with the ears of grain!
How tough with the spurs!
How tender with the dew!
How dazzling at the fair!
120 How tremendous with the final
banderillas of darkness!

But now he sleeps forever.
Now moss and grass
open with practiced fingers
the flower of his skull.
And now his blood appears singing:
singing across salt marshes and meadows,
sliding around frozen horns,
straying without its soul through the mist,
130 churned under by a thousand hooves,
a long, dark, sad tongue
forming a pool of agony
near the Guadalquivir of the stars.

O white wall of Spain!
O black bull of sorrow!
O hard blood of Ignacio!
O nightingale of his veins!

No.
I don't want to see it!
140 There's no chalice that can hold it,
no swallows that can drink it,
no frost of light that can cool it,
no song, no hard rain of lilies,
no glass to silver it.
No.
I refuse to see it!!

3. Cuerpo presente

La piedra es una frente donde los sueños gimen
sin tener agua curva ni cipreses helados.
La piedra es una espalda para llevar al tiempo
150 con árboles de lágrimas y cintas y planetas.

Yo he visto lluvias grises correr hacia las olas
levantando sus tiernos brazos acribillados,
para no ser cazadas por la piedra tendida
que desata sus miembros sin empapar la sangre.

Porque la piedra coge simientes y nublados,
esqueletos de alondras y lobos de penumbra;
pero no da sonidos, ni cristales, ni fuego,
sino plazas y plazas y otras plazas sin muros.

Ya está sobre la piedra Ignacio el bien nacido.
160 Ya se acabó. ¡Qué pasa! ¡Contemplad su figura!
La muerte lo ha cubierto de pálidos azufres
y le ha puesto cabeza de oscuro minotauro.

Ya se acabó. La lluvia penetra por su boca.
El aire como loco deja su pecho hundido,
y el Amor, empapado con lágrimas de nieve,
se calienta en la cumbre de las ganaderías.

¿Qué dicen? Un silencio con hedores reposa.
Estamos con un cuerpo presente que se esfuma,
con una forma clara que tuvo ruiseñores
170 y la vemos llenarse de agujeros sin fondo.

¿Quién arruga el sudario? ¡No es verdad lo que dice!
Aquí no canta nadie, ni llora en el rincón,
ni pica las espuelas, ni espanta la serpiente:
aquí no quiero más que los ojos redondos
para ver ese cuerpo sin posible descanso.

Yo quiero ver aquí los hombres de voz dura.
Los que doman caballos y dominan los ríos:
los hombres que les suena el esqueleto y cantan
con una boca llena de sol y pedernales.

3. The Laid-Out Body

Stone is a forehead where dreams groan
for lack of curving waters and frozen cypresses.
Stone is a shoulder for carrying away time
150 with its trees made of tears and ribbons and planets.

I've seen gray rains fleeing toward the sea
lifting tender, riddled arms,
trying to get away from stone
that unknits their limbs but doesn't soak up the blood.

For stone seizes seeds and clouds
and larks' skeletons and wolves of twilight;
but gives off no sound, no glass, no fire,
only bull-rings, bull-rings, and one last bull-ring without walls.

Now Ignacio, this quiet man, is laid out on the stone.
160 It's all over; what's happening? Look at him:
death has painted him in pale sulphurs
and put on him the head of a dark minotaur.

It's all over. Rain falls into his mouth.
Air in a panic escapes from his sunken chest,
and Love, soaked in tears of snow,
warms itself on the summits over the ranches.

What are they saying? Here lies a stenching silence.
We stand before a laid-out body that is fading,
a clear form that once held nightingales,
170 and see it filling with bottomless holes.

Who's rumpling the shroud? No, it's not true!
Nobody here is to sing, or weep in a corner,
or ring his spurs, or frighten off the snake.
Here I want everyone's eyes to grow round
to see this body that will never rest.

Here I want to see men of hard voice.
Those who break horses and master rivers;
men who, dancing, hear their skeletons and sing
with mouths full of sun and flints.

Aquí quiero yo verlos. Delante de la piedra.
Delante de este cuerpo con las riendas quebradas.
Yo quiero que me enseñen dónde está la salida
para este capitán atado por la muerte.

Yo quiero que me enseñen un llanto como un río
que tenga dulces nieblas y profundas orillas,
para llevar el cuerpo de Ignacio y que se pierda
sin escuchar el doble resuello de los toros.

Que se pierda en la plaza redonda de la luna
que finge cuando niña doliente res inmóvil;
que se pierda en la noche sin canto de los peces
y en la maleza blanca del humo congelado.

No quiero que le tapen la cara con pañuelos
para que se acostumbre con la muerte que lleva.
Vete, Ignacio: No sientas el caliente bramido.
Duerme, vuela, reposa: ¡También se muere el mar!

4. *Alma ausente*

No te conoce el toro ni la higuera,
ni caballos ni hormigas de tu casa.
No te conoce el niño ni la tarde
porque te has muerto para siempre.

No te conoce el lomo de la piedra,
ni el raso negro donde te destrozas.
No te conoce tu recuerdo mudo
porque te has muerto para siempre.

El Otoño vendrá con caracolas,
uva de niebla y montes agrupados,
pero nadie querrá mirar tus ojos
porque te has muerto para siempre.

Porque te has muerto para siempre,
como todos los muertos de la Tierra,

180 I want them to be here. Before this stone.
Before this body of broken reins.
I want them to show me a way out
for this captain tied down by death.

I want them to teach me a lament like a river
that has sweet mists and tall banks, that will bear
off the body of Ignacio and let him disappear
without hearing again the double snorting of the bulls.

Disappear into the round bull-ring of the moon,
who takes the shape, when a young girl, of a motionless, wounded bull;
190 disappear into the songless night of the fishes
and the white thicket of frozen smoke.

Let his face not be covered by handkerchiefs
so that he may get used to the death he carries.
Go, Ignacio. Forget the hot bellowing.
Sleep, soar, rest: Even the sea dies!

4. Absent Soul

The bull doesn't know you, nor the fig tree,
nor the horses, nor the ants of your own house.
The child doesn't know you, nor does the afternoon,
because you have died forever.

200 The face of the stone doesn't know you,
nor does the black satin in which your body breaks down.
Neither does the silenced memory of you know you
because you have died forever.

Autumn will come bringing sounds of conchs
and grapes of mist, and clustered hills,
but no one will want to look into your eyes
because you have died forever.

Because you have died forever,
like all the dead of the earth,

210 como todos los muertos que se olvidan
en un montón de perros apagados.

No te conoce nadie. No. Pero yo te canto.
Yo canto para luego tu perfil y tu gracia.
La madurez insigne de tu conocimiento.
Tu apetencia de muerte y el gusto de su boca.
La tristeza que tuvo tu valiente alegría.

Tardará mucho tiempo en nacer, si es que nace,
un andaluz tan claro, tan rico de aventura.
Yo canto su elegancia con palabras que gimen
220 y recuerdo una brisa triste por los olivos.

like all the dead who have been forgotten
on some heap of snuffed-out dogs.

No one knows you. No. But I sing of you.
I sing, for later on, of your profile and your grace.
The noble maturity of your understanding.
Your appetite for death and the taste of its mouth.
The sadness in your valiant gaiety.

There will not be born for a long time, if ever,
an Andalusian like him, so open, so bold in adventure.
I sing of his elegance in words that moan
220 and I remember a sad breeze in the olive grove.

[SONETOS DEL
AMOR OSCURO]

[*Joven y marinero, 1934*]

[SONNETS OF
DARK LOVE]

Translated by

Angela Jaffray

[Young Man and Sailor, 1934]

Soneto de la guirnalda de rosas

¡Esa guirnalda! ¡pronto! ¡que me muero!
¡Teje deprisa! ¡canta! ¡gime! ¡canta!,
que la sombra me enturbia la garganta
y otra vez viene y mil la luz de enero.

Entre lo que me quieres y te quiero,
aire de estrellas y temblor de planta,
espesura de anémonas levanta
con oscuro gemir un año entero.

Goza el fresco paisaje de mi herida,
10   quiebra juncos y arroyos delicados,
bebe en muslo de miel sangre vertida.

Pero ¡pronto!, que unidos, enlazados,
boca rota de amor y alma mordida,
el tiempo nos encuentre destrozados.

Soneto de la dulce queja

No me dejes perder la maravilla
de tus ojos de estatua, ni el acento
que de noche me pone en la mejilla
la solitaria rosa de tu aliento.

Tengo miedo de ser en esta orilla
tronco sin ramas; y lo que más siento
es no tener la flor, pulpa o arcilla
para el gusano de mi sufrimiento.

Si tú eres el tesoro oculto mío,
10   si eres mi cruz y mi dolor mojado,
si soy el perro de tu señorío,

no me dejes perder lo que he ganado
y decora las ramas de tu río
con hojas de mi otoño enajenado.

Sonnet of the Garland of Roses

That garland! Hurry! For I'm dying!
Weave quickly! Sing! Moan! Sing!
For shadow clouds my throat
and again, for the thousandth time, comes the light of January.

Between your love for me and mine for you
—air of stars and tremor of plant—
a thicket of anemones raises
with a dark moan an entire year.

Relish the fresh landscape of my wound,
break rushes and delicate rivulets,
drink blood poured on honeyed thigh.

But hurry! so united, entwined,
mouth broken by love and soul bitten,
time will find us destroyed.

Sonnet of the Sweet Complaint

Never let me lose the marvel
of your statue eyes or the accent
that by night the solitary rose of your breath
places on my cheek.

I'm afraid to be on this shore
a trunk without limbs, and what I most regret
is not to have flower, pulp or clay
for the worm of my suffering.

If you are my hidden treasure,
if you are my cross and my wet sorrow,
if I am the dog of your dominion,

do not let me lose what I have won
and adorn the waters of your river
with leaves of my alienated autumn.

Llagas de amor

Esta luz, este fuego que devora,
este paisaje gris que me rodea,
este dolor por una sola idea,
esta angustia de cielo, mundo y hora,

este llanto de sangre que decora
lira sin pulso ya, lúbrica tea,
este peso del mar que me golpea,
este alacrán que por mi pecho mora,

son guirnalda de amor, cama de herido,
donde sin sueño, sueño tu presencia
entre las ruinas de mi pecho hundido.

Y aunque busco la cumbre de prudencia
me da tu corazón valle tendido
con cicuta y pasión de amarga ciencia.

El poeta pide a su amor que le escriba

Amor de mis entrañas, viva muerte,
en vano espero tu palabra escrita
y pienso con la flor que se marchita
que si vivo sin mí, quiero perderte.

El aire es inmortal; la piedra inerte
ni conoce la sombra, ni la evita.
Corazón interior no necesita
la miel helada que la luna vierte.

Pero yo te sufrí; rasgué mis venas,
tigre y paloma sobre tu cintura
en duelo de mordiscos y azucenas.

Llena pues de palabras mi locura
o déjame vivir en mi serena
noche del alma para siempre oscura.

Wounds of Love

This light, this fire that devours,
this gray landscape that surrounds me,
this sorrow for one sole idea,
this anguish of sky, world and hour;

this lament of blood that adorns
a lyre now without pulse, lascivious torch,
this weight of the sea that pounds me,
this scorpion that dwells in my breast,

are a garland of love, bed of the wounded,
10 where without sleep, I dream of your presence
amid the ruins of my sunken breast.

And although I seek the peak of prudence
your heart gives me a valley spread
with hemlock and passion of bitter knowledge.

The Poet Asks His Love to Write Him

Love of my heart, living death,
in vain I await your written word
and think, with the flower that withers,
that if I live without myself, I wish to lose you.

The air is immortal; the inert stone
neither knows the shade nor avoids it.
The inner heart has no need
for the frozen honey poured from the moon.

But I suffered you, I ripped my veins,
10 tiger and dove on your waist,
in a duel of bites and lilies.

Fill, then, my madness with words
or let me live in my serene
night of the soul forever dark.

El poeta dice la verdad

Quiero llorar mi pena y te lo digo
para que tú me quieras y me llores
en un anochecer de ruiseñores
con un puñal, con besos y contigo.

Quiero matar al único testigo
para el asesinato de mis flores
y convertir mi llanto y mis sudores
en eterno montón de duro trigo.

Que no se acabe nunca la madeja
10 del te quiero me quieres, siempre ardida
con decrépito sol y luna vieja,

que lo que no me des y no te pida
será para la muerte que no deja
ni sombra por la carne estremecida.

El poeta habla por teléfono con el amor

Tu voz regó la duna de mi pecho
en la dulce cabina de madera.
Por el sur de mis pies fue primavera
y al norte de mi frente flor de helecho.

Pino de luz por el espacio estrecho
cantó sin alborada y sementera
y mi llanto prendió por vez primera
coronas de esperanza por el techo.

Dulce y lejana voz por mí vertida,
10 dulce y lejana voz por mí gustada,
lejana y dulce voz amortecida,

The Poet Tells the Truth

I want to cry my pain, and I tell you
so you will love me and will cry for me
in a dusk of nightingales
with a dagger, with kisses and with you.

I want to kill the only witness
to the assassination of my flowers
and turn my cry and my sweat
into an eternal heap of hard wheat.

Let the skein never end
10   of I love you you love me, ever burnt
with decrepit sun and old moon;

for whatever you don't give me and I don't ask of you
will be for death, which does not leave
even a shadow on trembling flesh.

The Poet Speaks with His Beloved on the Telephone

Your voice watered the dune of my breast
in the sweet wooden booth.
Toward the south of my feet it was spring
and to the north of my brow, flower of fern.

In the narrow space a pine tree of light
sang with no music of dawn, no seed bed,
and my cry caught for the first time
crowns of hope around the roof.

Sweet and distant voice poured out for me.
10   Sweet and distant voice I tasted.
Distant and sweet swooning voice.

lejana como oscura corza herida,
dulce como un sollozo en la nevada,
¡lejana y dulce, en tuétano metida!

El poeta pregunta a su amor
por la «Ciudad Encantada» de Cuenca

¿Te gustó la ciudad que gota a gota
labró el agua en el centro de los pinos?
¿Viste sueños y rostros y caminos
y muros de dolor que el aire azota?

¿Viste la grieta azul de luna rota
que el Júcar moja de cristal y trinos?
¿Han besado tus dedos los espinos
que coronan de amor piedra remota?

¿Te acordaste de mí cuando subías
10 al silencio que sufre la serpiente
prisionera de grillos y de umbrías?

¿No viste por el aire transparente
una dalia de penas y alegrías
que te mandó mi corazón caliente?

Soneto gongorino en que el poeta
manda a su amor una paloma

Este pichón del Turia que te mando,
de dulces ojos y de blanca pluma,
sobre laurel de Grecia vierte y suma
llama lenta de amor do estoy parando.

Su cándida virtud, su cuello blando,
en lirio doble de caliente espuma
con un temblor de escarcha, perla y bruma
la ausencia de tu boca está marcando.

Distant as a dark wounded doe.
Sweet as a sob in the falling snow.
Distant and sweet lodged within the marrow!

The Poet Asks His Love about the "Enchanted City" of Cuenca

Did you like the city that the water
carved drop by drop in the center of the pines?
Did you see dreams and faces and roads
and walls of grief lashed by the air?

Did you see the blue crack of broken moon
that the Júcar wets with crystal and trills?
Have your fingers been kissed by the hawthorns
that crown with love the distant stone?

Did you remember me as you climbed
10 to the silence that the serpent suffers,
prisoner of crickets and shady groves?

Did you not see in the transparent air
a dahlia of sorrows and joys
that my warm heart sent you?

Sonnet in the Manner of Góngora in Which the Poet Sends His Beloved a Dove

This young dove I send you from the Turia,
with sweet eyes and white feathers,
over Grecian laurel pours and subsumes
the slow flame of love where I am staying.

Its candid virtue, its soft neck
in double lily of warm foam
with a tremor of frost, pearl and brume
is marking the absence of your mouth.

Pasa la mano sobre su blancura
10   y verás qué nevada melodía
esparce en copos sobre tu hermosura.

Así mi corazón de noche y día
preso en la cárcel del amor oscura
llora sin verte su melancolía.

·

¡Ay voz secreta del amor oscuro!
¡Ay balido sin lanas! ¡Ay herida!
¡Ay aguja de hiel, camelia hundida!
¡Ay corriente sin mar, ciudad sin muro!

¡Ay noche inmensa de perfil seguro,
montaña celestial de angustia erguida!
¡Ay perro en corazón!, voz perseguida,
silencio sin confín, lirio maduro.

Huye de mí, caliente voz de hielo,
10   no me quieras perder en la maleza
donde sin fruto gimen carne y cielo.

Deja el duro marfil de mi cabeza,
apiádate de mí, ¡rompe mi duelo!,
¡que soy amor, que soy naturaleza!

El amor duerme en el pecho del poeta

Tú nunca entenderás lo que te quiero,
porque duermes en mí y estás dormido.
Yo te oculto llorando, perseguido
por una voz de penetrante acero.

Norma que agita igual carne y lucero
traspasa ya mi pecho dolorido,

Pass your hand over its whiteness
10 and you will see what snowy melody
it scatters in snowflakes over your beauty.

Thus my heart by night and day,
held in the dark prison of love,
cries its melancholy at not seeing you.

•

Oh secret voice of dark love!
Oh bleating without fleece! Oh wound!
Oh needle of gall, sunken camellia!
Oh current without sea, city without wall!

Oh immense night of sure profile,
celestial mountain erect with anguish.
Oh dog in the heart, pursued voice,
silence without bounds, ripe lily!

Flee from me, hot voice of ice,
10 don't seek to lose me in the brambles
where flesh and sky cry fruitlessly.

Leave the hard ivory of my head,
take pity on me, break my mourning!
For I am love, for I am nature!

The Beloved Sleeps on the Poet's Breast

You will never understand how much I love you
because you sleep in me and are asleep.
I conceal you crying, pursued
by a voice of penetrating steel.

Norm that shakes both flesh and morning star
now pierces my aching breast,

y las turbias palabras han mordido
las alas de tu espíritu severo.

    Grupo de gente salta en los jardines
10 esperando tu cuerpo y mi agonía
en caballos de luz y verdes crines.

    Pero sigue durmiendo, vida mía.
¡Oye mi sangre rota en los violines!
¡Mira que nos acechan todavía!

Noche del amor insomne

    Noche arriba los dos, con luna llena,
yo me puse a llorar y tú reías.
Tu desdén era un dios, las quejas mías
momentos y palomas en cadena.

    Noche abajo los dos. Cristal de pena
llorabas tú por hondas lejanías.
Mi dolor era un grupo de agonías
sobre tu débil corazón de arena.

    La aurora nos unió sobre la cama,
10 las bocas puestas sobre el chorro helado
de una sangre sin fin que se derrama.

    Y el sol entró por el balcón cerrado
y el coral de la vida abrió su rama
sobre mi corazón amortajado.

and turbid words have gnawed
the wings of your severe spirit.

    A group of people prances in the gardens
10 awaiting your body and my agony
on horses of light with green manes.

    But go on sleeping, my life.
Hear my broken blood in the violins!
Look, they are lying in ambush for us still!

Night of Sleepless Love

    Night up we two with the full moon,
I began to cry and you were laughing.
Your disdain was a god, my complaints
moments and doves in a chain.

    Night down we two. Crystal of pain,
you were crying over deep distances.
My sorrow was a group of agonies
above your weak heart of sand.

    Dawn drew us together on the bed,
10 mouths pressed to the frozen jet
of a blood without end that was spilling.

    And the sun entered through the closed balcony
and the coral of life opened its branch
above my shrouded heart.

OTROS SONETOS

1923–1936

[Autorretrato, 1931]

OTHER SONNETS

1923–1936

Translated by

Christopher Maurer

[*Self-portrait, 1931*]

El viento explora cautelosamente
qué viejo tronco tenderá mañana.
El viento, con la luna en su alta frente,
escrito por el pájaro y la rana.

El cielo se colora lentamente,
una estrella se muere en la ventana,
y en las sombras tendidas del Naciente
luchan mi corazón y su manzana.

El viento como arcángel sin historia
10 tendrá sobre el gran álamo que espía,
después de largo acecho, la victoria.

Mientras, mi corazón en la luz fría
frente al vago espejismo de la Gloria,
lucha sin descifrar el alma mía.

En la muerte de
José de Ciria y Escalante

¿Quién dirá que te vio, y en qué momento?
¡Qué dolor de penumbra iluminada!
Dos voces suenan: el reloj y el viento
mientras flota sin ti la madrugada.

Un delirio de nardo ceniciento
invade tu cabeza delicada.
¡Hombre! ¡Pasión! ¡Dolor de luz! Memento.
Vuelve hecho luna y corazón de nada.

Vuelve hecho luna: con mi propia mano
10 lanzaré tu manzana sobre el río
turbio de rojos peces y verano.

Y tú, arriba, en lo alto, verde y frío,
¡olvídame! Y olvida el mundo vano,
tristísimo Giocondo, amigo mío.

Cautiously the wind explores
which old tree trunk it will fell tomorrow.
The wind, inscribed by bird and frog,
with moon on her high brow.

Slowly the sky gains color,
a star dies in the window,
and in the stretching shadows of the East
my heart struggles with its apple.

Like an archangel with no history,
10 after a long wait, the wind will conquer
the huge aspen it is spying on.

Meanwhile my heart, in the cold light,
stares at the vague mirage of Glory,
and struggles, without deciphering my soul.

On the Death of
José de Ciria y Escalante

Who could say that he saw you, and when?
What pain of glowing shadow!
Two voices are heard—clock and wind—
while, with you gone, the early hours float by.

A frenzy of ashen spikenard
invades your delicate head.
Man! Passion! Pain of light! Memento.
Come back turned to moon and heart of nothing.

Come back turned to moon. With my own hand
10 I'll cast your apple onto the river,
cloudy with summer and red fish.

And you, on high, green and cold,
forget me! And forget the vain world,
oh sad, sad Giocondo, my friend.

Soneto de homenaje a Manuel de Falla
ofreciéndole unas flores

Lira cordial de plata refulgente
de duro acento y nervio desatado,
voces y frondas de la España ardiente
con tus manos de amor has dibujado.

En nuestra propia sangre está la fuente
que tu razón y sueños ha brotado.
Álgebra limpia de serena frente.
Disciplina y pasión de lo soñado.

Ocho provincias de la Andalucía,
10 olivo al aire y a la mar los remos,
cantan, Manuel de Falla, tu alegría.

Con el laurel y flores que ponemos,
amigos de tu casa, en este día,
pura amistad sencilla te ofrecemos.

A Carmela Condón,
agradeciéndole unas muñecas

Una luz de jacinto me ilumina la mano
al escribir tu nombre de tinta y cabellera,
y en la neutra ceniza de mi verso quisiera
silbo de luz y arcilla de caliente verano.

Un Apolo de hueso borra el cauce inhumano
donde mi sangre teje juncos de primavera.
Aire débil de alumbre y aguja de quimera
pone loco de espigas el silencio del grano.

En este duelo a muerte por la virgen poesía,
10 duelo de rosa y verso, de número y locura,
tu regalo renueva sal y vieja alegría.

Sonnet in Homage to Manuel de Falla
Offering Him Some Flowers

Cordial lyre of glowing silver,
of hard accent and supple nerve,
your hands of love have drawn
voices and fronds of an ardent Spain.

In our own blood is the fountain
that spurts your reason and your dreams.
Clean algebra of serene brow.
Discipline and passion for dreamt-of things.

Eight provinces of Andalusia—
10 olive tree in the air, oars in the sea—
sing your joy, Manuel de Falla.

With this laurel and these flowers,
friends of your family, we offer you
our pure, simple friendship.

To Carmela Condón,
Thanking Her for Some Dolls

A light of hyacinth illumines my hand
as I write your name of tresses and ink.
In the neuter ash of my verse I want
hot summer's clay and whistling light.

A bone Apollo wipes out the inhuman channel
where my blood weaves reeds of spring.
A weak breeze of alum and the needle of a chimera
madden with spikes the silence of the grain.

In this duel to the death with virgin poetry,
10 duel of rose and verse, number and madness,
your gift renews salt and old happiness.

¡Oh pequeña morena de delgada cintura!
¡Oh Perú de metal y de melancolía!
¡Oh España, oh luna muerta sobre la piedra dura!

Adán

A José Barbeito

Árbol de sangre moja la mañana
por donde gime la recién parida.
Su voz deja cristales en la herida
y un gráfico de hueso en la ventana.

Mientras la luz que viene fija y gana
blancas metas de fábula que olvida
el tumulto de venas en la huida
hacia el turbio frescor de la manzana,

Adán sueña en la fiebre de la arcilla
10 un niño que se acerca galopando
por el doble latir de su mejilla.

Pero otro Adán oscuro está soñando
neutra luna de piedra sin semilla
donde el niño de luz se irá quemando.

Soneto

Yo sé que mi perfil será tranquilo
en el norte de un cielo sin reflejo,
mercurio de vigilia, casto espejo
donde se quiebre el pulso de mi estilo.

Que si la yedra y el frescor del hilo
fue la norma del cuerpo que yo dejo,
mi perfil en la arena será un viejo
silencio sin rubor de cocodrilo.

O small dark girl of slender waist!
O Peru of metal and melancholy!
O Spain, O dead moon on hard stone!

Adam

To José Barbeito

A tree of blood soaks the morning
where the new mother groans.
Her voice leaves glass in the wound
and on the panes, a diagram of bone.

The coming light establishes and wins
white limits of a fable forgotten
by the tumult of veins in flight
toward the dim cool of the apple.

Adam dreams in the fever of the clay
of a child who comes galloping
through the double pulse of his cheek.

But a dark other Adam is dreaming
a neuter moon of seedless stone
where the child of light will burn.

Sonnet

I know that my profile will be serene
in the north of an unreflecting sky.
Mercury of vigil, chaste mirror
to break the pulse of my style.

For if ivy and the cool of linen
were the norm of the body I leave behind,
my profile in the sand will be the old
unblushing silence of a crocodile.

Y aunque nunca tendrá sabor de llama
10 mi lengua de palomas ateridas,
sino desierto gusto de retama,

libre signo de normas oprimidas
seré, en el cuello de la yerta rama
y en el sinfín de dalias doloridas.

Epitafio a Isaac Albéniz

Esta piedra que vemos levantada
sobre hierbas de muerte y barro oscuro,
guarda lira de sombra, sol maduro,
urna de canto sola y derramada.

Desde la sal de Cádiz a Granada,
que erige en agua su perpetuo muro,
en caballo andaluz de acento duro
tu sombra gime por la luz dorada.

¡Oh dulce muerto de pequeña mano!
10 ¡Oh música y bondad entretejida!
¡Oh pupila de azor, corazón sano!

Duerme cielo sin fin, nieve tendida.
Sueña invierno de lumbre, gris verano.
¡Duerme en olvido de tu vieja vida!

En la tumba sin nombre de Herrera y Reissig en el cementerio de Montevideo

Túmulo de esmeraldas y epentismo
como errante pagoda submarina,
ramos de muerte y alba de sentina
ponen loco el ciprés de tu lirismo.

Anémonas con fósforo de abismo
cubren tu calavera marfilina,

And though my tongue of frozen doves
10 will never taste of flame,
only of empty broom,

I'll be a free sign of oppressed norms
on the neck of the stiff branch
and in an ache of dahlias without end.

Epitaph for Isaac Albéniz

This stone that rises before us
from weeds of death and dark mud
holds a lyre of shadow, ripe sun,
and a lonely urn spilling song.

From the salt of Cádiz to Granada,
who builds in water her perpetual wall,
your shade moans for the golden light
on an Andalusian horse of harsh accent.

O sweet small-handed dead man!
10 O music and goodness intertwined!
O hawk's eye, sound heart!

Sleep sky without end, recumbent snow.
Dream winter firelight, gray summer.
Oh sleep without remembering your life!

At the Anonymous Tomb of Herrera y Reissig in the Cemetery of Montevideo

A tumulus of emeralds and of strangeness,
like a pagoda wandering beneath the sea,
branches of death, the bilge of dawn
are maddening the cypress of your lyricism.

Anemones with the phosphor of the deep
cover the ivory of your skull,

y el aire teje una guirnalda fina
sobre la calva azul de tu bautismo.

No llega Salambó de miel helada
ni póstumo carbunclo de oro yerto
que salitró de lis tu voz pasada.

Sólo un rumor de hipnótico concierto,
una laguna turbia y disipada,
soplan entre tus sábanas de muerto.

A Mercedes en su vuelo

Una viola de luz yerta y helada
eres ya por las rocas de la altura.
Una voz sin garganta, voz oscura
que suena en todo sin sonar en nada.

Tu pensamiento es nieve resbalada
en la gloria sin fin de la blancura.
Tu perfil es perenne quemadura.
Tu corazón, paloma desatada.

Canta ya por el aire sin cadena
la matinal fragante melodía,
monte de luz y llaga de azucena.

Que nosotros aquí de noche y día
haremos en la esquina de la pena
una guirnalda de melancolía.

and the breeze weaves a delicate crown
on the bald, blue spot of your baptism.

No Salammbô comes forth with frozen honey,
10   no posthumous carbuncle of stiff gold,
to saltpeter your voice again with lily.

Only the whisper of a hypnotic concert,
only a dim and faint lagoon
breathe on your winding sheets.

For Mercedes in Her Flight

On the high rocks you have turned
into a viola of stiff, frozen light.
Voice without throat, dark voice
that rings through everything and nothing.

Your thought is shifting snow
in an endless glory of whiteness.
Your profile, an unending burn;
your heart, an untethered dove.

Sing now, through the chainless breeze,
10   a fragrant morning melody:
hill of light, wound of an Easter lily.

While night and day,
here on the corner of pain,
we weave a wreath of melancholy.

POEMAS
SUELTOS

[Pera y dado con puntos que se desprenden, 1930]

UNCOLLECTED
POEMS

Translated by

Christopher Maurer

[*Pear and Die with Falling Spots, 1930*]

Voces
(Escaparate)

Nuestras voces
semejan
un bosque de feéricas
matasuegras
rematadas por plumas
de ideas.

Lombrices con anillos
de palabras
y virus
10 de miradas.

Columnas de cemento
metafísico.
¡Oh voz de catedrático
entre nieblas de puntos
suspensivos!

Hay voces que semejan
grises falos erectos
y otras que van manchadas
de cieno.
20 Hay algunas que mojan
como lenguas de perro
y hay voz que se destrenza
en el silencio.
La voz ala de mosca
de los viejos.

La voz agujereada
de la prostituta
y la voz de cosmético
de los curas
30 son hilos con que borda
la lechuza.

¡Rosa azul de palabras,
la voz de la niña!

Voices
(Shop Window)

Our voices
are like
a forest
of fey
paper serpents,
ending in tufts
of ideas.

Ringworms
of words
that carry the virus
of looks.

Columns of metaphysical
cement.
O voice of the professor
in clouds of
punctuation!

Some voices are like
erect gray phalluses,
others are
full of muck,
some of them slobber
like dogs' tongues.
Voices unbraided
in silence.
Old folks' voices
like flies' wings.

Voice of the prostitute,
riddled with holes,
cosmetic voice
of priests
are the thread-like voices
the owl needs
for its embroidery.

¡Riada de moaré,
la voz de la abuelita!

Hay voces pulpos
y topos
y otras
como cuellos
40   de palomas
y existe la voz *plebe*
ronca y negra.
Toda llena de dientes
de hembra.

En cuanto a las obras,
señores,
pueden encontrarlas
a poco coste
en el baratillo
50   de las voces.

Estampilla y juguete

El relojito de dulce
se me deshace en la lumbre.

Reloj que me señalaba
una constante mañana.

Azúcar, rosa y papel . . .
(¡Dios mío, todo mi ayer!)

En la cresta de la llama
(¡Señor, todo mi mañana!)

Cautiva

Por las ramas
indecisas

Blue rose of words:
voice of the little girl!
Granny's voice:
flood of moiré.

There are octopus voices
and mole voices,
40 and others
like the glittering necks
of pigeons.
And the vox populi,
black, hoarse,
full of women's teeth.

As for deeds,
gentlemen,
you can get them cheap
in the auction
50 of voices.

Candy Wrapper and Toy

The little candy clock
dissolves in the fire.

Clock that always pointed
to tomorrow.

Sugar, rose, wrapper . . .
(My God, my whole yesterday!)

At the tip of the flame
(Oh Lord, my whole tomorrow!)

Captive

Through the branches
hesitant,

iba una doncella
que era la vida.
Por las ramas
indecisas.
Con un espejito
reflejaba el día
que era un resplandor
10 de su frente limpia.
Por las ramas
indecisas.
Sobre las tinieblas
andaba perdida,
llorando rocío,
del tiempo cautiva.
Por las ramas
indecisas.

Canción de la desesperanza

Los olivos subían
y el río bajaba.

(Sólo yo me perdía
por los aires.)

Los Padres esperaban
el Santo Advenimiento
y las muchachas pintan
su corazón de verde.

(Sólo yo me perdía
por los aires.)

Canto nocturno de los marineros andaluces

De Cádiz a Gibraltar
¡qué buen caminito!

went a maiden
who was life.
Through the branches
hesitant,
she caught the day's reflection
in a little mirror:
the glow of her limpid brow.
10   Through the branches
hesitant.
Over the shadows
she went astray,
weeping dewdrops,
the captive of time.
Through the branches
hesitant.

Song of Despair

The olive trees were rising,
the river was falling.

(Only I
went astray on the breeze.)

The Parents were waiting
for Holy Advent,
and the girls were smearing
their hearts with green.

(Only I
10   went astray on the breeze.)

Night Song of the Andalusian Sailors

From Cádiz to Gibraltar,
what a fine little road!

El mar conoce mi paso
por los suspiros.

¡Ay, muchacha, muchacha,
cuánto barco en el puerto de Málaga!

De Cádiz a Sevilla
¡cuántos limoncitos!
El limonar me conoce
por los suspiros.

¡Ay, muchacha, muchacha,
cuánto barco en el puerto de Málaga!

De Sevilla a Carmona
no hay un solo cuchillo.
La media luna corta
y el aire pasa herido.

¡Ay, muchacho, muchacho,
que las olas se llevan mi caballo!

Por las salinas muertas
yo te olvidé, amor mío.
El que quiera un corazón
que pregunte por mi olvido.

¡Ay, muchacho, muchacho,
que las olas se llevan mi caballo!

Cádiz, que te cubre el mar,
no avances por ese sitio.
Sevilla, ponte de pie
para no ahogarte en el río.

¡Ay, muchacha!
¡Ay, muchacho!
¡Qué buen caminito!
Cuánto barco en el puerto
y en la playa, ¡qué frío!

The sea recognizes my steps
by my sighs.

Ah, girl, girl,
so many boats in Málaga's port!

From Cádiz to Seville,
so many little lemons!
The lemon grove knows me
by my sighs.

Ah, girl, girl,
so many boats in Málaga's port!

From Seville to Carmona,
there's not a single knife.
The half moon makes a cut,
and the wounded breeze goes by.

Ah, lad, lad,
the waves sweep away my horse!

By the dead salt pits
I forgot you, my love.
Whoever wants a heart
should ask why I forgot.

Ah, lad, lad,
the waves sweep away my horse!

Cádiz, the sea will flood you,
so take another path.
Seville, stand up
so you don't drown in the river.

Ah, girl!
Ah, lad!
What a fine little road!
How many boats in the port,
and how cold it is on the beach!

Abandono

¡Dios mío, he venido con
la semilla de las preguntas!
Las sembré y no florecieron.

    (Un grillo canta
    bajo la luna.)

¡Dios mío, he llegado con
las corolas de las respuestas,
pero el viento no las deshoja!

    (Gira la naranja
10   irisada de la tierra.)

¡Dios mío, Lázaro soy!
Llena de aurora mi tumba,
da a mi carro negros potros.

    (Por el monte lírico
    se pone la luna.)

¡Dios mío, me sentaré
con pregunta y sin respuesta!
a ver moverse las ramas.

    (Gira la naranja
20   irisada de la tierra.)

•

En tus ojos la serpiente
y en tu boca la manzana.

    (Cielo de nardos.
    Tierra de espigas.)

¡Por cada beso, te he dado
un gran racimo de lágrimas!

Abandoned

My God, I have come with
the seeds of questions.
I planted them, and they never flowered.

     (A cricket sings
     under the moon.)

My God, I have come
with the corollas of the answers,
but the wind does not strip them!

     (The earth turns:
10   iridescent orange.)

My God, I am Lazarus!
Fill my tomb with dawn,
give me black colts for my cart!

     (The moon is setting
     over the lyrical mountain.)

My God, I will sit down
with a question and no answer,
to watch the branches move.

     (The earth turns:
20   iridescent orange!)

   •

In your eyes, the serpent
and in your mouth, the apple.

     (Sky of nards.
     Earth of grain.)

For each kiss I gave you
a huge cluster of tears!

II

Voy solo por la alameda
como la niña de la estampa.

(Cielo sin luna.
Tierra sin viento.)

Y recuerdo tu mano en mi mano
y tu palabra en mi palabra.

III

Reflejas en tu cristal
el limón y la naranja.

(Cielo de sombra.
Tierra de ceniza.)

Verdes cicutas me dejan
tus caricias sobre el alma.

IV

¿Recuerdas aquel jardín
con la gran rosa del agua?

(Ni cielo
ni tierra.)

¡Tus labios crueles y fríos
sobre mi costado sangran!

Segundo aniversario

El alba nos trae un olor
de verdes lunas flotantes.

Finas agujas de escarcha
se clavan sobre mis sienes.

I go alone through the poplar grove
like the girl in the engraving.

    (Moonless sky,
10   Windless earth.)

I remember your hand in mine,
and your word in my word.

III

Your glass reflects
lemon and orange.

    (Sky of shadow.
    Earth of ash.)

Your caresses leave
green hemlock on my soul.

I V

Remember that garden
20 with the big water-rose?

    (No sky,
    no earth.)

Your cruel, cold lips
are bleeding on my side.

Second Anniversary

Dawn brings us the smell
of floating green moons.

Fine needles of frost
pierce my temples.

En los juncos la culebra
sueña un arco iris rojo.

Y yo vestido de luz
¡viendo morir al silencio!

Mosca

rriiiiiiiiii

(Revoltea fuera
de la ventana.)

Yo pienso en las gentes
que llaman.
Y levanto el cristal.

rriiiiiiiiii

(Revoltea dentro
de la ventana.)

10 Yo pienso en las gentes
encadenadas.
Y la dejo escapar.

rriiiiiiiiii

(Desesperada,
golpea otra vez por fuera
los iris de la ventana.)

rriiiiiiiiii

Margarita, tu tierno
corazoncillo araña
20 el cristal esmerilado
de mi alma.

rriiiiiiiiii

Down in the reeds, the serpent
dreams of a red rainbow.

And I dress up in light,
to watch the silence die.

Fly

zzzzzzzzzzzzz

(Buzzing outside
the window.)

I think of people
knocking.
And raise the glass.

zzzzzzzzzzzzz

(Buzzing inside
the window.)

10 I think of people
in chains.
And let it escape.

zzzzzzzzzzzzz

(Desperate
it knocks again
on the iridescent pane.)

zzzzzzzzzzzzz

Margarita, your tender
20 little heart scratches
the polished glass
of my soul.

zzzzzzzzzzzzz

Apunte para una oda

Desnuda soledad sin gesto ni palabra.
Transparente en el huerto, y untosa por el monte.
Soledad silenciosa sin olor ni veleta
que pesa en los remansos, siempre dormida y sola.

Soledad de lo alto toda frente y luceros
como una gran cabeza cortada y palidísima.
Redonda soledad que nos deja en las manos
unos lirios suaves de pensativa escarcha.

En la curva del río te esperé largas horas
10   limpio ya de arabescos y de ritmos fugaces.
Tu jardín de violetas nacía sobre el viento
y allí temblabas sola queriéndote a ti misma.

Yo te he visto cortar el limón de la tarde
para teñir tus manos dormidas de amarillo.
Y en momentos de dulce música de mi vida
te he visto en los rincones enlutada y pequeña.

Pero lejana siempre, vieja y recién nacida,
inmensa giraluna de fósforo y de plata.
Pero lejana siempre, tendida, inaccesible
20   a la flauta que anhela clavar tu carne oscura.

Mi alma como una yedra de luz y verde escarcha
por el muro del día sube lenta a buscarte.
Caracoles de plata las estrellas me envuelven
pero nunca mis dedos hallarán tu perfume.

Sombra, mujer y niño, sirena, lejanía.
Cisso llora en la ruina y Baco en el racimo.
Yo nací para ti, soledad de lo alto.
Cuelga una trenza tuya, hasta muro de fuego.

La fuente, la campana y la risa del chopo
30   cambio por tu frescura continua y delirante,
y el cuerpo de mi niña con la fronda del alba
por tu cuerpo sin carne y tus mimbres inmóviles.

Sketch for an Ode

1   Naked solitude with neither gesture nor word. Transparent in the orchard, smooth as oil on the hill. Silent solitude with neither fragrance nor weathervane, weighing on the backwaters, drowsy and alone.

2   Lofty solitude, all brow and bright stars, like a huge pallid head, lopped off. Round solitude that leaves in our hands soft lilies of pensive frost.

3   On the curve of the river I waited long hours for you. I was clean at last of arabesques and fleeting rhythms. Your garden of violets was budding somewhere over the wind, and you shivered there alone, loving yourself.

4   I have seen you cut the lemon of afternoon to dye your sleeping hands in yellow. And at times during my life, at moments of sweet music, I have seen you in the corners, small, dressed in mourning.

5   But always distant, old and newborn, huge moonflower of phosphorus and silver. But always alone, reclining, beyond the reach of the flute that yearns to needle your dark flesh.

6   Like ivy of light and green frost, my soul creeps up the wall of day, searching for you. The stars envelop me like silver snails, but my fingers will never find your perfume.

7   Shadow, woman and child, siren, distance. Cyssus cries in the ruins, Bacchus in a cluster of grapes. I was born for you, lofty solitude. Let your tresses down the wall of fire.

8   For your constant, delirious coolness I will exchange the fountain, the bell, the laughter of the poplar. And for your fleshless body and your unmoving reeds, the body of my girl with the frond of dawn.

•

Palabra de cera.
No te acuerdes más de ella.
Déjala que se torne brisa fresca.

Palabra de plomo.
Ésa se irá a lo hondo.
Sacude tu vestido sobre el pozo.

Sorprende por un rato
el tierno abecedario
que dibujan las ramas de aquel árbol
10 [en] la verde pizarra del remanso.

Mira y mira, hijo mío,
aquel lucero limpio,
y deja, satisfecho, en el olvido
tus mohosas palabras de bolsillo.

[*Chopo y torre*]

Chopo y torre.

Sombra viva
y sombra eterna.

Sombra de verdes voces
y sombra exenta.

Frente a frente piedra y viento
sombra y piedra.

•

Word of wax.
Forget your word of wax.
Let it turn to cool breeze.

Word of lead.
That one will sink completely.
Shake out your clothes over the well.

Surprise
the tender alphabet
those branches are sketching
10 on the green slate of the pool.

Stare long and hard, my child,
at that clean, bright star,
and be happy to forget
your musty pocket words.

[*Poplar and Tower*]

Poplar and tower.

Living shade
and eternal shade.

Shade of green voices
and barren shade.

Face to face, stone and wind,
shade and stone.

El mal corazón

I

Hace falta tener un jardín
y un mal corazón.
La luz está al otro lado.
El mundo es una espalda
de negra carne de mulo.

El corazón eléctrico del gato.
El corazón explosivo del toro.
En el mirador
y en la llanura
10   *¡vade retro!*

¡Oh mal corazón!

I I

¡Mal corazón!
Desnudo como un cero.
En una perspectiva
de mármoles y conceptos.

Corazón, capitel
que decore y soporte.
¡Nada más!
Mañana. Tarde. Noche.

20   La terca brújula.
Sol y luna.
El terco río . . .
Elige, amigo.
Estatua o vino.

Bad Heart

I

You need a garden
and a bad heart.
The world is a shoulder
of black mule's flesh.
The light is on the other side.

Electric heart of the cat.
Explosive heart of the bull.
Out the window
and on the plain,
10 *vade retro!*

Oh bad heart!

II

Bad heart!
Naked as a zero.
In a perspective
of marbles and concepts.

Heart like a capital,
for support and decoration.
And nothing more!
Morning, noon, and night.

20 The stubborn compass.
Sun and moon.
The stubborn river.
Take your choice, friend:
statue or wine.

La sirena y el carabinero
(Fragmentos)

A Guillermo de Torre

El paisaje escaleno de espumas y de olivos,
recorta sus perfiles en el celeste duro.
Honda luz sin un pliegue de niebla se atiranta
como una espalda rosa de bañista desnuda.

Alas de pluma y lino, barcas y gallos abren.
Delfines en hilera, juegan a puentes rotos.
La luna de la tarde se despega redonda,
y la casta colina da rumores y bálsamos.

En la orilla del agua cantan los marineros,
canciones de bambú y estribillos de nieve.
Mapas equivocados relucen en sus ojos,
un Ecuador sin lumbre y una China sin aire.

Cornetines de cobre, clavan sus agujetas,
en la manzana rosa del cielo más lejano.
Cornetines de cobre que los carabineros
tocan en la batalla contra el mar y sus gentes.
[. . . . .]

La noche disfrazada con una piel de mulo
llega dando empujones a las barcas latinas.
El talle de la gracia queda lleno de sombra
y el mar pierde vergüenzas y virtudes doradas.

Oh musas bailarinas, de tiernos pies rosados,
en bellas trinidades sobre el jugoso césped.
Acoged mis ofrendas dando al aire de altura,
nueve cantos distintos y una sola palabra.

•

Lento perfume y corazón sin gama,
aire definitivo en lo redondo,

The Siren and the Carabineer
(Fragments)

> *To Guillermo de Torre*

The scalene landscape of foam and olive trees
etches its profiles on the hard azure.
Deep light without a fold of mist pulls taut,
like the pink shoulder of a naked swimmer.

Cocks and boats open wings of feather and linen.
A chain of dolphins plays at broken bridges.
The round evening moon rises free,
and the chaste hill gives off murmurs and balsams.

On the shore the sailors sing
10 bamboo songs, refrains of snow.
Mistaken maps shine in their eyes:
a lightless Equator, a China without air.

Copper bugles needle
the pink apple of the farthest sky.
Copper bugles that the carabineers
play in the battle against the sea and its folk.
[. . . . .]

Night is here, disguised in a mule's skin,
shoving hard on the lateen sails.
The waist of grace fills with shadow
20 and the sea loses its shame and its golden virtues.

Oh dancing muses on tender pink feet,
in lovely trinities upon the juicy turf.
Accept my offerings, giving the high air
nine different songs and a single word.

•

Slow perfume, heart without a scale,
air definitive in its roundness,

corazón fijo, vencedor de nortes,
quiero dejaros y quedarme solo.

En la estrella polar decapitada.

En la brújula rota y sumergida.

Soledad insegura
[*Fragmentos*]

Rueda helada la luna, cuando Venus
con el cutis de sal, abría en la arena,
blancas pupilas de inocentes conchas.
La noche calza sus preciosas huellas
con chapines de fósforo y espuma.
Mientras yerto gigante sin latido
roza su tibia espalda sin venera.
El cielo exalta cicatriz borrosa
al ver su carne convertida en carne
10   que participa de la estrella dura
y el molusco sin límite de miedo.
[. . . . .]

Lirios de espuma cien y cien estrellas,
bajaron a la ausencia de las ondas.
Seda en tambor, el mar queda tirante,
mientras Favonio sueña y Tetis canta.
Palabras de cristal y brisa oscura
redondas sí, los peces mudos hablan.
Academia en el claustro de los iris
bajo el éxtasis denso y penetrable.
20   Llega bárbaro puente de delfines
donde el agua se vuelve mariposas,
collar de llanto a las arenas finas,
volante a la sin brazos cordillera.
[. . . . .]

Noche
Noche de flor cerrada y vena oculta.
—Almendra sin cuajar de verde tacto—.

fixed heart, conqueror of norths:
I want to leave you and be alone.

In the decapitated polar star.

In the broken, sunken compass.

Uncertain Solitude
[*Fragments*]

The frozen moon wheels in the sky
while salt-skinned Venus opens on the sand
the white eyes of innocent shells.
Night leaves precise footprints
on heels of phosphorus and foam,
while a stiff giant with no pulse
rubs his lukewarm, shell-less shoulder.
The sky exalts a smudgy scar
to see its flesh turned into flesh
10 participant in the hard star
and the boundless mollusk of fear.
[. . . . .]

A hundred stars, a hundred lilies of foam
went down to the absence of the waves.
Silken drum, the sea pulls taut
while Favonius resounds and Thetis sings.
Words of glass and dark breeze,
round ones, yes, are spoken by mute fish.
Academy in the iridescent cloister
beneath the dense, penetrable ecstasy.
20 A barbarous bridge of dolphins come,
where the water turns into butterflies,
a necklace of weeping for the fine sands,
flounce for the armless mountain range.
[. . . . .]

Night
A night of closed blossom and hidden vein,
an unformed almond green to the touch.

Noche cortada demasiado pronto,
agitaba las hojas y las almas.
Pez mudo por el agua de ancho ruido,
lascivo se bañaba en el temblante,
30   luminoso marfil, recién cortado
al cuerno adolescente de la luna,
y si el centauro canta en las orillas
deliciosa canción de trote y flecha
ondas recojan glaucas sus acentos
con un dolor sin límite, de nardos.
Lyra bailaba en la fingida curva,
blanco baile de inmóvil geometría.
Ojos de lobo duermen en la sombra
dimitiendo la sangre de la oveja.
40   En lado opuesto, Filomela canta
humedades de yedras y jacintos,
con una queja en vilo de Sur loco,
sobre la flauta fija de la fuente.
Mientras en medio del horror oscuro
mintiendo canto y esperando miedo
voz inquieta de náufrago sonaba:
«Desdichada nación de dos colores
(fila de soles, fila de granadas)
sentada con el mar en las rodillas
50   y la cabeza puesta sobre Europa.
Mapa sin eco en el vivir reciente.
Pueblo que busca el mar y no lo encuentra.
Oye mi doble voz de remo y canto
y mi dolor sin término preciso.
Trigo malo de ayer cubrió tu tierra.
La cicuta y la ortiga te envejecen.
Vulgo borracho canta en los aleros
la espada y el bigote, como norma.
Desdichada nación de catafalcos.»
[. . . . .]

A night cut too soon
was ruffling leaves and souls.
Mute fish in the broad noise of the water
bathes lasciviously in the trembling,
30 bright ivory cut recently
from the adolescent horn of the moon.
And if the centaur sings on the shore
his lovely song of trot and arrow
let the glaucous waves collect his accents
with a limitless pain of spikenards.
Lyra was dancing on the false curve,
motionless goal of motionless geometry.
Wolves' eyes slumber in the shadow
dismissing the blood of the sheep.
To the other side, Philomel is singing
40 dampnesses of ivies and hyacinth
with a drifting complaint of mad South
against the fixed flute of the fountain.
Meanwhile, in the dark horror,
feigning song and awaiting fear
the troubled voice of a shipwrecked man rang out:
"Wretched Nation of two colors—
a stripe of sunlight and a stripe of pomegranate
sitting with the ocean on its knees
50 and its head looming over Europe.
Map with no echo in recent life,
people who look in vain for the sea,
hear my double voice in oar and song
and my pain with no exact boundary.
Bad wheat of the past covered your land.
The hemlock and thistle make you old.
Your drunken people sing under the eaves
the sword and mustache that are your norm,
O wretched land of catafalques."
[. . . . .]

Dos normas

[*Dibujo de la luna*]

Norma de ayer encontrada
sobre mi noche presente.
Resplandor adolescente
que se opone a la nevada.
No pueden darte posada
mis dos niñas de sigilo,
morenas de luna en vilo
con el corazón abierto;
pero mi amor busca el huerto
10 donde no muere tu estilo.

[*Dibujo del sol*]

Norma de seno y cadera
bajo la rama tendida,
antigua y recién nacida
virtud de la primavera.
Ya mi desnudo quisiera
ser dalia de tu destino,
abeja, rumor o vino
de tu número y locura;
pero mi amor busca pura
20 locura de brisa y trino.

•

Tan, tan.
¿Quién es?
El Otoño otra vez.
¿Qué quiere de mí?
El frescor de tu sien.
No te lo quiero dar.
Yo te lo quitaré.

Tan, tan.
¿Quién es?
10 El Otoño otra vez.

Two Norms

[*Sketch of the moon*]

Yesterday's norm encountered
on my present night.
Glow of adolescence,
you oppose the snow.
The stealthy pupils of my eyes
do not want to take you in:
two brown girls of floating moon
and my open heart.
But my love looks for the orchard
10   where your style does not die.

[*Sketch of the sun*]

Norm of breast and hip
under the stretching bough;
old and newly born,
virtue of the Spring.
My naked body yearns to be
the dahlia of your destiny,
bee, murmur or wine
of your number and madness.
But my love goes on seeking
20   madness of breeze and trill.

•

Knock, knock!
Who's there?
Autumn again.
What do you want?
The coolness of your temple.
You can't have it.
I'll take it.

Knock, knock!
Who's there?
30   Autumn again.

Canción de cuna para Mercedes muerta

Ya te vemos dormida.
Tu barca es de madera por la orilla.

Blanca princesa de nunca.
¡Duerme por la noche oscura!
Cuerpo de tierra y de nieve.
Duerme por el alba ¡duerme!

Ya te alejas dormida.
¡Tu barca es bruma, sueño, por la orilla!

Cradle Song for Mercedes, in Death

We can see you even now, asleep,
your wooden boat along the shore.

White princess of never,
Sleep in the dark night.
Body of earth and snow.
Sleep in the dawn, sleep!

You wander off, asleep,
your misty boat of dream along the shore.

Notes to the Poems
by Christopher Maurer

These revised notes provide essential information about the texts (dates of composition, revision, and first publication) and attempt to clarify the least obvious of Lorca's literary and cultural allusions. I have tried not to assign meaning to Lorca's images, preferring to draw the reader's attention to parallel passages in other poems, the poet's own comments on his work, and relevant biographical data.

The names of series of poems or of divisions within a book are given in uppercase, for example: SUMMER HOURS. Names of poems published *in this book* are given in italics. Line numbers refer to the English text, except in direct quotations from the Spanish. Except as noted, all translations are my own. Works most frequently cited are abbreviated as follows:

AFGL   Archivo de la Fundación Federico García Lorca, Madrid.

B   Federico García Lorca. *Suites*. Ed. André Belamich. Barcelona: Ariel, 1983.

C   ———. *Conferencias*. Ed. Christopher Maurer. 2 vols. Madrid: Alianza Editorial, 1984.

Dibujos   ———. *Libro de los Dibujos de Federico García Lorca*. Ed. Mario Hernández. Madrid: Tabapress/Grupo Tabacalera/Fundación Federico García Lorca, 1990.

DS   ———. *Deep Song and Other Prose*. Tr. Christopher Maurer. New York: New Directions, 1980.

EC   ———. *Epistolario completo*. Ed. Christopher Maurer and Andrew A. Anderson. Madrid: Cátedra, 1997.

IGM   Francisco García Lorca. *In the Green Morning*. Tr. Christopher Maurer. New York: New Directions, 1986.

M   Federico García Lorca. *Canciones y primeras canciones*. Ed. Piero Menarini. Madrid: Espasa-Calpe, 1986.

OC   ———. *Obras completas*. Ed. Miguel García-Posada. 4 vols. Barcelona: Galaxia Gutenberg/Círculo de Lectores, 1997.

PI   ———. *Poesía inédita de juventud*. Ed. Christian de Paepe. Madrid: Cátedra, 1994.

PNY   ———. *Poet in New York*. Ed. Christopher Maurer. Tr. Greg Simon and Steven F. White. New York: Noonday Press, 1998.

PrI   ———. *Prosa inédita de juventud*. Ed. Christopher Maurer. Madrid: Cátedra, 1994.

SD   ———. *In Search of Duende*. Tr. Christopher Maurer. New York: New Directions, 1998.

SG   ———. *A Season in Granada*. Tr. Christopher Maurer. London: Anvil Press Poetry, 1998.

Other works mentioned are found in the Bibliography.

Libro de poemas / Book of Poems

Published 1921 in an edition paid for by Lorca's parents, at the printshop of his friend the painter and writer Gabriel García Maroto, Madrid. García Maroto remembers the poet telling him that he was to have the honor of publishing his first book, and proudly handing him the manuscript in an "old suitcase, with thousands of loose, unnumbered handwritten pages, mixed up, stained, badly treated, without so much as a pin [a staple], or a turned-down corner" (Maurer, " '¡Ay, Maroto!' . . . ," p. 32). Lorca's younger brother, Francisco, helped him select sixty-eight poems from several hundred written between 1918 and 1920. The Spanish text of the thirty-five poems presented here follows the edition of Mario Hernández (1998). Except for *Weathervane*, which serves as a prologue, the poems are given here in the approximate order of their composition. The dates in the subtitles, not always accurate, were added at the suggestion of García Maroto, probably to remind readers of 1921 that many of these were old poems and that Lorca had made much progress since 1918.

The first edition began with the following "Words of Justification":

In this book, which is filled with youthful ardor, torment, and unbounded ambition, I offer an exact image of the days of my adolescence and boyhood: days which link the present to my recent childhood.

In these disorderly pages lies the faithful reflection of my heart and spirit, colored by the pulsing life that came only recently into my field of vision.

Oh reader, oh you who hold this book in your hands: each of its poems was once a new shoot on the musical tree of my blossoming life.

Whatever its deficiencies of style, whatever its sure limitations, this book will at least have the virtue (and to me there are many others) of reminding me constantly of my passionate childhood, as I ran through the meadows of the Vega against the backdrop of the sierra.

By the time the book appeared, Lorca was hard at work on the *Suites* and felt somewhat distant from it. His friend Adolfo Salazar had published a favorable review on the front page of Spain's leading daily newspaper, *El Sol*, but had sent Lorca a letter tactfully reproaching him for certain lines of verse in which "I hear a voice that is not entirely your own" (*EC* 121). In early August 1921 the poet replied: "I agree totally . . . The bad parts are obvious, they leap out at you . . . But, dear Adolfo, when the book was at the printer, all the poems seemed (and still seem) equally bad . . . In my book I can't find myself; I'm lost in the terrible fields of the essay, carrying my tender, simple heart down the path of declamation, down the path of humor, down the *path of hesitation* [cf. *Crossroad*]; but now, at last, I think I've found an ineffable little road full of daisies and multicolored lizards" (*EC* 121).

Veleta / *Weathervane*. Published in *La Pluma* (Madrid), January 1921. Cf. *Memento* and *The Fallen Weathervane*. Lines 36–37: The "rose / with pyramid petals" is the one that appears on mariners' wind charts; cf. notes to VIGNETTES OF THE WIND.

¡Cigarra! / *Cicada!* Line 32: The wish to die consumed by light appears also in *Ghazal of the Flight*. Line 54: Lorca is probably remembering the woman depicted by Verlaine in "Mon rêve familier," *Oeuvres poétiques*, 63.

Mañana / *Morning*. One of several poems about water in *Book of Poems*: cf. "Lluvia" (Rain), "Meditación bajo la lluvia" (Meditation in the Rain), "Manantial" (Spring), and the two poems about the sea: *Ocean* and *Seawater Ballad*.

Elegia / Elegy. One of the earliest of Lorca's elegies about unfulfilled love and frustrated motherhood. The theme is developed most memorably in his plays *Yerma* and *Doña Rosita the Spinster.* Line 29: The *saeta* is a form of *cante jondo* music (see POEM OF THE *SAETA*).

Madrigal / Madrigal. Line 15: Allusion to the story of "Estrellita de Oro," a Spanish Cinderella, whose protector, the Virgin, puts a golden star on her forehead. A Castilian version of this tale is found in Espinosa, 227–31.

Aire de nocturno / Nocturne. A longer version dated November 4, 1919, is found in *PI* 530–32. The refrain (lines 9–13) is re-created in Act III of Lorca's drama *Once Five Years Pass*: "TYPIST: What's that I hear in the distance? / YOUNG MAN: Love, it's the day coming back / my love! . . . TYPIST: What's that I hear in the distance? / YOUNG MAN: Love, / it's the blood in my throat, / my love . . ." (tr. Logan and Gil, 153).

Canción primaveral / Spring Song. Lorca is remembering two poems by Antonio Machado: "Yo escucho los cantos / de viejas cadencias . . ." (I follow the songs / of children at play . . .) and "Yo voy soñando caminos / de la tarde . . ." (I dream my way / down evening roads . . .); see *Selected Poems*, tr. Trueblood, 76–79. Lines 5–8 of part 2 recall Miguel de Unamuno's great poem "En un cementerio de lugar castellano" (In a Castilian Country Cemetery). Text and commentary on the Unamuno poem by Juan Marichal in Burnshaw, 166.

Sueño / Dream. Published in *La Pluma* (Madrid), January 1921. The melancholy confidences to the spring and the assonant rhyme in *ía* suggest Lorca is imitating an early poem by Machado, "Fue una clara tarde, triste y soñolienta . . ." (The clear afternoon was drowsy and sad . . .); cf. Trueblood edition, 71–74.

Tarde / Evening. For an earlier, very different version, titled "Lluvia. Tarde de diciembre" (Rain. December Evening), from December 1917, see *PI* 83–84.

La sombra de mi alma / My Soul's Shadow. Published in *España* (Madrid), December 1920.

El camino / The Road. Line 17: Flammarion in the sense of "close observer of other worlds." Allusion to the popularizing French astronomer Nicolas-Camille Flammarion (1842–1925), known for his studies of double and multiple stars (the footprints). Line 50: Legendary bridge from a children's song: "Al pasar el puente / de Santa Clara / se me cayó el anillo / dentro del agua" (As I crossed the bridge / of St. Clara / my ring fell down / into the water).

El concierto interrumpido / The Interrupted Concert. Dedication: Salazar (1890–1958) was a gifted music critic, composer, and musicologist. David Z. Crookes (319–20) argues that the correct translation of line 12 is "has placed the mute on its barrel-organ" and that the mute is a cloud crossing the face of the moon.

La balada del agua del mar / Seawater Ballade. Published in Gerardo Diego's anthologies of 1932 and 1934. Unlike Juan Ramón Jiménez, Lorca uses dialogue in almost all the poems and prose pieces he titles "balada." The idealistic melancholy of Jiménez's *Baladas de primavera* (Spring Ballades) is at work throughout *Book of Poems.*

Deseo / Desire. Published in *La Pluma* (Madrid), January 1921. Lines 3–9: Five years later, in September 1926, Federico writes to his friend Guillén: "Just imagine, I would like to get married! Will I ever be able to? No. And this is the problem I want to solve. I am beginning to see that my heart is searching for a garden and a little fountain, as in my first poems. Not a garden of divine flowers and rich man's butterflies, but a garden with breezes and monotonous leaves where my five domesticated senses can stare at the sky" (*EC* 369).

Elegía del silencio / *Elegy: To Silence*. On the same topic, cf. *The Silence, Solitude*, and *Sketch for an Ode*. Inspired by those of Ramón Gómez de la Serna (see Introduction), Lorca was trying his hand at aphorisms on abstract themes. He wrote a similar poem the following month on "Presentiment" (Hernández ed., 105).

Encrucijada / *Crossroad*. See preliminary note, above. Published in *España* (Madrid), December 1920.

Prólogo / *Prologue*. Despite the title, this poem occurs halfway through the book. Lines 8, 91: Lorca's use of the epithet "lírico" (lyrical) throughout *Libro de poemas* is a mannerism he had acquired from Rubén Darío (Devoto, "García Lorca y Darío," 24). Lines 29, 91: Lorca was an avid reader of Goethe's *Faust*. Lines 53–58: In an early essay titled "Mística en que se habla de la eterna mansión" (Mystic Which Speaks of the Eternal Mansion), he complains bitterly: "Couldn't it be that we were created so that God could use us as toys? . . . It seems we are destined to be moved by the hands of an inflexible God who keeps us in a cage for his amusement. In moments of cataclysm people exclaim, 'How great God's power is!' Yes, to be sure, it is very great. But it is always the power of evil; that is, of suffering" (*PrI* 101–2).

Madrigal de verano / *Summer Madrigal*. Line 17: Allusion to Don Quixote (cf. *Minor Song*), the "knight of the sad countenance" (caballero de la *triste figura*). Line 18: "People have often spoken with great exaggeration of the physical clumsiness of Federico's movements. Certain biographical sketches depict him as slightly lame. The truth is that when he was older he had a very personal way of getting around, best described in his own words: '¡Oh mis torpes andares!' [Oh, my clumsy gait!]" (*IGM* 45).

Cantos nuevos / *New Songs*. On the same subject, cf. *Verlaine*.

Canción para la luna / *Song for the Moon*. Line 14, "anarchists": Waves of labor unrest, fomented in part by anarchist organizations like the C.N.T., swept all of Spain between 1919 and 1923. Lines 20–27: Probable allusion to Zoroastrianism. In "El cuervo" (The Crow), dated January 1918 (*PI* 129), Lorca writes: "The Parsees called you God of Purity. / Ahuramazda created you as a devourer. / To them you are a sacred animal, / who comes from an ideal, enchanted kingdom / to devour corruption."

Se ha puesto el sol / *The Sun Has Set*. Line 9: The precise meaning of "campo de pre-beso" (an image of the sky at dusk) is unclear. Lines 20–21 are faintly reminiscent of a Spanish Christmas carol, "Ya se van los pastores / de Extremadura. / Ya se queda la sierra / triste y oscura" (The shepherds are leaving / Extremadura. / The mountain is growing / sad and dark).

Consulta / *Inquiry*. Lines 7–10: On Venus, cf. *The Sun Has Set*, and the two poems titled *Venus* in SUITES. Line 22: The "insect of time" is, obviously, the clock, and the "butterfly," the poet's soul (for an early prose poem on the myth of Psyche, see *OC* I: 661–62).

El lagarto viejo / *The Old Lizard*. One of two "fables" in the book; the other is "Encuentros de un caracol aventurero" (The Encounters of an Adventurous Snail). The characters of Lorca's first dramatic production, *The Butterfly's Evil Spell* (1920), are animals. His devotion as a young man to St. Francis of Assisi and his interest in pantheism prompt him to insist, in an early essay: "In the forests there are gigantic loves, sublime sacrifices, and enormous souls. There are many men who are useless earth, and animals with delicate souls . . . We can never understand animals, never know for sure if they possess a soul, just as they, in their indescribable conversations, will never understand *us*" ("Mistica del dolor humano y de la sociedad horrible" [Mystic of Human Pain and of the Horror of Society], *PrI* 116). Line 34: The word "plateresque" refers to an ornate style of Spanish Renaissance architecture (e.g., the facade of the University of Salamanca), so called because it evokes the delicate work of silversmiths. Lines 52–53 refer to a folk belief that the lizard protects man from the snake.

Madrigal / Madrigal. Juan Ramón Jiménez arranged to have this poem published in *España* (Madrid), December 1920, along with *Crossroad* and *My Soul's Shadow*. Line 11: The "blue skull," which is *agujereada* (riddled with holes), is probably the starry sky. Line 19: "dolor salomónico" (spiral suffering) alludes to the *columna salomónica*, the twisted barley-sugar column popular in Spanish architecture of the style known as Churrigueresque (late seventeenth, early eighteenth centuries). Cf. CARACOL.

El diamante / Diamond. Years later, in a lecture recital on *The Gypsy Ballads*, Lorca would quote this poem as proof of his early interest in the ballad: "Formally, at least, [it] already shows the chiaroscuro of *The Gypsy Ballads* and the delight in mingling astronomical images with bugs and ordinary occurrences, a basic note of my poetic character" (*DS* 106). In the later version he omits lines 17–19.

Poema del cante jondo / Poem of the Deep Song

Lorca wrote over half the poems in this book, which was begun in August 1921, between November 11 and 21 of that year. He read several of them in public in Granada in 1922, shortly before the amateur festival that he organized with Manuel de Falla in order to vindicate the aesthetic value of *cante jondo* and to save it from commercial adulteration. Six poems were printed by Guillén in *Verso y Prosa* (Murcia) in April 1927, and a longer selection was published by the Instituto de las Españas at Columbia University during the poet's trip to New York, in 1930. Three early attempts to publish the complete book (1922, 1923, 1926) had come to naught. The first edition appeared in Madrid in May 1931 (Ediciones Ulises). For a detailed textual history, see Christian de Paepe's excellent critical edition, 7–100. Lorca's own lecture entitled "Deep Song" (1922) and the revised version (1930) entitled "Architecture of Deep Song" (*SD*, 1–25; *C* I:43–83; Maurer, *Federico García Lorca y su "Arquitectura . . ."*) shed much light on these poems. The Spanish text given here is from the editions of Mario Hernández (poems) and De Paepe (dialogues).

Lorca's earliest reference to the book comes in a letter to his friend the musicologist Adolfo Salazar, c. January 1, 1922: "I have gone back over the *Suites* for the last time, and am now putting the golden rooftiles on *Poem of the Deep Song*, which I am going to publish to coincide with the [*cante jondo*] festival. It is something different from the *Suites* and filled with suggestions of Andalusia. The rhythm is popular in a stylized way, and I bring out all of the old *cantaores* [singers of *cante jondo*], all the fantastic flora and fauna that fill these sublime songs. Silverio, Juan Breva, Loco Mateo, La Parrala, el Fillo . . . and Death! It is a great carved altarpiece [see Introduction, xlii], it's . . . a jigsaw puzzle, if you know what I mean. The poem [i.e., book] begins with a motionless sunset, and then the *siguiriya*, the *soleá*, the *saeta*, and the *petenera* come filing across it. The poem is full of gypsies, tapers, forges, and it even contains allusions to Zoroaster. It is the first thing I've done with a *completely different orientation*, and I still don't know what I can say about it . . . but it *does* have novelty. The only person who knows it is Falla, and he is enthusiastic, which you will readily understand, knowing *Manué* and how crazy he is about these things. Spanish poets have never even *touched* this theme, and I deserve a smile, at least, for my daring" (*EC*, 136–37).

Baladilla de los tres ríos / Ballad of the Three Rivers. Published in *Horizonte* (Madrid), 1923. On "the two rivers of Granada," the Darro (sometimes written Dauro) and the Genil, see *IGM* 7: "I have always suspected that this scene, with the Sierra Nevada in the background, is viewed from the plain on which we were born, where the two rivers branch off into a number of murmuring irrigation ditches." The "swift, arrowy" Darro (Ford, I:316), with its rosy clay bed, flows into the Genil in Granada not far from a house where the Lorca family once lived. The Genil, "increased by infinite mountain tributaries, unites, a noble stream, with the Guadalquivir, near Écija" (Ford, I:317). The *torrecillas* (little towers) and *estanques* (reflecting pools) in lines 21–22 are those of the Alhambra: in his lecture "How a City Sings from November to November" (*SG* 99), Lorca had written that the waters of Granada "lie down to die" there. The Darro and the Genil are compared in a long poem ("Prefacio") of June 17, 1918: the Moorish Darro, flanked by cypresses, which sings "in a minor key," is the river of sadness, and the Genil, flanked by poplars, is a "Christian river," a "river of sun," "strong and hardworking" (*PI* 306–12).

POEMA DE LA SIGUIRIYA GITANA / POEM OF THE GYPSY *SIGUIRIYA*. The gypsy *siguiriya* (phonetic deformation of *seguidilla*) is one of the basic forms of *cante jondo*. The lyrics, which Lorca admired for their emotional intensity, usually contain four lines of verse with assonant rhyme, with the following number of syllables: 6-6-11-6. On the *siguiriya*'s musical characteristics, see Katz, 627.

Paisaje / Landscape. This is both the "motionless sunset" Lorca had mentioned to Salazar (preliminary note, above) and the imaginary landscape suggested by the music and lyrics of the *siguiriya*. Barea (18) quotes an explanation of this poem by "a land worker, half Andalusian, half gypsy": "If you stand in the middle of an olive field between two trees, you look along a straight lane, like a fan that's shut. If you go behind a tree, all the rows between the lanes open up like a fan. And if you walk between the trees there's a big fan opening and shutting before you. And the olive fields are full of cries and calls. The fieldfares come in flocks and make a great noise, even in the night . . . Sometimes you'd think the whole tree is alive with wings and tails. They're a nuisance too, they're so greedy." Lines 15–18: Perhaps the trees' shadows in the dusk (*lo sombrío*).

La guitarra / The Guitar. Lines 19–20: "[To me] the gypsy *siguiriya* had always evoked (I am an incurable lyricist) an endless road, a road without crossroads, ending at the pulsing fountain of the child Poetry. The road where the first bird died and the first arrow grew rusty" (*SD* 4). Lines 26–27: The fingers? Allusion to religious images of the Virgin of Seven Sorrows, her heart transfixed by swords.

El grito / The Cry. Lorca is referring to the "vocalized melisma" that typically precedes the singing (see Katz, 627). "The gypsy *siguiriya* begins with a terrible scream that divides the landscape into two ideal hemispheres. It is the scream of dead generations, a poignant elegy for lost centuries, the pathetic evocation of love under other moons and other winds. Then the melodic phrase begins to pry open the mystery of the tones and remove the precious stone of the sob, a resonant tear on the river of the voice" (*SD* 4).

El silencio / The Silence. "The voice pauses and gives way to an impressive measured silence. A silence glowing with the trace of the hot iris which the voice has left in the sky" (*C* I:53). Cf. *Elegy: To Silence.*

El paso de la Siguiriya / The Passage of the Siguiriya. "Then the melody begins, an undulant, endless melody, but not in the same sense as in Bach. Bach's infinite melody is round, the phrase could go on repeating itself in an eternal circular motion; but the melody of the *siguiriya* loses itself horizontally, escapes from our hands as we see it withdraw from us toward a point of common longing and perfect passion where the soul will never disembark" (*C* I:53).

Después de pasar / Afterwards. The *cantaores* "sing as though fascinated by a point of light trembling on the horizon" (*C* I:82). Loughran (62) recalls "the absolute void and the silence that follows the rendition of a *siguiriya* in the country and among friends." Lines 6–7: Cf. lines 18–19 of *Madrigal* in *Book of Poems*; literally, "My pain, a spiral column, / bored through the moon" (p. 85).

POEMA DE LA SOLEÁ / POEM OF THE *SOLEÁ*. The *soleá* (the word is a contraction of *soledad*, "solitude" or "loneliness") has three or four lines of verse and is usually sung in ¾ or ⅜ time. "The melody is usually like a prolonged lament, and, in contrast to most forms of the *cante jondo*, the guitar accompaniment has always played a major role in its performance . . . In spite of its seriousness . . . the *soleá* rarely expresses the intense emotional dramas or the extremes of tragedy found in the *siguiriya gitana*" (Miller, 30).

Tierra seca . . . / Dry land . . . Untitled in the first edition. Titled "Evocación" (Evocation) in two of the manuscripts.

Pueblo. Line 6: The *hombres embozados* (i.e., with their capes covering part of their faces) add a dash of nineteenth-century Romanticism. Cf. the Young Man who does not show his face in the sixth scene of *The Tragicomedy of Don Cristóbal and Mistress Rosita* (tr. Honig, *Four Puppet Plays*, 60 ff.) As late as 1855, Richard Ford (I:119) advises travelers in Spain: "In the conduct of cloaks, remember, when you meet any one, being yourself *embozado* or muffled up, to remove the folds before you address him, as not to do a great incivility: again, when strangers continue to speak to you thus cloaked, and as it were disguised, be on your guard."

Encrucijada / Crossroads. "The crossroad suggests the presence of the cross: an exact location for pain and death" (De Paepe, 177).

Sorpresa / Surprise. On the melodramatic tone of this poem, see Introduction, p. xliv. Titled "Esquina" (Corner) in one of the manuscripts and "Copla" (Popular Song) in another two. Many of the *cante jondo* lyrics concern violent death. Machado y Álvarez (60), one of the first modern writers on *cante jondo*, notes that "street corners play a major part in the *coplas* about love."

La soleá / The Soleá. "One of the few [poems] in the [book] which attempt to reproduce not only the spirit and emotional atmosphere of the *cante* . . . but its actual metrical form as well—octosyllabic tercets rhyming in assonance" (Miller, 80). Another personification of "Solitude" occurs in *Ballad of Black Pain.*

Cueva / Cave. Probable allusion to the gypsy cave dwellers on the Sacromonte, Granada.

Encuentro / Encounter. Line 14: San Cayetano, or St. Cajetan (1480–1547), founder of the Theatine Order, is prayed to in hopeless situations (De Paepe, 188).

Alba / Dawn. Lines 1–4: De Paepe (189) relates these lines to lines 5–6 of the first poem of the section: the land of the olive groves (*Andalucía la baja*) is Córdoba, and the land of the sierra (*la alta*) is Granada.

POEMA DE LA SAETA / POEM OF THE *SAETA.* The *saeta* (literally, dart or arrow) is a spontaneous, unaccompanied cry of devotion to the Virgin or to Christ, sung by those watching the all-night Holy Week processions, especially those of Seville. Lorca saw these for the first time in 1922 together with his brother and Manuel de Falla. Lorca's sequence " 'takes place' in the streets of Seville and follows the progression from evocation of the 'landscape,' to the procession and religious floats, to the *saeta* itself sung from a balcony, and finally to the coming of dawn" (Loughran, *Federico García Lorca*, 70).

Arqueros / Archers. The "archers" are suggested by the "arrow" of the *saeta.*

Noche / Night. De Paepe (194) explains that the tapers are held by those marching in the procession; the oil lamps are burning before religious images inside the houses; the *faroles* (streetlights or lanterns) illumine the floats; and the fireflies signal "the participation of nature" in the event. The "swaying crosses" are those carried by the marchers.

Sevilla / Seville. "Seville is man in the full complexity of his sensuality and emotion. It is political intrigue and the triumphal arch. Don Pedro and Don Juan. It is full of the human element, and its voice brings tears, because anyone can understand it. Granada is like the narration of what already happened in Seville" (*SG* 67).

Procesión / Procession. De Paepe (198) believes Lorca is recalling, besides Ariosto's poem, a scene from Chapter 23 of the second part of *Don Quixote* (Durandarte bewitched in the Cave of Montesinos): Durandarte and Christ are both "victims of love."

Paso / Float. The statue-bearing floats, showing scenes from the Passion, are carried by the *cofradías* (brotherhoods). See note on *The Passage of the* Siguiriya above. Lorca made a lovely sketch of a similar scene (*Dibujos*, no. 65). Lines 1, 11: or "Virgin in a hoop skirt."

Saeta. The refrain is taken from popular *saetas* like "¡Miradlo por dónde viene, / el mejor de los nacidos!" (Look, he's coming by, / the best of men!) (Josephs and Caballero, 171). The "iris" of line 3 (translated as "lily") probably alludes to the wounds of Christ or to his purple vestments (De Paepe, 201); a certain type of Spanish iris is known as *lirio nazareno* (iris of Nazareth).

Balcón / Balcony. Line 15, "alberca": A sort of water trough. Loughran (*Federico García Lorca*, 73) draws attention to Lola's "narcissism of sorts" and to the " 'commonness' conferred upon her by the use of the demonstrative adjective *aquella*" in line 13; she has been changed for the better by singing the *saeta.*

Madrugada / Before Dawn. Lines 5–6: See note on *The Silence*, above.

GRÁFICO DE LA PETENERA / GRAPHIC OF THE *PETENERA.* De Paepe (124) believes Lorca's emphasis shifts here from the pure *cante* (chant) of the first three sections to dance with guitar. "The *petenera* is always accompanied by the guitar and is intended to be [danced]. It is a melancholy, sentimental song whose fundamental themes are similar to those of the *soleá*" (Miller, 37).

Campana / Bell. In the version which Lorca copied in New York, this poem is entitled "Clamor" (cf. *Death Knell*): mourning for the Petenera, the imaginary woman who personifies the lyrics called *peteneras.*

Camino / Road. Lines 7–8: Granada "sighs for the sea" because, in contrast to Seville, she is landlocked and her only harbor is her "high natural port of stars" (*SG* 100). Lines 12–13: The cemetery? The seven *ays* recall the Virgin of Seven Sorrows.

Danza / Dance. Line 2: Loughran (*Federico García Lorca,* 77) and De Paepe (215–16) believe these six gypsies correspond to the six strings of the guitar.

Muerte de la Petenera / Death of the Petenera. Line 2 is borrowed from popular lyrics about the Petenera—e.g., "Whoever named you Petenera / did not know what he was doing. / He should have named you / the ruination of men" (De Paepe, 217).

Falseta / Guitar Run. In the New York autograph ms. (1930), now in the Pierpont Morgan Library, the title is "False*te*," and this changes the meaning of the poem: Lorca would be referring to the whining falsetto voice of the *cantaor,* particularly shrill in "his wailing about the cemetery" (*DS* 24), as in the initial exclamations of this poem. "False*ta*" is found in the first edition, and if this is the definitive reading, Lorca is alluding to the improvised guitar interludes between strophes: "Because the guitarist's personality is as distinct as that of the singer, the guitarist too must sing, and this gives rise to the falseta, which is the strings' commentary, very beautiful when it is sincere, but often false, foolish, and full of senseless Italianisms" (*SD* 24).

Clamor / Death Knell. Cf. *Bell.* Lines 8–9: Death is traditionally pictured with a *vihuela* in Spanish representations of the dance of death. A crown of orange blossoms was formerly worn by Spanish brides. In an early poem, Lorca insists on the hidden sadness of these crowns: they remind him of the death of love and the inability of the tree to bear oranges ("El encanto del azahar" [The Enchantment of Orange Blossoms], *PI* 226–27).

Amparo. Lines 4–5: Literally: "Equator between jasmine [the color of her skin?] / and spikenard [the color of her dress?]." Cf. *The Gypsy Nun.*

VIÑETAS FLAMENCAS / FLAMENCO VIGNETTES. The dedication was written after Lorca had heard the *cantaor* Manuel Torres (1878–1933) remark: "In *cante jondo* what you must search for, and find, is the black torso of the Pharaoh" (Torres believed the *gypsies* to be of Egyptian origin). See *SD* 48. Torres, who participated in the *cante jondo* festival of 1922, was one of the first *cantaores* to sing "from the torso," rather than in a shrill nasal voice.

Retrato de Silverio Franconetti / Portrait of Silverio Franconetti. Renowned *cantaor* (1825–93) born of an Italian father and a Spanish mother. In his lecture "Deep Song" (*SD* 23), Lorca affirms of this "last Pope of *cante jondo*" that he "sang the song of songs [the *siguiriya*] better than anyone" and that his "scream opened quivering cracks in the moribund mercury of the mirrors," an allusion to an old *siguiriya* sometimes attributed to Silverio: "I don't know / what happened to the mercury / in the mirror I once used." Cf. lines 12–13.

Juan Breva. Professional name of Antonio Ortega (1835–1915), *cantaor* from Malaga, whom Lorca mentions in his lecture: "Juan Breva, who . . . sang *soleares* better than anyone else and invoked the virgin Pain in the lemon groves of Málaga or beneath the maritime nights of Cádiz" (*SD* 23). Lorca's brother, Francisco (*IGM* 29–30), observes that Lorca must have had "direct information" about Breva from his uncles, one of whom had actually met him. The expression "and the voice of a girl" is "too precise, too graphic not to be the echo of something Federico had heard by word of mouth. Among the *cantaores* one finds the husky, torn, dramatic voice that seems to be required for chants where pathos predominates. But one also finds those pure, transparent, more subtle voices that make Federico say . . . 'pain itself singing / behind a smile.' " Breva "sang blind," De Paepe explains, because he would close his eyes when singing, but in his lecture Lorca insists that *cante jondo* always "sings blind, like a nightingale without eyes, and is thus born of the night. It had nothing but the light of an abstract night, where one more star would throw things irresistibly off balance. It is a chant without landscapes and thus concentrated and terrible, like someone throwing golden javelins at people hiding behind the trees" (*C* I:70). Line 9: Literally, "of sleepy Málaga."

Café cantante / Cabaret. Another consciously historical allusion to the epoch of the flamenco "singing cabarets" in the second half of the nineteenth and early twentieth centuries. Dolores Parrales (alias "La Parrala") was renowned for her beauty. Lorca evokes her, together with Breva, as a singer of the *soleá* (*C* I:83).

Lamentación de la muerte / Death's Lament. "One of our uncles—I'm not sure whether it was Francisco or Enrique—told Federico and me of a conversation with [Juan] Breva. The singer (who had been expounding on the false and fleeting nature of success) said that for him everything came to an end with an oil lamp and a blanket on the floor. Tidy vision of death!" (*IGM* 28). Lines 16–19: *Carpe diem!*

Memento. Cf. *Leave-taking* in *Songs*. In his lecture on *cante jondo*, Lorca had marveled at a *copla* beginning: "If I should happen to die, / I order you, / tie up my hands / with your black tresses" (*SD* 20).

Malagueña. "The malagueña is never danced, and its lyrics, always of a serious, dramatic nature, frequently mention Málaga, its monuments and districts, or they relate events from the lives of mariners and others who make their living from the sea. Its *coplas* (stanzas) are normally composed of either four or five octosyllabic verses with the even lines rhyming in assonance" (Miller, 34).

Barrio de Córdoba (Tópico nocturno) / Neighborhood of Córdoba (Nocturnal Theme). *Tópico* in the subtitle means "commonplace," "cliché."

Baile / Dance. In the ms., this is titled "Dance (Old Woodcut)," and in the version published in *Verso y Prosa*, "Dance (Engraving, property of José Bergamín)."

Adivinanza de la guitarra / Riddle of the Guitar. De Paepe (255) notices that "Polyphemus is not merely the metaphorical incarnation of the golden opening—the eye—of the instrument; he also acts as the guard of the cave (*caja*), where he keeps the six maidens [the strings] as prisoners."

Candil / Oil Lamp. Line 3: Lorca and Falla believed that the gypsies had come to Spain from India in the fifteenth century.

Crótalo / Castanet. *Crótalo* is an ancient name for the castanet, and almost certainly has that meaning here. *Crótalo* can also mean rattlesnake.

Chumbera / Prickly Pear. The shape of the plant reminds Lorca of the "Laocoön Group" (first century B.C.) in the Vatican Museum. Lines 2, 5: Literally, "How handsome you look . . ."

Pita / Agave. The mention of cinches (agaves grow in belts around the mountain; cf. the "maguey spears" in *Sleepwalking Ballad*, line 20) is especially apt, according to De Paepe (261), because the fiber of the plant is used to make them. The "desfiladeros" (line 5) are defiles, ravines.

ESCENA DEL TENIENTE CORONEL . . . / SCENE OF THE LIEUTENANT COLONEL . . . Included in the first edition to fill out what would have been an extremely short book. The Civil Guard is a rural constabulary that patrols roads and beaches. See *Ballad of the Spanish Civil Guard*.

DIÁLOGO DEL AMARGO / DIALOGUE OF AMARGO. "I will say only a few words about the Andalusian force, the centaur of death and hatred that is called the Amargo [literally, "the Bitter One"]. When I was eight years old and was playing in my house at Fuente Vaqueros, a boy looked in the window. He seemed a giant, and he stared at me with scorn and hatred I shall never forget. As he withdrew he spat at me, and, from far away, I heard a voice calling, 'Amargo, come!' After that the Amargo grew inside me until I was able to decipher why he looked at me that way, an angel of death and of the despair that keeps the doors of Andalusia. This figure is an obsession in my poetic work. I no longer know whether I saw him or he was an apparition which I imagined, or if he has been waiting all these years to strangle me with his bare hands" (*DS* 117–18). *Song of Amargo's Mother*, line 9: Álvarez de Miranda (81) observes that here, as in primitive religions, the moon is "the final destiny and the country of the dead. The moon captures them and accompanies them, carries them toward herself." The same image occurs in *Lament for Ignacio Sánchez Mejías* (lines 185–89). In both cases, some consolation is implied: the moon dies but is reborn and provides man with hope of resurrection.

Suites

Written between early 1921 and August 1923. Published by the French Hispanist André Belamich in 1983, nearly half a century after Lorca's death. Neither the text nor the order of these poems can be considered definitive. Although Lorca spoke repeatedly between 1921 and 1936 of publishing *Suites* as a book, he did not leave a final, polished manuscript of the entire collection.

The texts published by Belamich and reedited here fall into four categories: (1) autograph copies (a few of which bear no indication of having been revised) from the AFGL or from the archives of friends; (2) versions published in poetry magazines of the 1920s and 1930s; (3) texts that Lorca quoted in his letters; (4) the three suites he published in the 1936 chapbook *Primeras canciones* (*First Songs*). This book begins with a note from the poet-publisher Manuel Altolaguirre: "The 'First Songs' (1922) of García Lorca, which, miraculously, have never been published, are taken from a book written during his adolescence, but which he has not yet ordered: an extremely important book for the later development of his poetic world. The poems are gathered here randomly, in anticipation of a longer and more representative edition."

Two textual problems affect almost all the poems published here: it is not always clear which of these series Lorca considered "suites," and it is quite impossible to know how he would have ordered the sequences and, in some cases, the poems within each one. An excellent doctoral dissertation by Melissa Dinverno, based on study of the manuscript and printed versions, suggests that there will never be a "final" text of *Suites*, only a faithful reconstruction of each suite and of the book itself at certain specific moments in their textual history. In this edition I have tried to present the suites in the approximate order of their composition (the dates must sometimes be deduced from the imagery or from the physical characteristics of the manuscripts). In the first edition of this book, study of the manuscripts in the AFGL made it possible to improve upon Belamich, who was working from photocopies. Research by Dinverno and new texts published by Mario Hernández, Christian De Paepe and others have allowed additional improvements here. No doubt the critical edition of *Suites* now being prepared by Dinverno will lead to further changes in the order and text of the poems.

As in the first edition, certain fragments published by Belamich (for example, those which Lorca rejected and those which, in my judgment, do not belong to the cycle of *Suites*) are omitted here. The few poems that Lorca removed from *Suites* to include in *Songs* are given here as well, in their original context in the *Suites*. Two typographical matters: (1) For stylistic reasons, the stanza breaks and use of italics in Jerome Rothenberg's English translation do not always correspond to those in the Spanish. (2) Missing lines of verse are indicated by a line of dots between brackets. Three dots in brackets mark the lacunae left by missing poems.

Title: On one of the ms. copies, made in 1926, Lorca gives the book a double title that would have connected the entire collection with a specific location: *Suites (o Cielo Bajo)*. *Low Sky* designates the glittering views at night of the gypsy quarter of the Albaicín, Granada, as seen from the Alhambra (Martín, *Federico García Lorca*, 116).

LA SUITE DE LOS ESPEJOS / MIRROR SUITE. Ms. dated April 15, 1921, at the Residencia de Estudiantes. Published by Juan Ramón Jiménez in *Índice* in early 1921. *Symbol*: Literally, "Christ / had a mirror / in each hand. / He used to multiply / his own specter. / He used to project his heart / in his black / looks (glances) / I believe!" *Rays*: Cf. *Floating Bridges* in IN THE GARDEN OF THE LUNAR GRAPEFRUITS (tr. Jerome Rothenberg): "And steadily our feet / keep walking & creating / —like enormous fans— / these roads in embryo." *Capriccio*, lines 5–6: Literally, "Behind each mirror / there is an eternal calm." *Eyes*: The "Castle of No Return" is mentioned in numerous folktales (e.g., Espinosa, 321), and the strange traveler and "Elenita" appear in a ballad sung by children, "Estando una niña / bordando corbatas . . ." (A girl was sitting / embroidering neckties . . .), which Lorca once re-created and choreographed (see Introduction, p. xliii). The traveler carries Elena off to the mountains and cuts off her head (Llorca, 48). A letter that Lorca wrote to his friend the guitarist Regino Sainz de la Maza in 1922 seems pertinent to lines 16–17 of *Confusion*: "I have discovered something terrible (don't tell anyone): *I haven't been born yet*. The other day I was meditating upon my past (I was sitting in my grandfather's easy chair) and none of the dead hours belonged to me. It wasn't I who had lived them: I hadn't lived either the hours of love or the hours of hate or the hours of inspiration. There were a thousand Federico García Lorcas, stretched out eternally in the attic of time. And in the storehouse of the future I beheld another thousand, all nicely pressed and folded and piled one on top of the other, waiting to be filled with helium and fly aimlessly away. I felt terribly afraid, my mother Mrs. Death had given me the key to Time, and for a second I understood everything. I live on borrowed things, what I have inside me isn't mine, and we'll see if I am born. My soul is still completely unopened. No wonder I sometimes think my heart is made of tin! In a word, dear Regino, I am sad and bored in my sham interior" (*EC* 158).

EL JARDÍN DE LAS MORENAS / GARDEN IN UMBER, or THE GARDEN OF THE BROWNHAIRED GIRLS. Undated: early 1921? Published by Juan Ramón Jiménez in *Índice* (1921). The ms. has not been found. The subtitle, which may have been added by Jiménez, raises the possibility that these "fragments" may have been culled from more than one series. *Acacia*, for example, appears also in WATER SUITE. *Encounter*: Devoto ("Notas," 37) reports that the refrain "¡Viva la rosa en su rosal!" is found in some versions of the popular children's ballad "Mambrú se fue a la guerra . . ." (Mambrú [=the Duke of Marlborough!] went off to war . . .); see SIX SONGS AT NIGHTFALL. In one version (Vigón, 65) it alternates with the refrain "¡Sor, viva el amor!" (Long live love!) and is uttered in reaction to news of the death of Mambrú. Read in this context, Lorca's poem acquires an even more funereal air. The feminine rhyme and the expression "junto a la fuentefría" (cf. *Dream* in *Book of Poems*) are also reminiscent of the ballad tradition. The mysterious "moonglove" (line 13) is mentioned years later in *Nocturne of Emptied Space* from *Poet in New York*.

NOCHE / NIGHT. The subtitle is literally "Suite for Piano and Emotional Voice." Written July 1921? Published by Juan Ramón Jiménez in *Índice* in 1921, the version followed here. This suite is probably the "tiny book in honor of our immortal father Sirius" mentioned in a letter of August 2, 1921, to the musicologist Adolfo Salazar (see MOMENTS OF SONG, below). The end of *Swath* evokes a well-known Spanish children's song first recorded in the early seventeenth century, "La pájara pinta" (The Painted Bird) which Lorca also quotes in his puppet play *The Tragicomedy of Don Cristóbal and Mistress Rosita* (tr. Honig, 60). Much admired by modern Spanish poets from Rafael Alberti to Gabriel Celaya, the song accompanies a circle game in which the child selects a girlfriend or boyfriend; thus Lorca's evocation of the "noche de mi amor." See Robertson, 83–86. *One*: The meaning of lines 1–3 may be "That star which appears [so] romantic / (to the magnolias / and to the roses)." *Memory*: The phrase "luna lunera" ("loony moon") occurs in many Spanish children's songs, including ones where the child makes some sort of wish (Newton, 281, and Rodríguez Marín, 59); Lorca glosses the expression in an early poem, "Noche de verano" (Summer Night) (AFGL ms. dated January 18, 1918). *At the Poorhouse*: The ironical refrain appears in certain versions of the ballad "Mambrú se fue a la guerra . . ." (e.g., Celaya 195–96). The title of *Comet* is probably a pun: "cometa" is both "comet" and "kite." The kite would prove there are children on Sirius, the Dog Star, the brightest one in the sky, guard of the heavens in the cosmogony of Zoroaster. Cf. notes to *Poem of the Deep Song*, p. 893, and MOMENTS OF SONG, below.

REMANSOS / BACKWATERS. One ms. is dated June 12, 1921. Published by Jorge Guillén in *Verso y Prosa* (Murcia) in April 1927 with the subtitle "(Diferencias)," a term used for "variations" in sixteenth-century Spanish music. The autograph ms. (dated August 1921 but made in 1927) followed by Guillén is now in the Houghton Library, Harvard University (Span. ms. 69M-12). Published again in 1936 in *Primeras canciones* (9–13) with the poems in a different order and one poem omitted: "Sigue" (Keep It Going): "Cada canción / es un remanso / del amor. // Cada lucero / es un remanso / del tiempo. / Un nido / del tiempo. // Y cada suspiro / un remanso / del grito" (tr. Rothenberg: "Each song's / a backwater / of love. // Each star's / a backwater / of time. / Of time tied / in a knot. // And each sigh's / the backwater / of a scream."). I have followed the version given in *Primeras canciones*, as emended by Mario Hernández (219–20). *Little Backwater*: On the oleander, see note to *Nu* (p. 918). *Half Moon*: García-Posada believes line 2 means: "How can the sky be so calm?" *(Poesiá 1*, 1st ed., 551). As early as the summer of 1918, Lorca was writing poetry about the "remansos" (backwaters, pools) of the Genil and comparing himself as a poet to the insects that skim their surface: "These insects [that hover] over the backwaters / and make such agile leaps / are hunters of the invisible. / Over the waters perhaps they dream / the deep tapestry of the river. / They embroider their fleeting nests / with the needles of their legs / from gentle threads of the fleeting breeze" ("Estos insectos . . . ," *PI* 337). Cf. note on DAYDREAMS OF A RIVER, p. 907.

CAPRICHOS / CAPRICCIOS. Ms. dated July 9, 1921.

MOMENTOS DE CANCIÓN / MOMENTS OF SONG. Ms. dated July 10, 1921. "I'm hard at work now, and think you'll like what I'm doing: much better, it seems to me, than the suites you already know. Would you like me to send you something? I call these pieces 'Songs with Reflections,' because that is all I want to do: allow my words to give the sublime feeling of the reflection, and take away from that which trembles the spiraling nature of a Baroque column ["quitando al temblor lo que tiene de *salomónico*"]. I'm also writing yellowing ballads ["baladas amarillentas"] and a tiny prayer book in honor of our immortal father Sirius : . . In a word, I'm working pretty hard" (from a letter to Adolfo Salazar, August 2, 1921, *EC* 123–24; it is to this Adolfo that *At Songfall* is dedicated). In the ms. Lorca has placed *Song Under Tears* in brackets, as though he had considered eliminating it. The ms. ends with "Canción muerta" (Dead Song) (*B* 215), crossed out, whose central image reappears in *Verlaine*: "A song has died / before it was born. / Where can I bury / my true song? / / While still a girl, it tried to reach the moon / without knowing / that on the moon there are no / flowers to make honey. / / My blue song has died / before it was born."

CUATRO BALADAS AMARILLAS / FOUR BALLADS IN YELLOW. July 1921? One of the mss. is dated August 20, 1922, but in view of the letter to Salazar, where Lorca says he is working on "yellowing ballads" (see note to MOMENTS OF SONG), this is probably the date of initial revision. Revised again in 1926 and published ten years later in *Primeras canciones,* the version followed here, as edited by Hernández (*Primeras canciones,* 56–59). The first line of poem I is taken verbatim from a traditional ballad, "En lo alto de aquel monte / un gran palacio había" (High up on the mountain / was a great palace) (Menéndez Pelayo, 262); many ballads begin with similar phrases (e.g., the poem about the loveless *pastorcillo*; ibid., 254). In poem III, Lorca describes oxen, not bulls. In the autograph ms. Lorca crosses out two verses before lines 19–20 of poem IV: "Jacobus de Voragine, / take up your quill!" *The Golden Legend* was one of his favorite books.

PALIMPSESTOS / PALIMPSESTS. An undated ms. (probably from the same period as FOUR BALLADS IN YELLOW) includes seven poems: *City, Corridor, Air, Madrigal,* "Camino" (Road) (crossed out), *Front Page,* and "El pecho" (The Chest) (crossed out). The series was published in 1936 in *Primeras canciones*

(22–36) without *Air* and *Madrigal*. The version followed here is a revised one from late 1926 or early 1927 (Dinverno, 263–66; punctuation mine). The poet's brother, Francisco (*IGM* 111–12), writes about these poems: "Federico had a habit of establishing connections between the past and the present. This never involved meditative reflection; it was instinctive, as though he felt the call of distant times. [In PALIMPSESTS] the poet gives plastic expression to the hidden but vital trace of the passage of time . . . And yet, in a way, Federico was an antihistorical being, at least in the years of his early youth. I believe that, back then, he was unable to feel time as history; he felt it as an elemental, shaping force. To him, the living mystery of a perishable individual flower or the rock beside the water were more vital manifestations of time than the flux of great events." The "Red Towers" ("Torres Bermejas") mentioned in *Madrigal* are part of the ramparts of the Alhambra. The libidinous "Melisendra" is the protagonist of a well-known traditional ballad.

TRES ESTAMPAS DEL CIELO / THREE PRINTS OF THE SKY. Probably written July 1921. The original title was "Estampas del azul" (Engravings of the Blue), and the series also included "Estampa roja" (Red Engraving) (*B* 224), which begins, " 'Throw a bomb / at every constellation,' / thought the surly star / whose light was dead." The suite was revised and dated May 7, 1923, at the Residencia de Estudiantes, Madrid, and further revised in 1926. The first poem was published by Jorge Guillén in *Verso y Prosa* in August 1927 and reprinted by the poet Gerardo Diego in an anthology of the silliest poems in modern Spanish literature (see *Lola*, supplement to *Carmen. Revista Chica de Poesía Española* [Santander], 6–7 [June 1928], n.p.). The text followed here was sent to the editors of *Verso y Prosa* in 1927 and first published by Jacques Comincioli (68–73). In *Venus* Lorca is alluding to several paintings by Titian and probably also to the "Rokeby Venus" of Velázquez.

ESTAMPAS DEL MAR / SEASIDE PRINTS. Written in July 1921. The original title was "Sea. Classical Themes." Retitled and revised (with the elimination of two poems), probably in 1926, and dedicated to Emilio Prados and Manuel Altolaguirre, the two poets who had offered to publish *Suites* and who brought out the first edition of *Songs* at "Litoral" in Málaga. In the first version of *Contemplation*, lines 5–8, Lorca had written: "The classical sea / that sings ever in summer / in the major key / of Aeschylus." In 1924 Lorca writes to Fernández Almagro that he is about to visit Málaga, "where I will behold the sea, the one force of nature that torments and perturbs me. More than the sky, much more! . . . Before the sea I forget my sex, my condition, my soul, my gift of tears . . . everything! The only thing that bites at my heart is the desire to imitate it and become like it: bitter, phosphoreal, in eternal vigil" (*EC* 240).

HORAS DE VERANO / SUMMER HOURS. Written in July 1921? A fair copy is dated August 10, 1921. On the Spanish text, see De Paepe ("Tres *Suites*," 16–19). Following De Paepe, I have corrected the text given in the first edition of this book. SUMMER HOURS was inspired by a sequence entitled "El reló de sombra" (Shadow Clock) by the Mexican José Juan Tablada (1871–1945) describing the passage of the hours from 6 p.m. to midnight; see Tablada, *Obras*, 445–48, and "Haiku of a Day" in Paz, ed., *Mexican Poetry*, 150–52. Lorca's first poem refers to an itinerant figure who makes his rounds with a grinding stone (the "catherine wheel" mentioned here), sharpening knives and scissors and announcing his presence with a panpipe.

FERIAS / FAIRS. Dated July 27, 1921, published by Soley, 1997. In the ms. of *Wooden Horses*, between lines 12 and 13, Lorca seems to have wanted to omit these stanzas: "And, back from the shadows, / man has chained you / to a wheel that spins / on summer nights. // When he was a boy / Don Quijote rode you, / sighing / for Dulcinea who rode / as now, through the stars. // Poor wounded Pegasuses, / as a child I dreamt / of a love dead like the moon / on your white back." In *Song in Brown*, Lorca drew a box around the following stanza (after line 11), as though to omit it: "I would lose myself / in your trembling breasts, / in the dark depths / of your soft body."

CANCIONES BAJO LA LUNA / SUBLUNAR CANTOS. Incomplete? Probably written in July 1921. Originally titled "Luna." The first poem was transferred to *Songs* in 1926 (pp. 496–98): Lorca had jotted in the manuscript: "I will write a song, finishing this." A final page (or pages) of the manuscript seems to be missing. Lines 15–16 of *Salome & the Moon* are illegible in the manuscript. Lorca had originally written: "The boundless love / of Salome for John / was because his head / was a blank moon."

SOMBRA / SHADOW. Ms. dated July 29, 1921. On revising this suite in 1926 Lorca jotted beside the title: "chromatic variations on this theme (I will add a few)." *Pueblo*, line 6: The tower is a "St. Lucy in stone" because of the empty openings (sockets) where bells used to hang: according to legend, St. Lucy's eyes were gouged out when she was martyred. *Bat*: See Introduction, p. xxxiii–xxxiv. Ursa Major is known in Spanish as "el carro" (line 2), "the Wain." In line 17, the "two big white bulls" (literally, "oxen") probably allude to Boötes, "Boyero" (ox driver).

EL REGRESO / THE RETURN. A ms. dated August 6, 1921, with a canceled dedication to the cinematographer Luis Buñuel, includes eleven poems. Revised in 1923: in October of that year Lorca copied out *The Return* and *Oxbow* for Fernández Almagro: "The suite 'The Return' is long, but I'm sending you its two most delicate little spangles" (*EC* 212–13). Published, after elimination of five poems, in *La Verdad* (Murcia) in May 1924. The first poem was revised in 1931 for use in Act I of *Once Five Years Pass* (tr. Logan and Gil, 58–59). In an early draft of this poem (Belamich, 108), entitled "The Known Road," Lorca writes: "I'm going back. / / Let me go back / to my source! / / I don't want to get lost / in the sea. / / I'm going to the pure breeze / of my childhood / so my mother can put / a rose in my lapel."

LA SELVA DE LOS RELOJES / IN THE FOREST OF CLOCKS. August 1921? The textual history is similar to that of WATER SUITE, and I have followed the copy hurriedly made by Genaro Estrada from Lorca's disordered mss. Following the version in *Taller*, Belamich publishes *One . . . two . . . three* as part of *The Sphinx Hour*. In Estrada's copybook it is presented as a separate poem (title illegible). In line 12 of *I entered the forest . . .* Lorca plays with the sound of "oro" (gold) and "hora" (hour), as though the "oro del amor" (gold of love) were a masculine hour; the same sort of wordplay goes on in poem II of THREE PRINTS OF THE SKY. *He* is mistakenly divided by Estrada and Belamich (158–59) into two poems. Line 11: The hands of the clock look like hieroglyphics of swallows' wings. *First/Last Meditation*: In the Estrada copybook the first three lines are separated by several pages from lines 4–12, making it doubtful this is all one poem.

ÁLBUM BLANCO / WHITE ALBUM. Two mss. exist: (1) an autograph dated August 8, 1921, which Lorca gave to his friend the poet Gerardo Diego, and which was published in facsimile by Miguel García-Posada in *Los Domingos de ABC* (Madrid), August 17, 1986; (2) a typewritten copy in the AFGL which was probably made in 1926 but is dated August 18, 1921. I have followed the latter. *Final Page*: José de Espronceda and Gustavo Adolfo Bécquer epitomize Spanish Romantic poetry; the latter has always been much admired by Spanish schoolgirls.

SECRETOS / SECRETS. Written in Asquerosa, August 11, 1921, at a moment when Lorca tells a friend he is "resting in this marvelous countryside, and working hard on a dramatic poem and on my poetry, which has a new norm and a new aesthetics" (*EC* 127). Five poems from this suite are published here for the first time in English. For the Spanish text, see Christian De Paepe, "Tres Suites," 13–14, and *OC* I: 234–38. *Woodcutter*, lines 6–10: Literally, "I returned with all of the stars on my back, / the whole bundle of the white night!" *Mirror*, line 1: *Cintillo* can also be a decorative hatband (as in *It's True*). *Journey*, line 3: For Lorca's drawing of the legendary griffin bird, see *Dibujos*, nos. 55, 56. Line 4: Delgadina is the tragic protagonist of one the most popular traditional ballads (often sung by children) of Spain and Latin America: her father, the king, makes love to her, and when she resists, she is confined to a tower, where she dies. Lorca had already written about her in an early poem, "Ensueño de romances" ("Daydream of Ballads") in *PI*, 112. For the text of the ballad, see Díaz Roig, 281. Lines 9–10: Allusion to the traditional song "Las tres cautivas," about three Christian girls taken captive by the Moors and found by "la fuente fría" (the cool fountain). Text in Alvar, pp. 231–32. *Doncella*: Maiden.

SEIS CANCIONES DE ANOCHECER / SIX SONGS AT NIGHTFALL. Ms. dated August 14, 1921. *Delirium*: On revising the poem in 1926 Lorca crossed out the end of the poem: "too tender / and chaste / too poetic / and vague / to be drunk / by this bad heart of mine / which has feasted too long on light / and song." *Memento*: The seven-syllable verses, refrain, and imagery recall the popular children's ballad "Mambrú se fue a la guerra . . ." and Lorca's Spanish readers would remember its lighthearted melody, sung by children holding hands in a circle. Compare lines 1–9 with those from the traditional ballad: "Que Mambrú ya se ha muerto / lo llevan a enterrar. / En caja de terciopelo / con tapa de cristal" (For Mambrú is dead / they are taking him to be buried / in a velvet coffin / with a glass lid) (Llorca, 43–45; Celaya, 195–97). Lorca has identified the moon with Mambrú's wife, "la Mambruna"; cf. Vigón, 66–67. The singing of "snakes at their fountains" (line 41; cf. *6:00 p.m.* in MOMENTOS DE LA TARDE) occurs in traditional ballads from Asturias in northern Spain (e.g., J. Menéndez Pidal, 156).

PAÍSES / COUNTRIES. The ms. appears to date from November 1921. Only the first page has been found.

SUITE DEL AGUA / WATER SUITE. Written fall 1921? Published in *Taller* (Mexico) in 1938 after a copy made in Spain during Lorca's lifetime by his friend the Mexican writer and diplomat Genaro Estrada (1887–1937). The original ms. is lost, and I have used a photocopy of the Estrada ms. (now in the AFGL) in correcting the text of Belamich, who, following *Taller*, includes nine poems: *Homeland, Tremor, Acacia, Curve, Beehive, North, South, East*, and *West. Acacia* also appears in GARDEN IN UMBER. Although *Curve*, with its mention of a "vereda azul" (blue footpath), might conceivably allude to a river (as well as to the night sky) and belong to WATER SUITE, *Beehive* seems thematically unrelated and might belong to a different series. The last four poems belong to CROSS. *Temblor*: Following García-Posada (*OC* I:899), I have corrected line 1 from *tendría* to *turbia*.

CRUZ / CROSS. Fall 1921? Published mistakenly in previous editions as part of WATER SUITE. The image of the arrow without a target occurs in *The Guitar* in *Poem of the Deep Song*, written in November 1921. The word "escala," translated as "diapason" in *East* and *West*, is the musical scale: the chromatic scale in line 4 of *West* and "set [literally, 'conjunct'] degrees" in *East* ("adjacent degrees of the staff representing successive tones of the scale").

TRES CREPÚSCULOS / THREE CREPUSCULAR POEMS. Written on the same day—November 11, 1921—as *Poem of the Gypsy* Siguiriya from *Poem of the Deep Song*: an astonishing example of Lorca's poetic versatility. Revised in 1926.

[RÍO AZUL] / [BLUE RIVER]. Date uncertain. Written late 1920 to early 1922. Similar imagery is found in a letter to the guitarist Regino Sainz de la Maza written around December 1920: "I am wildly happy over a series of things I'll tell you about when we see each other (hope it will be soon), and which give my life a high artistic meaning, a true, purely spiritual meaning. I am suffering from real *attacks* of lyricism, and am working away with the excitement of a child building a crèche . . . You know, Regino, curiosity has claws like a cat. Sharp little claws that scratch at the wall of the chest and make Lady Distraction close her one hundred odious, dizzy eyes . . . If you only knew what enthusiasm I feel! My hands are full of dead kisses (apples of snow with the trembling furrow of the lips), and I hope to toss them into the broken air and catch some new ones" (*EC* 93–94). Lines 15–25 of *Dreams* are remembered in a prose piece entitled "Paseo" (Promenade or Avenue) dated February 3, 1922: "Through the branches of the forest the round moon looked like an inert white muscle . . . Down the long promenade, open wide like a huge choir book, went the double procession of the benches, in search of other landscapes and other rhythms. The benches on this provincial promenade are as tender as mothers' laps and as dramatic and deep as old mirrors. They are on the outskirts of the city, where it flows out into the countryside, and they have saved many a shipwrecked person from a certain death. On this January night they are waving white sails of mist beneath the poplar trees and dreaming of a [illegible] of straight lines." In the same piece Lorca describes a vision of a "rare country where I met no one, a country that was floating down a bluish river." Looking into the nighttime sky, he discovers all the stars were blinking their luminous eyelids and sending telegraphic messages to one another. "More than any other star, Sirius was transmitting orange *tics* and green *tacs* [sound of the telegraph], to the astonishment of all" (*OC* I:664).

[SUITE]. Incomplete: pages 1 and 5 of the manuscript are missing. Dated December 7, 1921.

LA PALMERA / THE PALM TREE. Ms. dated March 25, 1922. Lorca had resumed work on *Suites* after composing most of *Poem of the Deep Song*. I have corrected the title ("Límites," not "Símiles") and text of the first two poems (cf. *B* 130–31). The only ms. is a rough draft. In *Limits*, Lorca crossed out these final lines (tr. Jerome Rothenberg): "The star floats in / the Mediterranean. / / (The blue is the forest / set free). / / (The sea is a palm tree / from a bird's / eye view.)" Lines 9–12 of the second poem were crossed out in 1926, but are restored here because syntactically necessary. In 1925, while he was visiting Salvador Dalí in Cadaqués, Lorca wrote out poem 3, probably from memory, and included only verses 10–14 and 21–28 (*B* 130).

NEWTON. Ms. dated March 26, 1922. As he sat in his garden in the moonlight, Newton saw an apple fall to the ground, asked himself why the moon did not fall also, and began to explore the question of gravity: this is the legend (popularized by Voltaire) to which Lorca alludes. *Question*: In his lecture on Góngora (1926) Lorca observes: "An apple means no less to [Góngora] than an ocean because he knows that each is infinite in its own world. The life of an apple, from when it is a tenuous blossom until it falls golden from the tree to the grass, is just as serious, just as grand as the periodic rhythm of the tides. And a poet ought to know this" (*DS* 69).

HISTORIETAS DEL VIENTO / VIGNETTES OF THE WIND. July 1922. The original title (crossed out in the ms.) was "July Poems." The first two and the last one were published in subsequent issues of *Verso y Prosa* (August and September 1927). Two others, "Rose" and *School*, were sent to Fernández Almagro in a letter of July 1922: "I am settling down to work and have done some prose, badly written but full of hope. In verse I am writing some 'historietas del viento' . . . We'll see . . . But how admirable, how full of perspective the wind is! Here they come—two little pastry puffs of wind" (*EC* 151–52). In a characteristic moment of self-censorship, Lorca crossed out the final stanza of poem III: "and it takes on the sweet / blush of mother of pearl / when it reaches the breasts / of my love" (*B* 86). Lines 7–10 had read: "The breeze / wells up like the white placenta / of dawn." The eliminated poem, "Rose," reads: "Wind rose! / / (Metamorphosis / of the black dot.) / / Wind rose! / / (Dot in bloom, / opened dot!)"

CÚCO-CUCO-CUCÓ / CÚCKOO-CUCKOO-CUCKÓO. A typewritten ms. (followed here) is dated July 25, 1923, but this must be the date of revision. In early August 1922 Lorca writes to Melchor Fernández Almagro: "I have *composed* several poems about the cuckoo (admirable, symbolic bird) . . ." (*EC* 155). Much of this "symbolism" relates to time, not only because of the cuckoo clock (*Cuckoo's Second Nocturne*) but also because the bird itself is associated in folklore with longevity: "seeing that the cuckoo is the annual herald of the spring and also that it disappears each year, it [is] easy to infer that the same bird always reappears each spring and sings its song in the same grove of trees year after year. It is but a little step forward to the further inference that the cuckoo never dies" (Field, 182). Lines 8–9 of the first poem reappear in a slightly different form in *Once Five Years Pass* (tr. Logan and Gil, 123–25): "El sueño va sobre el tiempo / flotando como un velero" (Dream flies over time / floating like a sailboat). The structure and refrain of *Cuckoo's First Nocturne* is similar to that of *And Then* in *Poem of the Deep Song*. *Cuckoo's Second Nocturne* is followed in the 1922 manuscript by an early draft of the poem entitled *Debussy* (in *Songs*), one stanza of which (later crossed out) seems vaguely related to the cuckoo poems: "This anguish of the hours / which is bound around my head / will dry up my sighs / in the final Springs" (*M* 135). This poem led directly into the following series, ENSUEÑOS DEL RÍO. Years later, Lorca detached *Last Nocturne* from the suite, eliminating lines 1–3 and 16–18 (*B* 121).

ENSUEÑOS DEL RÍO / DAYDREAMS OF A RIVER. Incomplete. In July and August 1922, Lorca returned to one of his favorite themes: water. He tells Fernández

Almagro that he has composed " 'ensueños del río,' emotional little poems that I feel deep inside me, in the darkest corner of my unhappy heart. You have no idea how I suffer when I see myself portrayed in the poems: I imagine I am a huge violet-colored dragonfly [*cinife*] skimming the backwaters of feeling. I work away, one stitch after another, like a shoemaker, and . . . it all comes to naught!" (*EC* 155; cf. BACKWATERS). Only the three poems given here can definitely be said to have belonged to this suite. Lorca sent *Lazy River* to Almagro, calling it "a stone from the portico which I am planning." In 1926, as he ordered the *Suites* for publication, he gave the first two poems the subtitles "Río Genil" and "En el Cubillas," the two rivers of his native village, Fuente Vaqueros. The first poem was retitled *Preludio* and used in *Songs* (*M* 206–7); see p. 529. Lorca had used the strange image of lines 17–18 of the first poem several times previously to describe his emotion as a pianist; e.g., "Cielo azul . . ." (*PI* 331): "Chopin . . . / on fingers of white Autumn / buds in my heart / to die in my hands."

MADRIGALES / MADRIGALS. Composed at the same time as DAYDREAMS OF A RIVER (July or August 1922). No doubt these are two more of the "emotional little poems" Lorca mentions in the letter to Fernández Almagro (see DAY-DREAMS . . .). I have restored several lines to the incomplete text presented in the Menarini edition of *Canciones* (315–16). Another love poem with water imagery composed around the same period, *Evening*, was used in *Songs*.

MEDITACIONES Y ALEGORÍAS DEL AGUA / MEDITATIONS & ALLEGORIES OF WA-TER. Written July–August 1922. Introduction to a series Lorca never completed. In the letter to Fernández Almagro (see note to DAYDREAMS OF A RIVER) Lorca continues: ". . . these days I feel pregnant. I have *seen* an admirable book that must be written and which *I* would like to write: 'Meditations and Allegories of Water.' What profound, living miracles one can tell about the water! The water poem of my book has blossomed in my soul. I see a great poem about the water, part Oriental and part Christian-European: a poem that sings, in ample verses or (*molto rubato*) in prose, the passionate life and the martyrdom of the water. A great Life of the Water with meticulous analysis of the concentric circle, the reflection, the drunken music (unblent with silence) of the currents. The river and the irrigation ditches have come deep inside me. Now one can truly say that the Guadalquivir or the Miño is born in Fuente Miña and empties out into Federico García Lorca, small-time dreamer and son of the water. I ask God to grant me sufficient strength and joy (yes, joy!) so that I can write this book . . . of devotion for those who travel through the desert . . . I can already see the chapters and the stanzas (there would be prose and verse), for example: The Looms of the Water, Map of the Water, The Ford of Sounds, Meditation on the Spring, Backwaters. And later, when I study (yes, study!) (pray to the saints to give me joy) the dead water, I will write an incredibly moving poem about the Alhambra, seen as the water's pantheon. I believe that if I were really to tackle this I could do something fine, and if I were a great poet, *really* a great poet, perhaps this would be my masterpiece" (*EC* 155). *Border*, line 1: "high desert" is *secano* in the original: drylands. Travelers are often astonished on entering the Vega of Granada (the "river valley" depicted here): "The line of irrigation, like a Rubicon, divides the desert from a paradise; while all within its influence is green and fruitful, all beyond it is barren and tawny" (Ford, I:291). The "border" or "dividing" line is the Cubillas River. See Gibson, *Lorca's Granada*, 246. For another translation of these prose poems, see *SG* 57–59.

CASTILLO DE FUEGOS ARTIFICIALES . . . / BARRAGE OF FIREWORK POEMS . . .
Ms. dated August 8, 1922, in Asquerosa, two months after Lorca's twenty-fourth birthday. Revised in 1926. In the third poem, Lorca eliminated these three final lines: "Six flowers / which scatter / their resounding pollen." He speaks proudly of Granada's firework manufacturers in his lecture "How a City Sings from November to November": "a legion of pyrotechnicians who build towers of noise, with an art equal to that of the Court of the Lions [in the Alhambra], to irritate the square water of the reflecting ponds" (*SG* 98).

RUEDAS DE FORTUNA / WHEELS OF FORTUNE. Incomplete. Ms. undated, on the same paper as BARRAGE OF FIREWORKS (dated August 8) and p. 20 of a ms. of *The Tragicomedy of Don Cristóbal and Mistress Rosita*, dated August 5, 1922. Probably written about the same time as *Merry-go-round* from *Songs*.

CARACOL / CARACOLS/SNAILS. Ms. dated November 1922 and revised in fall 1926. Dinverno gives both versions, and I have followed the second (258–60). In the first poem, Lorca alludes to the traditional children's lyric "Caracol, caracol, / Saca los cuernos al sol . . ." (Snail, snail / Bring your horns out into the sunlight); see Rodríguez Marín, 60, and Brenan, 110. The latter explains that in some Spanish villages songs like this were used as snail charms. "When rain had fallen women and children would go out after dark with lanterns to collect the big Roman snails that fed on the grass, and when they did this they sang it. The song is presumably intended to deceive the snail into thinking that the lantern is the sun and that it is time for it to get up and show itself." Lorca copies the third stanza of *Spiral* in a letter to a friend in 1928: the "pure lance without a knight" reminds him of Salvador Dalí, and the spiraling "Solomonic path" (i.e., a path that spirals like a Baroque column) is his own (*EC* 544).

[EPITAFIO A UN PÁJARO] / [EPITAPH FOR A BIRD]. Incomplete. Ms. dated November 1922. The erratic punctuation of the ms. (not a final draft) has been imitated here. In line 8 of the first poem, Lorca refers to a brother born in July 1900, who died of pneumonia when he was only two years old (see Stainton, 12).

SURTIDORES / WATER JETS. Incomplete. Ms. undated. November 1922? But perhaps begun as early as the summer of 1921. The first poem was retitled *Granada 1850* and used in *Songs*. The ms., which was given by Lorca to Luis Buñuel, is published in facsimile in Federico García Lorca, *Surtidores*, ed. Paul Rogers, 28–34. At least one page is missing: it would have contained the beginning of the poem before *Garden*.

HERBARIOS / HERBALS. December 1922. Published posthumously in *Taller*, December 1938 (see WATER SUITE). The text has been checked against a photocopy of Genaro Estrada's not very reliable copybook (see note to IN THE FOREST OF CLOCKS).

LUNAR GRAPEFRUITS POEMS. Published here are two drafts of the same poem: by early August 1923, Lorca had begun to revise and unify them. IN THE FOREST . . . is the earlier version (mentions of "el bosque," "the forest," are crossed out in several, but not all, of the GARDEN poems, and the word "jardín" [garden] is added in its place). Neither manuscript is complete, and the order of the poems (which differs here from that given by Belamich) is largely conjectural, for Lorca mixed one draft with another as he worked, did not number the pages carefully, set poems aside for revision or moved them to *Songs*, leaving gaps in the manuscript, and then suddenly abandoned the project. In this second edition I have reordered the poems following Dinverno (268–86).

Two letters of July–August 1923 tell of Lorca's progress on this series, the most ambitious of the suites. In the first he writes his friends Fernández Almagro and José de Ciria y Escalante: "I have finished a poem, 'The Garden of the Lunar Grapefruits,' and am willing to spend the whole summer working on it—I'm very anxious to get it exactly the way I've seen it. You could say that I have gone about it *feverishly*, for I've worked twenty days with their twenty nights . . . just to *pin it down*. The landscapes in this poem are absolutely motionless, with neither wind nor rhythm. I noticed that my verses were slipping out of my hands, and that my poetry was fleeting and *alive*. Reacting to that feeling, this poem is static [*extático*] and somnambulistic. My *garden* is the garden of possibilities, the garden of what is not, but could (and at times) *should* have been, the garden of theories that passed invisibly by and children who have not been born. Each word in the poem was a butterfly, and I have had to hunt them down one by one. / Later I fought off my two worldly enemies (the enemies of all poets): Eloquence and Common Sense; terrifying hand-to-hand combat, as in the battles of the *Poem of the Cid*. If you are true friends you'll write me quickly, and I will send you a song from the garden, for example the 'song of the seven-hearted boy' or the 'lament of the girl with no voice,' which seem to me to be pretty well *accomplished*" (*EC* 196–97).

In the second letter, mailed on July 30, 1923, Lorca tells Ciria y Escalante he is "polishing" his "extremely strange garden of lunar grapefruits": "I am sending you several 'engravings' from this poem, on condition you not read them to anyone, for they are not yet finished . . . Now more than ever I find that words have a phosphorescent glow and are full of mysterious senses and sounds. I feel real panic when I sit down to write! And what joy I feel when I read our old poets! [e.g., Fernando de Herrera and Lupercio Leonardo de Argensola]." He encloses a selection of seven poems, which he calls "estampitas" (little engravings), reiterating that the poems should not be shown to anyone, for "all of this will change." The poems are given in this order: *Song of the Seven-Hearted Boy*, *Portico*, *White Satyr*, *Engravings of the Garden (I)* (titled "Otra estampita": Another Engraving), *Frieze* (later transferred to *Songs*), *Little Song of the Unborn Child*, and *Wake Up/Ring Out* (identified as the final poem in the series). See *EC* 198–205.

EN EL BOSQUE DE LAS TORONJAS DE LUNA / IN THE FOREST OF THE LUNAR GRAPEFRUITS.

Prólogo / Prologue. Incomplete: final page missing. The word "extático" in the subtitle, prologue, and elsewhere in the poem has two meanings: not only "ecstatic," "enraptured," but also—and perhaps foremost in Lorca's mind—"static," "motionless" (from the homophonous "estático"). See the introductory note to LUNAR GRAPEFRUITS POEMS, above. In the *Prologue*, where he writes "I tried singing, keeping my voice big and tense in the air," he had originally written "I tried singing, so that my voice might have the ineffable, mysterious Italian background."

Reflexión / Reflection (in the sense of "meditation"). Incomplete? Two initial stanzas, later crossed out, betoken Lorca's yearning for a motionless poem, "with neither wind nor rhythm": "Wind who come and go, / look for your heart. / Tie yourself in a ring, / and pull up short, wind. / / Sun and Moon of time, / forget the road. / Draw up short and destroy / the tangle of rhythm."

Situación / Situation. "Tan-tan. / ¿Quién es?" (Literally: Knock knock! / Who's there?) is the beginning of a Spanish children's rhyme (see the untitled poem on p. 882–83). The narrator's transformation into a hundred-year-old man and his conversation with the devil in the next poem is reminiscent of one of Lorca's favorite stories, Victor Hugo's "Légende du beau Pécopin et de la belle Baldour," in *La Légende des Siècles*.

EN EL JARDÍN DE LAS TORONJAS DE LUNA / IN THE GARDEN OF THE LUNAR GRAPEFRUITS. Despite the clues provided by the letter to Ciria y Escalante and by *Prologue*, the order of the poems is uncertain. For the Spanish text I have followed Dinverno (274–86), who relates this suite to a perception of Maurice Maeterlinck, in "The Foretelling of the Future" (from *The Double Garden*, 1907): "There is no reason why we should not see that which does not yet exist, considering that which does not yet exist in its relation to us must needs already have its being and manifest itself somewhere." What Lorca drew from Maeterlinck, according to Dinverno (231), is the notion that " 'that which does not yet exist' always already resides in its own space parallel to ours, and although we may not be able to stay permanently in that area, by analogy, Maeterlinck contends that we should be able to visit the unrealized and inhabit that space for at least a time."

Pórtico / Portico. For Lorca's fanciful drawing of the griffin vulture (which inhabits the salt marshes of Huelva in southern Spain), see *Dibujos*, 55, 56, and pages 166–67.

Los puentes colgantes / Floating Bridges. Or "Suspension Bridges."

Estampas del jardín / Engraving of the Garden. There is no way to know for sure what poems were intended for this section. In his letter to Ciria y Escalante, Lorca uses the word "estampas" generically. The paper, ink, script, etc., of the ms. of *Widow of the moon . . .* matches that of the first *Engraving*, and the two poems may have been composed at the same time.

Glorieta / Pergola. Circled in the manuscript, but not eliminated. Lorca is remembering a traditional ballad about an apparition ("Paseábase Marbella / de la sala al ventanal": Marbella was pacing / from the room to the window), which he believed to epitomize Spain's obsession with death: "If you are my pretty friend, / why don't you look at me? / The eyes I looked at you with / I have given to the dark. / If you are my pretty friend, / why don't you kiss me? / The lips I kissed you with / I have given to the earth. / If you are my pretty friend, / why don't you hold me tight? / The arms I hugged you with / are covered now in worms" (*SD* 56).

Canción del muchacho de siete corazones / Song of the Seven-Hearted Boy. The "seven girls" are probably the seven colors mentioned in *Song of the Seven Maidens (Theory of the Rainbow)* in *Songs*. The phantom galley would remind Spanish readers of the ballad of Count Arnaldos (Smith, 208).

Arco de lunas / Moonbow. Lorca wrote "No" in the margin of the manuscript (as though he had considered eliminating this poem), but seems to have changed his mind, for he made a fair copy. See also the note to *From* NARCISSUS, below.

Duna / Dune. Lorca composed two endings for this poem, without crossing out either. The other reads (tr. Rothenberg): "Then the garden will follow / where time has its shore / will be beating like crazy / at the gateway of life."

Appendix *to* Suites

Viaje / Train Ride. Ms. dated November 1920. This poem and the next two are presented by Belamich (240–42) as an incomplete suite. Lorca gives a fantastic turn to a genre—the poem about a train trip—cultivated by Antonio Machado (see "Otro viaje" [Another Trip] in *Poesía y prosa,* ed. O. Macrí, 550–52) and, in a more prosaic narrative vein, by the nineteenth-century poet Ramón de Campoamor.

Después / Afterwards. August 1921? A first draft (crossed out) of IN THE FOREST OF CLOCKS begins at the end of the page.

Las tres / 3:00 p.m. From a one-page autograph ms. in the AFGL, the characteristics of which (paper, ink, handwriting, etc.) match that of SEASIDE PRINTS. Probably written July 1921. The poem may once have formed part of a series (see SUMMER HOURS).

Desde aquí / From Out Here. Undated. Probably related to THREE PRINTS OF THE SKY.

Tarde / Evening. Ms. dated November 1922.

DIURNO / DAY POEMS. Ms. dated December 27, 1922. The title plays upon the notion of "Nocturno" ("Nocturne"). Guillermo de Torre, to whom these poems are dedicated, was editor of *Hélices* (Helixes, Spirals; cf. lines 7, 21 of *The Reachon*), an Argentine literary journal with avant-garde pretensions.

De NARCISO / *From* NARCISSUS. Using manuscript evidence unnoticed by others, Dinverno (246) reconstructs a suite entitled NARCISO composed of the following poems: *Friso* (originally titled "Paisaje"), *Puerta, Yo, Arco de lunas, Altas torres,* and *Deposorio.* Three of these poems—*Friso, Altas torres* (later entitled *Scene*), and *Deposorio*—were moved by Lorca to *Songs.* One—*Arco de lunas*—was moved to the LUNAR GRAPEFRUITS series. Like the LUNAR GRAPEFRUITS poems, NARCISO involves a journey in which the speaker rejects societal norms and voices anguish over his inability to engender children.

Canciones / Songs

Published 1927. Although Lorca gave the years 1921–24 below the title, these poems were written between 1921 and 1926. Between December 1925 and February 1926, at a time when he felt disenchanted with his work in progress, Lorca went back over almost all of the poems he had composed over the preceding five years. Three books "emerged" from his papers: the series he had written in 1921 (*Poem of the Deep Song*); an open-ended collection of poetic sequences (*Suites*), and a cumulus of short lyrical poems (*Songs*). The "deep song" poems had an obvious thematic and structural unity, but as Lorca winnowed his manuscripts, revised poems, added titles and dedications, and made fair copies, he agonized over which poems to include in *Suites* and which in *Songs*: the same themes run through both books, and poems were transferred back and forth between them.

In October 1926 the poet Emilio Prados, who was running a small press (Litoral) in Málaga with Manuel Altolaguirre, visited Lorca in Granada and sequestered all of his handwritten originals, promising to publish three lovely editions. A month later, three poems from *The Gypsy Ballads* appeared with errata in Prados's literary magazine, *Litoral.* Lorca reproached Prados for the "ten enormous errata" which had destroyed the "hardness, the flinty *grace*" of his poems (*EC* 415). Prados scolded Lorca for his unintelligible handwriting and returned the mss., asking the poet to make the fair copies *himself*: "I am becoming a neurasthenic, translating you from the Chinese" (postcard, AFGL). In the end, only *Songs* was published at Litoral (May 1927; second edition, Madrid, 1929, at Revista de Occidente, directed by the philosopher José Ortega y Gasset).

The final ordering and selection of *Songs* caused Lorca "genuine anguish": "I have omitted [some of the] rhythmic songs despite their success because I want the book to have the high air of the sierra" (*EC* 417). By the time *Songs* appeared he felt himself "master" of the book, proud of his workmanship and editorial discernment: "*Songs* represents a sharp, serene lyrical effort, and to me it seems great poetry (great in the sense of nobility and quality, not of worth)" (*EC* 418). Even the long delay in publication seemed to have been beneficial. Fernández Almagro had warned Lorca that others were copying his unpublished poems. "Nothing could be further from the truth," he replies. "*They have come out unscathed, the poor things! But they have a certain something, and that something is what cannot be copied. I don't think music is everything, as do certain 'young poets'; I give my love to the word, and not to the sound. My songs are not of ash. How useful it was to have withheld them!*" (*EC* 318–19).

The Spanish text follows the edition of Mario Hernández. For chronological and textual information I have made use of the edition of Piero Menarini and of mss. in the AFGL and elsewhere.

Canción de las siete doncellas / Song of the Seven Maidens. 1923? The subtitle (added in 1926) and the questions posed in lines 11–12 (also added in 1926) connect this poem to *Suites*, where Lorca had explored the "garden of possibilities, the garden of what is not, but could (and at times *should*) have been, the garden of theories that went invisibly by, and children who have not been born" (*EC* 197). In a note to this poem Hernández (ed., 190) points out that the word *theory* in the subtitle and in the title of this section of *Songs* should be understood in its etymological meaning as a "procession." He adds that the word was used this way by Rubén Darío and other Modernist poets, and that in the fourteen poems in this section "a sense of procession, process, or transit prevails, as things or beings (colors, air, days, months, doves, hours, harlequin, or trees) succumb to the passage of time and to their consummation in death."

Nocturno esquemático / Nocturne in Outline. Ms. dated July 21, 1924. Carlos Bousoño (Alonso and Bousoño, 240) notices that the "outline" (or "scheme") is correlative: the *fennel* gives its aroma to the *air*, the *serpent* leaves its *trail* on the *earth*; the *rushes* are *apart* (or alone) in the *half-shadow*.

La canción del colegial / Schoolboy's Song. Fair copy dated February 1922.

El canto quiere ser luz . . . / Song would like to be light . . . Ms. dated 1925. Menarini aptly compares this poem to *Death* in *Poet in New York*.

Tiovivo / Merry-go-round. Written in 1922. In "How a City Sings from November to November," Lorca evokes the celebration of Corpus Christi in Granada each June. "Along come the dragon and dwarfs of Corpus Christi, and in the streets Granada's women with their lovely naked arms and wombs like dark magnolias suddenly open their green, orange and blue parasols, in a frenzy of lights, violins and carriages, in a carousel of love, gallantry and nostalgia, in the Castle-of-No-Return of the fireworks" (*SG* 108).

Balanza / Balance. "A poem tracing the decline of day and daytime movement, 'Balanza' [Scale] . . . is aptly titled because it describes the eventual balancing of night and day . . . day becomes as still (as death-like) as night . . . The title is self-reflexive, since the poem consists solely of parallel, balanced contrasts" (Quance, 258).

Canción con movimiento / Song with Movement. Probably August 1922.

Refrán / Proverb. The title alludes to a rich popular tradition of rhymed proverbs about the weather and the seasons.

Friso / Frieze. Sent to José de Ciria y Escalante on July 30, 1923, as a sample of IN THE GARDEN OF THE LUNAR GRAPEFRUITS (*EC* 204). See also the note to *From* NARCISSUS, above.

Cazador / Hunter. A fair copy was sent to Jorge Guillén in mid-February 1927 and published by him in *Verso y Prosa* the following April. On sending the ms., along with other poems, Lorca had complained: "None of these things are any good. I see I am good for nothing. They're from 1921, from when I was a child. Perhaps someday I'll be able to express the extraordinarily *real* drawings I am dreaming of. But for now, I'm far from that" (*EC* 435–36; mss. of letter and poem in *Papers of Jorge Guillén*, Houghton Library, Harvard University). In fact, *Hunter* appears to have been written in August 1922. In the Harvard ms., it is numbered "V" (later crossed out), suggesting that it once formed part of a longer sequence, perhaps one of the suites.

Fábula / Fable. 1921? Compare SEASIDE PRINTS. Lines 6–7: Lorca is recreating a verse from Rubén Darío's "Sinfonia en gris mayor" (Symphony in Gray Major): "El mar como un vasto cristal azogado / Refleja la lámina de un cielo de zinc" (The sea, like a vast mirror, / Reflects the lamina of a zinc-colored sky); *Prosas profanas,* 134.

Agosto . . . / August . . . Published in *Boletín del Centro Artístico de Granada* in September 1924, with the title "Cancioncilla" (Little Song). Menarini explains that "contraponientes" (line 2) is a neologism formed from *contra* (against) and *ponientes* (sunsets, western skies). Melon ("tasty moon") is sometimes eaten in Spain with dark bread.

Arlequín / Harlequin. Ms. dated 1923. For Lorca's pen-and-ink drawings of harlequins, see *Dibujos,* nos. 117, 122, 126, 127, etc.

Cortaron tres árboles / Three Trees Were Cut Down. Originally entitled "Elegy for Three Trees," the ms. is undated. 1926?

NOCTURNOS DE LA VENTANA / NOCTURNES FROM THE WINDOW. From the cycle of *Suites.* Typewritten ms. dated May 7, 1923, in the Residencia de Estudiantes, Madrid, but probably written earlier (summer 1922?). The same date and place appear on a fair copy of THREE PRINTS OF THE SKY. Poem 4: Cf. *Little Girl Drowned in the Well (Granada and Newburgh)* in *Poet in New York* and *Nocturne of the Drowned Youth* from *Six Galician Poems.* NOCTURNES probably formed part of *Suites.*

Canción china en Europa / Song of China in Europe. Ms. dated November 17, 1926. Translated into English during Lorca's lifetime by his friend Stanley Richardson. See "Chinese Song in Europe," *1616 (English & Spanish Poetry)* (London), 8 (1935), 162–63.

Cancioncilla sevillana / Sevillian Ditty. Both the *oro/moro* rhyme and the use of dialect (*naranjel*) are reminiscent of traditional poetry. Menarini (97) identifies a children's song echoed here: "Coche de oro / para el moro, / coche de plata / para la infanta" (A golden carriage / for the Moor; / A silver carriage / for the princess) (cf. Llorca, 101). Lorca is also imitating a well-known folk song glossed by Góngora (Cohen, 273–74) and Calderón de la Barca (Act II of *El alcalde de Zalamea*): "Las flores del romero, / niña Isabel, / hoy son flores azules, / mañana serán miel" (The flowers of the rosemary, / child Isabel, / are blue flowers today; / tomorrow they will be honey) (italics mine).

Caracola / Seashell. Ms. copy dated 1926.

El lagarto está llorando . . . / Mr. Lizard is crying . . . Ms. dated November 1925; dedicated and revised in 1926. Choreographed and staged at the Instituto Escuela in Madrid in 1933 or 1934, according to Robertson (79), who believes that the poem "derive[s] from a circle game [Lorca] probably played as a child in Granada, and which we find preserved in folklore collections of the late nineteenth century: 'La niña / que vino de Sevilla / y trajo / un delantal muy majo, / ahora / como se le ha perdido / la niña llora' (The girl / who came from Seville / brought / a pretty white apron. / Now / that it is lost / she's crying)."

Canción cantada / Song Sung. Sent to Fernández Almagro in a letter of September 1924 (*EC* 247), with the title "Cancioncilla" (Ditty). On the griffon bird, cf. *Portico*.

Canción tonta / Silly Song. This was the third poem in a ms. series of November 1925 entitled "Canciones tontas del niño y su mama" (Silly Songs of the Child and His Mother). For the first two poems, omitted from *Canciones*, see Menarini, 289–90. The poem *Mr. Lizard is crying . . .* seems to have formed part of the same series, and in a note on the manuscript, Lorca reminds himself to write others, including one about "the boy who lays an egg." A poetry of "silliness" and deliberate naïveté arises in Spain in the 1920s, the golden years of silent film comedy. Cf. *The Hen*. Rafael Alberti's *Marinero en tierra* (*Sailor on Land*) (1925) and *Yo fui un tonto . . .* (*I Was a Fool . . .*) (1928) and Dalí's and Lorca's own numerous drawings of "putrefactos" (socially rotten types) belong to the same genre. "[In contrast to the German satirist George Grosz], you and I have elevated idiocy to a *lyrical* category," Dalí writes Lorca in 1925. "We have arrived at a new lyricism of human stupidity; but with affection and tenderness . . ." (Santos Torroella, 16). The poem was reprinted, along with *Frieze*, by Gerardo Diego in 1928 in an anthology of "tontología" (silliness; both deliberate and involuntary) in *Lola* (Santander). See note to THREE PRINTS OF THE SKY.

Canción de jinete (1860) / Rider's Song (1860). Fair copy dated August 12, 1923. The year would evoke an era of contraband in the Sierra Morena, the formidable mountain range separating Andalusia from the north.

Adelina de paseo / Adeline Out Walking. Dated July 19, 1924. According to the poet's brother, the song is based on a popular tune: "I went to the sea to look for oranges, / but the sea has none, / and I came back soaked / by the waves that come and go" (Belamich, ed., *Oeuvres*, 1366). The title was added in 1926.

Zarzamora con el tronco gris . . . / Bramble gray of stalk . . . Ms. dated August 23, 1924. Suggested by a children's song, "Bramble, where are you going? / To look for what you give me not" (Ramos-Gil, 145).

Mi niña se fue a la mar . . . / My girl went down to the sea . . . Rough draft dated "October 5," probably 1923. Followed in the ms. by *Second Anniversary*. Line 10: In a prose poem about bullfighting (1935) Lorca compares Seville's cathedral tower, the Giralda, to a "mule decked out for the fair" ("enjaezada como una mula de feria") (*SG* 85).

Tarde / Evening. Fair copy dated July 1923, but the first draft is probably from the summer of 1922, when Lorca was composing MADRIGALS and DAYDREAMS OF A RIVER. Lucía, the "morenita de Granada," is also mentioned in PALIMPSESTS.

Canción de jinete / Rider's Song. Ms. dated July 4, 1924. Published in the *Boletín del Centro Artístico de Granada*, September 1924, and reprinted in Gerardo Diego's anthologies of 1932 and 1934. Lorca's brother, Francisco, writes memorably about this poem, comparing it with Góngora's sonnet to Córdoba (in *De Garcilaso a Lorca*, 222–24). *Rider's Song* reminded Roy Campbell (*Lorca*, 82–85) of "the Scotch-English border ballads, which concentrate a tragedy into one or two simple verses: 'Toom came his saddle all bloody to see, / Home came his good horse but never came he' (*Bonny George Campbell*) . . . In the consonants and the vowel sounds of this strange poem . . . one gets the rhythm of the canter of a horse . . . There results a frightened, furtive, hurried and sinister syncopation of hoofbeats and heartbeats that defies analysis." Lorca himself associated this poem with the emotion expressed in *Ballad of Black Pain* from *The Gypsy Ballads*, written the same month. *Rider's Song*, he said, "seems to picture that prodigious Andalusian Omar ibn-Hafsun exiled forever from his fatherland" (*DS* 112), a reference to the Muslim rebel who threatened the Caliphate of Córdoba in the ninth century. In the first draft (reproduced in facsimile in *Obras completas*, ed. del Hoyo, I:lii–liii) the final stanza begins with the line (crossed out): "¡Mi niña! ¡mi amor mi niña!," suggesting that the rider was trying to reach his beloved.

¡Es verdad! / It's True. Ms. dated August 22, 1924, and sent to Fernández Almagro that summer (*EC* 247).

Arbolé arbolé . . . / Tree, lifeless tree . . . Published by Melchor Fernández Almagro in *España*, October 13, 1923, and three years later in *El Estudiante. Revista de la Juventud Española* (Madrid), April 4, 1926. Written in 1923 and incorporated into the comic opera *Lola, the Actress*, which Lorca was working on with Falla. Cf. *Ballad of the Three Rivers* in *Poem of the Deep Song*. The phonetic deformation of *árbol* in the opening and closing lines is characteristic of folk songs.

Galán, / galancillo . . . / Suitor, suitor of mine . . . Ms. dated August 22, 1924. The rhyme, structure, refrain, and the image of words written on a ribbon (lines 8–9) make this an elegant imitation of traditional children's songs.

Verlaine. See note on MOMENTS OF SONG, p. 902. For an earlier "ars poetica," see *New Songs*. Verlaine had been a spiritual "traveling companion" of Lorca as an adolescent, and Sahuquillo, in examining this poem (243 ff.), suggests that Lorca associated him with homosexuality. At age twenty he describes himself to Adriano del Valle (*ZC* 47): "I am a poor, passionate, silent lad who, almost like the marvelous Verlaine, has within him a lily impossible to water." See Introduction, p. xxvii.

Baco / Bacchus. In small print in the first edition, as though this poem were the "shadow" of the preceding one. In his lecture on Góngora, Lorca explains: "In mythology, Bacchus suffers three passions and deaths. He is first a goat with twisting horns. For love of his dancer Cyssus, who dies and is turned into ivy, Bacchus changes into a vine. Lastly, he dies and is turned into a fig tree" (*DS* 78).

Juan Ramón Jiménez. Ms. dated October 3, 1924, a few months after the great Spanish poet (1881–1958) had visited the Lorca family in Granada. Hernández (ed., *Canciones*, 202) observes that "the portrait judges J.R.J. and his works from a distance, as though his magisterial influence over Lorca had come to an end." For a study of the three portraits, see Ilie, 25–40. Lines 1–2 and 7–8 are quoted by Álvarez de Miranda (80–81) as an example of the association between the moon and death that appears throughout Lorca's work: evidence, he argues, that Lorca's poetic vision coincides with that of primitive, naturalistic religions. Cf. *Ballad of the Moon Moon*.

Venus. Probably written July 1924 (Menarini, 132).

Debussy. Written July 1922 (see note on DAYDREAMS OF A RIVER, p. 907). The title occurred to Lorca several years later, in homage to the composer of "Reflets dans l'eau" and of *Soirée dans Grenade*, where "one can find all the emotional themes of the nighttime in Granada, the blue remoteness of the Vega, the Sierra greeting the tremulous Mediterranean, the enormous barbs of the clouds sunk into the distance, the admirable rubato of the city, the hallucinating play of its underground waters" (*SD* 9). Lorca was a fervent admirer of Debussy's piano music at least as early as the summer of 1917; see "Las reglas en la música" (The Rules of Music) (*PrI* 290).

Narciso / Narcissus. Ms. dated July 3, 1924.

A Irene García / To Irene García. In lines 7–10 Devoto (138) and Ramos-Gil (84) find echoes of an Asturian lullaby about snow and rain. The *carpe diem* theme is rare in Lorca's poetry.

Al oído de una muchacha / Whispered to a Girl. Ms. dated August 22, 1924. Another version, entitled "Cancioncilla" (Ditty), was sent to Fernández Almagro about the same time.

Las gentes iban . . . / People were leaving . . . Ms. dated July 1922. Trueblood explores the meaning of the image of concentric circles in Lorca's early work in "La geometría lírica de Federico García Lorca."

Canción del mariquita / Song of the Fairy. Fair copy dated 1924.

Naranja y limón . . . / Orange and lemon . . . Entitled "Polos" (Poles) in the undated AFGL ms. Fair copy dated May 1922. In February 1922 Lorca writes to Fernández Almagro: "I feel very distant from the poetic diarrhea that surrounds us, and dream of a future dawn with the ineffable emotion of primitive skies. I feel myself an Equator between the orange and the lemon. I love clear water and the murky star" (*EC* 143). Dalí reacted to this poem by reproaching Lorca for his lack of modernity: "We read Petrarch and we see him as a consequence of the times in which he lived . . . He uses materials from his own epoch. I read 'Orange and Lemon,' and I can't sense the painted mouths of mannequins. I look at Fernand Léger, Picasso, Miró, etc., and I know that machines exist, and new discoveries in natural science" (letter of June 1927, Santos Torroella, 59). Jorge Guillén (xxiii) writes of this poem: "An orange and a lemon? Let's play with these two fruits, and relate them to other beings: the girl, the sun, the water . . . The child in the poet—and they are one—is arranging [his] words in an [almost] arbitrary way . . . as though he were playing on the beach with pebbles and shells. That is the way that Federico played—using his imagination and his hands—with the world." Line 6: The "white girl" is mentioned in a well-known Asturian ballad (Hernández, ed., *Canciones*, 206).

La calle de los mudos / The Street of the Mute. A language of fans and, presumably, of handkerchiefs, was a necessary part of courtship in a society where young women were closely chaperoned. Every Spanish woman carries a fan, writes Richard Ford (I:112) in the 1855 edition of his *Handbook*: "It is the index of her soul, the telegraph of her chameleon feelings, her signal to the initiated, which they understand for good or evil as the wagging of a dog's tail. She can express with her dumb fan more than Paganini could with his fiddlestick. A handbook might be written to explain the code of signals."

La luna asoma / The Moon Appears. An earlier version appears in the suite SUBLUNAR CANTOS, probably written in July 1921. The third stanza seems to hint at an old superstition. In his 1855 *Handbook* Ford remarks of Seville oranges: "The natives are not very fanciful about eating them: they do not think them good before March, and poison if eaten after sunset" (I:214).

Dos lunas de tarde / Two Evening Moons. These poems were probably composed in July 1921, around the same time as SHADOW and SUBLUNAR CANTOS.

Lunes, miércoles y viernes / Monday, Wednesday, and Friday. Ms. dated June 1922.

Murió al amanecer / Dead at Daybreak. The only known ms., in the Houghton Library, Harvard University, was sent to Jorge Guillén for publication in *Verso y Prosa*; see note to *Hunter* (p. 914).

Primer aniversario / First Anniversary. Dated July 3, 1924. In the ms. it is the third poem in a series: the first two are *Narcissus* and *Whither bound, water?*

Segundo aniversario / Second Anniversary. This is probably one of the earliest poems in the book: summer 1921? The imagery is related to that of *The Sea* . . . in SEASIDE PRINTS. The rough draft of *The Sea* . . . had read: "Before the sea, / take up your lances, / and enter it, wounding it / as does the moon" (Belamich, 33).

EROS CON BASTÓN / EROS WITH A CANE (1925). The poet's brother, Francisco, suggested the title (Belamich, 1373). Toward the end of September 1925, Lorca confided to Fernández Almagro: "For the *first time in my life* I'm creating erotic poetry. An illustrious field of endeavor has suddenly opened up and is rewarding me in an extraordinary way. I don't understand myself, Melchorito. My mother tells me, 'You're still growing . . .' And yet I'm just now *getting into* problems that I should have faced long ago . . . Am I backward? . . . What *is* all this? It seems as though I've just reached adolescence. That's why when I'll be sixty I won't be old . . . I'm never going to be *old*" (*EC* 302). At least five of the poems in this section were written that summer.

Susto en el comedor / Fright in the Dining Room. First draft dated September 1925, with the title "Lucía Martínez" jotted on the back. Bousoño (iv) explains that "cranes, when they sleep, raise one of their legs. When they are awakening, they put their other foot down."

Lucía Martínez. September 1925?

La soltera en misa / The Unmarried Woman at Mass. Undated ms. (September 1925?) entitled "Prefacio" (Preface). This may have been meant as the first poem in the series.

Interior / Interior. September 1925? In the undated ms. the poem ends like this: "Open up! / And when I leave, dead, / don't anyone cry for me."

Nu. Two titles, both crossed out, are found in a ms. dated September 1925: "Georgette" and "Francesa desnuda" (Nude Frenchwoman). Hernández (ed., *Canciones*, 208) writes that Lorca understood the word *nu* "in the generic sense of a painting of a nude, rather than referring to the woman (the *nue*) in the poem. Brenan (135) explains that the rosebay (or oleander) "is the most striking of south Mediterranean plants. One meets it by every watercourse . . . In such surroundings its corymbs of rose-colored flowers seem mocking and sinister. They celebrate those cemeteries where the water lies dead and buried underground, too weak to rise and fertilize the parching soil. Besides, its taste is bitter and its leaves are poisonous both to men and cattle. 'Bitter as the oleander,' *como la adelfa amarga*, says a Spanish *copla* [popular song] when it wishes to describe the bitterness of unrequited love, and no image could be juster." Cf. *Little Backwater* in SUITES.

Serenata / Serenade. Homage to the greatest playwright-lover in all Spanish literature, and to his treatment of the traditional lyric in his plays and poems. Another, slightly different, version appears in the third scene of *The Love of Don Perlimplín for Belisa in Their Garden*, which Lorca sent to Fernández Almagro in January 1926 (*EC* 320).

En Málaga / In Málaga. Fair copy dated 1926. Lorca's vignette—black bathing suits, "pontifical flesh"—is reminiscent of the stage directions, in the style of prose poems, of the Spanish playwright Ramón del Valle-Inclán (1866–1936). On a fair copy sent to José Ortega y Gasset, Lorca wrote: "Don't call me a goose. This song is lovely." In that copy, the last two lines read: "along comes your behind: / Catholic, Apostolic and Roman."

Escena / Scene. July 1923. From IN THE GARDEN OF THE LUNAR GRAPEFRUITS; see pp. 391, 910. See also the note to *From* NARCISSUS, above.

Malestar y noche / Disquiet and Night. Ms. lost. Judging from the imagery, probably written in spring or summer 1925.

El niño mudo / The Voiceless Child. Date unknown, but the poem's genesis seems related to the LUNAR GRAPEFRUITS cycle. In July 1923 Lorca promises to send his friend Ciria y Escalante some of the more "accomplished" poems from that suite; among them was "Lament of the Girl with No Voice" (see p. 910).

El niño loco / The Crazy Boy. In October 1923, Lorca tells Fernández Almagro of his plans to "finish my poem 'Recreo del niño loco y el pájaro sin nido' " (Recreation of the Crazy Boy and the Nestless Bird) (*EC* 212). Some of Lorca's notes on the subject are published by Menarini (281–82). Judging from the mss. in the AFGL, the series was probably begun in July 1923. See also "Recreo del niño loco y el pájaro ciego" (Recreation of the Crazy Boy and the Blind Bird) (Menarini, 279).

Desposorio / Marriage Vow. July 1923? Ms. undated, but like *Scene*, the poem once belonged to the LUNAR GRAPEFRUITS series in *Suites*, where the narrator is transformed into a hundred-year-old-man. The title was added later. See also the note to *From* NARCISSUS above.

Despedida / Leave-taking. Date of composition unknown. Guillén (lxxvii) notices that although this poem follows the parallelistic structure of the medieval Galician-Portuguese lyric, Lorca is also half remembering the deep song repertoire—e.g., *siguiriyas* like the one beginning "Cuando yo muera / mira que te encargo . . ." (When I die / I ask you . . .); see *Memento*, p. 145.

Suicidio / Suicide. Ms. dated July 27, 1924.

Cancioncilla del primer deseo / Ditty of First Desire. 1922?

Eco / Echo. Written before October 1923 (see Menarini, 201). Probably a fragment from the LUNAR GRAPEFRUITS cycle (cf. *White Smell*).

Idilio / Idyll. Ms. dedicated to "Lucía, daughter of the Marquis," perhaps the "muchachita morena" mentioned in *Madrigal* (p. 216).

Narciso . . . / Narcissus . . . The image of the frogs and the "mirror" of the river also occurs in BACKWATERS.

Granada y 1850 / Granada 1850. Originally entitled "Interior," this poem was the first in the suite WATER JETS. In 1850 Granada's lingering Romanticism draws toward its close. It was in 1848 that the Russian composer Mikhail Ivanovich Glinka visited Granada. "Amid the eternal rhythm of Granada's waters [he] conceived the magnificent idea of creating his school and the courage to use the whole-tone scale for the first time" (*SD* 8). Théophile Gautier visited the city in 1840 and Alexandre Dumas several years later.

Preludio / Prelude. Composed, like *Debussy*, as part of DAYDREAMS OF A RIVER in 1922 but revised for inclusion in *Songs*. For the earlier version, see p. 343.

Soneto / Sonnet. A ms. subtitled "Narciso" (Narcissus) is dated July 1924: a time when Lorca was discovering that "there is a certain eternal sentiment to the sonnet which fits in no other vessel than this apparently cold one" (*EC* 240). It was around this time—perhaps the second half of July—that he wrote his sonnet *On the Death of José de Ciria y Escalante* (p. 845 and *EC* 239). Line 7: A similar phrase occurs in Góngora's sonnet 66: "aunque con lengua muda / suave Philomena ya suspira . . ." (though with muted tongue, / gentle Philomela now sighs). Philomela was turned into a nightingale after Tereus raped her sister Procne and cut out Procne's tongue. In some versions of the myth, their roles are reversed.

Agua, ¿dónde vas? / Whither bound, water? Dated July 3, 1924, when Lorca was writing "modern interpretations of figures from Greek mythology, something new in me, and which I find very entertaining" (*EC* 241). *Narcissus* and *Venus* form part of the same series. On revising the poem in 1926 Lorca added a dedication and title (suppressed in the book), "Acis," referring to the youth whom Galatea mercifully turned into a river after Polyphemus buried him under a huge stone.

Canción inútil / Useless Song. AFGL ms. dated September 1925; fair copy dated January 1926.

Dos marinos en la orilla / Two Sailors Ashore. Ms. undated. From a four-part series entitled, successively, "A Tavern of Sailors," "The Four Old Sailors," and "The Four Sailors." For the other two poems, see Menarini (96–97). Lorca is imitating Rubén Darío's vision of an old sea-wolf in "Sinfonía en gris mayor" (Symphony in Gray Major), *Prosas profanas*, 134.

Canción del naranjo seco / Song of the Dead Orange Tree. Composed in summer 1923 around the same time as IN THE GARDEN OF THE LUNAR GRAPEFRUITS, whose narrator expresses anguish over the children he might have engendered, but never did.

Canción del día que se va / Song of Departing Day. Ms. dated August 9, 1923. Lines 5–8 had read: "What a hard time I have / tracing on your bosom / the sleepless pages / of my lyrical almanac." Hernández (ed., *Canciones*, 214) compares the sentiment of this poem to that expressed in a letter from Lorca to the painter Benjamín Palencia in July 1925: "If you could see how long and golden these days are! The sunset seems never to end, never, never. There is a moment when the birds turn hard and brilliant as though they were metal, and the afternoon tries to become *eternal*. This unique, substantive light gives you the impression, each day, that *you have already died*" (*EC* 214).

Primer Romancero Gitano / The Gypsy Ballads

Written between 1921 and 1927; published in 1928 by the prestigious Revista de Occidente, Madrid. The book enjoyed a popular and critical success unprecedented in twentieth-century Spanish poetry, and six more editions appeared in Madrid and Buenos Aires during Lorca's lifetime (1929, two in 1933, two in 1935, and 1936). The title is literally *First Gypsy Ballad Book* but is usually shortened to *The Gypsy Ballads*.

The idea of a book of ballads on Andalusian themes seems to have occurred to Lorca in the summer of 1922 while he was still working on *Suites* (he had already written *Joke about Don Pedro on Horseback: Ballad with Lacunae and Lagoons*). In July 1922 he tells Fernández Almagro: "This summer I want to write something calm and serene. I'm thinking of constructing some ballads with lagoons, ballads with mountains, ballads with stars: a limpid, mysterious work like a flower (arbitrary and perfect as a flower), all fragrance! I want to bring out of the shadows the little Arab girls who play in these villages, and to lead astray, in the groves of my lyricism, the ideal figures of the anonymous *romancillos* [six- and seven-syllable traditional ballads]. Imagine a ballad with *skies* instead of lagoons. Nothing could be more exciting. This summer, if God helps me with his little doves [of inspiration], I will write a popular, extremely *Andalusian* work. I'm going to travel a bit through these marvelous villages, whose castles and whose people seem never to have existed for poets . . . And *enough of Castile!!*" (*EC* 147–48). See Introduction, pp. xviii–xix.

The "popular, extremely *Andalusian*" book written that summer turned out to be a puppet play, *The Tragicomedy of Don Cristóbal and Mistress Rosita*. Unlike *Poem of the Deep Song*, the *Ballads* would be written slowly over a period of years, and it was not until early 1926, when Lorca was going over the manuscripts of almost all of his poetry, that he decided to publish them as a book.

The Spanish text presented here follows the edition of Mario Hernández (rev. ed., 1998), with a few differences of punctuation and spacing. The *Ballads* are Lorca's best-studied book. English-speaking readers will learn much from Ramsden, *Lorca's* Romancero gitano; Harris, *Romancero gitano*; and Morris, *Son of Andalusia*. The most helpful discussions in Spanish are the editions of García-Posada, Josephs / Caballero, and Hernández; and the monograph by Fernández de los Ríos.

Romance de la luna, luna / Ballad of the Moon Moon. Ms. dated July 29, 1924. Published in *Proa* (Buenos Aires) in 1925; the daily newspaper *El Norte de Castilla* (Valladolid), April 9, 1926; and *Verso y Prosa* (Murcia), July 1927, with the title "Romance de la luna de los gitanos" (Ballad of the Moon of Gypsies). In his lecture recital on the *Ballads*, Lorca notes that his book "begins with two invented myths, the moon as a deathly ballerina and the wind as a satyr. A myth of the moon over lands of dramatic dance—concentrated, religious inner Andalusia; and a myth of the Tartesian beach where the air is as soft as the skin of a peach and all drama and dance are balanced on an intelligent needle of jest or irony" (*DS* 107). Line 1: Metalworking is one of the traditional livelihoods of the Spanish gypsies. Lines 31–32: Álvarez de Miranda (82) notices how Lorca coincides with primitive naturalistic religions in his conception of the moon as psychopomp, leading souls to the afterworld. Cf. note to DIALOGUE OF AMARGO (p. 899).

Preciosa y el aire / Preciosa and the Wind. Ms. dated January 28, 1926. Published that November in *Litoral* (Málaga). Lorca was fascinated with the personification of the wind in the lyrics of *cante jondo*: "The wind is a character who emerges in the ultimate, most intensely emotional moments. He comes into sight like a giant absorbed in pulling down stars and scattering nebulae. In no popular poetry but ours have I heard him speak and console" (*SD* 16). Cummins (64–67) provides numerous examples of traditional lyrics where the wind "acts like a playful, unruly lover, lifting the young girl's skirts; the man prays for a wind to blow him into those skirts; to be burned by the wind is a frequent metaphor for lovemaking, particularly for the loss of virginity." Ramsden (8) quotes several traditional lyrics in which the wind is a sexual threat, e.g. (translation mine): "Don't go alone to the field / when the wind is blowing hard; / because girls are flowers / and even the wind strips their petals," and "A bad little breeze / [is being] crazy with my skirts. / Away from me, bad wind! / Why lift my skirts?" Cf. *Tree, lifeless tree . . .* in *Songs*. The name of the gypsy girl and some of the poem's imagery were borrowed from Miguel de Cervantes's novella *La gitanilla* (*The Gypsy Girl*), e.g., the ballad that begins: "When Preciosa beats her tambourine . . ."; text in Cohen, 228–29; details in Ramsden. Guillén (1986) identifies another source: the Ovidian myth of Boreas, ravisher of Oreithyia. Forster believes that Lorca is superimposing *three* mythological figures: St. Christopher, Boreas, and Pan. Morris (100) writes that "the crude advances of the 'viento-hombrón' (wind-man) are no more than a reprise, in the context of Granada, of the persistence with which in classical lore satyrs harassed nymphs, often near rivers . . . Rape and attempted rape are, as Lorca knew, common classical themes." For Lorca's drawing of the saint, see *Dibujos*, no. 183. The exclamation of line 40 is borrowed from *cante jondo* lyrics (see note on *Saeta*, p. 896).

Reyerta / The Feud. Ms. dated August 6, 1926. Sent to Guillén the following month (*EC* 373–74) with the title "Reyerta de mozos" (Brawl [Feud, Dispute] Between Young Men). Published in *La Verdad* (Murcia), October 10, 1926; and, with the title "Gypsy Brawl," in the Catalan literary magazine *L'Amic de les Arts*, June 1927. According to Lorca, this poem "expresses a silent, latent struggle all over Andalusia and Spain among groups that attack each other without knowing why, for mysterious reasons: because of a look, a rose, a love affair two centuries old, or because a man suddenly feels a bug on his cheek" (*DS* 110). Line 2, Albacete: town between Madrid and Valencia famed for its *navajas*, with long blades that fold back into a handle. Ford (II:804) marvels that "where an unarmed Englishman *closes* his fist, a Spaniard *opens* his knife. Man, again, in this hot climate, is very inflammable and combustible; a small spark explodes the dry powder, which ignites less readily in damp England." Lines 5–8: Harris believes that "the reference to playing cards indicates a reason for the fight [. . .], while the verb *recortar* [cuts out] indicates that the horses and the horsemen of lines 7–8 are in silhouette. [. . .] They also allude to the game of cards, for the Spanish pack [. . .] contains a court card known as the 'caballo,' which is represented by a horseman silhouetted on the card." In lines 29–30 Lorca alludes to the Punic Wars for the possession of Spain but also, ironically, to classroom competition among Spanish children. In some schools, particularly Jesuit ones, the class was divided into competing teams, the "Romans" and the "Carthaginians" (Ramsden, 71; García-Posada, 118).

Romance sonámbulo / Sleepwalking Ballad. Ms. dated August 2, 1924. For

Lorca's illustration of this ballad (showing the house with its *barandas*, or railings), see *Dibujos*, no. 240.2. The poet's own commentary is willfully enigmatic: "It is one of the most mysterious [poems] in the book, and is thought by many to express Granada's longing for the sea and the anguish of a city that cannot hear the waves and seeks them in the play of her underground waters and in the undulous clouds with which she covers her mountains. That is true, but this poem is also something else. It is a pure poetic event, of Andalusian essence, and will always have changing lights, even for me, the man who communicated it. If you ask me why I wrote, 'A thousand crystal tambourines / were wounding dawn's dark sky,' I will tell you that I saw them, in the hands of angels and trees, but I will not be able to say more; certainly I cannot explain their meaning. And that is the way it should be. By means of poetry a man more rapidly approaches the cutting edge that the philosopher and the mathematician turn away from in silence" (*DS* 111–12). Dalí once remarked admiringly of this ballad, "It seems to have a story, but it doesn't" (Guillén, L). The thread of the narration seems to be this: a smuggler, badly wounded in a skirmish with the Civil Guard, returns shortly before dawn from the Passes of Cabra (mountain passes in the province of Córdoba, associated with brigandry), in search of his beloved, a gypsy girl, and converses with the girl's father. But, tired of waiting for him, the girl has fallen (or thrown herself) from the terraced roof of the house into an *aljibe* (a tank holding rainwater). Ramos-Gil (210) believes the girl is "the victim of the attraction, the spell cast by the dark water of the rain-tank"; a reading that would coincide with Lorca's (Granada's fascination with its underground waters, etc.). Line 1: Francisco García Lorca explores the ambiguity of this refrain, which can mean "I *want* you green," but also "I *love* you green": the "act of will" is more pronounced than the "act of love." "We can even suppose that the poet is anticipating not a particular green, but the very idea of green, not yet created. In this case, 'Verde que te quiero verde' would announce the creation of green . . . 'Let green exist, for I want it so.' This would be the *Fiat lux* of the entire poem. A green invoked, anticipated, still to be created. Green does not actually appear until the next verse: 'verde viento, verdes ramas.' . . . In [lines 3–4], the poet is ordering his poetic universe" (*De Garcilaso a Lorca*, 270). Envious of the line—all Spaniards recite it with admiration—Juan Ramón Jiménez insisted it was taken from a popular song: "Green, I love you green, / the color of an olive." On Lorca's use of the word *verde*, and the similarities between this poem and one by Jiménez himself ("El pajarito verde"), see also Díaz Plaja, 129. Line 14: The Spanish "estrellas de escarcha" is ambiguous: either star-shaped patches of frost or stars that look like frost. Lines 15–16: Shadow in the shape of a fish (e.g., that cast by a tree), descending the mountain as the sun rises, opening the way for dawn? Line 19: The sinister wildcat is mentioned in an early prose piece, "Largo apasionato" (*PrI* 400): At night, "a *gato garduño* comes out of the frightening poplar grove and rips apart a black toad with its claws." Lines 51–52: The *barandas*, or "railings," are suggested by traditional ballads and songs; e.g., the ballad of St. Catherine (Menéndez Pelayo, 305) speaks of "la baranda del cielo" (the railing of the sky). Lines 77–78: The moon's reflection on the rippling surface of the water tank.

La monja gitana / *The Gypsy Nun*. Ms. dated August 20, 1924. For Lorca's drawing of this nun, see *Dibujos*, no. 240.3. Even in his earliest writings, Lorca is aware of how life in the convent fails to still the temptations of the flesh: "the soul is still impassioned, and the good but unhappy men searching for God in these deserts of pain ought to have understood that it is useless to torture the flesh when the spirit asks for something else" (*Impressions and Landscapes*, 1918, *OC* III:25; see Ramsden, 31). García-Posada (121) believes that the convent is in the gypsy quarter of Granada, the Albaicín, of which Lorca had written in *Impressions and Landscapes*: "Streets with convents, perpetually closed, naïve and white, with their short belltowers, dusty high lattice windows almost touching the eaves of the roof . . . with pigeons and swallows' nests. Streets of serenades and with processions of innocent virgin nuns" (*OC* III:79). Ramsden remarks of lines 17–20 that "the making of crystallized fruits is a traditional occupation of nuns in Andalucía" (34), and García-Posada (132), apropos of the "wounds of Christ," that Lorca was fascinated by the religious names of these sweets: nuns' sighs, bacon of heaven, angel's hair, etc. (see *DS* 8, 60).

La casada infiel / The Unfaithful Wife. Ms. dated January 27, 1926. Published in *Revista de Occidente*, January 1928. The popularity of this poem was a source of anguish to Lorca, who sometimes refused to read it in public: it is "pure Andalusian anecdote . . . popular to the point of desperation . . . the most rudimentary, the most alluringly sensual and the least Andalusian [of the *Ballads*]" (*DS* 112). Andrés Soria Olmedo ("Éxito e ironía . . .," 234–35) argues persuasively that Lorca is smiling—with an irony overlooked by other critics—at the stereotypical Spanish male code of honor. "The reader encounters a self-definition of manhood (*hombría*), and its accompanying *decorum.*" The poem's sensuality "borders on parody and the comic." Francisco García Lorca quotes lines 1–3 to illustrate his brother's total assimilation of traditional poetry: "During an excursion to the Sierra Nevada, the mule driver who was leading sang to himself: 'So I took her to the river / thinking she was a maiden, / but she had a husband.' Sometime later, one day when we were speaking of the ballad of 'The Faithless Wife,' I reminded Federico of the mule driver's song. To my enormous surprise, he had completely forgotten it. He thought the first three lines of the ballad were as much his as the rest of the poem" ("Prologue" to Graham-Lijan and O'Connell, trs. *Three Tragedies*, 17). Line 4: The feast of St. James the Elder, patron of Spain, is celebrated on July 25. Lines 46–47: Devoto traces these lines to a wedding song in Lope de Vega: "Echen las mañanas, / después del rocío, / en espadas verdes / guarnición de lirios" (Let the mornings, / after the dew is gone, / guard [the couple] / with the swords of the lilies [or irises]) ("Lecturas," 520).

Romance de la pena negra / Ballad of Black Pain. Dated July 30, 1924, the day after *Ballad of the Moon Moon* and a few weeks after *Rider's Song.* In a letter to Fernández Almagro (*EC* 323), Lorca calls this poem "Ballad of Black Pain in Jaén," a picturesque Andalusian province—the "lands of olive trees" of line 21—otherwise absent from the *Ballads*. For the poet's drawing of Soledad Montoya, see *Dibujos*, no. 240.4. The name means "Solitude" or "Loneliness," and the surname is common among gypsies. "Set against the swaggering, ardent night of 'The Unfaithful Wife,' a night of the high vega and the reed in the penumbra, we have the night of Soledad Montoya, who embodies incurable pain, the black pain we cannot get rid of except by taking a knife and opening a deep buttonhole in the left side. The Pain of Soledad Montoya is the root of the Andalusian people. It is not anguish, because in pain one can smile, nor does it blind, for it never produces weeping. It is a longing without object, a keen love for nothing, with the certainty that death (the eternal care of Andalusia) is breathing behind the door" (*DS* 112). Years earlier Lorca had noticed how Pain is personified in the lyrics of *cante jondo*: "The woman of deep song is called Pain. / / It is admirable how sentiment begins to take shape in these lyrical constructions and quicken into an almost material thing. This is the case with Pain. / / In these poems Pain is made flesh, takes human form, and acquires a sharp profile. She is a dark woman wanting to catch birds in nets of wind" (*SD* 15). García-Posada (139) points out that the germinal image of this poem, black pain, does in fact occur in the lyrics of *cante jondo*, e.g.: "How do you expect me to feel? / I look for you and cannot find you. / Black pain has got a hold on me." Like Amparo in *Poem of the Deep Song* (p. 137), the Andalusian spinster in *Elegy* (p. 23), or Doña Rosita in Lorca's drama *Doña Rosita or the Language of the Flowers*, Soledad Montoya would be an image of the woman who waits in vain for love. The "linen nightgowns" of line 33 are her bridal trousseau, never to be used (García-Posada, 141). The image of a woman sweeping the floor with her long tresses as a sign of her grief (lines 27–30) is found in certain traditional ballads.

San Miguel (Granada) / St. Michael (Granada). Written in Lanjarón (a health spa to the south of Granada) in August 1926, and sent to Jorge Guillén on September 9 of that year (*EC* 372–73). Published in *Litoral*, November 1926. The poem describes the break of dawn on the feast of St. Michael (September 29), an occasion celebrated in Granada with a pilgrimage to the church of San Miguel el Alto on the hill (lines 2, 16) over the gypsy quarter of the Albaicín. Lorca could see the church from his home, the Huerta San Vicente. The mules are carrying sunflower seed, to be sold at the fair. The description of the Archangel (lines 17–24 and 45–48) is ekphrastic: Lorca is referring to a strange Baroque statue in the shrine. Ramsden (52) explains: "Behind the altar a glass screen (*vidrios*) separates the nave from the 'camarín' (*la alcoba de su torre*) where the statue of Saint Michael stands surrounded by four lights (*faroles*). The boyish figure of the saint (*efebo de tres mil noches*), sumptuously attired in female dress, a degenerate form of the Roman military tunic (*lleno de encajes . . . enseña sus bellos muslos*), and with a fine plume of feathers on his head (*plumas*), is treading, somewhat delicately, on the prostrate figure of a demonic, tailed Satan, his right arm upraised with three arrows in his hand (*el gesto de las doce*), threatening the demon beneath his feet." Drawing by Lorca in *Dibujos*, no. 244.4; photographs in García-Posada, between 156 and 157. Lines 29–30 read in the *Litoral* version: "The sea opens its balcony-windows / beneath the mountains," a reference to waves (resembling a curved balcony) or to the rocky inlets along the coast, which in fact is many miles to the south of Granada. Line 33: The "manolas" are city women of the lower classes, dressed up for the occasion. Line 35: Lorca's use of the word *culos* (arses) must have raised some eyebrows. Lorca's friend Cipriano Rivas Cherif tells him in February 1927 that he has had great success reciting "your ballad of the Camborios and the one about *culos*" (Sahuquillo, 63). Jorge Guillén writes to Juan Guerrero Ruiz, coeditor of a literary magazine, on September 13, 1926: "I had asked Federico for [some poems] with the crafty treacherous intention of sending them to *La Verdad*. 'Good God, let them be publishable,' I said to myself. And sure enough, he has sent me two ballads. One of them, about St. Michael, is impossible (*enseña sus bellos muslos*, etc.)" (Sala Zenobia y Juan Ramón Jiménez, University of Puerto Rico).

Line 41: The Bishop of Manila was one of the titles held by the Bishop of Granada. Line 50: The mention of odd numbers seems to allude to a lottery held on Michaelmas. As Harris (45–46) puts it, "The archangel who in the Calendar is the saint of the Church Militant has been turned by Lorca into the camp master of ceremonies of a local lottery." Of lines 51–52 Lorca remarks: ". . . that is Granada, seen from the Cerro del Aceituno. The song one hears is chaotic. It is all Granada singing at once: rivers, voices, ropes, foliage, processions, an ocean of fruits, the music of the swing rides at the fairs" (SG 112). Morris (381) points out that, in describing the pilgrimage to the shrine, Lorca is feeling some of the nostalgia he attributes to the "tall gentlemen" and "ladies of sad bearing." The pilgrimage to the shrine of St. Michael had been in decline for many years. "Lorca's poem, therefore, makes more sense as a picture of what he imagined the romería to have been" in the past.

San Rafael (Córdoba) / St. Raphael (Córdoba). Date unknown. García-Posada (145 ff.) believes the poem alludes to "a marginal world of homosexual relations": in the "closed carriages" are voyeurs, attracted by the naked children of Córdoba bathing in the Guadalquivir. Ramsden argues, convincingly, that Lorca is comparing the Córdoba that flourished under the Romans (ca. 200 B.C. to A.D. 400), native city of Seneca, Lucan, and several Roman emperors, to a second period of glory under the Muslims (e.g., the Caliphate of Córdoba from 929 to 1031). St. Raphael, tutelary saint of the city, symbolizes the fusion of the two. In his lecture on the Ballads, Lorca calls him a "peregrine archangel who lives in the Bible and the Koran, perhaps a better friend of the Muslims than of the Christians, and who fishes in the river of Córdoba" (DS 114). He is alluding to the story in the Book of Tobit, in which Raphael appears as companion and guide to Tobit's son, Tobias. "While Tobias was washing his feet in the River Tigris a huge fish leapt from the water and tried to devour him . . . At Raphael's bidding the young man caught the fish and killed it and later used its heart and liver to cast out devils from his bride and its gall to cure his father's blindness" (Ramsden, 58). The saint, who is "set over all the diseases and all the wounds of the children of men" (Enoch I:40), is commemorated in Córdoba by a series of statues, one of which is found on the Roman bridge alluded to in lines 39–42 and another on a column (line 42), located near the bridge, called the Triunfo. The great Baroque poet Don Luis de Góngora, known for his Latinate syntax and vocabulary, would form part of Córdoba's "Roman" heritage and is honored here with metaphors such as the "petals of frail tin" (the stars) that are "scaled on" the gray sky (lines 19–20) or the "ten . . . whispers" (the breeze?) that Neptune blows through the arches of the Roman bridge. The duality of Moorish and Roman elements was characteristic, Lorca thought, of Andalusia itself: "From the very first lines [of The Gypsy Ballads] we note that myth is mixed with what we might call the 'realistic' element. But in fact when this 'realism' touches the plane of magic it becomes as mysterious and indecipherable as the Andalusian soul, which is a dramatic struggle between the poison of the Orient and the geometry and equilibrium [cf. line 41] imposed by the Roman and Andalusian civilizations" (DS 107). Line 43: The adjective aljamiado applies to texts written in Spanish using Arabic characters. Drawings of St. Raphael (with a fish) in Dibujos, nos. 234.2, 269.4.

San Gabriel (Sevilla) / St. Gabriel (Seville). Undated. A poem of July 30, 1918, "La oración" (The Prayer), reflects Lorca's familiarity with St. Gabriel as depicted by Fra Angelico. Stressing the importance of neoprimitivism in the *Ballads*, Ramsden points out: "As Fra Angelico in the fifteenth century depicted his Annunciations in a wholly fifteenth-century context (dress, hairstyle, book of hours, Brunelleschi-type loggia) so Lorca, as an ostensible gypsy narrator, presents his Annunciation in local and contemporary gypsy terms: Saint Gabriel is a delightfully dandified Sevillian gypsy boy and the Virgen de los Reyes [patron saint of the Archdiocese of Seville] has become a local gypsy girl, Anunciación de los Reyes" (65). The ballad is prefigured in an early poem, "Santiago. Balada ingenua" (St. James. Naïve Ballad), written in 1918 and published in *Libro de poemas*, in which St. James pays a visit to an old woman. Line 28: The puzzling phrase "bien lunada" (literally, "well mooned") alludes to Anunciación's fertility. Álvarez de Miranda (97–98) explains that in archaic religions, the moon is often an impregnator of women. "[Here] the pregnant woman is 'well mooned' and her child will bear on his breast the symbol of his origins, the *lunar* [a mole or beauty mark]" (cf. line 54). García-Posada interprets "born under a good moon" and relates the phrase to the gestation of the Virgin. Line 38: "Campanillas" means both little bells (e.g., altar bells) and bellflowers; cf. lines 69–70, where the stars turn into ever-lastings or immortelles, associated with death (funeral crowns are made from them) both in Lorca's works and in popular belief.

Prendimiento de Antoñito el Camborio . . . / The Taking of Little Tony Camborio . . . Ms. dated January 20, 1926. Published in *Litoral*, November 1926. Lorca made at least three drawings of this figure, whom he dressed like a nineteenth-century *bandolero* (*Dibujos*, nos. 234.3, 240.6, 244.5). Fernández de los Ríos (137) and García-Posada (165) point out that the word "Prendimiento" in the title is used in connection with the arrest of Christ. Lines 1–4 are reminiscent of a popular song quoted by Forster: "A girl from Málaga / went to Seville to see the bulls / and halfway there / the Moors captured her." Line 22: "Capricorn night" alludes to olive-picking time in December. Lorca wrote melodies for this poem and the next (published in *OC* I:799–800).

Muerte de Antoñito el Camborio / The Death of Little Tony Camborio. Undated. "Given the renowned closeness of gypsy family ties, normally disrupted only in cases of offence against family honour, it seems reasonable to assume that the four Heredia cousins are here taking revenge for the betrayal of their lineage revealed in the previous poem" (Ramsden, 80). Lorca believed that Antoñito was one of the "purest heroes" of the *Ballads*, "the only one in the book who calls me by name at the moment of his death. A true gypsy, incapable of evil" (*DS* 117). As in the preceding poem, Ramsden calls attention to several allusions to the Passion of Christ. The "verónica" (line 16) dreamt of by the "erales" (two-year-old bulls) is a pass with the cape (the color of a scarlet gillyflower) which brushes the animal. Benamejí (line 26) is a town in Córdoba province near the border of Granada, ill famed for its bandits; it is also mentioned in *Scene of the Lieutenant Colonel . . .* Lines 45–46: The intervention of angels occurs also in a few traditional ballads (e.g., the angels who enshroud Delgadina in Menéndez Pelayo, 249).

Muerto de amor / Dead from Love. Published in *Litoral*, October 1927, in a special issue in honor of Góngora. Lines 1–2: Josephs and Caballero (268) believe Lorca is echoing a *saeta*: "What is that shining / up above the Sacro Monte? / It must be the Virgin Mary / who is going to heaven to get water." Another *saeta* (Aguilar y Tejera, 50) begins in much the same way: "¿Qué es aquello que reluce / en aquel monte florido? / Es Jesús de Nazareno / que con la cruz ha caído" (What is that shining / on that flowery mountain? / It is Jesus of Nazareth, / who has fallen with his cross). Line 41: Telegrams were blue in Spain.

El emplazado / Ballad of the Marked Man. Published in *Carmen* (Santander), January 1928. The theme of "heralded misfortune" is frequent in the traditional ballads (Ramsden, 90). Lines 23, 47: On "Amargo," see note on DIALOGUE OF AMARGO, p. 899. Lines 14–17 were suggested by a country expression which Lorca had admired in his lecture of 1926 on Góngora: "*Water-ox*, they call the deep channel of water that flows slowly across a field, thereby indicating its combativeness, its strength and volume" (*DS* 60; cf. Francisco García Lorca, "Prologue" to Graham-Lijan and O'Connell, trs., *Three Tragedies,* 17). Cf. *Nocturne of the Drowned Youth.* The metaphor horns/crescent moon is found in Góngora, who also speaks of the "hard bull" of the sea "charging at" a stream, and is further elaborated on here: the moons are reflected on the rippling water, as the boys bathe at night in the river. García-Posada (185) believes that the oleanders of line 25 will adorn Amargo's cadaver. Traditional songs allude to the plant's bitter and poisonous nature, and Lorca almost always associates it with death. See note to *Nu,* p. 918.

Romance de la Guardia Civil Española / Ballad of the Spanish Civil Guard. The Guard is a rural constabulary founded to patrol the highways and beaches and control banditry and smuggling. By the end of the nineteenth century, it had become an organ of power for the *caciques,* the local despots who ruled the Spanish provinces. The first sixty-two lines of this poem were sent to Guillén on November 8, 1926, with the remark: "I began it two years ago—remember? . . . This is what I have done so far. Now the Civil Guard arrives and destroys the city. Later they go back to their barracks and drink anise, toasting to the death of the gypsies. The scenes of the sack [of the city] will be lovely. At times, the Guards will inexplicably turn into Roman centurions. This ballad will be extremely long, but it will be among the best. The final apotheosis of the Civil Guard is very moving. / / Once I have finished this ballad and the 'Ballad of the Martyrdom of the Gypsy St. Eulalia of Mérida' I will consider the book finished. It will be marvelous. A good book, I think. And I will never again— *never! never!*—return to this theme" (*EC* 392–94).

In his lecture reading of the *Ballads,* Lorca calls this "one of the most difficult" poems in the book, for the theme is "incredibly anti-poetic" (*DS* 122). In a letter of 1926 to his brother, Francisco, he describes the cruelty of the Civil Guard in a remote mountainous district of Granada, the Alpujarras: "The countryside is ruled by the Civil Guard. A lieutenant from Carataunas, who was much annoyed by the gypsies, and wanted to make them disappear, called them into the barracks, took the tongs from the fireplace and pulled a tooth out of each one's mouth, saying, 'If you're not out of here by tomorrow, another tooth will *fall*' . . . This Easter in Cáñar, a fourteen-year-old gypsy boy stole five hens from the mayor. The Civil Guard tied his arms to a piece of wood and paraded him through the village, whipping him and forcing him to sing. I was told this by a little boy who saw the procession passing as he sat at his desk in school . . . All of this has a cruelty I had never suspected" (*EC* 330–31).

Line 8: The uniforms include a black patent-leather tricorn hat and belts. Line 12: Lorca explained the expression "miedos de fina arena" to one of his friends: "When the Civil Guards draw near to simple people who have heard terrifying things about them, their fear slips coldly down their backs, like a fine, slippery sand beneath their shirts" (García-Posada, 192). Lines 18, 100: As in other ballads, imagery borrowed from traditional poems (e.g., the "corners hung with banners") mingles here with borrowings from learned poets, e.g., the expression "salivilla de estrella." In his lecture on Don Luis de Góngora, Lorca quotes these lines from the *Second Solitude*, 294–97: ". . . The bee as queen who shines with wandering gold; / Either the sap she drinks from the pure air, / Or else the exudation of the skies / That sip the spittle from each silent star" (tr. by E. M. Wilson, *DS* 71). Line 26: reminiscent of traditional poetry, like the "luna lunera" in *Ballad of the Moon Moon*. Line 47: Owner of the great sherry house; the poem is presumed to take place in Jerez de la Frontera. Line 65: Civil Guards always patrol in pairs and are often referred to as "parejas" (couples). Lines 77–80 have long puzzled readers of the *Ballads*. García-Posada believes Lorca is referring to "a sweet, purplish syrup, a children's medicinal, called 'noviembre.' " Lines 105–8: As Harris (69) points out, Rosa de los Camborios "suffers the martyrdom of Saint Agatha."

Martirio de Santa Olalla / Martydom of St. Eulalia. Undated. Published in *Revista de Occidente*, January 1928. In the lecture recital Lorca calls this "a ballad of Roman Andalucía (Mérida is Andalusian, as is Tetuán, to the south) where the form, images and rhythm fit together as perfectly as building stones" (*DS* 122). His source is probably the hymn to the martyrdom of St. Eulalia in the *Peristephanon* of the Hispano-Roman poet Prudentius (348–410). The ruins of Mérida (Emerita Augusta, capital of Roman Lusitania)—including the *disjecta membra* of a Roman amphitheater, bridge, and aqueduct—are alluded to anachronistically throughout the poem, especially in lines 9–12. Line 5: Olive trees? The olive is sacred to Minerva. Lines 13–14: Not only crowing cocks but also Roman centurions? Line 23: Eulalia herself, seen as the Roman goddess. Ford was impressed, in the 1850s, with the pile-up of cultures in Mérida, especially in religion: "As is the creed, so are the temples, a pasticcio; and thus are the crumbs of Paganism served up again, thus Mars and Diana are now displaced, or metamorphosed into Santiago and Eulalia, in principle the same, *mutato nomine tantum*" (II:476). Line 24: The "little cascade stairs" (literally, "little stairs—or ladders—of water") may have been suggested by stairs leading down into a large Roman reservoir (a little north of Mérida) known as the Charca de la Albutera. Line 42: Eulalia was baked to death. Lines 73–74: Direct quotation from the Catholic liturgy (Ramsden, 104).

Burla de don Pedro a caballo (Romance con lagunas) / Joke about Don Pedro on Horseback (Ballad with Lacunae and Lagoons). Published in *Mediodía* (Seville), 1927. The subtitle plays upon the two meanings of "laguna": the gap in a document or a narration (lacuna) and a body of water (lagoon). In an interview, Lorca observes: "Songs . . . are like people. They live, they are perfected, and some of them degenerate and fall apart, until all that is left are palimpsests full of senseless lacunae" (*OC* III: 483). This is the most mysterious poem in the book, and the first that Lorca composed (see preliminary note, above): one ms. is dated December 28, 1921, the feast of the Holy Innocents, a day for practical jokes like the ones played in the United States on April Fools' Day. The joke is perpetrated here by withholding information from the reader; interpretations have been—will always be—comically at odds. The poem's position in the book—it is one of the three "Historical Ballads"—lends credence to the idea, argued most recently by García-Posada and Hernández, that Lorca's Don Pedro is based on the Spanish medieval king Peter I the Cruel, closely associated with Seville (see note on *Seville*, p. 896), whom Lorca had read about in numerous traditional ballads and several seventeenth-century plays. Don Pedro was slain by his brother Henry of Trastamara in 1369 on the Campo de Montiel near the "eyes of the Guadiana River," a series of lagoons, which are mentioned in some of the traditional ballads. In the ballads, Don Pedro, who has taken a lover (María de Padilla), imprisons his pregnant young wife, Doña Blanca de Borbón, and has her murdered. Some have argued, not very plausibly, that Don Pedro is the apostle St. Peter or the Baroque poet Pedro Soto de Rojas (see Martín, *Federico García Lorca*, 337 ff., who believes that Soto symbolizes the writer and that the lagoons contain amniotic fluid!).

Thamar y Amnón / Thamar and Amnon. Written 1926–27? Based on the story of incest in II Samuel 13, but Lorca's immediate sources were the numerous traditional ballads on this subject and plays by Tirso de Molina and Calderón. "The gypsies and all the Andalusian people sing the ballad of Tamar and Amnon, calling Tamar *Altas Mares* ("high seas")" (*DS* 122). Lines 23–24: The dove is associated with Venus; Góngora had called it "lascivious bird of the Cyprian goddess" (García-Posada, 213). Line 64: Lorca often speaks of the "needling" sound of the flute; e.g., in *Solitude*, p. 623. Line 68: Allusion to the deflowering of Thamar, seen as a gypsy rite. Lines 73–74 have a distinctly vulgar tone: Lorca is imitating the *romance de ciego* (the lurid ballads about crimes sung by blind men in public squares). Salvador Dalí, who wrote Lorca a letter sharply criticizing *The Gypsy Ballads* (see *Poet in New York*, xiv), found this poem "the best of the lot . . . chunks of incest" (Santos Torroella, 88).

[*Odas*] / [*Odes*]

In September 1928, Lorca tells his friend Melchor Fernández Almagro that he has "almost finished my book of Odes, poles apart from *The Gypsy Ballads* and, I think, with a more poignant lyricism" (*EC* 590). It is not known what poems would have formed part of this book, never published, which Lorca referred to repeatedly in interviews and letters between 1928 and 1936. García-Posada (*OC* I: 926) believes the collection would have included *Ode to Salvador Dalí*, *Ode to the Most Holy Sacrament of the Altar*, *Solitude (In Homage to Fray Luis de León)*, and "Oda y burla de Sesostris y Sardanápalo" (Ode and Jest of Sesostris and Sardanapalus, devoted to an Assyrian king notorious for his effeminacy and corruption). The latter poem was never completed, and the forty-eight extant lines have been omitted here. For the Spanish text, see *OC* I:744–46.

Oda a Salvador Dalí / Ode to Salvador Dalí. Begun summer 1925; finished March 1926; published in *Revista de Occidente* (Madrid) the following month. Lorca refers to this poem in a letter as "Didactic Ode to Salvador Dalí" (*EC* 336), a good description of its intent. He had met Dalí at the Residencia de Estudiantes in 1922 and had spent Holy Week of 1925 with the Dalí family in Cadaqués and Barcelona: his first taste of the cultural diversity and ebullience of Catalunya.

The reader should remember that the Dalí of 1925 and early 1926 was neither a Cubist nor the Surrealist of later years, but was at work on more or less "realistic" paintings in the spirit of what he called (borrowing a phrase from the

Catalan writer Eugenio D'Ors) "Holy Objectivity": "Basket of Bread," "Girl Sewing," "Port of Cadaqués," and the early portraits of his father and sister. To Lorca, his style, like that of Jorge Guillén and of Góngora (the lecture on the great Baroque poet was written around the same time), had come to symbolize an aesthetic of unsentimental clarity. "To me [Dalí] seems unique," the poet wrote several years later to the art critic Sebastià Gasch. "He possesses a *clarity* of judgment that is truly moving. He makes a mistake and it doesn't matter: *he is alive.* His razor-sharp intelligence combines with a disconcerting childishness in an astoundingly original, captivating way. What moves me most about him right now is his *delirious* yearning to construct (that is, to create) . . . Nothing more dramatic than this objectivity, this search for joy for its own sake. Remember that this has always been the Mediterranean canon. 'I believe in the Resurrection of the flesh,' says Rome. Dalí is the man who fights phantasms with a hatchet of gold" (*EC* 543–44). Line 3: For Lorca's negative judgments on Impressionism, see "Sketch de la nueva pintura" (A Sketch of the New Painting) (*OC* III:88–97). Line 6: Manuel de Falla praised Lorca for this image of Cubism (Maurer, *Epistolario*, 264), less an allusion to the art of Dalí than to the spirit of modern painting. Line 9: Dalí had written to Lorca in 1925: "There is nothing so marvelous as feet pressed to earth under the 'weight' of the body; more than in Poussin, in Egypt we find feet planted firmly on the ground . . . When I paint, I paint without shoes, I like to feel the earth very close to my 'two' feet" (Santos Torroella, 15). Line 16: Lorca uses the same phrase to evoke Cadaqués in a letter to Ana María Dalí, shortly after his visit in 1925: "I think of Cadaqués. To me it seems a perfect landscape, both present and eternal. The horizon rises up like a great aqueduct . . ." (*EC* 277). Dalí had told Lorca in 1925 of his concern for "the construction, the architecture of the landscape: I believe that painting is still a long way from Cézanne's ambition, 'faire du Poussin d'après nature' " (Santos Torroella, 13). Line 17: Cf. *The Siren and the Carabineer.* Line 27: During his first visit to Dalí, Lorca writes to a friend: "Witches from the Pyrenees come down to beg the sirens for a little light. In this landscape I have heard, for the first time in my life, the true, classic shepherd's flute" (*EC* 275). Line 31: Handkerchiefs of farewell?

Line 39: With the advent of Cubism, "dark grays, white, sienna, tobacco, and other muted, austere colors . . . conquer the greens, reds, many-shaded yellows, and mauve-colored deliquescences" of the Impressionists. "At last the orgy of color has been put to an end" ("Sketch," *OC* III:41). Line 41: Hygiene—both literally and figuratively, as a defense against the virus of sentimentality—was one of Dalí's obsessions in his rebellion against bohemian, neo-Romantic visions of art. His "Manifest Groc" of 1928 would call for an "estricta asepsia espiritual." Line 44: Eutimio Martín (*Antología comentada*, 81) points out that in September 1925 Dalí had written to Lorca: "I have painted the whole afternoon: 7 waves, hard and cold as are the waves of the sea . . . tomorrow I will paint 7 more [. . .] How fondly, I paint my windows open to the sea!" The fourteen parallel waves would suggest a sonnet. Lines 49 ff.: The first draft had read: "The current of time pools and orders itself / in the parallelograms dreamt by the centuries . . . / / You are afraid of flowers and the water of the river, / because they are fleeting and they pass like the breeze. / You love definite, exact matter, / indifferent to mysteries and deathly to the worm. / / (Your palette, timid as a foolish bird / pulses in your hands with the seven colors.)"

Line 71: Dalí writes to Lorca in 1925: "I am experimenting with the construction of the atmosphere, better said, the construction of the void; I am fascinated by the plasticity of empty spaces, a matter which never seems to have concerned anyone . . ." (Santos Torroella, 15). Lorca would put the concept to use in *Poet in New York* (e.g., *Nocturne of Emptied Space*). Line 90: Crossed out in the ms.: "I sing your beautiful struggle for Latin clarity" (see preliminary note). Line 93: Crossed out: "adorned with straight lines and without a single wound." The playing cards suggest harsh light without shadow, as in *The Feud*. Line 93: Martín (*Antología*, 83) observes that certain figures in the French deck of cards are shown with their hearts exposed. Lines 98–101: Lorca censored himself in line 103; the first draft read: "el culo [the behind] of Theresa," alluding, perhaps, to a well-known canvas of Dalí's sister, Ana María, standing at a window. On Lorca's self-censorship, brought to my attention by Mario Hernández, cf. notes to *In Málaga* and *St. Michael* (pp. 919, 925). Line 105: Crossed out: "our friendship, radiant with heart and with laughter." The line means literally: "our friendship painted like a game of snakes and ladders." *Oca* is played with dice, and the brightly colored game board shows geese, rivers, wells, etc. Line 107: An allusion to the Catalan flag (Martín, *Antología*, 84). Its four red bars on a field of gold are said to have been traced by the fingers, bloodied in battle, of a Catalan conqueror.

Soledad / Solitude. Published in *Carmen* (Santander), March 1928, in an issue in honor of Fray Luis de León (1527–91), one of Spain's greatest Renaissance poets. Both form and theme evoke Fray Luis's ode "To the Solitary Life," written, like this poem, in *liras* (alternating lines of 7-11-7-7-11 syllables) beginning: "What a restful life, / that of him who flees from worldly noise / and follows the hidden / path down which have gone / the few wise men who have existed in the world" (tr. Rivers, 91). The title "Soledad" evokes the two great pastoral poems of Don Luis de Góngora (cf. *Uncertain Solitude*, p. 879). The epigraph is from Jorge Guillén's "Noche de luna" (Moonlit Night), which Lorca published in *gallo* (Granada) in 1928; text in *Cántico*, 221. Line 18: The "knot" binding body and soul in the neo-Platonist system of Fray Luis. Line 29: Allusion to the "imperishable music," the harmony of the spheres, described by Fray Luis in his celebrated "Ode to Salinas" (tr. Rivers, 95). Cf., on the same subject, *Elegy: To Silence*, p. 55, and *Sketch for an Ode*, p. 871. Spanish text from *OC* I: 457–61.

Oda al Santísimo Sacramento del Altar / Ode to the Most Holy Sacrament of the Altar. Parts one and two were begun in January 1928 and published in *Revista de Occidente* eleven months later. "[A poem of] great intensity. Perhaps the greatest poem I have ever written," Lorca tells his Colombian friend Jorge Zalamea in autumn 1928 (*EC* 582). Parts three and four were finished in New York on September 17, 1929. Manuel de Falla, a fervent, orthodox Roman Catholic, found the first two sections profoundly shocking. "Were I to write on the same theme," he told Lorca on February 9, 1929, "I would do so with my spirit *on its knees*, and I would beg that all Humanity be made divine through the grace of the Sacrament. And then I would make my offering: gold, frankincense and myrrh. Pure and unalloyed" (*IGM*, 127–28).

Of an audience in Cuba (1930) that objected to this poem, Lorca remarked bitterly, "There are people who take a millstone for Communion but choke on the Host in poetry" (Martín, *Federico García Lorca*, 304). Spanish text from *OC* I: 463–69.

Exposición / Exposition. Epigraph: "Celebrate, [my] tongue, the mystery of the glorious body." From a hymn by St. Thomas Aquinas sung during the exposition of the Host.

Mundo / World. Epigraph: Prayer of penitence sung before Holy Communion. "Lamb of God who takest away the sins of the world, have mercy on us." The final sections of the poem are devoted to the three traditional enemies of the soul according to the Catholic catechism: the world, the flesh, and the devil. Lorca wrote to Jorge Zalamea apropos of line 59: "I like it very much. It has the indefinable poetic charm of half-heard conversation" (*EC* 577).

Demonio / Devil. Epigraph: "Thou, O God, art my refuge. Why hast thou rejected me? Why must I go like a mourner because my foes oppress me?" (Psalms 43:2; recited by the celebrant of the Mass). Lines 77–88: The images of "light" (*luz*) and "beauty" (*belleza*) are generated by Lucifer's Spanish name, Luzbel (Martín, *Federico García Lorca*, 305–6). Lorca sent lines 77–91 to Zalamea with the remark: "To me this Devil seems every inch a Devil. This part will grow progressively darker and more metaphysical, until at last the enemy emerges in all his cruel beauty: wounding beauty, inimical to love" (*EC* 583). Line 110: Allusion to Calderón de la Barca's drama of a student who surrenders his soul to the devil, *El mágico prodigioso.*

Carne / Flesh. The epigraph is from a song in Lope de Vega's one-act allegorical play *Auto de los cantares* (ed. Menéndez Pelayo, 389). The character who plays Christ has just removed his cape (*queda en cuerpo*) and wears only a white tunic symbolizing the whiteness of the Host. The mention of Lope, who wrote many poems to the Holy Eucharist, would have reminded Lorca's readers that the subject had been dealt with, even in "classical" poetry, with a good measure of conceptual liberty. Soria Olmedo (*Federico García Lorca*, 33) points out a more recent intertext: Unamuno's *El Cristo de Velázquez* (1920). Lines 15–16 of *Exposition*, for example, were suggested by Lope's tireless punning on *blanco* (both target and white—the whiteness of the Host): "Rush to the divine target/ whiteness," he exclaims in one ballad (ed. Blecua, 537). Dismissed by many as flippant "Surrealism," Lorca's ode—especially the first two parts—contains more than a few traditional poetic "conceits" (the decorative "needles" of the monstrance in lines 5–8; the whiteness of "spikenards under snow" in line 11, etc.). Line 156: Martín (*Federico García Lorca*, 266) believes as many as twenty verses may be missing between this line and the next. Line 158: Madroños are the small red berries of *Arbutus menziesii,* a shrub common in Spain. Lines 167–68: Cf. the sonnet *Adam.* Line 168: In the ms. Lorca writes both "niñas de *sangre*" (girls of *blood*) and "niñas de *lumbre*" (girls of *flame*), without crossing out either variant. Line 171: The line is incomplete in the ms.

Poeta en Nueva York / Poet in New York

A full introduction to this book, with notes, letters, photos, and Lorca's own commentary, are found in *PNY.*

Vuelta de paseo / After a Walk. Unpublished during Lorca's life. For Lorca's comments on this poem, see *PNY* 188–89.

1910 (Intermedio) / 1910 (Intermezzo). Unpublished during Lorca's life. For Lorca's commentary, see *PNY* 188.

Fábula y rueda de los tres amigos / Fable of Three Friends to Be Sung in Rounds.

Unpublished during Lorca's life. His friend Rafael Martínez Nadal believes the poet is remembering his love affair with Emilio Aladrén (Emilio) and adds coyly that he could identify the other two "friends" without difficulty. See Martínez Nadal, *Cuatro lecciones,* 30.

Tu infancia en Menton / Your Childhood in Menton. The title refers to the town on the French Riviera, and the epigraph is from Jorge Guillén's poem "Los jardines" (The Gardens) in section three of *Cántico,* 1928. Lorca's poem was published in *Héroe* (Madrid), 4 (1932), 4–5, and in *Sur* (Buenos Aires) 7, no. 34 (July 1937), 29–31, with the title "Ribera de 1910."

Norma y paraiso de los negros / Standards and Paradise of the Blacks. Unpublished during Lorca's life. Two manuscripts are extant, and in the earliest Lorca has rejected two titles: "La luna desierta y as de bastos" (Deserted Moon and Ace of Clubs) and "Paraíso quemado" (Burnt Paradise). The word "Paradise" may allude to the black cabaret, Smalls Paradise, mentioned in Lorca's lecture on this book, and *"Burnt* Paradise" is probably a reference to the persecution of the blacks by whites: one of the photos that Lorca wanted to include in *PNY* was a picture of a "burnt Negro."

El rey de Harlem / The King of Harlem. First published in *Los Cuatro Vientos* (Madrid), 1 (Feb. 1933), 5–10, as "Oda al Rey de Harlem." The black "king" recalls a poem by Juan Ramón Jiménez in *Diario de un poeta reciéncasado (Diary of a Newly Married Poet).* For Lorca's comments, see *PNY* 189–92.

Iglesia abandonada (Balada de la Gran Guerra) / Abandoned Church (Ballad of the Great War). Ms. dated November 29, 1929. First published in *Poesía* (Buenos Aires) 1, no. 7 (Nov. 1933), 28–29. Critics have pondered why this poem appears in the section about blacks. John K. Walsh notes that "Lorca might well have known the glowing legend of the Harlem blacks in the Great War" (Walsh, "The Social and Sexual Geography").

Danza de la muerte / Dance of Death. First published in *Revista de Avance* (Havana) 5, no. 45 (Apr. 15, 1930), 107–9. For Lorca's comments, see *PNY* 192–93.

Paisaje de la multitud que vomita / Landscape of a Vomiting Multitude. Published in *Poesía* 1, no. 7 (Nov. 1933); 25–26, and in *Noreste* (Zaragoza) 11 (1935), 6. One of the two extant manuscripts is dated December 29, 1929. The atmosphere, including the "fat lady," may have been suggested by Lorca's trip to Coney Island on July 4, 1929. (See his comments in *PNY* 193–94.)

Paisaje de la multitud que orina / Landscape of a Pissing Multitude. Unpublished during Lorca's life.

Asesinato / Murder. There are no less than five versions of this poem, first published in *Cristal* (Pontevedra) 2, no. 7 (Jan. 1933).

Navidad en el Hudson / Christmas on the Hudson. Unpublished during Lorca's life; ms. dated December 27, 1929.

Ciudad sin sueño / Sleepless City. Published in Diego, *Poesía española. Antologia: 1915–1931,* 320–22; ms. dated October 9, 1929.

Panorama ciego de Nueva York / Blind Panorama of New York. Unpublished during Lorca's life.

Nacimiento de Cristo / The Birth of Christ. Unpublished during Lorca's life.

La aurora / Dawn. Unpublished during Lorca's life. In the ms. Lorca has rejected two titles: "Obrero parado" (Unemployed Worker) and "Amanecer" (Daybreak). The ms. is undated, but the first title suggests it was written after the crash of the stock market in October 1929.

Poema doble del Lago Eden / Double Poem of Lake Eden. First published in *Poesía* 1, no. 7 (Nov. 1933), 26–28. A manuscript submitted in 1930 to the *Revista de Avance* (Havana), but not published, is reproduced and discussed in Marinello, *Contemporáneos*, 218–25. This manuscript contains autobiographical references omitted in the later versions, e.g., lines 37–48: "I want to cry speaking my name, / Federico García Lorca, on the shore of this lake, / to speak truly as a man of blood / killing in myself the mockery and the suggestive power of the word. // Here, before the most naked water, / I search for my freedom, my human love, / not my future flight, light or quicklime, / my present time, watching for me on the ball of crazed air. // Pure poetry. Impure poetry. / Vain pirouette, torn newspaper. / Tower of saltpeter, where words collide / and a smooth dawn which stays afloat with the anguish of exactitude." The epigraph is line 1146 of the second eclogue of Garcilaso de la Vega. Commentary by Lorca in *PNY* 197–98.

Cielo vivo / Living Sky. Published posthumously in Adolfo Salazar, "El mito de Caimito," *Carteles* (Havana) (Jan. 23, 1938), 24. The ms. is dated "cabaña de Dew-Kum-Inn. Eden Mills—Vermont—24 de agosto—1929," a reference to the lakeside cottage rented by the family of the poet Philip Cummings, whom Lorca visited in Vermont in summer 1929. Cummings told Kessel Schwartz that the poem (or perhaps only the title) "was inspired by a night of brilliant aurora borealis activity as the lake reflected the lights against a pitch-black Mount Norris" (Schwartz, "García Lorca and Vermont," 42).

El niño Stanton / Little Stanton. Unpublished during Lorca's lifetime. One of the two extant manuscripts is dated January 5, 1930. Another version was published by Adolfo Salazar in *Carteles* (Havana) (Jan. 23, 1938), 30. (See Lorca's comments on Stanton Hogan, a boy he had met while vacationing in Newburgh, New York, in *PNY* 194.)

Vaca / Cow. Published in *Revista de Occidente* (Madrid) 21, no. 91 (Jan. 1931), 24–25, with a dedication to Lorca's friend the architect Luis Lacasa.

Niña ahogada en el pozo / Little Girl Drowned in the Well. First published in Diego, *Poesía Española*, 1932. See Lorca's comments in *PNY* 197.

Muerte / Death. First published in *Revista de Occidente* 31, no. 91 (Jan. 1931), 21–22, with initial dedication to the journalist and critic Luis de la Serna.

Nocturno del hueco / Nocturne of Emptied Space. Text uncertain. Published in *Caballo verde para la poesía* (Madrid) 1 (Oct. 1935), 6–8 (the version followed here.) Ms. B offers a heavily corrected autograph version dated "New York / Sept. (Campo) 1929," written, apparently, during a visit to the country home of Lorca's friend Ángel del Río in Bushnellsville, near Shandaken, New York. Some corrections in Ms. B seem to postdate the *Caballo verde* version but cannot be included here: the original of B is still unavailable to researchers.

Paisaje con dos tumbas y un perro asirio / Landscape with Two Graves and an Assyrian Dog. First published in *1616* 7(1935), 4–5, a poetry magazine edited in London by Lorca's friend Manuel Altolaguirre.

Ruina / Ruin. Published in *Revista de Occidente* 31, no. 91 (Jan. 1931), 22, and in Diego, *Poesía española*, 1932, 318–20.

Luna y panorama de los insectos / Moon and Panorama of the Insects. The manuscript is dated January 4, 1930. Lorca's epigraph is from "Canción del pirata" (Pirate's Song) by the Romantic poet José de Espronceda, a poem every Spanish schoolchild knows by heart.

New York (Oficina y denuncia) / *New York (Office and Denunciation)*. First published in *Revista de Occidente* 31, no. 91 (Jan. 1931), 25–28.

Cementerio judío / *Jewish Cemetery*. Unpublished during Lorca's life. The ms. is dated January 18, 1930.

Crucifixión / *Crucifixion*. Unpublished during Lorca's life.

Grito hacia Roma / *Cry to Rome*. Unpublished during Lorca's life. The poem is widely believed to have been inspired by the signing of the Lateran treaties between Mussolini and Pius XI in February 1929. John K. Walsh believes that the poem refers to "the pope's failure to act humanely in the matter of the Cristeros rebellion in Mexico: on June 21, 1929, he issued the bland requisites of capitulation, leaving the Cristeros stranded in their cause, and their leader (Father Pedroza) to be killed brutally by the federalist army." ("The Social and Sexual Geography," 4).

Oda a Walt Whitman / *Ode to Walt Whitman*. Published in an edition of fifty copies by Ediciones Alcancía, Mexico, August 15, 1933. The ms. is dated June 15 [1930] and must, therefore, have been finished on board the ship that took Lorca from Havana back to New York and from there to Cádiz.

Pequeño vals vienés / *Little Viennese Waltz*. First published in *1616* 1 (1934). Another version is dated February 13, 1930. This poem and the next were to have formed part of a book that Lorca was planning in 1933: *Porque te quiero a ti solamente (Tanda de valses): Because I Love Only You (Waltz Album)*. In October 1933 he told the Argentine critic Pablo Suero: "In this book I speak of many things I like but which people say are out of fashion. Fashion I detest. Why shouldn't I admit that I like Zorrilla, that I like Chopin, that I like waltzes? . . . The book is written in waltz time . . . like *this*: sweet, lovable, vaporous" (*OC* III: 542–43).

Vals en las ramas / *Waltz in the Branches*. There is a ms. dated August 21, 1931, in the Huerta de San Vicente. Published by Manuel Altolaguirre in his magazine *Héroe* (Madrid) 1 (1932), 7–8, with the dedication "To Vicente Aleixandre for his poem *The Waltz*." Aleixandre's poem is from *Espadas como labios (Swords like Lips)*, 1932.

Son de negros en Cuba / *Blacks Dancing to Cuban Rhythms*. Written in Havana, this *son* (an Afro-Cuban chant) was dedicated to the Cuban anthropologist Fernando Ortiz (1881–1969) and published in *Musicalia* 11 (Apr.–May 1930). The poem alludes to a rail trip Lorca took to Santiago de Cuba in spring 1930. The images in lines 12–16 refer to the cigar boxes he had seen as a child: thus Romeo and Juliet, the blond hair of Fonseca, the paper sea and silver coins on the lids. Two of the labels are reproduced in Auclair, 216. See Lorca's commentary in *PNY* 200–1.

Trip to the Moon

Filmscript written during Lorca's visit to New York (1929); published posthumously in 1980 in a limited edition by Marie Laffranque. Filmed by Frederic Amat in 1998. Closely related to the cycle of New York poems and to the drama *El público (The Audience)*. Lorca's conversations with the Mexican artist Emilio Amero (who had recently made a short film entitled *777* using images of adding machines, drawings, photos, and numbers) about the possibilities of cinematographic movement, and his interest in *Un chien andalou* by Buñuel and

Dalí (a film that Lorca had not seen but had heard and read about) prompted him to write this scenario in a day and a half in his room at Columbia University (Stainton, 233). In his critical edition of this work, Antonio Monegal argues that it involves a metaphorical representation of desire and its frustration; a terrifying confrontation with feminine sexuality; and (in the final scenes) an ironic attack on the conventional cinema. Title: An allusion to Jules Verne's novel *De la Terre à la Lune* (1865); to Georges Méliès's film *Le voyage dans la lune* (1902); and to a well-known cyclorama at Luna Park, Coney Island, New York: A Trip to the Moon. 13: The sexual symbolism is obvious. Fish are on the verge of "penetrating" round objects in several drawings by Lorca (*Dibujos* nos. 107, 112, 208). 34: Monegal observes that the same name (suggesting archetypal woman) appears in *The Audience*, one of whose masculine characters equates it to "Selene" (the moon). 38: Two drawings by Lorca of St. Radegunda are extant (*Dibujos* nos. 161, 162) and p. 747. Lorca's interest in this sixth-century saint, Queen of the Franks, to whom he gives a martyrdom of his own invention, has never been satisfactorily explained. In one of the drawings "the body [of the saint] is vomiting, seems to have four wounds in its chest, and bleeds from its genitals. In the second . . . there is no vomiting, but the figure also bleeds from its genitals and is accompanied by a strange, lion-like beast that appears in other New York drawings, by a flying angel bearing a lyre . . . and by another personage who carries a lighted candle" (Gibson, *Federico García Lorca*, 276). 42: The figure with exposed veins was frequently depicted in Salvador Dalí's work of the later 1920s. 45: Female genitals, probably. For drawings by Lorca, see *Dibujos*, nos. 290.4, 290.5.

"Infancia y muerte" / Poemas de *Tierra y luna*
"Childhood and Death" / Poems from *Earth and Moon*

With the exception of the first, which was never given a final revision, these poems were intended for a collection entitled *Tierra y luna*, which Lorca was working on in mid-1933 but later abandoned. For a discussion of *Tierra y luna*, whose contents were later assigned to *Poet in New York* and *The Tamarit Divan*, see PNY 290–91.

Infancia y muerte / Childhood and Death. Rough draft of a poem from the New York cycle (dated October 7, 1929). Facsimile version (followed here) in Hernández, ed., *Manuscritos neoyorquinos*, 220–23. Lorca's friend Rafael Martínez Nadal, who edited the manuscript posthumously, recalls that a despondent Lorca sent it to him from New York with the comment: "So you can see my state of mind" (*Autógrafos*, xxxv). When Martínez Nadal reminded Lorca of this poem years later, he did not want to look at it again. The *anda* (streamer) mentioned in line 31 was carried by children on either side of the coffin in funeral processions (the streamers were attached to the coffin) (Zambrano, 189).

Tierra y luna / Earth and Moon. Ms. dated August 28, 1929. The title poem of the collection. Written in Eden Mills, northern Vermont, during Lorca's visit to the young American poet Philip Cummings and his family. Published in *El Tiempo Presente* (Madrid) in March 1935. Line 19, "Pharaoh": See note to FLAMENCO VIGNETTES, p. 897. The text followed here is Hernández, *Manuscritos neoyorquinos*, 212–17.

Pequeño poema infinito / Little Infinite Poem. Ms. dated January 10, 1930. Written in New York. Spanish text from Hernández (*Manuscritos neoyorquinos,* 218–19), who follows the autograph manuscript. In the ms., the title "Pequeña narración china" (Small Chinese Tale) is crossed out.

Omega (Poema para muertos) / Omega (Poem for the Dead). Probably written summer 1931, when Lorca tells his friend Regino Sainz de la Maza: "I have written a book of poems, *Poems for the Dead,* one of the most intense that has ever come from my hand. I have been like a fountain, writing morning, noon and night. Sometimes I have run a fever, like the old Romantics, but without ever ceasing to feel the intense conscious joy of creation" (*EC* 716). Plans for this book were abandoned. *Omega* was first published in 1935 in the poetry magazine *1616* (London). As in *Landscape with Two Graves and an Assyrian Dog* one dead man appears to be addressing another. Text from *OC* I: 580–81.

Canción de la muerte pequeña / Song of a Little Death. Spanish text from Martín, *Poeta en Nueva York,* 280–81, who follows the version that appears in Gerardo Diego's 1934 anthology. An earlier, very different version was published in *La Nación* (Buenos Aires) of October 20, 1933, during Lorca's visit to Argentina. The earlier version is as follows: "Song of a Little Death / / Mortal sky of moons / and blood beneath the earth. / Sky of old blood. / / Mortal meadow of moons / and night beneath the earth. / Meadow of old blood. / / I happened into Death. / Mortal sky of grass. / A small death. / / The dog [was] on the roof. / Only my left hand / went through unending hills / of dry flowers. / / Cathedral of ash. / The snow moans and trembles / behind the door. / / A death, and I, a man. / A man alone, and she, / a small death. / / A death, and I a man. / A man alone and she. / Meadow. / Love. / Light / and sand." Martín (*Poeta en Nueva York,* 84) believes this poem was to form part of *Tierra y luna,* but the documentary evidence is slight.

El poeta pide ayuda a la Virgen / The Poet Prays to the Virgin for Help. Spanish text in Hernández, *Poeta en Nueva York,* 224–25. Date of composition uncertain. See *PNY* 195–96. For the Virgin's reply (incomplete), see Hernández, 227. Simon and White translate as follows: "The Holy Virgin Replies: But I pluck out my eyes of the giraffe. / And I replace them with the crocodile's eyes. / Because I am the Virgin Mary. / The flies see a cloud of black pepper. / But they are not the Virgin Mary. / I watch the crimes of the leaves, / the stinging pride of the wasps, / the indifferent mule driven crazy by the double moon / and the stable where the planet eats all its tiny offspring. / Because I am the Virgin Mary. // Solitude lives stuck in the mud." A more complete manuscript of the poem was apparently given by Lorca to the French Hispanist Mathilde Pomès, but it has since been lost.

Diván del Tamarit / The Tamarit Divan

Written 1931–34; published posthumously in 1940 in a special issue of *Revista Hispánica Moderna,* Columbia University. The book was to have been published by the University of Granada, and the page proofs had already been pulled (they are still extant) when the project was interrupted, probably by the outbreak of the Civil War in July 1936.

Qasida 5 was written in Granada in August 1931. Anderson believes that qasidas 6 and 9 were also written that month. Five poems (ghazals 8 and 10 and qasidas 1, 2, and 6) were written April 4–5, 1934, aboard the *Conte Biancamano* as Lorca returned to Spain from Buenos Aires. The *Divan* was revised and finished by September of that year.

The Spanish text follows the critical edition of Andrew A. Anderson. For a detailed commentary see Anderson, *Lorca's Late Poetry*.

In a prologue written for the Granada edition, the Arabist Emilio García Gómez explains: "In Arabic the word *qasida* refers to a fairly long poem of a certain internal architecture (the details are not important here), with a single rhyme. The *ghazal*—employed principally in Persian lyric poetry—is a short poem, preferably with an erotic theme . . . with more than four verses and fewer than 15. *Diván* is the poet's collected verse, generally arranged in the alphabetical order of the rhymes" (Anderson edition, 183–84).

The "Tamarit" was a *huerta* (or small farm) "which belonged to the father of one of [Lorca's] favorite cousins . . . The word Tamarit means 'abundant in dates' in Arabic, and the poet used to say that he loved [this] *huerta*, with its wonderful views of the Sierra Nevada and the poplar groves of the Vega" (Gibson; *Federico García Lorca*, 386).

Gacela primera. Del amor imprevisto / Ghazal of Love Unforeseen. Anderson (*Diván*, 192) believes lines 11–12 are reminiscent of a traditional ballad about the Duke of Alba, which Lorca quotes in his lecture "How a City Sings from November to November": "They tried to open his chest / to see what he had died from. / On one side of his heart / he had two words of gold. / One said 'Duke,' / and the other, 'dearer than life' " (*SG* 110–11).

Gacela II. De la terrible presencia / Ghazal of the Terrible Presence. Probably written between April and September 1934 (Anderson, *Diván*, 193). Published in *Quaderns de Poesía* (Barcelona) in October 1935.

Gacela III. Del amor desesperado / Ghazal of Desperate Love. Probably written between June and September 1934 (Anderson, *Diván*, 196).

Gacela IV. Del amor que no se deja ver / Ghazal of the Love That Hides from Sight. Lines 1–2 are from the lyrics of a flamenco piece, a *tanguillo*: "I want to live in Granada / only to hear / the bell of the Vela / when I go to sleep" (Anderson, *Diván*, 198). In his *Handbook for Travellers in Spain*, Richard Ford explains (I:303) that the "*torre de la Vela* is so called, because on this watchtower hangs a silver-tongued bell, which, struck by the warder at certain times, is the primitive clock that gives notice to irrigators below. It is heard on a still night even at Loja, 30 m. off, and tender and touching are the feelings which the silver sound awakens. This bell is also rung every January 2, the anniversary of the surrender of Granada; on that day the Alhambra is visited by crowds of peasantry. Few maidens pass by without striking the bell, which ensures a husband, and a good one in proportion as the noise made, which it need not be said is continuous and considerable. The fete is altogether most national and picturesque." The crown of vervain ("verbena") in line 3 would be appropriate for a future husband (or wife). The rhyme *verbena / Cartagena* was suggested by a children's song alluded to also in *Book of Poems*: "Ay! Ay! Ay! / When will my love come? / Verbena, verbena, / garden of Cartagena" (Anderson, *Diván*, 199). Line 8 could also be translated: "I tore out my garden of Cartagena."

Gacela V. Del niño muerto / Ghazal of the Dead Child. Cf. *Qasida of One Wounded by Water.*

Gacela VI. De la raíz amarga / Ghazal of the Bitter Root. Published in *Héroe* (Madrid) 6 (1933). Anderson (*Diván*, 205) explains that the image of the "bitter root" occurs in the Epistle of St. Paul to the Hebrews, 12:14–16: "Follow peace with all men . . . / / Looking diligently lest any man fail of the grace of God; lest any root of bitterness springing up trouble you, and thereby many be defiled; / / Lest there be any fornicator, or profane person, as Esau, who for one morsel of meat sold his birthright." Lines 6–7: García-Posada (*Poesía, 1,* 63) asks: "What can these 'thousand windows' be but the stars? The poet calls them 'livid bees' because he has imagined the sky as a huge beehive—'a thousand' is hyperbole—whose stars seem to be in combat and whose lividness is a probable image of their more or less deathly glow."

Gacela VII. Del recuerdo de amor / Ghazal of the Memory of Love. Line 7, "For a plaster heart": or "For a heart of gypsum" (see line 1 of *Ghazal of Marvelous Love*). Line 19, "Grass": or "The weeds . . ."

Gacela VIII. De la muerte oscura / Ghazal of Dark Death. Published in *Floresta de Prosa y Verso* (Madrid) 2 (Feb. 1936). Lines 17–18: Cf. *Ballad of the Marked Man.*

Gacela IX. Del amor maravilloso / Ghazal of Marvelous Love. Line 1: Literally: "With all the gypsum . . ." but with the suggestion of "Despite . . ."

Gacela X. De la huida / Ghazal of the Flight. Published in *Almanaque Literario* (Madrid) in January 1935 with the title "Casida de la muerte clara" (Qasida of a Clear Death); cf. line 17 and *Ghazal of Dark Death.* The *Almanaque* version was dedicated to Lorca's friend the journalist Miguel Pérez Ferrero. Cf. the luminous death the poet yearns for in *Cicada!*

Gacela XI. Del amor con cien años / Ghazal of the Hundred-Year-Old Love. Published in *Almanaque Literario* (Madrid), January 1935. Line 13: Literally: "Through the myrtles . . ." Anderson points out that the plant is associated with Venus and is therefore emblematic of love. The "myrtle" referred to here is not periwinkle (*vinca*) but the tall evergreen shrub with aromatic foliage; myrtle bushes grow in the gardens of the Alhambra in Granada.

Casida primera. Del herido por el agua / Qasida of One Wounded by Water. Cf. *Little Girl Drowned in the Well (Granada and Newburgh)* in *Poet in New York* and *Nocturne of the Drowned Youth* in *Six Galician Poems.* Lines 7–8: Cf. *Garden* in WATER JETS, where Lorca compares the *jets d'eau* to swords.

Casida II. Del llanto / Qasida of the Weeping. Published in Gerardo Diego's anthology of 1934.

Casida III. De los ramos / Qasida of the Branches. In his lecture on *duende* Lorca had written of artistic inspiration: "The duende does not come at all unless he sees that death is possible. The duende must know beforehand that he can serenade death's house and rock those branches we all wear: branches that do not have, will never have, any consolation" (*SD* 58). Lines 14–15: Literally: "Seated with the water on their knees / two valleys were waiting for Autumn."

Casida IV. De la mujer tendida / Qasida of the Woman Prone. Published in *Almanaque Literario,* January 1935, 254. Lorca's vision of Earth in lines 1–4 recalls Rafael Alberti's "Tres recuerdos del cielo" (Three Memories of Heaven) in *On the Angels* (1929).

Casida V. Del sueño al aire libre / Qasida of the Dream in Open Air. Published in *Héroe* (Madrid) 5 (1933). In the first four lines images of nature seem to flow together as in a dream: the bleeding "bull" of the sunset suggests the "chart" or map (for Spain is commonly said to be shaped like a bull's hide), and the "infinite pavement" of line 2 suggests a "hall." The latter suggests a "harp," and the sound of "Arpa" and the thought of the sunset leads to "Alba" (dawn). Line 12:

Anderson suggests Lorca is referring to the moon, in the "infinite pavement" of the dark sky.

Casida VI. De la mano imposible / Qasida of the Impossible Hand. The image of the hand occurs in two other compositions of the same period. In his "Elegy" for the painter María Blanchard, Lorca writes: "No one caressed her monstrous waist, except that great dead hand, just unnailed from the Cross and still spurting blood. This was the arm that . . . helped her in terrible 'childbirth' [i.e., death] when the huge dove of her soul could hardly squeeze through her sunken mouth" (*DS* 6). In *Once Five Years Pass*, the hand comes onstage to guide a dead child to the other world. Line 15: Cf. the final line of *Lament for Ignacio Sánchez Mejías.*

Casida VII. De la rosa / Qasida of the Rose. In his lecture on Góngora, Lorca writes: "The greatness of a poem does not depend on the grandness of its theme . . . [T]he form and fragrance of just one rose can be made to give the impression of infinity" (*DS* 69).

Casida VIII. De la muchacha dorada / Qasida of the Golden Girl. Both the theme of the maiden bathing at night and the comparison of the girl to a heron are common in Spanish traditional verse (see Cummins, 77, 80–82).

Casida IX. De las palomas oscuras / Qasida of the Dark Doves. Published in *Héroe* (Madrid) 2 (1932), in *La Nación* (Buenos Aires), October 29, 1933, and in *Primeras canciones* (*First Songs*), 1936. The *qasida* contains reminiscences of at least two folk songs. Daniel Devoto (*Introducción*, 114) has written that lines 3–4 recall "De tu cara sale el sol, / de tu garganta la luna; / morenas he visto yo; / pero como tú, ninguna" (The sun comes from your face, / from your throat, the moon; / I have seen dark women, / but none like you). Brenan (119) quotes and translates a traditional song from Granada province: "Pajarito de la nieve, / dime, ¿dónde tienes el nido? / Lo tengo en un pino verde / en una rama escondida" (Little bird of the snow, / Tell me, where have you built your nest? / I have made it in a green pine tree / on a safely hidden branch). See also Fuentes Vázquez, 193.

Gacela del mercado matutino / Ghazal of the Market in the Morning. It was Lorca's Argentine editor, Guillermo de Torre, who added this poem to the *Divan*, and it is given here in appendix. The "Arch of Elvira" or "Gate of Elvira" leads to the gypsy (formerly Moorish) quarter of the Albaicín, Granada. John K. Walsh (unpublished notes) suggests that, throughout the *Diván*, Lorca is "wary of overly specific homoeroticism: when the time came to publish the entire set of poems, he apparently removed the *Ghazal of the Morning Market,* where the beloved was clearly a young man and the image of cactus penetrating crystal was too exposed."

Seis poemas galegos / Six Galician Poems

Written 1932–34. Published in Santiago de Compostela by Editorial Nós toward the end of 1935. Lorca traveled on four occasions—first (1916) as a student and years later as lecturer and as director of the amateur theater troupe La Barraca—to Galicia, the rainy, hilly farming region that forms the northwestern angle of the Iberian Peninsula. Home of an important school of lyric poetry (the so-called Galician-Portuguese lyric) in the fourteenth century, Galicia enjoyed a literary renaissance in the nineteenth and early twentieth centuries.

How these poems came to be "produced" in Galician is a matter of some dispute. Andrew Anderson, whose critical edition is followed here, argues convincingly that they were "composed originally, in written or oral form, in Castilian or defective Galician. Thereafter, they were translated or copied out, certainly with linguistic and possibly also aesthetic corrections by [Lorca's close friend] Ernesto Guerra da Cal and possibly another. Finally, they were transcribed again with further orthographic, linguistic, and aesthetic revisions by [the noted Galician author] Eduardo Blanco Amor. The received text is the result of an accretion of several redactions and versions, and certainly not all of these were supervised, corrected, or directly checked and approved by Lorca himself" ("Who Wrote *Seis poemas gallegos* . . . ?" 139). For a detailed commentary see Anderson, *Lorca's Late Poetry.*

Madrigal â cibdá de Santiago / Madrigal for the City of Santiago. Published at least seven times during Lorca's lifetime.

Romaxe de Nosa Señora da Barca / Ballad of Our Lady of the Boat. Lorca refers to a nocturnal pilgrimage to a shrine near Muxia, in the province of La Coruña. Dedicated to the Virgin, the hermitage sits on a flat boat-shaped rock (Anderson, *Lorca's Late Poetry,* p. 248). Line 11: both the living and the dead participate in certain Galician religious processions; the dead are thought to take the form of reptiles and insects. See *SD* 57, 98. Line 15: Literally, "the flowers of the shrouded woman."

Cántiga do neno da tenda / Song of the Shop Boy. Written 1933–34 during Lorca's trip to Buenos Aires, home to thousands of Galician immigrants known for their *morriña,* a melancholy longing for the motherland. The title—not an accurate one, since this is a ballad—evokes the medieval Galician-Portuguese lyric. Line 1: The bagpipe is a traditional instrument among Galicians, who are of Celtic origins. Line 14, "muiñeira": a popular Galician dance performed to the wail and shriek of the bagpipes, "a courting dance in the form of a dialogue of hands and feet" (Starkie, 28).

Noiturnio do adoescente morto / Nocturne of the Drowned Youth. Line 15: The image is from Góngora; Lorca had admired lines 417–18 of the *First Solitude,* where the West "draws round the Sun, on the blue couch of the sea, / turquoise curtains." Lorca took these curtains to refer to the wind (*DS* 66). Line 16: On the expression "water-oxen," see note to line 14 of *Ballad of the Marked Man.*

Canzón de cuna pra Rosalía Castro, morta / Lullaby in Death for Rosalía de Castro. The poetry of Rosalía de Castro (1837–85) had attracted Lorca's interest as early as March 1919. In "Salutación elegíaca a Rosalía de Castro" (Elegiac Greeting to Rosalía de Castro), full of melancholy reflection upon Spain's political and cultural decline, he tells the greatest of modern Galician poets (prose translation): "To open your books is to see your soul. The dust of an old pain rises from them . . . Pain of mothers who sow the seed of disenchantment in the furrows. Pain of children abandoned. Pain of dry fields, lit by the black torch of emigration. To open your books is to open Spain, a Spain full of decay and sorrow" (*PI* 514). The refrain of this lullaby echoes a song by Rosalía: "Cantan os galos pr'o día; / érguete, meu ben, e vaite" (The cocks crow at daybreak. / Arise, my love, and go) (Feal Deibe, 580).

Danza da lúa en Santiago / Dance of the Moon in Santiago. The refrain (literally: "in the Quintana of the dead") refers to a small plaza in Santiago, next to the cathedral, the former cemetery of the canons (Ford, II:611).

Llanto por Ignacio Sánchez Mejías /
Lament for Ignacio Sánchez Mejías

Written October 1934, published in March or April 1935 by Cruz y Raya, Madrid. The *Lament* commemorates Lorca's friend the bullfighter Ignacio Sánchez Mejías (Seville 1891–Madrid 1934), who was gored in a provincial ring at Manzanares and died two days later of gangrene poisoning, on August 13, 1934. Sánchez Mejías had retired from the ring in 1927 to pursue a career as a playwright and to manage the career of the dancer Encarnación López Júlvez, "La Argentinita," to whom the poem is dedicated. A connoisseur of poetry and of *cante jondo* (the poet Jorge Guillén called him one of the most lucid and intelligent people he had ever met), Sánchez Mejías had invited Lorca, Guillén, and other writers to Seville in December 1927 to celebrate the three hundredth anniversary of the death of Góngora. He was in New York in 1930 at the same time as Lorca, and the poet introduced him when he lectured at Columbia University.

Sánchez Mejías's return to bullfighting at age forty-three, after seven years of retirement, surprised and dismayed his friends. He appears to have been spurred on by the memory of his brother-in-law, Joselito, who had died in the ring. "The only danger in bullfighting," he told a journalist in 1934, "is the danger of ceasing to exist. Joselito is alive. More alive than Belmonte or I because he *did* die valiantly in the bull-ring, while we, like cowards, are tucked away at home. We cease to exist, while *his* presence is felt in every bullfight." Of Sánchez Mejías's death, Lorca told a friend: "It is like my own death, an apprenticeship for my own death. I feel an astonishing sense of calm . . . There are moments when I see the dead Ignacio so vividly that I can imagine his body, destroyed, pulled apart by the worms and the brambles, and I find only a silence which is not nothingness, but mystery" (Auclair, 28–29).

The *Llanto* (the title, from the Latin *planctus*, suggests a "lament" or "lamentation" more visceral and intense than an "elegy") was published in an edition of two thousand copies by the poet's friend the writer José Bergamín (publisher of *Poet in New York*) at Cruz y Raya, Madrid. The Spanish text followed here is from Anderson's 1988 edition (*Diván*). See also the edition of Mario Hernández (Madrid: Ayuntamiento de Madrid, 1997), which includes an excellent introductory essay.

1. *La cogida y la muerte / The Goring and the Death.* In the *Llanto*, the poet officiates over a liturgical form (with elements of the Holy Mass and of the litany) of his own invention. Francisco García Lorca writes that section 1 is "the first time in the history of Spanish meter that the [hendecasyllabic] line, of learned Renaissance tradition, is joined to the older octosyllable" (*Federico y su mundo*, 207). Line 5: Quicklime was used as a disinfectant in the infirmaries of bullrings and was often used at burials (García-Posada, *Primer romancero*, 223; Anderson, *Diván*, 285). Line 15: Sánchez Mejías was deeply gored in the right thigh; cf. line 43, where the horn has left a wound in the shape of a lily. Line 17: Literally, "bass strings of the guitar begin to sound." Line 23: Presumably the bull is rejoicing in his triumph: Lorca's expression recalls the Latin *sursum corda* ("Lift up your hearts"), from the Mass. Line 41: Sánchez Mejías insisted on having the wound bandaged and being transported to Madrid. There was a long delay in getting him to the hospital, and penicillin had not yet been developed. Line 43: Anderson (1986) believes Lorca may also be alluding to Adonis, who died after

being wounded in the groin by the tusks of a boar. On the cult of Adonis in Roman Spain, see Josephs, 108 ff. Line 47: José Bergamín, who was with Sánchez Mejías in the infirmary at Manzanares, writes that "the little room . . . had a tiny barred window, like a jail cell, which barely let in the dusty, burning air on that hottest of August afternoons. I opened the shutters from time to time, and outside the window there was always a sunburnt peasant face asking the same anxious question: 'Did he die yet?' " (García-Posada, *Primer romancero*, 225).

2. *La sangre derramada / The Spilled Blood*. Line 1: Lorca refused to attend Sánchez Mejías's bullfights. He went to the clinic where his friend was being treated but refused to enter the room where Sánchez Mejías was dying. Lines 58–61: "The moon—'wide open': either at the full or brightly gleaming—is like a horse amidst the quiet clouds . . . [p]robably in that the clouds are scudding before the wind and so creating the common optical illusion that while *they* are still the moon is racing" (Jones and Scanlon, 101). Line 67: An allusion to the moon, associated, in mythology and in primitive religious beliefs, with the bull and the cow. In a prose poem on the bullfight, Lorca had written: "Man sacrifices the brave bull, offspring of the sweet cow, goddess of the dawn, who is alive in the dew. And the huge heavenly cow, a mother whose blood is always being shed, demands that man, too, be sacrificed" (*SD* 83). Lorca's allusion to the dawn and the dew makes it clear he is referring, in the prose passage just quoted, to the Sevillian "Virgin of the Dew," celebrated in a pilgrimage to the edge of the marsh of the Guadalquivir delta at Pentecost (see Josephs, 120). On the moon's "absorption" of blood, see Álvarez de Miranda (90). Line 71: The "bulls of Guisando" are crudely carved granite figures from the second century B.C., in what is now the province of Ávila. Line 77: An allusion to Calvary. The term "gradas" (steps) would be appropriate for those leading to the altar. Line 91: The "thirsting crowd," is reminiscent of those who call for the crucifixion of Christ in Luke 23:13–25 (Anderson, *Diván*, 293). Christological imagery too obvious to require annotation is found throughout the *Llanto*. Hernández (*Llanto*, line 71) points out that the bulls were so excellent that the crowd called for the bull-rancher to stand up. Line 96: The "terrified [literally, terrifying or terrible] mothers" are probably the Fates (Moirai or Parcae) whose influence is exerted at birth. Martínez Nadal (*Cuatro lecciones*, 82) believes Lorca is remembering *Faust*, Part II, Act I, Scene V. Line 100: The zodiacal constellation Taurus? The "*niebla*" (mist) would be the white starshine (cf. *Night*), and the "mayorales" (foremen on the bull ranches) probably allude to the constellation Boötes, called Boyero (ox driver) in Spanish. Line 109: Literally, "his well-sketched prudence." Line 110: The Roman Baetica. The emperor Trajan was born at Italica, near modern Seville. Lines 114–21: Reminiscent of Jorge Manrique's "Verses on the Death of His Father" (Cohen, 48–75), a poem Lorca emulates throughout the *Llanto*. Line 127: The "marismas" (salt marshes) near the mouth of the Guadalquivir, in the Andalusian province of Huelva, produce some of the finest fighting bulls in Spain. Line 133: Literally, "by the Guadalquivir of the stars," a metaphor for the Milky Way. Line 141: Swallows are thought to have removed the crown of thorns and to have drunk up the blood of the crucified Christ; both legends are alluded to in *saetas* sung during Holy Week processions (Aguilar y Tejera, 125). Line 144 alludes to the monstrance where the consecrated Host is displayed for veneration.

3. *The Laid-Out Body*. Lorca's meter shifts to the fourteen-syllable alexan-

drines he had used in *Odes* and, often, in *Book of Poems*. The title, "Cuerpo presente"—literally, "Present Body," but meaning funeral wake, or viewing—contrasts with the title of the final section, "Absent Soul." Lorca told his friend the painter José Caballero that he was thinking in this section not only of the slabs found in morgues but also of "the long, rough slab of stone that serves as an operating table in the infirmaries of the oldest bullrings" (Auclair, 26). Line 159: The epithet "el bien nacido" (well-born, noble) is reminiscent of the Spanish epic *Poem of the Cid*. Anderson (*Diván*, 301) observes that the lines 172–73 can be read either as an imperative: "Nobody here is to sing . . ." or as a statement: "Here, no one sings . . ." Lines 188–89: An image, in the manner of Góngora, of the bright, slender "horns" of the moon.

4. *Alma ausente / Absent Soul*. Line 218: "Claro" (noble, distinguished), used in Manrique's *Coplas* in the fifteenth century, has a slightly archaic ring.

Sonetos / Sonnets

Lorca wrote many sonnets between 1917 and 1936 and, like Juan Ramón Jiménez, was able to avoid the air of pastiche that weakened the genre in twentieth-century Spanish literature. There was renewed interest in the sonnet in Spain in the 1930s. In an interview near the end of his life, Lorca says that, like himself, certain young poets (he was probably thinking of Miguel Hernández and Luis Rosales) were "crusading" for a return to "traditional forms, after a wide-ranging and sunny stroll through the freedom of meter and rhyme" (*OC* III:633). In the same interview, he lists a book entitled *Sonetos* among four he is preparing to publish. While in hiding at the home of Luis Rosales, days before he was assassinated, Lorca was working on a collection entitled *Jardín de los sonetos* (*Garden of Sonnets*). No table of contents has survived, but the book would surely have included the eleven love sonnets written in 1935, inspired by Rafael Rodríguez Rapún, the young engineering student with whom Lorca had fallen in love in 1933. These eleven poems constitute a cycle, whose title has been much debated. Several of Lorca's friends, including the poets Vicente Aleixandre and Luis Cernuda, heard Lorca refer to it as *Sonetos del amor oscuro* (*Sonnets of Dark Love*). This title is used in the present edition but is given in brackets because it does not appear in any autograph manuscript. Many of these eleven poems remained unpublished in Spanish until December 1983, when they were printed, probably in Madrid, by the scholar and bibliophile Victor Infantes in an anonymous limited edition, unauthorized by the poet's family (for further information, see Hernández, "Jardín"; Eisenberg, "Reaction"; Infantes, "Lo 'oscuro' "; (71–82); and Anderson, who points out that ten of the eleven love sonnets were written during a brief trip to Valencia, Nov. 9–12, 1935 ("New Light," p. 112). An "authorized" version of all eleven poems was published in a special supplement to the Madrid daily *A.B.C.* on March 17, 1984.

It should be emphasized that *not all of these texts are final versions*. Lorca usually made his final changes by correcting a typewritten manuscript, but no authorized typescript containing the [*Sonnets of Dark Love*] is extant. The Spanish text given here is taken from Andrew Anderson's excellent unpublished edition and commentary, based on the mss. in the AFGL. See also Anderson, *Lorca's Late Poetry*, 275–399. I am also grateful to the late John K. Walsh for allowing me to consult his notes on these sonnets; and to Jeffrey Miller of Cadmus Editions.

[*Sonetos del amor oscuro*] / [*Sonnets of Dark Love*]

Soneto de la guirnalda de rosas / *Sonnet of the Garland of Roses.* Anderson (*Lorca's Late Poetry*, 311) explains a web of allusion to the myth of Venus and Adonis. Line 7: Lorca often associates the anemone with sleep and dream (it is the flower of Morpheus). John K. Walsh suggests: "The breaking of delicate reeds and rivulets in line 10 might refer to interior veins broken in furious lovemaking. In the poem, then, the poet would be placing himself in a passive role."

Soneto de la dulce queja / *Sonnet of the Sweet Complaint.* Spanish text from Hernández, *Antología*, 125.

Llagas de amor / *Wounds of Love.* Title: Anderson (*Lorca's Late Poetry*, 329) observes that the word *llagas* (rather than *heridas*) brings to mind the wounds of Christ. The definition of love through an enumeration of its symptoms and effects is common in the sixteenth- and seventeenth-century Spanish and Portuguese sonnet. See, for example, Camões's sonnet "Amor é um fogo que arde sem se ver, / é ferida que dói, e não se sente" (Love is a fire that burns and is not seen, / a wound which hurts and is not felt) in Mendes Paula, 479.

El poeta pide a su amor que le escriba / *The Poet Asks His Love to Write Him.* On the complicated textual history of this sonnet, see Anderson ("New Light," 112–120). Line 1: The oxymoron "living death" is characteristic of both Petrarchan and mystic poetry. Line 4: Lorca alludes to a well-known poem glossed by both St. Teresa of Ávila and St. John of the Cross. The latter's version, entitled "Verses of the Soul That Pines to See God" (Cohen, 222–23) begins: "Vivo sin vivir en mí, / y tan alta vida espero / que muero porque no muero" (I live and do not live in myself, and so strong are my hopes that I am dying of not dying). Lines 5–6: Regarding the "inert" stone, cf. the opening of section 3 of *Lament for Ignacio Sánchez Mejías.* Line 8: As in *At the Anonymous Tomb of Herrera y Reissig,* Lorca departs from the expression "luna de miel" (honeymoon). Line 13–14: The expression "noche serena" recalls verse 189 of St. John's *Spiritual Canticle.* Line 14: Allusion to the *noche oscura del alma* or "dark night of the soul" of John of the Cross: a state preliminary to union with God, in which the senses are blind to what surrounds them. See "Song of the Ascent of Mount Carmel": "In a dark night, inflamed by love's desires—oh, lucky chance—I went out unnoticed, all being then quiet in my house" (Cohen, 218).

El poeta dice la verdad / *The Poet Tells the Truth.* Lines 9–11 might also mean: a "skein . . . woven from decrepit sun and old moon."

El poeta habla por teléfono con el amor / *The Poet Speaks with His Beloved on the Telephone.* Line 12: Lorca remarks in an interview: "Once they asked me what poetry was, and I remembered a friend of mine and said: 'Poetry? Well, it is the union of two words that one never supposed could be joined, and which produce a sort of mystery; and the more one pronounces them, the more mysterious they become.' For example . . . 'ciervo vulnerado'" (wounded stag). The "wounded doe" mentioned here recalls St. John of the Cross's image of Christ: "Vuélvete, paloma, / que el ciervo vulnerado / por el otero asoma" (Return, dove, / for the wounded deer / has come to the hill). St. John explains in the commentary to his *Spiritual Canticle*: "The Husband [Christ] is compared to the deer . . . and when He is wounded He runs quickly to seek relief in the cold waters; and if He hears His mate complaining and senses that she is wounded, He goes to her and comforts and caresses her." (Cruz, *Vida y obras*, 403, 737)

Both in traditional poetry and in amatory verse of the sixteenth century, the lover is often compared to a deer wounded by a hunter.

El poeta pregunta a su amor por la "Ciudad Encantada" de Cuenca / The Poet Asks His Love about the "Enchanted City" of Cuenca. "The 'ciudad encantada' is a tourist attraction a little outside the town located in the pine forests of the Serranía de Cuenca [in central Spain, 260 km southeast of Madrid]. It is a curious and remarkable formation of eroded limestone which covers a substantial area. Its huge, variously shaped blocks of stone have been said to resemble the ruins of the palaces, temples, bridges, arches, columns, houses and squares of some colossal ancient city. Lorca visited Cuenca . . . during Easter Week of 1932" (Anderson, *Diván*). Line 6: The deep ravine of the river Júcar, which flows through Cuenca. Line 11: A pun: *grillo* means both "cricket" and "shackles."

Soneto gongorino . . . / Sonnet in the Manner of Góngora . . . Gibson (*Federico García Lorca*, 419) explains the circumstances in which this poem was written: "When the Barraca [the amateur theater troupe which Lorca directed] visited [Valencia] in 1933 Lorca had met briefly a young and exquisitely elegant poet from the nearby town of Alcoy, Juan Gil-Albert, whose father was a rich industrialist. Now [in early November 1935 in Valencia] he saw him again. Gil-Albert, who was about to publish a book of sonnets in which he made no effort to disguise his homosexuality, . . . had the idea of sending Lorca the present of a dove in a cage, which he had just bought at the local market. Gil-Albert knew nothing of [Lorca's lover] Rodríguez Rapún, or indeed of [his] private life in general, and was surprised to discover the following spring in Madrid that Federico had written a sonnet in the style of Góngora in which the poet delivers a pigeon in a cage to his beloved." Line 1: The river Turia flows through Valencia. Lines 5–6: A "Gongoristic" allusion to the myth of Venus, born from the foam. In his lecture on Góngora (*DS* 78) Lorca had admired Góngora's line about the dove: "Taking away its normal epithet, *cándida* [white and pure], he writes: 'Ave lasciva de la cipria Diosa' (lascivious fledgling of the Cypriote queen)" (*DS* 78). Line 8: Because the dove is associated with the kiss (see *DS* 81), the bird reminds the poet of the absent mouth of his beloved.

Ay voz secreta del amor oscuro . . . / Oh secret voice of dark love . . . The series of exclamations opening this sonnet recalls St. John of the Cross's "Song of the Living Flame of Love" (Cohen, 222–23): "Oh, gentle cautery! oh, delicate wound! oh, soft hand! oh, gentle touch that tastes of eternal life . . . !" Line 8: As happens often in Lorca's poetry, *lirio* might mean either iris or lily. Line 9: Lorca's habit of not using accent marks has led to two readings of the ms.: (1) *Huye de mi . . . voz* (Flee from my . . . voice) and (2) *Huye de mí . . . voz* (Flee from me, . . . voice). See Hernández, "Jardín," 196–97, who prefers the first of these readings. I understand the voice mentioned in line 9 to be the same as the one in line 1. Line 13: Anderson (*Lorca's Late Poetry*, 380) writes that several senses of *duelo*—including mourning and duel—may well be relevant here.

El amor duerme en el pecho del poeta / The Beloved Sleeps on the Poet's Breast. The title alludes to a stanza from St. John of the Cross's "Dark Night of the Soul" (Cohen, 220–21), wherein the soul remarks of Christ: "En mi pecho florido, / que entero para él sólo se guardaba, / allí quedó dormido" (In my burgeoning heart, which kept itself wholly for Him alone, there He stayed asleep). Line 2: Anderson (*Lorca's Late Poetry*, 382) notices that the participle *dormido* is "the one overt indication in the entire cycle that the beloved is male." Lines 9–11: An allusion to Christ's agony in the garden of Gethsemane, where his disciples slept (cf. line 2) and where he was accosted by "a great multitude with swords and staves" (Mark 14:43).

Noche del amor insomne / Night of Sleepless Love. In lines 1 and 5 Lorca has created neologisms (*noche arriba, noche abajo*) that play on colloquial expressions like *calle arriba, calle abajo* (up the street, down the street), *monte arriba, monte abajo* (up or down the hill), *boca arriba, boca abajo* (face up, face down), etc. The sense of these lines can only be guessed at. Perhaps: The night face up . . . The night face down . . .

Otros Sonetos / Other Sonnets, 1923–1936

El viento explora cautelosamente . . . / Cautiously the wind explores . . . Written August 1923, first published by Anderson in *Antología poética*, 195. The AFGL ms. bears the title (crossed out) "Canción del alma en acecho" (Song of the Soul Lying in Wait), and lines 5–7 (also canceled) read: "En mi puesto desde la madrugada / espero al ángel negro que me turba / con la flecha de acero preparada" (At my post from early morning / I await the black angel who troubles me / with the steel arrow he has prepared). On the same page, Lorca has copied two lines pertinent to line 13. The first is from an elegy of the sixteenth-century poet Fernando de Herrera (ed. Cuevas, 360): "En el silencio de la noche fría / me hiere el miedo del eterno olvido" (In the silence of the cold night, / I am wounded by the fear of being eternally forgotten). The second is from a love sonnet by the Aragonese poet Lupercio Leonardo de Argensola (d. 1613): "La sombra sola del olvido temo" (I fear only the shadow of oblivion) (ed. Blecua, 50). See also the introductory note to the LUNAR GRAPEFRUITS poems (p. 909).

En la muerte de José de Ciria y Escalante / On the Death of José de Ciria y Escalante. Written July 1924, in memory of a friend from the Residencia de Estudiantes who had died the month before of typhus, at the age of twenty-one. On sending the poem to Fernández Almagro, Lorca writes: "These days I've had a tough time of it, for I wanted to write something tender and *authentic* in memory of our Ciria. And yet, no matter how much I struggled I wasn't able to get my fountain (my fountain!) to flow for him. Yesterday, as I stood in a dark, cool poplar grove, I said, 'Pepe, why don't you want me to evoke you?' And I felt my eyes filling with tears. And then, in an instant, after 10 days of constant effort, I gave birth to the sonnet I'm sending you . . . This sonnet, naturally, has a great feeling of containment and stasis [un sentimiento contenido y extático]. I am happy with it, although I will have to polish it a bit. I want to dedicate three or four to him, and I want them to be sonnets, for the sonnet has a feeling of eternity that fits only in this seemingly cold vessel . . . Goodbye, and console yourself thinking that our friend is with God, in a divine environment of unending air and sky. Down with cold silence! Long live mysticism and love and friendship!" (*EC* 238–39). The poem was included in Gerardo Diego's anthologies of 1932 and 1934. Lines 5–6: Cf. this image of pallor with lines 161–62 of *Lament for Ignacio Sánchez Mejías*: "death has painted him in pale sulphurs / and put on him the head of a dark minotaur." Line 14: Lorca is said to have originally ended the poem with the words "novio mío" (my bridegroom); see Ayála, 116–17. Spanish text from *OC* I:635.

Soneto de homenaje a Manuel de Falla . . . / Sonnet in Homage to Manuel de Falla
. . . Written in February 1927 (fair copy dated February 12) to celebrate Falla's
fiftieth birthday. Lorca met the composer in Granada in 1919 and collaborated
with him on a number of projects (see the chapter on Falla in *IGM*). Spanish
text from *EC* 425.

Soneto a Carmela Condón . . . / To Carmela Condón . . . Written in the spring
of 1929 at the boarding house in Madrid where Lorca was living with his
brother. Published 1937 by Pablo Neruda and Nancy Cunard, together with
"Song of Spain" by Langston Hughes, in *Les poètes du monde défendent le peuple
espagnol*. Carmela Condón has never been identified. Line 3: Cf. what Lorca
tells Fernández Almagro about his *Songs* in early 1926: "I give my *love* to the
word! And not to the sound. My songs are not of ash" (*EC* 319). Lines 5–8:
The mention of Apollo, of bone, and of the "needle of a chimera" suggests
Lorca is imagining a rustic flute (more than once in his work, the sound of the
flute is compared to a needle). Line 9: Similar imagery occurs in a speech Lorca
gave in Granada around the time he wrote this sonnet: "Now, more than ever,
I need the silence and spiritual density of the air of Granada, to carry on *my duel
to the death* with my heart and with poetry. With my heart, to free it of the im-
possible passion that is destroying it and of the false shadow of the world, which
sows it with sterile salt; with poetry, *who defends herself like a virgin*, in order to
construct the poem that is wide awake and true . . ." (*OC* III:195; italics added).
Line 11: The happiness and grace ("salt") of his own childhood. Spanish text
from Rozas (167), but I have followed Hernández (*Diván*, 179) in correcting
line 14 ("dura" for "fría").

Adán / Adam. Ms. dated "December 1, 1929. New York." Published in *Héroe*
(Madrid) in 1932, in *Poesía* (Buenos Aires) in 1933 (with the dedication: "For
Pablo Neruda, surrounded by phantasms"), and again in the chapbook *Primeras
canciones*, 1936. For a rhymed translation, see Campbell (86). Spanish text from
OC I: 637. Line 2: The "new mother," obviously, is Eve. José Ángel Valente
(196) explains this sonnet in relation to "the non-germinative nature of homo-
sexuality," a frequent theme in Lorca's poems and plays. Line 9, "Adán sueña":
"And the Lord God *caused a deep sleep to fall upon Adam, and he slept*: and he took
out one of his ribs, and closed up the flesh instead thereof" (Genesis 2:21).

Soneto / Sonnet. First draft dated "New York. 1929. December." Published in
Revista de Avance (Havana) in April 1930 and, with variants, in *Cristal* (P—onteve-
dra) in 1932. In the manuscript, line 2 reads: "en el musgo de un norte sin re-
flejo" (in the moss of an unreflecting north). Lines 9–11: Cf. Lorca's image of
childhood in *Double Poem of Lake Eden* (*Poet in New York*), p. 683: "when all the
roses spilled from my tongue . . ." Line 11: Literally: "the deserted taste of
broom." Lines 12–14: Cf. *Two Norms*, p. 883. Spanish text from Anderson, *An-
tología poética*, 199, but I have followed García-Posada and others in substituting
"rama" for "llama" in line 13.

Epitafio a Isaac Albéniz / Epitaph for Isaac Albéniz. Recited by Lorca at the
dedication of a statue of Albéniz in the cemetery of Montjuic, Barcelona, on
December 14, 1935. Published that evening in the daily newspaper *La Noche*
(Barcelona). Also read was an "Ode to Albéniz" by Juan Ramón Jiménez (Ro-
drigo, 392). In his lecture on deep song, Lorca had praised the pianist and com-
poser (1860–1909) for having plumbed "the lyrical depths of Andalusian song
in his work" (*SD* 10). Some of the music that Federico himself composed for

the piano is reminiscent of that of Albéniz. Lines 5–6: Cádiz is on the Atlantic coast (thus the mention of "salt"). Granada's "wall" is built from *jets d'eau* and fountains, celebrated everywhere in Lorca's work. Albéniz's *Suite española* includes pieces devoted to both these cities. In the 1920s Lorca and his friends had put up a commemorative tile in Granada "In Honor of Isaac Albéniz, who lived in the Alhambra. Spring 1882" (Rodrigo, 146). Spanish text from *OC* I: 638–39.

En la tumba sin nombre de Herrera y Reissig . . . / At the Anonymous Tomb of Herrera y Reissig . . . Spanish text from Anderson, *Antología poética*, 200, who published the poem for the first time and dated it to the end of 1935 or the first half of 1936. Probably written for a special issue (never published, due to the Civil War) of Pablo Neruda's literary magazine, *Caballo verde para la poesía* (Madrid). Herrera y Reissig (1875–1910), translator of Baudelaire and master of the Modernist sonnet, was born and died in Montevideo. Lorca must have discovered his work when writing his earliest poems. Neruda and Lorca seem to have visited his grave on Lorca's trip to Uruguay in 1934. In a speech given in 1935, Federico praises his "extravagant, adorable, overwhelmingly, affectedly sentimental and phosphorescent voice" (*OC* III:465). This sonnet is a skillful pastiche of Symbolism (e.g., the sunken pagoda) and of the *fin de siècle* Hispanic Modernism to which it led. Among the Modernist traits to which this sonnet alludes are the use of Latinisms (*túmulo*), Gallicisms (*lis*), and words accented on the antepenultimate syllable (*póstumo, hipnótico*); the fondness for precious stones and metals (*esmeraldas, carbunclo, oro*); neologisms like *salitrar*, and the insistence on the spirituality of the color blue (*azul*). Line 1: From the grammatical term *epenthesis* (insertion of a sound in the body of a word), Lorca coined the noun *epentismo* and the adjective *epéntico* and used them in his conversation and letters in connection with homoeroticism. Sáenz de la Calzada (189) reports Lorca's own definition: "There are three kinds of person: the *ente* (ent), the *subente* (sub-ent) and the *epente* (ep-ent). The first is a normal person, us, for example: the government worker, the professor, etc. The sub-ent is the fairy, the queer . . . the miserable being that a man can turn into when he cohabits with a woman . . . finally, we have the *epente*, who, unlike the other two, creates, but does not procreate." Line 9: Herrera y Reissig wrote a short series of poems entitled *El collar de Salambó* (Salammbô's Necklace).

A Mercedes en su vuelo / For Mercedes in Her Flight. Mario Hernández (*Antología poética*, 154) explains that this sonnet, written in 1936, "is dedicated to a daughter of the Counts of Yebes [friends whom Lorca had met in Madrid], who had left their autograph album with the poet a few days before the death of Mercedes, who was a child. When Lorca learned on the telephone of the girl's death, he wrote this sonnet for the album." See *Cradle Song for Mercedes, in Death,* p. 885.

Poemas sueltos / Uncollected Poems

Voces / Voices. Dated October 27, 1920. First published by Menarini, 262–63.

Estampilla y juguete / Candy Wrapper and Toy. Undated. Published posthumously from an early manuscript, numbered 1, as though this poem were the first in a series. Text from Hernández, *Primeras canciones*, 117.

Cautiva / Captive. Undated, published in *Primeras canciones*. Text from Hernández, 65.

Canción de la desesperanza / Song of Despair. The undated ms. is published in facsimile by Rogers, 45. 1921? The image in line 8 occurs in *Wind Gust* in THE RETURN.

Canto nocturno de los marineros andaluces / Night Song of the Andalusian Sailors. First published in *La Nación* (Buenos Aires), December 24, 1933, but probably written in 1922. The first twelve lines are sung by a smuggler, one of a "classic gang . . . wearing velvet, with beards and blunderbusses, throwing dice and singing," in *The Tragicomedy of Don Cristóbal and Mistress Rosita* (tr. Honig, 49). Spanish text from *OC* I:477–78. Ford (I:143) took the road "from Cádiz to Gibraltar" in the 1850s and found it "a wild and dangerous ride, especially at the *Trocha* pass, which is infested with smugglers and charcoal-burners, who occasionally become *rateros* [thieves] and robbers." The road from Seville to Carmona, "the Moorish Karmunah, with its Oriental walls, castle, and position" has a "magnificent view over the vast plains below" (Ford, I:222).

Abandono / Abandoned. November 1922. Published by Belamich as a fragment from *Suites*, 154–55.

En tus ojos la serpiente . . . / In your eyes, the serpent . . . First published by Menarini, 311–12. 1923?

Mosca / Fly. First published by Menarini, 300–1. 1924?

Apunte para una oda / Sketch for an Ode. Ms. dated July 3, 1924. Published posthumously. Spanish text from *OC* I:743–44. See *Solitude*. On Cyssus (paragraph 7), see note on *Bacchus*, p. 916.

Palabra de cera . . . / Word of wax . . . Ms. dated August 4, 1924. First published by Menarini, 277.

[Chopo y torre] / [Poplar and Tower]. Written on a postcard sent to Jorge Guillén from La Granja (royal palace with fountains and gardens, near Segovia) in summer 1925. The poplar is one of the most frequently mentioned trees in Lorca's poetry. Gerald Brenan (15) gives a fine description of those that grow in the Alpujarras (province of Granada): "They line the watercourses and they also grow in irrigated groves whose fine green grass invites one to lie down and act the part of a Giorgione shepherd until one notices that they squelch with water. These poplars belong to a foreign species, native to Virginia, and introduced during the last century to provide poles for building: they have sticky, aromatic buds and a heart-shaped leaf and, though never allowed to grow large, they make a delicate pattern like perpendicular stitchwork on the huge, little-diversified mountainside."

El mal corazón / Bad Heart. First published by Menarini, 319–20. Written September 1925, when Lorca writes wistfully to Fernández Almagro: "My poetry is a pastime. / / My life is a pastime. / / But I am not a pastime. / / The world is a shoulder of dark flesh (black flesh of an old mule). And the light is on the other side. / / I would like to be as naked as a zero and *contemplate*. / / I want to travel at length, but not to foolish, mysterious Japan or dirty India, recently and eternally discovered. I want to travel through Europe, where one finds the coin tossed into the depths of love" (*EC* 300).

La sirena y el carabinero / The Siren and the Carabineer. Ms. dated December 1925. Published in *La Gaceta Literaria* (Madrid) in March 1927. Cf. *Ballad of the Spanish Civil Guard* and *Scene of the Lieutenant Colonel.* On March 2, 1926, Lorca sends a slightly different version of these lines to Jorge Guillén with the comment: "These days I'm working on a *long poem.* The 'Didactic Ode to Salvador

Dalí is already 150 [sic] alexandrines long, but this poem will surely reach 400. In it I tell how a carabineer shoots a little siren to death with his rifle. It is a tragic idyll. At the end there will be great wailing from the sirens, a wailing that rises and falls at the same time, like the seawater, while the carabineers take the siren to the barracks. All this will have great lyrical impact. The same lyricism for the carabineer as for the siren. A flat light, and *love and serenity* in the form. It will be a *huge bore*, but I am profoundly moved by this story. It is the myth of the useless beauty of the sea. Then I would like the water to grow calm, so I can meticulously describe one wave (the first) and then a second one, and then the third, until we come upon a little boat—boat where the poet will dream his last dream. This ending, with the moving water, will be admirable if I can bring it off. Don't tell anyone about any of this . . ." (*EC* 336). Lines 21–24: Lorca is remembering the opening lines of Hesiod's *Theogony*, which he read as a young man.

Lento perfume . . . / Slow perfume . . . Sent to Jorge Guillén on September 9, 1926, along with *The Feud* and *St. Michael* (*EC* 376).

Soledad insegura / Uncertain Solitude. Fragments of an unfinished poem. The title, mythological references, and use of metaphor are meant to evoke the two *Solitudes* of Don Luis de Góngora. Lorca sent several fragments of this poem to Jorge Guillén in February 1927 with the comment: "Now I'm writing a Solitude which, as you know, I began long ago. It is what I am sending to the ceremonies in honor of Góngora . . . that is, if it turns out well" (*EC* 427; cf. *EC* 337–38). Of lines 1–11 he comments: "Isn't this a lovely allusion to the myth of Venus? And [the line] 'the mollusk without limit of fear' I like, for it is true" (*EC* 429). Line 15: Favonius is the west wind and Thetis a marine divinity, sister of the Nereids, who dwell in the depths of the sea. Line 18: Literally, "Academy in the cloister of the irises," an allusion to the eyes of the fish but also, perhaps, to the water's iridescence. Line 36: Lyra is probably the star. Lorca had planned to adorn the cover of *Songs* with his own drawing of the constellation Lyra. Lines 47–59 were not sent to Guillén but were published posthumously by Manuel Fernández-Montesinos García (1987, 45). A first draft of this poem in the AFGL is dedicated to Juan Ramón Jiménez. Spanish text from *OC* I:482–84.

Dos normas / Two Norms. Written March 1928, published in *Parábola* (Burgos) several months later with a dedication: "To the great poet Jorge Guillén." Another version (the one followed here) appeared posthumously in *Revista Hispánica Moderna* (New York), July–October 1940. Written in a metrical form—the *décima*—which Guillén had cultivated with much success. In the manuscript, the first norm begins with a sketch of the moon, and the second with a sketch of the sun (Martín, *Federico García Lorca*, 77).

Tan, tan . . . / Knock, knock! . . . Written 1933? Lorca includes this poem in his lecture "How a City Sings from November to November" (*SG* 113). Based on a children's rhyme (Llorca, 16).

Canción de cuna para Mercedes, muerta / Cradle Song for Mercedes, in Death. Written summer 1936, published posthumously in *Revista Hispánica Moderna* (New York), July–October 1940. See note to *For Mercedes in Her Flight* (p. 950). Spanish text from *OC* I:645.

Bibliography

Editions of Poetic Works of García Lorca

Complete Works

Belamich, André, ed. *Oeuvres complètes*. Vol. 1. Paris: Gallimard (Pléiade), 1981.

García-Posada, Miguel, ed. *Obras completas*. 4 vols. Barcelona: Galaxia Gutenberg/Círculo de Lectores, 1996–97.

Hernández, Mario, ed. *Obras*. Madrid: Alianza, 1981–present. See under individual works.

Hoyo, Arturo del, ed. *Obras completas*. 3 vols. Madrid: Aguilar, 1986.

Anthologies

Anderson, Andrew A., ed. *Antologia poética*. Granada: Edición del Cincuentenario, 1986.

Hernández, Mario, ed. *Antología poética*. Madrid: Ediciones Alce, 1978.

Martín, Eutimio, ed. *Antologia comentada*. Vol. 1, *Poesía*. Madrid: Ediciones de la Torre, 1988.

Letters

Maurer, Christopher, and Andrew A. Anderson, eds. *Epistolario completo*. Madrid: Cátedra, 1997.

Lectures

Maurer, Christopher, ed. *Conferencias*. 2 vols. Madrid: Alianza Editorial, 1984.

Drawings

Hernández, Mario, ed. *Libro de los dibujos de Federico García Lorca*. Madrid: Tabapress / Grupo Tabacalera / Fundación Federico García Lorca, 1990.

———. *Line of Light and Shadow: The Drawings of Federico García Lorca*. Tr. Christopher Maurer. Durham: Duke University Press, 1991.

Book of Poems

Gibson, Ian, ed. *Libro de poemas (1921)*. Barcelona: Ariel, 1982.

Hernández, Mario, ed. *Libro de poemas [1918–1920]*, rev. ed. Madrid: Alianza Editorial, 1998.

Massoli, Marco, ed. *F.G.L. e il suo "Libro de poemas": Un poeta alla ricerca della propria voce. (Introduzione. Testo critico. Commento.)* Pisa: C. Cursi Editore, 1982.

Poem of the Deep Song

De Paepe, Christian, ed. *Poema del cante jondo*. Madrid: Espasa-Calpe, 1986.

Hernández, Mario, ed. *Poema del cante jondo (1921) seguido de tres textos teóricos de Federico García Lorca y Manuel de Falla*, rev. ed. Madrid: Alianza Editorial, 1998.

Josephs, Allen, and Juan Caballero, eds. *Poema del cante jondo. Romancero gitano*. 7th ed. Madrid: Cátedra, 1984.

Suites

Belamich, André, ed. *Suites*. Barcelona: Ariel, 1983.

Comincioli, Jacques. *Federico García Lorca. Textes inédits et documents critiques*. Lausanne: Éditions Rencontre, 1970.

Dinverno, Melissa A. *Listening Through Mirrors: Representing García Lorca's Suites*. Ph.D. dissertation, University of Michigan, 2000.

Hernández, Mario, ed. *Primeras canciones. Seis poemas galegos. Poemas sueltos. Colección de canciones populares antiguas*. Madrid: Alianza Editorial, 1981.

Rogers, Paul, ed. *Surtidores. Algunas poesías inéditas de Federico García Lorca*. México: Editorial Patria, 1957.

Soley, Ramón, ed. *Ferias*. Barcelona: Edicions Delstre, 1997.

Songs

Hernández, Mario, ed. *Canciones (1921–1924)*. Madrid: Alianza Editorial, 1982. Revised edition, 1998.

Menarini, Piero, ed. *Canciones y primeras canciones*. Madrid: Espasa-Calpe, 1986.

Gypsy Ballads

García-Posada, Miguel, ed. *Primer romancero gitano. Llanto por Ignacio Sánchez Mejías. Romance de la corrida de toros en ronda y otros textos taurinos*. Madrid: Castalia, 1988.

Harris, Derek, ed. *Romancero gitano*. London: Grant & Cutler, 1991.

Hernández, Mario, ed. *Primer romancero gitano (1924–1927)*. Madrid: Alianza Editorial, 1983. Revised edition, 1998.

Josephs, Allen, and Juan Caballero, eds. See under *Poem of the Deep Song*.

Trip to the Moon

Monegal, Antonio, ed. *Viaje a la luna. Guión cinematográfico*. Valencia: Pre-Textos, 1994.

Poet in New York

Bergamín, José, ed. *Poeta en Nueva York*. Mexico: Editorial Séneca, 1940.

Hernández, Mario, ed. *Manuscritos neoyorquinos: Poeta en Nueva York y otras hojas y poemas*. Madrid: Tabapress/Fundación Federico García Lorca, 1990.

Humphries, Rolfe, tr. *The Poet in New York and Other Poems of Federico García Lorca*. New York: W. W. Norton, 1940.

Martín, Eutimio, ed. *Poeta en Nueva York / Tierra y luna*. Barcelona: Ariel, 1981.

Maurer, Christopher, ed. *Poet in New York*. Tr. Greg Simon and Steven F. White. New York: Noonday Press, 1998.

Millán, María Clementa, ed. *Poeta en Nueva York*. Madrid: Cátedra, 1987.

The Tamarit Divan, Six Galician Poems, Lament for Ignacio Sánchez Mejías

Anderson, Andrew A., ed. *Diván del Tamarit. Seis poemas galegos. Llanto por Ignacio Sánchez Mejías. Poemas sueltos*. Madrid: Espasa-Calpe, 1988.

Hernández, Mario, ed. *Diván del Tamarit. Llanto por Ignacio Sánchez Mejías. Sonetos*. Madrid: Alianza Editorial, 1981.

———, ed. *Llanto por Ignacio Sánchez Mejías, con dos grabados de José Hernández y otros textos de Ignacio Sánchez Mejías, Francisco Garciá Lorca, y José Bergamín*. 2 vols. Madrid: Ayuntamiento de Madrid, 1997.

Sonnets of Dark Love

Anderson, Andrew A., ed. *Sonnets* (manuscript).

[Infantes, Victor, ed.] *Sonetos del amor oscuro (1935–1936)*. Granada, 1983. Privately and anonymously printed first edition.

Hernández, Mario, ed. *Sonetos del amor oscuro, con dibujos de Miguel Rodríguez-Acosta Carl-*

ström, introducción de Jorge Guillén y notas de Mario Hernández. Barcelona: Maeght, 1980.

Ruiz-Portella, Javier, ed. *Sonetos del amor oscuro. Poemas de amor y erotismo. Inéditos de madurez.* Barcelona: Ediciónes Áltera, 1995.

Other Editions

De Paepe, Christian, ed. *Poesía inédita de juventud.* Madrid: Cátedra, 1994.

Martínez Nadal, Rafael, ed. *Autógrafos.* Vol. 1, *Facsímiles de ochenta y siete poemas y tres prosas.* London: Dolphin Book Club, 1975.

Maurer, Christopher, ed. *Prosa inédita de juventud.* Madrid: Cátedra, 1994.

García-Posada, Miguel, ed. *Poesía, 1.* 2nd ed. Madrid: Akal, 1982. (1st ed. 1980.)

Selected Poetry, Drama, and Prose of García Lorca in English

Allen, Donald M., and Francisco García Lorca, eds. *The Selected Poems of Federico García Lorca.* New York: New Directions, 1955.

Barnstone, Willis, tr. *Six Masters of the Spanish Sonnet . . .* Carbondale: Southern Illinois University Press, 1993.

Bauer, Carlos, tr. *Ode to Walt Whitman & Other Poems.* San Francisco: City Lights Books, 1988.

————, tr. *Poem of the Deep Song / Poema del cante jondo.* San Francisco: City Lights Books, 1987.

————, tr. *The Public and Play Without a Title: Two Posthumous Plays.* New York: New Directions, 1983.

Belitt, Ben, tr. *The Audience* (excerpts). *Evergreen Review* 2, no. 6 (Autumn 1958):93–107.

————. "Fourteen Lyrics." *Quarterly Review of Literature* 4, no. 1 (1950):5–13.

————, ed. *Poet in New York.* New York: Grove Press, 1955.

Blackburn, Paul, tr. *Lorca/Blackburn. Poems of Federico García Lorca.* San Francisco: Momo's Press, 1979.

Bly, Robert, tr. *Lorca and Jiménez. Selected Poems,* rev. ed. Boston: Beacon Press, 1997.

Brilliant, Alan, tr. *Tree of Song.* Santa Barbara: Unicorn Press, 1971.

Campbell, Roy, tr. *Lament for the Death of a Matador.* Seville, 1954.

————. *Lorca. An Appreciation of His Poetry.* New Haven: Yale University Press, 1952.

Cobb, Carl W., tr. *Lorca's Romancero gitano: A Ballad Translation and Critical Study.* Jackson: University Press of Mississippi, 1983.

Cooper, Julian, tr. *Federico García Lorca. Some of His Shorter Poems.* London: A.F.X. Demaine, 1955.

Cummings, Philip, tr. *Songs.* Ed. Daniel Eisenberg. Pittsburgh: Duquesne University Press, 1976.

Dewell, Michael, and Carmen Zapata, trs. *Three Plays.* Ed. and intro. Christopher Maurer. New York: Farrar, Straus and Giroux, 1993.

Edmunds, John, tr. *Four Major Plays.* New York: Oxford University Press, 1997.

Edwards, Gwynne, tr. *Plays: One.* Portsmouth, N.H.: Heineman, 1988.

————, tr. *Plays: Two.* London: Methuen, 1990.

Edwards, Gwynne, and Henry Livings, trs. *Plays: Three. Mariana Pineda, The Public, Play Without a Title.* London: Methuen, 1994.

Edwards, Gwynne, and Peter Luke, tr. *Three Plays. Blood Wedding, Doña Rosita the Spinster, Yerma.* London: Methuen, 1987.

Forman, Sandra, and Allen Josephs, trs. *Only Mystery: Federico García Lorca's Poetry in Word and Image.* Gainesville: University Press of Florida, 1992.

García Lorca, Francisco. *See* Donald M. Allen.

Gershator, David, ed. and tr. *Selected Letters.* New York: New Directions, 1983.

Gili, J. L., tr. *Lorca.* Harmondsworth: Penguin Books, 1960.

Gili, J. L., and Stephen Spender. *See* Spender.

Graham-Lujan, James, and Richard L. O'Connell, trs. *Collected Plays of Federico García Lorca.* London: Sacker and Warburg, 1976.

———, tr. *Five Plays. Comedies and Tragicomedies.* New York: New Directions, 1963.

———, tr. Prologue by Francisco García Lorca. *Three Tragedies. Blood Wedding, Yerma, Bernarda Alba.* New York: New Directions, 1947.

Hartnett, Michael, tr. *Gipsy Ballads: A Version of the Romancero Gitano (1924–1927) of Federico García Lorca.* Dublin: Goldsmith Press, 1973.

Havard, Robert G., ed. *Gypsy Ballads / Romancero gitano.* Warminster: Aris and Phillips, 1990.

Honig, Edwin, tr. *Four Puppet Plays. Divan Poems and Other Poems. Prose Poems and Dramatic Pieces. Play Without a Title.* New York: Sheep Meadow Press, 1990.

———, ed. *García Lorca.* New York: New Directions, 1963.

Hughes, Langston, tr. *Gypsy Ballads. The Beloit Poetry Journal* 2, Chapbook no. 1 (Fall 1951).

Hughes, Langston, and W. S. Merwin, trs. *Blood Wedding and Yerma.* New York: Theatre Communications Group, 1994.

Hughes, Ted, tr. *Blood Wedding.* London: Faber and Faber, 1997.

Humphries, Rolfe, tr. *From the Spanish. Poetry. García Lorca.* Monterrey: Ediciones Sierra Madre, 1960.

———, tr. *The Gypsy Ballads of Federico García Lorca.* Bloomington and London: Indiana University Press, 1953.

Johnston, David, tr. *The Love of Don Perlimplín for Belisa in the Garden and Yerma.* London: Hodder and Stoughton, 1990.

———, tr. *Blood Wedding.* London: Hodder and Stoughton Educational, 1989.

Kennelly, Brendan, tr. *Blood Wedding.* Newcastle upon Tyne: Bloodaxe Books, 1996.

Kirkland, Will, tr. *The Cricket Sings. Poems and Songs for Children.* New York: New Directions, 1980.

Klibbe, Lawrence, tr. *Impressions and Landscapes.* Lanham / New York / London: University Press of America, 1987.

Lewis, Richard, tr. *Still Waters of the Air. Poems by Three Modern Spanish Poets.* New York: Dial Press, 1970.

Lloyd, A. L., tr. *Lament for the Death of a Bullfighter, and Other Poems in the Original Spanish with English Translation.* 1937; reprint, Westport: Greenwood Press, 1977.

Logan, William Bryant, and Ángel Gil Orrios, eds. and trs. *Once Five Years Pass and Other Dramatic Works.* Barrytown, N.Y.: Station Hill Press, 1989.

London, John, tr. *The Unknown Lorca. Dialogues, Dramatic Projects, Unfinished Plays and a Filmscript.* London: Atlas, 1996.

Loughran, David K., tr. *Gypsy Ballads, Songs / Romancero gitano, Canciones.* Hanover, N.H.: Ediciones del Norte, 1994.

———, tr. *Sonnets of Love Forbidden.* Missoula, Mont.: Windsong Press, 1989.

Macpherson, Ian, and Jacqueline Minett, trs. *Yerma.* Warminster: Wiltshire, Aris and Phillips, 1987.

Mallan, Lloyd, tr. *Selected Poems.* Prairie City, Ill.: James A. Deckler, 1941.

Mann, Emily, tr. *The House of Bernarda Alba. A Drama About Women in Villages of Spain.* New York: Dramatists Play Service, 1999.

Maurer, Christopher, ed. and tr. *A Season in Granada.* London: Anvil Press Poetry, 1998.

————. *Federico García Lorca, 1898–1936.* CD-ROM. Madrid: Imago Mundi/ Fundación Federico García Lorca, 1998.

————, tr. *In Search of Duende.* New York: New Directions, 1998.

————, ed. and tr. *Selected Verse.* New York: Farrar, Straus and Giroux, 1994.

————, tr. *Deep Song and Other Prose.* New York: New Directions, 1980.

Merwin, W. S. *See* Langston Hughes.

Neiman, Gilbert, tr. *Blood Wedding.* Norfolk, Conn.: New Directions, 1939.

Owens, Rebecca, tr. *Ten Poems.* Church Hanborough, Oxford: Hanborough Parrot Press, Didcot Press, 1988.

Pavón, Max T., tr. *Andalusian Poems / Romancero Gitano.* Morris Publishing, 2000.

Raine, Kathleen, and Rafael Martínez Nadal, eds. and trs. *Sun and Shadow.* London: Enitharmon, 1972.

Rexroth, Kenneth, tr. *Thirty Spanish Poems of Love and Exile.* San Francisco: City Lights Books, 1968.

Rothenberg, Jerome, tr. *Suites.* Los Angeles: Green Integer Books, 2001.

Sawyer-Lauçanno, Christopher, tr. *Barbarous Nights. Legends and Plays from the Little Theater.* San Francisco: City Lights Books, 1991.

Simont, Marc, tr. *The Lieutenant Colonel and the Gypsy.* New York: Doubleday, 1971.

Skelton, Robin, tr. *Songs and Ballads.* Montreal: Guernica, 1992.

Smith, William Jay, tr. *Federico García Lorca. Songs of Childhood.* Roslyn, N.Y.: Stone House Press, 1994.

Spender, Stephen, and J. L. Gili, trs. *Selected Poems of Federico García Lorca.* London: Hogarth Press, 1943.

————, trs. *Poems.* London: Dolphin, 1939, 1942.

Spicer, Jack. *After Lorca.* 1957; reprinted in *The Collected Books of Jack Spicer,* ed. Robin Blaser. Los Angeles: Black Sparrow Press, 1975.

Stafford, William, and Herbert Baird, trs. "Quarrel," *Kenyon Review* 29 (1967), 662–63.

Svich, Caridad, tr. *Impossible Theater. Five Plays and Thirteen Poems by Federico García Lorca.* Hanover, N.H.: Smith and Kraus, 2000.

Turnbull, Eleanor L., tr. *Contemporary Spanish Poetry.* Baltimore: Johns Hopkins University Press, 1945.

Waldrop, Keith, tr. *Poem of the Gypsy Seguidilla.* Providence: Burning Deck, 1967.

Williams, Merryn, tr. *Selected Poems.* Newcastle upon Tyne: Bloodaxe Books, 1992.

Wright, James, tr. "Afternoon." *Sixties* 4 (1960): 18–19.

————, tr. "Gacela of the Remembrance of Love." *Poetry* 96, no. 3 (June 1960): 151–52.

Other Works Cited

Aguilar y Tejera, Agustín. *Saetas populares.* Madrid: CIAP, 1930.

Alonso, Dámaso, and Carlos Bousoño. *Seis calas en la expresión literaria española (Prosa—Poesía—Teatro).* Madrid: Gredos, 1963.

Alvar, Manuel. *Romancero viejo y tradicional.* Mexico: Editorial Porrúa, 1979.

Alvarez de Miranda, Ángel. *Obras.* Vol. 2. Madrid: Ediciones Cultura Hispánica, 1959.

Amat, Frederic. "Notes on *Trip to the Moon.*" In Caridad Svich, *Impossible Theatre,* 159–62.

Anderson, Andrew A. "Bibliografía lorquiana reciente" (1984–present). Appears in each issue of *Boletín de la Fundación Federico García Lorca,* Madrid.

————. "New Light on the Textual History of García Lorca's *Sonetos del amor oscuro.*" In David T. Gies, *Negotiating Past and Present: Studies in Spanish Literature for Javier Herrero.* Charlottesville: Rookwood Press, 1997. 109–26.

————. *Lorca's Late Poetry: A Critical Study.* Leeds: Francis Cairns, 1990.

————. "Who Wrote *Seis poemas gallegos* and in What Language?" In C. Brian Morris, ed., *"Cuando yo me muera . . ." Essays in Memory of Federico García Lorca.* Lanham, Md.: University Press of America, 1988. 129–46.

Argensola, Lupercio Leonardo de. *Rimas.* Ed. José Manuel Blecua. Madrid: Espasa-Calpe, 1972.

Auclair, Marcelle. *Enfance et mort de García Lorca.* Paris: Éditions du Seuil, 1968.

Ayala, Francisco. *Recuerdos y olvidos.* Vol. 1. Madrid: Alianza Editorial, 1982.

Barea, Arturo. *Lorca: The Poet and His People.* Tr. Ilsa Barea. New York: Cooper Square, 1973.

Binding, Paul. *Lorca: The Gay Imagination.* London: GMP Publishers, 1985.

Bousoño, Carlos. "Metáforas lorquianas." *El País* (Madrid), August 19, 1986, iv.

Brenan, Gerald. *South From Granada.* 1957; reprint, New York: Octagon Books, 1976.

Burnshaw, Stanley. *The Poem Itself. 45 Modern Poets in a New Presentation.* New York: Holt, Rinehart and Winston, 1960.

Celaya, Gabriel. *La voz de los niños.* Barcelona: Editorial Laia, 1972.

Cohen, J. M. *The Penguin Book of Spanish Verse.* London: Penguin, 1988.

Crookes, David Z. "Pythagoras by Moonlight: A Translation and Explication of Lorca's *El concierto interrumpido.*" *Neophilologus* 74 (1990): 318–20.

Cruz, Juan de la. *Vida y obras.* Ed. Crisógono de Jesús, Matías del Niño Jesús, and Lucinio Ruano. 6th ed. Madrid: Biblioteca de Autores Cristianos, 1972.

Cummins, J. G. *The Spanish Traditional Lyric.* New York and Oxford: Pergamon Press, 1977.

Dalí, Salvador. *The Secret Life of Salvador Dalí.* 1942; reprint, London: Vision Press, 1968.

Darío, Rubén. *Prosas profanas.* Madrid: Mundo Latino, 1917.

Dempsey, Andrew. *A Life of Lorca. Drawings, Photographs, Words.* Norwich, Eng.: University of East Anglia, 1997.

Dennis, Nigel. *Vida y milagros de un manuscrito de Lorca: En pos de* Poeta en Nueva York. Santander: Sociedad Menéndez Pelayo, 2000.

De Paepe, Christian. *Understanding Federico García Lorca.* Charleston: University of South Carolina Press, 1995.

————. "Tres *Suites* recompuestas y siete poemas inéditos de Federico García Lorca." *Boletín de la Fundación Federico García Lorca* (Madrid), 16 (1994): 7–28.

Devoto, Daniel. *Introducción a "Diván del Tamarit" de Federico García Lorca.* Paris: Ediciones Hispanoamericanas, 1976.

————. "Notas sobre el elemento tradicional en la obra de Federico García Lorca." In Ildefonso-Manuel Gil, ed., *Federico García Lorca.* Madrid: Taurus, 1975. 25–72.

————. "García Lorca y Darío." *Asomante* 23, no. 2 (Apr.-Jun. 1967): 22–31.

————. "Lecturas de García Lorca." *Revue de Littérature Comparée* 33, no. 4 (Oct.-Dec. 1959): 518–28.

Díaz Plaja, Guillermo. *Federico García Lorca. Su obra e influencia en la poesía española.* 4th ed. Madrid: Espasa-Calpe, 1968.

Díaz Roig, Mercedes, ed. *El romancero viejo.* Madrid: Cátedra, 1985.

Diego, Gerardo, ed. *Poesía española. Antología: 1915–1931.* Madrid: Signo, 1932.

————, ed. *Poesía española. Antología (Contemporáneos).* Madrid: Signo, 1934.

Doggart, Sebastian, and Michael Thompson, eds. *Fire, Blood and the Alphabet: One Hun-*

dred Years of Lorca. Durham, Eng.: Durham, Modern Languages Series/University of Durham, 1999.

Eisenberg, Daniel. "Reaction to the Publication of the *Sonetos del amor oscuro.*" *Bulletin of Hispanic Studies* 65 (1988): 261–71.

———. "A Chronology of Lorca's Visit to New York and Cuba." *Kentucky Romance Quarterly* 24 (1977).

Espinosa, Aurelio M. *Cuentos populares españoles recogidos de la tradición oral de España.* Vol. I. Madrid: Consejo Superior de Investigaciones Científicas, 1946.

Falla, Manuel de. *Escritos sobre música y músicos.* Madrid: Espasa-Calpe, 1972.

Feal Deibe, Carlos. "Los *Seis poemas galegos* de Lorca y sus fuentes rosalianas." *Romanischen Forschungen* 83 (1971): 555–87.

Federico García Lorca (1898–1936). Madrid: Comisión Nacional del Centenario de Federico García Lorca / Museo Nacional Centro de Arte Reina Sofia / Fundación Federico García Lorca, 1998.

Fernández de los Ríos, Luis Beltrán. *La arquitectura del humo. Una reconstrucción del "Romancero gitano" de Federico García Lorca.* London: Tamesis Books, 1986.

Fernández-Montesinos García, Manuel. "La preocupación social de García Lorca." In Piero Menarini, ed., *Lorca, 1986*, 15–33. Bologna: Atesa Editrice, 1987.

———."Descripción de la biblioteca de Federico García Lorca (Catálogo y estudio)." "Licenciatura" thesis presented to the Universidad Complutense, Madrid, September 13, 1985.

Field, John Edward. *The Myth of the Pent Cuckoo: A Study in Folklore.* London: Elliot Stock, 1913.

Ford, Richard. *A Handbook for Travelers in Spain.* 2 vols. 3d ed. London: John Murray, 1855.

Forster, Jeremy C. "Aspects of Lorca's St. Christopher." *Bulletin of Hispanic Studies* 43 (1966): 109–16.

Fry, Edward. *Cubism.* New York: McGraw-Hill, 1966.

Fuentes Vázquez, Tadea. *El folklore infantil en la obra de Federico García Lorca.* Granada: Universidad de Granada, 1991.

García Lorca, Francisco. *In the Green Morning. Memories of Federico.* Tr. Christopher Maurer. New York: New Directions, 1986.

———. *De Garcilaso a Lorca.* Ed. Claudio Guillén. Madrid: Istmo, 1984.

———. *Federico y su mundo.* Ed. Mario Hernández. 2d ed. Madrid: Alianza, 1981.

Gautier, Théophile. *Travels in Spain.* In F. C. de Sumichrast, ed., *The Works of Théophile Gautier.* Vol. 4. New York: George D. Sproul, 1901.

Gibson, Ian. *Lorca's Granada. A Practical Guide.* London: Faber and Faber, 1992.

———. *Federico García Lorca: A Life.* New York: Pantheon, 1989.

Gibson, Ian, Rafael Santos Torroella, Fèlix Fanés, Dawn Ades, and Agustín Sánchez Vidal. *Salvador Dalí: The Early Years.* Ed. Michael Raeburn. New York: Thames and Hudson, 1994.

Gómez Baquero, E. de. *Pen Club I: Los poetas.* Madrid: CIAP, 1929.

Guillén, Jorge. "Federico en persona." In Arturo del Hoyo, ed., *Obras completas.* Madrid: Aguilar, 1986. I:xvii–lxxxiv.

Harris, Derek, ed. *García Lorca. Poeta en Nueva York.* London: Grant and Cutler, 1978.

Hernández, Mario. "Jardín deshecho: Los 'sonetos' de García Lorca." *El Crotalón. Anuario de Filología Española* 1 (1984): 193–228.

Herrera, Fernando de. *Poesía castellana original completa.* Ed. Cristóbal Cuevas. Madrid: Cátedra, 1985.

Huidobro, Vicente. *The Selected Poetry.* Ed. and introd. by David M. Guss. New York: New Directions, 1981.

Ilie, Paul. "Three Shadows on the Early Aesthetic of Lorca." In C. Brian Morris, ed., *"Cuando yo me muera . . ." Essays in Memory of Federico García Lorca.* Lanham, Md.: University Press of America, 1988. 25–40.

Infantes, Víctor. "Lo 'oscuro' de los 'Sonetos del amor oscuro' de Federico García Lorca." In Gabriele Morelli, ed., *Federico García Lorca. Saggi critici nel cinquentenario della morte.* Fasano: Schena Editore, 1988. 59–88.

Johnston, David. *Federico García Lorca.* Somerset, Eng.: Absolute Press, 1998.

Jones, R. O., and G. M. Scanlon. "Ignacio Sánchez Mejías: The 'Mythic Hero'." In Nigel Glendenning, ed., *Studies in Modern Spanish Literature and Art Presented to Helen F. Grant.* London: Tamesis Books, 1972. 97–108.

Josephs, Allen. *White Wall of Spain. The Mysteries of Andalusian Culture.* Ames: Iowa State University Press, 1983.

Katz, Israel J. "Flamenco." In Stanley Sadie, ed., *The New Grove Dictionary of Music and Musicians,* Vol. VI. London: Macmillan, 1980. 625–30.

Llorca, Fernando. *Lo que cantan los niños.* Madrid: Editorial Llorca, n.d.

Loughran, David K. *Federico García Lorca. The Poetry of Limits.* London: Tamesis Books, 1978.

Machado, Antonio. *Poesía y prosa.* 3 vols. Ed. Oreste Macrí and Gaetano Chiappini. Madrid: Espasa-Calpe / Fundación Antonio Machado, 1988.

———. *Selected Poems.* Tr. Alan S. Trueblood. Cambridge, Mass.: Harvard University Press, 1982.

Machado, Manuel. *Alma. Museo. Los cantares.* Madrid: Librería de Pueyo, 1907.

Machado y Álvarez, Antonio (Demófilo). *Cantes flamencos.* Madrid: Ediciones Cultura Hispánica, 1975.

Marinello, Juan. *Contemporáneos: Noticia y memoria.* Havana: Universidad Central de las Villas, 1964.

Martín, Eutimio. *Federico García Lorca, heterodoxo y mártir. Análisis y proyección de la obra juvenil inédita.* Madrid: Siglo XXI, 1986.

———. "Federico García Lorca: Un poema inédito y algunas variantes." *Annals S. Humanitats* 1 (1985): 109–21.

Martínez Nadal, Rafael. *Cuatro lecciones sobre Federico García Lorca.* Madrid: Fundación Juan March / Cátedra, 1980.

———. *Federico García Lorca. Mi penúltimo libro sobre el hombre y el poeta.* Madrid: Editorial Casariego, 1992.

Maurer, Christopher. "¡Ay, Maroto!: Noticias de una amistad." In Angelina Serrano de la Cruz Peinado, ed., *Gabriel García Maroto y la renovación del Arte Español Contemporáneo.* Junta de las Comunidades Castilla-La Mancha, 1999. 31–39.

———. *Federico García Lorca y su "Arquitectura del cante jondo."* Granada: Comares, 2000.

———. "Epistolario: Federico García Lorca y Manuel de Falla." In Laura Dolfi, ed., *L'imposible / posible di Federico García Lorca. Atti del convegno di studi, Salerno, 9–10 maggio 1988.* Naples: Edizioni Scientifiche Italiane, 1989. 251–66.

———. "Apostillas textuales sobre *Suites y Canciones.*" In Dolfi, ed. *L'imposible/posible di Federico García Lorca,* 77–90.

———. "De la correspondencia de García Lorca: Datos inéditos sobre la transmisión de su obra." *FGL. Boletín de la Fundación Federico García Lorca* 1 (1987): 58–85.

———. "Lorca y las formas de la música." In Andrés Soria, ed., *Lecciones sobre Federico García Lorca.* Granada: Edición del Cincuentenario, 1986. 235–50.

Mendes Paula, Beatriz, and M. Ema Tarracha Ferreira. *Textos literários século XVI.* Lisbon: Editorial Aster, 1960.

Menéndez Pelayo, Marcelino. *Antología de poetas líricos castellanos.* Vol. 9. Santander: Aldus, 1945.

Menéndez Pidal, Juan. *Poesía popular. Colección de los viejos romances que se cantan por los asturianos.* Madrid: Hijos de J. A. García, 1885.

Menéndez Pidal, Ramón. *Discurso acerca de la primitiva poesía lírica española leído en la inauguración del curso de 1919.* Madrid: Ateneo de Madrid, 1919.

Miller, Norman C. *Garcia Lorca's* Poema del cante jondo. London: Tamesis Books, 1978.

Morris, C. B. *Son of Andalusia. The Lyrical Landscapes of Federico García Lorca.* Nashville, Tenn.: Vanderbilt University Press, 1997.

Newton, Candelas M. *Lorca, una escritura en trance*: Libro de Poemas y Diván del Tamarit. Amsterdam: John Benjamins, 1992.

Paz, Octavio, ed. *Mexican Poetry. An Anthology.* Tr. Samuel Beckett. New York: Grove Press, 1985.

Predmore, Richard L. *Lorca's New York Poetry: Social Injustice, Dark Love, Lost Faith.* Durham, N.C.: Duke University Press, 1980.

Quance, Roberta. "Lorca's *Canciones*: The Poetics of Desire." In Gregorio C. Martin, ed., *Selected Proceedings, 32nd Mountain Interstate Foreign Language Conference*, Winston-Salem, N.C.: Wake Forest University, 1984. 255–63.

Quesada Dorador, Eduardo, and Yolanda Romero Gómez, coordinators. *Federico García Lorca y Granada.* Madrid: Centenario de Federico García Lorca, 1998.

Ramos-Gil, Carlos. *Claves líricas de García Lorca. Ensayos sobre la expresión y los climas poéticos lorquianos.* Madrid: Aguilar, 1967.

Ramsden, H. *Lorca's* Romancero gitano: *Eighteen commentaries.* Manchester, Eng.: Manchester University Press, 1988.

Río, Ángel del. "El poeta Federico García Lorca." *Revista Hispánica Moderna* (New York) 1 (1935): 1–15.

Rivers, Elias L. *Renaissance and Baroque Poetry of Spain with English Prose Translations.* New York: Scribner's, 1966.

Robertson, Sandra. *Lorca, Alberti, and the Theater of Popular Poetry.* New York: Peter Lang, 1991.

Rodrigo, Antonina. *Memorias de Granada. Manuel Ángeles Ortiz. Federico García Lorca.* Barcelona: Plaza and Janes, 1984.

Rodríguez Marín, Francisco. *Cantos populares españoles.* Vol. 1. Seville: Francisco Álvarez, 1882.

Rozas, Juan Manuel. "El soneto 'A Carmela, la peruana.' " *Trece de Nieve* (Madrid) 1–2, 2d series (1976): 165–72.

Rueda, Salvador. *El cielo alegre.* Valencia: Pascual Aguilar, n.d.

Sáenz de la Calzada, Luis. *"La Barraca." Teatro universitario.* Madrid: Revista de Occidente, 1976.

Sahuquillo, Ángel. *Federico García Lorca y la cultura de la homosexualidad: Lorca, Dalí, Cernuda, Gil-Albert, Prados y la voz silenciada del amor homosexual.* Alicante: Instituto de Cultura "Juan Gil Albert" / Diputación de Alicante, 1991.

Santonja, Gonzalo. *Al otro lado del mar: Bergamín y la Editorial Seneca (México, 1939–1949).* Barcelona: Círculo de Lectores, 1996.

Santos Torroella, Rafael. *Salvador Dalí escribe a Federico García Lorca [1925–1936].* Special issue of *Poesía. Revista Ilustrada de Información Poética* 27–28 (1987).

Schwartz, K. "García Lorca and Vermont." *Hispanic* 12 (1959).

Smith, C. Colin. *Spanish Ballads*. Oxford: Pergamon Press, 1964.

Smith, Paul Julian. *The Theatre of García Lorca*. Cambridge: Cambridge University Press, 1998.

Soria Olmedo, Andrés. "Éxito e ironía en García Lorca: El ejemplo de 'La casada infiel.'" In Gabriel Morelli, ed., *Ludus. Cine, arte y deporte en la literatura española de vanguardia*. Valencia: Pre-Textos, 1998. 223–36.

————. Federico García Lorca. Madrid: Editorial Eneida, 2000.

Stainton, Leslie. *Lorca: A Dream of Life*. New York: Farrar, Straus and Giroux, 1999.

Stanton, Edward F. *The Tragic Myth. Lorca and Cante Jondo*. Lexington: University Press of Kentucky, 1978.

Starkie, Walter. *Spain. A Musician's Journey Through Time and Space*. Vol. 2. Geneva: René Kister, 1958.

Tablada, Juan José. *Obras*. Vol. 2, *Poesía*. Ed. Héctor Valdés. México: Universidad Nacional Autónoma de México, 1971.

Trueblood, Alan S. "La geometría lírica de Federico García Lorca: Los círculos concéntricos." In Birutė Ciplijauskaité and Christopher Maurer, eds., *Voluntad de humanismo. Homenaje a Juan Marichal*. Barcelona: Anthropos, 1990.

Valente, José Ángel. "Pez luna." *Trece de Nieve* (Madrid) 1–2, 2d series (1976), 191–201.

Vega Carpio, Lope de. *Obras poéticas*. Ed. José Manuel Blecua. Vol. 1. Barcelona: Planeta, 1969.

————. *Poesías líricas*. Ed. José F. Montesinos. Vol. 1. 1925; reprinted Madrid: Espasa-Calpe, 1968.

————. *Obras de Lope de Vega*. Vol. 6, *Autos y coloquios*. Ed. M. Menéndez Pelayo. Madrid: BAE, 1963.

Verlaine, Paul. *Oeuvres poétiques complètes*. Ed. Y.-G. Le Dantec and Jacques Borel. Paris: Gallimard, 1962.

Vigón, Braulio. *Juegos y rimas infantiles*. Villaviciosa: Imprenta de la Opinión, 1895.

Walsh, John K. "Las cintas del vals: Three Dance-Poems from Lorca's *Poeta en Nueva York*." *Romanic Review* 79, no. 3 (1988): 502–16.

————. "The Social and Sexual Geography of Lorca's *PNY*," paper read at a symposium on García Lorca at UCLA, May 2, 1986.

————. Unpublished notes on Lorca's *Sonnets* and *Divan*.

Zambrano, María. "El viaje: Infancia y muerte." *Trece de Nieve* (Madrid) 1–2, 2d series (1976), 181–90.

The Translators

CATHERINE BROWN is an associate professor of Spanish at the University of Michigan, Ann Arbor.

COLA FRANZEN is the translator of Alicia Borinski, Saúl Yurkievich, Marjorie Agosín, Jorge Guillén, and other Spanish and Latin American poets, novelists, and critics.

ANGELA JAFFRAY recently received her doctorate from Harvard University in medieval Arabic philosophy. She specializes in translating philosophical and mystical texts.

GALWAY KINNELL is the author of numerous books of poetry, essays, and criticism and a translator of Rilke. He is the winner of a Pulitzer Prize and has received both a MacArthur Fellowship and the National Book Award.

WILL KIRKLAND, a San Francisco Bay area poet and writer, is the translator of *The Cricket Sings* (an anthology of children's poems by Lorca) and of contemporary poets and novelists. His most recent book is *Gypsy Cante: Deep Song of the Caves.*

WILLIAM BRYANT LOGAN, a writer and teacher, is the translator of Lorca's *Once Five Years Pass* and of *Wild Works* by Ramón de Valle-Inclán.

ROBERT NASATIR is the author of *Burning Shadow*, a study of Lorca's influence on British and American poets.

JEROME ROTHENBERG is the author of more than fifty books of poetry and translations, including *Poems for the Game of Silence* and *Poland 1931*, and the editor of a number of anthologies of experimental and traditional poetry. He is a member of the department of visual arts and the department of literature at the University of California–San Diego.

GREG SIMON, a writer and translator, lives and works in Portland, Oregon.

ALAN S. TRUEBLOOD is professor emeritus of Hispanic studies and comparative literature at Brown University. He is the translator of Góngora, Sor Juana Inés de la Cruz, Lope de Vega, and Machado.

STEVEN F. WHITE teaches Spanish at St. Lawrence University. His most recent books include *Fire that Engenders Fire* and *Ayahuasca Reader: Encounters with the Amazon's Sacred Vine.*

CHRISTOPHER MAURER, professor of Spanish at the University of Illinois–Chicago, has also edited Lorca's lectures and correspondence. He is a translator of Baltasar Gracián and Juan Ramón Jiménez and author of *Dreaming in Clay on the Coast of Mississippi: Love and Art at Shearwater.*

Index of Titles and First Lines

INDEX OF TITLES AND FIRST LINES

Índice de Títulos y Primeros Versos